LEARNING CHRIST

LEARNING CHRIST

IGNATIUS OF ANTIOCH & THE MYSTERY OF REDEMPTION

GREGORY VALL

The Catholic University of America Press
Washington, D.C.

Copyright © 2013
The Catholic University of America Press
All rights reserved

Library of Congress Cataloging-in-Publication Data
Vall, Gregory, 1961–
Learning Christ : Ignatius of Antioch and the mystery of redemption /
Gregory Vall.
    pages cm
Includes bibliographical references and index.
ISBN 978-0-8132-3478-6 (pbk)   1. Ignatius, Saint, Bishop
of Antioch, —approximately 110.   I. Title.
BR65.I34V35 2013
270.1—dc23   2013020069

To Francis Martin

CONTENTS

Acknowledgments	ix
Abbreviations	xi
Introduction	1
1. Scripture and Economy	27
2. Issues in Ignatian Scholarship	52
3. Jesus and the Father	88
4. Flesh and Spirit	118
5. Faith and Love	159
6. Judaism and Christianity	200
7. Word and Silence	256
8. A Luminous Mystery	284
9. Christ and the Church	301
10. Unity and Eschatology	359
Bibliography	377
Index of Primary Sources	387
Index of Greek Words and Phrases	394
General Index	397

ACKNOWLEDGMENTS

Devoting three years of my life to the letters of Ignatius of Antioch has been a great privilege and a labor of love. I am grateful to the many colleagues and students at Ave Maria University who encouraged me along the way. Special thanks are due to Fr. Matthew Lamb and Dr. Michael Dauphinais, who have fostered my development as a scholar in practical ways. Jeremiah Vallery read an early draft of this book, made numerous helpful suggestions for its improvement, and inspired me with his own work on Ignatius. Stephen Hildebrand and Thomas A. Robinson reviewed the penultimate draft and offered many valuable criticisms. Sarah DeVille of Canizaro Library located difficult-to-find books and articles. Paul Shields and Teresa Vall helped with the indexes. James Kruggel and Theresa Walker of the Catholic University of America Press, and Philip Gerard Holthaus, freelance copy editor for the press, have been a pleasure to work with. I am grateful for Andrew Olson's proofreading. His keen eyes found several errors at a late stage of the final manuscript. To my parents, siblings, and in-laws I owe an incalculable debt of gratitude. Above all, I thank them for their prayers. My wife, Lourdes, and our children—Teresa, Thomas, Ezra, and Mark—have been unfailing in their love, patience, and good humor. I hope they know that they are the joy of my life. Finally, I wish to dedicate this book to my mentor and dear friend, Fr. Francis Martin.

ABBREVIATIONS

Primary Texts

Barn.	Epistle of Barnabas
1 Clem.	Clement of Rome, Letter to the Corinthians
Dem.	Irenaeus, Demonstration of the Apostolic Preaching
Dial.	Justin Martyr, Dialogue with Trypho the Jew
Did.	Didache of the Twelve Apostles
Diog.	Epistle to Diognetus
Eph.	Ignatius, Letter to the Ephesians
Haer.	Irenaeus, Adversus haereses
Magn.	Ignatius, Letter to the Magnesians
Mart.	Martyrdom of Polycarp
Phil.	Polycarp, Letter to the Philippians
Phld.	Ignatius, Letter to the Philadelphians
Poly.	Ignatius, Letter to Polycarp
Rom.	Ignatius, Letter to the Romans
sal.	salutation (as an unnumbered chapter in each letter)
Shep.	Hermas, The Shepherd
Smyr.	Ignatius, Letter to the Smyrnaeans
STh	Thomas Aquinas, Summa theologiae
Tral.	Ignatius, Letter to the Trallians

Reference Works and Series

BDAG	W. Bauer, F. W. Danker, W. F. Arndt, and F. W. Gingrich, Greek-English Lexicon of the New Testament and Other Early Christian Literature

BDF	F. Blass, A. Debrunner, and R. W. Funk, *A Greek Grammar of the New Testament and Other Early Christian Literature*
CCC	*Catechism of the Catholic Church*
CCSL	Corpus Christianorum Series Latina
LSJ	H. G. Liddell, R. Scott, and H. S. Jones, *A Greek-English Lexicon*
NIGTC	New International Greek Testament Commentary
PG	J.-P. Migne, Patrologia Graeca
PL	J.-P. Migne, Patrologia Latina
SC	Sources chrétiennes
TDNT	G. Kittel, G. Friedrich, and G. W. Bromiley, eds., *Theological Dictionary of the New Testament*

LEARNING CHRIST

INTRODUCTION

This book is a theological exploration of the economy of redemption, based on a historically informed exegesis of the seven authentic letters of the second-century bishop and martyr Ignatius of Antioch. Since my approach to early Christian literature does not fit neatly into any established methodology, this introduction will lay before the reader (1) my thesis and method, (2) an explanation of my hermeneutic and its bearing on historical theology, (3) some initial observations about Ignatius's communicative intention and mode of discourse, (4) four principles for the theological interpretation of early Christian texts, and (5) an overview of the book's contents.

Thesis and Method

My main thesis is that Ignatius of Antioch articulates a cohesive, penetrating, and relatively comprehensive vision of the economy of redemption and that his letters represent one small but important witness to the great theological tradition that runs from the New Testament to the church fathers and beyond. In support of this thesis, I shall demonstrate that Ignatius was well acquainted with several of the writings later incorporated into the New Testament canon, that he understood these well and made apt use of them, and that his theology represents a penetrating synthesis of Pauline, Johannine, and Matthean elements.[1] Having pondered the mystery of Christ in the light of these sources for years, and faced with the urgent pastoral need to address doctrinal errors, he quite consciously advanced the church's reflection on the person and event of

---

1. In the case of Johannine theology, where the influence on Ignatius is especially profound but the evidence of direct literary dependence less than compelling, it is possible that Ignatius depended on oral tradition rather than on the written Gospel of John.

Jesus Christ, the new life of grace, and the nature of the church itself, often in the direction of later theological developments. In making my case, I shall also demonstrate that Ignatius's letters are carefully and skillfully composed. They are not, as is often claimed, slipshod or lacking in coherence. In sum, I hope to rehabilitate and advance Ignatius's reputation as theologian, exegete, and epistolographer.

The method employed in this book is predominantly exegetical and descriptive. Most of my attention is given to a close reading of the Greek text of the seven letters in an effort to understand Ignatius's conceptual horizon and communicative intention as far as possible. To a significant extent, then, my method corresponds to the classic historical-critical attempt to reconstruct the author's intended meaning in its original historical context. This objective, while not constituting the sum and substance of interpretation, remains an indispensable and foundational component in any serious effort to understand ancient texts. Naturally, I interact with previous Ignatian scholarship throughout the book. On this exegetical and descriptive level at least, I hope that my work is of interest and value even to scholars who do not share my hermeneutical, epistemological, or theological convictions. Each can judge from his or her own vantage point whether my interpretation of the letters makes good overall sense of their contents.

As important as it is to make every effort to reconstruct an ancient author's conceptual horizon and intended meaning, however, this effort by itself falls short of interpretation. Moreover, the notion that we should search for this meaning with strictly disinterested historical neutrality is not only an unrealistic ideal but a false one. In Hans-Georg Gadamer's terms, we arrive at real "understanding" (Verstehen), not by attempting to isolate the author's horizon, but by bringing it into dialogue with other horizons, including, but not limited to, our own.[2] Further, we always read texts within interpretive traditions and various overlapping conversations. And it is good that we do so, for we would not get very far otherwise. In the present case, I have made a deliberate and by no means disinterested decision to read the Ignatian letters not only within the conversation and interpretive tradition that we call modern scholarship but also and at the same time within the Christian and especially Roman Catholic theological tradition.

2. For an introduction to Gadamer's notion of Verstehen, see Jean Grondin, "Gadamer's Basic Understanding of Understanding," in The Cambridge Companion to Gadamer, ed. Robert J. Dostal (New York: Cambridge University Press, 2002), 36–51.

In chapter 1 I shall introduce and explain a schema for viewing the economy of creation and redemption as a whole and for relating its various dimensions to each other. This schema is based on five classic distinctions derived from the theological tradition: (1) between θεολογία (God's inner life) and οἰκονομία (the divine economy), (2) between creation and redemption, (3) between old covenant and new covenant, (4) between the mission of the Son and the mission of the Spirit (or between the life of Christ and the life of the church), and (5) between the life of grace and the vision of glory. Some of these distinctions are explicit in Scripture (e.g., between old covenant and new covenant), while others are only implicit (e.g., between "theology" and "economy"). Some of the terminology is from later authors such as Augustine and Aquinas, in whose writings each of these distinctions receives considerable attention and careful elaboration. The schema as a whole, and the diagram with which I shall present it in chapter 1, are my own. They represent my working understanding of the *analogia fidei*, the overarching unity and coherence of the truths and mysteries of the faith.

Although Ignatius himself sometimes makes similar, possibly related, distinctions (e.g., between "old practices" and "newness of hope" in *Magn.* 9:1), I make no claim that my schema represents his conceptual horizon.[3] In fact, I employ it as a kind of standard for assessing his theology. The schema is also a heuristic device, in that it helps generate and organize a series of questions about Ignatius's thought that will be taken up in the ensuing chapters. Most of these questions have been asked in Ignatian scholarship many times before. For example, does Ignatius teach a radically realized eschatology, or does his eschatology include a significant future dimension? In other words, does he clearly distinguish between grace and glory? But the schema brings old questions into a new light and places them in relation to each other, so that we may better take stock of Ignatius's theology as a whole.

While the schema of five distinctions is not intended to represent Ig-

---

3. Unless otherwise indicated, all translations of ancient or medieval texts are my own. For the Ignatian letters and the other subapostolic writings, my base text is the Greek text of Michael W. Holmes, ed. and trans., *The Apostolic Fathers: Greek Texts and English Translations*, 3rd ed. (Grand Rapids, Mich.: Baker Academic, 2007). Wherever I depart from this edition (usually by way of rejecting a conjectural emendation in favor of an attested reading) or otherwise base my argument on a disputed reading, this is indicated in a footnote. As a matter of principle, I strive not to give undue interpretive weight to any passage for which the text is highly uncertain. For citations from *Smyrnaeans* 6–8, I do not follow Holmes's idiosyncratic chapter divisions but those found in all other editions.

natius's conceptual horizon, I do not think it merely coincidental that it came to me while I was engaged in an intensive study of his letters. For thirty years I had devoted myself to the study of Scripture, on the one hand, and, less assiduously, to the church fathers and later theologians, on the other. I discerned points of continuity between the two groups of texts, of course, but to a large extent still felt that I was moving between parallel universes. When I took up the letters of Ignatius in earnest, it was as if I had discovered the missing link. More to the point, I began to see the big picture of the divine economy itself with a new clarity. The pieces in the theological puzzle began to come together. What Ignatius offered me was his own very profound and unified vision of the mystery of redemption in Jesus Christ, and that vision helped me arrive at a new level of understanding of the proper object of theology: God and all things in relation to God.[4]

Obviously there is a certain circularity involved here. If I take the schema that came to me while studying Ignatius's letters, place it at the beginning of my book, and use it as a standard against which to judge Ignatius's theology, one can expect that he will do fairly well! Nevertheless, this is a properly hermeneutical circularity, not a merely logical or epistemological one. I came to Ignatius's letters with a prior understanding of the divine economy, an understanding that was informed by Scripture, the fathers, the doctors, and a few modern theologians. Naturally, since I wanted to know what Ignatius too had to say about the divine economy, I endeavored to make sense of his dense and elliptical discourse and to grasp his conceptual horizon. More vitally, however, I was interested in what light he could throw on the thing itself. Through studying Ignatius's letters I wanted to come to a deeper understanding of the mystery of redemption, and I did.

To use another of Gadamer's well-known concepts, the schema of five distinctions represents a "melting together" of several horizons (*Horizontverschmelzung*): not only Ignatius's and mine, but also those of Scripture, Augustine, Aquinas, and many others (as each of these has been taken up, no doubt very imperfectly, into my horizon). In a certain sense, the same could even be said of this book as a whole. It represents not only my decipherment of Ignatius's meaning, but my understanding of the divine economy precisely insofar as I have benefited from Ignatius's understanding of the same reality. That is one of the elements

---

4. Thomas Aquinas, STh I, q. 1, a. 7.

that makes this volume, I hope, a work of historical *theology*, rather than merely a historical work *about* theology.

In making this admission I do not wish to be construed as having abandoned the historical-critical task, and still less am I looking to be absolved of responsibility in that regard. When it comes to the descriptive work of identifying Ignatius's intended meaning and conceptual horizon, which is the bulk of the book by far, I have certainly endeavored to get it right, and I expect to be criticized where I have not. Any significant failure in that regard must certainly compromise the whole structure of "understanding" that I have built up. Still, I do not view the historical-critical effort to explicate Ignatius's meaning as an end in itself, nor do I regard my theological effort to understand better the mystery of redemption through the reading of his letters as an extrinsic second step of mere application, personalization, or "theologizing." Explication and understanding together constitute the integral act of interpretation.

Naturally, for the sake of clarity and scholarly objectivity, there must be some effort to keep distinct even things that are ultimately inseparable. When occasionally I attempt to cast light upon aspects of Ignatius's theology by quoting the *Summa Theologiae* or even the *Catechism of the Catholic Church*, I have obviously moved well beyond Ignatius's conceptual horizon, and I usually acknowledge that fact explicitly. But it would be artificial and even detrimental to exegesis of the letters, not to mention theology, were we to try to say precisely where Ignatius's horizon begins and ends, so that his theology could be rigorously isolated from the rest of the tradition and viewed in its radical "singularity." No matter how much study we give to his letters, moreover, there will always be much residual uncertainty about exactly what he has in mind in this or that passage, as well as significant gaps in our reconstruction of his theological horizon. Recognizing this, some scholars suppose that methodological rigor requires us to exclude from our reconstruction of Ignatius's conceptual horizon everything but what he states with clear and distinct ideas. This is a counsel of despair, for extreme minimalist approaches can be as distortive as maximalist approaches and in any case forestall real understanding. The alternative I have chosen is to start with a reasonable working hypothesis about how Ignatius fits into the theological tradition and to test that hypothesis by attempting to read him within that tradition.

Historical Theology and the Hermeneutic of Understanding

In this section I shall try to ground my approach more firmly in a hermeneutic of understanding and empathy and suggest how such a hermeneutic can remedy what I perceive to be methodological shortcomings in modern historical theology.

According to Gadamer, understanding comes about through conversation, and a conversation is carried along by "the law of the subject matter."[5] In an authentic dialogue—namely, one in which each interlocutor is genuinely seeking truth and not simply pressing for the acceptance of his or her own ideas—the focus is not on words and ideas as such but on "the matter at hand" *(die Sache selbst),* that which the conversation is about.[6] As the participants bring their horizons together, allowing various observations, insights, and perspectives to play off each other, the conversation—now taken over by a dynamic that is more than the sum of its parts—wends its way, by however tortuous a path, closer and closer to the truth of the matter at hand, drawn onward as if by a gravitational pull. For the most part, words and meanings remain within what Michael Polanyi calls the interlocutors' "subsidiary awareness," while their "focal awareness" is on the topic of conversation, the matter at hand.[7] Naturally, there will be moments when their focal awareness shifts temporarily to words and meanings, as when one participant asks another to explain an unfamiliar expression or to clarify exactly how a term is being used. But the progress of the conversation depends on getting the focus back to the matter at hand and keeping it there as much as possible.

By wedding elements of Gadamer's hermeneutical model of *Verstehen,* in particular its recognition of the primacy of the subject matter, to Polanyi's distinction between subsidiary and focal awareness, one thus arrives at a modest and workable hermeneutic of understanding. A simple illustration may be helpful. Let us say that my sister and I are having a conversation about our father's health. As we talk, my focal awareness is not on the meaning of her words and sentences but on the matter at hand: our father's health. Because her "intended meaning" does not

---

5. Hans-Georg Gadamer, *Philosophical Hermeneutics,* trans. and ed. David E. Linge (Berkeley and Los Angeles: University of California Press, 1976), 66.
6. Günter Figal, "The Doing of the Thing Itself: Gadamer's Hermeneutic Ontology of Language," in *Cambridge Companion,* 106–8.
7. For the epistemological and hermeneutical distinction between subsidiary awareness and focal awareness, see Michael Polanyi and Harry Prosch, *Meaning* (Chicago: University of Chicago Press, 1975), 33–41.

normally present me with interpretive difficulties, much less a hermeneutical gap, I do not need to apply a conscious "method" to it. And as long as my "exegesis" of her words remains on the level of my subsidiary awareness, I have what Polanyi calls a "tacit" or "nonexplicit" knowledge of her intended meaning.[8] And that is all I need or want, since my real concern and focus, like hers, is not on meaning as such but on the matter at hand. Now, if in the course of the conversation she should use a medical term with which I am unfamiliar, we may need to divert our focal awareness away from the subject matter temporarily so that she can explain the term's meaning to me. But that would only be "a kind of detour." When this model is applied to the interpretation of texts, we see that, in that case too, "understanding is primarily related to the issue at hand and not to the author's intention as such."[9]

This hermeneutical model has important implications for the study of early Christian literature. When Ignatius of Antioch writes of "the present grace" (Eph. 11:1), "the ordinances of the apostles" (Tral. 7:1), or "the passion of my God" (Rom. 6:3), he directs the attention of his readers to extratextual realities that he knows by experience and with which he is deeply concerned. He assumes that they too have some experiential knowledge of these realities, or at least access to such knowledge, and he invites them to be as passionately invested in them as he is. His communicative intention is not only to get across his ideas but also that his readers would consider these realities for themselves, view them in a new light, enter more deeply into them, or act on them in a specific way. His letters are didactic, and he teaches with implicit authority, but he addresses his readers as "my fellow students" (Eph. 3:1), inviting them to sit alongside him, as it were, in order to ponder with him the matter at hand: the mystery of Jesus Christ and all that it entails. This is what Ignatius is writing *about*, and we have not yet really understood him or his letters until we have come to a deeper understanding of this reality ourselves. Absent this, we may do much fine and helpful historical-critical work that *contributes* to understanding, but we have not achieved understanding in the Gadamerian sense.

We modern readers, however, can hardly sit down with Ignatius of Antioch and without further ado have a conversation about "the matter at hand"! Even if we have extensive linguistic and historical training

---

8. Ibid., 34.
9. Grondin, "Gadamer's Basic Understanding," 40.

and have spent years studying his letters, we shall find ourselves pausing frequently to consider the precise sense of this or that Greek phrase or perhaps to raise anew a text-critical issue once considered settled. The mere semantic construal of his sentences, which presumably required for the most part only the subsidiary awareness of his first readers, will be the preoccupation of our focal awareness. It may consume 90 percent or more of our time. Moreover, if and when we finally come around to a consideration of *die Sache selbst*, Ignatius's whole cast of mind may still be so foreign to us, his religious sensibilities so off-putting, that his letters may seem, at least for a time, more a hindrance to our understanding of the mystery of Christ than an aid. It may even seem impossible to achieve a "fusion" of his horizon with our own.

Faced with these very real difficulties, it is understandable that modernity would develop a deliberate and self-conscious approach to ancient texts, one that emphasizes our historical and cultural distance from the ancient authors and places a premium on correct semantic construal of their words. The classic historical-critical method makes reconstruction of the author's originally intended meaning the main focus and primary goal of interpretation. And given that the results it achieves in this regard are almost always tentative and revisable, it is not surprising that practitioners of the method have been, at least until recently, reticent to press beyond this primary task. This ethos of sobriety and reserve is, of course, one of the great virtues of the historical-critical method, for in its emphasis on solving exegetical difficulties and its unwillingness to come to a facile understanding of the subject matter, it rediscovers and guards the foreignness of the ancient text and thus opens new avenues to authentic understanding. Apart from some element of strangeness, texts, whether ancient or modern, have no capacity to teach us or to lead us to conversion.

If I find that an ancient Christian text immediately resonates with me in a powerful and personal way, even before I have devoted careful study to it, this may be due to the instincts of faith, but then again it may not. Perhaps I should step back and consider whether what seems to be instant understanding might not rather be the product of my own facile association of the author's words with something very different in my experience, something that perhaps has little or nothing to do with the author's communicative intention. Such an easy assimilation of the text's horizon to my own is not the same as a true fusion of horizons, which generally requires some intellectual and spiritual labor. The historical-critical method is often faulted for sweeping away cherished traditional interpretations that have developed over centuries, leaving what once seemed a familiar and edifying text scarcely recognizable from across a yawning chasm, an ancient artifact to which only the experts have access. There is, to be sure, a real problem here, but there is also something salutary. Some traditional interpretations need to be swept away like cobwebs, so that the ancient text can speak afresh from across the centuries and renew our understanding of the mystery of the faith.

Nevertheless, a method that makes reconstruction of the author's mere "meaning" an end in itself cannot deliver anything like a complete interpretation. For starters, the author's communicative intention involves much more than meaning per se. Inseparable from his or her intended meaning is a reference to extratextual realities (the "matter at hand"), implicit or explicit truth-claims about these realities, and an implicit or explicit invitation to the reader to engage these realities in new ways. Texts are meant to be interactive and are composed to elicit a whole range of responses in the reader. This hermeneutical observation stands in considerable tension with the classic modern ideal of disinterested historical neutrality, especially when it comes to the study of texts of a religious or theological nature. The canons of modern "historical theology" demand that the scholar bracket the text's truth-claims and prescind from his or her own faith convictions when making historical and exegetical judgments. The historical theologian's task is understood to be strictly descriptive, especially when it comes to religious beliefs and truth-claims, which are in any case often viewed as a matter of private numinous experience and nonrational subjectivity. Can such a method really disclose the ancient author's communicative intention?

A work of historical theology in this purportedly strictly descriptive vein will endeavor to tell us what Ignatius of Antioch thought and believed to be true about Jesus Christ, salvation, and the church, but will, at least in theory, refrain from passing judgment concerning the truth or falsity of what Ignatius thought and believed. It is assumed that the realms of religious faith and historical knowledge can and must be kept quite discrete. The problem is that, even if the modern reader were able to approach the text with perfect neutrality, relatively few texts, certainly none in the corpus of early Christian literature, are actually written with disinterested readers as the target audience. Ignatius must have envisioned that some of his readers would passionately disagree with him and reject what he was saying in his letters, but he could hardly have imagined a reader who would as a matter of methodological principle defer indefinitely the whole question of the truth or falsity of the gospel, thinking that such a procedure would somehow yield a lucid perception of his meaning! What I am trying to sketch out in this introduction is a clearer sense of what Ignatius did expect of his readers and a hermeneutic that is better suited to the sort of texts we have in front of us when we study his letters.

Actually, a fair amount of recent scholarship appreciates that Ignatius was not writing for disinterested readers and recognizes that this consideration must be factored into any comprehensive attempt to discern the communicative intention embodied in his letters. Much of this scholarship, which strongly accents the rhetorical dimension of early Christian literature, no longer feels itself bound by the old scruple against judging an ancient author's religious truth-claims. The old historicism, which ruled out of court all metaphysical questions and religious truth-claims from the outset, has increasingly given way to a more radical historicism that brings metaphysics and religious faith back into the courtroom—for sentencing! If the nineteenth-century hermeneutic of historical-criticism made a more or less sincere attempt to refrain from passing judgment on faith's truth-claims, while romanticism even left open the possibility that humanity's universal religious orientation might provide some sort of natural access to transcendence, the trend in recent decades has been toward a hermeneutic of suspicion, with the result that theology has come to be identified more and more with "ideology," a term which almost always retains at least overtones of a false consciousness employed in the interests of power. This trend toward ideological criticism is evident not only in feminist and liberationist approaches but in sociocritical approaches generally.[10]

These developments have had a palpable effect on Ignatian scholarship. Not a few scholars of the early to mid-twentieth century regarded

---

10. On the sociocritical theory undergirding these approaches, see Anthony C. Thiselton, *New Horizons in Hermeneutics: The Theory and Practice of Transforming Biblical Reading* (Grand Rapids, Mich.: Zondervan, 1992), 379–409. I speak here only of trends and do not mean to suggest that sociological approaches are inextricably linked to a hermeneutic of suspicion. For an empathetic and keenly insightful sociological reading of a difficult Ignatian passage, see Margaret Y. MacDonald, "The Ideal of the Christian Couple: Ign. Pol. 5:1–2 Looking Back to Paul," *New Testament Studies* 40 (1994): 105–25.

Ignatius of Antioch as high-strung, grandiose, and perhaps emotionally imbalanced. Some faulted him for his morbid death wish, while others opined that his doctrine had deviated from the pure Pauline gospel of grace and had "veered off" into early catholicism. With few exceptions, however, Ignatius's critics of a couple generations ago still treated him with a degree of respect and admired at least the sincerity and deep conviction with which he puts forth his views, even if they considered some of these to be erroneous. Nowadays, however, Ignatius's rhetorical extravagancies are interpreted rather less innocently. He is, we are told, a "spin-doctor" who employs "the rhetoric of coercion" in order to force through his political agenda and "construct" a new social reality.[11] And whereas the old historicism treated Ignatius's claim to prophetic inspiration as a religious phenomenon that the historian was not competent to judge, the new historicism assumes that such a claim must be bogus and strongly suspects that it is a manipulative ploy.

Near the end of chapter 2, I shall summarize and critique one such reading of the Ignatian letters. This will serve as a foil for my own approach, which employs, not a hermeneutic of suspicion, but one of understanding and empathy. In a sense, my project is to see what I can get from the letters by giving Ignatius the benefit of the doubt, morally and intellectually. If he speaks with emotionally charged rhetoric, I assume that he is sincere before I try the alternative hypothesis. If he says something confusing or appears to contradict himself, my working assumption is that he knows what he is saying and is making sense but that I need to work a little harder to get at his meaning. I do not too quickly jump to the conclusion that he has become "caught in his own rhetoric."[12] Of course, my hermeneutic may turn out to be naïve and ill-suited to the task of interpreting the Ignatian letters. It is theoretically possible that the bishop of Antioch was as manipulative and crassly political as some scholars claim. It will be up to the reader to decide which working presuppositions lead to a more plausible overall interpretation of the letters.

---

11. Allen Brent, *Ignatius of Antioch: A Martyr Bishop and the Origin of Episcopacy* (London: T. & T. Clark Continuum, 2009), 58–59; David M. Reis, "Following in Paul's Footsteps: Mimēsis and Power in Ignatius of Antioch," in *Trajectories through the New Testament and the Apostolic Fathers*, ed. Andrew F. Gregory and Christopher M. Tuckett (New York: Oxford University Press, 2005), 305.

12. Judith M. Lieu, *Image and Reality: The Jews in the World of the Christians in the Second Century* (London: T. & T. Clark Continuum, 1996), 32.

Letters Written for the Sake of Understanding

If we wish to apply a hermeneutic of understanding to the Ignatian letters, we must provide preliminary answers to three basic questions about them. First, what is the subject matter of the letters, and how does Ignatius orient himself and his readers epistemically to that subject matter? Second, what sort of appeal does Ignatius make to his readers, and what sort of effect does he want his letters to have on them? And third, what mode of discourse and writing style does he employ in discussing this subject matter and making this appeal?

With respect to the first question, Ignatius writes about a number of topics—church order and Christian unity, true and false doctrines, the virtues of faith and love, his impending martyrdom, and so forth—and he seems to jump from topic to topic almost spontaneously. All these topics, however, are closely interrelated aspects of a single reality: the mystery of Jesus Christ. The gospel, as Ignatius presents it, is fundamentally concerned with the person and event of Jesus and the new life that members of the church have in union with him. The seven letters of Ignatius of Antioch draw us into a conversation in which Jesus Christ is "the matter at hand."

As for Ignatius's epistemic orientation to the subject matter of his letters, he is keenly aware that he is dealing with a "mystery" (*Magn.* 9:1). The person and event of Jesus Christ is nothing less than the self-manifestation of the one true God and as such far exceeds Ignatius's or anyone else's conceptual horizon (8:2). His letters proclaim this mystery, direct the reader's attention to this mystery, and articulate profound insights into this mystery, but they in no way pretend to nail it down with human concepts. In fact, Ignatius's use of the word-and-silence paradox, which we shall examine in chapter 7, reflects his clear recognition that such a thing is out of the question. In this context we might apply to the Ignatian letters a comment that Gadamer makes about the New Testament. He observes that "we do the New Testament authors a false honor" when we limit the "meaning" of their texts to the actual "horizon of understanding" of the authors. "Their honor should lie precisely in the fact that they proclaim something that surpasses their own horizon of understanding—even if they are named John or Paul."[13] Or, we may add, Ignatius. To reduce the communicative intention of Ignatius's let-

---

13. Gadamer, *Philosophical Hermeneutics*, 210.

ters to his conceptual horizon fails to reckon with the nature of what he is talking about and his epistemic orientation to that reality.

Turning to the second question, we can say that Ignatius's appeal to his readers is rhetorical, intellectual, and authoritarian. Ideological criticism is not mistaken to call attention to the significantly rhetorical character of the letters. The bishop of Antioch writes to persuade, and he employs various literary devices to that end. It would be incorrect, however, to suppose that Ignatius expects or even wants any of his readers to be won over to his views by sheer brunt of rhetoric. As the treatment of the Ignatian concepts of "faith" and "love" in chapter 5 will show, the bishop of Antioch has a great respect for the role that the individual's intellect and freedom play in the Christian life. And I hope that this book as a whole will demonstrate that Ignatius engages the intellect and freedom of his readers in a serious manner.

At the same time, it would be misleading to say that Ignatius thinks to sway his readers with rigorous logic or sustained argumentation. He is a real thinker, to be sure, and he brings his penetrating intellect to bear on the mystery of redemption. I could not disagree more with C. C. Richardson's characterization of the letters as "popular rather than deep."[14] Nevertheless, the sort of rational appeal that Ignatius makes in his letters is suited to the "mysterious" nature of their subject matter. His affirmations tend to be synthetic and suggestive rather than analytic and conceptually precise. And as we shall see momentarily, this mode of reasoning especially befits his rather early chronological position in the "conversation" that we call the history of Christian theology. In saying that Ignatius's formulations lack conceptual precision in comparison to later theology, however, I do not at all mean that he is a fuzzy thinker or a careless writer. My whole project aims to demonstrate that the opposite is true. The point here is rather that his very carefully worded formulations, some of which he no doubt developed over many years of teaching and preaching, draw the reader's attention to mysterious and paradoxical aspects of the gospel.

Ignatius's appeal to authority is more intricate and subtle than is generally recognized, having several intertwined strands. He insists on the authority of the bishops and is confident that they have the mind of Christ (Eph. 3:2), but he does not emphasize their teaching role. He assumes

---

14. Cyril C. Richardson, trans. and ed., *Early Christian Fathers* (New York: Macmillan, 1970), 74.

that the local churches have access to various authoritative writings and traditions, including "the prophecies and the law of Moses" (*Smyr.* 5:1) and "the precepts of the Lord and of the apostles" (*Magn.* 13:1), and he explains that these are reducible to one source and one truth. As God's self-manifestation, Jesus Christ is both "our only teacher" and the truth that we are to learn (8:2, 9:1). The person and event of Jesus Christ constitute the church's official "archives," so that "learning Christ" is the sum and substance of Christianity (*Phld.* 8:2). The believer encounters the person and event of Christ not only through words of instruction but also, in a remarkably concrete manner, in the eucharist (*Smyr.* 7:1). Furthermore, the authority of the gospel is not merely external but has an interior dimension too, for each believer has "received the knowledge of God, which is Jesus Christ" and has within himself or herself the "gift" (χάρισμα) of the Holy Spirit (*Eph.* 17:2). Ignatius is confident that his readers "have Jesus Christ within" (*Magn.* 12:1), and he no doubt relies on the "living and speaking water" of the Spirit to draw them inwardly to the Father (*Rom.* 7:2). He is deeply concerned that false teachers have infiltrated the churches of Asia Minor, and one of the central purposes of his letters is to provide these churches with principles and criteria for distinguishing true from false doctrine. Ignatius himself teaches with authority but never invokes his episcopal office in a didactic context. He stakes his credibility as teacher and the enduring authority of his letters on his willingness to die as a model of Christian discipleship and as a witness to the realities about which he writes.[15]

It is important to note in this regard that Ignatius does not expect his letters to have their effect in isolation. His authoritative instruction is clearly meant to function within the multidimensional life of the church and in conjunction with other witnesses to the truth of the gospel, including his own martyrdom (*Smyr.* 5:1). Basically, he is trying to confirm his readers in the faith, draw them more deeply into the life of Christ, and secure the unity of each church under its bishop. The letters are not meant to accomplish this on their own but together with the celebration of the eucharist, the reading of Scripture, the leadership of the bishop, and the life of prayer. They are written in such a way as to realize their communicative effect upon the reader within that ecclesial context and dynamic, not in abstraction from it. At a minimum, the modern

---

15. Robert F. Stoops Jr., "If I Suffer . . . : Epistolary Authority in Ignatius of Antioch," *Harvard Theological Review* 80 (1987): 161–78.

scholar must reflect on this fact and its hermeneutical implications with a degree of empathy, even if he or she does not choose to read the letters from within an analogous modern ecclesial context or dynamic of faith.

Now we may pose the third question. What mode of discourse and writing style does Ignatius employ in teaching about the mystery of Jesus Christ and in making his appeal to the churches? Since this is a rather complex topic, aspects of which will be dealt with in chapter 2, here I shall touch on only a few features pertinent to the present discussion.

We may begin with Ignatius's marked fondness for fixed pairs of terms.[16] Some of these are synthetic, as when the phrase ὁρατά τε καὶ ἀόρατα ("things visible and invisible") serves as a merism for all of reality (Tral. 5:2). Similarly, the virtues "faith and love," which Ignatius identifies as "the beginning and end of life," respectively, represent the totality of Christian existence under its teleological aspect (Eph. 14:1). Other pairs, including some with a Johannine ring, are antithetical, such as "life and death," or "God and the world." Several of the most frequently occurring pairs can be used either way. For example, Ignatius typically uses "flesh and spirit" synthetically, to express the totality of the human person or human existence, but he occasionally employs the same two terms in a more antithetical, quasi-Pauline manner (Eph. 8:2). When speaking about the paschal mystery, Ignatius likes to employ the merism "passion and resurrection," two terms which in another context might be heard as antithetical. That he is probing the profound paradox at the heart of this mystery is especially evident in the phrase "true life in death" (Eph. 7:2). For our purposes, it is crucial to note that Ignatius employs pairs of terms in suggestive and thought-provoking ways, not in order to make fine conceptual distinctions.

Another striking feature of Ignatian discourse is the way he uses predications of identity (always with ἐστιν) to express a variety of analogous, participatory, or causal relationships. For example, when Ignatius speaks of the church "breaking one bread, which is the medicine of immortality" (Eph. 20:2), he implies a four-term analogy: the eucharist is to everlasting life what medicine is to biological life. On the other hand, when he says that to possess an unwavering spirit "is Jesus Christ," he probably means roughly that it is a participation in the grace of Jesus

---

16. Here I depend in part on the fine discussion of Ignatian style in José Pablo Martin, "La pneumatología en Ignacio de Antioquia," *Salesianum* 33 (1971): 382–86.

Christ (*Magn.* 15:1). And when he says that Jesus' passion "is our resurrection," he evidently means that it is the cause of our resurrection (*Smyr.* 5:3). Some of his predications of identity are still more provocative and open to interpretation, either because they are stated so baldly—"God promises unity, which is himself" (*Tral.* 11:2)—or because they are complex and elliptical: "Regain yourselves in faith, which is the flesh of the Lord, and in love, which is the blood of Jesus Christ" (8:1). It is important to note here that Ignatius's discourse is interactive, inviting the reader to ponder the realities spoken of, to consider their interrelationships, and to go beyond what Ignatius has said explicitly.

More than one scholar has noted the "peculiar density" of Ignatius's writing and his "intriguing ability ... to suggest more than he says."[17] Nowhere is this pregnancy of expression more in evidence than in his many striking Christological affirmations. Most of these are rather concrete, gathering the key moments in the historical Christ event into a quasi-creedal narrative, especially in antidocetic contexts (*Tral.* 9:1–2). Others are more abstract and schematic: "one Jesus Christ, who came forth from one Father, and was toward one, and departed" (*Magn.* 7:2). Ignatius's Christological formulae may be symmetrical, stringing together synthetic and antithetic pairs of terms in a quasi-poetic manner (*Eph.* 7:2), or they may employ daring abstract language in an elliptical and highly provocative fashion (*Poly.* 3:2). But without exception they are inherently geared toward stimulating the reader's own reflection on the person and event of Jesus Christ. In other words, they serve the central dynamic of the life of grace: "learning Christ" (*Phld.* 8:2).

Ignatius's Christological affirmations reflect the mind of one who is keenly aware that he is dealing with a mystery of unfathomable plenitude and who wishes to advance the church's understanding of this mystery by sharing his own profound insights in carefully crafted formulae. It is remarkable in this regard how many of these formulations anticipate later Christological reflection and even dogma. Aloys Grillmeier notes, for instance, how Ignatius, by predicating "the divine and the human of one and the same subject" (in *Eph.* 7:2) anticipates the dogmatic formula εἷς καὶ ὁ αὐτός ("one and the same") promulgated by the Council of Chalcedon.[18]

---

17. William R. Schoedel, *Ignatius of Antioch: A Commentary on the Letters of Ignatius of Antioch*, Hermeneia (Philadelphia: Fortress Press, 1985), xiii; Donald F. Winslow, "The Idea of Redemption in the Epistles of St. Ignatius of Antioch," *Greek Orthodox Theological Review* 11 (1965): 130.

18. *Christ in Christian Tradition*, vol. 1, *From the Apostolic Age to Chalcedon (451)*, 2nd ed., trans. John Bowden (Atlanta: John Knox Press, 1975), 546.

Olavi Tarvainen aptly describes Ignatius's thought as "dynamic" and "pressing forward."[19] In pressing forward, however, the bishop of Antioch does not leave behind the apostolic traditions. In the words of Thomas G. Weinandy, "Ignatius has both intrinsically linked his Christology to that apostolic tradition and simultaneously nudged it vigorously down the doctrinal road to Nicaea and, ultimately, to Chalcedon."[20] Again and again we shall see Ignatius combine traditional elements in original ways that anticipate the writings of later church fathers. He is, to cite but one example, the first of many to juxtapose the titles "Son of Man" and "Son of God" as biblical shorthand for Christ's humanity and divinity, respectively (Eph. 20:2).

In the New Testament books and Ignatius's letters we glimpse theology in its embryonic stage, in what, borrowing an expression from Hans Urs von Balthasar, we might call its "infolded," that is, not-yet-unfolded, state.[21] The density of thought and expression that is characteristic of these writings is appropriate to the very early place they occupy in the centuries-long conversation that we call the Christian theological tradition. If the one true God has revealed himself definitively in the person of his incarnate Word and in the events of his brief earthly life—which is what John, Paul, and Ignatius all believe to have occurred in Jesus Christ—it makes good sense that the first attempts at proclaiming this unfathomably rich mystery in words would be primarily concerned with the concrete fact of its occurrence and would, in a compact style more suggestive than analytical, take only the crucial first steps toward unfolding the significance of that mystery conceptually, leaving it to later generations to tease it out further and with greater conceptual precision. This, I take it, is roughly what Gadamer has in mind when he describes the New Testament writings as *Urliteratur*.[22]

The Ignatian letters represent a kind of second phase in the church's *Urliteratur*. When we consider their place within the long development of the theological tradition, they are quite close to the New Testament

---

19. *Glaube und Liebe bei Ignatius von Antiochien*, Schriften der Luther-Agricola-Gesellschaft 14 (Joensuu, Finland: Pohjois-Karjalan, 1967), 16 ("dem dynamischen, vorwärtsdrängenden Denken des Ignatius").

20. "The Apostolic Christology of Ignatius of Antioch: The Road to Chalcedon," in *Trajectories*, ed. Gregory and Tuckett (New York: Oxford University Press, 2005), 77.

21. See E. A. Nelson's brief comment on Balthasar's use of the words *einfalten* and *Einfaltungen* in Hans Urs von Balthasar, *Convergences: To the Source of the Christian Mystery*, trans. E. A. Nelson (San Francisco: Ignatius Press, 1983), 9.

22. *Philosophical Hermeneutics*, 210.

books in terms of presenting a still largely "infolded" theology. When we zoom in on the first two centuries of Christianity, however, we see Ignatius taking a series of small but decisive steps beyond the New Testament writings in the theological unfolding of the mystery of Christ and his church. Therefore, when we apply a hermeneutic of understanding to Ignatius's letters, we need to keep in mind their almost unique place in this larger conversation.

The central point I have attempted to develop in this section is that Ignatius's letters are inherently geared toward theological reflection on, and elaboration of, the mystery of Christ. Their subject matter is God's self-manifestation in Jesus Christ as well as the whole economic and ecclesial mystery that surrounds the person and event of Christ. Ignatius orients himself and his readers to this reality precisely as to a mystery, and his rhetorical, intellectual, and authoritative appeal is that his readers would attend to this mystery, understand it more deeply, and live it more fully. His mode of discourse, moreover, serves the interactive intent of the letters. Ignatius's compact, synthetic, elliptical, and suggestive style invites the reader's active intellectual engagement. His communicative intention is not simply to transmit to his readers his own ideas about the mystery of Jesus Christ, or in other words, his own theological horizon. His letters are intrinsically dialogic or "conversational," and as such they belong both to the early second-century conversation between Ignatius of Antioch and the churches of southwestern Asia Minor and Rome, and to the church's centuries-long theological conversation about the content of revelation. They are written for the sake of *Verstehen*, written with the goal of "learning Christ" in mind.

Four Principles of Theological Interpretation

Thus far I have made the case that a hermeneutic of understanding is well suited to the interpretation of the Ignatian corpus of letters. But a similar case might be made for many nontheological texts as well. Gadamer's hermeneutic of understanding is a general hermeneutic that comprises a series of helpful insights into verbal communication and human existence as such. Given what we have learned about the Ignatian letters, is there a special hermeneutic that is suited to them specifically as theological texts and yet still compatible with the hermeneutic of understanding? My proposal is that the classic approach to theology found in the fathers and doctors of the church supplies us with the additional hermeneutical principles we need in order to bring a hermeneutic of understanding fully to bear on the interpretation of Ignatius's letters. Using two classic definitions of theology, I shall sketch out the most important of these principles and in the process suggest their compatibility with the hermeneutic of understanding.

Viewing theology from the standpoint of its object, Thomas Aquinas defines it as the study of God and all things in relation to God, or more precisely, God and all things as "ordered to God as their beginning and end."[23] In a complementary fashion Anselm of Canterbury, viewing theology more from the standpoint of the subject, defines it as "faith seeking understanding."[24] From these two definitions we may derive four principles for the properly theological interpretation of early Christian texts, including nonbiblical texts such as Ignatius's letters.

The first principle is that theological interpretation is primarily concerned, not with words and ideas as such, but with realities or "things" (*res*), especially "divinely revealed things" (*divinitus revelata*).[25] Realities such as Jesus Christ, who is "God in man" (*Eph.* 7:2), the deeds "truly and surely accomplished" by him (*Magn.* 11:1), and the "catholic church" (*Smyr.* 8:2) comprise the primary subject matter of Ignatius's letters. Theological interpretation seeks not merely to comprehend what Ignatius has written about these things but to understand the things themselves in light of what Ignatius has written. This principle (especially as it applies to Scripture) was widely agreed upon for the first millennium or so of Christian theology but since the dawn of nominalism has become increasingly difficult for us moderns to accept, given our epistemological insecurities. It is, however, quite compatible with the hermeneutic of understanding, which gives primacy to *die Sache selbst*, provided we play that hermeneutic in the key of epistemological realism, joined to faith.[26] To make use of this principle requires one to accept that the words of Scripture and the symbol of faith refer to extratextual realities that have been accessible to believers down through the ages. As Aqui-

23. STh I, q. 1, a. 7 (omnia autem pertractantur in sacra doctrina sub ratione Dei, vel quia sunt ipse Deus; vel quia habent ordinem ad Deum, ut ad principium et finem). My translations and citations of Aquinas's works are based on the Latin text as presented by Enrique Alarcon at the University of Navarre website (www.corpusthomisticum.org).

24. *Proslogium* 1 (fides quaerens intellectum).

25. *Dei Verbum* 11.

26. According to Brice Wachterhauser, Gadamer himself was "an uncompromising realist" ("Getting It Right: Relativism, Realism, and Truth," in *Cambridge Companion*, 52–78, quote from 66). In any case, Gadamer's hermeneutic of understanding appears to be at least amenable to a realist interpretation and application.

nas puts it, "the act of the believer terminates not in the proposition, but in the reality."²⁷ From this perspective the history of Christian theology is not simply the evolution of a series of religious ideas and systems but the church's ongoing conversation about, and developing understanding of, abiding realities.

The second principle is that theological interpretation seeks to understand these divinely revealed realities according to their overarching unity and coherence. My schema of five classic distinctions, discussed above and presented more fully in chapter 1 below, is an attempt to outline this unity and coherence, which is sometimes called the *analogia fidei* or the *ordo veritatum fidei*.²⁸ Because the schema includes God's inner life (θεολογία) as well as the entire economy of creation and redemption (οἰκονομία), it comprehends the proper object of theology: God and all things in relation to God. Moreover, by beginning with God's inner life and ending with the rational creature's highest participation in that life ("glory"), the schema indicates broadly how all things come forth from God and return to God. This answers Aquinas's concern that theology view creatures precisely as "ordered to God as their beginning and end." And as we shall see, Ignatian theology too has some elements of an *exitus-reditus* scheme, notably in its presentation of God the Father as primal origin and ultimate end.²⁹

In order to understand the realities of faith according to their unity and coherence, it is helpful to view them under the aspect of "mystery," a biblical and patristic category the recovery of which is vital for the renewal of biblical exegesis and theology in our day.³⁰ As Gottlieb Söhngen notes, "The mysteries of the faith form a mysterious structure in which we can, and should, relate them to each other and thereby form a rich account of the individual mysteries in the midst of all their connections."³¹ As we shall see, especially in chapter 8, the letters of Ignatius of Antioch have a significant contribution to make in this regard.

---

27. STh II-II, q. 1, a. 2, ad 2 (actus credentis non terminatur ad enuntiabile sed ad rem).

28. On this use of the phrase *analogia fidei* (which is used in several other ways as well), see Gottlieb Söhngen, "The Analogy of Faith: Unity in the Science of Faith," trans. Kenneth Oakes, Pro Ecclesia 21 (2012): 179–86.

29. Ferdinando Bergamelli, "Dal Padre al Padre: Il Padre come principio e termine del Cristo e del cristiano in Ignazio di Antiochia," Studia Patristica 36 (2001): 168–76. The letters of Ignatius, however, lack anything resembling Aquinas's fully developed doctrine of creation.

30. Hans Boersma, *Nouvelle Théologie and Sacramental Ontology: A Return to Mystery* (Oxford: Oxford University Press, 2009).

31. Söhngen, "Analogy of Faith," 179.

The third principle is that theological interpretation presupposes the truth and stable content of the Christian faith and employs the rule of faith as its standard. There is no question in the present context of entering into the many thorny questions that hover around this principle, concerning, for example, the relationship between Scripture and tradition, the authority of the councils, or the development of doctrine. Suffice it to say that the definition of theology as "faith seeking understanding" presupposes that faith has an objective content (*fides quae creditur*), to which Christians have adhered, however imperfectly, from the apostolic age to the present time. My working assumption is that Ignatius intends to teach what the Lord and his apostles taught and that we can learn a great deal from him. At the same time, we can safely assume that there are gaps, obscurities, and possibly errors in his presentation of the gospel. Since his letters are noncanonical texts, his truth-claims and theological opinions are to be judged according to the rule of faith.

It is obvious, not least from the polemics contained in Ignatius's letters, that second-century Christians were not in complete agreement about the content and correct understanding of the faith, but Ignatius himself frequently expresses the conviction that the gospel does have an essential, indispensable, and unchanging content that has been handed down by the apostles, and that revealed truth can be known, lived, and taught. We need to agree with him on this point if we are to interpret his letters (or any other text) theologically. Here as elsewhere, I am swimming against the current of contemporary scholarship, much of which is committed to the idea that expressions such as "orthodox Christianity" or "the common faith" are sheer anachronisms when applied to the early second century, which allegedly knew only "multiple Christianities."[32] Again, I ask the reader only for the opportunity to make my case that the Ignatian letters, whatever their limitations, represent one important witness to the deep organic theological continuity that runs from the New Testament writings to the church fathers and beyond.

Provided we do not conceive of the objective content and continuity

---

32. According to Michael J. Svigel, who also bucks this trend, the early second-century churches already possessed "a distinct sense of catholic identity based on a shared christological confession" when there was as yet "no set credo, canon, and cathedra": "This central incarnational narrative helps explain the eventual solidification of credo, canon and cathedra not as tenets of a late developing catholicity, but as the practical means of defending and promoting the confessional narrative center of an earlier catholic Christianity" ("The Center of Ignatius of Antioch's Catholic Christianity," *Studia Patristica* 45 [2010]: 367–71, quotes from 371).

of the faith in too mechanical and impersonal a fashion, reducing it to a series of propositions, this third principle meshes well with a hermeneutic of understanding. Gadamer holds that for a conversation to achieve "understanding" (*Verstehen*), there must be a prior basic "agreement" (*Verständigung*) about the subject matter on the part of the interlocutors.[33] In the model of theological interpretation that I am sketching out here, the whole rich mystery of Jesus Christ is the objective content of the faith and therefore the "subject matter" of the centuries-long conversation that we call the theological tradition. The rule of faith represents the essential "agreement" about this subject matter on the basis of which the participants in the conversation "seek understanding." The mystery of Christ is the same, yesterday, today, and forever, but the church gradually unfolds this mystery by living it out and reflecting on it.

The fourth principle is that theological interpretation takes as its starting point, not only the objective content of faith, but also the virtue, act, and subjective experience of faith (*fides qua creditur*). This subjective aspect of faith seems to be what Anselm especially has in mind in the phrase *fides quaerens intellectum*. Of course, this principle was axiomatic long before Anselm. When explaining the relationship between faith and understanding, Augustine, on whom Anselm depends, quotes Isaiah 7:9 according to the Old Latin version: "Unless you believe, you will not understand" (*nisi credideritis non intellegetis*).[34] This verse of Scripture was a commonplace among the fathers in such contexts.

Unlike the modern discipline of historical theology, which requires its practitioners, if they have any faith, to check it at the door, the classic notion of theological praxis presupposes a fully engaged faith and a deep spiritual life on the part of the theologian. "If you are a theologian, you truly pray; if you truly pray, you are a theologian," runs the axiom of Evagrius Ponticus.[35] The "seeking" involved in theological interpretation is, first of all, the earnest and frequent petition for the illumination of one's intellect by the Holy Spirit, both in order to make correct judgments about the communicative intention of the author's words, and to understand the realities to which those words refer. Naturally, prayer does not compensate for every defect of intellect, education, or charac-

---

33. Grondin, "Gadamer's Basic Understanding," 39–42.
34. E.g., *De magistro* 11.
35. *Chapters on Prayer* 60 (Evagrius Ponticus, *The Praktikos, Chapters on Prayer*, trans. John Eudes Bamberger, Cistercian Studies 4 [Kalamazoo, Mich.: Cistercian Publications, 1981], 65, punctuation modified).

ter that might impede understanding, but, all things being equal, it can help a great deal. Nor would I wish to suggest for one moment that a spiritual approach to studying ancient Christian texts could in any way substitute for linguistic expertise or careful historical research, which are indispensable. The point is simply that faith and the life of prayer are essential to the practice of theology in the proper sense of the term.

Overview of the Book

Since the argument that unfolds over the following ten chapters is dense and intricate, it may be advisable to conclude this somewhat unconventional introduction in the conventional manner, namely, by providing a bird's-eye view of the book's contents.

1. Scripture and Economy   This chapter lays a foundation for the theological interpretation of the Ignatian letters in three steps. First, using the famous "archives" passage (Phld. 8:2) as a point of departure, I explain why Ignatius subordinates Scripture to the mystery of Christ himself and why this does not represent a "denigration" of Scripture. Second, I present my schema of five classic distinctions as a framework for the study of the divine economy, and I generate a series of questions and concerns that arise when we place Ignatius's theological horizon alongside this schema. And third, I display Ignatius's familiarity with the Pauline, Matthean, and Johannine writings (or traditions) and the creative manner in which he weaves this source material into his letters.

2. Issues in Ignatian Scholarship   This chapter takes up three issues in modern scholarship that have a particular bearing on this project. First, with respect to Ignatius's epistolary style, I demonstrate how the letters are built up largely out of aphorisms, creedal formulae, and brief topical discourses, all woven together in a skillful and coherent manner. Second, I take up the question of which heretical teaching(s) Ignatius addresses in the polemical letters, as well as the question of his possible relationship to incipient gnosticism. And third, under the rubric of Ignatius's "agenda," I summarize and critique the hypothesis of Allen Brent, whose overall approach to the letters will serve as a foil for my own.

3. Jesus and the Father   Ignatius views the economy of redemption as a *mysterium unitatis* comprising several interlocking dimensions of unity.

Guided by the programmatic formulations of *Magnesians* 1:2 and 13:1, chapters 3, 4, and 5 take up the three aspects of unity that Ignatius lists in both passages. Exploring the unity of "Jesus and the Father," which Ignatius calls the "most essential" dimension of unity, chapter 3 considers Ignatius's Christology, his nascent Trinitarianism, and his understanding of the economic missions of the Son and the Spirit.

4. Flesh and Spirit   Though Ignatius's use of the terms "flesh" and "spirit" is not quite what we find in Galatians or Romans, his soteriological anthropology is essentially biblical and Pauline. To maintain this thesis in face of what at times appears to be an incipiently gnostic view of man and salvation, it is necessary to take an extended look at Ignatius's cosmology (including the relationship between the church and the non-Christian "world"), his understanding of spiritual warfare and martyrdom, and the epistolary aims and rhetorical strategy of his *Letter to the Romans*, where all these themes converge.

5. Faith and Love   This chapter expounds and defends Ignatius's teaching on "the union of faith and love," which some have viewed as a dangerous departure from "pure Pauline trust." Ignatius stresses adherence to orthodox doctrine and the noetic dimension of faith, but these are entirely compatible with personal adherence to Christ and faith's fiduciary dimension. Faith and love possess a special economic relation to the Christ event and enable the Christian to "suffer with" Christ. Ignatius's dynamic and teleological view of redemption—faith is the ἀρχή and love the τέλος of the Christian life (*Eph.* 14:1)—discloses the bond between these two virtues.

6. Judaism and Christianity   The remaining five chapters of the book inquire into Ignatius's presentation of the economy of redemption under its historical aspect, beginning with his understanding of the relationship between Judaism and Christianity. Since modern scholarship tends to conflate a variety of views under the label "supersessionism," I sketch out a spectrum of second-century approaches by examining four texts—the *Epistle to Diognetus*, the *Epistle of Barnabas*, Justin Martyr's *Dialogue with Trypho*, and Irenaeus's *Demonstration of the Apostolic Preaching*—and then locate Ignatius's letters along this spectrum. His teaching about the relationship between Judaism and Christianity, while not without lacunae, is carefully nuanced and theologically vital.

7. Word and Silence   The word-and-silence paradox is a key to Ignatius's thought, but it has often been misunderstood. His description of Jesus Christ as God's "Word come forth from silence" (*Magn.* 8:2), which has been interpreted as an expression of gnostic or modalist emanationism, is in fact fully compatible with the New Testament and anticipates elements of orthodox Trinitarian theology. Ignatius's commendation of "silent" bishops, far from reflecting an early stage in the development of the episcopacy during which the bishop was an administrator but not necessarily a teacher, grounds the "good" of the ecclesial teaching ministry in the Lord's own ministry as the "one teacher" who "silently" performed deeds "worthy of the Father" (*Eph.* 15:1).

8. A Luminous Mystery   This chapter undertakes a theological exegesis of the Lord's baptism in the Jordan as it is presented in the canonical gospels and in two of Ignatius's creedal formulae: *Smyr.* 1:1b–2 and *Eph.* 18:2. This "mystery of light" illuminates two important aspects of the historical economy: the interrelation of the distinct moments that comprise the Christ event, and the relationship between the Christ event and the events that precede and follow it in the economy's temporal unfolding. The baptism of the Lord can be viewed as a kind of hinge between the incarnation and the paschal mystery, helping us to grasp the soteriological unity of the life of Christ, while it also suggests how the Christ event is connected to the creation of the world, God's covenant with Israel, and the sacramental life of the church.

9. Christ and the Church   Ignatius's ecclesiology has been variously interpreted and sometimes harshly criticized by modern scholars, who have not always placed it in its proper relation to his broader understanding of the economy of redemption. This chapter considers the mission of the Holy Spirit and the gift of "imperishability," the mission of the apostles and the "apostolic character" (*Tral.* sal.), the relationship between the "catholic church" and the local churches (*Smyr.* 8:2), the ecclesiological typology by which Ignatius illuminates the threefold hierarchy of the local church, and the appointment and validation of bishops.

10. Unity and Eschatology   Ignatius is sometimes thought to favor a Hellenized concept of realized eschatology over the Jewish concept of future eschatology and to exaggerate the personal dimension of eschatology at the expense of its communal dimension, but this assessment entails

false dichotomies that obscure Ignatius's actual teaching. This chapter establishes that his eschatology does in fact have a future orientation and a communal dimension, and then it asks whether it also has a properly historical dimension. The volume concludes with a final demonstration that Ignatius's letters provide us with a cohesive vision of the divine economy.

1

SCRIPTURE AND ECONOMY

The Philadelphia Incident

Led through Asia Minor in the summer of A.D. 113 on the way to his martyrdom in Rome, Ignatius of Antioch stopped in the city of Philadelphia (modern Alaşehir, Turkey), where he was allowed to visit the local church and its bishop.[1] During his stay Ignatius found that some members of the community had fallen under the sway of teachers who were "interpreting Judaism" to them, that is, marshaling exegetical arguments for a Judaized form of Christianity. It is not clear exactly which Jewish practices these teachers were insisting on, but circumcision does not seem to have been one of them (Phld. 6:1). Possibly they were convening a weekly assembly on the Sabbath to rival the "one eucharist" that was celebrated with the authority of the "one bishop" each Sunday.[2] In any case, they were "schismatics" who had caused a "division" in the community with their "evil doctrines," and this brought them into inevitable conflict with the bishop of Antioch.[3] Writing to the Philadelphians from Troas some weeks after his visit, Ignatius recalls what seems to have been a brief and

---

1. Ignatius informs us that he wrote to the Romans from Smyrna on "the ninth day before the calends of September" (August 24), but unfortunately fails to mention the year (Rom. 10:3). Eusebius (Historia ecclesiastica 3:36) places Ignatius's martyrdom within the reign of Trajan (A.D. 98–117), and most scholars since Lightfoot accept this as providing a reliable approximate date (cf. J. B. Lightfoot, The Apostolic Fathers, part 2, S. Ignatius, S. Polycarp, 3 vols., 2nd ed. [London: Macmillan, 1889], 2.435–72). Stevan L. Davies proposes a plausible scenario whereby Ignatius's arrest and journey may be fixed more precisely to A.D. 113 ("The Predicament of Ignatius of Antioch," Vigiliae Christianae 30 [1976]: 175–80). I have adopted this date merely for the sake of convenience and to supply a touch of verisimilitude. My interpretation of Ignatius's letters does not in any way depend on such exactitude.
2. Phld. 4:1; cf. Magn. 9:1.
3. Phld. 3:3, 2:1.

27

inconclusive dialogue between himself and some members of this Judaizing faction.

> I exhort you to do nothing out of factiousness but according to the learning of Christ. For I heard some say, "If I do not find it in the archives, I do not believe it in the gospel." And when I said to them, "It is written there," they answered me, "That is the question." But to me Jesus Christ is the archives. The inviolable archives are his cross, death and resurrection, and the faith that comes through him. It is by these, through your prayers, that I wish to be justified. (Phld. 8:2)

The "archives" or "original documents" (ἀρχεῖα) to which the Philadelphian Judaizers appealed as their final authority were the Jewish Scriptures or Old Testament (presumably in Greek translation), while "the gospel" here probably refers to the Christian proclamation as represented by whatever combination of authoritative written texts and oral traditions was circulating in Asia Minor in the early second century, along with Ignatius's own teaching.[4] For those who "interpreted Judaism," the more ancient sacred writings of Israel trumped the novelties of the gospel. While in Philadelphia Ignatius "did [his] part as a man constituted for unity" to secure the community's submission to the three-tiered hierarchy of bishop, presbyters, and deacons, insisting above all that the Philadelphians "do nothing apart from the bishop."[5] But when the Judaizers were unable to find this and other elements of Christian teaching in the Old Testament, they felt justified in rejecting them.

Ignatius must have found himself in an awkward position in Philadelphia. He was filled with anxious concern for his own episcopal see in Syrian Antioch, which for the time being had to manage without a visible shepherd (Rom. 9:1), and he may have had no way of knowing how he would be received by the churches in Asia Minor. Philadelphia was the first stop on Ignatius's itinerary of which we have any knowledge, and his letter to that church contains several hints that the reception he had there was not unanimously enthusiastic. He found it necessary to come to the defense of the godly but taciturn bishop of Philadelphia,

---

4. On the semantics and interpretation of this difficult text, see William R. Schoedel, "Ignatius and the Archives," *Harvard Theological Review* 71 (1978): 97–106; and Schoedel, *Ignatius of Antioch: A Commentary on the Letters of Ignatius of Antioch*, Hermeneia (Philadelphia: Fortress Press, 1985), 207–9. Charles E. Hill sees a reference here to one or more written gospels ("Ignatius, 'the Gospel,' and the Gospels," in *Trajectories*, ed. Gregory and Tuckett, 273), while Matthew W. Mitchell explicitly denies that "gospel" here refers to a written gospel ("In the Footsteps of Paul: Scriptural and Apostolic Authority in Ignatius of Antioch," *Journal of Early Christian Studies* 14 [2006]: 38).

5. Phld. 8:1, 7:2; cf. sal. 4:1, 7:1.

who appears not to have had the full cooperation of his flock. There was an inherent tension in this situation. Were Ignatius to assert his own authority too forcefully, he would appear to be meddling and thus would undercut the authority of the local bishop, the very thing he earnestly wished to promote.

Ignatius himself was a man of few words, or at least he aspired to be so, and as a matter of principle he would have been reticent to speak with anyone whom he considered to be promoting a false doctrine.[6] But the situation in Philadelphia was delicate and required tact. The Judaizers had made inroads into the community, winning adherents, and Ignatius sincerely hoped for their repentance (Phld. 3:2, 8:1). When he heard their axiom—"If I do not find it in the archives, I do not believe it in the gospel"—he responded with a single Greek word: γέγραπται ("it is written [there]"; 8:2). By this technical term Ignatius probably meant that the truth of Christ could in fact be established from a proper exegesis of the "archives." In responding so briefly, Ignatius was probably exercising emotional restraint, wishing to avoid the heat of anger and the exacerbation of an already tense situation. As he says in the same context, "Where there are division and anger, God does not dwell" (8.1). But, rightly or wrongly, Ignatius's interlocutors probably sensed an insult in his curt and elliptical reply. Their riposte likewise consisted of a single Greek word: πρόκειται (literally, "it lies before"), which idiomatically means, "That is just the question."[7] In other words, the Judaizers challenged Ignatius to show them exactly where "it is written."

As far as we know, the conversation ended right there. Some scholars suppose that Ignatius backed off because he was not especially skilled in the Christological exegesis of the Old Testament and could not in fact demonstrate his point.[8] In other words, the Judaizers had called his bluff. According to Paul J. Donahue, "Ignatius could not win his exegetical argument with his opponents, so he changes the rules." By identifying Jesus Christ as the archives, "he appeals to a higher, more decisive

---

6. Tral. 6:1; Smyr. 4:1, 5:3.

7. BDAG (Walter Bauer, Frederick William Danker, W. F. Arndt, and F. W. Gingrich, eds., *Greek-English Lexicon of the New Testament and Other Early Christian Literature*, 3rd ed. [Chicago: University of Chicago Press, 2000]), 871. Alternatively, πρόκειται can be taken literally: "They [the archives] lie before us" (with the neuter plural noun taking the singular form of the verb). If so, the Judaizers would be referring deictically to actual texts of Jewish Scripture lying before them on the table (cf. the somewhat similar sense of this verb in *Magn.* 5:1). Either way, they would be challenging Ignatius to prove his point.

8. E.g., C. P. Hammond Bammel, "Ignatian Problems," *Journal of Theological Studies* 33 (1982): 83.

standard."⁹ I disagree with the low opinion of Ignatius's exegetical ability presupposed in this comment, as well as with the insinuation that he was engaging in evasive tactics of argumentation. Near the end of this chapter and at various points throughout the volume I shall demonstrate that Ignatius's use of the Old Testament, while circumscribed, is learned and sophisticated. Donahue is, however, correct when he says that Ignatius "appeals to a higher, more decisive standard." Whether Ignatius attempted on the spot to demonstrate his point exegetically or not, at least by the time he wrote *Philadelphians* he recognized that the real issue lies at a deeper level than mere exegesis. His considered response to the Judaizers' axiom shifts the ground of the debate to the level that we would call fundamental theology: "But to me Jesus Christ is the archives. The inviolable archives are his cross, death and resurrection, and the faith that comes through him" (8:2).

According to John J. O'Keefe and R. R. Reno, Ignatius's assertion may strike modern readers as "profoundly unsatisfactory" because of the way it seems to forestall any real exegetical discussion. Moreover, they maintain that to "equate" a person with a text is "obscure, to say the least"; whatever point Ignatius is making by this statement is made "opaquely." Indeed, they find Ignatius's entire narration of the incident "cryptic."¹⁰ Nevertheless, O'Keefe and Reno are quite confident that they know just what Ignatius means when he says that "the archives are Jesus Christ." He means very simply that "knowing the identity of Jesus Christ is the basis for right reading of the sacred writings of the people of Israel." Put even more simply, "The cross, death, and resurrection of Jesus Christ, and 'the faith that came by him,' provide the interpretive key" to the Old Testament.¹¹

According to this interpretation, Ignatius is making a very simple point but has expressed himself rather poorly. I propose instead that he is making a profound point and has expressed himself well, albeit tersely. Ignatius would, no doubt, agree that knowledge of Jesus Christ is essential to the correct interpretation of the Scriptures of Israel. But in this passage of *Philadelphians* he is not really concerned with interpretive strategies. His claim that "Jesus Christ is the archives" is not simply another way to say that Christ is the hermeneutical key to the Old Tes-

---

9. Paul J. Donahue, "Jewish Christianity in the Letters of Ignatius of Antioch," *Vigiliae Christianae* 32 (1978): 86.
10. John J. O'Keefe and R. R. Reno, *Sanctified Vision: An Introduction to Early Christian Interpretation of the Bible* (Baltimore: Johns Hopkins University Press, 2005), 27–28.
11. Ibid., 28.

tament.¹² William R. Schoedel (echoing Donahue) is closer to the mark when he says that here "Ignatius appeals to an even higher authority" than Scripture itself.¹³ In other words, Ignatius subordinates Scripture to the person and work of Jesus Christ, who is God's definitive revelation.¹⁴

I would like to advance this point one step further and suggest that Ignatius is, in effect, affirming an analogical relation between Christ and Scripture (here, the Old Testament).¹⁵ According to Ignatius, Jesus Christ is the preexistent Logos through whom God has "manifested himself" in human history (*Magn.* 8:2), "the mouth that cannot lie, by which the Father has spoken truthfully" (*Rom.* 8:2), and the "one teacher" whose words and deeds are "worthy of the Father" (*Eph.* 15:1). Put simply, he is "the knowledge of God" (17:2). Among those realities that can be called λόγος θεοῦ, Jesus Christ is the prime analogate. He alone is Word of God in a definitive and unqualified sense, while Scripture is the "word of God" by virtue of its economic participation in the mystery of Christ.¹⁶ "Scripture is the word of God that bears witness to God's Word" and that "only has meaning in relation to Christ's words, acts and being."¹⁷

Ignatius's subordination of Scripture to the person and work of Christ by no means entails "a denigration of scriptural authority."¹⁸ On the contrary, it indicates Scripture's proper place and vital role within the economy of redemption. Ignatius understands the life of Christ to constitute the fundamental "mystery" (μυστήριον) by which "our only teacher, Jesus Christ" has enabled us to believe in the true God and come to eternal life (*Magn.* 9:1). The principal moments of the Christ event—

---

12. *Pace* Daniel Hoffman, "The Authority of Scripture and Apostolic Doctrine in Ignatius of Antioch," *Journal of the Evangelical Theological Society* 28 (1985): 75.

13. Schoedel, *Ignatius of Antioch*, 209.

14. It is not simply a question of "subordination to the Christian *message*," as Matthew W. Mitchell would have it ("In the Footsteps of Paul," 42; emphasis added). Were that his point, Ignatius might simply have insisted that "the gospel" is more definitive than "the archives," as he does in the very next chapter (*Phld.* 9:1–2). But here in chapter 8 he makes the more basic and more profound point that divine revelation is located first and foremost in a *person* and in the *event* of his life, death, and resurrection.

15. For the moment, I will leave aside the question of how the writings later to be included in the New Testament fit into this picture.

16. That is to say, by virtue of the role it plays in the economy of redemption. Because the economy has the person and event of Christ at its center and is summed up in Christ, every other element or facet of the economy must in some way participate in the mystery of Christ and serve this mystery. This may be called its "economic participation," a phrase I borrow from Francis Martin, *Sacred Scripture: The Disclosure of the Word* (Naples, Fla.: Sapientia Press of Ave Maria University, 2006), 241.

17. Han Urs von Balthasar, *Explorations in Theology*, vol. 1, *The Word Made Flesh*, trans. A. V. Littledale with Alexander Dru (San Francisco: Ignatius Press, 1989), 11, 52.

18. *Pace* Mitchell, "In the Footsteps of Paul," 39.

especially the incarnation, death, and resurrection—are the "mysteries" by which "God was manifesting himself humanly" (Eph. 19:1–3). In the chapters to follow, I hope to unfold what Ignatius means by "mystery." For the moment, it is important to recognize that, according to Ignatius, the Old Testament prophets did not simply foresee the coming of Christ but participated in his mystery proleptically. As Peter Meinhold correctly notes, they were partakers in the events of salvation by the grace of the Holy Spirit. For Ignatius "the primary reality is not the holy Book but the saving facts of Christianity, in which the authors of the Old Testament participated through Spirit and grace."[19]

When the Old Testament Scriptures are taken up into the life of the church, therefore, the prophets proclaim the gospel of Christ to us with great immediacy, while they themselves are seen to be "saints worthy of love and worthy of admiration ... numbered together with us in the gospel of the common hope" (Phld. 5:2). When Ignatius says that "Jesus Christ is the archives," he is not using a clumsy expression that seems to equate a person with a text. Rather, he is employing analogical language in order to affirm a relationship of economic participation. The Jewish Scriptures are appropriately called ἀρχεῖα ("archives") because they are ancient and possess great authority by virtue of containing authentic revelation of the one true God. But these qualities are possessed supremely and transcendently by Jesus Christ, who "was with the Father before the ages" and came into the world as God's final and definitive self-manifestation (Magn. 6:1). Within the economy of redemption Scripture derives its authority and revelatory character from Christ and plays a subservient but vital role (in conjunction with the sacraments, the rule of faith, the hierarchy, and other elements of ecclesial life) in the mediation of the definitive revelation,

---

19. Peter Meinhold, *Studien zu Ignatius von Antiochien* (Wiesbaden: Franz Steiner Verlag, 1979), 43 ("Das Primäre sind also bei ihm nicht das heilige Buch, sondern die christlichen-Heilsfakten, die durch Geist und Gnade den Verfassern des Alten Testamentes zuteil geworden sind"). Similarly, Robert M. Grant says that Ignatius's point in Phld. 8:2 is that "the true foundation of Christian faith is not the Old Testament as such but Jesus Christ, to whom the Old Testament points" ("Scripture and Tradition in St. Ignatius of Antioch," *Catholic Biblical Quarterly* 25 [1963]: 322). Almost immediately, however, Grant shifts his position when he equates the person of Christ with "the cardinal revelatory events of Christian history" and then equates the latter with oral tradition. The point thus becomes that Ignatius "valued tradition more highly than scripture" (323), and this is reaffirmed in the article's conclusion, with specific reference to Phld. 8:2 (334). The confusion in Grant's argument stems, in part, from a failure to recognize that both Scripture and tradition give access to the person of Christ and to the revelatory events of his life, and it is compounded by the fact that Grant takes a conclusion drawn from Ignatius's "traditional" use of (what will become) New Testament materials and applies it to the statement in Phld. 8:2, where it is a question rather of his view of the Old Testament.

which is Christ. Naturally, Ignatius would not have conceptualized the matter in this way. I am using later precisions in an attempt to get at what is incipient and densely expressed in the formulation of *Philadelphians* 8:2.

To be more precise, Israel's Scriptures are subordinate to Jesus Christ in two respects. First, as we have already seen, he is the Word, whereas they consist of "words about the Word." But second, they are subordinate inasmuch as they contain the old covenant, whereas Christ's coming into the world inaugurates a new covenant. At first glance, this second contrast would appear to be of relatively little significance for Ignatius, who seems to treat Israel's prophets as full-fledged Christians who happened to live a few centuries before Christ's historical advent. Moreover, when the Philadelphian Judaizers argue on the premise that Israel's Scriptures have more authority than the gospel precisely because they are old, Ignatius does not immediately offer the counterclaim that the gospel is superior to the ancient Scriptures precisely because it is new. Instead, he subordinates the Old Testament to the person and event of Christ, and thereby implicitly subordinates all "words about the Word" to the Word itself. Presumably this would include the words of the gospel in its oral and written modalities. On the other hand, Ignatius does make a qualitative distinction between the Old Testament and the gospel in the very next chapter of *Philadelphians*. Even as he extols the "beloved prophets" of Israel, he notes that "the gospel possesses a distinct advantage," namely, "the advent of the Savior, our Lord Jesus Christ, his passion, and the resurrection" (Phld. 9:2). Within the economy of redemption, then, the words of the gospel have a more intimate relationship to the person and life of the incarnate Word than do the words of Israel's Scriptures. This theoretical privileging of the gospel over the Old Testament is, moreover, matched by Ignatius's praxis. His knowledge of books and traditions that will eventually be canonized in the New Testament plays a far more pervasive and significant role in his theology than does his use of the Old Testament.

Ignatius and the Economy

The present volume aims to be a theological exploration of the economy of redemption, based on a historical exegesis of the letters of Ignatius of Antioch. At the heart of the economy, as Ignatius views it, is God's self-manifestation in Jesus Christ, who is the preexistent Word of God and humanity's "one teacher" (Eph. 15:1). All other elements of the economy

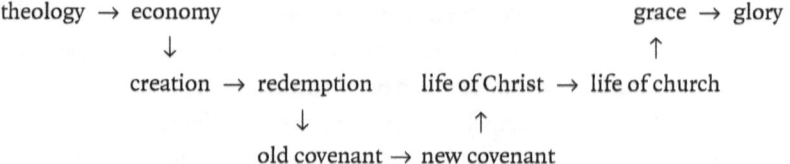

FIGURE 1. Schema of Five Classic Distinctions

hover around this central mystery and participate in it. We have already seen how this is the case with Sacred Scripture. It is also true of the episcopacy and of Ignatius's own ministry as bishop, epistolary theologian, and would-be martyr. Nothing is more fundamental to Ignatius's self-understanding than his sense of participating in the redemptive mystery of Jesus Christ.

I am interested, then, in what Ignatius can teach us about the economy of redemption, and I am interested simultaneously in what he can show us about being a theologian. The sort of theological praxis that Ignatius models for us does not attempt to detach itself from the economy of redemption in order to examine it at arm's length. The theologian reflects upon and attempts to illuminate the divine economy as that in which he or she participates. One important aspect of Ignatius's participation in the mystery of the incarnate Word is his handling of the written word—that is, of the texts that later came to be canonized in the two testaments of the Christian Bible. Throughout this volume, therefore, we shall pay particular attention to the way Ignatius interprets and utilizes Sacred Scripture. But the fundamental object of our inquiry remains the divine economy itself.

By way of laying out a broad theological framework for the elaboration of our topic, we might think in terms of a series of binary distinctions visualized as a descending and ascending staircase (see figure 1 above). As noted in the introduction, these are classic distinctions from the theological tradition and do not represent Ignatius's conceptual horizon as such. The schema as a whole is my own.

At the top of the stairs to the left is the most fundamental distinction, namely, between "theology" and "economy," that is, between the eternal mystery of God (θεολογία) and his master plan in its temporal execution (οἰκονομία). Here it is important to recall that God's *ad extra* activity is based on who he is *in se* and constitutes his self-revelation. There is thus a real ontological bond between theology and economy.

Moving down to the second level, we note that the economy, which is a kind of divine "condescension" (συγκατάβασις), consists in two distinct though inseparable orders: creation and redemption. In this pair too, the second element is, according to its own manner, founded on the first element, even as it reveals the latter's ultimate end and brings it to that end, according to the axiom, "Grace presupposes nature and perfects it" (*gratia supponit naturam et perficit eam*).[20]

Next, descending to a third level on our schema, the order of redemption manifests itself in two distinct but intrinsically connected phases: old covenant and new covenant. The first of these comprises the historical approaches of Yahweh to Israel, which are partial in nature and occur in a variety of modalities (πολυμερῶς καὶ πολυτρόπως), while the second consists of God's definitive act of self-revelation and redemption in his Son (Heb 1:1–4). We can distinguish, therefore, between many imperfect, provisional *vetera* and a single, transcendently superior *novum* (cf. Is 43:18–19). In important respects this "new thing" presupposes, fulfills, and perfects the "old things." It gathers them up into itself and in so doing discloses their true end. Moreover, the *novum* already lies hidden in the *vetera*. The relationship between the two covenants is, therefore, quite complex.

In the new covenant we see both the depths of God's condescension and that by which he lifts humanity up to himself, and so it is fitting that our schema begins its ascent at this point. Moving up a level, therefore, we find that the *novum* itself consists in two moments: the economic missions of the Son and of the Spirit, which issue in the life of Christ and the life of the church, respectively. The Father sends the Son into the world at the incarnation in order to redeem humanity through the paschal mystery, and following upon the Son's glorification, he sends the Holy Spirit upon the church and into the hearts of baptized believers (Gal 4:4–6). As with the other distinctions, the second item of this pair in some sense presupposes and completes the first item, but here we must be careful to note that the Holy Spirit's mission adds nothing substantive to the Son's work. It completes it only in the sense of bringing it to fruition in the life of the church. Nor does the Spirit reveal anything of its own but only what the Son has already revealed. As Gregory of Nyssa puts it, "there is no distance between the Son and the Holy Spirit."[21]

---

20. The order of creation is not, however, reducible to "pure nature," since our first parents were given the grace of original justice; cf. CCC 374–76 (*Catechism of the Catholic Church*, 2nd ed. [Vatican City: Libreria Editrice Vaticana, 1997]).

21. *Adversus Macedonianos* 16; PG 45.1321 (τὸ μηδὲν διάστημα μεταξὺ τοῦ υἱοῦ καὶ τοῦ ἁγίου πνεύματος); cf. Jn 14:26, 16:13–15; CCC 689–90.

Finally, ascending one more level, we find that the church's life consists in two distinct but intrinsically related stages: grace and glory. The former is a foretaste of the latter, while the latter is the perfection of the former. As Thomas Aquinas puts it, "grace is nothing other than a certain beginning of glory in us."[22] It is fitting that this last step returns us to the level on which the schema began, inasmuch as heavenly glory is the creature's fullest possible participation in God's eternal life.

What this schema does not immediately disclose is the centrality of Jesus Christ. It would seem, rather, to confine his activity to a single moment within the economy of redemption, the moment that we usually refer to as "the Christ event." When Jesus Christ is understood to be God's co-eternal Logos, however, we find that the entire economy is united in his person and that the economy itself is rooted in the inner life of God. The Logos who is eternally with God is the same Logos through whom the world has been made and through whom the world is redeemed. Moreover, because the Son perfectly reveals the Father through his incarnation, the Holy Spirit's activity within the old covenant must lead up to and anticipate this one definitive revelation, while the same Spirit's activity within the life of the church must unfold that one definitive revelation in order to bring it to perfect fruition in the life of glory.

Now, it will be obvious to anyone who reads Ignatius's letters that his theology is Christocentric, at least in the general sense of placing a strong emphasis on the person and event of Jesus Christ, especially in the realms of soteriology, ecclesiology, and personal piety.[23] Above all, Jesus is manifestly the object of Ignatius's faith, love, and hope. He believes in Christ, loves Christ, and hopes to "attain Jesus Christ" (Rom. 5:3). But does Ignatius's Christocentrism amount to a coherent and unified vision of the divine economy?

When we read Ignatius's letters against the backdrop of the systematic theological schema sketched out above, we find that important and challenging questions emerge at each step. To begin with, we might ask whether he distinguishes clearly between θεολογία and οἰκονομία, and whether he in fact roots his Christ-centered view of the economy in God's inner life. Some have found the very passage in which Ignatius

---

22. *STh* II-II, q. 24, a. 3, ad 2 (*gratia nihil est aliud quam quaedam inchoatio gloriae in nobis*).

23. Eduard Freiherrn von der Goltz writes eloquently on this point, noting that the central place that the historical person of Jesus Christ occupies in the "thought and feeling" of Ignatius sets his letters apart from the other subapostolic writings and aligns them closely with the canonical books of the New Testament (*Ignatius von Antiochien als Christ und Theologe: Eine Dogmengeschichtliche Untersuchung* [Leipzig: J. C. Hinrichs, 1894], 11–12).

identifies Jesus as the Logos to be expressive of a sort of modalism, if not an incipiently gnostic emanationism, since he speaks of the Word's having "come forth from silence" (*Magn.* 8:2). We shall consider this question in chapter 7.

Moving down to the second step of our schema, it may be asked whether Ignatius's view of redemption is adequately rooted in a biblical understanding of creation. On the one hand, his nonpejorative "flesh and spirit" anthropology, along with his decided emphasis on the humanity of Christ, suggests an affirmative answer to this question. One might even say that he anticipates Irenaeus and Aquinas in according such importance to the material creation. On the other hand, Ignatius never explicitly refers to God the Father as Creator, and his one fleeting allusion to the creation of the world seems to identify Christ as the sole agent of creation (*Eph.* 15:1). Does he, then, view the Logos as a demiurge? In addition, his frequent references to Satan as "the ruler of this aeon," his occasional allusions to cosmic warfare, and the seemingly irreconcilable hostility he posits between God and "the world," taken together may seem to smack of cosmic dualism. This issue will be broached in chapter 4.

Descending to the bottom step of the schema, we encounter the problem that Ignatius seems to "Christianize" the prophets and thus to lack a properly salvation-historical view of the relationship between old covenant and new covenant. His great enthusiasm for Paul and relative lack of interest in the Old Testament might even suggest that Ignatius had something in common with his younger contemporary Marcion of Pontus. While he certainly stops short of Marcionism, Ignatius is generally taken to be a supersessionist who denigrates Israel's covenant with God. This difficulty will be addressed in chapter 6.

Ascending to the level at which we distinguish between the life of Christ and the life of the church, a host of interesting questions and several potential problems emerge, of which we may mention just a few here. While Ignatius speaks often enough of Jesus' death and resurrection "for us," he has an underdeveloped hamartiology and says nothing of atonement as such. Moreover, many have found him to use words such as "flesh," "faith," and "justify" in a disturbingly non-Pauline fashion. This set of issues will be dealt with in chapters 4 and 5. Further difficulties surround Ignatius's ecclesiology. He seems to privilege office over charism, and his promotion of a very specific hierarchical structure for the local church (one bishop, a council of presbyters, and deacons) seems to be founded on little more than a garbled typology that correlates earthly realities with their heavenly archetypes. There is also the question of what exactly he means by "the catholic church" and how he conceives of its relation to the local churches (*Smyr.* 8:2). I shall tackle these and other ecclesiological issues in chapter 9.

Finally, with respect to the last step on our schema, which distinguishes between grace and glory, Ignatius has been criticized for promoting an individualistic, ahistorical, and radically "realized" eschatology. I shall address this issue in chapter 10.

While I hope in the following pages to rehabilitate Ignatius's reputation as a serious theologian, I am willing to concede at the outset that there are lacunae and deficiencies in his theology, even after we have taken account of the fact that we are dealing with a tiny corpus of occasional documents of a pastoral nature. His emphasis on economy over theology and on redemption over creation is so lopsided that it is only on the basis of a handful of mostly incidental references that we can even demonstrate that his view of the economy of redemption presupposes some appreciation for the realm of θεολογία and for the order of creation. Because two of his letters deal directly with the Judaizing heresy, we have more to go on when it comes to his view of the relationship between old and new covenants, but the difficulties on this score are no less real. He judges the old covenant rituals to be intrinsically "good" (*Phld.* 9:1–2) but ultimately fails to articulate their role in the economy of redemption. As a Roman Catholic I find Ignatius's ecclesiology and his teaching on faith and love to be less problematic than many Protestant scholars do, but I wish to distance myself from the exaggerated claims sometimes made for him in popular "Catholic apologetics."[24] Ignatius says nothing about apostolic succession, and his *Letter to the Romans* hardly lends unambiguous support to Roman, much less papal, primacy.[25] If Ignatius knew there to be a sole bishop over the church in Rome, his failure to greet or even mention him—after having gushed over the bishops of Ephesus, Magnesia, Tralles, Philadelphia, and Smyrna—must be judged one of the great gaffes in epistolary history.[26]

---

24. E.g., Stephen K. Ray, *Upon This Rock: St. Peter and the Primacy of Rome in Scripture and the Early Church* (San Francisco: Ignatius Press, 1999), 72, 121–22, 132–44.

25. For an even-handed treatment of this question, see James F. McCue, "The Roman Primacy in the Second Century and the Problem of the Development of Dogma," *Theological Studies* 25 (1964): 171–75.

26. Ignatius would not likely have had access to the sort of current information about the church of Rome that he possessed with regard to the churches in southwest Asia Minor, but one

Naturally, most of the lacunae in Ignatius's theology are just the sort we should expect to find in an author of the early second century. If, for example, he refers constantly to the Father and the Son but only now and then to the Holy Spirit, what near contemporary of his does not similarly suffer from an underdeveloped pneumatology? Indeed, what has more often than not surprised modern scholars about Ignatius is not what he omits but how much he does say and how developed certain aspects of his theology are vis-à-vis the New Testament. His Christology explicitly thematizes the coincidence of humanity and divinity in Christ. He is the first to use the noun πάθος to refer to the "passion" as a distinct event. He confesses the eucharist to be the flesh and blood of Christ. He is the first on record to promote monepiscopacy and the first to speak of "Christianity" and "the catholic church." It is in part the advanced nature of Ignatius's theology that has led some scholars to hypothesize that his letters are actually forgeries from a later period.[27] All such hypotheses have been convincingly refuted, however, and Ignatius's place within the first three decades or so of the second century is secure. From within that historical context he occupies an important place in the history of theology. Together with the other apostolic fathers but foremost among them, he represents an important link between the New Testament and the later church fathers.

Despite the lacunae in Ignatius's thought, he possesses, as I hope to demonstrate, a fundamentally coherent and cohesive theology that represents an imperfect but nonetheless valuable grasp of the whole. He has, in other words, a sense of the *analogia fidei*, that is, "the coherence of the truths of the faith among themselves and within the whole plan of revelation."[28] Even and especially where Ignatius's letters present theological difficulties, they elicit just the sort of questions that help one contemplate the economy of redemption as a whole. As noted in the introduction, in Ignatius's letters we glimpse theology in its embryonic or "infolded" stage. Not only have exegesis, dogmatics, pastoral theology,

---

would certainly expect him to have included some generic greeting or commendation of the Roman bishop, unless he had some reason to doubt that the church in Rome had by this time embraced a monepiscopal structure. Cf. Lightfoot, *Ignatius, Polycarp*, 1.398–99. According to traditional lists, Alexander I would have been bishop of Rome at the time of Ignatius's martyrdom (cf. Eusebius, *Historia ecclesiastica* 4:1, 4).

27. This argument plays a major role, for example, in the hypothesis of Robert Joly, according to which all seven letters were forged at Smyrna in the late second century (*Le dossier d'Ignace d'Antioche*, Université libre de Bruxelles, Faculté de philosophie et lettres 69 [Brussels: Éditions de l'Université de Bruxelles, 1979]).

28. CCC 114.

and mystical theology not yet been separated out from each other at this stage, but even within what will later be delimited as the realm of dogmatics the various elements of the economy of redemption cohere and interpenetrate in the compact unity of the one *mysterium fidei*.

The point is not that the later unfolding of this mystery is a regrettable development. Quite to the contrary, it is a sure sign of the church's vitality. The presence of the Holy Spirit guarantees both faithful preservation of the *depositum fidei* and authentic theological and doctrinal development. But development is only authentic to the extent that theology ceaselessly renews itself by its *recursus ad fontes*, its return, that is, to the more or less "infolded" expressions of theology in the writings of the church fathers, and above all to the remarkably compact unity of Scripture itself. Of all the subapostolic authors, Ignatius is arguably the closest to Scripture in this regard. His letters do not echo the books of the future New Testament as precisely or frequently as does Polycarp's *Letter to the Philippians*, but this may be because Ignatius has internalized these writings more deeply, has synthesized the principal currents of New Testament tradition (Pauline, Johannine, and Synoptic), and knows how to express himself, not just in apostolic words, but "in the apostolic character" (*Tral.* sal.).[29]

Ignatius and the New Testament

This claim raises the question of which early Christian writings Ignatius actually knew. As this issue is an important prolegomenon to my project, I would like to dwell on it here. The minimalist position holds that Ignatius had read 1 Corinthians and possibly one or two other Pauline letters and that he had some familiarity with oral traditions akin to the canonical gospels of Matthew and John.[30] My working hypothesis is

---

29. Noting that Ignatius's allusions to the later New Testament writings "flow from his pen as though the words were his own," Milton Perry Brown concludes that Ignatius "appears to be characteristically independent as a thinker and writer. His obligations are relatively few, as far as we can now determine, and even those few are very intimately and for the most part appropriately woven into the fabric of his thought. He seems to have assimilated much of the Pauline viewpoint and certain of Paul's expressions, but still, when they are run through the mill of his own mind, they come out in his letters as [Ignatius] and not Paul" (*The Authentic Writings of Ignatius: A Study of Linguistic Criteria* [Durham, N.C.: Duke University Press, 1963], 95).

30. Mitchell, "In the Footsteps of Paul," 27–45; Schoedel, *Ignatius of Antioch*, 9–10. Paul Foster holds that Ignatius probably knew four Pauline epistles (1 Corinthians, Ephesians, and 1–2 Timothy) and the Gospel of Matthew, but he considers his dependence on the Gospel of John far less likely ("The Epistles of Ignatius of Antioch and the Writings That Later Formed the New Testament," in Andrew F. Gregory and Christopher M. Tuckett, eds., *The Reception of the New Testa-*

that he knew the written Gospel of Matthew and very possibly also the Gospel of John, and that he had studied most, if not all, of the Pauline epistles.[31] After presenting some of the evidence for Ignatius's knowledge of Matthew and John, I will give a few examples of how he utilizes the Pauline epistles and how he synthesizes the various New Testament traditions. It is important to work with a defensible hypothesis regarding which books Ignatius knew, but such a hypothesis is illuminative of his letters only to the extent that we also cultivate a sense of *how* he uses these writings.

Ignatius's knowledge of Matthew is evident principally in the way he echoes dominical logia that are distinctive of the First Gospel.[32] Below are a few of the clearest examples, each preceded by its Matthean parallel. I have rendered these texts somewhat woodenly, so that both the similarities and the differences will be evident even in translation.

Permit it for now, for thus it is fitting for us to fulfill all righteousness. (Mt 3:15)
... baptized by John, in order that all righteousness might be fulfilled by him. (Smyr. 1:1)

Be wise as the serpents and innocent as the doves. (Mt 10:16)
Be wise as the serpent in all things and innocent as the dove. (Poly. 2:2)

---

ment in the Apostolic Fathers [New York: Oxford University Press, 2005], 159–86). Those who adopt a highly skeptical approach to this question tend to assume that they occupy the methodological high ground, but this is not necessarily so. Charles E. Hill demonstrates how Ignatius's "doctrine of the apostolate" and his several references to apostolic teaching and writing place the matter in a different light ("Ignatius and the Apostolate: The Witness of Ignatius to the Emergence of Christian Scripture," *Studia Patristica* 36 [2001]: 226–48).

31. Essentially the same position, stated more cautiously, is taken in Hermut Löhr, "The Epistles of Ignatius of Antioch," in *The Apostolic Fathers: An Introduction*, ed. Wilhelm Pratscher (Waco, Texas: Baylor University Press, 2010), 101–2. At various points in the chapters to follow I will supply indications of Ignatius's possible dependence on several other texts, including the Wisdom of Solomon, the Epistle to the Hebrews, the book of Revelation, and 1 *Clement*.

32. Partly for this reason some scholars hold that Ignatius used a pre-Matthean version of the special "M" source rather than canonical Matthew (J. Smit Sibinga, "Ignatius and Matthew," *Novum Testamentum* 8 [1966]: 263–83; Christine Trevett, "Approaching Matthew from the Second Century: The Under-Used Ignatian Correspondence," *Journal for the Study of the New Testament* 20 [1984]: 59–67). Three considerations especially tell against this unnecessarily complicated hypothesis: (1) The strongest parallel between Matthew and Ignatius (Mt 3:15; Smyr. 1:1b) is clearly from Matthew's redaction of Mark, not from "M"; (2) in all significant parallels, the differences between Matthew and Ignatius are easily explained in terms of Ignatius's adaptation of the given saying to his epistolary context; and (3) we have every reason to believe that the Gospel of Matthew, which many scholars believe to have originated in Antioch, had been in circulation for at least twenty years at the time of Ignatius's journey to Rome, whereas we have no evidence or reason to believe that a "pre-Matthean" version of "M" was still in circulation (if it ever was widely circulated).

For from the fruit the tree is known. (Mt 12:33)
Manifest is the tree by its fruit. (Eph. 14:2)

Every planting that my heavenly Father has not planted will be uprooted. (Mt 15:13)
For they are not a planting of the Father. (Tral. 11:1; cf. Phld. 3:1)

Let the one who can accept, accept. (Mt 19:12)
Let the one who accepts, accept. (Smyr. 6:1)

... and he bore [our] diseases [καὶ τὰς νόσους ἐβάστασεν]. (Mt 8:17)
Bear the diseases of all [πάντων τὰς νόσους βάσταζε]. (Poly. 1:3)[33]

While Ignatius never quotes Matthew verbatim, the differences are slight, and most of them can easily be explained in terms of Ignatius's adaptation of a given saying to his specific purpose. In the first passage cited above, for example, he makes the grammatical changes necessary to incorporate the Lord's words to John the Baptist into one of his creed-like formulations. Similarly, in the second passage he changes plurals to singulars because he is addressing Polycarp individually, and he adds "in all things" in order to insist on the applicability of the saying to all facets of Polycarp's ministry.

The evidence for Ignatius's direct dependence on the Gospel of John is less impressive, at least at first blush.[34] The strongest echo is the following.

... but you know not whence it [the Spirit] comes or whither it goes. (Jn 3:8)

... for it [the Spirit] knows whence it comes and whither it goes. (Phld. 7:1)

---

33. This is not a dominical logion but does constitute a striking parallel. Matthew quotes Is 53:4 in a form quite different from LXX, so that Ignatius's echo cannot be explained as his independent use of the latter (cf. Lightfoot, *Ignatius, Polycarp*, 2.334). For details, see Maarten J. J. Menken, "The Source of the Quotation from Isaiah 53:4 in Matthew 8:17," *Novum Testamentum* 39 (1997): 313–27.

34. The most thorough and carefully argued studies of this question have come down strongly on the side of Ignatius's literary dependence on the Fourth Gospel: see Paul Dietze, "Die Briefe des Ignatius und das Johannesevangelium," *Theologische Studien und Kritiken* 78 (1905): 563–603; Walter J. Burghardt, "Did Saint Ignatius of Antioch Know the Fourth Gospel?" *Theological Studies* 1 (1940): 1–26, 130–56 (Burghardt leaves open the slight possibility that Ignatius was familiar with John's thought by way of oral tradition or a Johannine School [156]); Christian Maurer, *Ignatius von Antiochien und das Johannesevangelium*, Abhandlungen zur Theologie des Alten und Neuen Testaments 18 (Zurich: Zwingli Verlag, 1949), 100; and Charles E. Hill, *The Johannine Corpus in the Early Church* (Oxford: Oxford University Press, 2004), 421–43. Paul Foster's recent examination of the question, which concludes that "Ignatius' use of the Fourth Gospel cannot be established with any degree of certainty" ("Epistles of Ignatius," 183–84), is by comparison quite brief and, frankly, superficial. For example, he discusses the relationship between Phld. 7:1 and Jn 3:8 without so much as mentioning Jn 8:14 or the possibility of a composite quotation.

Ignatius's transformation of this logion, which makes the Spirit the subject of the verbs, may have been influenced by another passage in the Fourth Gospel, where the Lord says about himself, "I know whence I have come and whither I go" (Jn 8:14). Elsewhere Ignatius uses distinctively Johannine phrases such as "living water," "the bread of God" (with eucharistic overtones), and "the gift [δωρεά] of God," as well as the more vaguely Johannine expression "the door of the Father."[35] The imagery of shepherd, sheep, and wolves in *Philadelphians* 2:1–2 is reminiscent of John 10:11–14. Ignatius's affirmation that "the Lord did nothing apart from the Father" echoes not only the diction but one of the central ideas of the Fourth Gospel.[36] In the same context Ignatius explicitly affirms Christ's preexistence "with the Father," refers to him as God's "Logos," and says that he "pleased the one who sent him in all things."[37] As I will demonstrate in chapter 3, it is especially in *Magnesians* 6–8 that Ignatius utilizes the basic Johannine summary of the Christ event: The Son came forth from the Father, accomplished the will of the Father, and returned to the Father. Ultimately, answering the question whether Ignatius knew the written Gospel of John or only Johannine oral tradition is not as important as the recognition that Johannine theology has deeply penetrated his thinking about the mystery of redemption.

The fact that Ignatius never explicitly cites either the Gospel of Matthew or the Gospel of John, and that not one of his apparent echoes of these books reproduces an entire logion verbatim, does not amount to a convincing argument against the hypothesis that he had read these two gospels. The fact is, apart from two citations from the book of Proverbs, each introduced with the formula "it is written" (γέγραπται), Ignatius never explicitly cites any text.[38] His modus operandi is not to cite authoritative texts but to adapt and weave them into the fabric of his own discourse. This is especially true of his use of the Pauline letters. No one doubts that Ignatius knew 1 Corinthians, and yet he never explicitly cites it and never reproduces an extended statement from it in precisely Paul's words.

The easiest explanation for this phenomenon of inexact borrowing

---

35. "Living water": *Rom.* 7:2 (Jn 4:10, 7:38). "Bread of God": *Eph.* 5:2; *Rom.* 7:3 (Jn 6:33). "Gift of God": *Smyr.* 7:1 (Jn 4:10). "Door of the Father": *Phld.* 9:1 (cf. Jn 10:7 and 9, 14:6).

36. *Magn.* 7:1; cf. Jn 5:19, 8:28.

37. *Magn.* 6:1, 8:2; cf. Jn 1:1, 8:29.

38. He cites Prv 3:34 at *Eph.* 5:3 and Prv 18:17 at *Magn.* 12:1. On the nonexplicit citation of Is 52:5 at *Tral.* 8:2, see Schoedel, *Ignatius of Antioch*, 150–51.

is that Ignatius was quoting from memory, which is probably true in any case. While I do not ascribe to the view that Ignatius dashed off his letters in such "extreme haste" that he was not always quite sure what he was saying,[39] it is reasonable to suppose that what time he did find for epistolary composition during the stopovers at Smyrna and Troas would not have been best spent thumbing through copies of the gospels or Paul's epistles (even assuming such were available) in order to secure the exact wording of the passages he wished to utilize. Some of the incidental differences between Ignatius's borrowings and his source texts (e.g., inconsequential variations in word order and the use of synonyms) may indeed be the result of imperfect memorization.

Still, if Ignatius's utilization of New Testament sources is not a matter of verbatim repetition, neither can it be characterized as sloppy. It is actually rather precise and quite sophisticated, as is evident especially when Ignatius draws together words and phrases from two or three source texts in composing a single statement. I would like to demonstrate this point with a few examples.

The first line of *Philadelphians* 8:2 affords a convenient place to begin.

παρακαλῶ δὲ ὑμᾶς μηδὲν κατ' ἐριθείαν πράσσειν, ἀλλὰ κατὰ χριστομαθίαν.

I exhort you to do nothing out of factiousness but according to the learning of Christ.

This carefully crafted statement is composed of three pieces. The first piece, the phrase παρακαλῶ δὲ ὑμᾶς ("I exhort you"), is an expression characteristic of Paul. With minor variations it occurs twelve times in Paul's letters and is placed in Paul's mouth by Luke in Acts 27:34.[40] The verb παρακαλῶ admits of a range of senses, but C. E. B. Cranfield underscores the special "note of authority" it conveys in Paul's letters, where it often serves "as a technical term for Christian exhortation, the earnest appeal, based on the gospel, to those who are already believers to live consistently with the gospel they have received."[41] This is also how the term is normally used by Ignatius,[42] whose letters are essentially authori-

---

39. Lightfoot, *Ignatius, Polycarp*, 2.159.

40. Rom 12:1, 15:30, 16:17; 1 Cor 1:10, 4:16, 16:15; 2 Cor 2:8, 10:1; Eph 4:1; 1 Thes 4:10, 5:14; and Phlm 10. The only other New Testament occurrence is at Heb 13:22.

41. C. E. B. Cranfield, *A Critical and Exegetical Commentary on the Epistle to the Romans*, International Critical Commentary (Edinburgh: T. & T. Clark, 1979), 597. The verb occasionally has this technical sense elsewhere in the New Testament (Acts 11:23, 14:22, 15:32, 16:40, 20:1–2; Heb 3:13, 10:25).

42. Eph. 3:2; Magn. 14:1; Tral. 6:1, 12:2; Poly. 1:2, 7:3.

tative exhortations to pursue Christian authenticity. The second piece, the phrase μηδὲν κατ' ἐριθείαν ("nothing according to factiousness"), is taken verbatim from Philippians 2:3, where it is part of the preamble to the famous kenosis hymn (2:6–11). Ignatius has added the word πράσσειν ("do") in order to fill out the sense of Paul's characteristically elliptical expression. This infinitive serves as the grammatical complement of παρακαλῶ and thus also has the effect of stitching together the first two parts of Ignatius's statement.

The noun ἐριθεία is difficult to translate inasmuch as it combines the idea of "selfish ambition" with that of "factiousness."[43] The link between these two aspects of its meaning is that one who seeks political office or a position of ecclesiastical leadership out of self-interested motives tends thereby to cause divisions within a community. For Paul the term thus denotes a self-seeking spirit of divisiveness that runs directly counter to the "mind of Christ" as expressed in the kenosis hymn. Ignatius understands Paul's words in exactly this way and borrows them to express the concern that lies at the very heart of his letters to the churches of Asia Minor. While still in Philadelphia, he exhorted the community to "love unity" and "flee divisions" (Phld. 7:2), not simply because the love of unity has the pragmatic consequence of keeping a community together, but because it is a disposition that places one close to the heart of God. The "unity" that Ignatius wishes to inculcate in the Philadelphians is no less than a participation in the "unity of God" (8:1, 9:1). By the same token, "division" is not simply a practical problem but a defective condition of the human heart and of the community that will render the indwelling presence of God impossible (8:1).

The third and final piece of the statement that we are analyzing is the phrase ἀλλὰ κατὰ χριστομαθίαν ("but according to the learning of Christ"). Here Ignatius does not so much borrow Paul's words as summarize one of his major ideas. The word χριστομαθία is an Ignatian coinage, and a brilliant one. It denotes learning that has the person of Christ as its object, or in other words, discipleship to Christ. Ignatius's immediate Pauline inspiration for coining this word was no doubt Ephesians 4:20, where an elaborate description of the darkened mind and debauched life of the pagan is followed by this clause: "but you did not thus learn Christ" (ὑμεῖς δὲ οὐχ οὕτως ἐμάθετε Χριστόν). Christian catechesis is not merely a matter of learning *about* Christ but of learning the

---

43. BDAG, 392; Ceslas Spicq, *Theological Lexicon of the New Testament*, trans. and ed. James D. Ernest, 3 vols. (Peabody, Mass.: Hendrickson, 1994), 2.70–72.

person of Christ and how to live in him. Christian morality is not merely a matter of conforming to the commands of Christ but of "having the mind that was in Christ" and of assimilating his character. Ignatius has summarized all this in a single word, which he has fashioned as the perfect antonym for ἐριθεία.

The terms χριστομαθία and ἐριθεία denote the two fundamentally opposed modes of existence between which the Philadelphians must choose. Like other early Christian writers, Ignatius recognizes that "there are two ways, one of life and one of death, and a great difference between the two ways."[44] While Ignatius uses the term χριστομαθία only once, he refers to authentic Christian existence by means of similar expressions elsewhere. He calls it "living according to Jesus Christ," "becoming a disciple [μαθητής] of Jesus Christ," "learning to live according to Christianity," and "living according to the Lord's day."[45] Since Ignatius sees divine revelation to lie at the center of the economy of redemption and views Jesus Christ as "our only teacher" (*Magn.* 9:1), it is none too surprising that he thinks of the Christian life as fundamentally a matter of "learning Christ." And while doctrine plays an essential role in this life of learning, Ignatius is promoting no mere intellectualism but rather a holistic Christianity in which intellect, will, affectivity, words, and actions are all deeply integrated. This will become particularly clear when we examine his use of the terms "faith" and "love" in chapter 5.

As a second example of Ignatius's creative recombination of New Testament materials, we may consider a portion of an oracle that he delivered in the assembly at Philadelphia.

| μιμηταὶ γίνεσθε Ἰησοῦ Χριστοῦ | Be imitators of Jesus Christ, |
| ὡς καὶ αὐτὸς τοῦ πατρὸς αὐτοῦ. | even as he is of his Father. (Phld. 7:2) |

This is the third of three rhyming couplets in a quasi-poetic text that amounts to a précis of Ignatius's preaching. The idea that we find in the first half of the couplet, that Christians are to be "imitators of God" and "imitators of the Lord," occurs frequently in Ignatius's letters and is likely a borrowing from the Pauline epistles.[46] On the other hand, the precise notion that we find in the second half of the couplet, that Jesus himself was an "imitator" of the Father, is to my knowledge unparalleled in early Christian literature, though it certainly recalls the words of the

---

44. Did. 1:1; cf. Barn. 18:1; Magn. 5:1.
45. Tral. 2:1; Phld. 3:2; Rom. 4:2; Magn. 9:1, 10:1.
46. Eph. 1:1, 10:3; Tral. 1:2; Rom. 6:3; cf. Eph 5:1; 1 Thes 1:6; 1 Cor 11:1.

Johannine Jesus: "Amen, amen, I say to you, the Son can do nothing of himself, but only what he sees the Father do."⁴⁷ Evidently, then, Ignatius has taken the Johannine concept of the Son's dependence on the Father and rephrased it in the Pauline language of "imitation," and this translation of the Johannine idea into Pauline diction has facilitated its being coupled with the Pauline idea that Christians are to be imitators of the Lord Jesus.

Further, the structure of Ignatius's couplet, as well as the generic notion of *imitating the imitator*, seems to derive from a specific passage in Ignatius's favorite Pauline letter: "Be imitators of me, even as I am of Christ" (μιμηταί μου γίνεσθε, καθὼς κἀγὼ Χριστοῦ).⁴⁸ Unlike Paul, Ignatius does not ask his readers to imitate him, but instead asks them to imitate the Lord Jesus just as the latter imitated the Father. As we shall see in chapter 3, the idea that our relationship to Jesus parallels his relationship to the Father, and that we thus relate to the Father through Jesus, is found throughout Ignatius's letters and constitutes one of the most basic building blocks in his theology of unity. It is a characteristically Johannine idea, which Ignatius has wedded to the Pauline notion of *imitatio Christi*. The resulting lapidary formula—"Be imitators of Jesus Christ, as he is of the Father"—affords a fine example of the way "two spiritual 'currents' converge in Ignatius," the Pauline and the Johannine.⁴⁹

Like other early Christian writers, Ignatius also drew upon sources that would ultimately not make it into the New Testament. In composing the following narrative he appears to have reworked and recombined a variety of canonical and noncanonical materials.

And when [the risen Jesus] came to those around Peter, he said to them, "Take, handle me, and see that I am not a bodiless phantom." And immediately they touched him and believed, being mingled with his flesh and spirit. (*Smyr*. 3:2)

The verb "he came" (ἦλθεν) and the imperative "take" (λάβετε) recall the Johannine account of Jesus' first appearance to the disciples in the

---

47. Jn 5:19; cf. 5:30; 8:28 and 38.
48. 1 Cor 11:1. If we compare the first part of this statement (μιμηταί μου γίνεσθε) with the first half of Ignatius's couplet (μιμηταὶ γίνεσθε Ἰησοῦ Χριστοῦ), we see that even the change in word order (placing γίνεσθε immediately after μιμηταί) is purposeful, since it enables Ignatius's couplet to rhyme (Χριστοῦ ... αὐτοῦ).
49. Pope Benedict XVI, *Church Fathers: From Clement of Rome to Augustine* (San Francisco: Ignatius Press, 2008), 2. The basic idea that we are to relate to Jesus as he related to the Father is also found in the Epistle to the Hebrews, which solemnly affirms that Jesus "learned obedience through what he suffered" and thus "became the cause of eternal salvation for all who obey him" (Heb 5:8–9).

locked room (Jn 20:19–23), while the reference to the disciples as "those around Peter" (τοὺς περὶ Πέτρον) occurs elsewhere only in the canonically marginal "shorter ending" to the Gospel of Mark, where it is found in a similar context. The phrase "handle me and see" (ψηλαφήσατέ με καὶ ἴδετε) is found verbatim also in Luke 24:39, but since Ignatius nowhere else shows dependence on Luke, he may have known the phrase from another source. Origen tells us that the logion "I am not a bodiless phantom" (οὐκ εἰμὶ δαιμόνιον ἀσώματον) goes back to the *Doctrine of Peter*, while Jerome identifies it as coming from the *Gospel of the Hebrews*.[50] In any case, Ignatius no doubt chose this phrase, which has no close parallel in the canonical gospels, because it served his antidocetic polemic so well. The next statement, "And immediately they touched him and believed," looks like Ignatius's own free reworking and generalized summary of the Johannine appearance to Thomas (Jn 20:24–29). It may be aimed at countering those gospel traditions that suggest that the disciples were "still unbelieving" even after having seen the risen Lord, or that they never actually touched him.[51] The diction and thought of the narrative's final phrase, "being mingled with his flesh and spirit," is thoroughly Ignatian.[52]

Other examples of Ignatius's recombination and synthesis of source materials will be provided sporadically throughout this volume, where and when they serve our primary goal of exploring the economy of redemption in the light of Ignatius's letters. The point of the foregoing

---

50. For the relevant texts, see Kurt Aland, ed., *Synopsis Quattuor Evangeliorum: Locis parallelis evangeliorum apocryphorum et partum adhibitis*, 14th ed. (Stuttgart: Deutsche Bibelgesellschaft, 1995), § 356 (pp. 502–3), and for discussion, see Lightfoot, *Ignatius, Polycarp*, 2.294–96; and Schoedel, *Ignatius of Antioch*, 226–27. Pier Franco Beatrice argues vigorously for regarding all of *Smyr.* 3:1–2 as a direct quote from the *Gospel of the Hebrews* ("The 'Gospel according to the Hebrews' in the Apostolic Fathers," *Novum Testamentum* 48 [2006]: 147–63). His insistence that this already tenuous hypothesis, which he considers "impossible to refute," should be "the starting point" for assessing "all the evangelical and apocryphal material available in Ignatius's epistles" (163) is methodologically unsound, and his macrohypothesis (163–95), which makes all four canonical gospels, the apostolic fathers, Justin Martyr, and Melito of Sardis largely dependent for their Jesus material on but two sources—the Aramaic *Gospel of the Hebrews* (= Aramaic *Gospel of Matthew* = *Gospel of the Nazoraeans* = *Gospel of the Ebionites*) and the Greek *Gospel of Peter* (= *Kerygma Petrou* = *Didaskalia Petrou* = *Secret Gospel of Mark*)—is beyond the pale of plausibility.

51. Lk 24:41; Mt 28:17. Both Luke and John say that Jesus "showed" the disciples his wounds, and both place the accent on what the disciples "saw" (Lk 24:39–40; Jn 20:20). Neither says that they "touched" him. Even John's account of the appearance to Thomas leaves the impression that in the end the doubting disciple needed only to "see," not actually to touch the Lord's wounds, in order to believe (20:27–29). On the other hand, Ignatius's affirmation finds a kind of support in Matthew's statement that the women who encountered Jesus as they returned from the empty tomb "laid hold of his feet" (Mt 28:9; cf. Jn 20:17).

52. Cf. *Eph.* 5:1; *Magn.* 1:2.

demonstration is not to insist that Ignatius was consciously thinking in terms of splicing together specific source texts as he composed his letters. On the contrary, what we find in the letters suggests a procedure that is by no means artificial or mechanical but a mode of theological discourse born of years of study, meditation, and preaching. Ignatius pondered the mystery of Christ with an active and creative intellect. "I think about many things in God," he tells the Christians at Tralles (*Tral.* 4:1). As various authoritative texts cross-pollinated in his mind, it probably became second nature for him to synthesize the ideas of Paul, John, Matthew, and others. It should also be noted that Ignatius was not overly dependent on the theological vocabulary and formulations of any of these authors. He speaks in his own voice and expresses many original insights. As the apostolic traditions were sown deeply in his mind, verbal echoes of New Testament materials appear as an organic element in his discourse. Above all, it must be recognized that the principle of synthesis in Ignatius's theology is not his or anyone else's words or ideas, but the mystery of Christ itself. Pondering the "things" (*res*) of redemption made Ignatius's theological reflection fruitful.

An Old Testament Allusion

To round out this chapter, let us return to the question of Ignatius's regard for the Scriptures of Israel. Because the bishop of Antioch does not quote the Old Testament often, and especially because he does not seem to have accepted the Philadelphian Judaizers' challenge to supply exegetical proofs for his opinions on disputed matters, many scholars simply assume that he lacked skill in the area of Old Testament exegesis. This is an erroneous assumption, however. First, as explained above, Ignatius has a good theological reason for not meeting the Judaizers on their own turf. His identification of the person and event of Jesus Christ as the true "archives" is not an evasive tactic but the indispensable foundation for Christian exegesis of the Old Testament. Second, Ignatius uses the Old Testament more extensively than is generally recognized. In the Ignatian corpus of letters we find two explicit citations, one nonexplicit citation, three patent allusions, and several other statements that reflect at least a general knowledge of the Old Testament.[53] Third, while two of the cita-

---

53. See Eph. 5:3 (explicit citation of Prv 3:34), 15:1 (double allusion to Ps 33:9 and Gn 1:3), 19:2–3 (possible dependence on Gn 37:5–11 and several passages from the Wisdom of Solomon), *Magn.* 8:2 (description of the ministry of Israel's prophets), 9:2 (reference to the prophets), 12:1

tions are conventional, the other passages display originality and skill. I shall give one example here, with others to follow in later chapters.

Ignatius exhorts the church at Magnesia,

Be earnest, therefore, to be confirmed in the ordinances of the Lord and of the apostles, in order that *in all that you do you may prosper*, in flesh and spirit, in faith and love, in the Son and the Father and in the Spirit, in the beginning and in the end.... (*Magn.* 13:1)

The words in italics are taken verbatim from Psalm 1:3, except that Ignatius has altered the inflection of the verbs to fit his context. He is well aware that this psalm is an exhortation to study and observe "the law of the Lord" (i.e., the Mosaic law) day and night (1:2) and that "prospering in all one does" is the result that the psalmist promises to the person who takes this advice. Ignatius, however, has removed this advice and promise from the context of the "old practices" of Judaism and transposed it to the "newness of hope" found in Christianity (*Magn.* 9:1). He counsels diligent study and observance of "the ordinances of the Lord and of the apostles," a phrase that in all likelihood refers to written documents such as the Gospel of Matthew and the epistles of Paul.[54] While these texts have not yet acquired their full canonical status, they are already beginning to take precedence over the law and the prophets in the letters of Ignatius (as also in Polycarp's *Philippians*).

Ignatius, moreover, has given some serious thought to why this should be so. He views the relationship between Judaism and Christianity, not in terms of a sharp contrast between law and freedom, but, as we shall see in chapter 6, in carefully nuanced terms of old and new, good and better, and imperfect and perfect. The "grace of God" that has come into the world does not represent a departure from law as such but has its effect in and through "the law of Jesus Christ" (*Magn.* 2:1). This new law is now the "law of the Lord" that the Christian should study day and night. This does not mean, however, that the law of Moses and the books of the prophets have been replaced or rendered obsolete. Rather, they have been taken up into the new and more perfect dynamic of the gospel (*Smyr.* 5:1).

(explicit citation of Prv 18:17), 13:1 (allusion to Ps 1:3); *Tral.* 8:2 (nonexplicit citation of Is 52:5); *Phld.* 5:2 (reference to the prophets), 8:2 (disagreement over the "archives"), 9:1–2 (references to Israel's priests, high priest, patriarchs, and prophets); *Smyr.* 1:2 (composite allusion to Is 5:26, 11:10, 49:22, 62:10), 5:1 (reference to "the prophecies and the law of Moses"), 7:2 (reference to the books of the prophets). Ignatius thus draws on the Old Testament in the five heavily theological letters, and especially in the two letters that polemicize against Judaizers.

54. Hill, "Ignatius and the Apostolate," 234–48.

Ignatius's delicate allusion to Psalm 1 in *Magnesians* 13 is suggestive of the way the old Scriptures may be taken up into the fabric of Christian parenesis and transformed in the process. This passage hardly represents a "denigration" of the Old Testament. In the immediately preceding verse Ignatius quotes a line from the book of Proverbs as authoritative Scripture, introducing it with the formula: "As it is written ..." (12:1), and here he takes up a line from Psalm 1 ("all that he does will prosper") in a manner that reflects both an awareness of its Old Testament context (where it is linked to the study of "the law of the Lord") and of its transformation in the new context of the gospel. Israel's Scriptures have been subordinated to "the ordinances of the Lord and of the apostles" and, even more so, to the person and event of Jesus Christ, who is the true "archives" (Phld. 8:2), but by being subordinated in this way they have been taken into a higher reality and thus raised to a new level. The "law of the Lord" has become the "law of Jesus Christ."

ISSUES IN IGNATIAN SCHOLARSHIP

Because God has revealed himself and redeemed humanity in and through a historical economy, the true theologian will want to make use of every legitimate means of access to that reality. Sifting through the mountains of accumulated textual, linguistic, and historical research into early Christianity, while developing a hermeneutic that will enable one to bring this research into a fruitful dialogue with the wisdom of the ancients and medievals, may be a laborious task, but it is indispensable to the theological endeavor in our day. Each age makes its own contribution to the advancement of human knowledge and thus "necessarily poses new questions to the Christian tradition."[1] An attempt to sidestep these questions by divorcing theology from history would be disastrous.

Anyone who doubts the value of historical-critical research into the Bible and early Christianity ought to look into what has been accomplished in the case of Ignatius of Antioch. For the better part of church history, from the fourth century to the early seventeenth, the letters of Ignatius circulated primarily in a heavily interpolated "long recension" and were accompanied by six forged letters. After three centuries of manuscript discoveries and debate, during which the "middle" and "short" recensions were published, scholars of the late nineteenth century, led by Theodor Zahn and J. B. Lightfoot, arrived at a consensus that affirms the authenticity of seven (and only seven) letters, identifies the middle recension as that which most nearly approximates their original

---

1. Francis Martin, *The Feminist Question: Feminist Theology in the Light of Christian Tradition* (Grand Rapids, Mich.: Eerdmans, 1994), 174.

Greek text, and reaffirms Ignatius of Antioch's identity as a historical figure of the early second century.[2] This Lightfoot-Zahn consensus has been challenged several times, including very recently, but appears to be more securely founded than ever.[3] Accordingly, it forms a working presupposition of the present volume. Textual criticism of Ignatius's letters, building on the foundation of Lightfoot's magisterial work, has continued to advance over the past 125 years with the discovery of a previously unknown Arabic version and of a fifth-century papyrus codex that contains most of *Smyrnaeans* in the Greek middle recension. Our understanding of Ignatius's Greek usage has been aided, not only by advances in Greek lexicography as such, but by a vast body of new information about the historical context and cultural-religious milieu in which he lived and wrote. This textual, lexical, and historical research has in turn served as the groundwork for hundreds of valuable studies of aspects of Ignatius's thought. It is no exaggeration to say that the vast majority of what we know about Ignatius and his letters has been learned over the last four centuries, and that this is largely the fruit of the historical-critical method.[4]

Obviously, none of this means that we should accept the views of modern Ignatian scholarship uncritically. I have begun to engage this scholarship appreciatively but critically in chapter 1 and will continue to do so throughout the volume. The present chapter will take up three major issues that require extensive treatment before we move ahead with our theological interpretation of the letters. The first of these concerns Ignatius's epistolary style, which in my opinion has been significantly underestimated and misunderstood, contributing to a general undervaluation of his ability as a theologian. The second issue is Ignatius's

---

2. Theodor Zahn, *Ignatius von Antiochien* (Gotha: Perthes, 1873); Lightfoot, *Ignatius, Polycarp*.

3. For summaries and able refutations of the most prominent forgery theories proffered since the time of Lightfoot, see Hammond Bammel, "Ignatian Problems," 62–79; William R. Schoedel, "Are the Letters of Ignatius of Antioch Authentic?" *Religious Studies Review* 6 (1980): 196–201; and Brent, *Ignatius of Antioch*, 95–143. Recently Roger Parvus has argued that the letters were written in the middle of the second century by a follower of Apelles, the erstwhile disciple of Marcion, and then heavily reworked by a "proto-Catholic" editor/interpolator (*A New Look at the Letters of Ignatius of Antioch and Other Apellean Writings* [Bloomington, Ind.: iUniverse, 2008]). Parvus's methodology is arbitrary in the extreme. First, any phrases, words, or parts of words that do not fit Apellean doctrine are assigned to the editor/interpolator. Then, wherever it is difficult to explain why the editor/interpolator would have made such an addition to the text, Parvus simply describes it as a "clumsy" insertion (cf. 3, 4, 8, 10, 21, 25, 31, etc.). This procedure could "prove" almost any redaction-critical hypothesis about almost any text.

4. For an up-to-date and judicious historical-critical introduction to the Ignatian letters, see Löhr, "Epistles of Ignatius," 91–115.

involvement with heresy. Here two questions must be dealt with: Does Ignatius confront two distinct heresies in the letters, or just one? And what, if any, relationship do his letters have to emergent gnosticism? The third issue pertains to the circumstances of Ignatius's arrest and journey to Rome and his agenda in writing the letters. Here I will summarize and critique the hypothesis of Allen Brent, whose overall approach to the letters will serve as a foil for my own.

Epistolary Style

Aphorisms

I hope to demonstrate that Ignatius of Antioch was not merely a rhetorically gifted pastor with a vibrant piety but a serious theologian, a deep thinker, and a careful author. In taking this position, I am going against the grain of much Ignatian scholarship. Even many of Ignatius's greatest admirers view him as a theological welterweight, a fuzzy thinker, and a haphazard epistolographer. According to C. C. Richardson, Ignatius's letters are "popular rather than deep," and their style is "compressed and turbulent, reflecting the brusque and impetuous nature of their author."[5] This view is romanticized by Pierre-Thomas Camelot, for whom Ignatius's letters are an utterly personal and spontaneous outpouring of the heart. *Romans* in particular is "the vibration of a soul 'constrained' by the anguish of love."[6] Similarly, according to James Moffatt, because "Ignatius becomes lyrical as he describes his personal religion," we ought not to treat his words as "theological formulas and arguments," but rather recognize that he is "speaking from his heart and experience, not caring to measure his terms."[7] Even Virginia Corwin, who takes Ignatius seriously as a theologian, accepts the oft-repeated idea that the "trying circumstances" under which Ignatius wrote his letters "would account in large measure for their lack of coherence and form." His mind "passes quickly from one suggested and only half-explicated point to another," revealing a temperament that is "vigorous, impulsive, energetic."[8] B. H.

---

5. Richardson, *Early Christian Fathers*, 74.

6. P.-Th. Camelot, *Ignace d'Antioche, Polycarpe de Smyrne: Lettres, Martyre de Polycarpe: Texte Grec, introduction, traduction et notes*, 4th ed., SC 10 (Paris: Cerf, 1969), 17 ("la vibration d'une âme «étreinte» par l'angoisse de l'amour"), alluding to *Rom.* 6:3.

7. James Moffatt, "Ignatius of Antioch—A Study in Personal Religion," *Journal of Religion* 10 (1930): 178.

8. Virginia Corwin, *St. Ignatius and Christianity in Antioch* (New Haven, Conn.: Yale University Press, 1960), 19, 21.

Streeter is less complimentary. In his view, because Ignatius was a person of "neurotic temper" who wrote "under circumstances of great nervous strain," his letters are "instinct with excitement and exaggeration, and must be interpreted with due allowance made for the mentality of the writer."[9]

It is undeniable that Ignatius's letters are characterized by abrupt transitions and are "somewhat staccato in style."[10] I am not convinced, however, that either his difficult circumstances or his supposedly fiery temperament had much to do with this. It seems to me likely that Ignatius would have written in much the same style even if he had had more leisure, and probably did in fact write in a similar style on other occasions. If the abrupt transitions in his discourse reflect an aspect of his character, this is more likely to be his intellectual humility and reserve than his alleged impetuosity and brusqueness. In any case, the salient feature of Ignatius's style is not so much abrupt transition, and certainly not "lack of coherence and form," but what Schoedel aptly terms "the peculiar density of his language."[11] Richardson is correct to describe Ignatius's letters as "compressed," but it is misleading to say they are "turbulent." Much of what appears, upon a superficial reading, to be turbulence can be accounted for by the recognition that Ignatius constructs his letters largely out of aphorisms, creedal formulations, and brief discourses or homilettes on various subjects. We shall consider each of these types of building material briefly and then look at the overall structure of one of the letters.

Ignatius was evidently a great lover of aphorisms. It is no coincidence that the two Old Testament passages he cites explicitly are from the book of Proverbs and that his echoes of the gospels consist almost entirely of adaptations of dominical logia. His great fondness for Paul's letters may in part be due to the fact that they are laced with gnomic sayings. Above all, Ignatius seems to have enjoyed fashioning his own aphorisms. As Jesus Ben Sira says, "Those who understand sayings become wise themselves and pour forth keen proverbs" (Sir 18:29). Note the use of alliteration in our first example, which gives lapidary expression to a timeless truth: "Where there is much toil, there is great gain" (ὅπου πλείων

---

9. Burnett Hillman Streeter, *The Primitive Church: Studied with Special Reference to the Origins of the Christian Ministry* (New York: Macmillan, 1929), 169.

10. Michael A. G. Haykin, "'Come to the Father': Ignatius of Antioch and His Calling to Be a Martyr," *Themelios* 32 (2007): 26.

11. Schoedel, *Ignatius of Antioch*, xiii.

κόπος, πολὺ κέρδος; Poly. 1:3). Ignatius also knows that incorporating a vivid simile into an aphorism makes it more memorable and effective: "Stand firm, like an anvil when it is struck" (3:1).

Some of Ignatius's gnomic sayings are similar in thought and structure to those found in the New Testament epistles. Here is one reminiscent of the First Letter of John: "No one who professes faith sins, nor does anyone who has acquired love hate."[12] Inviting the Smyrnaeans to withdraw their minds from speculations about angels and archons in order to give thought to performing a charitable deed for another church, Ignatius gently chides, "Since you are perfect, think also about doing perfect deeds" (τέλειοι ὄντες τέλεια καὶ φρονεῖτε; Smyr. 11:3). To which we may compare Paul's words to the Galatians: "If we live by the Spirit, let us also walk in step with the Spirit" (εἰ ζῶμεν πνεύματι, πνεύματι καὶ στοιχῶμεν; Gal 5:25).

On the other hand, some of Ignatius's finest aphorisms are highly original, slightly cryptic, and expressive of his distinctive insights into Christian existence. Explaining to the Trallians that God does not bestow upon us all the charisms and spiritual knowledge that we might like to have, lest we should become inflated with pride and miss out on the goal of our existence, Ignatius writes: "For we lack many things, in order that we may not lack God" (πολλὰ γὰρ ἡμῖν λείπει, ἵνα θεοῦ μὴ λειπώμεθα; Tral. 5:2). Alluding perhaps to Paul's contrast between rhetorical persuasion (πεισμονή) and the power of the gospel, Ignatius reminds the Romans, "The work is not one of persuasion; rather, Christianity achieves its greatness when it is hated by the world."[13] This statement combines Ignatius's concern for human authenticity (words are futile unless completed by actions) with his development of the Johannine teaching that Christianity only overcomes the world by suffering at its hands.[14] Evidently Ignatius does not mean, however, that Christians are not to employ the art of persuasion, for Romans itself is a rhetorical masterpiece.

Much of the bumpiness one experiences reading Ignatius's letters is due to their being sprinkled with such pithy sayings. Indeed, large segments of his discourse are composed almost entirely of aphorisms. This is generally recognized with regard to the exhortation found in *Polycarp* 1:2–4:3, but it is also true, for example, of his discourse on silence and authenticity in *Ephesians* 15, which begins as follows.

---

12. Eph. 14:2; cf. 1 Jn 2:9–11, 3:6, 3:15, 4:20.
13. Rom. 3:3; cf. 1 Cor 2:4; Gal 1:10, 5:8; Schoedel, *Ignatius of Antioch*, 173.
14. These themes are developed in *Ephesians* 15 and 10, respectively.

It is better to be silent and be, than to speak and not be. Teaching is good, if the one who teaches acts. There is one teacher, who spoke and it came to be. Even the things he did in silence were worthy of the Father. (Eph. 15:1)

When Ignatius rose to speak in the Spirit to the congregation at Philadelphia, it was hardly an emotional "outburst."[15] On the contrary, he summed up his message to the churches of Asia Minor neatly in twenty-eight Greek words, arranged in three rhyming couplets.

χωρὶς τοῦ ἐπισκόπου μηδὲν ποιεῖτε,	Do nothing apart from the bishop,
τὴν σάρκα ὑμῶν ὡς ναὸν θεοῦ τηρεῖτε.	keep your flesh as a temple of God.
τὴν ἕνωσιν ἀγαπᾶτε,	Love unity,
τοὺς μερισμοὺς φεύγετε.	flee divisions.
μιμηταὶ γίνεσθε Ἰησοῦ Χριστοῦ,	Be imitators of Jesus Christ,
ὡς καὶ αὐτὸς τοῦ πατρὸς αὐτοῦ.	even as he is of his Father. (Phld. 7:2)

We have already seen how carefully crafted the third of these couplets is, and the same could be shown of the other two.

Ignatius's fondness for aphorism does not, however, reflect an inability to compose longer sentences with a coherent structure and clear meaning. The *Philadelphians* salutation, for example, has a Trinitarian structure reminiscent of the great hymn with which the Pauline Ephesians opens (1:3–14). It begins with a reference to God the Father, focuses on Jesus Christ throughout the bulk of the sentence, and closes with a reference to the Holy Spirit. This salutation, comprising a single sentence of eighty-five Greek words, establishes a tone of solemnity and adumbrates some of the themes with which Ignatius will deal in the body of the letter (e.g., unity with the bishop, presbyters, and deacons). To cite but one further example, *Magnesians* 9 contains a seventy-word rhetorical question that articulates in an effective manner Ignatius's understanding of the relationship between the rites of the old covenant (especially Sabbath observance) and what it means to live the Christian mystery. We shall have opportunity in later chapters to give both of these carefully worded sentences the attention they deserve. For the present it is enough to note that Ignatius chooses his words carefully, whether he employs a gnomic saying or composes a longer sentence. I do not wish to exaggerate the point, however. Ignatius's style never rises to the elegance of the Epistle to the Hebrews or the *Epistle to Diognetus*. His discourse is often elliptical, and not a few of his sentences suffer from anacoluthon. Recognition of these deficiencies (which are present also in Paul's undisputed

---

15. Pace Brent, *Ignatius of Antioch*, 41.

epistles) ought not, however, to blind us to the rhetorical artistry and serious theological nature of the Ignatian corpus.

Creedal Formulae

We may now consider a second building block of Ignatius's epistolography: his creedal formulae. These dense Christological formulations are embedded in every letter and occur with such variety that it is impossible to suppose that Ignatius has simply lifted them verbatim from a liturgical source. By "creedal" I mean only that they are creedlike expressions of the rule of faith. There is no reason to suppose that they are based on fixed formulations.[16] While Ignatius must be drawing on primitive kerygmatic traditions of some sort and obviously intends his creedal formulae to express the church's common faith, it seems that he has handcrafted each of these to serve its particular context. They incorporate some of his most characteristic expressions (e.g., "flesh and spirit") and are woven almost seamlessly into the fabric of his discourse. As most of Ignatius's creedal formulations will receive extended analysis in the chapters to follow, we shall look briefly at but two of them here. I have chosen one from an antidocetic letter (*Trallians*) and one from an anti-Judaizing letter (*Philadelphians*) in order to illustrate the way Ignatius adapts creedal material to different purposes.

The first example is displayed stichometrically in order to present its structure more clearly.

> Be deaf, then, when anyone speaks to you without Jesus Christ,
> the one from the stock of David, the one from Mary,
> who truly was born, and both ate and drank,
> truly was persecuted under Pontius Pilate,
> truly was crucified and died,
> while beings in heaven, on earth, and under the earth looked on;
> who also truly was raised from the dead, his Father having raised him;
> whose Father will in like manner raise us who believe in him,
> raise us in Christ Jesus, without whom we have not the true life. (*Tral.* 9:1–2)

---

16. Cf. J. N. D. Kelly, *Early Christian Creeds*, 3rd ed. (New York: Continuum, 2006), 68–70. During the second century the emergent rule of faith was fixed in outline but malleable in detail, and individual authors were evidently free to summarize it in original ways. There was a common faith, but there seems to have been no "verbally fixed confession of faith" before the fourth century (Wolfram Kinzig and Markus Vinzent, "Recent Research on the Origins of the Creed," *Journal of Theological Studies* 50 [1999]: 539). In light of recent research on the origins of the Creed (see ibid., 537), it is also noteworthy that Ignatius's Trinitarian formulae are generally found apart from the Christological passages in question here (*Eph.* 18:2 is an exception) and are less explicitly confessional in nature (9:1, 17:2; *Magn.* 13:1; *Phld.* sal.).

Ignatius has framed this creedal formula by means of an *inclusio*. The phrase "without Jesus Christ" in the first line is echoed by the words "Christ Jesus, without whom" in the final line. Ignatius warns the Trallians that the result of listening to a heretic who speaks "without Jesus Christ" is that one will end up, in fact, *without Jesus Christ* and thus without true life. Within this framing device, Ignatius lists some of the fundamental affirmations about Jesus. Unlike most of his creedal formulae, this one makes no reference to Christ's divinity or origin in God (e.g., contrast Eph. 7:2), so concerned is Ignatius to insist on Jesus' real humanity in face of those who teach that he merely "seemed to have suffered" (Tral. 10:1). The repeated use of the adverb "truly" (ἀληθῶς) is likewise characteristic of Ignatius's antidocetic polemic (cf. Smyr. 1:1–2). As a rule, Ignatius's creedal formulations focus on the two great poles of the Christ event: incarnation (conception and birth) and paschal mystery (passion, death, and resurrection). The glancing allusion here to the period between these poles, in the words "both ate and drank," serves to present the life of Jesus as a continuous whole, even as it drives home the fact of Christ's fleshly humanity. The reference to "beings in heaven, on earth, and under the earth," taken nearly verbatim from Philippians 2:10, is included for the particular benefit of the Trallians, who, like the Smyrnaeans, seem to be overly interested in astral speculations (Tral. 5:1–2). Ignatius wants them to realize that all rational beings in the cosmos, no matter how glorious or powerful, will be held accountable for how they respond to Jesus' death on the cross (cf. Smyr. 6:1). Finally, Ignatius emphasizes the link between Christ's resurrection and our own, perhaps indicating that the docetists of Asia Minor (like those whose views Paul refutes in 1 Corinthians 15) either denied the general resurrection outright or thought in terms of a merely spiritual "resurrection" (cf. 2 Tm 2:18).

Our second example shows how differently Ignatius uses creedal material when he is dealing with the Judaizing heresy.

> The priests also are good, but better is the high priest entrusted with the most holy things, who alone has been entrusted with the hidden things of God; being himself the door of the Father, through which enter Abraham and Isaac and Jacob and the prophets and the apostles and the church, all these, into the unity of God. But the gospel has a distinct advantage: the advent of the Savior, our Lord Jesus Christ, his passion, and the resurrection. For the beloved prophets proclaimed him in advance, but the gospel is the perfection of imperishability. All things together are good, if you believe with love. (Phld. 9:1–2)

Strictly speaking, the traditional creedal material in this passage is confined to the reference to Christ's advent, passion, and resurrection, a concise summary of the Christ event. Faced with the challenge presented by the Judaizing faction at Philadelphia, Ignatius supplements this core affirmation with reflection on the old covenant and its relation to the new covenant in order to present a more elongated overview of the historical economy. The antidocetic creedal formulation of *Trallians* 9, which we have just examined, certainly roots the Christ event in history, particularly with its reference to Pontius Pilate, but it alludes to the gospel's Old Testament antecedents only in its brief mention of "the stock of David." Here in *Philadelphians* 9, by contrast, Ignatius displays the sweeping panorama of salvation history, from Abraham to the contemporary church, while clearly indicating that Jesus Christ is its centerpiece. The "unity of God," which each local church finds in submission to its bishop and which belongs to the "catholic church" by virtue of its union with Jesus Christ (*Smyr.* 8:2), here discloses its historical dimension. In this text Ignatius shows some awareness of the biblical notion of one pilgrim people of God moving through history. His chief point here is that Jesus Christ provides the unique access to this unity. He is "the door of the Father."

Once again, Ignatius has employed the technique of *inclusio*, in this case framing his creedal formula with affirmations about what is "good" (καλός). He does not respond to the Judaizers' preference for the law and the prophets by denying or diminishing the divine authority of these Scriptures but shows how a Christian can recognize their essential goodness only within a proper view of the economy as a whole. Ignatius's typological argument regarding the priests and high priests of the old covenant is sophisticated and shows that he was not completely out of his depths when it came to interpreting the "archives." The relationship between priests and high priests *under* the old covenant is itself a prefigurement of the relationship *between* old covenant and new covenant. The old-covenant high priest, who alone enters the holy of holies (on the Day of Atonement), prefigures Christ, who as preexistent Son alone has access to the hidden things of God. Moreover, the economic relationship between the two covenants, which Ignatius elsewhere speaks of in the Pauline terms of "old" and "new" (*Magn.* 9:1–2), is here described in terms of "good" and "better." Both the typological argument and the contrast between "good" and "better" are reminiscent of the Epistle to the Hebrews (9:1–10) and may indicate Ignatius's dependence on that text.

Having clarified the analogical relationship between Jesus Christ and the archives in *Philadelphians* 8, Ignatius is now in a position to return to the original question, namely, that of the relationship between the archives and the gospel. His answer to this question—namely, that the gospel possesses "a distinct advantage" (ἐξαίρετον τι)—hardly has the character of an off-the-cuff remark from a writer who jumps randomly from one half-baked idea to another, but is the considered opinion of one who wishes to be as precise as possible about the relationship between Judaism and Christianity (as the very similar use of the adverb ἐξαιρέτως at *Smyr.* 7:2 clearly shows). The "distinct advantage" that the gospel possesses is a definitive event with three principal moments: the advent, passion, and resurrection of the Savior. This event brings what was begun under the old covenant to completion, and so the gospel is "the perfection of imperishability." Elsewhere Ignatius refers to the same reality as "the newness of eternal life" (*Eph.* 19:3).

Finally, Ignatius rounds out the creedal formulation of *Philadelphians* 9 with a deceptively simple aphorism, which actually contains in germ a great deal of his theology: "All things together are good, if you believe with love." It would be an exaggeration, though not entirely misleading, to say that my entire project amounts to an exposition of this statement. The phrase "all things together" refers to the entire economy of redemption, while "believing with love" is one of the ways Ignatius summarizes Christian existence as the appropriation of the gift of redemption. In any case, we shall have opportunity to examine the relationship between faith and love in chapter 5, the relationship between old covenant and new covenant in chapter 6, and the Christ event in chapters 7 and 8. For the time being, it is hoped that these two examples give some indication of how carefully Ignatius fashions his creedal formulae and works them into the texture of his letters.

Topical Discourses and Homilettes

Next, we turn to Ignatius's short topical discourses and homilettes, which we shall consider briefly. Ignatius warns Polycarp, "Flee the evil arts. Instead, give a homily [ὁμιλία] about them" (*Poly.* 5:1a). It is uncertain which "evil arts" Ignatius has in mind. To some scholars the context suggests magical practices associated with sex and marriage.[17] According to others, Ignatius warns against taking up "low trades" that pan-

---

17. BDAG, 501.

der to pleasure.[18] In either case the admonition supplies a suitable segue from the warning against "slavery to desire" at the end of the preceding chapter to Ignatius's own instruction on marriage and celibacy.

Tell my sisters to love the Lord and to be content with their life partners in flesh and spirit. Likewise, charge my brothers in the name of Jesus Christ to love their life partners, as the Lord loves the church. (5:1b)

Ignatius is drawing on the New Testament Epistle to the Ephesians here, as the echo of Ephesians 5:25 in the phrase "as the Lord loves the church" especially indicates. He by no means merely parrots his Pauline source, however, but adapts it creatively to the needs of the community he is addressing.[19] Recognizing that the Smyrnaeans are a bit too preoccupied with "heavenly things" (cf. *Smyr.* 6:1), Ignatius calls them down to earth. Rather than speak of "husbands" and "wives," he chooses the word σύμβιος ("life partner"), a term suggestive of the demands of everyday living (βίος). Ignatius does not demand submission on the part of wives but simply asks for contentment, perhaps sensing that the Smyrnaean women have overspiritualized marriage and entertain unrealistic expectations regarding their husbands. The phrase "flesh and spirit," as we shall see, is a constant refrain in Ignatius's letters, serving to drive home the point that the Christian way of life encompasses the whole of human existence and must not be reduced to the supramundane realm. Naturally, Ignatius does not swing the pendulum too far in the opposite direction and thereby reduce Christianity to an intramundane reality. His skillfully hewn statement begins with the demand to love the Lord Jesus and ends by reminding his readers that Christian charity is a participation in the Lord's own love for the church.

Continuing his instruction, Ignatius takes up the issue of celibacy.

If anyone is able to remain in purity for the honor of the Lord's flesh, let him remain free of boasting. If he boasts, he is lost. And if it becomes known to anyone beyond the bishop, he is corrupted. (*Poly.* 5:2a)

Here too, Ignatius fears an overspiritualized view of Christian existence and the boasting that may result from it. Everything must be grounded in

---

18. Schoedel, *Ignatius of Antioch*, 271; MacDonald, "Ideal of the Christian Couple," 113.

19. The letter is formally addressed to Polycarp but is obviously meant to be read to the whole church at Smyrna. In chapter 5 Ignatius transitions from an exhortation of Polycarp to taking up matters of concern to the community as a whole. Beginning at 6:1 he shifts to the second person plural and addresses the community directly, moving back and forth between singular and plural throughout the remainder of the letter.

the real historical humanity of Jesus Christ and in the visible structure of the local church. Celibacy is indeed a good, a special way of cultivating purity, but it must not be a flight from the material realm. One ought to embrace celibacy "for the honor of the Lord's flesh." Nor does a vow of celibacy confer a special spiritual privilege upon a person, enabling him or her to act independently of the bishop.

Having alluded to the oversight that the bishop is to exercise even over the realm of personal vocation, Ignatius now returns to the subject of marriage, this time dealing not with those who are already married but with those who plan to get married.

> It is proper for men who would get married and for women who would be given in marriage[20] to contract their union with the approval of the bishop, in order that the marriage might be according to God and not according to lust. Let all things be to the honor of God. (5:2b)

The Pauline Epistle to the Ephesians 5:32 identifies Christian marriage as a "great mystery" (*sacramentum magnum*) that signifies Christ's love for the church, but Ignatius is concerned that *signum* and *signatum* not be viewed as extrinsically related to each other. The contracting of marriage is brought under the umbrella of episcopal jurisdiction, and thus the marriage itself is, at least to an extent, incorporated into the life of the church. Marriage is a "union" (ἕνωσις, an important concept for Ignatius, as we shall see) that has its proper place within, and presumably contributes to, "the unity of the church," which is nothing less than "the unity of Jesus Christ" and "the unity of God."[21] Ignatius's warning against disordered desire or "lust" (ἐπιθυμία) may hearken back to the prohibition of "evil arts" with which he began his instruction on marriage and celibacy (*Poly.* 5:1), and in any case links it with the preceding instruction concerning slaves, which likewise concludes with a reference to the danger of ἐπιθυμία (4:3). There is ultimately only one principle of right order and unity, God himself, and so no realm of a Christian's life may float free. "A Christian does not have authority over himself but devotes his time to God" (7:3). Sexuality may be a private affair, but it is not absolutely so. Everything must be brought into the structure and dynamics of ecclesial life, so that the members of the church may "abide in the unity and oversight [ἐπισκοπή] of God" himself (8:3). Finally, Ignatius

---

20. Reading γαμουμέναις ("be given in marriage") with Codex Mediceo-Laurentianus and most other witnesses. Holmes reads γαμούσαις ("get married") with the Greek manuscripts of the long recension (*Apostolic Fathers*, 266).

21. Phld. 3:2, 5:2, 8:1.

rounds out his instruction on marriage and celibacy with an aphorism that articulates a universal principle of conduct: "Let all things be to the honor of God."

Many other short topical discourses occur throughout the Ignatian corpus. For example, *Ephesians* 10 is a homilette on how Christians are to relate to those outside the church, and *Ephesians* 14 is an instruction on the relationship between faith and love. In *Magnesians* 5 Ignatius takes up the early Christian commonplace of the "two ways" and develops it into a homilette under the image of "two coinages." In *Polycarp* 6, which is an exhortation to unity, athletic images give way to a military metaphor, which Ignatius develops at some length, in part by giving his own take on the Pauline "armor of God" motif.

The Structure of an Ignatian Letter

Ignatius's preference for brief discourses of this sort is not indicative of an inability to treat a topic in a more sustained manner, nor is it the case that an Ignatian letter is merely a pastiche of smaller pieces lacking a coherent overall structure. Both points can be demonstrated by means of a brief look at how Ignatius unfolds his argument in *Trallians*. At the center of the salutation to this letter lies a reference to the "flesh and blood of Jesus Christ" and his resurrection, which anticipates the central purpose of the letter: a refocusing of the Trallians' faith on the true humanity of Christ and the reality of his paschal mystery, in refutation of the docetic teachings that threaten the community. Ignatius's claim to be writing "in the apostolic character" (*Tral*. sal.) launches a leitmotif of six references to the apostles that extends throughout the letter.[22] Adherence to the "precepts of the apostles" will keep the Trallians rooted in the historical revelation of Jesus Christ and protect them from doctrinal error (7:1).

Moving into the body of the letter, Ignatius thanks the Trallians for the act of kindness they have shown him in sending their bishop Polybius to meet him in Smyrna and explains that in the person of the bishop he has in fact "seen" the entire congregation (1:1–2). This statement achieves the dual purpose of making an important ecclesiological point about the episcopacy and of indicating the grounds on which Ignatius

---

22. The remaining five references are at *Tral*. 2:2, 3:1, 3:3, 7:1, and 12:2. These give Trallians almost as many references to the apostles as are found in the other six letters combined. Since presbyters have a special correspondence to the apostles in Ignatius's ecclesiological typology, Charles E. Hill plausibly connects the special emphasis on the apostles in this letter to the apparent failure of the Trallian presbyters to accompany their bishop Polybius to Smyrna ("Ignatius and the Apostolate," 232–33).

addresses a letter to a community of Christians that he has not actually visited. In the next two chapters (2–3) Ignatius exhorts the Trallians to submit to their bishop and presbyters and to show reverence for their deacons, but he does so in a way that roots his practical concern for right order in a profound ecclesiology and ultimately in the paschal mystery itself. Ignatius's personal commendation of Polybius and his humility (3:2) links this part of the letter back to the reference to Polybius's visit in chapter 1, while it simultaneously anticipates the main theme (humility) of the next section (chapters 4–5).[23] In that section, Ignatius broaches the problem of the Trallians' preoccupation with "heavenly things," explaining that, while he is certainly capable of writing on such matters, he will refrain from doing so out of consideration for his own need for humility and the Trallians' lack of readiness for such advanced doctrine. Ignatius rounds off this section, and the first half of the letter (i.e., the salutation through chapter 5), with one of the aphorisms we have already mentioned: "For we lack many things, in order that we may not lack God" (5:2).

The juncture between chapters 5 and 6 marks the main point of transition in the letter. Up to this point, Ignatius has carefully prepared for his chief topic: the danger that the docetic heresy poses. Now he launches into a sustained parenesis on this subject (chapters 6–11), which he introduces with the Pauline phrase παρακαλῶ οὖν ὑμᾶς ("I exhort you, then ..."). This phrase, along with the aphorism that immediately precedes it, thus serves as a kind of hinge on which the two main parts of the letter swing like the two panels of a diptych.[24] The same verse contains the letter's guiding metaphor: food. The Trallians ought to partake "only of Christian nourishment" and "avoid exotic vegetation, which is heresy" (6:1). Ignatius has already warned them that, were he to feed them even with legitimate teaching about "heavenly things," they might "choke" on it (5:1). Now he compares heretical teaching to a "lethal drug" (θανάσιμον φάρμακον) mixed with "honeyed wine" (6:2). By way of inclusio, he will return to this domain of images near the end of the exhortation. The docetic teachers are "not a planting of the Father" but

---

23. Note the references to πραότης ("humility") in 3:2 and 4:2, as well as the resumption of this theme by means of the virtual synonym πραϋπάθεια ("meakness") in 8:1.

24. Not coincidentally, the identical phrase functions in the identical way in the Pauline Ephesians (4:1), which likewise has the structure of a diptych (chapters 1–3 and 4–6 forming two panels). On the epistolographical function of παρακαλῶ in the Pauline and Ignatian corpora, see Hermann Josef Sieben, "Die Ignatianen als Briefe: Einige formkritische Bemerkungen," *Vigiliae Christianae* 32 (1978): 1–18.

"evil offshoots that bear deadly fruit," and "if anyone tastes this fruit, he will die suddenly" (11:1). True teachers of the faith, by contrast, are "branches of the cross," which bear "imperishable fruit." This glancing allusion to the cross as the tree of life (a commonplace among the later fathers of the church) quickly gives way to the complementary Pauline image of Christians as "members" of Christ "the head" (11:2).

Between these two bookends (chapters 6 and 11), Ignatius tells the Trallians that the authentic nourishment by which they can restore themselves to health consists "in faith, which is the flesh of the Lord, and in love, which is the blood of Jesus Christ" (8:1). This statement obviously evokes the eucharist, which Ignatius elsewhere describes as the "medicine of immortality" (φάρμακον ἀθανασίας) and the "antidote" that enables us to escape death (Eph. 20:2); but for Ignatius the eucharistic flesh is the historical flesh in which Christ lived, suffered, and was raised (Smyr. 6:3), and so his main concern in the present context is that the Trallians be renewed in the true faith and in the love to which that faith is inseparably linked. Accordingly, the centerpiece of the entire exhortation is the creedal formulation of chapter 9, which, as we have already seen, accents the humanity of Christ. In the last two chapters of the letter (12–13), Ignatius offers final greetings to the church at Tralles, requests their prayers for himself and for the church at Antioch, and reminds them once again to submit themselves to their bishop and his presbyters. Hopefully these few observations will suffice to indicate that *Trallians*, with its antidocetic polemic, is no rant, but a carefully structured text. The same point could be demonstrated with regard to any of the other six letters.

In light of the foregoing survey of Ignatius's aphorisms, creedal formulae, and short discourses, along with our analysis of the structure of *Trallians*, Ignatius's letters hardly appear to be the spontaneous effusion of an exuberant heart, and still less the bluster of an impetuous nature. We seem rather to be dealing with a man who chose his words carefully and habituated himself to verbal restraint. It is worth noting in this connection that the entire Ignatian corpus of seven authentic letters is only about the length of 1 *Clement* by itself, which is to say, a bit shorter than the Gospel of Mark. Ignatius's longest letter, *Ephesians*, is shorter than the New Testament epistle of the same name and less than a third the length of the *Epistle of Barnabas*. As I hope to make clear over the course of this study, the relative brevity of Ignatius's letters and the "peculiar density of his language" are intimately linked to his understanding of the economy of redemption itself and to his self-understanding as bishop and would-be martyr. Jesus Christ, the incarnate Logos, is God's self-revelation and the "one teacher," not only by means of the words he spoke but also in the deeds he did "silently," deeds "worthy of the Father" (Eph. 15:1)—above all in his death on the cross, which was a mystery "accomplished in the silence of God" (19:1). Ignatius emulates bishops who imitate the Lord Jesus by cultivating silence and who exercise authentic ecclesial power by ruling their flocks in meekness.[25] He wishes to proclaim the gospel more with his life and death than with words, and indeed wants to *become* a "word" (*Rom.* 2:1), but charity obliges him to speak and write (*Eph.* 3:2). His tiny corpus of letters exemplifies the efficacy of teaching "with few words" and is intended to be a complement to, even a commentary on, his approaching martyrdom at Rome.[26]

Nor do the circumstances of Ignatius's journey, which must have been physically unpleasant and emotionally stressful indeed (cf. *Rom.* 5:1), seem to have required him to dash off his letters in such a haphazard manner that he was unable to compose them thoughtfully.[27] It is reasonable to assume that Ignatius was able to write such substantive letters and give succinct expression to his ideas, even under difficult conditions, because he wrote about matters to which he had previously given serious thought. Even if Ignatius's interaction with the churches of Asia Minor on his way to Rome may have required him to think on his feet a bit, as was probably the case in his encounter with the Judaizers at Philadelphia, he was able to do so effectively because he could draw upon years of prayerful study and preaching. In all likelihood he had already encountered varieties of docetism and Judaization while still in Syria and, with his background in the Matthean, Johannine, and Pauline writings, had long since recognized these views to be incompatible with the gospel. Evidently his previous efforts in opposition to these heresies had already left a deep stamp on his theology, which we can recognize especially in his great appreciation for the historical humanity of Christ and the integral role he understood the physical body to play in the economy of redemption, as well as in the fairly sophisticated and well-thought-out position he takes with regard to the relationship between Judaism and Christianity. In giving theological instruction and pastoral exhortation to the churches of Asia Minor, Ignatius was not shooting from the hip.[28]

---

25. Eph. 6:1; Phld. 1:1; Tral. 3:2.   26. Rom. 8:2–3; Poly. 7:3; Magn. 14:1.
27. Joly actually cites the manifest literary character of the letters as evidence of their being written at leisure by a forger rather than by a man led away under guard (*Le dossier*, 94–96).
28. Corwin, *St. Ignatius and Christianity*, 29; Donahue, "Jewish Christianity," 82.

I do not by any means wish to suggest that Ignatius's letters are lacking in personal expression or deep feeling. Nothing could be further from the truth. Like his hero Paul, Ignatius wore his heart on his epistolary sleeve, and there is no author in the first hundred years of Christian literature, save Paul himself, who reveals more of his personality to us than does Ignatius.[29] But uninhibited verbal spontaneity is not the only, or even the best, way to communicate the truth of oneself in words. It may be, in fact, that one can do this more effectively through the discipline of choosing one's words carefully. In any case, that seems to have been true for Ignatius.

His *Letter to the Romans* does strike the reader as having more of a free-flowing quality than the other letters, but this is not because it is "the vibration of a soul constrained by the anguish of love." Actually, *Romans* is the most disciplined and carefully constructed of the seven letters. Belying the notion that Ignatius's mind "passes quickly from one suggested and only half-explicated point to another," *Romans* is proof positive that he could remain focused on a single point for ten chapters. Everything in it is subordinated to his single-minded goal of "attaining God" and his fear that the Romans may do him "an unseasonable kindness" by attempting to forestall his martyrdom (4:1). If the depth of Ignatius's personal feeling comes across more powerfully in *Romans* than elsewhere, if his passionate love for Jesus Christ seems to flow like a rushing torrent, it is largely because it has been channeled through a very narrow conduit. What makes *Romans* a true masterpiece is not that its author knew how to disburden himself emotionally, but that he knew how to bring the resources of language and rhetoric to the service of communicating a truth that mattered more to him than anything else in the world. Had Ignatius composed his plea to the Roman Christians in the gushing romantic style of, say, Beethoven's "Letter to the Immortal Beloved," it is unlikely it would have come to be regarded as one of the most powerful and moving texts in all of Christian literature.

Ignatius and Heresy

How Many Heresies?

A vitally important question about which modern scholarship has yet to reach a firm consensus concerns the number and nature of the her-

---

29. Corwin, *St. Ignatius and Christianity*, 30.

esies opposed by Ignatius. Nearly everyone agrees that Ignatius polemicizes against some form of docetism in *Trallians* and *Smyrnaeans*, while he takes aim at Judaizing tendencies in *Magnesians* and *Philadelphians*. But this initial observation raises a number of questions. Are we dealing with two distinct heresies, or with two aspects of the same heresy? Is the docetic tendency also gnostic? Which Jewish practices are the Judaizers promoting? Do Ignatius's polemics reflect prior engagement with the same or similar heresies at Antioch? What sort of heresy, if any, is in view in *Ephesians*? Lightfoot was convinced that Ignatius opposed a single heresy, which he refers to as "Docetic Judaism" or "Gnostic Judaism."[30] While Lightfoot and his one-heresy hypothesis have not been without their defenders, probably the greater number of subsequent scholars has favored some variation on the two-heresy hypothesis, with only a few defying Ockham's razor to the point of positing three or more heresies.[31] Since I have adopted the two-heresy view as a working hypothesis, I shall offer a brief defense of that position here.[32]

The relevant evidence from the New Testament (Colossians, 1 and 2 Timothy, Revelation 2–3, and possibly the Johannine Letters) indicates that a variety of heterodox teachings and groups troubled the churches of southwest Asia Minor in the late first century. As we shall see in chapter 6, there is a significant grain of truth in the view that the docetic and Judaizing heresies represent "the far ends of the Christian spectrum" during this period.[33] Docetism denies the true humanity of Christ and can lead to a nonhistorical view of redemption, while Judaization sees Christ as merely one in a long historical sequence of inspired prophets and teachers. It may even be possible to understand Ignatius's theology as an attempt to navigate between Scylla and Charybdis in this regard. While this schema has heuristic value, there seem also to have existed hybrid heresies that cannot be located so neatly along a single spectrum. As the evidence from Colossians especially indicates, there is nothing inherently improbable in the idea that a given group may have combined docetic and Judaizing tendencies in their brand of Christianity. Perhaps

---

30. Lightfoot, *Ignatius, Polycarp*, 1.373–88.
31. For a succinct overview of the debate, see Thomas A. Robinson, *Ignatius of Antioch and the Parting of the Ways* (Peabody, Mass.: Hendrickson, 2009), 113–17. For a plausible attempt to identify a "third error" in the Ignatian letters, see Christine Trevett, "Prophecy and Anti-Episcopal Activity: A Third Error Combatted by Ignatius?" *Journal of Ecclesiastical History* 34 (1983): 1–18.
32. My argument has several points in common with that of Donahue, "Jewish Christianity," 82–87.
33. Robinson, *Parting of the Ways*, 81–82.

Ignatius knew that such a group was threatening the churches of Asia Minor. Still, it must be borne in mind that Colossae was approximately one hundred kilometers from the nearest churches addressed by Ignatius (Philadelphia and Tralles) and, more importantly, that, even if we take Colossians to be deutero-Pauline and date it rather late, it bears witness to a situation that obtained at least a quarter century prior to Ignatius's journey. Each of the other New Testament texts mentioned above presents its own difficulties and limitations if we attempt to use it as evidence for reconstructing the situation in Asia Minor in Ignatius's day.[34] In any case, for our purposes, we need not reconstruct the broad historical picture but simply ask a more modest question. What heterodox teachings did Ignatius understand himself to be facing? And to answer that question, we need to turn to his letters.

Unless we take Ignatius to be an entirely unreliable witness, we can accept two reasonably certain facts as providing a firm point of departure. First, Ignatius actually encountered a group of Judaizers within the community at Philadelphia and had reason to believe, presumably on the testimony of Bishop Damas, that similar teachings and practices also threatened the church at Magnesia. Second, Ignatius's stay at Smyrna convinced him that the church in that city was imperiled by a group of docetists whose names he actually knew (*Smyr.* 5:3), and he had reason to believe, presumably on the testimony of Bishop Polybius, that similar teachings had already influenced the church at Tralles. While some scholars plausibly find elements of antidocetic polemic within the anti-Judaizing *Magnesians*, it is important to note that the two heretical tendencies are in any case kept entirely separate when it comes to letters addressed to the two churches Ignatius had actually visited: Philadelphia and Smyrna.

Lightfoot maintains that Ignatius addresses a single heresy from its Judaic "side" in *Philadelphians* and *Magnesians* and from its docetic "side" in *Smyrnaeans* and *Trallians*, but he never suggests why Ignatius may have done such a thing. This is the point on which the one-heresy hypothesis falters. As we have already seen in our overview of *Trallians*, Ignatius regarded docetic teaching as a deadly poison that strikes at the very heart of the Christian faith. If he had any inkling that the Philadelphian Judaiz-

---

34. Lightfoot greatly simplifies the picture by baldly asserting that Colossians, the pastoral epistles, the catholic epistles, and Revelation all bear witness to a single "category" of heresy, which he further identifies with the teaching of the Cerinthians, that is, the same "Doceto-Judaism" that Ignatius attacks in all his letters to the churches in Asia Minor (*Ignatius, Polycarp*, 2.124–25).

ers also embraced a docetic view of Christ, why on earth would he fail to warn the church at Philadelphia against this mortal danger? Conversely, Ignatius considered the practice of Judaism to be entirely incompatible with the profession of Christ and, like Paul, believed that Christians who turn to the practice of Judaism risk falling from grace. If he thought for one moment that the docetists who threatened the churches at Smyrna and Tralles also encouraged Jewish observances, why would he not alert those churches to this perilous error? The selectivity by which Ignatius, according to Lightfoot's hypothesis, focuses now on the docetic side of docetic Judaism, now on the Judaic side of the same heresy, appears quite arbitrary.

Nor is this problem adequately dealt with in more recent variants on the one-heresy hypothesis. According to John W. Marshall, for example, Ignatius opposes "a single group of Jewish Christians who understand Jesus to be an angel." They claim that Jesus only "seemed" to die but are not "docetists" in the usual sense.[35] By demonstrating that the "resources" for developing an angel-Christology were "plentiful within Second Temple Judaism," Marshall no doubt puts forward a more plausible single-heresy hypothesis than Lightfoot's "Docetic Judaism."[36] But when he attempts to demonstrate "the integration of Ignatius' arguments" in the various letters, Marshall proves too much. He notes, for example, that in *Smyrnaeans* Ignatius "surrounds" his argument against a τὸ δοκεῖν ("seeming") view of Jesus' death with references to Jesus' fleshly descent from David, the authority of "the prophecies and the law of Moses," and the church's inclusion of "Jews and Gentiles"—all of which, according to Marshall, brings both Ignatius and his opponents into the realm of Jewish Christianity (where an angel-Christology might appear attractive).[37] But these are precisely the *sort* of references to Judaism that one never finds in *Philadelphians* or *Magnesians*, where they would tend to take the edge off Ignatius's sharp contrast between "Judaism" and "Christianity" (terms that never occur in *Smyrnaeans* or *Trallians*).

---

35. "The Objects of Ignatius' Wrath and Jewish Angelic Mediators," *Journal of Ecclesiastical History* 56 (2005): 1–23 (quotation from 18).

36. Ibid., 12.

37. Ibid., 18–20. See Smyr. 1:1–2, 5:1. The appeal in 5:1 is to the authority of the Old Testament Scriptures, including "the prophecies," whereas in *Magnesians* and *Philadelphians* Ignatius praises "the prophets" themselves as disciples of Jesus but hardly needs to recommend the Old Testament as authoritative to his readers. Indeed, as we have seen, he seeks to qualify its authority vis-à-vis the gospel (Phld. 8:2–9:2). As for Jesus' descent from David, it is striking that Ignatius confesses it in every letter other than *Magnesians*, *Philadelphians*, and *Polycarp*.

In the end Marshall himself must admit that "the letters usually described as addressing a docetic problem [*Smyrnaeans* and *Trallians*] cannot stand as a key which subsumes the clear polemic against Jewish practice and belief" in *Magnesians* and *Philadelphians*. He rightly notes that "Ignatius spares no effort to distinguish himself from the Judaisers" but never suggests a reason why Ignatius does so in two letters only. Conversely, Marshall complains that "elaborate methodological strictures" have been used "to isolate those letters which deploy the phrase τὸ δοκεῖν from those that do not."[38] The truth of the matter, however, is that only a strained exegesis can prevent *Smyrnaeans* and *Trallians* from standing out among the letters by virtue of their sharp polemic against the τὸ δοκεῖν heresy, whether one identifies that heresy as docetism, angel-Christology, or something else.

The weightiest counterargument in favor of the one-heresy hypothesis lies in an appeal to the apparent admixture of anti-Judaizing and antidocetic elements within the polemic of *Magnesians*. The anti-Judaizing character of this letter is beyond question, but it also contains two brief phrases allegedly suggestive of an antidocetic polemic. The first of these involves a corrupt text, which Lightfoot plausibly emends in such a way that Ignatius may be understood to say that "some people" (which in context must refer to the Judaizers) deny Jesus' death (9:1).[39] If we understand this to mean that they deny the physical reality of his death, these Judaizers are thus also docetists (at least in Marshall's loose sense). This text, however, even when emended in the manner suggested by Lightfoot, may just as easily be taken to mean that the Judaizers deny Jesus himself or the whole "mystery" of his person and life-giving death. In countering the Philadelphian Judaizers, as we have seen, Ignatius insists on the absolute centrality and supreme importance of Jesus Christ and of his cross, death, and resurrection (*Phld*. 8:2). Any failure to recognize this amounts to a denial of the gospel. Though the Judaizers of Magnesia must have made some positive affirmations about Jesus Christ, Ignatius considers their Jewish observances to constitute a de facto denial of Christ (*Magn*. 10:3).

The second seemingly antidocetic passage in *Magnesians*, the passage that provides the lynchpin of the one-heresy hypothesis, is a creedal formula in which the birth, passion, and resurrection are said to have occurred within a specific historical period and to have been "truly and

---

38. "Objects of Ignatius' Wrath," 20 (all three quotes).
39. *Ignatius, Polycarp*, 2.130.

surely accomplished by Jesus Christ" (11:1). The phrase "truly and surely" (ἀληθῶς καὶ βεβαίως) recalls Ignatius's similar use of ἀληθῶς in passages that are unquestionably antidocetic.[40] In taking up the stock argument from *Magnesians* 11 against the two-heresy hypothesis, Thomas A. Robinson asks, "Why does Ignatius comment about the birth, passion, and resurrection of Jesus—themes that normally have an anti-docetic ring?"[41]

The force of Robinson's rhetorical question relies on the mistaken assumption that Ignatius appeals to the historical humanity of Christ and the events of his life only when he wishes to wield these as weapons against docetism. In fact, however, Ignatius employs creedal formulae and emphasizes the historical flesh-and-blood humanity of Jesus Christ and the core events of his life in all his letters, including *Romans*, a letter that is patently nonpolemical.[42] Robinson treats Ignatius's references to the birth, passion, and resurrection of Jesus as so many antidocetic talking points. In fact, the historical reality of Jesus Christ and the events of his life constitute the heart and soul of Ignatius's theology, and this theology informs every aspect of his understanding of Christian existence. It is a little hard to imagine Ignatius writing any letter to any church under any circumstances without referencing this creedal core.

Furthermore, Ignatius has a specific and very good reason for insisting on the factual-historical occurrence of the Christ event, not only in his antidocetic polemic, but in his anti-Judaizing polemic as well. As we shall see in chapter 6, Ignatius's view of the relationship between Judaism and Christianity depends on his appreciation for the historical-covenantal structure of the economy of redemption. His anti-Judaizing polemic thus hinges on the *fact* that Jesus Christ has come into the world, has suffered and died, and has risen from the dead. Indeed, the reference to these three key moments of the Christ event in *Magnesians* 11 finds a close parallel within the anti-Judaizing polemic of *Philadelphians*, where Ignatius explains that the gospel's superiority over the old covenant lies in "the advent of the Savior, our Lord Jesus Christ, his passion, and the resurrection" (9:2).

The same mistaken assumption whereby *Magnesians* 11 is sometimes thought to be antidocetic has led some scholars to conclude that *Ephesians* too is an antidocetic letter since it contains creedal formulae that

---

40. Tral. 9:1–2; Smyr. 1–2.
41. Robinson, *Parting of the Ways*, 119–20.
42. Rom. 6:3, 7:3, 8:2.

stress the historical humanity of Christ.[43] Actually, these creedal formulae possess a strikingly symmetrical character, each of them indicating that Jesus Christ is both human and divine. While *Ephesians* contains strong warnings against "evil doctrine," it is not in the strict sense a polemical letter since it does not directly confront a specific heterodox teaching.[44] In many respects it is the most "neutral" and comprehensive presentation of Ignatius's theology.

On the other hand, *Ephesians* is no academic treatise, but like the other letters is written out of deep pastoral concern for the specific community that it addresses. Ignatius has learned that some believers in Ephesus, possibly Johannine Christians, do not accept the episcopal authority of Onesimus, do not regularly attend his eucharistic assembly, and are resisting the emergent monepiscopal version of ecclesiastical structure more generally.[45] Still, this faction "lives in accord with the truth" and thus does not constitute a heretical group (Eph. 6:2). Ignatius addresses this situation early in the letter, explaining in Johannine terms that Onesimus has been "sent" by the Lord Jesus (6:1) and that a community's unified submission to the bishop and his presbytery is one important aspect of what it means to "glorify Jesus Christ, who has glorified you" (2:2).

Ignatius knows that heretical teachers have already passed through Ephesus, and he is pleased to learn that the church there refused to give them a hearing (9:1). He confidently affirms that "no heresy resides" among the Ephesian Christians (6:2). Still, he expresses concern that individuals within the community may yet be deceived (8:1). Moreover, he is at pains to indicate the close connection between evil teaching and evil deeds, between heresy and immorality, especially immorality of a sexual nature (16:1-2). He is convinced that the Ephesians have a solid understanding of the faith and is eager to supplement this understanding with advanced teaching about the divine economy, even proposing to write them a second letter on the subject (20:1). But he is concerned that they may be vulnerable to the "wicked guile" of those who "bear about the name but practice things unworthy of God" (7:1), and this concern is the thread that runs through the seemingly haphazard series of topical discourses and homilettes that comprise this longish letter. Those who are spiritual must not live carnal lives (8:2) but must "remain in Jesus

---

43. Eph. 7:2, 18:2, 20:2.
44. Eph. 9:1, 16:2–17:1.
45. Paul Trebilco, *The Early Christians in Ephesus from Paul to Ignatius* (Grand Rapids, Mich.: Eerdmans, 2008), 645–83.

Christ in all purity and self-control" (10:3), "either fearing the coming wrath or loving the present grace, one of the two" (11:1). They must learn how to complete their faith with love, practice what they preach, recognize that the Lord knows the secrets of the heart, and live as his temples (14:1–15:3). All of Ignatius's letters are exhortations to Christian authenticity, but *Ephesians* has this character par excellence.

To summarize, *Trallians* and *Smyrnaeans* contain an antidocetic polemic (with no hint of anti-Judaizing polemic), *Magnesians* and *Philadelphians* contain an anti-Judaizing polemic (with no antidocetic polemic), and *Ephesians* contains a general warning against heterodox teaching and the sexual immorality that accompanies it. It is important to note the distinctive character of each of Ignatius's letters and to appreciate the role theological truth plays within his polemics and pastoral exhortations. Some scholars draw more or less indiscriminately upon the seven letters, which after all are addressed to Christians in southwest Asia Minor and Rome, in order to reconstruct the situation Ignatius left behind in Syria. Sometimes Ignatius's letters are even thought to tell us *more* about the church in Antioch than about the churches in Asia Minor. As noted earlier, because Ignatius seems well prepared to deal with docetism and Judaization, it is reasonable to assume that he had already encountered these heresies previously, presumably in or around Antioch. We may even have corroboration of this supposition in the recognition that Saturninus, a Christian gnostic with a docetic Christology, lived in Antioch around the time of Ignatius, and (more tentatively) in the possibility that the Gospel of Matthew, which is sharply anti-Judaic, originated in Antioch.[46] But, as I will illustrate with an example below, elaborate reconstructions of the situation in Antioch at the time of Ignatius sometimes rest on dubious historical methodology.

The problems here run deeper than mere methodology, however. A web of flawed presuppositions attends much of the historical scholarship that deals with Ignatius's letters. It is perfectly legitimate to use the letters as evidence for historical research, but just as theologians must respect the historical dimension of these documents, so historians need to respect their theological character. Even some scholars who do not put much stock in the latest sociological theories adopt an implicit so-

---

46. For Saturninus, see Birger A. Pearson, *Ancient Gnosticism: Traditions and Literature* (Minneapolis: Fortress Press, 2007), 34–35. For Antioch as the place of origin of the Gospel of Matthew, see John P. Meier, "Matthew, Gospel of," in *Anchor Bible Dictionary*, ed. David Noel Freedman, 6 vols. (New York: Doubleday, 1992), 4.624.

ciopolitical model for understanding the life of the early church while they also tend to reduce theology to ideology. The doctrines that Ignatius espouses in his letters are viewed less as truth convictions that inform every aspect of life than as pragmatic means for achieving political ends. Although several valuable studies have illuminated the close interrelation among the various elements of Ignatius's theology,[47] historians continue to treat these elements in atomistic and functional terms, while they also view them as extrinsically related to Ignatius's practical "agenda" (i.e., his pastoral and ecclesial concerns).

I hope to demonstrate in this volume that Ignatius's polemics against docetism and Judaization, his concern for ecclesial unity, his promotion of the three-tiered hierarchy, his exhortations to moral purity, his understanding of the eucharist, and his personal aspiration to martyrdom are all deeply rooted in a single theological vision. At the heart of this vision is a grasp of the historical economy of redemption, and at the heart of that economy Ignatius places the person and event of Jesus Christ. This is why all of Ignatius's letters, whether polemical or not, contain creedal formulae. It is not merely the case that Christian "praxis" makes use of theology as "theory," but that Christian existence is radically and thoroughly theological. Christian existence is χριστομαθία, learning the person of Christ.

Relationship to Emergent Gnosticism?

Whatever one makes of Marshall's hypothesis about an angel-Christology, it is clear that Ignatius's polemic in *Trallians* and *Smyrnaeans* targets a group that denied the real physical birth, life, death, and resurrection of Jesus Christ while explicitly maintaining that he only "seemed to have suffered."[48] The similarity between this doctrine and that of Saturninus, combined with the Trallians' and Smyrnaeans' apparent curiosity regarding angels and archons, may suggest that the opponents' brand of docetism was also incipiently gnostic.[49] Still, nothing in the letters indicates that Ignatius is countering a full-blown gnostic system. He does not condemn speculation about heavenly matters as inherently dangerous but actually professes himself to have knowledge of "the places assigned to angels and the archontic constellations" (*Tral.* 5:2). He hesitates to discourse upon

---

47. Especially strong in this regard are Goltz, *Ignatius von Antiochien*, and Corwin, *St. Ignatius and Christianity*.
48. *Tral.* 9–10; *Smyr.* 1–3.
49. *Tral.* 5:1–2; *Smyr.* 6:1.

such matters when writing to the tyronic Trallians but speaks freely of Christ's manifestation "to the aeons" in his letter to the more proficient Ephesians (Eph. 19:2).

These observations raise the question whether Ignatius's own theology might be incipiently gnostic. Already in the late nineteenth century, Lightfoot noted that Ignatius's vocabulary is "tinged" with gnosticism, but he did not judge this coloring to penetrate to the core of Ignatius's theology.[50] Early in the twentieth century, representatives of the history of religions school, led by Heinrich Schlier and Hans-Werner Bartsch, spawned a fruitful debate about Ignatius's relationship to emergent gnosticism.[51] The dust is far from settling on the broader question of gnosticism's origins and its relationship to Judaism and early Christianity, especially in the wake of the 1945 discovery of the Nag Hammadi codices,[52] but there is now widespread agreement with regard to Ignatius's letters that, while they contain some intriguing parallels to gnostic vocabulary, Schlier and Bartsch have exaggerated the number and importance of these parallels. This point constitutes something of a leitmotif running through the major works of Corwin, Schoedel, and Robert M. Grant.[53] Most would probably agree with L. W. Barnard's assessment that the essence of Ignatius's thought is closer to being antignostic than gnostic.[54]

It may not be wise, however, to dismiss Ignatius's possible affinities to emergent gnosticism as a nonissue. His terminology is indisputably less conventional than what one finds in 1 Clement, the Didache, or Polycarp's Philippians, and to ignore this fact would not be any more illuminative of Ignatius's theology than it is to press the alleged gnostic parallels too hard. We should note, first of all, that some of Ignatius's gnosticlike expressions may have been taken from books that later came to be included in the New Testament, while others could not have been.

---

50. Lightfoot, *Ignatius, Polycarp*, 1.388.

51. Heinrich Schlier, *Religionsgeschichtliche Untersuchungen zu den Ignatiusbriefen* (Giessen: Alfred Töpelmann Verlag, 1929); Hans-Werner Bartsch, *Gnostisches Gut und Gemeindetradition bei Ignatius von Antiochien* (Gütersloh: Bertelsmann, 1940).

52. Contrast, e.g., the equally well informed but divergent views of Alastair H. B. Logan, *Gnostic Truth and Christian Heresy: A Study in the History of Gnosticism* (Peabody, Mass.: Hendrickson, 1996), and Pearson, *Ancient Gnosticism*.

53. Corwin, *St. Ignatius and Christianity*; Schoedel, *Ignatius of Antioch*; Robert M. Grant, *Ignatius of Antioch*, vol. 4 of *The Apostolic Fathers: A New Translation and Commentary*, ed. Robert M. Grant (Camden, N.J.: Thomas Nelson & Sons, 1966).

54. L. W. Barnard, *Studies in the Apostolic Fathers and Their Background* (New York: Schocken Books, 1966), 26–30.

On the one hand, the expression θεοῦ γνῶσις ("knowledge of God") is thoroughly biblical, and Ignatius uses the word πλήρωμα ("fullness") in a manner not dissimilar to the way the term is used in the Pauline Ephesians and Colossians.⁵⁵ On the other hand, Ignatius sometimes uses the word αἰών ("aeon, age, world") in a way that finds no clear precedent in the New Testament and may have some affinity to its gnostic use.⁵⁶ Still other gnosticlike expressions found in the Ignatian letters—for example, "archontic constellations," "filtered out," and "pure light"—do not occur in the New Testament at all.⁵⁷ A reasonable working hypothesis is that Ignatius, in articulating his insight into the economy of redemption, drew upon currents of thought, both biblical and nonbiblical, that were, at about the same time, contributing also to the early development of gnosticism. There is, however, no compelling reason to suppose that he drew directly upon a well-formed gnostic myth or system.

I do not possess the requisite expertise in gnostic studies to offer a direct defense of this modest hypothesis, but I can demonstrate how Ignatius's various affirmations, including those that seem to have a gnostic ring, fit together within a cohesive and eminently orthodox theology. As we shall see throughout this volume, one of the keys to Ignatius's understanding of the economy of redemption is the way he interrelates its vertical-transcendent and horizontal-temporal dimensions. Generally speaking, it seems that when he employs gnosticlike expressions, whether these are also attested in the New Testament or not, it is in order to safeguard the vertical-transcendent dimension. But I will also make the case that he never does this at the expense of the horizontal-temporal dimension. Three passages that have justifiably invited comparison to gnostic thought will require special attention in this regard. In *Romans* 6:2 Ignatius expresses a strong desire to resist the enticement of "matter," to leave the "world," and to attain the realm of "pure light." In *Ephesians* 19:2–3 he presents a quasi-mythical narrative concerned with the sun, moon, and stars in order to explain how the incarnate Son of God "was manifested to the aeons." And in *Magnesians* 8:2 Ignatius describes

---

55. For "knowledge of God" and similar expressions, see Eph. 17:2; Hos 4:1, 6:6; Prv 2:5; Wis 2:13, 8:4, 14:22; Jn 17:3; 1 Cor 15:34; 2 Cor 2:14, 10:5; Gal 4:9; Eph 1:17, 4:13; Col 1:10; 1 Thes 4:5; 2 Pt 1:2–3; 1 Jn 2:14, 4:6–8, 5:20. For "fullness," see Eph. sal.; Tral. sal.; Eph 1:23, 3:19, 4:13; Col 1:19, 2:9–10; Jn 1:16.

56. Eph. 8:1, 19.2; Smyr. 1:2.

57. "Archontic constellations": Tral. 5:2. "Filtered out": Rom. sal. and Phld. 3:1. "Pure light": Rom. 6:2. The phrase "the perfect man" (τοῦ τελείου ἀνθρώπου; Smyr. 4:2), sometimes thought to have a gnostic ring, finds a close parallel in Eph 4:13 (ἄνδρα τέλειον).

Jesus Christ as God's "Word come forth from silence" (λόγος ἀπὸ σιγῆς προελθών). I will deal with the *Romans* and *Ephesians* passages in chapter 4 and with the *Magnesians* passage in chapter 7.

Ignatius's Agenda

Perhaps the single greatest benefit to accrue from the twentieth-century debates regarding Ignatius's polemics and his relation to gnosticism lies in the fact that they have challenged scholars to grapple seriously with his theology, and to a significant extent this has mitigated the prejudicial effects of Ignatius's prior reputation for authoring slipshod letters that merely give expression to popular piety. In the half century since the appearance of Corwin's *St. Ignatius and Christianity in Antioch*, the tendency has been to take Ignatius somewhat more seriously as a thinker and theologian.[58]

Old prejudices die hard, however. The idea that Ignatius is more rhetorically persuasive than theologically profound, combined with the notion that his volatile temperament is responsible for the peculiar style of his letters, reemerges in an extreme form in a recent volume by Allen Brent, a prominent figure in contemporary Anglophone Ignatian scholarship. In *Ignatius of Antioch: A Martyr Bishop and the Origin of the Episcopacy*, Brent opines that Ignatius may have been "disturbed" and dangerously close to losing touch with reality.[59] Ignatius conducted himself "strangely as one possessed by the Spirit" and was "apt to burst forth with new revelations."[60] This "strange and enigmatic figure" was, however, "capable of eliciting awe" among simple-minded believers.[61] Moreover, his "idealized vision" of how things ought to be convinced him that "that is how they actually are."[62] As Ignatius composes his letters, his "highly strung and, one might even say, disturbed temperament flits from actual

---

58. In addition to the above-mentioned works of Corwin, Grant, Meinhold, and Schoedel, see Karin Bommes, *Weizen Gottes: Untersuchungen zur Theologie des Martyriums bei Ignatius von Antiochien*, Theophaneia: Beiträge zur Religions- und Kirchengeschichte des Altertums 27 (Cologne: Peter Hanstein Verlag, 1976); and Henning Paulsen, *Studien zur Theologie des Ignatius von Antiochien* (Göttingen: Vandenhoeck & Ruprecht, 1978). Among earlier works that take Ignatius seriously as a theologian, Goltz, *Ignatius von Antiochien*, deserves special mention.

59. *Ignatius of Antioch*, 58. In this compendious presentation of his hypothesis, Brent integrates elements from several of his earlier studies, including "Ignatius and the Imperial Cult," *Vigiliae Christianae* 52 (1998): 30–58, and *Ignatius of Antioch and the Second Sophistic: A Study of an Early Christian Transformation of Pagan Culture*, Studien und Texte zu Antike und Christentum 36 (Tübingen: Mohr Siebeck, 2006).

60. *Ignatius of Antioch*, 41.   61. Ibid., 59.
62. Ibid., 18.

to imagined reality."⁶³ Surprisingly, however, this very trait was the key to Ignatius's ultimate success—and for Brent, one might add, an interpretive key to Ignatius's letters. According to Brent's hypothesis, there was no monepiscopacy—not in Antioch, not in the churches of Asia Minor, not in Rome—until Ignatius *invented* it.

Ignatius, according to Brent, was faced with a crisis involving "competing systems of authority" in the church at Antioch. A faction that favored "an egalitarian, purely charismatic authority" was pitted against a group that respected the authority of a body of previously appointed presbyters (sometimes called "bishops") and deacons, who nonetheless could not even agree among themselves. Ignatius's response was to "reconceptualize church order in terms of pagan religious cults."⁶⁴ Promoting himself as Antioch's sole "bishop," who conveniently happened also to be a charismatic, he launched a campaign for a new three-tiered hierarchy of bishop, presbyters, and deacons.⁶⁵ Initially the Christians of Antioch were reluctant to accept this new idea, particularly given its source. Brent explains:

> Ignatius cut a strange figure in the eyes of the Antiochene community, and we must sympathize with them. He was not the sort of bishop with whom people would be comfortable at a Buckingham Palace garden party. Apt in the course of a heated exchange to change his appearance and with it his voice, he begins speaking "in the Spirit." He claims hidden revelations in support of a controversial policy that he demands the Church accept.⁶⁶

Soon the Christian community in Antioch was in an uproar. When the violence spilled into the streets, the Roman magistrates intervened, put Ignatius on trial, and sent him off to Rome to be thrown to the beasts.⁶⁷ His attempt to "force through a radical change in the structure of ecclesial authority" seemed to have failed.⁶⁸

But this is where Ignatius's gift for "constructing social reality rather than reflecting it" proved especially handy.⁶⁹ Taking his show on the road, Ignatius bribed his imperial guards in order to gain access to the churches en route and "choreographed" his journey "as a sacrificial procession in which he was the scapegoat victim on his way to sacrifice on a pagan altar at Rome."⁷⁰ When embassies of presbyters and deacons from Ephesus, Magnesia, and Tralles met him at Smyrna, he surprised

63. Ibid., 19.
64. Ibid., 34–35, 160.
65. Ibid., 39–40.
66. Ibid., 40.
67. Ibid., 42.
68. Ibid., 32.
69. Ibid., 58.
70. Ibid., 50–51.

them by singling out a de facto leader from among the presbyters of each church and referring to him as the sole "bishop" of that church. Taken aback at first, Onesimus, Damas, Polybius, and Polycarp soon grew accustomed to their promotion to a higher rank, and so the monepiscopacy was born.

Thus, when Ignatius refers in his letters to a tidy, three-tiered hierarchy, consisting of a single bishop, a body of presbyters, and a number of deacons in each church, he is "not describing an established church order in an existing historical situation" but is "creating a new social reality."[71] In promoting his agenda, Ignatius was not drawing upon the living tradition of the church or unfolding something inherent in the gospel. He may well have capitalized on Matthew's Petrine model of leadership, Brent suggests, but Matthew's presentation of Peter was itself no more than an "idealized portrait" serving the pragmatic function of bringing "order out of the charismatic chaos at Antioch."[72] No, Ignatius proved himself a "master of missionary persuasion" by couching his proposal to the churches of Asia Minor in the pagan discourse that his contemporaries found really convincing. "Such, after all, is the general method of spin-doctors in creating any movement for political change."[73]

Meanwhile, back in Antioch, the scapegoat mechanism was taking its effect. As "contemporary social-psychological studies and theories" teach us, a subgroup torn by internal strife will initially experience a kind of "therapy" and relief when they can gang up against an individual who has been demonized as the source of tensions, but afterward they may experience remorse over that person's fate. Sure enough, the Antiochene Christians who had united against Ignatius now experienced "feelings of guilt" and regretted that things had gone so far. Intuitively sensing this "change of mood" from afar, Ignatius quickly learned how to "play the martyr card" in order to gain sympathy for himself and support for his agenda.[74] In "a dazzling piece of enacted rhetoric," Ignatius gave his martyr procession "the character of a mystery play" in which one imitates the actions of a god or goddess in order to experience union with that deity.[75] Explaining that a bishop is "an image of the Father," Ignatius led his own procession as "the image of his suffering Father-god," referring to himself in the salutation of each letter as "God-bearer" (Θεοφόρος).[76] Simultaneously he imitated "an Attis rite" in which "the

71. Ibid., 151.
73. Ibid., 59.
75. Ibid., 158, 72.
72. Ibid., 29–30.
74. Ibid., 45–47.
76. Ibid., 80; cf. Tral. 3:1; Eph. sal.; etc.

mutilation of the priest" enabled the other members of the procession to gaze upon the blood of the god.[77] Responding to this pagan imagery, those Christians of Asia Minor who had run together to join Ignatius's procession were "stirred to ecstasy" and "inflamed by the blood of God."[78] As subsequent church history proves, Ignatius had successfully employed "the image of the scapegoat martyr" in order to "unite the divided community in collective guilt for what had transpired, and make them accept his particular definition of ecclesial unity."[79]

Brent's hypothesis makes for interesting reading. It also serves to illustrate the considerable challenge facing anyone who attempts to bring contemporary scholarship on early Christianity to the service of a theological project. It would be a mistake, I think, to dismiss Brent's work out of hand. His hypothesis skillfully weaves together a number of suggestions made by earlier scholars and has the merit of offering solutions to several real conundrums simultaneously.[80] What was the reason for Ignatius's arrest? How was it related to the Antiochene church's temporary loss of "peace," which seems to have caused Ignatius considerable anxiety during the early stages of his trip? What exactly does Ignatius mean by saying (later, in a letter written from Troas) that the church of Antioch was again at peace and had been restored to its "own bodily integrity" (Smyr. 11:2)? Why does Ignatius incorporate pagan religious imagery into his letters? Why does he call himself Θεοφόρος? Why (in every letter but Romans) does he need to insist so vehemently on submission to the bishop? When and how did monepiscopacy and the three-tiered hierarchy originate, and what was Ignatius's role in this process?

This last question is Brent's central concern, and while his claim that

---

77. Brent, *Ignatius of Antioch*, 153.   78. Ibid., 83; cf. Eph. 1:1.
79. Brent, *Ignatius of Antioch*, 56.
80. Streeter, writing in the 1920s, already combines the view of Ignatius as "a man of abnormal psychology" with the idea that "the consolidation of an ecclesiastical discipline centered in the monarchical bishop was the ideal for which Ignatius had lived, and which he hoped by a martyr's death firmly to rivet on the Church at large" (*Primitive Church*, 168–82; quotes from 171 and 181). Walter Bauer makes Ignatius the leader of an orthodox minority who attempts to seize power over the church in Antioch by promoting himself as its sole bishop in order to set up "a dictatorship that would establish the supremacy of his own party" (*Orthodoxy and Heresy in Earliest Christianity*, ed. Robert A. Kraft and Gerhard Krodel [Philadelphia: Fortress Press, 1971], 61–65; quote from 62), and Hammond Bammel hypothesizes that it was the "disputed election" of Ignatius that caused the unrest leading to his arrest ("Ignatian Problems," 79). Patrick Burke goes a step further and "argues that there were no bishops in Asia Minor until Ignatius passed through and that various individuals were raised to this position when Ignatius simply applied the label 'bishop' to them" (Robinson, *Parting of the Ways*, 101, n. 51, summarizing Patrick Burke, "The Monarchical Episcopate at the End of the First Century," *Journal of Ecumenical Studies* 7 [1970]: 499–518).

Ignatius was "not describing an established church order in an existing historical situation" but "creating a new social reality" may seem unlikely, it is really no less problematic than John Zizioulas's bald assertion of the opposite view, namely, that Ignatius's references to a sole bishop "corresponded to an historical state of affairs."[81] Anyone who accepts the latter view must attempt to explain why there are no patent references to monepiscopacy in the New Testament, the *Didache*, 1 *Clement*, or even Polycarp's *Philippians*.[82] Almost certainly the truth lies somewhere between the opinions of Brent and Zizioulas.[83]

Brent's argument might be critiqued from a number of angles. I shall mention a couple of problems by way of example. First, he seems so eager to find pagan religious imagery in Ignatius's letters that he frequently overlooks the biblical background to Ignatius's vocabulary. For instance, when Ignatius refers to himself as a θυσία ("sacrifice"; *Rom.* 4:2), Brent remarks that "Ignatius does not shrink from using a characteristically pagan word for sacrifice."[84] He fails to mention, however, that θυσία refers to sacrifices enjoined by the Torah hundreds of times in the Septuagint and the New Testament. When this term refers to Christ's self-offering or figuratively to the sacrificial charity of Christians, the background and overtones are decidedly Mosaic, and in the few texts where θυσία does refer to pagan or otherwise illicit sacrifices, this is spelled out clearly.[85] In any case, Ignatius's sacrificial imagery (in *Romans* 4 and elsewhere) skillfully blends biblical and pagan motifs.[86]

---

81. Brent, *Ignatius of Antioch*, 151; John D. Zizioulas, *Eucharist, Bishop, Church: The Unity of the Church in the Divine Eucharist and the Bishop during the First Three Centuries*, trans. Elizabeth Theokritoff (Brookline, Mass.: Holy Cross Orthodox Press, 2001), 159.

82. Lightfoot finds indirect testimony to the monepiscopacy in the fact that *Philippians* is sent from "Polycarp and the presbyters with him," rather than "Polycarp and the other presbyters" (Ignatius, *Polycarp*, 1.394–95).

83. Frederick W. Norris offers a plausible middle position: "The strong case which Ignatius made for the theological and organizational significance of the bishop probably was new, but prior to his writing, the offices existed and were distinguished from each other in Asia Minor, and probably in Western Syria" ("Ignatius, Polycarp, and 1 Clement: Walter Bauer Reconsidered," *Vigiliae Christianae* 30 [1976]: 35). Similarly, Paul Trebilco cites evidence from within the letters to suggest that "Ignatius was trying to consolidate and extend the authority of the bishop over the life of the church" ("Christian Communities in Western Asia Minor into the Early Second Century: Ignatius and Others as Witnesses against Bauer," *Journal of the Evangelical Theological Society* 49 [2006]: 31). See also Trebilco's fuller discussion in *Early Christians in Ephesus*, 658–68.

84. Brent, *Ignatius of Antioch*, 48.

85. Christ's self-offering: Eph 5:2; Heb 9:26. Sacrificial charity of Christians: Phil 4:18. Pagan or illicit sacrifices: 1 Cor 10:18; Acts 7:41.

86. The "pure bread" image of *Rom.* 4:1 is a case in point (see Lightfoot, *Ignatius, Polycarp*, 2.207). In a generally favorable review of Brent's *Ignatius of Antioch and the Second Sophistic*, Pieter G. R. de Villiers notes that "Brent's analysis requires further work in terms of Jewish texts that relate

Second, there are problems with Brent's historical methodology, particularly when it comes to reconstructing the events leading up to Ignatius's arrest. There is a strong trend in recent scholarship to suppose that Ignatius was taken into custody due to the role he played in a disturbance within the Christian community at Antioch, and not as the result of a persecution as such.[87] This is a plausible and attractive way of construing the handful of tantalizing hints that Ignatius drops about the situation in Antioch, but the way Brent fills in the details is simply stunning. What other scholars have offered as a tenuous hypothesis—namely, that the Gospel of Matthew and the *Didache* were composed in Antioch and supply us with information about the internal politics of that church during the decades just prior to Ignatius's arrest—Brent treats as the historical bedrock on which to build his hypothesis.[88] Furthermore, as I have hinted above, a host of sociological presuppositions regarding how groups resolve power struggles is operative in the interpretation of this "evidence."

Finally, a number of speculative leaps enable Brent to relate his already tendentious interpretation of Ignatius's behavior at Philadelphia

---

to the key motifs he investigates" ("Ignatius of Antioch in His Pagan Context," *Studia Historiae Ecclesiasticae* 33 [2007]: 405).

87. Of this hypothesis, Corwin writes: "It is possible, though it can be only a matter of speculation; we simply do not know why he was condemned" (*St. Ignatius and Christianity*, 25). *Smyrnaeans* 11 can certainly be read as implying that some sort of dissension occurred within the church at Antioch, but Ignatius's protests of unworthiness and his calling himself the "last" member of the church at Antioch (Eph. 21:2; Magn. 14:1; Tral. 13:1; Rom. 9:2; Smyr. 11:1) can be explained otherwise than by the supposition that he was the cause of the dissension as such and that a large part of the community had turned against him. Corwin notes that as bishop Ignatius would have felt responsible for the dissension no matter how it was caused and that he would have agonized over leaving the church before having been able to bring about a restoration (*St. Ignatius and Christianity*, 28).

88. For the use of Matthew as the missing link between the church of Antioch during the days of Barnabas, Paul, and Peter and the church of Antioch at the time of Ignatius, Brent is heavily dependent on the hypothesis of John Meier, in Raymond E. Brown and John P. Meier, *Antioch and Rome: New Testament Cradles of Catholic Christianity* (New York: Paulist Press, 1983), 11–72. Brown and Meier insist on "the tentative character of much of what [they] propose" and "are painfully conscious of weak links in the chain of evidence, particularly in the second generation," i.e., the generation for which Matthew is summoned as the sole witness to developments in the church of Antioch (213). As for the *Didache*, Meier acknowledges its apparent dependence on the Gospel of Matthew and suggests that it might have originated "somewhere in Syria," but he thinks it "impossible" to place its final form at Antioch and strongly advises against using it to fill in the gap between Matthew and Ignatius (83), which is the very thing Brent does. Meier briefly entertains the "possibility that at the very end of the first century the college of prophets and teachers at Antioch developed briefly into the two-tier system of bishops (or elders) and deacons as a transitional stage on the way to the threefold hierarchy," but concludes that while this may be "suggested by the data in the *Didache*, it must remain a pure surmise" (84). This pure surmise is the lynchpin in Brent's reconstruction (cf. *Ignatius of Antioch*, 26–30).

to the question of what "must" have transpired at Antioch. On the basis of all this, Brent is able to identify the precise nature of the (alleged) conflict at Antioch, the factions involved, how they felt about Ignatius, what he said to them, how they responded, how the authorities intervened, and how the various parties felt about his arrest both initially and subsequently. Brent is not shy in his advocacy of historical-critical methodology, which has brought about "the liberation of late medieval consciousness from its ahistorical dream world," nor in his disdain for a postmodernist approach to texts, which seems "fated simply to lapse into the pre-historical consciousness witnessed in the late Middle Ages."[89] But to be candid, I find his reconstruction of the situation at Antioch to resemble the playful musings of the postmodernist more than the sober analysis of the critical historian.

At the same time, whatever the merits or defects in Brent's approach, his book is properly historical in the sense of investigating a legitimate and important historical question: the origins of the episcopacy. Near the very end of the volume he briefly suggests that the results of his inquiry may have some relevance for contemporary struggles within the Anglican Communion, in which he is an ordained priest, but he never claims to be doing theology.[90] He is therefore not to be faulted for failing to adopt a theological approach, only for underestimating the depth and seriousness of Ignatius's theology, as well as for the sort of lapses in lexical and historical methodology that I have already mentioned.

My own interest in Ignatius's letters is quite different. The present investigation is meant to be properly theological in the sense of having for its principal object God himself and all things "according to their relation to God" (*secundum ordinem ad Deum*).[91] Specifically, I aim to study the economy of redemption as a divinely revealed reality. For this project, Ignatius as a historical figure and his letters as the object of interpretation are thus not ends in themselves but means toward an end. While it is certainly legitimate to view Ignatius's letters as a source of historical evidence in the investigation of a historical object, there is a sense in which they lend themselves more readily to a properly theological investigation. Ignatius composed his letters with a number of interrelated personal and pastoral concerns in view: to promote unity within and among the churches of Asia Minor, to insist on the three-tiered hierarchy, to refute the docetic and Judaizing heresies, to see the church in An-

---

89. Ibid., 6.
91. STh I, q. 1, a. 7.
90. Ibid., 159–62.

tioch restored to "its proper bodily integrity," and, above all, to "attain God" by means of martyrdom in Rome. One might, in this sense, say that Ignatius had an agenda. But at an even more fundamental level, his letters are concerned with "the economy of God" (Eph. 18:2, 20:1), for he understood that each of the items on his agenda would be accomplished to the extent that he himself and his readers entered more deeply into the mystery of redemption by way of "believing [the truth of revelation] with love" (Phld. 9:2). I take up Ignatius's letters, not merely to determine what Ignatius thought or what he meant to say, but to learn from him about the things whereof he wrote.

We might, then, call Ignatius our teacher, were it not for the fact that he eschews that title, reserving it for Christ alone.[92] Instead, Ignatius addresses us, his readers, as his "fellow students" (συνδιδασκαλίται; Eph. 3:1), a term that suggests that theology is properly an ecclesial activity and not merely the function of isolated individuals. Our place, then, is to sit alongside Ignatius and contemplate the mystery of redemption with him. This is, in a sense, the most natural way to read his letters. It is to respect their literary genre and to read them according to the spirit in which they were written. What Jean-Pierre Jossua expresses beautifully with regard to the church fathers in general is certainly true of Ignatius. "For the Fathers, redemption is a fact, an event of the 'economy,' before which they place themselves in order to attempt to comprehend and express something of its meaning."[93]

Now, this properly theological endeavor, whereby one inquires into the fact of redemption by means of the intellect and attempts, under the light of divine faith, to form correct judgments about it, is greatly enhanced by the "sympathy for divine things," which, as Aquinas tells us, is the result of that charity that unites us to God.[94] One who "does theology" in this sense does not attempt to stand aloof from the object of inquiry in order to judge it on the basis of extrinsic criteria but, on the contrary, draws near to it with faith and love. Naturally, since neither Ignatius nor his letters are per se the object of theological inquiry, it is perfectly legitimate for the theologian to criticize Ignatius for any

---

92. Eph. 15:1; Magn. 9:1; cf. Mt 23:8.

93. J.-P. Jossua, *Le salut: Incarnation ou mystère pascal, chez les Pères de l'Église de saint Irénée à saint Léon le Grand* (Paris: Éditions du Cerf, 1968), 5 ("Pour les Pères, la rédemption est un fait, un événement de l'« économie », devant lequel ils se placent pour tenter de comprendre et d'exprimer quelque chose de son sens").

94. STh II-II, q. 45, a. 2 (huiusmodi autem compassio sive connaturalitas ad res divinas fit per caritatem, quae quidem unit nos Deo).

deficiencies there may be in his grasp of the rule of faith, his interpretation of Scripture, his reasoning, or his epistolary self-expression. Still, the person who approaches Ignatius's letters with sympathy for divine things will also have a kind of sympathy for this ancient brother in the Lord and will judge his letters with Christian charity. And this is precisely what Ignatius asks of his readers. "I hope that you hear me in love [ἐν ἀγάπῃ]," he writes to the church at Tralles (Tral. 12:3), while to the Roman Christians he says, "If anyone has [Christ] in him, let him recognize what I want and sympathize with me [συμπαθείτω μοι], knowing the things that constrain me" (Rom. 6:3).

It is my contention that Ignatius has been judged unfairly by some scholars with regard to his epistolary style, his theological acumen, and his understanding of Scripture. I have found, time and again, that if I give Ignatius the benefit of the doubt and study his letters carefully, he shows himself to be a fine writer, a skillful exegete, and a superb theologian. As we have seen, Allen Brent goes much further in his criticism of Ignatius than do most earlier scholars, judging him personally and rather harshly, maintaining as he does so that "we must sympathize" with Ignatius's *opponents* within the Christian community at Antioch.[95] Leaving aside the fact that we do not know for certain whether Ignatius had any opponents within his own church, I suggest that we will get much better traction in our attempt to understand Ignatius's letters, and thus benefit from his insights into the economy of redemption, if we accord him the sympathy he asks of us. In his own attempt to understand the divine economy, Ignatius did not view Israel's prophets as bizarre and mentally imbalanced figures of a remote age, but as "saints worthy of love and worthy of admiration," who belong to "the unity of Jesus Christ" (Phld. 5:2). We might do well to regard Ignatius in the same way.

95. Brent, *Ignatius of Antioch*, 40.

3

JESUS AND THE FATHER

Doctor Unitatis

If Ignatius of Antioch were given an honorific title like those bestowed upon the doctors of the church, it might be Doctor Unitatis.[1] Indeed, he describes himself as "a man constituted for unity" (Phld. 8:1). In the six letters sent to Christian communities in southwest Asia Minor, Ignatius's overriding pastoral concern is to establish the unity of each local church under the authority of its bishop and over against the heretical teachers who threaten to divide the community. The unity of those who are "mingled" with the bishop derives from, and is a local manifestation of, the unity of the universal church in Jesus Christ, which in turn is rooted in Jesus' union with the Father.[2] In the remaining letter, Romans, which has a unique epistolary purpose, the theme of ecclesial unity is pushed to the periphery (alluded to briefly in the salutation but never mentioned thereafter), and its place is taken by the theme of Ignatius's personal hope for "attaining God" through martyrdom.[3] These two concerns are not unrelated, however. The attainment of God is, presumably, the definitive personal realization of that union with God and with other Christians that one experiences within the church already prior to death.

A close inspection of Ignatius's letters reveals that he views the economy of redemption in terms of several interlocking dimensions of unity. Redemption is a *mysterium unitatis*. Among these dimensions each of the following has a certain prominence in Ignatius's letters and plays an integral role in his theology: Jesus' unity with the Father (Magn. 1:2), the

---

[1]. Pope Benedict XVI, Church Fathers, 16. [2]. Eph. 5:1; Smyr. 8:2.
[3]. Rom. 1:2, 2:1, 4:1, 9:2.

unity of the human person as a creature who is both "fleshly and spiritual" (Poly. 2:2), the personal unity of Jesus Christ himself as both "God in man" (Eph. 7:2) and "the perfect man" (Smyr. 4:2), the unity of the "catholic church" in Jesus Christ (Smyr. 8:2), the doctrinal unity of those who gather with "one mind" to confess "one Jesus Christ" (Magn. 7:1–2) in the "unanimity of faith" (Eph. 13:1), the sacramental unity of "one eucharist" offered on "one altar" under the authority of "one bishop" (Phld. 4:1), and the unity of faith and love (Eph. 14:1). While Ignatius's desire to "attain God" may be rhetorically central to Romans, and the unity of the local church may be pastorally central to the other six letters, neither of these concerns is theologically central for Ignatius. They are but dimensions of a single unity of all reality in Jesus Christ, and it is he, in his union with the Father, who is central in Ignatius's theology.

Since unity is the dominant leitmotif of the Ignatian corpus, examining this topic carefully may lead us to an appreciation of the basic contours and deep patterns of Ignatius's thought. Such an examination may even grant us access to core aspects of his view of reality and thus afford a beachhead from which to explore other less developed dimensions of his theology. Accordingly, the next three chapters of this book will be devoted to the aspects of unity and certain related matters. After a few preliminaries, the present chapter focuses on the unity of "Jesus and the Father," which Ignatius considers the "most essential" dimension of unity (Magn. 1:2). This will involve us in an exploration of Ignatius's theology of God, his Christology, and his understanding of the economic missions of the Son and the Spirit. Chapter 4 considers the unity of "flesh and spirit," which is the foundational concept in Ignatius's soteriological anthropology. The same chapter also tackles the difficult topic of Ignatius's cosmology and his view of Christian existence as spiritual combat. Chapter 5 is devoted to the unity of "faith and love."

Ignatius thematizes his concern for unity in various ways. It will be helpful at the outset to survey a few of the most significant terms by which he does so. Foremost among these are the virtual synonyms ἑνότης ("unity") and ἕνωσις ("union"),[4] along with the factitive verb ἑνόω ("to unify,

---

4. These terms are not entirely interchangeable. In my opinion, Ignatius generally uses ἑνότης to denote an objective and already established condition or fact of "unity" (e.g., Phld. 2:2, 3:2, 5:2, 8:1, 9:1), whereas he uses ἕνωσις to refer to a "union" or "unification" that is in process, wished for, or in the future (e.g., Magn. 1:2, 13:2; Tral. 11:2; Phld. 8:1; Poly. 5:2). Corwin, on the other hand, thinks that Ignatius generally uses ἑνότης for the "unity" that exists among the members of the church (on earth) while he usually reserves ἕνωσις for "a transcendent reference," to denote "what seems to be the ultimate in human experience," that is, union with God (St. Ignatius and Christianity, 259–60).

make one"). These three cognates, which are derived from ἕν ("one"), occur a total of twenty-four times in Ignatius's letters, as compared to just twice in the entire New Testament.[5] Ignatius also frequently uses the numeral "one" itself (εἷς, μία, ἕν) to express the idea of unity. In an especially striking passage he outstrips his Pauline model (the sevenfold use of "one" in Eph 4:4–6) by employing the word "one" no less than nine times in the span of two verses.

But when you are together, let there be one prayer, one petition, one mind, one hope.... All of you should hasten together as to one temple of God, as to one altar, to one Jesus Christ, who came forth from one Father, and was toward one, and departed. (*Magn.* 7:1–2)

Ignatius also imitates, and outdoes, Paul in the employment of the prefix συν- ("together, with") to express collaboration and unity among Christians.[6] For example, he attaches it to six different verbs within a brief exhortation: "Train together, vie together, run together, suffer together, sleep together, rise together" (*Poly.* 6:1).

Indeed Ignatius's creative use of συν-terms is almost unbounded. By way of illustration we may confine ourselves to the instances found in a single letter. Ignatius addresses the Ephesians as his "fellow learners" (συνδιδασκαλίται) and calls their deacon Burrhus his "fellow slave" (σύνδουλος).[7] He exhorts them to "run together" (συντρέχω) in the will of God and in the will of their bishop, with whom Ignatius himself has enjoyed intimate spiritual "fellowship" (συνήθεια).[8] Indeed the Ephesian presbyters are already "in tune with" (συναρμόζομαι) the bishop, like strings on a lyre, while the congregation hymns Jesus Christ in "harmonious" (σύμφωνος) love (Eph. 4:1–2), and to that extent all things are "harmonious" (σύμφωνος) in unity (5:1). The Ephesians are like "fellow pilgrims" (σύνοδοι) in a religious procession, and Ignatius "congratulates" (συγχαίρω) them (9:2). They have always "lived in accord with" (συναινέω) the apostles (11:2) and are "fellow initiates" (συμμύσται)

---

5. The term ἑνότης is found in Eph. 4:2, 5:1, 14:1; Phld. 2:2, 3:2, 5:2, 8:1, 9:1; Smyr. 12:2; and Poly. 8:3; ἕνωσις is found in Magn. 1:2, 13:2; Tral. 11:2; Phld. 4:1, 7:2, 8:1; Poly. 1:2, 5:2; and ἑνόω is found in Eph. sal.; Magn. 6:2, 7:1, 14:1; Rom. sal.; and Smyr. 3:3. Only ἑνότης is found in the New Testament (Eph 4:3, 4:13; and, in some manuscripts, Col 3:14).

6. Some examples from the Pauline epistles: συγκοινωνοί ("fellow participants" in grace; Phil 1:7); συμπολῖται ("fellow citizens" in the kingdom of God; Eph 2:19); σύμψυχοι ("united in spirit"; Phil 2:2); συνεργός ("coworker" in the gospel; 2 Cor 8:23, 1 Thes 3:2); συγκακοπαθέω ("to suffer hardship [for the gospel] with"; 2 Tm 1:8, 2:3).

7. Eph. 3:1, 2:1.

8. Eph. 3:2, 4:1, 5:1.

of Paul in particular (12:2). Ignatius exhorts them to "come together" (συνέρχομαι) for the eucharist often and in one faith.[9]

Dimensions of Unity

While Ignatius does not explore unity in a systematic manner, his statements about unity do presuppose a coherent structure of thought, even as they disclose his grasp of the *analogia fidei*, that is, the deep interrelations among the truths of the faith. To begin to appreciate Ignatius's insight in this regard, it will be instructive to consider two programmatic passages that frame the body of his *Letter to the Magnesians*. The first of these is especially important because it is Ignatius's clearest general statement about what he hopes to accomplish by visiting and writing to the churches as he passes through Asia Minor on his way to Rome.

> Having been honored with a godly name and bearing about these chains, I sing the praises of the churches and pray that there will be in them a union [ἕνωσις] of flesh and spirit of Jesus Christ, our everlasting life, of faith and love, to which nothing is preferable, and most essentially of Jesus and the Father, in whom, if we endure all the abuse of the ruler of this aeon and escape, we shall attain God. (Magn. 1:2–3)

This passage provides us with what seems to be almost an outline of the levels or dimensions of ecclesial unity. Ignatius wishes the churches to possess a unity: (1) of flesh and spirit of Jesus Christ, (2) of faith and love, and (3) of Jesus and the Father. If we can but grasp what these three phrases signify, we will have, as it were, the structure of Ignatius's thought on the subject of unity. Furthermore, this passage places Ignatius's concern for unity within the context of his ministry to the churches of Asia Minor and within the context of spiritual warfare and personal eschatology, which is to say, within the context of a teleological view of Christian existence. Indeed, it brings together as clearly as any passage in the Ignatian corpus the bishop of Antioch's two most fundamental concerns, the unity of the churches and the success of his own martyrdom, and indicates their close interrelationship.

---

9. Eph. 13:1, 20:2. Occurring less frequently than ἐν-words or συν-words but nevertheless important are a trio of ὁμο-words employed by Ignatius: ὁμοήθεια ("sameness of character"), ὁμολογέω ("to confess"), and ὁμόνοια ("unanimity, concord"). The last of these terms occurs eight times in Ignatius's letters and seems to have been of special importance to him. In a recent monograph John-Paul Lotz illuminates the rich political and cultural background of ὁμόνοια and its use by Ignatius (*Ignatius and Concord: The Background and Use of the Language of Concord in the Letters of Ignatius of Antioch*, Patristic Studies 8 [New York: Peter Lang, 2007]).

The goal of ecclesial unity and the goal of martyrdom are one and the same: the attainment of God. Ignatius opens the statement in the first person singular and closes it in the first person plural. At the beginning he refers to the chains that "I" bear about, and at the end he speaks of how "we" may attain God by enduring the devil's torments. In this way Ignatius includes his readers, as it were, in his martyr procession and its goal. Or rather, he shows them that their own road to the attainment of God will be found in the cultivation of ecclesial unity. We must, then, by no means conceive of the unity Ignatius wants for the churches as a static equilibrium. As shall become increasingly clear as we proceed with this study, Ignatius views everything that pertains to the divine economy under its dynamic and teleological aspect.

The ambiguous phrase "a unity *of* flesh and spirit *of* Jesus Christ" can be plausibly understood in several ways, depending in part on how one construes the two Greek genitives involved. We could, for example, take the first as a genitive of domain and the second as a genitive of source, thus: "a unity *in the domain of* flesh and spirit that *comes from* Jesus Christ." Alternatively, we could take the first as a genitive of source and the second as a genitive of possession, thus: "a unity *that comes from* the flesh and spirit *that belong to* Jesus Christ." It may not, however, be wise to attempt to nail down the grammatical sense too precisely when Ignatius has chosen to employ such imprecise language. It is more important and helpful to attend both to the immediate context and to the way Ignatius speaks throughout his letters. As we shall see in chapter 4, the categories of "flesh and spirit" are basic to Ignatius's view of the human person, especially as human persons live together in Christ. So, just as the Trallians have refreshed Ignatius "both in flesh and in spirit" (*Tral.* 12:1) and the Roman Christians are "united according to flesh and spirit" (*Rom.* sal.), so in the present passage we should refer "flesh and spirit" in the first instance to the Magnesians themselves. Ignatius wishes them to enjoy a unity that encompasses and involves the whole human person, flesh and spirit. Of course, this begs the question of what Ignatius means by "flesh and spirit," and to that issue we shall have to return.

In any case, this reading of *Magnesians* 1:2 need not preclude all reference to the flesh and spirit *that belong to* Jesus Christ. Even if we construe the grammar such that Ignatius speaks of "a unity *in the domain of* flesh and spirit *that comes from* Jesus Christ," we need to ask why he should specify Jesus Christ as the source of the unity of flesh and spirit in particular. The obvious answer to this question is that Ignatius is directing our attention to a kind of parallelism and causal connection between the incarnation as a union of "flesh and spirit" and Christian unity as involving a renewed integration of the human person composed of "flesh and spirit." As Virginia Corwin puts it, "The unity within the human being is thought of as presaged by and dependent upon the unity of flesh and spirit that marked Jesus Christ."[10] Jesus Christ is the "one healer," able to confer a unity of flesh and spirit upon his disciples, precisely because he himself is "fleshly and spiritual" (Eph. 7:2). If "flesh" and "spirit" are Ignatius's favorite anthropological terms, why should he not refer them also to the one who is "perfect man" (Smyr. 4:2)?

Thus the formulation of *Magnesians* 1:2 probably implies that the intrapersonal and interpersonal unity available to Christians by grace is in some sense a participation in the prior unity of "flesh and spirit" that exists in "the new man Jesus Christ" (Eph. 20:1). Elsewhere Ignatius says of the apostles who saw and touched Jesus after his resurrection that they were "mingled with his flesh and spirit" (Smyr. 3:2).[11] Presumably this grace is extended, in a sacramental manner, to Christians of every age. We need to be cautious here, however. One could easily suppose that Ignatius applies the expression "flesh and spirit" *univocally* to Jesus Christ and to human persons. But, when we consider "flesh and spirit" within the dual contexts of Christology and anthropology, we shall see that this is not the case. Jesus Christ is "flesh and spirit" in a unique sense.[12]

Ignatius never considers the human person strictly according to the order of creation (much less in terms of "pure nature"). In keeping with the pastoral purpose of his letters, his concern is with repentance, renewal, and salvation. Accordingly, he always views man within the context of the economy of redemption, which he calls "the economy concerning the new man Jesus Christ" (Eph. 20:1). Therefore our examination of his anthropology will of necessity lead into some consideration of his hamartiology and soteriology. For example, we shall need to ask how his use of the terms "flesh" and "spirit" compares to Paul's use of the same terms. It is in this realm that Ignatius's theology is thought by

---

10. Corwin, *St. Ignatius and Christianity*, 258.

11. Reading πνεύματι ("spirit") with the Greek, Latin, and Coptic witnesses to the middle recension. Holmes reads αἵματι ("blood") with the Armenian version (*Apostolic Fathers*, 250).

12. For Ignatius's use of σάρξ and σαρκικός in Christological and anthropological contexts, see especially Horacio E. Lona, "Der Sprachgebrauch von σάρξ, σαρκικός bei Ignatius von Antiochien," *Zeitscrift für katholische Theologie* 108 (1986): 383–408. For his use of πνεῦμα and πνευματικός in Christological and anthropological contexts, see Martin, "La pneumatología en Ignacio," 387–405.

some scholars to have serious deficiencies and even to represent a fundamental departure from the teaching of the New Testament. In chapter 4 I will present their criticisms and attempt to offer a more generous interpretation of what Ignatius has to say about flesh and spirit and about sin and salvation.

This will lead us in chapter 5 into a consideration of the unity "of faith and love," the second level of unity according to the formulation of *Magnesians* 1:2. Because the pairing off of "faith and love" is ubiquitous in Ignatius's letters and is therefore universally recognized to be one of the keys to understanding his theology, these terms have not been neglected in Ignatian scholarship. I will attempt to illuminate two aspects of Ignatius's teaching that have not, however, garnered enough attention. First, a focus on the intellectual dimension of faith (but not to the exclusion of the fiduciary and other dimensions) will help us relate the unity of faith and love both to Ignatius's emphasis on Christ as revealer of the Father and teacher of man and also to the great importance he attaches to the figure of the bishop and to authentic doctrine. Second, the teleological relation between faith and love with respect to "life" (ζωή)—"faith is the beginning and love the end ... of life" (Eph. 14:1)—will help us to relate Ignatius's exhortation to unity both to the Christ event as redemptive and to the eschatological goal of Christian existence, namely, the attainment of God.

The third and "most essential" (κυριώτερον)[13] dimension of unity in the formulation of *Magnesians* 1:2 is the unity "of Jesus and the Father." Once again the phrase may be variously construed, but given the Johannine cast of Ignatius's thought and the great importance that Jesus' relation to the Father has throughout his letters, it seems tolerably clear that Ignatius is praying that the Magnesians will in some sense participate in the union that the Son has with the Father. Indeed, Ignatius seems to echo Jesus' own prayer: "Holy Father, keep them in your name, which you gave to me, in order that they may be one even as we are ... that they all may be one, even as you, Father, are in me and I am in you, in order that they also may be in us."[14]

In his effort to rid Ignatius's letters of anything that smacks of mystical union, William R. Schoedel maintains that *Magnesians* 1:2 "should not be taken as referring to union *with* Jesus and the Father." Instead,

---

13. In Koine Greek the comparative has largely taken over the role of the superlative (BDF §§ 60 and 244).

14. Jn 17:11b, 21a.

Ignatius is merely indicating that "the union of Father and Son is a *model* for the perfect concord of the Christian community."¹⁵ But this reductive interpretation flies in the face of the way Ignatius speaks throughout his letters. He knows that the Magnesians "have Jesus Christ within" themselves (12:1) and are "filled with God" (14:1). Likewise, when the "members of his Son" live "in blameless unity," they "always participate [μετέχω] in God" (Eph. 4:2). The church is "mingled" with Jesus Christ, just as he is with the Father (5:1). Even Ignatius's references to "imitation" imply much more than mere copying. "Imitators of God" are the sort who "enflame themselves in the blood of God" (1:1), and "imitators of the Lord" are those who "abide in Christ Jesus in flesh and in spirit" (10:3). Only the person who has Jesus Christ "within himself" can sympathize with Ignatius's desire to "imitate the passion" of his God (Rom. 6:3). This is to mention but a few of the expressions by which Ignatius refers to the Christian's present mystical union with God, to say nothing of the fact that he speaks of the eschatological goal of the Christian life in terms of "attaining God" no less than seventeen times.¹⁶ Of course, it remains to be seen what Ignatius means by all these expressions, but Schoedel's sanitized interpretation would require us to regard them as so much extravagant rhetoric.

Near the end of *Magnesians* Ignatius tells his readers that if their lives are founded on the commands of the Lord Jesus and the apostles, they will prosper "in flesh and spirit, in faith and love, in the Son and the Father and in the Spirit, in the beginning and the end" (*Magn.* 13:1). Like the statement in 1:2–3, this formulation is immediately followed by a reference to the threefold hierarchy of bishop, presbyters, and deacons, while the larger context indicates that here too Ignatius is explicitly concerned with ecclesial ἕνωσις (13:2). When we place the two formulations alongside each other, their similarity in structure (as well as a couple of interesting differences) becomes apparent.

Magnesians 1:2	*Magnesians* 13:1
... that there may be in them a unity	... that you may prosper
of *flesh and spirit* of Jesus Christ	in *flesh and spirit*,
our everlasting life,	
of *faith and love*,	in *faith and love*,

---

15. Schoedel, *Ignatius of Antioch*, 105 (emphasis added).
16. The phrase "to attain God" (θεοῦ ἐπιτυχεῖν or similar) occurs in Eph. 10:1, 12:2; Magn. 1:3, 14:1; Tral. 12:2, 13:3; Rom. 1:2, 2:1, 4:1, 5:3 (bis), 8:3, 9:2; Smyr. 9:2, 11:1; Poly. 2:3, 7:1. Related expressions are found in Eph. 1:2; Tral. 5:2, 12:3; Phld. 5:3.

to which nothing is preferable,	
and most essentially	
of Jesus and the Father ...	in the Son and the Father and in the Spirit
	in the beginning and the end ...

Ignatius's listing of three dimensions of unity in the same order in both texts—flesh and spirit, faith and love, and Son and Father—is no mere coincidence but reflects a nascent systematization in his thinking and one of his core insights into the mystery of redemption. As already indicated, this schema will provide the framework for the present exploration. I shall devote one chapter to each of these three dimensions. But instead of taking them in the order in which Ignatius lists them, I shall begin with the dimension that he identifies as "most essential": the unity of Jesus and the Father. The reference to Jesus as "Son" and the inclusion of the Holy Spirit in Ignatius's second formulation may suggest that he did not think of this dimension of unity as a purely economic reality but as something rooted in God's Trinitarian being. I shall touch on this question toward the end of the present chapter within a consideration of Ignatius's use of the term "the unity of God" (ἑνότης θεοῦ) and his pneumatology. Finally, the phrase "in the beginning and the end" (ἐν ἀρχῇ καὶ ἐν τέλει) supports my earlier supposition that Ignatius views ecclesial unity teleologically. This topic will concern us especially in chapter 5, where we shall attempt to understand the precise relationship between faith and love, which Ignatius identifies respectively as the ἀρχή and τέλος of life in Christ (Eph. 14:1).

Christology

As we have just seen, Ignatius occasionally refers to Father, Son, and Holy Spirit in triadic formulae, but for the most part his discourse about God is dominated by dyadic references to God the Father and Jesus Christ.[17] Since Ignatius tells us that the relationship between Jesus and the Father is the "most essential" dimension of unity, we shall begin our systematic treatment of unity by looking at what he has to say about the person and work of Jesus Christ and his relationship to the Father insofar as these pertain to the theme of unity, deferring discussion of the Holy Spirit to the last part of this chapter.

17. Triadic formulae: *Magn.* 13:1; *Eph.* 9:1; *Phld. sal.* Dyadic references: *Eph. sal.*, 3:2, 4:2, 5:1, 15:1, 20:2, 21:2; *Magn. sal.*, 1:2, 5:2, 7:1, 7:2, 8:2; *Tral.* 1:1, 3:1, 9:2, 12:2, 13:3; *Rom. sal.*, 2:2, 3:3, 8:2; *Phld.* 1:1, 3:1, 3:2, 7:2b; *Smyr. sal.*, 7:1, 8:1; *Poly. sal.*, 8:3.

The great importance that Christology has for Ignatius is reflected in the fact that each of his seven letters contains at least one solemn creedal statement about Jesus Christ.[18] Ignatius embraces a high Christology. Before the creation of the world Jesus Christ was already "with the Father" (*Magn.* 6:1). Prior to his conception in the virgin's womb, he was "timeless ... invisible ... intangible ... impassible," but upon taking flesh in the temporal realm he became "visible" and "passible" for the sake of our salvation (*Poly.* 3:2). Like the New Testament authors, Ignatius refers to Jesus as "the Lord" (over thirty times) and "Son of God" (six times), but unlike many of them, he does not hesitate to refer to Jesus also as "our God" or "my God." At least this is true with respect to three letters: *Ephesians*, *Romans*, and *Polycarp*.[19] It is probably not coincidental that references to Christ as "God" (θεός) are entirely absent from the two anti-Judaizing letters (*Magnesians* and *Philadelphians*) and virtually absent from the two antidocetic letters (*Trallians* and *Smyrnaeans*).[20] In the former case Ignatius is presumably guarding against being interpreted as having abandoned biblical monotheism (by introducing a "second God"), while in the latter case he naturally places the accent more on Jesus' humanity than on his divinity.[21]

At any rate, Ignatius's references to Christ as "God," properly interpreted, serve neither to confuse Jesus with the Father nor to give the impression of two Gods. In chapter 7 I shall answer the charge that Ignatius's references to Jesus Christ's having "come forth" from the Father (*Magn.* 7:2) or from "silence" (8:2) express a sort of modalism or economic emanationism. A crystal-clear relational distinction between Jesus and the Father permeates Ignatius's theology of God, and he indicates that this relational distinction existed "before the ages" (6:1). Moreover, he carefully safeguards the absolute uniqueness of the relationship between the Father and the Son. God is "the Father of Jesus Christ" (*Tral.* sal.), and Jesus is "the Son of the Father" (*Rom.* sal.). Despite the influence of Paul and John on Ignatius's theology, he never refers to Christians as "sons" or "children" of God.[22] And despite Ignatius's apparent

---

18. Eph. 7:2, 18:2, 20:2; Magn. 6:1, 7:2, 8:2; Tral. 9:1–2; Rom. 6:1, 7:3; Phld. 9:2; Smyr. 1:1–3:3; Poly. 3:2.

19. Eph. sal., 15:3, 18:2; Rom. sal. (bis), 3:3, 6:3; Poly. 8:3.

20. *Smyrnaeans* does, however, refer to "Jesus Christ, the God who made you so wise" (1:1), and in some witnesses we find a reference to "Christ God" at 10:1.

21. In *Ephesians*, which contains a more general warning against heresy, Ignatius freely refers to Jesus as "our God" but qualifies this usage by means of expressions such as "the blood of God" (1:1), "God in man" (7:2), and "God manifesting himself humanly" (19:3).

22. Naturally, Paul and John have their own ways of maintaining a distinction between Je-

familiarity with the Gospel of Matthew and his intimate sense of mystical union with God, he never refers to God as "our Father."

Father-Son language is strictly reserved for the relationship between "the Father Most High and Jesus Christ his only Son" (Rom. sal.). Ignatius refers to God as "Father" over forty times in his small corpus of letters, but he is scrupulously careful always to relate God's Fatherhood to Jesus Christ. The Christian, to be sure, is summoned by the Spirit to "come to the Father" (7:2), but one makes that journey only in and through Jesus Christ, the unique Son. Christians "sing in one voice through Jesus Christ to the Father" (Eph. 4:2), and they acquire the "imprint of God the Father through Jesus Christ" (Magn. 5:2).

At the same time, the relationship between the Father and the Son is a perfect unity in "one God" (8:2), who is "unity" (Tral. 11:2). Ignatius's frequent and consistent use of the terms "Father" and "Son" enables him to maintain a relational distinction within God, while his fluid use of the word θεός, to refer either to the Father or to the Son, or even simply to "God" in his unity, helps him safeguard God's oneness. As one might expect from a second-century author, there are lacunae in Ignatius's theology of God. For example, he never explicitly affirms the eternal generation of the Son. Indeed, when he describes Jesus Christ as "born and unborn" (γεννητὸς καὶ ἀγέννητος), it is the latter term that refers to his preincarnational existence (Eph. 7:2).[23] Nonetheless, given that Ignatius does not enjoy the benefit of later dogmatic definitions, he does quite well in maintaining both the unity of Father and Son and their relational distinction.

If Ignatius promotes a high Christology—by calling Jesus Christ "God"; by confessing his preexistence in a timeless, invisible, intangible, and impassible state; and by stressing his unique filial relation to God the Father—none of this is to the detriment of Christ's true humanity. On the contrary, Ignatius vigorously denounces those who refuse to acknowledge that Jesus Christ is "flesh-bearing" (σαρκοφόρος), who regard him as "a bodiless phantom," and who say that he merely "seemed" to suffer.[24] We would be mistaken, however, to view Ignatius's emphasis

---

sus' divine filiation and the grace of filiation enjoyed by Christians. Paul speaks of the latter as an "adoptive sonship" (υἱοθεσία; Rom 8:15, 23; Gal 4:5; Eph 1:5). John, for his part, reserves the word "Son" (υἱός) for Jesus while speaking of Christians as God's "children" (τέκνα; 1 Jn 3:8–10).

23. On these terms, see Lightfoot, *Ignatius, Polycarp*, 2.90–94, and Camelot, *Ignace d'Antioche*, 27–28.

24. Smyr. 2:1, 3:2, 5:2.

on Christ's humanity merely in terms of its function within his polemic against docetism. The true, historical, flesh-and-blood humanity of Jesus Christ factors significantly into all seven letters and impacts every level of Ignatius's theology. What is more remarkable for such an early Christian author, and of particular importance for understanding Ignatius's teaching on unity, is the conscious and explicit manner by which he affirms not only the coexistence of divinity and humanity in the person of Christ but their unity as well. Note, for example, how he brings together two of Christ's biblical titles (in a way that will become standard practice among the later church fathers) to indicate that the "one Jesus Christ" is both "Son of Man and Son of God," that is, human and divine.[25]

Ignatius's carefully crafted creedal formulae sometimes employ rhetorical symmetry in order to make this point emphatically. It will be instructive to take a careful look at the formulation of *Ephesians* 7:2, which, when it is laid out schematically, following the Greek word order as far as possible, exhibits a precise structure.

- A There is one healer,
- B fleshly and spiritual,
- C born and unborn,
- D in man God,
- D' in death true life,
- C' both from Mary and from God,
- B' first passible and then impassible,
- A' Jesus Christ our Lord.

This solemn creedal affirmation consists of eight phrases arranged as a chiasmus. The opening and closing phrases (A and A'), which identify the "one" whom the church confesses, serve to frame six descriptive pairs (B through B'). In each of these pairs the first element pertains to Christ's true humanity ("fleshly ... born ... in man ... in death ... from Mary ... passible") while the second element pertains to his divinity or, as I shall explain presently, to his divinity's effect upon his humanity ("spiritual ... unborn ... God ... true life ... from God ... impassible"). Superimposed upon this broad parallelism is the more precise inverted parallelism that gives the formula its chiastic structure. For example, phrase C ("born and unborn") is echoed by C' ("both from Mary and from God").[26] A chiastic structure often serves to focalize the central ele-

---

25. Eph. 20:2; cf. Dem. 92. Contrast Barn. 12:10 (οὐχὶ υἱὸς ἀνθρώπου ἀλλὰ υἱὸς τοῦ θεοῦ)!
26. I shall explain the parallelism between B and B' below.

ment. The centerpiece of this chiasmus is the fascinating parallelism between phrases D and D', which are further set off from the other phrases by their common syntactic structure ("in X, Y"). Phrase D alludes to the incarnation ("in man God") and phrase D' to the paschal mystery ("in death true life"), so that together these two phrases constitute a thumbnail sketch of the Christ event. The parallelism between them reminds us that Jesus' being *man* makes possible his real *death*, whereas his being *God* enables him to be the source of *true life* through his death and resurrection. J. N. D. Kelly's disparaging reference to this passage as a "dry-as-dust enumeration of facts" overlooks its intricate structure.[27]

To appreciate this creedal formula and its relation to the theme of unity more fully, we need to place it in its epistolary context, which is a strict warning not to be deceived by those who speak falsely about Jesus and who practice immorality (*Eph.* 6:1–9:2). As Ignatius views the matter, the fact that heterodox teachers lead carnal lives is hardly a coincidence, for immorality and heresy both pertain to division. While heresy divides the community, immorality divides the self. Man is created to be a unity of "flesh and spirit," but immoral persons are simply "fleshly" (σαρκικοί; 8:2). The "evil guile" with which they act reveals a divided mind and leads to the hypocrisy of "bearing the name" of Christ while "doing things unworthy of God" (7:1). Indeed, their humanity is so compromised that Ignatius describes them (here and elsewhere) in bestial terms. They are "rabid dogs" whose bite is "difficult to cure" (7:1). Jesus Christ is the "one healer" who has the remedy for both intrapersonal and interpersonal division. He is able to bring about the unity of flesh and spirit, in and among his disciples, because in his own person he is already a perfect unity of flesh and spirit (σαρκικὸς καὶ πνευματικός).

As we shall see in the next chapter, when Ignatius uses the phrase σαρκικὸς καὶ πνευματικός anthropologically, he refers to two complementary dimensions *of the human person* (more specifically, of the human person in Christ): a material or physical dimension and an immaterial or spiritual dimension. For example, he says that Polycarp is "fleshly and spiritual" (*Poly.* 2:2) and as such is well constituted to attend to all the concerns of his flock, "both fleshly and spiritual" (1:2). One might suppose, then, that the phrase σαρκικὸς καὶ πνευματικός has the same meaning in the Christological context of *Ephesians* 7:2. In other words,

---

27. *Early Christian Creeds*, 3rd ed. (New York: Continuum, 2006), 69. For a more appreciative and probing examination of this "fine passage," see Grillmeier, *Christ in Christian Tradition*, 1.87–89.

we might take both terms together to refer to the *humanity* of Jesus Christ, a humanity constituted of body and soul. And this interpretation would seem to find support in Ignatius's reference to Christ as "the perfect man" (*Smyr.* 4:2).

But there are at least three good reasons to reject this interpretation of *Ephesians* 7:2. First, as we have already noted, this creedal formula employs rhetorical symmetry in order to indicate the unity of *humanity and divinity* in the person of Christ, not the unity of body and soul within the humanity of Christ. In each of the other pairs of terms, the first pertains to his humanity and the second to his divinity (or to his divinity's effect upon his humanity). Thus σαρκικός ought by itself to refer to his humanity and πνευματικός to his divinity. Second, when Ignatius refers unambiguously to the humanity of Christ elsewhere in his letters, he speaks either in terms of "flesh" alone or in terms of "flesh and blood."[28] Both usages are rooted in the Johannine literature, where "flesh" by itself can designate the humanity of Christ and where "flesh and blood" (rather than "body and blood") is the distinctively Johannine way to refer to Christ's presence in the eucharist.[29] Third, Ignatius's Christological formulations conform to what we generally find among orthodox authors prior to the condemnation of Apollinarianism in the late fourth century. During this period so much attention was given to the unity of the divine Word with a true bodily humanity that the question of whether Christ had a human soul was sometimes overlooked. In Ignatius's case this is hardly surprising, given that the term "soul" (ψυχή) plays virtually no role in his anthropology to begin with.[30] To sum up then, Ignatius refers to the humanity of Christ as "fleshly" but refers to the humanity of Christians as "fleshly and spiritual." Jesus was nailed to the cross "in the flesh," but Christians are, as it were, nailed to his cross "in both flesh and spirit" (*Smyr.* 1:1–2).

Does all of this mean that in *Ephesians* 7:2 Ignatius uses the word "spiritual" (πνευματικός) to refer to what later will be called Christ's

---

28. He refers to Christ's "flesh" in *Magn.* 13:2; *Phld.* 5:1; *Smyr.* 1:1–2, 3:1, 5:2. 7:1; and *Poly.* 5:2; and to his "flesh and blood" in *Tral.* 8:1; *Rom.* 7:3; *Phld.* 4:1; and *Smyr.* 12:2. We should perhaps also include here *Tral.* sal. ("at peace in the flesh and blood of Jesus Christ"), but a number of textual variants make this reading uncertain. The reference to the postresurrection "flesh and spirit" of Christ in *Smyr.* 3:2 will be dealt with below.

29. For "flesh" referring to the humanity of Christ, see Jn 1:14; 1 Jn 4:2; and 2 Jn 7; and for "flesh and blood" referring to the eucharist, see Jn 6:53–56. Ignatius for his part can use either expression to designate Christ's historical humanity and eucharistic humanity simultaneously (*Rom.* 7:3; *Smyr.* 7:1).

30. The term occurs only in *Phld.* 1:2, 11:2.

"divine nature"? It is probably not quite that simple. Without charging Ignatius with adoptionism, it might be fair to say that he has a somewhat more dynamic notion of the unity of humanity and divinity in Christ than we find in some later dogmatic formulations.[31] Already for Ignatius, to be sure, the conception of Jesus in Mary's womb has become a clear focal point for Christology.[32] In the present passage, accordingly, he expresses the unity of humanity and divinity in terms of origin "both from Mary and from God." But Ignatius also incorporates into this Christological confession references to the paschal mystery, such as: "in death true life." Based on what he says elsewhere, we might gloss this phrase roughly this way: "Put to death in his humanity, he was raised by divine power and became the source of new life for those who conform their own living and dying to his passion." Much as Paul says of Jesus Christ that through his resurrection he became "a life-giving spirit" (1 Cor 15:45), so Ignatius understands something soteriologically vital to have *happened* to Jesus Christ in his resurrection.

This change, which is the culmination of what I referred to above as the effect of his divinity upon his humanity, is alluded to in any number of passages but is particularly clear in the final pairing of our passage: "first passible and then impassible" (Eph. 7:2). At first blush this formulation would seem to contradict Ignatius's reference elsewhere to Christ as "the impassible one, who for our sake became passible" (Poly. 3:2). There is no contradiction, however, provided we recognize that the latter passage refers to the change that took place at the incarnation while the former refers to the change that took place at the resurrection. Thus one could combine the two statements in one coherent formulation as follows. Prior to the incarnation God's Son was strictly and in every respect impassible; through the incarnation he became passible, that is, capable of suffering in his humanity; and through the resurrection he became once again "impassible," not as if leaving his humanity behind, of course, but inasmuch as that humanity had been transformed by divine power and rendered incapable of further suffering.[33] Thus, however much one right-

---

31. "Though the static character of a 'two nature' christology may become visible as early as Ignatius, a full, living dynamic is evident throughout his writings. This has its source in his all-pervading view of the economy of salvation and the basic soteriological-anthropological tone of this christology" (Grillmeier, *Christ in Christian Tradition*, 1.89).

32. Eph. 18:2; Tral. 9:1.

33. Cf. Paul, Rom 6:9. Corwin attempts to harmonize the two Ignatian passages by maintaining that "in neither case is the order significant" (*St. Ignatius and Christianity*, 93). But Ignatius explicitly says "first ... then" in Eph. 7:2, indicating that the order of the historical events of redemption is not irrelevant to his point.

ly insists that the hypostatic union was perfect and indissoluble from the first moment of Christ's conception in his mother's womb, one can also say that the transformative effect of this union on the humanity of Christ was not complete until he was glorified. Now, if we are correct in our analysis of the Christological formula of *Ephesians* 7:2 as having a chiastic structure, the phrase "fleshly and spiritual" (B) would be the counterpart of the phrase "first passible and then impassible" (B´). And if that be the case, "spiritual" might not mean simply "possessing a divine nature" but might also include the notion of Christ's having been spiritualized, that is, glorified or "divinized," in his humanity.

This hypothesis finds support in certain statements that Ignatius makes about the postresurrection condition of Christ within the context of his antidocetic polemic in *Smyrnaeans*. First, Ignatius makes the nearly unprecedented statement that Jesus "raised himself" (ἀνέστησεν ἑαυτόν), which suggests that the glorification of his humanity had its source not outside of himself but in his own divinity and that it came about by virtue of the union between humanity and divinity in his own person.[34] Next, Ignatius expresses his solemn conviction that Christ was still "in the flesh after the resurrection" and supports this affirmation by means of his own narration of gospel-like traditions (*Smyr.* 3:1–3). He who according to his divinity "could not be handled" (*Poly.* 3:2) commanded the apostles to "handle" him, in order that they might see that he was "not a bodiless phantom." When they "touched him and believed," they were "mingled with his flesh and spirit" in such a way that they themselves were now "found to be beyond death" (*Smyr.* 3:2). Clearly the point is not merely that Jesus was still in the body but that in his risen state of "flesh and spirit" he is able to communicate the new life of grace to those who come into contact with him and believe. (For believers of subsequent generations this contact would be primarily sacramental, as the eucharistic overtones in Ignatius's narration intimate.)

Ignatius also recalls that after the resurrection Jesus ate and drank with his disciples "as if in the flesh" (ὡς σαρκικός), although in fact he was "spiritually united" (πνευματικῶς ἡνωμένος) to the Father (3:3). At this point he seems in serious danger of undermining his own polemic. Wrested from their context, these last two expressions could easily be given a docetic interpretation. It seems unlikely that Ignatius would have risked speaking this way at all had he not been attempting to make an important point. He knows that the word "flesh" has biblical overtones

---

34. *Smyr.* 2:1; cf. Jn 10:17–18.

of weakness and mortality that do not apply to Christ's risen body, for the paschal mystery has accomplished "the dissolution of death" (*Eph.* 19:3). He is unwilling to exchange the docetic error for a crass view of the resurrection as the resuscitation of a corpse to its previous mortal existence. Later in the letter he will describe the resurrection as a reality that is "both fleshly and spiritual" (*Smyr.* 12:2).

What is most important for our purposes is to recognize that a participation in Christ's spiritual union "with the Father" is communicated to believers by means of the "fleshly and spiritual" union of humanity and divinity in the person of Christ. This union is, to be sure, present from the first moment of the incarnation but is most perfectly realized through the passion and resurrection of "the new man, Jesus Christ" (*Eph.* 20:1). By the "newness" of life that Christ brings into the world (19:2–3) believers can in turn experience an intrapersonal and interpersonal "union" that is "both fleshly and spiritual" (*Magn.* 13:2).

We might therefore describe Jesus Christ's union with the Father as having three stages, with the second stage building upon the first, and the third building on both the first and the second. The first stage consists in the fact that prior to the incarnation, and even prior to the creation of the world, the Son was "with the Father" (*Magn.* 6:1). This perfect divine unity is never abrogated but is the basis for the two subsequent stages of union. The second stage begins with Jesus' conception in Mary's womb and continues through his death on the cross. During this stage the Son continues to live out the same perfect divine union with the Father that he has always enjoyed but does so now "in the flesh," that is, through a concrete bodily and historical human life culminating in death. This new mode of union with the Father is made possible by means of the unification of divinity and humanity in the person of the incarnate Son. The third stage of union with the Father begins with the resurrection. It is not a return to the first stage (though the divine union of the first stage has never been lost) but involves a full spiritualization or glorification of Christ's humanity. He who was once weak and vulnerable to suffering (παθητός) is now immune to suffering (ἀπαθής), not only in his divinity but in his humanity as well. And in this glorified condition he is able to communicate the "newness of eternal life" (*Eph.* 19:3) to those who believe in him, rendering them (already in this life, in a certain sense) "beyond death" (*Smyr.* 3:2).

Were we to ask Ignatius whether Jesus was both "fleshly and spiritual" (σαρκικὸς καὶ πνευματικός) already during stage two, we can be confident that he would answer affirmatively. He is no adoptionist. But when he employs this phrase in the Christological formulation of *Ephesians* 7:2, he probably has in mind especially the risen, stage-three Christ, the "one healer" of all division who has "breathed imperishability into the church" (17:1) and offers her "the medicine of immortality" in the eucharist (20:2).

It may be worth mentioning in passing that the same three stages are implicit in the way Ignatius speaks about Christ's relation to temporality in *Polycarp* 3:2. Prior to the incarnation he was "timeless" or "outside time" (ἄχρονος), but through the incarnation, presumably, he entered into the flow of time and was in a sense subject to it. Through the resurrection he did not return to the state of being "timeless" but is instead now "beyond time" (ὑπὲρ καιρόν), a phrase that invites comparison to the description of the apostles as "beyond death" (ὑπὲρ θάνατον) in *Smyrnaeans* 3:2. The risen and still-incarnate Christ can hardly leave time altogether, but he does transcend the limitations of earthly temporality even in his humanity. This renders him mystically available to his church in all places and times even while it transforms the believer's orientation to temporality. Ignatius thus exhorts Polycarp to "take note of the times" and to "await him who is beyond time" (*Poly.* 3:2). The Christian does not attempt to escape temporality but "redeems the time."[35]

This hardly scratches the surface of what we can learn from Ignatius about human temporality as the theater of redemption, a subject to which we shall return in several of the remaining chapters. We also have more to say about "the union of flesh and spirit." Up till now we have approached Ignatius's use of the terms σάρξ and πνεῦμα primarily from the vantage point of Christology. In the next chapter we shall consider them within the context of Ignatius's anthropology, hamartiology, and soteriology. At present, I would like to pursue still further that "most essential" unity of Jesus and the Father by considering Ignatius's presentation of the Son's redemptive mission.

Mission of the Son

Ignatius's understanding of the Son's economic mission is built on a basic Johannine schema: Jesus came forth from the Father, accomplished the will of the Father, and returned to the Father.[36] Ignatius develops this

---

35. Col 4:5; Eph 5:16.   36. Cf. Jn 13:1–3, 16:28.

schema most fully in *Magnesians* 6–8, which is, not coincidentally, an exhortation to ecclesial unity in face of the Judaizing heresy, and where we find a high concentration of Johannine and quasi-Johannine expressions. The Son is God's "Logos" (8:2), who was "with the Father before the ages" (6:1). Having "come forth" into the world, he "did nothing without the Father, remaining united to him," but "in all things pleased the one who sent him," until finally he "departed" (7:1–8:2). Were we to ask Ignatius the purpose of the Son's mission, his answer would be that "the one God manifested himself through Jesus Christ his Son" (8:2). And here we come to what is arguably the heart of Ignatius's theology: the Son as revealer of the Father. Jesus Christ is "the mouth that cannot lie, in whom the Father has spoken truthfully" (*Rom.* 8:2). He is "the mind-set [γνώμη] of the Father" (*Eph.* 3:2), "the knowledge [γνῶσις] of God" (17:2), and "our only teacher" (*Magn.* 9:1). The Son began to teach and to reveal the Father with the creation of the world, for he is "the one teacher, who spoke and it came to be" (*Eph.* 15:1), and he continued to teach through the prophets (*Magn.* 9:2). But God's perfect self-revelation came through the incarnation, and this is why Christ's true humanity is so important to Ignatius. In Jesus "God was manifesting himself humanly [ἀνθρωπίνως]" (*Eph.* 19:3). This last formulation is important not only because of its accent on Christ's humanity but also because, without collapsing the relational distinction between Father and Son, it eliminates any imagined distance between the revealer and the one whom he reveals. Jesus Christ *is* God manifesting *himself*. He is the "Word" who issues forth from the depths of eternal "silence" (*Magn.* 8:2). This is why, in the strict sense, there can be no other teacher!

But *how* does the Son reveal the Father? Jesus manifested his own preincarnational union with the Father through the way he related to the Father throughout his life among us and especially in his passion. Jesus "followed" the Father (*Smyr.* 8:1), "did nothing apart from" the Father (*Magn.* 7:1), "pleased" the Father (8:2), and "submitted" to the Father (13:2). He was able to do this because, though he had taken flesh, he remained "united" to the Father (7:1). Ignatius's most succinct articulation of this point places it squarely within the Johannine framework mentioned above. There is "one Jesus Christ, who came forth from one Father, *and was toward one*, and departed" (7:2). The phrase in italics (καὶ εἰς ἕνα ὄντα) suggests that Jesus remained "turned toward" the Father during his temporal life, just as he had been "with the Father before the ages" (6:1).

Later in the same letter, however, when he describes Jesus' "submission" to the Father, Ignatius qualifies it as being "according to the flesh" (13:2) and in this way avoids a crass subordinationism. With the hindsight of the condemnation of monothelitism by the Third Council of Constantinople (A.D. 680–681), we can see that obedience or submission became possible and necessary for the Son once he had assumed a human soul, which included a human will that needed to be subordinated to the divine will (cf. Jn 6:38). His human life of obedience *usque ad mortem* reflects and reveals his preexistent relationship to the Father but cannot be identified with the latter without remainder.

Still, the formulation of *Magnesians* 7:2 quoted above, with its language of "one Jesus Christ" coming forth from "one Father" and remaining turned "toward one," suggests that this revelation is as perfect and complete as it can be, especially when Ignatius follows it up by restating the point in terms of the biblical affirmation of "one God."

> There is one God, who manifested himself through Jesus Christ his Son, who is his Word come forth from silence, who in all things pleased the one who sent him. (8:2)

God did not simply provide a limited or partial revelation by means of a being lesser than himself (as was the case when he revealed the old law through Moses). He manifested *himself* through his only Son Jesus Christ, who is both "God" and "from God" (*Eph.* 7:2).

It has become common in systematic theology in the last century or so to speak of God's "self-revelation" in Jesus Christ. We have become so confident that the notion of a personal self-manifestation captures the distinctively biblical understanding of revelation that we easily forget that the New Testament itself never quite speaks this way.³⁷ What God has revealed in Christ is never in the Bible explicitly said to be "himself." Already in creating the world God manifested "his own eternal power

---

37. The Old Testament, for its part, does occasionally use reciprocal verb forms (Hebrew Niphal or Hithpael) to express the idea that Yahweh "revealed himself" to certain individuals or groups (Gn 35:7; 1 Sm 2:27, 3:21; Is 22:14). These somewhat unguarded expressions hardly suggest a definitive self-revelation, however. When Yahweh says, "In a vision I make myself known [to a prophet]," this level of revelation is considered inferior to the "mouth to mouth" communication he has with Moses (Nm 12:6–8). More solemn and theologically weighty is the expression by which it is implied that God has made himself known by his sacred name, Yahweh, in a manner that surpasses his self-revelation to the patriarchs as El-Shaddai (Ex 6:3). In any case, later Old Testament passages will speak somewhat more circumspectly of Yahweh's having revealed "his righteousness" (Ps 98:2) or "his holy arm" (Is 52:10, 53:1). Still later passages will anticipate the New Testament by speaking of God as the revealer of "mysteries" (Dn 2:28, 47). One Old Testament statement comes close to Ignatius's formulation: "He manifests himself [ἐμφανίζεται] to those who do not disbelieve him" (Wis 1:2).

and deity," and now he has manifested "the mystery hidden for ages and generations."³⁸ God's "grace" and "word," which already existed "before eternal ages," have been "manifested now through the appearance [ἐπιφανεῖα] of our Savior Christ Jesus."³⁹ The "eternal life that was with the Father" and the "love of God" have been manifested "because God has sent his only Son into the world."⁴⁰ "The mystery of godliness," identified with Jesus Christ himself, has been "manifested in the flesh" (1 Tm 3:16). In his life among us Jesus Christ manifested his own glory, which is the glory he shared with the Father before the foundation of the world, even as he manifested the Father's "name."⁴¹ By faith we behold "the glory of Christ, who is the image of God."⁴² By these and dozens of other expressions the New Testament authors *imply* that Jesus Christ is God's definitive self-revelation, but it took the astute theological mind of Ignatius of Antioch to recognize this, and his bold diction to express it in just so many words: "There is one God, who has manifested himself [ὁ φανερώσας ἑαυτόν] through Jesus Christ his Son" (*Magn.* 8:2).⁴³

This statement deserves to be recognized as a significant moment in the history of theology. It enables us to perceive a profound paradox that lies at the heart of the economy of revelation. If, on the one hand, God wills to reveal *himself*, this revelation cannot ultimately be a partial one but must be infinite, unified, and total. Revelation must be one, as God is one. But if, on the other hand, human beings, who are finite bodily

---

38. Rom 1:19–20; Col 1:26; Rom 16:25–26; Eph 3:4–5.
39. 2 Tm 1:9–10; Ti 1:2–3.   40. 1 Jn 1:2, 4:9.
41. Jn 2:11, 17:5–6.   42. 2 Cor 4:4; cf. 3:18.
43. Ignatius uses a similar phrase in *Eph.* 19:3: θεοῦ ἀνθρωπίνως φανερουμένου ("God was manifesting himself humanly"). As expressing the idea of self-revelation, this formulation is somewhat less pointed than that of *Magn.* 8:2. The difference is that in the former passage Ignatius employs a middle-voice participle (in a genitive absolute construction), whereas in the latter he employs an active-voice participle with the reflexive pronoun ἑαυτόν ("himself"). It should also be noted that Ignatius prepares for the statement of *Magn.* 8:2 by speaking of Jesus Christ just a few lines earlier as he "who was with the Father before the ages and appeared [ἐφάνη] at the end" (6:2). Among the other apostolic fathers, the doctrine that Jesus Christ is the definitive revealer of the Father is more or less clearly expressed in three texts, all of which are probably later than Ignatius's letters. First, according to the *Epistle to Diognetus*, God "has demonstrated himself" (ἑαυτὸν ἐπέδειξεν) by making known his "wise plan" and the "things prepared from the beginning" through his "beloved Child" (8:5–11). Second, the fragmentary homily that is now appended to *Diognetus* as chapters 11–12 (but is almost certainly composed by a different author) maintains that the Logos has revealed the "mysteries of the Father" (11:2). And third, *2 Clement* says that "the only God, invisible, the Father of truth" has sent the Savior and through him "manifested to us the truth and the heavenly life," so that we have come to know "the Father of truth" himself (20:5, 3:1). The *Epistle of Barnabas*, which is roughly contemporary to Ignatius's letters, says that Jesus Christ "was manifested in the flesh" (5:6, 6:9, 6:14) and that "he manifested himself to be the Son of God" (5:9), but it does not clearly present the Son as the self-manifestation of the Father.

creatures embedded in temporality, are to receive this revelation, it must come to them *in time* and *over time*. It must come to them piecemeal and gradually, for they cannot receive it in a single timeless instant.⁴⁴

The resolution to this paradox lies in the traditional notion of *mysterium*. In the incarnation, God himself, in the person of the Son, enters the dimensions of space and time and becomes an actor within human history. God himself is fully and personally present in Jesus Christ and definitively and perfectly reveals himself in the Christ event, but even the Christ event has a temporal thickness (extending from annunciation to ascension), so that God's self-revelation does in fact come to man in time and over time. But does this mean that the individual moments of Christ's life are mere pieces in the puzzle, mere parts of the whole? No, this cannot be, for such an understanding of the specific words and actions of Christ would not do justice to the first part of the paradox, namely, that revelation must be infinite and one. Rather, we must recognize that the whole of God's self-revelation, which is God himself, is perfectly present at every moment in the Christ event. Naturally, some moments are more luminous than others, and it is these especially that we term *mysteria vitae Iesu*. But they are "mysteries" because in each of them something of the mystery may be glimpsed and because we know that in each of them the whole mystery is truly and personally present.⁴⁵

Moreover, this notion of mystery can and must be extended beyond the Christ event properly speaking and must encompass the entire economy of creation and redemption. If the events of the Old Testament and Yahweh's speaking to Israel through Moses and the prophets are to be accepted as authentic revelation, as God's self-revelation, then it will be necessary to say that Jesus Christ was truly and personally present in those events too. They too are *mysteria*. Naturally he cannot have been present in the same manner as he would be subsequent to the incarnation, but he must have been present and acting nonetheless. Ignatius's way of handling this is to view the Old Testament prophets and saints as "disciples" of Jesus Christ "by the Spirit" (*Magn.* 9:2), as "believers" who belonged to "the unity of Jesus Christ" and "were saved" (*Phld.* 5:2). Because they were "inspired by his grace," they can truly be said to have "lived according to Christ Jesus" (*Magn.* 8:2).

---

44. The recognition of this paradox governs Aquinas's treatment of the object of faith in STh II-II, q. 1.

45. See Christian Schütz, OSB, "The Mysteries of the Life of Christ as a Prism of Faith," *Communio* 29 (2002): 28–38.

While the theology of mystery may do justice to the paradox of God's self-revelation to finite, embodied creatures, it raises any number of vexing questions. These pertain to the relationship between the old covenant and the new covenant, the relationship between the incarnation and the paschal mystery, the relationship between the Christ event and the sacramental life of the church, and the relationship between the present life of grace and the future life of glory. As I hope to show in chapters 6 through 10, these are questions that can be profitably explored within the context of the study of Ignatius's letters. I have touched on the theology of mystery here in order to lay some of the groundwork for those chapters, in which I hope also to indicate how the theme of unity relates to other aspects of Ignatius's theology.

Unity of God and Pneumatology

The phrase "unity of God" (ἑνότης θεοῦ) appears four times in Ignatius's letters, and here again we must wrestle with the ambiguities of the Greek genitival construction.[46] In this case there are at least three possibilities: "unity *from* God" (genitive of source), "unity *with* God" (objective genitive), or "unity *within* God" (subjective genitive). Schoedel favors the first of these for all four passages, and for the most part he has good contextual reasons for doing so.[47] Within the context of *Philadelphians* the phrase ἑνότης θεοῦ clearly refers to economic-ecclesial unity broadly conceived. By means of his one salvation-historical plan God has established a unity into which patriarchs, prophets, apostles, and the contemporary church have all entered. Because all these enter through "the door of the Father" (9:1), this same unity may be called "the unity of Jesus Christ" (5:2). Because it is an ecclesial unity under the visible authority of the "council of the bishop" (8:1), it may also be termed "the unity of the church" (3:2). Finally, because the eucharist in some sense effects, expresses, and preserves this unity, Ignatius calls it "union in his blood" (4:1). In all these passages there is no doubt that Ignatius is speaking of the unity that members of the church have with one another. And since this economic-ecclesial unity certainly has God as its ultimate source, it seems reasonable to interpret the phrase ἑνότης θεοῦ in *Philadelphians* (and also in *Poly.* 8:3) to mean unity *from* God.

But when Ignatius greets the church in Smyrna ἐν ἑνότητι θεοῦ καὶ

---

46. Phld. 8:1, 9:1; Smyr. 12:2; Poly. 8:3.
47. Schoedel, *Ignatius of Antioch*, 21, 206, 252, 280.

ὑμῶν, this is most naturally rendered "in unity *with* God and *with* you" (*Smyr.* 12:2), and Schoedel forces the issue a bit when he interprets this phrase to mean "in unity *from* God and *among* you."[48] As with the genitives in *Magnesians* 1:2, we must ask, with regard to the four occurrences of ἑνότης θεοῦ, whether Ignatius has not purposely employed imprecise language in order to express a multifaceted reality. In other words, is it not possible, even likely, that God is the source of a unity that binds us not only to one another but also, and at the same time, to himself? As we already noted in our discussion of *Magnesians* 1:2 above, the many other expressions by which Ignatius speaks of the believer's present participation in God and the way he orients the whole of Christian existence toward the eschatological attainment of God make this conclusion inescapable.

God is, then, both the *source* and the *object* of unity. There remains the question of whether he is furthermore the *subject* of unity. In other words, Ignatius clearly speaks of an economic unity from God and with God, but does he at the same time refer to a theological unity that is eternally within God? Corwin raises this question and answers it in the affirmative.[49] More clearly than Schoedel, she recognizes that the unity of which Ignatius speaks is multidimensional. After discussing the interpersonal, intrapersonal, mystical, and eschatological dimensions of unity, she notes that God is able to supply this unity because "union is the nature of God himself."[50] Further, she correctly observes that, while this properly theological dimension of unity cannot easily be inferred from the four ἑνότης θεοῦ passages alone, Ignatius does affirm it in at least two other passages. He informs the Ephesians that if they possess faith and love together in unity, "it is God" (*Eph.* 14:1), and even more straightforwardly he tells the Trallians that "God promises union, which is himself" (*Tral.* 11:2). These statements are typical of the way Ignatius employs predications of identity in order to express relations of economic participation.[51] The unity available to Christians "is" God analogically, which is to say that it is a real participation of the creature in God's own

---

48. Ibid., 252. With regard to this text, Corwin notes: "The 'unity of God' is something more than the unity of the group, or the two would have no place in these pairs of concepts, where there is affirmed the unity of what is at least partly distinguishable" (*St. Ignatius and Christianity*, 260).

49. Ibid., 259.   50. Ibid., 268.

51. Cf. *Magn.* 7:1 ("in blameless joy, which is Jesus Christ") and 15:1 ("having obtained an unwavering spirit, which is Jesus Christ"); *Tral.* 8:1 ("regain yourselves in faith, which is the flesh of the Lord, and in love, which is the blood of Jesus Christ"); *Smyr.* 5:3 ("until they repent into the passion, which is our resurrection").

unity. Finally, Corwin rightly intimates that Ignatius's identification of God as the source and goal of ecclesial unity requires God to have unity in himself.[52] How can God give what he does not already possess? We can bolster Corwin's argument by appealing to still one more text. In a passage focused intensely on unity, and just before one of the occurrences of the phrase ἑνότης θεοῦ, Ignatius says, "Where there is division and wrath, God does not dwell" (Phld. 8:1). The implication is clear. Disunity is contrary to God's nature.

Can we say anything further, on the basis of Ignatius's letters, about the precise nature of this unity as it exists in God eternally? Here Corwin drops the ball. She maintains that the "God" who is unity is "neither the Father God nor the Incarnate Lord of the church, but God as suprapersonal."[53] Her reasoning seems to be that the personal distinction between Father and Son amounts to a "separation" and is thus ultimately incompatible with unity. Although she does not spell it out in so many words, Corwin's view would require the Son to be an economic emanation from God, such that the suprapersonal God is "split" into the persons of Father and Son at the time of the incarnation (if not earlier). Presumably this split is only temporary, to be resolved in an eschatological collapse of the distinction between Father and Son, since there could be no definitive and final unity as long as that "separation" remained. In defending her position exegetically, Corwin maintains that the phrase "union ... of Jesus and the Father" in Magnesians 1:2 could not possibly refer to Jesus' union with the Father since it would be "meaningless" for Ignatius to pray for something that already exists.[54]

This misses the point that Ignatius is praying (in good Johannine fashion) that the churches will participate in the unity that Jesus already has with the Father. This is tolerably clear from another passage, where Ignatius congratulates those who are "mingled with" their bishop "as the church is with Jesus Christ and as Jesus Christ is with the Father, so that all things may be in harmonious unity" (Eph. 5:1). And as we have seen, Ignatius's identification of Jesus as the one "who before the ages was with the Father" (Magn. 6:1) implies that the personal distinction between Father and Son preexists creation and time.[55] Therefore, the best

---

52. Corwin, St. Ignatius and Christianity, 262.
53. Ibid.
54. Ibid., 261. She is thus able to keep the interpretation of this passage separate from those passages in which Ignatius says that God "is" union (Eph. 14:2; Tral. 11:2).
55. It is theoretically possible that Ignatius, like the fourth-century Arians, holds that the Son existed "before the ages" but is nevertheless not coeternal with the Father. However, since he

way to put *Magnesians* 1:2 together with *Trallians* 11:2 is to say (with Corwin) that "union is the nature of God himself," while at the same time maintaining (against Corwin) that this divine union is not "suprapersonal" but *interpersonal*. Corwin seems to be working with a conception of unity according to which ultimate unity requires the negation of personal identity, but the Johannine, Ignatian, and fundamentally Christian view of God's unity is that of an eternal interpersonal and relational unity.[56] God, then, is not simply the subject of unity but the intersubjective principle of unity.

Since Jesus is both God and man, his union with the Father must be both eternal and economic. It is eternal prior to the incarnation and both eternal and economic from the moment of his conception in the virgin's womb. The incarnate Logos is united to the Father both in his divinity and in his humanity. Put differently, the union of divinity and humanity in the person of Christ brings about also a union of the God-man *with* the Father, and this union is manifested in the way Jesus lives. "The Lord did nothing apart from the Father, remaining united to him" (*Magn.* 7:1). Moreover, the union of divinity and humanity that begins with the incarnation transforms the humanity of Christ within the dynamic structure of the Christ event, such that this transformation culminates in the glorification of his humanity in the resurrection. Following the resurrection, Jesus Christ remains economically (as well as eternally) united to the Father. Thus we have the three stages of the Son's union with the Father discussed above: (1) prior to the incarnation, (2) from conception to resurrection, and (3) subsequent to the resurrection.

Since Ignatius (following Mt 1:20) assigns the Holy Spirit a vital role in Christ's conception in Mary's womb (*Eph.* 18:2) and specifies that after the resurrection Jesus was "spiritually [πνευματικῶς] united to the Father" (*Smyr.* 3:3), it may be wise at this juncture to take an initial look at Ignatius's pneumatology.[57] This will serve to round out our discussion of the union "of Jesus and the Father" while also laying the groundwork for the next two chapters, where we relate this "most essential" dimen-

---

refers to Jesus in a confessional context as "the timeless one" (*Poly.* 3:2), it seems more likely that he would understand preexistence to imply strict timelessness or eternity.

56. It is interesting to note in this regard that, after the publication of *St. Ignatius and Christianity*, Corwin gravitated toward the study of Eastern religions (see Michael Cooper, "Virginia Corwin Brautigam, 95, Pioneer in Comparative Religion," *New York Times*, August 24, 1996; available online at http://www.nytimes.com/1996/08/24/us/virginia-corwin-brautigam-95-pioneer-in-comparative-religion.html).

57. The magisterial treatment of this topic is Martin, "La pneumatología en Ignacio," 379–452 (esp. 405–18 and 446–52).

sion of unity to the other dimensions of economic-ecclesial unity. Two questions concern us here. First, how does Ignatius understand the Holy Spirit's economic role, particularly as this pertains to unity? Second, does Ignatius understand the Spirit to be involved also in the eternal unity of Father and Son? In other words, is his understanding of this dimension of unity ultimately Trinitarian (rather than binitarian)?

The Ignatian corpus contains upward of a dozen references to the Holy Spirit. Strikingly, while all of these statements pertain to the Spirit's economic mission, the vast majority of them also employ some sort of Trinitarian formula, or at least an evocation of the Trinity. Moreover, Ignatius sees the Holy Spirit as active at each of the principal stages in the economy of redemption, spanning the Old Testament period, the life of Christ, and the age of the church. Israel's prophets were "inspired" (ἐμπνεόμενοι) by the grace of Christ to convince unbelievers that there is one God and were thus Jesus' disciples in the Spirit (Magn. 8:2–9:2). In a creedal formula, Ignatius tells us that "Jesus Christ was conceived by Mary according to the economy of God, from the seed of David and the Holy Spirit" (Eph. 18:2). Jesus breathed (πνέω) imperishability upon the church through his paschal mystery (17:1), and he remained "spiritually [πνευματικῶς] united to the Father" after the resurrection (Smyr. 3:3). Christians are "temple stones prepared for the edifice of God the Father, borne up to the heights by means of the crane of Jesus Christ, which is the cross, making use of the Holy Spirit as a cable" (Eph. 9:1). The Holy Spirit is the gift sent by the Lord Jesus to give us knowledge of God (Eph. 17:2) and the "living water" that speaks within Christians beckoning them to "come to the Father" (Rom. 7:2). In "the church of God the Father," bishops, presbyters, and deacons are appointed according to the will of Jesus Christ and confirmed "by his Holy Spirit" (Phld. sal.), and when a Spirit-filled leader such as Ignatius rises to preach in the assembly, it is in fact the Spirit who speaks through him (7:2). Like the Johannine "Spirit of truth," the Ignatian Spirit "is not deceived" and "exposes [ἐλέγχει] hidden things."[58] In other words, the Holy Spirit is at work within the church to root out the falsehood that is the main cause of disunity. In sum, Ignatius's pneumatology might be characterized as an economic Trinitariansim, in which the Holy Spirit is active throughout the history of redemption. Clearly the Spirit has a vital role in bringing about the multidimensional ecclesial unity that Ignatius is promoting and in a

---

58. Phld. 7:1; cf. Jn 16:8–13.

particular way is associated with the believer's progress "to the Father" through Jesus Christ.⁵⁹

Does Ignatius go further than this and implicate the Holy Spirit in the eternal union of the Father and the Son? Is his pneumatology not only economically but also theologically Trinitarian? Ignatius comes closest to a properly theological affirmation about the Holy Spirit when he says that "the Spirit is not deceived, being from God [ἀπὸ θεοῦ ὄν]" (Phld. 7:1). This statement is not simply a reference to the Spirit's economic mission but to its ontological origin in God and implicitly to its divine nature. It does not, however, further illuminate the Spirit's "place" within the Trinity, that is, the Spirit's precise relation to the Father and the Son.

Perhaps there is a hint in that regard in *Magnesians*, however. As we have already seen, Ignatius's reference to the "most essential" union "of Jesus and the Father" (1:2) is paralleled later in that letter by a Trinitarian formula, which literally reads, "in Son and Father, and in Spirit" (ἐν υἱῷ καὶ πατρὶ καὶ ἐν πνεύματι; 13:1). The parallelism between these two passages probably indicates that the economic union of Jesus and the Father is rooted in a prior theological-Trinitarian unity. The peculiar wording of the Trinitarian formula, whereby "Son" and "Father" are governed by a single preposition while "Spirit" is relegated to its own prepositional phrase, may suggest that the Spirit's relation to the Son and Father is not strictly symmetrical to their relationship to each other. Ignatius does not, as it were, view the Trinity as a triangle or a three-legged stool. The relationship between Father and Son is most basic. It is the eternal union. Where, then, does that leave the Holy Spirit? Some later systematic theology will identify the Spirit as the very "bond" (*nexus*) uniting Father and Son.⁶⁰ Ignatius does not say this, but his nascent Trinitarian theology seems to be heading in that direction. In any case, the eternal union between Father and Son is manifested economically in the Christ event, where we find Jesus "spiritually united to the Father" (πνευματικῶς ἡνωμένος τῷ πατρί).⁶¹

Unus Doctor

We began this chapter by noting that Ignatius of Antioch might be fittingly invoked as Doctor Unitatis. In fact, however, he would probably

---

59. *Rom*. 7:2; *Eph*. 9:1.
61. *Smyr*. 3:3; cf. *Magn*. 7:1.

60. *STh* II-II, q. 1, a. 8, ad 3.

reject any such honorific. Although his letters are obviously didactic, he eschews the title "teacher" and repeatedly presents himself instead as a learner and the "fellow student" of his readers.[62] These statements are not merely rhetorical expressions of humility, whether false or genuine, but flow from what we identified above as the core of Ignatian theology.[63] Because Jesus is the definitive revealer of the Father, he must be "our only teacher" (*Magn.* 9:1). Naturally, it is not a question of placing a taboo on any other use of the word "teacher." Ignatius recognizes that Christians are called to teach the gospel to each other and to the world, and he commends the Roman church for doing just that (*Rom.* 3:1). "Teaching is good," provided one put into practice what he or she teaches and always remember that in the strict sense there is only "one teacher."[64] But Ignatius is keenly aware of the perilous tendency of teachers to lose sight of precisely this truth, and he warns against anyone who "speaks without Jesus Christ" (*Tral.* 9:1). Most of the explicit references to teaching in Ignatius's letters concern the "evil teaching" of heretics,[65] who spread the "foul odor of the teaching of the ruler of this aeon" and thus cause disunity (*Eph.* 17:1). Ignatius encourages his fellow Christians to think of themselves, not as teachers, but foremost and always as students and disciples of Jesus Christ. "Since we are his disciples, let us learn to live according to Christianity" (*Magn.* 10:1). Christianity is after all essentially a matter of "learning Christ" (*Phld.* 8:2).

What does the *unus doctor* teach? What does the revealer reveal? God has "manifested himself" through Jesus Christ his Son, but *who* has he manifested himself to be? Based on what we have seen thus far, the answer to this question must be that God has revealed himself to be eternal, interpersonal unity. Through the Christ event the Son has revealed his eternal union with the Father in the Holy Spirit. But God's self-revelation is not merely a self-disclosure. He communicates to us, and gives us a share in, that which he reveals. "God promises union, which is himself" (*Tral.* 11:2). In other words, the economy of revelation is also an economy of redemption. Unlike John, Ignatius never explicitly says that "God is love" (1 Jn 4:8, 4:16), but as we shall see in chapter 5, he makes it clear

---

62. *Eph.* 3:1; *Magn.* 10:1; *Rom.* 4:3.
63. According to Matthew W. Mitchell, "Ignatius is sounding a note of false humility" in *Rom.* 4:3 ("In the Footsteps of Paul: Scriptural and Apostolic Authority in Ignatius of Antioch," *Journal of Early Christian Studies* 14 [2006]: 36).
64. *Eph.* 15:1; cf. Mt 23:8.
65. *Eph.* 9:1, 16:2; *Phld.* 2:1; *Poly.* 3:1.

that the ἀγάπη by which Christians love one another comes from God and leads back to God. We shall also see how closely linked love is with the faith by which we lay hold of divine truth with our intellects. Furthermore, faith and love are the beginning and end of "life" (ζωή; Eph. 14:1). By apprehending God's truth in faith and participating in divine love, Christians possess that life which originates in God and enables human beings to "attain God." And to possess this life is nothing less than unity in all its dimensions. In fact, it is probably safe to suppose that the Ignatian concept of unity encloses the Johannine notions of truth, love, and life.

As we ponder these realities further, it will become clear why Ignatius places such stress on Jesus Christ as revealer of the Father, the intellectual dimension of faith, the preservation of authentic doctrine, and submission to the local bishop. Through faith, doctrine, and ecclesial authority, human beings are able to receive and appropriate the revelation of the true God and thus enter into a unity that is intrapersonal, interpersonal, mystical, and eschatological, a unity that is a real participation of the creature in God. As "children of the light of truth," believers must "flee division and evil doctrines" and follow their bishop as sheep follow a shepherd. The "wolves" who teach heresy have no part in this unity (Phld. 2:1–2). From the cynical and rather simplistic perspective of one recent interpreter, in all such statements Ignatius is merely employing the "rhetoric of coercion" in order to "elevate the authority" of his cronies in the episcopacy by imposing a "theological sameness" and ecclesiastical conformity that "marginalizes otherness and demonizes difference."[66] The truth of the matter is actually far more profound and certainly more beautiful.

---

66. So David M. Reis, "Following in Paul's Footsteps: Mimēsis and Power in Ignatius of Antioch," in *Trajectories*, ed. Gregory and Tuckett, 287–305 (quotes from 301–5).

FLESH AND SPIRIT

In the previous chapter we noted that Ignatius identifies the "union of flesh and spirit of Jesus Christ" as one of the primary dimensions of the unity that he wishes the churches to enjoy (*Magn.* 1:2), and we interpreted that statement to mean that Christians can, by grace, possess a union in their own flesh-and-spirit humanity that flows from, and participates in, the flesh-and-spirit union that exists in Jesus Christ. Indeed, the economic-Christological union of "flesh and spirit" brings about the soteriological-anthropological union of "flesh and spirit" that is constitutive of "the newness of eternal life" (*Eph.* 19:3). Having noted further that the expression "flesh and spirit" has a unique sense when it refers to Jesus Christ, we proceeded to expound this usage within a broad discussion of Ignatius's Christology and nascent Trinitarianism.

Continuing our investigation of the various dimensions of unity outlined in *Magnesians* 1, the agenda for the present chapter is as follows. First, I shall situate Ignatius's anthropological use of the terms σάρξ and πνεῦμα within his broadly biblical view of reality and indicate the distinctly soteriological character of his anthropology. While granting that Ignatius's use of σάρξ is not identical to what we find in Galatians or Romans, I will defend his anthropology as essentially biblical and Pauline. This apologia encounters some difficulty in what seems at first glance to be an incipiently gnostic formulation at *Romans* 6:2, where Ignatius describes salvation in terms of overcoming the allure of "matter," departing from "the world," and arriving at "pure light." Since he implies that this sort of deliverance is required for one to become a "man" (ἄνθρωπος), is it possible to maintain that Ignatius's anthropology is authentically biblical? To answer this important question and to get a firm handle on the relationship between anthropology and soteriology in Ignatius's letters, it will be necessary to broaden our investigation a bit in order to take in elements of his cosmology, his understanding of spiritual warfare and martyrdom, and the epistolary aims and rhetorical strategy of *Romans*. The second item on our agenda, accordingly, will be a lengthy exposition of the star narrative of *Ephesians* 19, which is a key text for understanding Ignatius's cosmology and its place within his overarching vision of the divine economy. Third, I shall transition from cosmology to the topic of spiritual warfare—traditionally viewed as an attempt to overcome three enemies: the world, the flesh, and the devil—by considering Ignatius's teaching on the church's relationship to the non-Christian world, especially as this is found in *Magnesians* 5 and *Ephesians* 10. Fourth, our attention will turn back to *Romans*, where the topics of spiritual warfare, Ignatius's martyrdom, and personal eschatology ("attaining God") all converge. Here I shall attempt to explain why Ignatius speaks of his death as a disappearance from the *world*, what he means by the crucifixion of *desire*, and why he is so worried that the Roman Christians may cooperate with the "envy" of the *devil* by forestalling his execution. In a final section I shall attempt to draw together the strands of the argument.

It is worth recalling that Ignatius concludes the passage about the dimensions of unity by reminding his readers that "if we endure all the abuse of the ruler of this aeon and escape, we shall attain God" (*Magn.* 1:3). This statement contains Ignatius's understanding of spiritual warfare in a nutshell, even as it raises the ticklish question of what he means by "escape." In this chapter I hope to illuminate Ignatius's "flesh and spirit" anthropology and his economic cosmology as foundational elements in his understanding of how human persons vanquish evil and come to salvation in Jesus Christ. As noted in the previous chapter, Ignatius views unity dynamically and teleologically. Our intrapersonal and interpersonal participation in the union of Jesus and the Father, which we certainly can experience now by faith and love, will be fully realized only after death, when "we shall attain God." And for Ignatius, the attainment of God comes only by way of a battle of cosmic proportions. To analyze his teaching on the dimensions of unity in abstraction from what he says about cosmology and spiritual warfare, perhaps in order to sidestep difficult questions, is not therefore an option.

A Soteriological Anthropology

The letters of Ignatius of Antioch express an essentially biblical view of reality. The one God has "willed all things that exist" and created them by his Word.[1] The created universe comprises "things visible and invisible," a material realm and a spiritual realm.[2] There are rational beings in heaven, on earth, and under the earth, including glorious angels and "rulers, both visible and invisible."[3] Many of these beings are aligned against God and his kingdom and thus belong to "the old kingdom," which is the domain of "the ruler of this aeon" (Eph. 19:1–3). Man, as a creature of "flesh and spirit," stands at the juncture of the material and immaterial realms and in a sense unites them in his person, but when human beings abandon the truth and live in a merely carnal fashion, they are like "beasts in human form" (Smyr. 4:1). It is above all "the new man Jesus Christ" who unites the realms of matter and spirit "in his faith and in his love, in his passion and resurrection," in one all-embracing economy of redemption (Eph. 20:1). Indeed, he not only unites the material and immaterial realms of creation; he also reconciles the whole creation to its Creator. As eternal Son of God, he is "the timeless one"; as Son of Man he has entered our temporal realm. He is "the invisible one, who for our sake became visible ... the impassible one, who for our sake became passible" (Poly. 3:2). He is both "the perfect man" (Smyr. 4:2) and "God in man" (Eph. 7:2).

This biblical understanding of reality and Ignatius's firm adherence to the apostolic kerygma concerning Jesus Christ inform his polemics against docetism and Judaization, and the marshaling of his forces against docetism in particular must have required him to reflect deeply on the relationship between material and spiritual realities. Man's own composition as a creature of "flesh and spirit" is at the forefront of Ignatius's thinking as he works out the "fleshly and spiritual" implications of redemption at various levels. Christians abide in Jesus Christ "in a fleshly and spiritual manner" (σαρκικῶς καὶ πνευματικῶς), that is, with both the material and the immaterial dimensions of their personhood (Eph. 10:3). They must carry out Christ's commands "according to flesh and spirit" (Rom. sal.). Polycarp must fulfill the demands of the episcopacy "with attention to every fleshly and spiritual concern" (Poly. 1:2). Indeed, God has placed the bishop, a being "of flesh and spirit," over the local church precisely so that he can deal both with visible and invisible realities (2:2).

---

1. Magn. 8:2; Rom. sal.; Eph. 15:1.   2. Tral. 5:2; Rom. 5:3; Poly. 2:2.
3. Tral. 9:1; Eph. 13:2; Smyr. 6:1.

Married persons, for their part, are to be content with their spouses "in flesh and spirit" (5:1). The church at Tralles enjoys peace "in flesh and spirit" (*Tral. sal.*) and has refreshed Ignatius "both in flesh and spirit" (12:1). These examples could be multiplied indefinitely, as Ignatius never ceases to remind the churches that Christianity is not merely a "spiritual" endeavor but involves the whole person.

The words σάρξ ("flesh") and πνεῦμα ("spirit") are, then, the bread and butter of Ignatius's anthropology. He also employs several related adjectives and adverbs: σαρκικός ("fleshly"), πνευματικός ("spiritual"), σαρκικῶς ("in a fleshly manner"), and πνευματικῶς ("in a spiritual manner"). Occasionally he mentions the "soul" (ψυχή) but never in a theologically significant context, and his use of "body" (σῶμα) as an anthropological term is similarly infrequent and relatively insignificant.[4] Notably, he never uses these two terms together to speak of the human person as comprised of body and soul but prefers to speak in terms of flesh and spirit. While both sets of terms are biblical, they are not strictly interchangeable. "Body and soul" might have expressed more of a concern with man's nature according to the order of creation, whereas Ignatius's preference for "flesh and spirit" reflects his focus on the drama and dynamics of redemption. Ignatius is not so much concerned with anthropology in an abstract sense as he is with man-without-Christ and man-in-Christ, with man's choice between "death and life" and his ultimate destiny (*Magn.* 5:1). When Ignatius uses the term "flesh" by itself, it usually refers to man left to his own resources and deceived by the wiles of the devil into living a merely carnal life, whereas "flesh and spirit" together reflects a graced spiritualization and unification of the whole human person and of all the dimensions of human life. "Spirit" is thus not merely the immaterial dimension of the person but is that dimension brought to "life" (ζωή) in such a way that the whole person, including the flesh, and the whole of human "life" (βίος), including "fleshly matters," are transformed in Christ. The key to Ignatius's soteriological anthropology lies in recognizing that he never envisions a purely "spiritual" state of man as the goal of redemption. The goal is rather an intrapersonal and interpersonal "unity" that is "both fleshly and spiritual" (*Magn.* 13:2).[5]

---

4. "Soul": Phld. 1:2, 11:2. "Body": Rom. 4:2, 5:3. There are also specialized uses of ἀσώματος ("bodiless") in a Christological context (Smyr. 2:1, 3:2) and σωματεῖον ("bodily integrity") in an ecclesiological context (11:2).

5. "The goal is that the self, composed of flesh and spirit in unity, shall be dominated by

The following paragraphs will defend and develop the interpretation of Ignatius's anthropological use of σάρξ and πνεῦμα that I have just sketched out. Some scholars question whether Ignatius's use of these terms reflects an authentically biblical grasp of redemption. According to L. W. Barnard, for example, Ignatius "knows nothing of the Pauline idea of the salvation wrought by Christ from σάρξ, conceived as the seat of sin, or of the activity of the indwelling Spirit."[6] There is a significant element of truth in this criticism. Ignatius does not in fact employ σάρξ and πνεῦμα with the full range of subtle nuances that we find in Paul's Epistle to the Romans in particular. On the other hand, it is reductive to speak of *the* Pauline idea of salvation or *the* Pauline use of σάρξ and πνεῦμα. Ignatius's distinctive utilization of anthropological terms does find precedent in some Pauline passages. Notably, his use of the words σαρκικός, πνευματικός, and ἄνθρωπος ("man, human person") is virtually identical to what we find in 1 Corinthians 3:1–4, and his use of σάρξ and πνεῦμα can to some extent be viewed as an extension and development of that specific Pauline usage. It must be remembered that Ignatius did not, as far as we can tell, have a canonical list of Paul's letters that gave Romans pride of place, nor was he riding in the wake of the Western theological tradition of Augustine, Aquinas, and Luther, a tradition that has placed Romans and Galatians near the center of the New Testament canon and of theological discourse. It seems that 1 Corinthians and Ephesians are the Pauline letters to which Ignatius gave the most attention, and to fault him for doing so would be anachronistic.

Ignatius uses the word σάρξ in two ways, one neutral and the other somewhat pejorative. In the former case "flesh" denotes the visible, material realm as distinct from the spiritual world, without any pejorative connotation. Ignatius's "journey according to the flesh" is his physical-geographical route from Antioch to Rome (*Rom.* 9:3). Onesimus is the Ephesians' "bishop in the flesh" (*Eph.* 1:3), as distinct from their unseen Bishop in heaven (*Magn.* 3:2). Jesus' own submission to the Father is described as "according to the flesh" (κατὰ σάρκα), certainly not because it was worldly or carnal in any pejorative sense but because it was carried out in the somatic, historical realm (*Magn.* 13:2). Building on this usage, however, "flesh" can also denote that which is merely physical or worldly to the neglect of the spiritual dimension. Thus to love another person's

---

spirit and united with God. There is here no flesh-spirit dualism like that which characterizes later gnostic thought" (Corwin, *St. Ignatius and Christianity*, 162).

6. Barnard, *Studies in the Apostolic Fathers*, 28.

"flesh" is to love him in a superficial or worldly way, failing to keep his greater good (i.e., eternal salvation) in mind (Rom. 2:1). To look upon one's neighbor "according to the flesh" is to view him or her in a reductive manner and to fail in Christian charity (Magn. 6:2). Ignatius insists that he has written to the Romans "not according to the flesh but according to the mind-set of God" (8:3). His opponents in Philadelphia underestimated him because they viewed him in a merely human or worldly manner. They thought to deceive him "according to the flesh," not recognizing that he possessed "the Spirit," which, "being from God, is not deceived" (Phld. 7:1). Likewise, they suspected that he had learned about the divisions in their community "from human flesh," whereas in fact he possessed prophetic knowledge from the Holy Spirit (7:2). We should note in these last few examples that even activities that transcend the merely physical—such as composing a letter, attempting to deceive, or acquiring information—are done "according to the flesh" when they are done apart from God's will or without the Holy Spirit. This indicates that Ignatius does not strictly limit "flesh" to the physical or material realm but can refer it to mental or intellectual activities that are carried out in an unspiritual manner. This usage at least tends in the direction of the more typically Pauline notion of σάρξ.

Perhaps the single most important passage for grasping Ignatius's understanding of the fleshly and spiritual realms is Ephesians 8:2.

> Those who are fleshly [οἱ σαρκικοί] cannot do spiritual things [τὰ πνευματικά], nor can those who are spiritual [οἱ πνευματικοί] do fleshly things [τὰ σαρκικά]. In the same way, faith cannot practice the things that belong to unbelief, nor can unbelief practice the things that belong to faith. But even those things you do according to the flesh [κατὰ σάρκα] are spiritual [πνευματικά], for you do all things in Jesus Christ.

Borrowing a rhetorical stratagem from Paul (1 Cor 3:1–4), Ignatius initially seems to accept the incipiently gnostic distinction between those who are fleshly (οἱ σαρκικοί) and those who are spiritual (οἱ πνευματικοί). But by the former designation he means those who live according to their own merely human resources, whereas the latter live by the power of grace and the illumination of the Holy Spirit. The authentically "spiritual" life does not attempt to dissociate itself from the body and the realm of matter but sanctifies every mundane and bodily action, so that "even what you do according to the flesh [κατὰ σάρκα] is spiritual." This is obviously not the way Paul normally uses the phrase κατὰ σάρκα, but Ignatius does express here an authentically biblical and Pauline understanding of redemption.[7] When Ignatius exhorts the Philadelphians to "keep your flesh as the temple of God," his thought, and to some extent even his language, echoes Paul's.[8] What is more, the recognition that the physical and historical realm is integral to redemption and that mundane and bodily activities can and must be sanctified is one of the basic building blocks of Ignatius's pastoral theology. Rooted in his understanding of redemption as involving a historical economy with the incarnate Word as its centerpiece, this conviction is foundational for Ignatius's exhortations concerning ecclesial life, the sacraments, marriage and celibacy, the corporal works of mercy, and the proper Christian attitude toward outsiders. Christian faith and love, to be authentic, must be "both fleshly and spiritual" (Smyr. 13:2).

Ignatius's use of σάρξ is paralleled to some extent by his use of the term ἄνθρωπος ("man, human person"). He generally uses this word in the plural, occasionally with a neutral meaning (Eph. 10:1) but more often pejoratively. In the latter case ἄνθρωποι means "mere men," exactly as Paul uses it in 1 Corinthians 3:4. To "live according to men" is to live in a merely human fashion, which is the opposite of living "according to Jesus Christ" (Tral. 2:1). To acquire an ecclesial ministry "through men" would be to do so by merely political means and with merely human motives rather than "in the love of God the Father and the Lord Jesus Christ" (Phld. 1:1). To "please men" is the opposite of pleasing God (Rom. 2:1). The fellowship that Ignatius enjoyed with Onesimus was "not human but spiritual" (οὐκ ἀνθρωπίνην οὖσαν ἀλλὰ πνευματικήν), that is, not merely human but imbued with revealed truth and divine love (Eph. 5:1). Of course, if Jesus Christ only appeared to be human, as the docetists held, each of these statements would imply a denigration of what is human, but in fact according to Ignatius Jesus is the "perfect man" in whom the fleshly and the spiritual are most perfectly united (Smyr. 4:2). Christian perfection is achieved, therefore, by imitating the Lord and abiding in him in flesh and spirit (Eph. 10:3), being conformed to "the new man" (20:1). This goal is reached, however, only by way of the mystery of suffering and death. One must "die into Jesus Christ" in order to "attain Jesus Christ" and thereby to become, finally and truly, a "man" (ἄνθρωπος; Rom. 5:3–6:2). Somewhat paradoxically, Ignatius adds, almost in the same breath, "I no longer wish to live according to men [κατὰ

---

7. Paul too is capable of using the phrase in a neutral manner, even in Romans (9:3, 9:5).
8. Phld. 7:2; cf. 1 Cor 6:19–20; 2 Cor 6:16, 7:1.

ἀνθρώπους]" (8:1), which is to say, "I no longer wish to live in a merely human fashion."

Ignatius never uses the word σάρξ in the fully pejorative Pauline sense by which "the flesh" designates the human personality as dominated by sin. This does not represent so much a failure to understand Paul as it does a selective use of Paul's terminology. Ignatius's theology, it must be remembered, combines Pauline, Johannine, and Matthean elements. In particular, his distinctive insight into the mystery of redemption synthesizes an essentially Johannine understanding of the incarnation with the Pauline theme of suffering with Christ. The utilization of anthropological terms that I have outlined above serves that insight well. Moreover, Ignatius's encounters with docetism seem to have led him to focus on the created goodness and redemptive role of physical reality. He may have judged that the fully pejorative Pauline use of the word "flesh" could too easily be taken to imply that material reality, or the physical body in particular, is the evil from which Christ delivers us. That would hardly be consonant with Ignatius's teaching that the Son of God came "bearing flesh" (σαρκοφόρος) in order that human beings might be transformed by a love that is "both fleshly and spiritual."[9]

Admittedly, however, there are passages in *Romans* that present difficulties for the interpretation of Ignatius's soteriological anthropology that I have been offering here. The following passage is arguably the most problematic.

> Do not give back to the world one who wishes to belong to God, nor entice him with matter. Permit me to receive pure light. When I arrive there, I will be a man. (*Rom.* 6:2)

Ignatius claims that his goal is to become a true "man" (ἄνθρωπος), yet it is by resisting the allurement of "matter" (ὕλη), leaving the "world" (κόσμος), and arriving in the realm of "pure light" (καθαρὸν φῶς) that he intends to reach this goal of authentic humanity! This statement seems to play right into the hands of the docetists. According to Lightfoot, Ignatius is "trenching upon Gnostic ground" here.[10]

To be correctly understood, the troubling passages in *Romans* need to be read within two contexts. One of these is, of course, the epistolary purpose and rhetorical strategy of that rather unusual letter. Later in this chapter we shall attempt to understand how Ignatius views his

---

9. *Smyr.* 5:2, 13:2.
10. Lightfoot, *Ignatius, Polycarp*, 1.388.

situation as he approaches Rome and what he is trying to accomplish by communicating with the Roman Christians ahead of his arrival. It will be recalled that his anthropology is concerned with the dynamics of soteriology and personal eschatology, or, to put it in his words, with "attaining God." This dimension, while not lacking in the other letters, is obviously to the fore in *Romans*. The other context that we need to establish, which is even more basic and will therefore be dealt with first, may be broadly termed Ignatius's "cosmology." Under this rubric I would gather several interrelated items: his view of reality as consisting of both a material and a spiritual realm, his theology of creation, his understanding of the relationship between the church and the non-Christian "world" (κόσμος), and the place spiritual warfare has in his approach to the Christian life. We shall not be able to penetrate below the surface of Ignatius's letters, least of all *Romans*, if we ignore the fact that he quite seriously understands himself to be involved in a cosmic battle.

An Economic Cosmology: *Ephesians* 19

Our best point of entry for the exploration of Ignatian cosmology is, however, not *Romans* but *Ephesians*. In the latter epistle Ignatius casts his net more widely than elsewhere. If he refrains from discussing "heavenly matters" in *Trallians* and *Smyrnaeans*, fearing that he and his hearers may become puffed up with knowledge, he is relatively uninhibited in this regard in *Ephesians*. Ignatius considers the Ephesian church, which is "renowned to the aeons" (*Eph.* 8:1), to have a special importance among the churches of Asia Minor, and his ambition (never fully realized) is to lay out for them a more or less comprehensive view of the divine economy (20:1). It is interesting to note that *Ephesians* contains Ignatius's only explicit reference to the creation of the world, all three instances of the word οἰκονομία ("economy") in his corpus, four explicit references to Satan (double the number in any other letter), three of his four references to the virgin Mary, an entire chapter on how Christians should relate to non-Christians, and what seems to be a puzzling detour into astral mythology.

By this last phrase I refer to the famous star narrative of *Ephesians* 19. While this passage presents a formidable exegetical challenge, the temptation simply to ignore it must be resisted. Within the structure of *Ephesians* it constitutes the grand crescendo of Ignatius's presentation of the divine economy, and it may well hold a valuable key to his thought. Hopefully it will repay a patient and empathetic analysis. To get a running start, we pick up the thread of Ignatius's argument at 18:1, where he echoes Paul's teaching in 1 Corinthians 1-2 in order to remind the Ephesians that divine wisdom and eternal life are to be found in the scandal of the cross. To elucidate this mystery, Ignatius next supplies one of his characteristically dense creedal formulae.

> Our God, Jesus the Christ, was conceived by Mary according to the economy of God, from both the seed of David and the Holy Spirit. He was born and baptized in order that by his passion he might cleanse the water. (Eph. 18:2)

This confession of faith, which will occupy us at length in chapter 8, presents Jesus' conception in the womb of the virgin as the moment in God's master plan when humanity and divinity converge in the person of Christ. This affirmation seems to target any adoptionist scheme that might identify that moment with Jesus' baptism in the Jordan, while it also prepares for the theological core of the star narrative, namely, the fact that "God was manifesting himself humanly" in Jesus Christ (19:3). Ignatius's formula further implies that the Christ event had a comprehensive effect on the physical world. Through his incarnation, baptism in the Jordan, and passion, Jesus Christ cleansed the waters of the world so that grace might be conferred through the water of sacramental baptism. As we shall see in chapter 8, some of the church fathers think of the Jordan as a "cosmic" river and understand Christ to have descended into the Jordan in order to take on and defeat the powers of darkness. That Ignatius thinks in similar terms is perhaps indicated by the fact that his next statement refers to the defeat of Satan.

> And these escaped the notice of the ruler of this aeon: the virginity of Mary and her childbirth, as also the death of the Lord—three mysteries of a cry, which were accomplished in the silence of God. (19:1)

Deferring till chapter 7 the central exegetical problem posed by this statement (i.e., the meaning of the phrases "mysteries of a cry" and "silence of God"), we note in the present context that with this passage Ignatius begins a sort of commentary on the immediately preceding creedal formula. His explicitly theological focus on the virgin Mary is quite remarkable for such an early author. Ignatius does not present her as merely a role player in the mystery of salvation but as someone who is near its center. First he tells us that she conceived Christ "according to the economy of God," and then he places her virginity and her childbirth alongside

Christ's passion as central mysteries of the faith. Obviously Ignatius does not always accent Mary's role in this way, and this raises the question why he does so here. Two reasons suggest themselves. First, by focusing on the one from whom the Word took flesh Ignatius continues to relate the Christ event to the physical creation as he leads up to the cosmic narrative of 19:2–3. Second, the intimation of cosmic battle already present in the reference to the cleansing of the water in 18:2 is now heightened as Ignatius places the pure and silent virgin directly opposite "the ruler of this aeon."

"The ruler of this aeon" (ὁ ἄρχων τοῦ αἰῶνος τούτου) is Ignatius's favorite and most distinctive epithet for the evil one.[11] Once again he has constructed his idiom out of Johannine and Pauline components, combining John's "ruler of this world" (ὁ ἄρχων τοῦ κόσμου τούτου)[12] with Paul's frequent use of αἰών ("age, aeon") in phrases such as "the god of this age" (referring to Satan in 2 Cor 4:4) and "the rulers of this age" (referring to earthly rulers in 1 Cor 2:6–8). As αἰών is always, or nearly always, a temporal term in the Pauline letters, it is generally translated "age" in Ignatius's letters as well. But since it has a nontemporal, or at least not exclusively temporal, meaning in *Ephesians* 8:1 and 19:2, it may be better to leave the question open by using the transliteration "aeon" wherever there may be any doubt about the precise meaning of the term. "This aeon" may mean this spatiotemporal sphere in which we now live, as distinct from both "the coming age" and the outer, extraterrestrial spheres. These latter may be what Ignatius intends by "the aeons" in 8:1 and 19:2.[13]

The point would then be that both the fame of the Ephesian church (8:1) and, more importantly, the mystery of Christ (19:2) have been made known to the spiritual beings who inhabit those heavenly realms, so that they too are faced with a choice regarding Christ. This interpretation harmonizes nicely with what Ignatius says elsewhere. Jesus suffered and died "while those in heaven and on earth and under the earth looked on" (*Tral.* 9:1). Thus all rational creatures, including the most glorious angels

---

11. It occurs at *Eph.* 17:1, 19:1; *Magn.* 1:3; *Tral.* 4:2; *Rom.* 7:1; and *Phld.* 6:2. Elsewhere Ignatius refers to "Satan" (*Eph.* 13:1) or "the devil" (10:3; *Tral.* 8:1; *Rom.* 5:3; *Smyr.* 9:1).

12. Jn 12:31, 14:30, 16:11.

13. It is difficult to say whether the term is "personified" here, as Hermann Sasse maintains (TDNT 1.207). If so, it would more directly refer to the spiritual beings who inhabit the heavenly places, whereas I am suggesting that it refers directly to the heavenly places and indirectly to their inhabitants, which amounts to much the same thing. A personification of the aeons would make Ignatius's usage more akin to later gnostic usage, though hardly identical.

and "the rulers, both visible and invisible," must "believe in the blood of Christ" if they are to escape eschatological condemnation (Smyr. 6:1). Ignatius's understanding of these matters may have been influenced by the Pauline claim that God's wisdom, as revealed in "the economy of the mystery," is being "made known now to the rulers and the authorities in the heavenly places through the church" (Eph 3:9–10).

The value of this whole discussion lies in the light it sheds on the passage we are about to consider, where the epiphany of Christ "to the aeons" by way of the appearance of a new star causes "astonishment," "consternation," and "commotion" in the heavens, presumably because battle lines are being drawn.

> How then was he manifested to the aeons? A star shone in the heavens, bright beyond all the stars. Its light was indescribable, and its newness caused astonishment. All the rest of the stars, together with the sun and the moon, formed a chorus around the star. And there was consternation regarding the source of the newness that was so dissimilar to them. Consequently all magic and every spell were being broken. The ignorance that accompanies malice was vanishing. The old kingdom was being destroyed, being ruined because God was manifesting himself humanly for the newness of eternal life. And that which had been perfected with God was receiving its beginning, whence all things [τὰ πάντα] were in commotion because the destruction of death was being taken care of. (Eph. 19:2–3)

Early Christians found this unusual passage attractive, but moderns are wont to dismiss it as a quaint relic of ancient lore. With a hint of condescension, Schoedel comments that Ignatius is rejecting popular magic "in the name of a higher magic."[14] I prefer to adopt the working assumption that this text communicates Ignatius's grasp of the cosmic significance of the Christ event as this is mediated by the prescientific worldview and literary-theological traditions of his age and culture. This does not mean, of course, that we accept Ignatius's cosmology at face value, but neither does it mean that we can neatly separate off, and dispose of, his references to sun, moon, and stars in order to obtain a pure, demythologized form of the kerygma.[15] Our knowledge of the extraterrestrial realm is in many respects far superior to that of Ignatius, but it may be that he

---

14. *Ignatius of Antioch*, 93. Similarly, according to Hammond Bammel, "Ignatius himself no doubt shares with his opponents a background in which magical superstition and speculation about angels and heavenly powers were rife" ("Ignatian Problems," 84).

15. See R. M. Grant's critique of H.-W. Bartsch's attempt to do just this with regard to our passage (Grant, *Ignatius of Antioch*, 51; Bartsch, *Gnostisches Gut*, 156–58), as well as J.-P. Jossua's comments about "mythisation" and "sur-symbolisation" as cultural phenomena and their integral role in patristic theology (*Le salut*, 385).

still has something to teach us about the relationship between the created universe (τὰ πάντα) and the Christ event, and that he communicates his insights by means of (not despite) a quasi-mythological cosmology.

It is generally recognized that Ignatius drew upon a number of biblical and perhaps parabiblical texts and traditions in composing his star narrative.[16] With some confidence we can pinpoint at least four canonical texts that find echoes in this passage: Genesis 37:5–11, the Wisdom of Solomon (various passages), Matthew 2:1–15, and Revelation 12:1–17. In what follows I shall venture to read Ignatius's star narrative intertextually by comparing and contrasting it with these possible source texts.

Genesis 37:5–11 concerns two dreams of the young Joseph that foretell the future subjection of Joseph's brothers to him even as Joseph's recounting of the dreams increases their present hostility toward him. The two dreams are obviously meant to be taken together and reinforce each other. By simply combining the image of the brothers' sheaves encircling Joseph's sheaf (from the first dream) with the parallel image of the sun, moon, and stars worshipping him (from the second dream), Ignatius was able to produce the central image of his own narrative. The sun, moon, and stars form a chorus around the new star, which represents Christ.[17] In Genesis the sheaves and the stars represent the brothers, who along with Joseph become eponymous ancestors of the twelve tribes, while the sun and moon represent Jacob and Rachel, patriarch and matriarch of the people. The imagery in both dreams thus points to Israel, the people of God. The symbolism itself is significant. Elsewhere in Scripture Israel is frequently symbolized by the agricultural products of the holy land or compared to the stars of the sky.[18] In God's redemptive plan Israel stands in as the chosen representative of all creation, the heavens and the earth.[19]

Joseph rises up from the midst of his brothers, is gifted with divine

---

16. For a possible common background between *Ephesians* and the *Ascension of Isaiah* and an illuminative intertextual reading, see Robert G. Hall, "Astonishment in the Firmament: The Worship of Jesus and Soteriology in Ignatius and the *Ascension of Isaiah*," in *Jewish Roots of Christological Monotheism: Papers from the St. Andrews Conference on the Historical Origins of the Worship of Jesus*, Supplements to the *Journal for the Study of Judaism*, ed. Carey C. Newman, James R. Davila, and Gladys S. Lewis (Leiden: Brill, 1999), 148–55.

17. Ignatius may also have been influenced by Clement of Rome's reference to "the sun and the moon and the choruses of stars" (1 *Clem.* 20:3).

18. Gn 15:5, 22:17, 26:4; Ex 32:13; Nm 24:17; Dt 1:10; 1 Chr 27:23; Neh 9:23; Ps 80:9–17; Sir 44:21; Is 5:1–7, 27:2–6, 60:21, 61:3; Jer 8:13, 11:16, 24:1–10, 32:41, 42:10; Ez 19:10–14; Dn 12:3; Hos 2:25, 9:10, 14:6; Am 9:15; Mi 7:1; 2 Mc 1:29.

19. Cf. Clement's apt collocation of Gn 13:16 (which likens Abraham's descendants to "the dust of the earth") and 15:5 (which likens them to "the stars of the sky") in 1 *Clem.* 10:4–6.

wisdom, and is God's chosen instrument for the salvation of his people. But before he is acknowledged as ruler, he is rejected by his brothers, falsely condemned, and suffers much. His career is characterized by descent—into the cistern, down to Egypt, into the dungeon—before Pharaoh elevates him to a position of authority "over all the land of Egypt" (41:43). In Ignatius's narrative the epiphany of the star at the time of the incarnation foretells the glorious kingship of Christ, but the consternation and tumult in heaven foreshadow the fact that Christ will first be rejected by some of his own.

The Wisdom of Solomon, which was composed in Greek in Alexandria toward the end of the Old Testament period, is intensely interested in the interrelations among the following realities: God the Creator, divine wisdom (personified as Sophia), the created cosmos, and God's holy people, Israel. Here we shall merely touch on those aspects of this book's rich imagery and rather complex theology that seem to be echoed in Ignatius's star narrative. Advancing a motif found in Proverbs 8 and Sirach 24, the Wisdom of Solomon presents Sophia as a divine hypostasis: the "reflection of eternal light," the "image" of God's goodness, and the "fashioner of all things" (7:21, 7:26). This is essentially how Ignatius views the *preincarnate* Logos.[20] According to Wisdom 7:29–30, the splendor of Sophia is greater than the sun and "beyond every constellation of stars" (ὑπὲρ πᾶσαν ἄστρων θέσιν), and "malice" (κακία) does not prevail over Sophia. In Ignatius's narrative the new star shines bright "beyond all the stars" (ὑπὲρ πάντας τοὺς ἀστέρας) and brings to an end the "ignorance of malice" (κακίας ἄγνοια).

A subtle but important difference between these two texts is to be noted. In the former, Sophia is greater than all celestial bodies because she is not part of creation, while in Ignatius's text the *incarnate* Logos is represented by a star among stars that nonetheless surpasses every star in glory. It is not that Ignatius blurs the distinction between Creator and creation. Rather, he recognizes that the definitive entrance of the Creator into his creation brings about a transcendent "newness" *within* creation. This difference between *Ephesians* and the Wisdom of Solomon may also be seen in the way the latter text polemicizes against those who suppose "the circle of the stars" and "the luminaries of heaven" (i.e., the sun and the moon) to be "gods" (13:2), whereas in *Ephesians* 19 the sun, moon, and stars encircle and worship the new star, thus confessing it to be truly divine.

20. *Magn.* 6:1, 8:2; *Eph.* 15:1.

Wisdom of Solomon 11–19 is devoted to a typological midrash (an imaginative and highly interpretive retelling) of the exodus event, in which the central theme is that "the whole creation in its nature was fashioned anew" in order both to punish the Egyptians and to assist and glorify the Israelites (19:6).[21] The plague of cosmic darkness that comes upon the Egyptians reflects the darkness of ignorance into which their idolatry, magic arts, and immorality have plunged them, while the cosmic light that Israel experiences reflects the fact that the "imperishable light" of God's law is to come into the world through them (18:4). The final plague, the death of the firstborn, is the occasion of a sort of epiphany of God's people, through which the Egyptians, "though they had disbelieved everything because of their magic arts," are compelled to acknowledge Israel as "the son of God" (18:13). This requires an especially dramatic intervention on God's part. "While gentle silence [ἥσυχος σιγή] enveloped all things [τὰ πάντα]," God's "all-powerful word [λόγος] leaped from heaven, from the royal throne ... and stood and filled all things with death, and touched heaven while standing on the earth" (18:14–16). This immediately leads to apparitions and dreams that "greatly troubled" (ἐξετάραξαν) the Egyptians (18:17).

In this strange narrative, then, Israel as God's "son" is juxtaposed to the divine Logos who bridges heaven and earth. The latter descends to deal death not life, but creation itself comes to the assistance of the Creator in order that God's holy people might be saved through the very things by which the wicked are punished.[22] Indeed Israel itself is touched by "the experience of death" in the wilderness and would be entirely consumed by divine wrath except for the intercession of Aaron (18:20–23). Only in the symbolism of Aaron's high priestly garments do we finally see the convergence of cosmos, Israel, and divine majesty (18:24).

In Ignatius's narrative, by contrast, the Word descends into his creation to bring, not death, but the "newness of eternal life," indeed the "dissolution of death" (Eph. 19:3). The sun, moon, and stars that form a chorus around the new star presumably represent heavenly beings who recognize Christ's glory and honor him. Curiously, however, they are also said to experience "consternation" or "confusion" (ταραχή) at the star's arrival (19:2), which almost seems the opposite of a "chorus" (χορός).[23]

---

21. The typological dimension of this midrash, by which the Hebrews enslaved to the Egyptians in the days of Moses prefigure the Jews living in Alexandria at the time of the author (circa 25 B.C.), is not pertinent to Ignatius's reuse of this text and will not concern us here.

22. Wis 11:5, 13, 16:24, 18:8.

23. The former term is sometimes used of the confusion of a defeated army, while the latter

Just possibly Ignatius refers to two groups of heavenly beings with two quite different responses to the star, but this is far from clear. In any case, his narrative is not merely an allegory or parable. Ignatius and the author of the Wisdom of Solomon share the conviction that, due to man's special place within the universe, God's economic dealings with humanity must have a real impact on the cosmos, and Ignatius presumes that the glory of the one by whom God was "manifesting himself humanly" must have been "manifested to the aeons," setting "all things" into commotion (19:2–3).

At this point, however, another subtle but important difference between the two writers emerges. While the author of the Wisdom of Solomon holds that "through the envy of the devil death entered the world" (Wis 2:24), the only members of the devil's party who are of concern to this author are unrighteous human beings, especially unjust earthly rulers. He presents the nonhuman cosmos quite positively as the eager servant of its Creator and maintains that death exercises its dominion only in Hades, not on earth.[24] For Ignatius, by contrast, death seems to have taken a deeper hold on the cosmos, including the heavenly powers. Magic seems to constitute a real bondage (δεσμός, "spell") that needs to be "loosed" (λύω), and the "old kingdom" is not merely Pharaonic Egypt, or even the sum total of unrighteous human beings, but the state of thralldom in which Satan holds virtually the entire universe (Eph. 19:3). There are, of course, graced individuals, such as the virgin Mary, who are well disposed to God's economic action, but the tenor of Ignatius's letters suggests that the universe as such stands in need of redemption. When God's Logos descends into creation in the Wisdom of Solomon, it finds "gentle silence" enveloping "all things" (Wis 18:14), but in *Ephesians* the incarnation sets "all things" into commotion (Eph. 19:3).

Only surrounding Mary and Jesus himself do we find the "silence of God" within creation (19:1). In these two persons creation stands ready and eager to serve its Master by cooperating fully in the economy of redemption. Ignatius will describe the cooperation of the incarnate Son as his "submission" to the Father "according to the flesh" (*Magn.* 13:2), not because Christ's humanity was in any sense rebellious but because

---

term often refers to dancing in a ring (LSJ, 1758, 1999). Hall plausibly suggests that the heavenly "aeons" see the star's glory but are confused because they do not understand its source. Like the ruler of the terrestrial aeon, they have no access to God's silence and are thus unaware of the incarnation and passion of Jesus, deeds "wrought in the silence of God" ("Astonishment in the Firmament," 153–54). This seems inconsistent with *Tral.* 9:1, however.

24. Wis 1:14, 5:17, 5:20, 16:24, 19:6.

it is principally in that sacred humanity that we see the creation serving its Creator. The glorification of Christ's physical body in the resurrection anticipates the eschatological transformation of the entire cosmos, but this transformation is already mysteriously anticipated in the cosmic events surrounding the incarnation.

Next we turn to a third source upon which Ignatius is likely to have drawn in composing his star narrative, namely, Matthew's magi narrative (Mt 2:1–15), which, like the Wisdom of Solomon 11–19, is a typological midrash on the exodus story. Here Matthew employs traditional motifs to create dramatic irony. In the book of Exodus the magicians are dupes of Pharaoh, and in the Wisdom of Solomon the Egyptians' magic arts are concomitant with pagan ignorance, but Matthew's μάγοι are portrayed positively.[25] Their examination of the heavens, which leads them to the birthplace of the Christ child, functions as a sort of natural mode of revelation, running parallel to, and completed by, the chief priests' and scribes' inquiry into the prophetic Scriptures of Israel (Mt 2:2–9).[26] The arrival of the star over the house where Jesus is to be found fills them with "an exceedingly great joy," and when they enter and find him with Mary, they worship him and present him with gifts (2:10–11). By contrast, the Jewish king Herod and the citizens of Jerusalem, who are ironic antitypes of Pharaoh and the Egyptians, are "troubled" (ἐταράχθη) by news of the birth of a new king (2:3), and Herod plots to kill the child. At a second level of Matthew's sophisticated typology, the antagonism of Herod and the Jerusalemites foreshadows Judaism's generally negative response to the Christ event, while the magi represent the more favorable response of the gentiles.[27]

Ignatius, for his part, is less interested here in this contrast between Jews and gentiles than he is concerned with the way Christ's entrance into the world demands a response and leads to the division of all rational beings into two camps: those who accept Christ and those who reject him, in other words, the church and the "world." For both Matthew and Ignatius it is a question of two kingdoms and of a contrast between the old and the new. The "old kingdom" of powers who assert themselves

---

25. Ex 7:11, 22; 8:7, 18, 19; 9:11; Wis 17:7, 18:13. "In our text the Magi are not sketched negatively. They are not converted by the child Jesus from their godless arts but they are wise and pious Gentiles who from the beginning seek that which is right, namely, to worship the child Jesus" (Ulrich Luz, *Matthew 1–7: A Commentary*, trans. Wilhelm C. Linss [Minneapolis: Augsburg Fortress, 1989], 135).

26. Raymond E. Brown, *The Birth of the Messiah: A Commentary on the Infancy Narratives in the Gospels of Matthew and Luke*, 2nd ed., Anchor Bible Reference Library (New York: Doubleday, 1993), 178.

27. Ibid., 182–83.

over against God and his reign must give way to the rule of the "new king," who upon his arrival brings the old to naught.[28] As the book of Revelation puts it, "The kingdom of the world has become the kingdom of our Lord and of his Christ" (Rv 11:15). In this context, Ignatius's reference to the destruction of "magic" (μαγεία) probably indicates that he understood Matthew's μάγοι to have been converted from their magic practices to faith in Jesus Christ.[29]

Finally, it should be noted that, whereas Joseph the husband of Mary is the main protagonist in Matthew's infancy narrative, Matthew also places a subtle but clear accent on Mary herself, who maintains a silent presence throughout the narrative. When the magi enter the house, they see "the child with Mary his mother" and prostrate themselves in worship before him (Mt 2:11). As Ignatius reads the First Gospel, he may discern two closely interrelated reasons for Matthew's mentioning Mary here. First, the magi seek out the new king by following a cosmic sign, "his star" (2:2), and so they fittingly find him in the arms of the one through whom he has entered the cosmos and has in a sense become part of it. Second, as representative gentiles, the magi do not worship Christ independently of faithful Israel. As mother of the Messiah, Mary represents the faithful remnant of Israel through whom Christ comes into the world. Or to put it in Pauline terms, Jesus and Mary, together with faithful Israelites of every age, constitute the olive tree onto which the gentiles are grafted (Rom 11:17–24). Matthew indicates this typologically by noting that Joseph follows very precise angelic instructions in taking "the child and his mother" down to Egypt and in returning them to the land of Israel again[30] and by quoting Hosea 11:1, "Out of Egypt I have called my son," in reference to the Christ child (Mt 2:15). Jesus, "with Mary his mother," is the true Israel. In sum, Mary is most closely associated with her son in his relation to the cosmos and in his relation to Israel. And if we recall that Israel stands in for the whole cosmos in their covenant with the Creator, we can appreciate the fact that Mary represents Israel and cosmos simultaneously.

---

28. This "old kingdom" is not, however, to be identified with Israel or the old covenant. It is comprised of all rational beings who are opposed to God.

29. This places Ignatius's interpretation of Mt 2:1–12 on a trajectory toward that given by Justin Martyr, who views the magi as under the thrall of a demonic power and given over to all manner of evil practices prior to their encounter with the Christ child (Dial. 78:9). This is pointed out by Cullen I. K. Story, whose treatment of Ignatius's rereading of the magi narrative, somewhat different from my own, is worth consulting ("The Christology of Ignatius of Antioch," *Evangelical Quarterly* 56 [1984]: 175–76).

30. Mt 2:13–14, 20–21 (where the phrase "the child and his mother" occurs four times).

That which is intimated in the subtle shadings of Matthew's magi narrative is depicted in bold strokes and bright colors in Revelation 12, the fourth and final biblical text that seems to lie behind Ephesians 19.[31] Somewhat as in Matthew 2, a "great sign" appearing "in the heavens" reflects an event on earth that has significance for the entire cosmos (Rv 12:1). The adornment of the woman with sun, moon, and twelve stars draws its imagery from the second dream of Joseph the patriarch (Gn 37:9) in order to indicate that the woman represents Israel precisely in the latter's cosmic dimension. The great red dragon of the second sign represents, as we are explicitly informed later in the chapter, "the ancient serpent, who is called the devil and Satan" (Rv 12:3, 12:9), and this suggests that the woman is also an Eve-like figure. In other words, she represents Israel, humanity, and cosmos simultaneously. While the dragon is initially a heavenly figure who draws a third of the stars down to earth with him, the apocalyptic imagery of seven heads, ten horns, and seven diadems indicates that he expresses his opposition to God's rule by means of his sway over the kingdoms of the earth (12:3). He is "the one who leads the entire world astray" (12:9).

Next, John the Seer tells us that the woman's child "will shepherd all the nations with a rod of iron" (12:5). This patent allusion to Psalm 2 identifies the woman as mother of the Messiah and her child as God's Son, while it strengthens the intimation that her son's installation as God's terrestrial viceroy will stir up the latent hostility of the kings of the earth "against the Lord and against his anointed" (Ps 2:2). Indeed, the Christ event provokes an all-out cosmic war, which pits the archangel Michael and his hosts against Satan and his angels (Rv 12:7). The woman's labor pains (12:2) seem to reflect her mysterious participation in her son's suffering, spanning his entire life from birth to death. Long after her son has been caught up to the throne of God, the woman remains the special object of Satan's "persecution," while the earth itself comes to her defense (12:13–16). The intimation here, that the woman is also mother of the church and its representative member, is confirmed near the end of the chapter when the seer refers to Christians as "the

---

31. For a thorough treatment of Revelation 12, see G. K. Beale, *The Book of Revelation: A Commentary on the Greek Text*, NIGTC (Grand Rapids, Mich.: Eerdmans, 1999), 621–80. Behind Matthew's infancy narrative, the vision of Revelation 12, and ("in a much softened form") the story of Joseph and his brothers, Austin Farrer discerns "a very old mythic pattern," according to which: "A true prince is to be born. He is fated to overthrow a usurper. The usurper tries to kill him at birth, but the child is providentially snatched away and hidden. The prince comes to maturity, kills the usurper and takes the throne" (*The Revelation of St. John the Divine: A Commentary on the English Text* [Oxford: Clarendon Press, 1964], 141).

rest of her seed" (12:17). In sum, the mother of the Messiah, by virtue of her pivotal role in the economy of redemption, represents both Israel and the church, that is, the one people of God spanning the old and new covenants. Furthermore, she is simultaneously present in celestial glory and in terrestrial exile (12:1, 12:6, 12:14). As the new Eve, and as Israel/church, she stands in as a representative for all of humanity and all of creation.

Ignatius's presentation of Mary in *Ephesians* 18–19 is not as elaborately developed as is the presentation of the mother of the Messiah in Revelation 12, but there are significant parallels between the two texts.[32] Ignatius's creedal formula confesses Jesus to be the Davidic Messiah, "conceived by Mary according to the economy of God" (Eph. 18:2).[33] In other words, Mary plays a vital role as mother of the Messiah at the pivotal moment in God's great historical plan of redemption. Through her, God's Son enters the cosmos. Like John the Seer, Ignatius presents Mary as the opponent of Satan while he hints at an intimate but mysterious connection between her childbirth and Jesus' passion (19:1). *Ephesians* also parallels the Apocalypse in recounting a heavenly sign—involving sun, moon, and stars—that accompanies the Christ event (19:2).

While Ignatius does not explicitly involve Mary in this heavenly event, the implicit connection between his references to her (18:2 and 19:1) and the star narrative that immediately follows (19:2) lies in the cosmic-creaturely dimension of the incarnation. The Son of God enters creation through Mary, and his entrance impacts the entire cosmos. If we place the star narrative of *Ephesians* 19:2 alongside the heavenly sign of Revelation 12:1–2, the new star of the former text parallels *the woman* of the latter text. Both are surrounded by sun, moon, and stars. We might be tempted, then, to take Ignatius's star to symbolize Mary rather than Jesus. But since the woman of Revelation 12 is already pregnant—that is, she "surrounds" the Christ child even while she herself is clothed with the cosmos—it would be better to take Ignatius's star to represent Jesus

---

32. Though modern scholars are reticent to identify the woman of Revelation 12 with Mary the mother of Jesus, that would not have been the case with Ignatius. For a consideration of possible points of contact between Ignatius's letters and the book of Revelation, and between *Ephesians* 19 and Revelation 12 in particular, see Christine Trevett, "The Other Letters to the Churches of Asia: Apocalypse and Ignatius of Antioch," *Journal for the Study of the New Testament* 37 (1989): 117–35.

33. Like the New Testament authors, Ignatius very often refers to "Jesus Christ" ('Ιησοῦς Χριστός), treating Χριστός almost as part of the Lord's name. But here in Eph. 18:2 he writes "Jesus the Christ" ('Ιησοῦς ὁ Χριστός), which is to say, "Jesus the Messiah," and identifies the Lord as coming "from the seed of David."

and Mary together. The star is Christ in his cosmic dimension. The Son of God joined himself to his creation in the virgin's womb. He clothed himself in flesh. But Mary's role in "surrounding" Jesus Christ does not begin and end with nine months of gestation. She is the culmination of the faithful remnant of Israel that Yahweh formed and purified over the course of the Old Testament period, so that through that faithful remnant the Messiah might come into the world. "For Yahweh has created a new thing on the earth: A woman will surround a man" (Jer 31:22). She is, moreover, the mother and representative member of the church, the people who form a "chorus" around Jesus Christ to sing praise to the Father through him (Eph. 4:2).

Finally, we should note that the motif of cosmic battle, which dominates Revelation 12, is by comparison muted in *Ephesians* 19. In the former text the dragon stands menacingly before the woman in anticipation of her child's birth, that he might gobble him up; and after the child is "snatched away to God and to his throne" and the dragon is cast down to earth, the latter viciously pursues the woman and "the rest of her offspring."[34] But in Ignatius's narrative Satan seems not even to realize that he is in a battle until its outcome has been decided. Mary's virginity and childbirth and Jesus' death escape his notice, apparently because he is insensitive to the purity, love, and humility by means of which these mysteries have been "accomplished in the silence of God" (Eph. 19:1). The Christ event, then, constitutes a sort of surprise invasion of Satan's territory. The centerpiece of Revelation 12 is an all-out war between two heavenly armies, but in *Ephesians* the star's appearance merely causes "astonishment" and "consternation" in the heavens (19:2). Obviously the point is not that Ignatius wishes to deny the cosmic importance or efficacy of the Christ event. On the contrary, this event brings about the destruction of the "old kingdom" and the "dissolution of death" (19:3). But for Ignatius the cosmic battle is quite lopsided. Satan is no match for Jesus Christ and his virgin mother.

Ignatius acknowledges that there is a cosmic dimension to spiritual combat, but throughout his letters he wishes to draw attention more to the way this warfare plays out in the lives of Christians on earth. The Christ event has indeed been "manifested to the aeons," but Satan is "the ruler of *this* aeon," and that is where Ignatius usually focuses his readers' attention. The attacks of the devil are to be taken seriously, but paradoxically the Christian overcomes these attacks by enduring and ab-

---

34. Rv 12:4–5, 13–17.

sorbing them, as it were (*Magn.* 1:3). The enemy's point of vulnerability is "the ignorance that accompanies malice" (*Eph.* 19:3). He is congenitally blind to the love and humility that constitute the true wisdom of the cross, as are those whom the world regards as "wise" (σοφός; 18:1). Ignatius warns us that since we have received this authentic "knowledge of God" through Jesus Christ, we ought to be truly "wise" (φρόνιμοι) and not "perish foolishly" (17:2). By embracing the utter ignobility of martyrdom, Ignatius makes his own spirit a "lowly offering" (περίψημα) on behalf of the cross, "which is a scandal to unbelievers, but to us salvation and eternal life" (18:1). John the Seer, for his part, certainly grasps that Satan now wages his war on earth, and like Ignatius he appreciates that Christians win the victory by sharing in Christ's passion through martyrdom (Rv 12:10–12), but it may be that Ignatius articulates a somewhat deeper penetration into the spiritual dynamics of this victory. I hope to expound some of the elements of his insight in the remainder of this chapter.

I have interpreted Ignatius's star narrative within its immediate context in *Ephesians* and by comparing it to four biblical texts that Ignatius seems to have drawn upon. This procedure has illuminated important aspects of Ignatian cosmology, two of which I would like to specify more precisely. First, Ignatius views the cosmos, not as static and timeless, but as an economic and teleological reality. It was created by God in the beginning (*Eph.* 15:1) to be the theater of the economy of redemption. The Christ event marks the decisive turning point in that economy, when the "old kingdom" of death gives way to the "newness" of eternal life (19:3). As a result, we now live in the "last times" (11:1). This economic aspect of Ignatius's cosmology corresponds to the dynamic and soteriological character of his anthropology, which we noted earlier in this chapter. This observation leads to the second point, which is that man occupies a special place in the cosmos. Human beings such as David, Mary, and, of course, Jesus play the central roles in the historical economy of redemption. Ignatius acknowledges other participants in the drama, notably Satan, and other "aeons" than the one in which we live, but he keeps the focus on the human realm. The point of the star narrative itself is not that terrestrial events are mere reflections of more important and more real supramundane events, but that the definitive and most important event, which has taken place "humanly" and in the human realm, has ramifications for the entire cosmos. In sum, we may say that Ignatius's cosmology is economic and anthropocentric.

Spiritual Warfare and Martyrdom
Christians in the World

The incarnation throws the cosmos into commotion because its strange "newness" constitutes an assault upon "the old kingdom" (Eph. 19:2–3). As we have seen, the Christ event is a surprise invasion of Satan's realm, aimed at exploiting his main point of vulnerability. In his prideful malice the devil fails to appreciate the power of Jesus' humility and love. The followers of Christ can make use of the same strategy in their own spiritual combat. For example, the Christ-like "meekness" of Bishop Polybius of Tralles is paradoxically his "power" in dealing with the godless (Tral. 3:2), and Ignatius recognizes his own need of this virtue, "by which the ruler of this aeon is destroyed" (4:2). Similarly, if the devil's dominion is energized by anger, division, and deceitful doctrine, Christians can counteract these forces by assembling for eucharistic worship "with an undivided heart."[35]

> For when you come together frequently, the powers of Satan are thrown down and his destructiveness is undone by your unanimity in the faith. Nothing is better than peace, by which all warfare of those in heaven and on earth is nullified. (Eph. 13:1b–2)

Most paradoxically, Christians overcome evil and "attain God" precisely by "enduring every abuse of the ruler of this aeon" in imitation of their Savior's victory on the cross (Magn. 1:3). This is Ignatius's own strategy as he anticipates his martyrdom in Rome.

> Fire and cross, battles with beasts, mutilation, dismemberment, wrenching of bones, hacking of limbs, grinding up of the whole body, cruel punishments of the devil—let them come upon me, only let me attain Jesus Christ! (Rom. 5:3)

As Ignatius's parenetic letters to the churches touch on various aspects of the economy of redemption, the cosmic scope of this drama is never far from view. But Ignatius's primary concern is with the sublunary realm. According to him, there is real opposition to God present in the universe, not only among the principalities and powers in high places but among human beings here below. There is "warfare" in both the heavenly and the earthly realms (Eph. 13:2). To the extent that human society embodies this enmity toward God, it is called "the world" (ὁ κόσμος), in the pejorative sense found often in the New Testament.[36] Ignatius tells

---

35. Phld. 6:2, 8:1.
36. Jn 7:7, 8:23, 12:31, 14:17, 27; 15:18–19, 16:8, 11, 20, 33; 17:9, 14–16, 18, 25; 18:36; 1 Cor

the Magnesians that there are "two coinages, one of God and one of the world," and that each has its own "imprint" (χαρακτήρ). "Unbelievers" bear the imprint of the world, while those who "believe with love" have the imprint of God the Father stamped upon them through their willing participation in the passion of Jesus Christ (*Magn.* 5:2). Which imprint one bears has eschatological consequences. It is a matter of "life and death" (5:1). Here we see the unity of flesh and spirit, and of knowledge and love, in Ignatius's thought. Faith is not merely a matter of being called a Christian but of actually being one.[37] "Believing with love" makes one the sort of creature who is apt for everlasting union with God. It constitutes an "imprint" upon the person, an imprint that is eternal life. This is a decidedly nondocetic and nongnostic view of redemption.

In *Ephesians* 10, Ignatius gives an instruction on how Christians are to deal with those outside the church. Here he does not use the pejorative term "world," and his approach is surprisingly positive. Christians are to "pray unceasingly" for unbelievers in hope of their repentance and eventual salvation, and they are to kill them with kindness, so to speak, by countering anger with meekness, boasting with humility, blasphemy with prayers, deceit with firmness in the faith, and savagery with mildness. While Christians obviously should not imitate unbelievers, they should prove to be "their brethren" by dealing gently with them (*Eph.* 10:1-3). This use of ἀδελφοί ("brethren") is remarkable, since elsewhere in early Christian literature this term so often designates members of the body of Christ over against non-Christians.[38] The context, however, suggests that Ignatius is not so much promoting chumminess with nonbelievers as he is inculcating the recognition of essential human solidarity and the universality of God's salvific will. He goes on to recommend the radical *imitatio Christi* by which Jesus' followers can overcome evil by allowing it to fall upon them. Indeed, Ignatius encourages the Ephesians to compete with each other, as it were, to see "who may be the more wronged, who the more defrauded, who the more rejected"! Above all, he is concerned that no one in the Christian community conform to the world's moral standards and thus prove to be a "weed of the devil" within the church.

1:20, 2:12, 3:19, 5:10, 11:32; 2 Cor 5:19, 7:10; Gal 6:14; Eph 2:2; Col 2:20; Jas 1:27, 4:4; 2 Pt 1:4, 2:20; 1 Jn 2:15-17; 3:1, 13, 4:5, 17; 5:4, 19.

37. *Magn.* 4:1; *Rom.* 3:2.

38. See TDNT 1.145-46; BDAG, 18. Alvyn Pettersen understands Ignatius to be referring specifically to heretics as "brothers" in *Eph.* 10:3 ("Sending Heretics to Coventry? Ignatius of Antioch on Reverencing Silent Bishops," *Vigiliae Christianae* 44 [1990]: 343), but this is most unlikely. Ignatius refers explicitly to "the rest of mankind" (τῶν ἄλλων ἀνθρώπων; *Eph.* 10:1).

Thus he concludes the chapter by exhorting the Ephesian Christians to "purity and self-control" (10:3).

Schoedel observes how many themes and expressions *Ephesians* 10 shares with passages where Ignatius discusses his impending martyrdom, and he rightly concludes that "martyrdom represents a special focusing of the Christian stance in the world."[39] It is probably safe to take this one step further and say that martyrdom represents an intensification of Christian existence *tout court*. In any case, it is no surprise to find that Ignatius's most profound insights into spiritual combat and the Christian's relationship to the world are found in *Romans*, a letter devoted almost entirely to the significance of his own martyrdom. Having explored Ignatius's cosmology through our study of *Ephesians* 19, as well as his understanding of the relationship between the Christian community and the "world" in *Magnesians* 5 and *Ephesians* 10, we are perhaps now in better position to interpret his statements about personal eschatology, spiritual combat, and martyrdom in *Romans*.

Disappearance from the World

It is not the sheer endurance of pain or death that effects or completes the believer's union with God. The authentic imitation of Christ involves a moral transformation, or more precisely, a purification of desire, so that Christians "love nothing according to the life of men, but only God" (Eph. 9:2), and are actually able to "rejoice in the passion of our Lord" (Phld. sal.). As we have seen, Ignatius understands salvation to involve the whole person, both flesh and spirit. At the same time, however, he realizes that man must subordinate the physical to the spiritual and that "matter" (ὕλη) can present an alluring distraction to one who has an opportunity to attain "pure light" (Rom. 6:2). Ignatius himself is "learning not to desire [ἐπιθυμεῖν] anything" (4:3) and even claims that through his union with Christ his own "desire [ἔρως] has been crucified" and that no "matter-loving fire" (πῦρ φιλόϋλον) continues to burn within him (7:2). He has been so transformed that now he can truthfully say that he "loves [ἀγαπάω] to suffer" (Tral. 4:2) and "desires [ἐράω] to die," not because suffering and death are per se desirable but because they constitute the way by which Ignatius can "come to the Father" (Rom. 7:2).

Still, because the Son of God came among us "bearing flesh" (σαρκοφόρος) in order to save us (Smyr. 5:2), the journey to God can never be salvation from the body or a deliverance from the material realm.

---

39. Schoedel, *Ignatius of Antioch*, 70.

Nor could Ignatius's ἔρως be so "spiritualized" as to be directed toward God in a way that is unmediated by material reality, for that would amount to the denial of man's true nature as created by God and the denial of Jesus Christ "the perfect man" (*Smyr.* 4:2). Ignatius's desire is to become an authentic "man" (ἄνθρωπος), not an angel (*Rom.* 6:2). To be sure, he no longer desires "perishable food or the pleasures of this life," but he does long for "the bread of God, which is the flesh of Christ, who is from the seed of David," and for drink he wants "his blood, which is an imperishable love-feast" (7:3). In this characteristically rich passage we find ourselves near the core of Ignatius's understanding of redemption, in which God's historical act of salvation in the person of Christ, its sacramental and ecclesial mediation, and the mysticism of a genuinely charismatic soul all converge. Ignatius's human love, purified of every inordinate desire (4:3), has found its resting place in the one reality that is both fully concrete and fully transcendent—the person and event of Jesus Christ—as this reality is made present to the Christian in the visible church, its doctrines, and its sacraments.

With his poetic imagination and prophetic sense for finding meaning in concrete circumstances, Ignatius reflects on the fact that his journey from Antioch to Rome is taking him from the eastern part of the empire to the western part, where he will disappear from the world's sight. He likens this to the sun's circuit across the sky and its sinking below the horizon in order to rise again the next day, and he remarks that it is good for him to "set" on the world in order to "rise" to God (*Rom.* 2:2). This image leads, in turn, to an intriguing reflection on what it means to "appear" or "not appear" to the world. Ignatius claims that he will have proved "faithful," that is, a true believer, when he "no longer appear[s] to the world" (3:2), and then he makes one of his characteristically abrupt and arresting statements: "Nothing that appears is good" (οὐδὲν φαινόμενον καλόν; 3:3).

This epigram, which could easily be taken to mean that nothing visible or material is good, is probably not the sort of thing Ignatius would have dared to write to the churches in Smyrna or Tralles, where he feared the influence of docetism. Correctly understood, however, it is actually an antidocetic axiom. Schoedel notes that "in Greek literature 'appearing' (τὸ φαινόμενον) is frequently synonymous with 'seeming' (τὸ δοκοῦν)."[40] According to Ignatius, the docetists, who deny the reality of Christ's physical body, likewise fail to appreciate the importance of cor-

---

40. Ibid., 173.

poral works of mercy (*Smyr.* 6:2). We might say that their Christological docetism tends to lead to moral docetism, that is, to the attitude that what the Christian does in the body is of little or no consequence. Ignatius is vehemently opposed to such a conception of Christianity, for it runs directly counter to his emphasis on personal integrity and Christian authenticity, which is to say, the concrete living out of the gospel "in flesh and spirit." In the very passage with which we are dealing, he asks the Roman Christians to pray for him that he will have strength "interiorly and exteriorly," that he will not only speak about dying for Christ but actually will it, and that he will not only be "called a Christian" but actually prove to be one (*Rom.* 3:2). As Schoedel puts it, "mere appearance is the Christian's worst enemy," and Ignatius will not be "free of any doubt as to whether he truly is what he now only appears to be (namely, a Christian)" until he has seen "his martyrdom through to the end."[41]

Schoedel's explanation of this passage is compelling, but there are deeper levels here worth probing. First of all, there is a Christological basis for what Ignatius is saying about his own death. He glosses his axiom ("Nothing that appears is good") with an equally enigmatic statement about Christ: "For our God Jesus Christ, now that he is in the Father, is more apparent" (3:3). In his fondness for paradox Ignatius explains a statement in which "appearing" connotes a wholly negative thing by means of a statement in which "appearing" is a positive thing. His meaning is nonetheless tolerably clear and may be expounded as follows. While Jesus was in the mortal and weak flesh of his preresurrection existence, he was available (visible and tangible) to relatively few people over a short period of time, and his identity as eternal Son of God was not fully "apparent." When, however, through the paschal mystery, he returned to the Father with the humanity that he had assumed and that humanity was transformed through its assimilation to Trinitarian glory ("in the Father"), he became available to the world more universally, that is, to people in all places and times, and in such a way that his identity as God's Son was "more apparent."

This new mode of availability or presence is realized in and through the church, that is, through the action of the Holy Spirit; the proclamation of the gospel; the ministry of bishops, presbyters, and deacons; and the church's liturgical-sacramental life. In *Smyrnaeans*, Ignatius insists that Jesus was still "in the flesh" after his resurrection, and his narration

41. Ibid.

of the risen Lord's appearance to the apostles contains ecclesial and eucharistic overtones.

> And when he came to those around Peter, he said to them, "Take, handle me, and see that I am not a bodiless phantom." And immediately they touched him and believed, being mingled with his flesh and spirit. (Smyr. 3:2)[42]

The point here is that the resurrection—that is, the glorification of Christ's humanity, as opposed to its being left behind at some point—makes possible Christ's eucharistic presence to the church ("those around Peter"), and that his eucharistic presence is an extension (through time and space) of his historical presence.

Ignatius, it seems, is looking for a parallel transformation of his own existence through his imitation of the passion of Jesus. With a touch of gallows humor worthy of Alfred Hitchcock, he imagines the beasts in Rome making such complete work of him that there is nothing left to bury, so that they become his "tomb." The significance of this scenario, apart from the practical consideration that Ignatius would not be a "burden" to anyone after his death, is that he would literally disappear from the world. "Then I shall truly be a disciple, when the world no longer sees my body" (Rom. 4:2). In the same context he calls himself "God's wheat" and speaks of the beasts "grinding" him up with their teeth so that he becomes "a pure loaf of bread" (4:1). In other words, Ignatius's ecclesial-sacramental existence in this life is to be consummated by martyrdom in such a way that he himself, in some sense, becomes eucharist. He even takes this one step further and suggests that he would in that case become "a sacrifice to God" (θεοῦ θυσία; 4:2). While there is a bit of playfulness in Ignatius's tone at this point in Romans, it would be a mistake to toss these expressions aside as mere hyperbole and metaphor. The overall tenor of the letter is, after all, one of great urgency and earnestness. Ignatius's images direct our attention to a profound mystery that deserves careful reflection.

There is a deep paradox in the fact that the body-soul unity needs to be broken for a human being to achieve the full integrity to which he or she is called, to become consummately an ἄνθρωπος and "attain God."

---

42. The imperative "take" (λάβετε) evokes both the institution of the eucharist (Mt 26:26) and the risen Lord's conferral of the Spirit upon the church (Jn 20:22). There may also be a eucharistic overtone in Ignatius's affirmation that Jesus ate *and drank* with the apostles after his resurrection (Smyr. 3:3). The canonical gospels mention only eating; but see Acts 10:41, which is similar in wording to Ignatius's account. Finally, the Armenian version of Smyrnaeans contains a further eucharistic overtone, as it reads "mingled with his flesh *and blood*" (3:2).

Often a thing needs to be destroyed, "dis-integrated," in order to serve a higher purpose or to be taken up into a higher order of existence. For example, a tree is felled, stripped of its bark, cut into chips, and ground into pulp to be used in the production of paper, which when written upon becomes a medium of ideas. Thus one might think of a book as a spiritualized tree. To cite another example, animals are butchered and cooked, and grains are winnowed and milled, to serve man's need for nourishment, and all foods are broken down through digestion, in order to be taken up into the body-soul unity that is the human person.

This spiritualization of the material realm takes on a more explicitly symbolic dimension in the practice of immolation, through which animals and grain are sacrificed by being destroyed in fire. The reduction of these goods to ashes and rising smoke is a symbolic spiritualization, whereby the creation is rendered back to its transcendent Creator. This is implicit, for example, in the Hebrew term 'ôlâ, which denotes a whole burnt offering but literally means "that which ascends." Furthermore, rites of immolation, and also of libation, are suggestive of self-denial and trust in the Creator, and they have the symbolic quality of being irreversible and definitive. Insofar as the worshiper offers not merely a surplus but the best of what he or she has to live on, the gesture of sacrifice is not merely symbolic but embodies a real act of trust and devotion.

This link between interior act and exterior gesture is, of course, most perfect when a human being freely makes an offering of his or her own bodily life. Moreover, only in death can one make a definitive act of self-donation. All these considerations, and more, factor into Ignatius's understanding of his approaching martyrdom, which he views as a unique opportunity to pour himself out as a libation to God (2:1–2). He anticipates the disintegration of his body—divided up, limb from limb—as the consummation of a life lived in imitation of the passion of Jesus Christ and as the point of entry into a higher state of existence. He will be "ground up" like wheat to become a "pure loaf" and a "sacrifice to God" (4:1–2; 5:3).

The Crucifixion of Desire

Near the center of *Romans* lies a cluster of interrelated themes: desire, love, and will. Ignatius is writing to the churches, and to the Romans in particular,to assure them that he is going to his death "willingly" (ἑκών; 4:1), but he is anxious to obtain the grace not merely to speak about this but to "will" it (θέλω) to the end (3:2). He hopes, moreover, that it is the divine "will" (θέλημα) that he should reach his goal but is not presumptuous in this regard (1:1). What if the beasts themselves do not "want [θέλῃ] one who is willing [ἑκόντα]" (5:2)? Above all, Ignatius is concerned with the willingness of the Roman Christians. Will they allow the martyrdom to take place, or will they attempt to interfere?

> I no longer want [θέλω] to live in a human fashion. And this will be so, if you want it [θελήσητε]. So, *want* it [θελήσατε], that you also may be wanted [θεληθῆτε]. (8:1)

The one remaining earthly pleasure that the bishop of Antioch seems to have permitted himself was the joy of playing with words!

The issue of human willingness will not be decided in a vacuum but will be played out within a theater of spiritual forces. Satan "wishes" (βούλεται) to corrupt Ignatius's "mind-set toward God," that is, his spiritual understanding of the situation and firm resolve to "attain God" (7:1). The devil's greatest ally in this endeavor is "the world," that is, the chaotic mix of disordered human desires and competing wills that he, as "ruler of this aeon," manages to orchestrate into a unison of opposition to God and his plan. The paradox of a chaotic unison is significant. It is precisely the disorder of sinful desires and the chaos of competing wills that "unites" them in opposition to every true unity: the Trinitarian unity *in se*, the unity of God's *ad extra* activity forming one economy of creation and salvation, the unity of the human person as flesh and spirit, the solidarity of the human race, and in a particular way the unity of the church in Jesus Christ. The "world" is the realm of "delights" (τέρπνα) and "pleasures" (ἡδοναί)—that is, those things whose salient feature is that they make an appeal to the senses and hold an attraction for one who is occupied with "this life" (τοῦ βίου τούτου)—and it is the realm over which men attempt to establish "the kingdoms of this aeon" (6:1, 7:3). Ignatius does not vanquish the world by an absolute death to all desire, but through "faith and love." And as we shall see in the next chapter, neither of these virtues is a matter of sheer will. Rather, they combine knowledge, desire, and will. The authentic Christian victory over the three spiritual enemies—the disordered desires of one's own personality, the world and its pleasures, and the ruler of this aeon—comes only by way of a deeper attraction and a greater love.

Ignatius knows this love in its incarnational and Trinitarian aspects. It is first of all a passionate love for Jesus Christ.

Neither the delights⁴³ of this world nor the kingdoms of this aeon will profit me. It is better for me to die for Jesus Christ than to rule over the ends of the earth. Him I seek, who died on our behalf; him I want [θέλω], who rose for us. (6:1)

This love is the result of an interior action of the Holy Spirit that engenders trust and affection for God the Father: "There is living and speaking water in me, saying from within, 'Come to the Father!'" This greater love, this living water, douses the "matter-loving fire" that previously dominated Ignatius's personality, so that he can honestly say that his "desire [ἔρως] has been crucified" (7:2). The crucifixion of Ignatius's human desire is one important aspect of his participation in the passion. He is led to his martyrdom by the same motive that led Jesus Christ to Golgotha: love for the Father.

Origen of Alexandria understood the word ἔρως in this passage to refer to Jesus Christ himself, who is objectively Ignatius's "desire" and who, of course, was crucified.⁴⁴ Though modern scholars dismiss this interpretation out of hand,⁴⁵ it contains an important grain of truth. Given Ignatius's fondness for wordplay, he may well have intended a double entendre here. The primary referent of the statement, read in its context, is certainly that Ignatius's desire for worldly pleasures has been put to death. But by describing this mortification of desire in Pauline terms as a "crucifixion," while perhaps also playing on the idea that Jesus Christ himself has replaced the pleasures of this life as the object of Ignatius's desire, the bishop of Antioch indicates what is distinctive of and essential to Christian asceticism, namely, that it is not a denial of desire as such, but an attachment to Jesus Christ that purifies and elevates desire. The believer must indeed die to the deeply disordered drives of his or her personality, but does so in union with Christ, such that one's desire is purified and transformed by being directed toward Jesus and the Father. This purification is not, moreover, a denial of man's constitution as flesh and spirit but is made possible precisely by the real historical and sacramental humanity of Jesus Christ. The believer is able to direct the fullness of human desire toward the eucharistic flesh and blood of

---

43. I accept the reading τέρπνα found in the Greek manuscripts of the middle recension and the Acts of the Metaphrast. Following Lightfoot (*Ignatius, Polycarp*, 2.217), Holmes reads πέρατα ("ends [of the earth]") on the basis of the Latin version of the middle recension, the Greek long recension, and other witnesses (*Apostolic Fathers*, 230).

44. Origen, *Commentarium in Canticum Canticorum*, prologus 2:36; SC 375.116–17.

45. Lightfoot, *Ignatius, Polycarp*, 2.222–23; Grant, *Ignatius of Antioch*, 93; Schoedel, *Ignatius of Antioch*, 184.

Christ, which Ignatius describes in Johannine terms as "bread of God" and "drink."[46]

A further advantage to hearing Romans 7:2 as a *double entendre* is that this reading brings out the Trinitarian structure of Ignatius's statement more clearly.

> My desire (Jesus Christ) has been crucified,
> and there is in me no matter-loving fire;
> but there is in me living and speaking water (the Holy Spirit),
> saying from within, "Come to the Father!"

The historical economy of redemption, in which the passion of Christ makes possible the outpouring of the Holy Spirit, who in turn draws all men and women to eschatological union with the Father, is paralleled by the personal economy of redemption, whereby the believer's union with Christ crucified so purifies and transforms desire that the believer can hear and respond to the interior voice of the Spirit beckoning him or her to the Father. In typically Ignatian fashion, this teaching combines Pauline and Johannine elements. It recalls the Trinitarian formula in which Paul describes the interior action of "the Spirit of [God's] Son" as prompting the believer to cry out "Abba, Father," as well as the Johannine description of the indwelling Spirit as "living water" that enables the believer to "worship the Father in spirit and truth."[47] Finally, it recalls the Johannine principle that "the world" and its threefold concupiscence, "the lust [ἐπιθυμία] of the flesh and the lust of the eyes and the pride of life," can never be overcome by mere asceticism but only by "the love of the Father" (1 Jn 2:15–17).

Anxiety, Rhetoric, and Envy

There remain important aspects of Ignatius's understanding of spiritual warfare and martyrdom, especially as disclosed in *Romans*, that we have yet to penetrate. The next step in our investigation requires a careful consideration of what we might call Ignatius's twofold anxiety: his concern over how he himself will deal with the situation that awaits him in Rome, and his concern over how the Roman Christians will deal with it. These two interrelated concerns dominate the letter. Understanding them is one of the keys to its interpretation. Given the confidence with which

---

46. Rom. 7:3; cf. Jn 6:33, 55.
47. Gal 4:6; Rom 8:15; Jn 4:10, 23.

Ignatius speaks of the crucifixion of his desire and the interior presence of the Holy Spirit beckoning him to the Father, the great uncertainty he betrays (throughout *Romans* and elsewhere) about his own ability to seal the deal and "attain God" is a bit puzzling at first. A complete solution to this problem will have to await our investigation of the relationship between faith and love in chapter 5, but we can begin to make some headway in the present context. We are in a little better position to appreciate his great anxiety over how the Roman Christians will deal with his impending martyrdom, and so that will be our primary focus throughout the remainder of this chapter.

We need not be detained, however, by the cultural-historical question: How could a minority group in second-century Rome have interfered with a state execution? Whether they could have obtained the prisoner's release by paying a ransom or by some other form of personal or political influence, the entire thrust of the letter depends on a common understanding between Ignatius and his addressees in Rome that a stay of execution was a real possibility. Ignatius goes as far as to suggest that it would be "easy" for the Roman Christians to obtain one (Rom. 1:2).[48] The real question for us, the question that will advance our investigation into Ignatius's understanding of spiritual warfare and martyrdom, is why he thinks they might be motivated to do so.

A selective reading of *Romans* might suggest that Ignatius has a low opinion of the spiritual condition of the Roman Christians. If they attempt to impede his martyrdom, it will be because they are "men-pleasers" (2:1), helpers of the devil, and hypocrites who "speak Jesus Christ but desire [ἐπιθυμεῖν] the world" (7:1). Ignatius even seems to suspect that the Christians of Rome "hate" him (8:3) and harbor "malignant envy" (βασκανία) toward him (3:1, 7:2). Noting that this last term carries overtones of "bewitchment" and the "evil eye," Schoedel supposes that Ignatius suspected that the Romans were resentful of him personally and of "his glorious

---

48. Schoedel's discussion of this point (ibid., 168–69) is helpful, but his conclusion that "Ignatius instinctively exaggerates the possibility as he contemplates the enormity of the struggle that lies before him" (169) is unsatisfying. According to Timothy McConnell, the best the Roman Christians could hope to accomplish would be to have Ignatius's sentence commuted, from the gruesome public spectacle of being thrown to the beasts to a private and less painful execution by the sword. And this precisely is Ignatius's concern in *Romans*: not whether he will suffer and die, but how; and whether or not his execution will give public witness ("Ignatius of Antioch: Death Wish or Last Request of a Condemned Man?" Studia Patristica 45 [2010]: 385–89). This hypothesis cannot be sustained, however. Many passages make it patently clear that Ignatius's primary concern is whether or not he will suffer and "get to God," not the manner of execution (e.g., Rom. 4:3, 5:2–6:2, 7:2, 8:3; Smyr. 4:2).

martyrdom in their own city."⁴⁹ Presuming that this was not actually true of the Roman Christians, Schoedel's reading suggests that Ignatius suffered from a combination of grandiosity and paranoia. And this diagnosis would seem to be confirmed by the fact that he considers anyone who opposes him to be opposing God and taking sides with the devil (7:1).

This entire line of interpretation is mistaken, however, because it fails to situate these individual statements within the overall rhetorical strategy of the letter. Ignatius begins by extolling the church at Rome and the quality of its Christianity in unqualified terms. Unlike the other churches to which Ignatius writes, this one does not seem to be threatened by heretical influence; nor do its members seem to be holding any liturgical events or other meetings without their leaders' permission. Instead, this is a church "filtered clear of any strange hue" (sal.). And unlike the docetists, who neglect the demands of Christian charity (Smyr. 6:2), the Roman Christians "preside over love [ἀγάπη]" (Rom. sal.). Presumably this means that they have a reputation among the churches for their practice of the corporal works of mercy. Next, Ignatius tells the Roman Christians that this is exactly what he is worried about: "I fear your love [ἀγάπη], lest it do me wrong" (1:2). This is one of several passages in his letters where Ignatius personifies the ἀγάπη of one or the other church.⁵⁰ Inasmuch as love is the animating principle of Christian life, a phrase such as "the ἀγάπη of the brethren who are at Troas" (Phld. 11:2), for example, seems to designate the "spirit" of that community, the binding force that gives it authentic unity in Christ and the particular quality of its Christian existence. Thus Ignatius is very far from considering the Roman church to be especially worldly or carnal. Rather he fears that they will attempt to interfere with his martyrdom out of the purest of Christian motives.

The remainder of the letter is aimed at convincing the Romans that their well-intentioned act of fraternal charity would actually be an "unseasonable kindness" (Rom. 4:1). Paradoxically, it would do him the greatest harm. In making this point, Ignatius frequently resorts to the rhetorical use of irony. For example, he writes, "It is difficult for me to attain God, unless you spare me" (1:2). Ignatius wants the Roman Christians to "spare" him precisely by not sparing him the suffering of martyrdom. Similarly he says (to cite but one more example), "Do not impede me from living; do not will me to die" (6:2). The "living" Ignatius

---

49. Ibid., 184.
50. Rom. 9:1, 9:3; Tral. 13:1; Phld. 11:2; Smyr. 12:1.

has in mind is the sort that comes only through dying, and the "dying" that he fears is the sort that would result from his remaining alive. The statements about being men-pleasers, lovers of the world, and helpers of the devil have a similar rhetorical force. I am not suggesting, however, that they are exaggerations. There is a difference between irony and hyperbole. Ignatius is dead serious when he makes these statements. But he does not suspect the Roman Christians of impure motives. It is exactly the opposite. He is convinced that they are well disposed toward him but regards precisely this as the real danger.[51] He writes to persuade them that any attempt to secure a stay of execution in his case would be a tragic mistake, and an ironic one. In their attempt to "believe with love," they would in effect be acting as men-pleasers and lovers of the world. They would in effect be assisting the devil.

Ignatius's statements about envy require an additional clarification. Employing a variety of lexical items, Ignatius refers to envy four times in his letters, and three of these references are in *Romans*.[52] What Ignatius has in mind in these passages can be illuminated by the one reference to envy found outside *Romans*. Here, "the envy" (τὸ ζῆλος) is clearly a demonic force, and it is present particularly where there are temptations to spiritual boasting and pride (*Tral.* 4:2).[53] When people speak in such a way as to "puff up" Ignatius, they are actually laying "scourges" of the devil upon him. He fears that he lacks the humility necessary to be worthy of martyrdom and to defeat the prince of this world (4:1–2). Here Ignatius is probably alluding to Satan's primordial envy of mankind, by which "death came into the world" (Wis 2:24).[54] Only those with true spiritual insight are able to perceive this satanic envy, which Ignatius knows to be "warring" against him personally (*Tral.* 4:2).[55] "The envy," then, would be a way of summing up Satan's active hostility toward God and man, and a way of referring to any and every force that attempts to

---

51. The term εὔνοια (translated "kindness" in *Rom.* 4:1) refers to an action flowing from a "good disposition" or "benevolence" (BDAG, 409).

52. *Rom.* 3:1, 5:3, 7:2; *Tral.* 4:2.

53. Schoedel, *Ignatius of Antioch*, 144, n. 5; Lightfoot, *Ignatius, Polycarp*, 2.162–63. Far less likely is the interpretation that understands τὸ ζῆλος to refer to Ignatius's own "burning zeal for martyrdom" (Grant, *Ignatius of Antioch*, 74) or his "impatience" (Camelot, *Ignace d'Antioche*, 99).

54. The word translated "envy" in Wis 2:24 is φθόνος, not ζῆλος. But the latter is found in place of φθόνος in Clement's patent allusions to Wis 2:24 in *1 Clem.* 3:4 and 9:1. Ignatius may well have been familiar with *1 Clement* (Schoedel, *Ignatius of Antioch*, 172), and, if so, would likely have had this work in mind especially when composing his letter to the church at Rome.

55. Ignatius's assertion that "the envy does not appear to many" (*Tral.* 4:2) should be read in light of his advice to Polycarp: "Ask that the invisible things be made manifest to you" (*Poly.* 2:2). One needs to pray for the ability to perceive the unseen spiritual forces at work in the world.

keep man from "attaining God." Thus Ignatius solemnly declares, "May nothing of things visible or invisible envy [ζηλόω] me my attaining Jesus Christ!" (Rom. 5:3).

In raising the possibility that the Romans might unwittingly end up participating in this diabolic envy, Ignatius employs an even more pejorative pair of terms from the same semantic domain: the verb βασκαίνω ("to bewitch, malign, envy, begrudge") and its cognate noun βασκανία ("bewitchment, malignant envy"). The former lexeme is notable for having been used by Paul in the heat of exasperation: "O stupid Galatians! Who has bewitched [ἐβάσκανεν] you, before whose eyes Jesus Christ was depicted as crucified?" (Gal 3:1). Exactly which tonalities of βασκαίνω we are supposed to hear in this Pauline passage is a difficult question.[56] The explicit reference to the Galatians' "eyes" might suggest that the "evil eye" of the Judaizing heresy has "caught their eye," placing them under a spell and causing them to lose their focus on Christ crucified.[57] It is in any case clear that Paul is speaking of what he considers to be a most baleful force that threatens to divert the Galatians from the true faith, such that they would be "severed from Christ" and "fallen from grace" (5:4). Whether the Judaizers realize it or not, they are complicit with demonic forces in their attempt to convince the Galatians to be circumcised. Ignatius is similarly concerned that the Roman Christians might unwittingly do something that would prevent him from attaining salvation. He even hints that they might "entice" him with "matter" (Rom. 6:2), that is, that they might attempt to talk him out of martyrdom by appealing to his natural desire to preserve his life and to remain in this world a bit longer.

Ignatius reminds the Romans that up till now they "have never envied [ἐβασκάνατε] anyone" (3:1).[58] That is, they have never done anything to lead anyone away from faith in Christ or to prevent anyone from attaining the goal of faith. On the contrary, they have instructed many in true discipleship (3:1). Later in the letter he reminds them not to al-

---

56. Because Paul uses the accusative of the object (ὑμᾶς) rather than the dative (ὑμῖν), it is better to translate "bewitched" than "envied." How literally Paul means "bewitched" is what I mean by the question of tonality. See the discussion and literature cited in James D. G. Dunn, *A Commentary on the Epistle to the Galatians* (London: A. & C. Black, 1993), 151–52.

57. F. F. Bruce translates: "Who has hypnotized you?" (*The Epistle to the Galatians: A Commentary on the Greek Text*, NIGTC [Grand Rapids, Mich.: Eerdmans, 1982], 147–48).

58. Here a textual problem affects the translation. Some authorities give the personal object in the accusative (οὐδένα), while others give it in the dative (οὐδενί). In the former case we should probably translate "bewitched," in the latter "envied" (see LSJ, 310). For textual details, see Holmes, who favors the dative (*Apostolic Fathers*, 228).

low "malignant envy" (βασκανία) to dwell among them (7:2). Here the context makes it quite clear what Ignatius is talking about. It is not that he supposes for one moment that the Roman Christians actually harbor feelings of rancor toward him or begrudge him the glory of martyrdom, as Schoedel imagines. Ignatius knows that the Christians of Rome are motivated by a deep affection for him as a brother in Christ and admiration for him as a wise and courageous leader of the church. (Even this motive is ironically characterized as "loving my flesh" [2:1].) But if they do anything to prevent him from taking advantage of "such an opportunity to attain God" (1:2), they will in fact be aiding and abetting the ruler of this aeon in his endeavor to corrupt Ignatius's "mind-set toward God" (7:1). The rhetorical force of these passages, and the rhetorical strategy of the letter, depends entirely on Ignatius's confidence that the Roman Christians would be aghast at the very thought of doing such a thing.

The whole purpose of *Romans* is to enable the Roman Christians to see Ignatius's impending martyrdom in a new light, or to be more precise, from a prophetic perspective. Ignatius is convinced that at this moment, as he writes the letter, he has a clear spiritual perception of the matter. He is committing this perspective to writing so that, even if his own mind should, by the time he reaches Rome, become clouded by fear of suffering or love for this life, the letter will speak authoritatively on behalf of the prophetic clarity that he "now" enjoys.

> Let no malignant envy dwell among you. Even if I myself, upon my arrival, should attempt to counsel you otherwise, do not be persuaded by me. Rather, believe what I am now writing to you. Though alive, I write as one desiring to die. (7:2)

If the Romans have Jesus Christ dwelling within them, they will be able to put themselves in Ignatius's shoes and view his martyrdom from the same spiritual perspective.

> Permit me to be an imitator of the passion of my God. If anyone has him in himself, let him understand what I want and sympathize with me, knowing the things that constrain me. (6:3)

Actions and Their Telos

Having surveyed Ignatius's soteriological anthropology, his economic cosmology, and his understanding of spiritual combat and martyrdom, we are now somewhat better able to sympathize with him and to understand "the things that constrain" him. In concluding this chapter, then,

I shall attempt to draw together some of the important strands of our investigation in order to disclose more precisely the relationship between man's constitution as flesh and spirit, his situation in the "world," and his existential decision for or against God.

Ignatius would no doubt enthusiastically endorse Tertullian's axiom, "The flesh is the hinge of salvation" (*caro salutis est cardo*).[59] As an embodied spirit, man is able to exercise his freedom within the spatiotemporal realm in concrete actions that have interpersonal significance and historical consequences. Redemption is not deliverance from the flesh but occurs in and through the flesh. It takes place objectively in the flesh and blood of Jesus Christ and must be appropriated subjectively by believers "in a fleshly and spiritual manner" (σαρκικῶς καὶ πνευματικῶς). Still, the material dimension of existence must be subordinated to, and transformed by, higher realities. The flesh is not evil, but it must be spiritualized, so that "even those things you do according to the flesh are spiritual, for you do all things in Jesus Christ" (*Eph.* 8:2). This is why the flesh cannot be viewed as a neutral sphere. One is either sanctifying life in the flesh, or not. The person who does not "do all things in Jesus Christ" is living a merely carnal existence, which is to say, heading for perdition.

Though Ignatius says nothing explicit on the subject, he no doubt recognizes the goodness of creation and the solidarity of the human race based on man's having been created in the image of God. When, for example, he writes, "It is better for me to die for Jesus Christ than to rule over the ends of the earth" (*Rom.* 6:1), the use of the comparative "better ... than" (καλόν ... ἤ) suggests that we are dealing here with relative goods, not with an ontological dualism of good and evil.[60] The kingdoms of the world certainly encompass many created goods. Still, the coming of God's Logos into the world discloses the teleology of all human actions and in so doing compels every rational creature to a definitive decision with eschatological consequences.

> Since our actions [πράγματα] have an end [τέλος], these two also lie side by side before us: death and life. And each of us will depart to his own place. (*Magn.* 5:1)

Human life has a definite structure. It is *vita usque ad mortem*. Every action derives its significance and moral gravity from its being part of this whole and from its orientation to the end. All of life's moments lead up

---

59. Tertullian, *De resurrectione mortuorum* 8:2; CCSL 2.931.
60. The use of the positive adjective (καλόν) with ἤ to express comparison is due to Semitic influence (BDF § 245a).

to, prepare for, and participate in the one great opportunity (καιρός) that embodied spirits have to make a definitive act of love and self-donation. To "do things" (πράσσω) in Jesus Christ is, therefore, to imitate his obedience unto death, and it is only through death that one can "come to the Father."

Ignatius's statement about actions having an end begins the chapter on the "two coinages" and is as close as he comes to giving us an explanation for why there must ultimately be a complete opposition between God and the "world," and between those who are "of God" and those who are "of the world." Like the flesh, the world cannot be viewed as a neutral sphere of activity. Because human life and history have a teleological structure, they demand a definitive act of allegiance. It may seem odd that early Christian literature uses the word κόσμος to refer both to the world as created and loved by God and to "the world" in the pejorative sense, but it is important to recognize that, while these may be two distinct senses of the word, the two referents are not separable. The world created and loved by God becomes "the world" by default when human beings ignore the invitation of the gospel. The positive tone of *Ephesians* 10—Ignatius's exhortation regarding the way Christians should relate to nonbelievers, including the surprising statement that the former should show themselves to be the "brethren" of the latter—does not at all represent a compromise with the world. The instruction given in that chapter is predicated entirely on the "hope of repentance." In other words, non-Christians are the object of brotherly love precisely insofar as they have the potential to be "made disciples," leave the sphere of "the world," and ultimately "attain God" (10:1).

But how are non-Christians to be "made disciples" (μαθητευθῆναι) by Christians? The word itself suggests a process of "learning" (μανθάνω)— "learning to live according to Christianity" (*Magn.* 10:1), or simply, "learning Christ" (*Phld.* 8:2)—and the natural conclusion to draw is that Christians are to instruct them. Indeed, Ignatius mentions that the Roman Christians have done just that: "You have taught others ... making them disciples [μαθητεύοντες]" (*Rom.* 3:1). But a few lines later he reminds them that neither rhetorical persuasion nor even words themselves constitute the primary and most effective mode of instruction.

The work is not one of persuasion; rather, Christianity achieves its greatness when it is hated by the world (3:3).

Here Ignatius combines a Johannine axiom, according to which Christians will be hated by the world just as Jesus was, with the Pauline principle that the gospel of the cross is proclaimed in power when the preacher experiences weakness through afflictions and persecutions.[61] In *Ephesians* 10, where Ignatius mentions the "works" by which Christians might hope to make new converts, he says nothing about preaching or teaching but places all the emphasis on meekness, humility, and suffering at the hands of the world. Similarly, a bishop's true power lies in meekness, which presents a "great lesson" (μεγάλη μαθητεία), especially to the "godless" (*Tral.* 3:2).

Such meekness may win the bishop a degree of "respect" among outsiders (3:2), but precisely in its capacity as μαθητεία it must ultimately provoke them to a decision. Any time Christians live out the gospel with anything approaching authenticity, some tension between Christianity and the world will be apparent. But when Christians live out the gospel so radically that the world can no longer tolerate their presence, the true identities of both world and church are manifest. When the world singles out individuals and groups of Christians for persecution and execution, the true nature of the conflict and the identity of the participants involved are revealed. As Schoedel puts it, "martyrdom represents a special focusing of the Christian stance in the world."[62] Moreover, martyrdom is not simply one "witness" among others. It is the Christian witness par excellence. Viewed in this light, Ignatius's ardent desire to be fed to the beasts is hardly a self-centered preoccupation. The path by which he can personally attain God is also the means by which he can "become a word" that proclaims the gospel powerfully to the world (*Rom.* 2:1).

A host of theological questions follows in the wake of Ignatius's statements about "the world"—regarding the relationships between the order of creation and the order of redemption, between this age and the next, between the kingdom of God and the church, and between the church and human society—questions that have emerged and provoked debate over two millennia. For Ignatius, however, there is a moment of theological and existential clarity as he writes from Smyrna to the Roman church. His life has come to a fork in the road. Before him lies a golden "opportunity" (καιρός) to attain God, to "be truly a disciple of Jesus Christ," to "be a man," to "be someone."[63] Seizing this opportunity requires a definitive renunciation of the world. "Do not give back to the world one who wants to belong to God," he begs the Roman Christians (6:2). This is not a rejec-

---

61. Jn 15:18–19, 17:14; 1 Jn 3:13; 1 Cor 1:23–29, 4:9–13; 2 Cor 4:7–12, 6:3–10, 11:21–12:10.
62. Schoedel, *Ignatius of Antioch*, 70.
63. *Rom.* 2:1, 4:2, 6:2, 9:2.

tion of creation or of material reality per se. A careful examination of Ignatian anthropology and cosmology does not permit such a conclusion. It is, however, a "bidding farewell to this life" (ἀποταξάμενος τῷ βίῳ). This is the phrase that Ignatius himself applies to Rheus Agathopus, who followed him from Syria (Phld. 11:1). Anyone who wishes to cooperate so closely with Ignatius in his sacral procession from Antioch to Rome must share in his renunciation of the world to a significant extent. This is true also of the Roman Christians who will be present when Ignatius finally arrives at the arena of martyrdom. They need to recognize that they will be players in the final act of a spiritual drama of cosmic proportions.[64] The stakes are high. A man's eternal destiny and his enduring witness to Jesus Christ hang in the balance.

[64]. "The Roman believers are not mere bystanders who are simply expected to allow something to happen. Both Ignatius and the believers at Rome must choose either to act out the implications of Christ's passion or to desire the world" (Michael A. G. Haykin, "'Come to the Father': Ignatius of Antioch and His Calling to Be a Martyr," *Themelios* 32 [2007]: 32–33).

FAITH AND LOVE

The nouns πίστις ("faith") and ἀγάπη ("love"), along with their cognate verbs and adjectives, are ubiquitous in the Ignatian letters, occurring a grand total of 132 times.[1] Within the corpus of early Christian literature only the Pauline epistles contain a comparably dense concentration of these terms.[2] Moreover, Ignatius couples "faith" with "love" sixteen times, sometimes explicitly commenting on their correlation, and, as we have seen, he identifies the union of faith and love as one of the principal dimensions of unity in the programmatic formulations of *Magnesians* 1:2 and 13:1. Obviously no attempt to grasp his theology could hope to succeed apart from a correct understanding of his use of these terms.[3]

We begin the present chapter, accordingly, with a thorough investigation of Ignatius's concept of faith, comparing it to Paul's, identifying its various dimensions, and stressing that there is no opposition between intellect and will in the act of faith. We shall pay special attention to how Ignatius relates the gift of faith to the Christ event, finding that the mystery of Christ is not only the object of faith but the means

---

1. This tally includes all instances of the following lexemes (with the number of each given in parentheses): ἀγαπάω (20), ἀγάπη (46), ἀγαπητός (5), ἀξιαγάπητος (2), ἀξιόπιστος (2), ἀπιστέω (1), ἀπιστία (2), ἄπιστος (4), πιστεύω (18), πίστις (27), and πιστός (5). In addition, there are textually doubtful occurrences of the following: καταξιοπιστεύομαι (*Tral.* 6:2), πιστεύω (*Rom.* 7:2), and πίστις (*Smyr.* 10:2).

2. The Pauline corpus of thirteen letters, which is about three times the length of the Ignatian corpus, contains a grand total of 385 occurrences, distributed as follows: ἀγαπάω (31), ἀγάπη (75), ἀγαπητός (27), ἀπιστέω (2), ἀπιστία (5), ἄπιστος (16), πιστεύω (54), πίστις (141), πιστόομαι (1), and πιστός (33).

3. Of enduring value is the judicious study of Olavi Tarvainen, *Glaube und Liebe bei Ignatius von Antiochien*, Schriften der Luther-Agricola-Gesellschaft 14 (Joensuu, Finland: Pohjois-Karjalan, 1967).

by which "the faith of God" has come into the world. Next, we shall examine the distinctive character of Christian love, as Ignatius presents it, noting its "vertical" and "horizontal" dimensions (love of God and love of neighbor), and discovering that love has a special relation to the passion of Christ and to the purification of desire. Having considered faith and love each on its own, the remainder of the chapter will be devoted to the way Ignatius relates them to each other. After demonstrating how his teaching on the "union of faith and love" both draws upon the Pauline epistles and adumbrates the classic understanding of the theological virtues, we shall consider his studied use of the term γνώμη ("mind-set"), which forms a sort of conceptual bridge between faith and love, and the way he relates faith and love to the mystery of συμπάθεια ("suffering with" Christ). Finally, in order to put together all the pieces of this puzzle, we shall examine the way Ignatius relates faith and love to his teleological understanding of human temporality—he identifies faith as the "beginning" and love as the "end" of the Christian life—and take a look at his "ergology," or theology of works.

The Dimensions of Faith

Ignatius's understanding of faith has invited frequent comparison with Paul's and is usually judged to be a theologically decadent version of the latter. C. C. Richardson, for example, views the bishop of Antioch as intensifying the gradual shift away from "pure Pauline trust" and toward the practical concern with safeguarding correct doctrine that is so characteristic of the second century.[4] T. F. Torrance likewise notes that in Ignatius's letters "faith takes on the connotation of holding for true a sum of holy tradition."[5] And according to L. W. Barnard, Ignatius has "no real appreciation" for the Pauline doctrine of justification by faith.[6] Since this last charge can only be answered after we have considered the relationship between faith and love in Ignatian theology, I shall return to it at the end of this chapter. For the present, it will suffice to say that while Ignatius uses the terms "faith" (πίστις) and "believe" (πιστεύω) with distinctive emphases that differ from Paul's use of the same terms, it would

---

4. Cyril Charles Richardson, *The Christianity of Ignatius of Antioch* (1935; reprint, New York: AMS Press, 1967), 7.

5. Thomas F. Torrance, *The Doctrine of Grace in the Apostolic Fathers* (Edinburgh: Oliver & Boyd, 1948), 68.

6. *Studies in the Apostolic Fathers*, 28. Similarly, Walter H. Wagner, *After the Apostles: Christianity in the Second Century* (Minneapolis: Fortress Press, 1994), 145.

be a crass exaggeration to view this as a complete rupture.⁷ Richardson himself qualifies his statement about "pure Pauline trust" by correctly pointing to elements of continuity between these two early Christian epistolographers: "In the first place the intellectual element by no means exhausts Ignatius's idea of faith, and in the second place it is not altogether absent from Paul."⁸

It is beyond question that, as one moves from the undisputed Pauline letters to the pastoral epistles and then on to the apostolic fathers and the second-century apologists, the concept of faith gains an increasing emphasis on firm adherence to orthodox doctrine. Obviously the growing threat of heresy and Christianity's need to define itself clearly vis-à-vis Judaism played a major role in this development, and it is equally obvious that Ignatius belongs in the family portrait of second-century Christianity. But I see a few modern presuppositions operative in Ignatian scholarship blurring the focus on this portrait a bit. To begin with, there is a tendency not merely to distinguish the intellectual dimension of faith from other dimensions, such as the fiduciary, but to view it as the antithesis of authentic "religious feeling." Even in the most judicious and accurate treatments of Ignatius's concept of faith there lingers in the air the idea that to the extent that one intellectualizes the Christian faith one diminishes that fervor of devotion to the person of Christ that accompanies "pure trust" and "perfect receptivity." The fallacy in this principle ought to be apparent from the deeply intellectual nature of Paul's own faith, as Richardson seems to realize when he notes that "to attempt to separate the two (the affective and the mental qualities of faith in Paul) is to introduce modern psychological categories and distinctions where possibly none existed." But when he turns to Ignatius, Richardson lapses back into the dichotomy he has just resisted: "Faith in these letters is taking upon itself an intellectual rather than an emotional content."⁹ Even Virginia Corwin, who recognizes that "faith-belief" and "faith-trust" are not mutually opposed but complementary, feels it necessary to apologize for Ignatius's heavy emphasis on the former by making reference to "the desperateness of the situation which he faced" in combating heresy.¹⁰

It is easy to contrast the apostolic verve of Galatians or 2 Corinthi-

---

7. Goltz supplies a more evenhanded and appreciative assessment of Ignatius's understanding of faith and its continuity with Pauline theology (*Ignatius von Antiochien*, 41–47).
8. *Christianity of Ignatius*, 11.   9. Ibid.
10. *St. Ignatius and Christianity*, 239.

ans with the stereotyped expressions of the pastoral epistles or the placid moralism of 1 *Clement*, but Ignatius's letters pose something of a puzzle for the reader who accepts this alleged opposition between the fervor of pure trust and the aridity of intellectual assent to doctrine. Ignatius seems to have preserved something of Paul's passionate love for Jesus Christ despite his promotion of a dogmatic and authoritarian brand of Christianity. Richardson marvels that Ignatius, having lost the distinctively Pauline *meaning* of the word "faith," somehow manages to retain "much of its warm content."[11] The solution to this enigma lies in the recognition that it was precisely Ignatius's intellectual apprehension of the mystery of the faith that kindled and fed the fire of devotion within him. Richardson is unable to see this, in part, because he views Ignatius as merely a popular theologian, indeed as "no theologian" when compared to Paul. In Richardson's opinion, Ignatius lacked "profound religious insight" but had "a throbbing personal faith." He "understood the mysteries of religion less clearly than Paul" but "felt them as genuinely."[12] According to this view, then, Ignatius combined a shallow intellectualism with warm devotion, presumably by keeping the two more or less separate.

As indicated in chapter 2, I have a much higher estimation of Ignatius's theological acumen, and I would argue that his heart lived off of a deeply intellectual appropriation of the truth of revelation. Moreover, in his letters Ignatius expresses an avid desire to share his understanding of the Christian mystery with the churches of Asia Minor. He has good reason to be careful not to give the Trallians too much too quickly, lest they "choke" on it (*Tral.* 5:1), but he obviously feels that the Ephesians are ready for a generous helping right away. He sends them a long letter rich in doctrine and plans to supplement it with a second letter expounding further the economy of redemption (*Eph.* 20:1). Ignatius's letters are filled with intricately woven creedal formulae, not because he had a pragmatic interest in preserving the power of his cronies in the episcopacy by keeping their subordinates in dogmatic lockstep, but because the "love of Jesus Christ" compelled him to feed the flock with "Christian nourishment" (*Tral.* 6:1). Richardson's description of Ignatius as "more an administrator than a thinker" is grossly unfair. Ignatius viewed Christians as "children of the light of truth" (*Phld.* 2:1), "beloved" by God and

---

11. *Christianity of Ignatius*, 7.
12. Ibid., 5.

"illuminated" in baptism (*Rom. sal.*), who require authentic doctrine to strengthen faith and build up love. It is quite true that Ignatius moored faith to orthodox doctrine and stressed its noetic dimension, but the whole thrust of his teaching is that faith, precisely as intellectual assent and unwavering adherence to the truth of revelation, is the motive power (δύναμις) of the Christian life and thus could not possibly be more intimately linked to love (*Eph.* 14:2).

Ignatius's insistence on adherence to traditional or apostolic doctrine brings into play a couple of other modern presuppositions, closely related to the one just discussed and equally problematic. First, there is the assumption that unbending adherence to the propositional truth of doctrine necessarily compromises personal adherence to Christ. Second, there is the assumption that the acceptance of doctrine on authority, especially the authority of ecclesiastical tradition, tends to stultify the intellect and render creative thinking about theology impossible. Naming these presuppositions helps resolve the mild paradox by which the same author who speaks of "pure Pauline trust" has no trouble viewing Paul's own faith in terms of "keen intellectual genius" and "profound religious insight."[13] The immediacy of Paul's experience of Christ and the originality of his thought make him, it is supposed, the exemplar of a faith that is in no way dependent upon doctrine, tradition, or human authority. Be that as it may, I would like to suggest that studying the letters of Ignatius of Antioch, and his teaching on faith in particular, affords us a fine opportunity to perceive the fallacy of both presuppositions.

With respect to the first, Ignatius himself gives living witness to the principle, so precisely articulated by Thomas Aquinas, that "the act of the believer terminates not in the proposition, but in the reality."[14] This principle is lost to many moderns, who assume that to understand faith as intellectual assent limits the object of faith to doctrines or ideas. Were that the case, one would need to reduce the role of the intellect and diminish the importance of doctrine in order to make a deeply personal act of faith (i.e., "pure trust") in Jesus Christ. But this view of the matter will hardly make good sense out of Ignatius's letters, where we find that faith in traditional doctrine seems quite compatible with vibrant personal adherence to Christ. Schoedel has the scent of the fox when he says that for Ignatius "faith refers to the body of Christian truth or (perhaps some-

---

13. Ibid.
14. STh II-II, q. 1, a. 2, ad 2 (*actus credentis non terminatur ad enuntiabile sed ad rem*).

what more accurately) the reality of the Christian revelation that determines the Christian way of life as a whole."[15]

It is important to note in this connection that, while the *gesta Christi*—the things "truly and certainly done by Jesus Christ" (*Magn.* 11:1)—lie at the heart of Ignatius's creedal affirmations, the realities that these statements propose for faith are not bare "historical facts" in the modern sense. Much modern scholarship treats the historical facts of Christ's life as intrinsically mute things, onto which the early Christians have imposed layers of meaning or interpretation. But when Ignatius speaks of "an immovable faith" that is "fully convinced concerning our Lord" that he was "truly" descended from David, born of a virgin, baptized by John, crucified, and raised from the dead (*Smyr.* 1:1–2), he means more than the simple conviction that these things actually took place, and certainly more than that Christians have found them meaningful. Jesus Christ is a real historical personage, and the events of his life occurred during a specific period in the historical past, "under Pontius Pilate and Herod the Tetrarch" (1:2). But they are not merely in the past. Through the exaltation of Christ in the resurrection, he and the events of his life are now also sacramentally and mystically present to his church.[16] The act of faith terminates in the person, words, and actions of Jesus Christ, historical realities present in mystery.

As for the remaining presupposition, concerning the acceptance of revealed truth on the authority of ecclesiastical tradition, Ignatius's letters constitute a beautiful example of how thinking about the content of faith from within the tradition, far from inhibiting insight and theological development, actually fosters these. A careful study of Ignatius's letters reveals time and again that precisely where he is most indebted to the apostolic kerygma (usually as this is mediated by the Pauline, Johannine, and Matthean writings) he shows himself most perceptive and original. This creative fidelity, which is a hallmark of genuine theological craft, consists in unfolding a mystery that is both unchanging and ever new. At the same time, however, Ignatius's frequent references to the apostles alongside his many statements about the ecclesial hierarchy raise difficult questions concerning how he conceives of the connection between the two, questions that bear upon the issue of unity. He is obvi-

---

15. *Ignatius of Antioch*, 26.
16. I have touched upon this delicate point (not one to be affirmed glibly) already in previous chapters and hope to continue to elucidate it under the rubric *mysterium* in the remainder of this volume.

ously instructing the churches from within an apostolic tradition, and yet he never appeals to tradition as such. At least the concept never appears explicitly in his letters. In a single breath he demands obedience both to "the ordinances of the Lord and of the apostles" and to the local hierarchy of bishop, presbyters, and deacons,[17] but the connections he draws between these two sources of authority seem on first sight to be merely symbolic and rhetorical. We shall have to return to this problem in chapter 9, which deals with Ignatius's ecclesiology. For the moment it is enough to recognize that Ignatius's understanding of faith includes an implicit appeal to authority. For Ignatius the supreme authority of faith is Jesus Christ, "our only teacher" (*Magn.* 9:1). The difficulty lies in the question of how exactly Christ's teaching authority is mediated to the church in every generation and to each local church.

The basic components of Ignatius's concept of faith are widely agreed upon. As we have noted, he especially accents the intellectual-doctrinal aspect. Faith is closely associated with knowledge of, and firm adherence to, the basic truths of the gospel. "I know and believe that [Jesus] was in the flesh even after the resurrection," Ignatius writes (*Smyr.* 3:1). Christians are often said to be "firmly convinced" (πληροφορέω in the passive voice) with regard to the basic creedal affirmations about Jesus.[18] The objective propositional content of faith creates "the unanimity of faith" (ἡ ὁμόνοια τῆς πίστεως) among Christians (*Eph.* 13:1). They gather "in one faith and one Jesus Christ, who is from the stock of David according to the flesh, Son of Man and Son of God," and this gives them the "undisturbed understanding" by which they can "break one bread" of the eucharist together (20:2). Indeed, they have "one mind" (*Magn.* 7:2). None of this diminishes the fiduciary aspect of faith, however. When Ignatius says, "I believe in the grace of Jesus Christ, who will free you from every bond" (*Phld.* 8:1), this is obviously an expression of trust. At most it might be said that Ignatius does not especially accent the fiduciary dimension of faith.

One other aspect of faith that needs to be mentioned is fidelity, and this pertains especially to the adjective πιστός, which can mean either "believing" or "faithful," or both. When Ignatius says, "The Father is πιστός in Jesus Christ to fulfill my request and yours" (*Tral.* 13:3), we should translate πιστός "faithful" or "trustworthy." Ignatius sometimes

---

17. *Magn.* 13:1–2; *Tral.* 7:1.
18. *Smyr.* 1:1; *Phld.* sal.; *Magn.* 8:2, 11:1.

uses the plural πιστοί as a substantive, denoting "believers, faithful ones," a virtual synonym for "Christians."[19] Heretics are both ἄπιστοι ("unbelievers," i.e., those who err in their beliefs) and ἀξιόπιστοι (only seemingly "worthy of trust").[20] When Ignatius reaches his goal of martyrdom, he will not only be called a Christian but actually be one, and likewise he will "also then be a πιστός" (Rom. 3:2). This statement clearly indicates that for Ignatius faith cannot be limited to adherence to doctrine but entails a life of fidelity that endures unto the end. We shall return to this teleological dimension of faith when we consider its relationship to love.

It is vital that we not think of these dimensions of faith as held together in tension such that an emphasis on one would detract from another. They are rather integral aspects of a single reality that require each other. I will illustrate this point with an example of human faith, which, while it differs from divine faith in several important respects, has the same essential structure.[21] Let's imagine that I am driving in an unfamiliar part of town, looking for a store I have never shopped at, and I become hopelessly lost. When I see a woman doing yard work in front of her house, I pull over and ask her how to get to the store. She gives me a detailed set of specific directions that involves a series of turns and several landmarks. I decide to accept her testimony as authoritative and trustworthy and begin to follow her directions. I have already made an act of faith. To put it in the terms of Scholastic theology, my will has moved my intellect to accept her testimony as truth. And what was my decision based on? She gave the impression of being intelligent, spoke articulately, and seemed to know the neighborhood well. What is more, her friendliness and pleasant demeanor gave me no reason to suspect that she would mislead me maliciously. My act of faith is thus not a blind leap. I have more or less good reasons to believe, or "motives of credibility."[22]

It is also important to recognize that by means of her testimony and

---

19. Eph. 21:2; Smyr. 1:2.

20. For the former term, see Eph. 18:1; Tral. 10:1; Smyr. 2:1, 5:3; for the latter, see Phld. 2:2; Poly. 3:1.

21. By "human faith" I mean the human act of assenting to a truth-claim proposed by merely human authority. Such acts require no grace, and we make them frequently throughout the day. By "divine faith" I mean the human act of assenting, by grace, to divinely revealed truth, especially as this is mediated to us by Scripture and tradition.

22. In the case of divine faith too, the believer has "a sufficient motive for believing" (STh II-II, q. 2, a. 9, ad 3).

my acceptance of it I have acquired knowledge that I did not possess previously. I now know where the store is and how to get there. This is not the same mode of knowledge as direct experience brings, but it is a genuine mode of knowledge nonetheless. Generically it is the same mode of knowledge by which I know that Jupiter has at least sixty-seven moons or that a molecule of water contains two atoms of hydrogen and one of oxygen (truths that I accept on the authority of others), but it differs from the mode by which I know that there is an oleander in my garden (something I know empirically), and again from the mode by which I know that two plus two equals four (a truth that reason itself compels me to accept).

Now, as I follow the woman's directions, I will have any number of opportunities to renew my act of faith or to retract it. And here too it is not a matter of sheer will, as voluntaristic accounts of faith might suggest. If I find that the first few landmarks and intersections are just as she described them, my faith in her directions (and in her personally) will grow stronger, and I am more likely to persevere in my quest even if I subsequently experience a setback or two. But if I find that her directions seem to be confused and have little correspondence to the reality of the streets in that part of town, my faith is likely to weaken. I may begin to doubt whether she is a competent authority on this matter, or even whether she is personally trustworthy. But for the sake of completing the illustration, let's assume the former scenario, namely, that her directions prove accurate and helpful.

As I move from the spot in front of her house, where I received the directions, toward the goal of my journey, there is an intricate interplay between faith and experience. Initially my knowledge of the store's location and how to arrive there was based entirely on faith, but as I continue along the way, experience plays an ever increasing role. Faith makes a certain type of experience possible and guides it. This experience in turn confirms faith and enhances the journey lived by faith, giving me a certain satisfaction and joy in proceeding on the road of faith. When I arrive finally at the store and attain the "vision" of what I have been seeking, faith is no longer necessary or even possible. This observation points to the fact that faith is not a static reality but has its proper place within the dynamics of the teleological structure of a journey or quest. As Ignatius says with regard to divine faith, it is the ἀρχή ("beginning, guiding principle"), whereas love is the τέλος ("goal, end") of the Christian life (Eph. 14:1).

The thrust of the foregoing illustration is that human faith has a coherent structure that accounts for its various component parts and their interrelationship. There is no opposition between will and intellect in the act of faith. They work together. Nor is there any opposition between trust and knowledge. This same structure obtains *mutatis mutandis* in the case of divine faith. Nowhere does Ignatius suggest that God requires us to make a blind leap of faith in Jesus Christ. When the risen Christ came to the apostles, he commanded them to "take" and "handle" him, so that they might "see" that he had truly been raised in the flesh; and they accordingly "touched him and believed" (Smyr. 3:2). Now all persons are called to heed a long historical train of witnesses to Christ comprising the prophets, the law of Moses, the gospel, and the sufferings of contemporary Christians (5:1). Non-Christians are to be won over to repentance by the good deeds and patient suffering of Christians (Eph. 10:1–3), and this human instrumentality in no way contradicts the conviction that repentance can only occur by the grace of Christ (Smyr. 4:1). It would be anachronistic to imagine that Ignatius conceptualized the act of faith in a fully elaborated theory such as we find in Thomas Aquinas's treatise on the virtues,[23] but if we come to Ignatius's letters with the classic understanding of the *actus credendi* in its broad contours, we are able to make good sense out of his various statements about faith.

Faith and the Mystery of Christ

Next, I would like to turn to a somewhat neglected aspect of Ignatius's teaching about faith, namely, its precise relationship to the Christ event. This will help us relate his understanding of faith to other aspects of his theology, which is centered on the person and actions of Jesus Christ, especially the passion and resurrection. Although he only rarely mentions forgiveness or justification, Ignatius clearly views Christ's passion and death in terms of its soteriological efficacy. Jesus Christ is "our Savior."[24] He was nailed to the cross in the flesh "for us" and "suffered all these things for us, that we might be saved" (Smyr. 1:2–2:1). In the eucharist we receive "the flesh of our Savior Jesus Christ, which suffered for our sins, and which the Father by his kindness raised" (7:1). In all such passages the death and resurrection of Christ are intimately linked, and in

---

23. STh II-II, qq. 1–16.
24. Eph. 1:1; *Magn.* sal.; Phld. 9:2.

one passage both are explicitly said to have been accomplished "for us" (Rom. 6:1). And just as we find throughout the New Testament, so in Ignatius's letters, that which has been done "for us" is the object of faith. Jesus Christ "died for us, in order that, *believing in his death*, we might escape death" (Tral. 2:1). Ignatius solemnly warns all rational creatures in heaven and on earth that they are obligated to "believe in the blood of Christ" if they wish to avoid condemnation (Smyr. 6:1). Ultimately, of course, the object of faith is not only the death or the blood, but the person, of Christ himself.[25]

We should by no means consider Ignatius to be merely parroting the kerygmatic tradition in these passages. The soteriological efficacy of the paschal mystery, its relationship to faith, and, yes, even the justification of the sinner, are integral to his understanding of the gospel (Phld. 8:2). This is evident, for example, in the unaffected but skillful manner by which he weaves a traditional creedal formula into a very personal and intimate expression of his own faith in Jesus.

> Him I seek, who died for our sake;
> him I desire, who rose for us. (Rom. 6:1)

If Ignatius fails to elaborate on these specific aspects of faith, it is no doubt because the situation that prompted his letters did not call for that. At the same time, we should readily admit that he prefers to view the paschal mystery more in terms of deliverance from death than deliverance from sin. He is much more inclined to speak of "imperishability" and "life" than he is of atonement or forgiveness, and in this respect, of course, he adumbrates one of the distinctive emphases of Eastern theology. Ignatius is fond of presenting the truth of redemption in terms of the paradoxical relationship between life and death. Jesus Christ is "true life in death" (Eph. 7:2), and his passion is our resurrection (Smyr. 5:3). By "believing in his death" we "escape death" (Tral. 2:1). The cross is a stumbling block for unbelievers but "salvation and eternal life for us" (Eph. 18:1). It is a tree of life (Tral. 11:2) or, more imaginatively, a "crane" that hoists the "stones" of God's temple (i.e., Christians) "up to the heights" (Eph. 9:1).

More distinctive and intriguing than the statements that make the death of Christ the object of faith are those that speak of Christ or his paschal mystery as the means through which faith has come into the world.

---

25. Tral. 9:2; Phld. 5:2.

Jesus' death and resurrection constitute "the mystery through which we have received the faith" (*Magn.* 9:1). This statement and the others we are about to cite indicate how reductive it is to think of faith essentially as "our response" to what God has done. "The faith" is first of all something that has come to us from God, and it has come to us through events that constitute a "mystery."[26] Elsewhere Ignatius compares heretics to "home wreckers" (οἰκοφθόροι). As the latter destroy families through adultery, so the former "with evil teaching corrupt the faith of God [πίστις θεοῦ], for the sake of which Jesus Christ was crucified" (*Eph.* 16:1–2). Whether we understand πίστις θεοῦ to mean "faith *in* God" (objective genitive) or "faith *from* God" (genitive of source), faith is an objective reality that has come into the world through the cross of Christ. For Ignatius the supreme rule of life consists in Jesus' "cross and death, and his resurrection, and the faith that is through him" (*Phld.* 8:2).

How then does Jesus bring "the faith of God" into the world? We can be sure that at least part of the answer is that he does so as revealer of the Father, for without revelation there can be no divine faith, no πίστις in the biblical sense of the term. In the person of Jesus, and above all in his passion and death, "God was manifesting himself humanly," and he did this precisely in order to dispel "the ignorance that accompanies malice" (κακίας ἄγνοια; *Eph.* 19:3). Jesus Christ is "the mouth that cannot lie, by whom the Father has spoken truthfully" (*Rom.* 8:2). As we saw in chapter 3, this Johannine principle of the Son's revelation of the Father is central to Ignatius's theology.

But it is possible that when Ignatius speaks of faith coming into the world through Jesus, he also has in mind Jesus' subjective "faithfulness" (πίστις) to the Father.[27] Jesus is the true high priest "who alone has been entrusted [πεπίστευται] with the hidden things of God" (*Phld.* 9:1). He reveals and makes available these divine mysteries through his life of faithfulness and love, which Ignatius elaborates elsewhere by saying that Jesus "followed" the Father (*Smyr.* 8:1), "did nothing apart from" the Father (*Magn.* 7:1), oriented his life "toward" the Father (7:2), "pleased" the Father (8:2), and "submitted" to the Father (13:2). The virtues of faith and love by which humanity will be renewed come into the world

---

26. Rather than the usual noun πίστις, in *Magnesians* 9.1 Ignatius uses the articular infinitive τὸ πιστεύειν (literally, "the believing"), perhaps to indicate the manifold reality of faith: the objective content of revealed truth, the grace to believe, and the whole ecclesial dynamic of the life of faith.

27. Ferdinando Bergamelli, "'Fede di Gesù Cristo' nelle lettere di Ignazio di Antiochia," *Studia Patristica* 40 (2006): 339–51.

through Jesus Christ by being tangibly present in his human life, especially as it culminates in the paschal mystery. Thus Ignatius describes the economy of redemption as pertaining to "the new man Jesus Christ, in his faith and in his love, in his passion and resurrection" (Eph. 20:1).[28] And since Ignatius refers at least once to the Father's own faithfulness (Tral. 13:3), we might take this interpretation one step farther and suggest that Jesus' fidelity to the Father was an aspect of his imitation of the Father. Thus our faithfulness to Jesus imitates his faithfulness to the Father, which is in turn an imitation of the Father's own faithfulness. As Ignatius exhorts the Philadelphians, "Be imitators of Jesus Christ, even as he is of the Father" (Phld. 7:2).

Above we noted that faith is a dynamic reality within the teleological structure of the individual life, but its role may also be viewed from the broader perspective of the historical teleology of the economy of redemption. Since Jesus Christ is the one in whom God definitively manifests himself, such that faith in Christ is necessary for eternal salvation, it must be that Israel's prophets were somehow already his disciples, that they in some sense preached the gospel proleptically, and that they "were saved" by "believing in him" (Phld. 5:2). At the same time, Christ's historical advent marked a great turning point in the historical economy such that Judaism "came to believe" (ἐπίστευσεν) in Christianity (Magn. 10:3). The considerable tension between these two statements, seemingly between a timeless conception of the Christian gospel and a salvation-historical conception, is a problem to which we shall turn in the next chapter. For the moment it is enough to recognize that a definitive self-revelation of God necessarily makes faith in that self-revelation a universal requirement for salvation, and it is the universal call to faith in a single revelation that gives the economy unity along the historical axis. It is precisely by faith in Christ that the prophets entered into "the unity of Jesus Christ" (Phld. 5:2). Jesus is "the door of the Father, through whom enter Abraham and Isaac and Jacob and the prophets and the apostles and the church, all these, into the unity of God" (9:1). Christ's coming into the world also marks the point at which this universalism opens out onto the axis of geography and ethnicity, such that "every tongue has come to believe" in Christ and so "has been gathered to God" (Magn. 10:3). The "one body of his church" thus comprises both Jews and gentiles (Smyr. 1:2).

---

28. There may be references to Jesus' subjective faith and love also in Rom. sal. and Tral. 8:1.

Christian Love

Like Paul and other early Christian writers, Ignatius uses the noun ἀγάπη ("love"), the verb ἀγαπάω ("to love"), and the adjective ἀγαπητός ("beloved") to refer to the love that is distinctive of life in Christ. In most of these instances Christians are both the subject and the object of love. In other words, it is above all a question of the Johannine *mandatum novum* to "love one another" (*Tral.* 13:2). But while Ignatius says relatively little about the vertical axis of love—God's love for us and our love for God—it is nonetheless clear that he does not think of ἀγάπη as a love that originates in the human subject or terminates in the human object. Rather he has in mind a love that flows forth from God the Father as its eternal source, enters the world through Jesus Christ, and is returned to God the Father likewise through Jesus Christ. The Lord Jesus is in a unique sense "the beloved" of God the Father (*Smyr.* sal.), and he in turn loves the church (*Poly.* 5:1). The local churches are thus "loved by God the Father of Jesus Christ" (*Tral.* sal.). Christians are to "love nothing except God alone" (*Eph.* 9:2), that is, love him in a unique and unqualified sense, and so they "rightly love" the Lord Jesus since he is "our God" (15:3). Even the love by which Christians love one another is not merely horizontal (between humans) but constitutes a participation in "the love of God the Father and of the Lord Jesus Christ" (*Phld.* 1:1). They cannot possibly keep the new commandment on the basis of mere human affections (κατὰ σάρκα) but can only love one another "in Jesus Christ" (*Magn.* 6:2).

The dual principle of loving "God alone" and loving one another "in Christ" purifies and orders human affections, and it is this rightly ordered love that is properly designated ἀγάπη. Ignatius refrains from using ἀγάπη, ἀγαπάω, or ἀγαπητός to refer to any love that is tainted by lust or is merely human in its source or goal.[29] When it is a question of "loving the flesh" or "loving the world," he employs ἐπιθυμέω or ἐράω, either verb suggesting a disordered love or concupiscence;[30] and he uses the corresponding nouns ἐπιθυμία and ἔρως in a similar manner. Christian marriages must be lived out "according to God and not according to lust [ἐπιθυμία]" (*Poly.* 5:2), and in all the dimensions of life Christians

---

29. In *Eph.* 9:2 Ignatius does use the verb ἀγαπάω to refer to unspiritual love, but only hypothetically, rejoicing that the Ephesians do not in fact love anything in a worldly manner. Moreover, it is clear that he has chosen this verb here in order to apply it to the love of God in the completion of the statement.

30. *Rom.* 2:1, 7:1; *Poly.* 4:3.

must guard against becoming "slaves of desire [ἐπιθυμία]" (4:3). Ironically, it is especially while bound with chains that Ignatius is "learning not to desire [ἐπιθυμέω] anything," so that through martyrdom and resurrection from the dead he may become "a freedman of Jesus Christ" (Rom. 4:3). This purification of desire takes place through conscious union with the passion of Christ. Now that Ignatius's "desire [ἔρως] has been crucified," and the flames of "matter-loving fire" have been doused by the "living water" that wells up within him, he says, "I love [ἀγαπάω] to suffer" (Tral. 4:2) and "desire [ἐράω] to die" (Rom. 7:2).

Ignatius draws a close correlation between Christian love and the passion of Jesus Christ, presumably because the latter is the special locus of encounter with the divine love that purifies and animates the Christian life. The Father's love is visible and available at the cross, and the Christian reciprocates God's love by conforming his or her life to the passion. Ignatius virtually identifies ἀγάπη with "the blood of Jesus Christ."[31] And since the reality of the passion is present to the church sacramentally, the use of ἀγάπη as a technical term for the "love feast" that was the context of the eucharist in the early church has a special appropriateness in Ignatius's letters.[32] As the shedding of his blood on the cross was the goal of Jesus' life, so "love is the end" (τέλος δὲ ἀγάπη) of our life in Christ (Eph. 14:1). Love is that by which one "pours oneself out" for others (Phld. 5:1) and makes oneself, finally, "a libation to God" (Rom. 2:2). Love is the "way" by which one ascends to God (Eph. 9:1). As it was necessary for Jesus to pass through suffering in order to attain glory, so Christians must "love in order that they may also rise" from the dead (Smyr. 7:1).

Ignatius uses the word ἀγάπη to refer to love both as moral action and as the interior dynamism or virtue that motivates and animates that action. Love is first of all something one has received from God and in some sense has appropriated, on the basis of which one is able to perform specific moral actions "in love" (Poly. 1:2). Thus, "one who has obtained love does not sin" (Eph. 14:2). The specific content and character of Christian love is informed by faith, so that those who "believe with love" bear the "imprint [χαρακτήρ] of God the Father through Jesus Christ" (Magn. 5:2). Conversely, false doctrine, which is in accord with the "mind-set" of the devil, has the effect of "wearing away" (θλίβω) this imprint, so that one is gradually "weakened in love" (Phld. 6:2). For all this attention to the interior dimension of love as a virtue, how-

---

31. Tral. 8:1; Smyr. 1:1.   32. Smyr. 8:2; Rom. 7:3.

ever, Ignatius by no means neglects the practical exterior dimension. He cites a dominical logion and then spells out its meaning: "'The tree is manifest from its fruit,' so those who profess to belong to Christ will be seen through what they practice."[33] Authentic Christian love is "eager" (ἄοκνος) to perform even arduous service to the church for the glory of God (Poly. 7:2). By "love" Ignatius sometimes means specifically the corporal works of mercy (Smyr. 6:2). At the same time, there is no danger that he will reduce love to an intramundane reality. The specific act of Christian charity to which Ignatius refers most often is intercessory prayer, by which Christians are actually able to help each other "attain God."[34]

Adapting Pauline teaching (cf. Eph 5:25) in his own distinctive style, Ignatius views Christian marriage as a special point of intersection between divine and human love.

Tell my sisters to love the Lord and to be content with their life partners in flesh and spirit. Likewise, charge my brothers in the name of Jesus Christ to love their life partners, as the Lord loves the church. (Poly. 5:1)

In this one passage we see Christ's love for the church, the church's love for Christ, and the love of the *mandatum novum* exemplified in the mutual love of spouses. Love flows up and down between heaven and earth, even as it simultaneously flows back and forth among Christians.

Not surprisingly, Ignatius promotes love within specifically ecclesial contexts—for example, when he exhorts a congregation to love its bishop (Eph. 1:3), or asks one church to perform an act of charity for another church (Poly. 7:2)—for he knows that "harmonious love" is the very substance of unity (Eph. 4:1). But love is not simply something that occurs within the life of the church. It is the life of the church. Nowhere is this clearer than in the seven passages in which Ignatius virtually hypostatizes the word ἀγάπη. When he says, "I exhort you—not I, but the love of Jesus Christ" (Tral. 6:1), or, "Love does not permit me to be silent concerning you" (Eph. 3:2), we may almost regard ἀγάπη as a synonym for the Holy Spirit.[35] In the remaining passages ἀγάπη is the unifying and animating principle of one or more local churches, personified as sending greetings to another church (Tral. 13:2), or even as exercising some manner of pastoral care for another church (Rom. 9:1). It is "the love of the churches" or "the love of the brethren."[36]

33. Eph. 14:2; cf. Mt 12:33.
35. Cf. Phld. 5:1, 7:2.
34. Magn. 14:1; Tral. 12:3.
36. Rom. 9:3; Phld. 11:2; Smyr. 12:1.

In a related usage, Ignatius receives an "exemplification" of the ἀγάπη of a given church in the embassy they have sent to meet him (Tral. 3:2), thus making it possible for him to "see" the entire community "in the modality of love" (κατὰ ἀγάπην; Eph. 2:1). It is important to note here that these ambassadors have communicated ecclesial love to Ignatius not simply by way of their symbolic presence but by concrete acts of charity, by "refreshing" him "both in flesh and spirit."[37] Ignatius's frequent acknowledgment of their expressions of love and his even more frequent protestations of his own love for the churches are not merely a function of epistolary good manners. They serve to present his entire procession from Antioch to Rome in terms of that which constitutes the church qua church, namely, love. Above all, he insists that his epistolary exhortation of the churches is itself an ecclesial act of ἀγάπη,[38] and he therefore asks that his letters be heard "in love" (Tral. 12:3).

The Union of Faith and Love

Having looked at how Ignatius uses the terms "faith" and "love" separately, we may now turn to the relationship between these two, especially as it bears on the question of unity. What precisely does it mean to describe Christian unity as "a union of both faith and love" (Magn. 1:2)? Sixteen times in his letters Ignatius establishes a clear and exclusive correlation between these two virtues, most often by using them in a single dyadic phrase, such as κατὰ πίστιν καὶ ἀγάπην ("according to faith and love"; Eph. 1:1), and in all but two cases the order is first faith, and then love.[39] In only two passages does Ignatius form a triad by adding a third term, either ὁμόνοια ("unanimity"; Phld. 11:2) or ὑπομονή ("endurance"; Poly. 6:2). Despite the fact that "hope" (ἐλπίς) is also a fairly important category in Ignatius's theology, he never directly correlates it with faith and love. Like "all other things that make for excellence," hope presumably "follows upon" faith and love (Eph. 14:1). We can be quite sure that Ignatius's decided preference for the dyadic "faith and love" over any other formulation is not merely stylistic or rhetorical because of the exclusive claims that he makes for these two virtues. "Nothing is preferable" to faith and love (Magn. 1:2). "The whole is faith and love" (Smyr. 6:1). "Faith

---

37. Tral. 12:1; cf. Eph. 2:1.
38. Eph. 3:2; Magn. 6:1; Tral. 3:3, 6:1, 8:1; Phld. 5:1; Smyr. 4:2.
39. Eph. 1:1, 9:1, 14:1–2, 20:1; Magn. 1:1, 1:2, 5:2, 6:1, 13:1; Tral. 8:1; Rom. sal.; Phld. 9:2; Smyr. sal., 1:1, 6:1, 13:1. The two passages in which "love" precedes "faith" are Magn. 1:1 (where the correlation is mostly stylistic) and Phld. 9:2 (where "love" may be placed first for emphasis).

is the beginning, and love is the end; and if these two exist in unity, it is God" (Eph. 14:1).

In formulating his teaching on faith and love Ignatius has picked up hints from the Pauline epistles and developed them in an insightful and distinctive manner. The dyadic phrase "faith and love" occurs twice in the Pauline corpus—plus once in the reverse order: "love and faith"—and faith and love are paired off in a handful of other passages in various ways.[40] More famously, Paul sometimes adds "hope" or "endurance" as a third member to form the classic triad of theological virtues.[41] Other triadic formulations have "peace" or "grace" as the first member, followed by faith and love (in either order) as the second and third members.[42] Finally, the pastoral epistles include faith and love in *Tugendlisten* that comprise up to seven items.[43] In general, then, faith and love are coupled in a more varied and less exclusive manner in the Pauline epistles than they are in the Ignatian letters, where the phrase "faith and love" has more the character of a fixed formula purposefully employed. Moreover, whereas Paul calls attention (once) to the triadic formulation "faith, hope, and love" (1 Cor 13:13), he never calls attention to the dyadic "faith and love." Ignatius, by contrast, does this frequently, and he even offers something along the lines of an explanation of the relationship between faith and love (Eph. 14:1–2).

On the other hand, there are two Pauline passages that may have contributed specific theological content to Ignatius's understanding of the relationship between faith and love. First, the famous phrase "faith working through love" (πίστις δι' ἀγάπης ἐνεργουμένη; Gal 5:6) may have provided the basic framework by which Ignatius accents the noetic aspect of faith and the practical aspect of love and views them as complementary and inseparable dimensions of the Christian life.[44] Lifting a similar phrase verbatim from the Wisdom of Solomon (3:9), Ignatius virtually defines Christians as "those who are faithful in love" (οἱ πιστοὶ ἐν ἀγάπῃ).[45] Second, a Pauline text that situates faith and love within the "economy of God" and identifies love as the "end" (τέλος) of the com-

---

40. "Faith and love": 1 Thes 3:6; 2 Tm 1:13. "Love and faith": Phlm 5. "Faith" and "love" paired off in various ways: 1 Cor 16:13–14; Gal 5:6; Eph 3:17; 1 Tm 1:4–5.

41. 1 Cor 13:13; Col 1:4–5; 1 Thes 1:3, 5:8; Ti 2:2.

42. Eph 6:23; 1 Tm 1:14.

43. 1 Tm 2:15, 4:12, 6:11; 2 Tm 2:22, 3:10.

44. According to Graydon F. Snyder, "faith" and "love" in the Ignatian letters correspond to "ethics" and "theology," respectively ("The Historical Jesus in the Letters of Ignatius of Antioch," *Biblical Research* 8 [1963]: 9). In what follows I hope to show that it is just the other way around!

45. *Magn.* 5:2; cf. *Phld.* 9:2.

mandment (1 Tm 1:4–5) may have inspired the programmatic formulation by which Ignatius identifies faith and love as the "beginning and end [τέλος] of life" within his broader presentation of the "economy of God."[46]

In important respects Ignatius's presentation of πίστις and ἀγάπη adumbrates the classic understanding of *fides* and *caritas* (along with *spes*) as theological virtues. According to the *Catechism of the Catholic Church*, the theological virtues are "infused by God into the souls of the faithful" in order to "adapt man's faculties for participation in the divine nature." They "animate" Christian moral activity, giving it its "special character," and they enable human persons to attain eternal life (CCC 1812–13). Similarly, according to Ignatius, faith and love originate in God, belong properly to Jesus Christ, and are graciously bestowed upon the church in their "fullness" (*Smyr.* sal.), so that "those who are faithful in love" possess "the imprint of God the Father through Jesus Christ" (*Magn.* 5:2). If they persevere "in the power of faith unto the end" (*Eph.* 14:2), they will "attain God" (*Magn.* 1:3). According to later Scholastic theology, the two spiritual faculties of the soul, intellect and will, operate in unison both in the act of faith (where the will moves the intellect to assent to revealed truth) and in the act of charity (where the intellect informs and guides the will with the content of revealed truth).[47] Nonetheless, there is a special correlation of faith and love to intellect and will respectively. Faith perfects the intellect, while charity (in conjunction with hope) perfects the will.[48] Again, there is no question of finding this sort of conceptual precision in Ignatius's letters, but he does associate faith with knowledge of the truth of the gospel, and love with freely living out the gospel, even while he regards faith and love as inseparable dimensions of the Christian life.

If we are to grasp Ignatius's insight into the relationship between faith and love, it is crucial to establish firmly that no antithesis between mind and will, or between intellectual virtue and moral virtue, exists in his theology. Naturally, Ignatius recognizes that ruptures do exist within the hu-

---

46. *Eph.* 14:1, 18:2. The latter verse and 1 Tm 1:4 contain the sole instances of the exact phrase οἰκονομία θεοῦ in the corpus of apostolic fathers and the New Testament, respectively. (The phrase occurs with definite articles and in a different sense in Col 1:25.) It is also interesting to note that all three instances of οἰκονομία in the Ignatian corpus are in *Ephesians* (6:1, 18:2, 20:1).

47. On the one hand, "to believe pertains to the intellect inasmuch as it is moved by the will to give its assent" (*STh* II-II, q. 2, a. 2), but on the other hand, "it is necessary that the final end be in the intellect before it is in the will, for the will cannot be inclined to anything except inasmuch as it is apprehended by the intellect" (q. 4, a. 7).

48. *STh* II-II, q. 1, a. 3, ad 1.

man personality wounded by sin. He is well aware of the "hypocrisy" and "evil guile" of those who "bear about the name" but "do things unworthy of God," who "speak Jesus Christ but desire the world."[49] Above all, he is anxious that he himself will "not only speak" the truth "but also will it" (Rom. 3:2). But such breeches and inconsistencies are not constitutive of the human person, and it is the singular effect of grace to heal them. Christians can find strength "in Jesus Christ" to believe and love "with an undivided heart."[50] By grace they may possess an "unwavering spirit" and a "blameless and unwavering mind," which is nothing less than an authentic participation in Jesus Christ, who is "our unwavering life."[51] Ignatius thus strives for and extols the harmony of the inner man with the outer man (Rom. 3:2), of speech with action (Eph. 4:2), and of teaching with practice (15:1). He explains that the person who really apprehends the truth of revelation with his mind cannot continue to sin against this truth willfully without thereby diminishing the quality of his faith (14:2). "Faith cannot perform the things that belong to unbelief, nor can unbelief perform the things that belong to faith" (8:2). The correspondence between intellectual virtue and moral virtue present in the life of the authentic Christian is thus paralleled by the correspondence between "evil teaching" (κακοδιδασκαλία) and "evil desire" (ἡδονὴ κακή) in the life of the heretic (Phld. 2:1–2).

Mind-set

It will be helpful at this point to introduce another of Ignatius's favorite words, to which reference will be made frequently throughout the remainder of this chapter. The noun γνώμη ("mind-set, firm purpose, will, approval"), which occurs fifteen times in the Ignatian corpus, lies roughly at the semantic interface between "faith" and "love," though it is more closely related to the former term. As its etymological relation to γνῶσις ("knowledge") suggests, the noetic dimension has a certain primacy in γνώμη. Even in contexts where one might justifiably trans-

---

49. *Eph.* 7:1; *Magn.* 3:2; *Rom.* 7:1.
50. *Tral.* 13:2; *Phld.* 6:2.
51. *Magn.* 15:1; *Tral.* 1:1; *Eph.* 3:2. Literally, Ignatius says that an unwavering mind "is" Jesus Christ (*Magn.* 15:1). As elsewhere, he uses the verb "to be" in order to express not absolute identity but true ontological and economic participation. The "unwavering" (ἀδιάκριτος, which can also mean "not doubting") mind or spirit is one that adheres to the object of faith, Jesus Christ, steadfastly and in a morally "blameless" manner (note also the use of the adverb ἀδιακρίτως in *Rom.* sal. and *Phld.* sal.).

late it "will," γνώμη denotes a firm purpose that is based on one's prior knowledge of a matter. At the same time, the volitional dimension of "resolve" is also integral to the concept of γνώμη. The term thus designates a kind of unison of intellect and will, which is captured fairly well by the English word "mind-set." Not surprisingly, Ignatius roots the notion of γνώμη as a Christian attribute in God himself, and he relates it back to God at every point. God's γνώμη is his eternal counsel or wise plan, which is not arbitrary but based upon and synonymous with eternal truth. It is fully present, revealed, and realized in Jesus Christ and may be accessed by the faithful by means of their obedience to the "mind-set" of the local bishop.

This is all expounded with remarkable precision in the following passage, in which the word γνώμη occurs four times.

> But since love does not permit me to be silent concerning you, I have undertaken to exhort you to run together in the mind-set of God. For it is Jesus Christ, our unwavering life, who is the mind-set of the Father, as also the bishops designated throughout the world are in the mind-set of Jesus Christ. Therefore it is fitting for you to run together in the mind-set of the bishop, as you are in fact doing. (Eph. 3:2–4:1a)

The double occurrence of the verb συντρέχω ("run together") in this text is purposeful. The first instance indicates that the conformity of many lives to the will of God will bring unity to the local church community, and its repetition indicates that running together in the mind-set of God translates into running together in the mind-set of the bishop. In effect, Ignatius is saying, "If you want to be sure that you are living according to God's will, submit to the bishop's will." But it is significant that he does not speak here simply in terms of "will" (θέλημα) but rather in terms of γνώμη. Ignatius is promoting neither blind obedience to the bishop's whims nor submission to the arbitrary will of an inscrutable God. God's will is his truth, and he has revealed that truth in Jesus Christ. In this schema Jesus Christ and the local bishop constitute the crucial links between the mind-set of God and the lives of the faithful, and what is communicated to the faithful through this linkage is neither arbitrary will, nor gnosis, but a mind-set: a firm resolve and orientation of one's life that is based on knowledge of revealed truth. To say that Jesus Christ is the mind-set of the Father means both that his own mind-set ("the mind-set of Jesus Christ") is identical to that of God the Father and that he has revealed and enacted God's mind-set by what he taught and the way he lived. Both his words and his deeds are "worthy of the Father" (15:1).

It is imperative to recognize that Ignatius understands God's mind-set, as it is communicated to the church in Jesus Christ, to have real noetic and moral content. We have no hope of grasping Ignatius's theology of unity if we neglect this point. He urges the Smyrnaeans to "take note of those who hold heterodox views concerning the grace of Jesus that has come to us—how contrary to the mind-set of God they are!" How is this contrariety manifested? Ignatius specifies first the heretics' neglect of charity (ἀγάπη) toward widows, orphans, and prisoners, and second, their absence from the eucharist, which "they do not confess to be the flesh of our Savior Jesus Christ." With this last remark Ignatius smoothly transitions into a creedal formula, which goes on to affirm that this very flesh "suffered for our sins" and was raised by the "loving-kindness" of the Father (Smyr. 6:2–7:1). In short, then, the heretics show themselves to be contrary to God's γνώμη precisely in the realms of faith and love, with the eucharist as the point of convergence between the two. God the Father manifested his loving-kindness (χρηστότης) to the world by sending his Son to die for our sins and by raising him up. This historical self-communication of God is made sacramentally present in the eucharistic assembly, where the church confesses its faith in Jesus Christ and is united in love. With this same faith and love the members of Christ go forth to care for the disadvantaged and suffering, which is nothing less than an expression of the heart of the Father.

This point, that the "mind-set of God" is a communication of real noetic and moral content, can be established even more forcefully from *Ephesians* 4, if we pick up right where we left off in the passage cited earlier. This chapter, which is replete with musical imagery, is something of an encomium on unity. When Christians are "in tune" with their bishop, Jesus Christ himself is "sung" by their "unanimity" (ὁμόνοια) and their "harmonious love" (σύμφωνος ἀγάπη; 4:1b). Ignatius employs ὁμόνοια here and elsewhere as a near synonym for πίστις. It denotes *faith* as the appropriation of revealed truth, but faith viewed precisely under the aspect of effecting unity. The term ὁμόνοια, then, serves as a perfect counterpart for σύμφωνος ἀγάπη, which is to say, *love* under the same aspect of effecting unity. Ignatius goes on to indicate that the church is able to sing this hymn because it has "received the tone color of God" (χρῶμα Θεοῦ λαβόντες; 4:2a). In other words, the terms of unity do not come "from below," but neither are they an arbitrary imposition from on high. The ultimate basis for unity is the nature and character of God himself.

Ignatius completes the thought with admirable economy of expression.

> In unity you sing to the Father through Jesus Christ, in order that he may both hear and recognize you through the things you do well, being members of his Son. So then, it is advantageous for you to live in blameless unity, so that you may also always participate in God. (4:2b)

Lives unified by faith and love constitute a song "to the Father" because he has revealed himself as Father. They are sung "through Jesus Christ" because this revelation came through the incarnate Son. God is able to "hear and recognize" those who have been incorporated into the body of his Son because he recognizes his own "tone color" in the way they live.[52] When it is lived in blameless unity, ecclesial life is nothing less than a participation in God! What Ignatius teaches the Ephesians by means of musical imagery is the same truth he teaches the Magnesians via a numismatic image: "Those who are faithful in love bear the imprint [χαρακτήρ] of God the Father through Jesus Christ" (*Magn.* 5:2).

If faith and love amount to a participation in the life and character of God, it is no surprise if Ignatius often speaks of these virtues as providing a firm foundation for the lives of believers and stability in the life of the local church. Ignatius wishes, for example, that the household of Tavia in Smyrna will be "firmly established in faith and love" (*Smyr.* 13:2). Faith in particular, which is a participation in God's own fidelity, and which with its objective doctrinal content constitutes the governing principle (ἀρχή) of the Christian life (*Eph.* 14:1), is a kind of foundation (cf. Heb 6:1). Christians should oppose the deceit of outsiders by being "firmly established in faith" (*Eph.* 10:2). But if life is ordered by its principle, it is also ordered by the "end" or "goal" (τέλος) toward which it is directed, which Ignatius identifies as love (14:1). Accordingly, the "good order" of the Magnesian church is determined precisely by its "love for God" (*Magn.* 1:1). Never at a loss for a vivid and arresting image, Ignatius adapts the Pauline notion of "co-crucifixion"[53] in order to commend the Smyrnaeans for the stability they have in faith and love.

> I perceived that you were established in an unshakable faith—nailed, as it were, to the cross of the Lord Jesus Christ in both flesh and spirit—and firmly grounded in love in the blood of Christ. (*Smyr.* 1:1)

---

52. The image is apt since tone color, or timbre, is the quality that enables the hearer to distinguish one instrument or voice from another playing the same notes.

53. Rom 6:6; Gal 2:19.

Ignatius then segues into a long creedal affirmation concerning Jesus Christ, about which the Smyrnaeans are "fully convinced" (1:1–2).

It is in this connection that the concept of "mind-set" (γνώμη) serves Ignatius especially well. He employs it by way of indicating how faith and love in unison give stability to Christian existence and ecclesial life, and how heretical doctrines threaten this stability. One who has "acquired the mind-set of God" maintains his or her own mind-set "in God" and directs it "toward God."[54] This is to possess a clear knowledge of revealed truth and to be firmly resolved to base one's life and teaching upon that truth, "as if on an immovable rock" (*Poly.* 1:1). Such a one was Polycarp, whom Ignatius could expect to "stand firm" against strange doctrines "like an anvil when it is struck" (3:1). The ruler of this aeon aims to corrupt the Christian's "mind-set toward God" (*Rom.* 7:1). Indeed the devil has his own "mind-set," the deceit of false doctrines, which wears down the Christian's resolve and weakens his love (*Phld.* 6:2). Anyone who follows a schismatic "walks by a strange mind-set" and does not conform himself to the passion of Christ (3:3). The mind-set of the evil one breeds divisions and instability, just as God's mind-set fosters unity and stability.

Suffering with Christ

It is no coincidence that most of Ignatius's references to γνώμη concern bishops: Polycarp, Onesimus, the unnamed bishop of Philadelphia, or Ignatius himself. As noted above, the bishop is a vital link in the chain by which God's mind-set becomes known to the faithful. That a particular bishop possesses a "mind-set toward God" is not something Ignatius affirms glibly, however. The personal assimilation of God's own holiness that this phrase connotes demands a spiritual life of extraordinary quality, as Ignatius's depiction of the bishop of Philadelphia suggests.

I am especially struck by his mildness [ἐπιείκεια]. He is able to do more silently [σιγῶν] than those who speak futile words, for he has attuned himself to the commandments as a zither to its strings. Therefore my soul blesses his mind-set toward God, recognizing it to be virtuous [ἐνάρετος] and perfect [τέλειος]. It is his serenity [τὸ ἀκίνητον] and his freedom from anger [τὸ ἀόργητον] in all the mildness [ἐπιείκεια] of the living God. (*Phld.* 1:1–2)

Ignatius lauds the character of this bishop in terms reminiscent of Stoicism.[55] The governing concept here is ἐπιείκεια ("mildness"), which

---

54. *Poly.* 8:1, 1:1; *Phld.* 1:2.   55. Lightfoot, *Ignatius, Polycarp*, 2.253.

occurs twice, functioning as a framing device (inclusio) around this brief panegyric. The first instance of ἐπιείκεια makes reference to the bishop's own mildness, which has made a deep impression on Ignatius, while the remainder of the description serves to spell out what is meant by mildness. The second occurrence of ἐπιείκεια rounds out the passage by indicating that all the bishop's attributes are rooted "in the mildness of the living God." Ignatius could hardly have chosen a more perfect word to indicate the character of a bishop who is genuinely godlike. In the Septuagint and in Hellenistic Judaism ἐπιείκεια is first of all an attribute of God the divine ruler, who shows kindness and clemency toward human beings, and then it is an attribute befitting men who have been placed in authority by God (Moses, judges, kings, and prophets). It suggests both their temperate mode of life and also the reasonableness and leniency with which they rule.[56] In the Pauline letters ἐπιείκεια is the particular attribute of Christ in imitation of which Paul exhorts the brethren (2 Cor 10:1), and therefore an attribute desirable in a bishop (1 Tm 3:3). The bishop of Philadelphia shows his deep penetration of the *mysterium fidei* and his nearness to God and Christ in his silence (a theme we shall explore in chapter 7) and in the conformity of his life to the commandments. His "mind-set toward God," which is to say, the orientation of his mind toward God and the firm resolve of his will, renders him, as we might expect, free from passion and anger.

Schoedel finds, not without reason, that Ignatius describes the bishop of Philadelphia as imitating "a somewhat Hellenized God devoid of passion." The apparent reference to the biblical "living God" therefore "seems out of place here."[57] For this reason Schoedel follows Lightfoot's suggestion and construes the participle ζῶντος ("living") such that it refers to the bishop, not to God.[58] One could then translate the conclusion of the passage along these lines: "living in all the mildness of God." This interpretation is grammatically possible but not compelling, as it misses the real thrust of Ignatius's statement. Schoedel seems still to be in the thrall of the old Tübingen antithesis between Hellenism and Judaism, whereas Ignatius's thought is steeped in the writings of Hellenistic Judaism and Christianity (e.g., 4 *Maccabees*, Wisdom of Solomon, the Gospel of John, and the Pauline corpus), which represent an ongoing synthesis of biblical faith and Greek thought, a synthesis that had been in the

56. TDNT 2.588–90.
57. Schoedel, *Ignatius of Antioch*, 196.
58. Ibid.; cf. Lightfoot, *Ignatius, Polycarp*, 2.253.

works for centuries by the time Ignatius wrote his letters. For Ignatius there is no contradiction between the "living God" of Scripture and the Hellenistic notion of a God of perfect serenity.

Any tension he might have felt between the two he would no doubt have referred to the supreme mystery of "the passionless one" (ὁ ἀπαθής) who became "subject to passion" (παθητός) for our sake (Poly. 3:2). His description of the bishop of Philadelphia suggests a man who had entered deeply into this mystery. Ignatius was learning from experience, as he approached his martyrdom, that the Christian who becomes "an imitator of the passion of [his] God" does not merely embrace a Stoic ideal of dispassion (ἀπάθεια), but "suffers with" (συμπαθέω) Jesus Christ.[59] The attempt to attain dispassion by means of a flight from all passion will always fall short of the ideal, but the distinctive grace of Christianity affords the opportunity to purify and perfect passion by willingly directing one's living and dying "into" the passion of Christ (Magn. 5:2). Authentic freedom from passion is found only in union with the total passion of Jesus.

This is the paradox of the cross. What greater deprivation of human freedom is there than to have one's hands and feet nailed down? What greater vulnerability than to hang naked before one's foes, with arms spread wide, so that they might mock you, spit upon you, and strike you? Crucifixion is coerced passivity. Nearly anyone in such a situation would be like a worm wriggling on a hook, doing anything possible to resist or retaliate if even in some small way. But the Lord's passion is perfect. "Reviled, he did not revile in return; suffering (πάσχων), he did not threaten; but he handed himself over to the one who judges justly" (1 Pt 2:23). In making himself an offering for others, he acts in perfect freedom. No one takes his life from him; he lays it down of his own accord (Jn 10:18). In suffering love, action and passion coincide. Jesus is fixed to the cross, handing over his life in the perfect freedom of love. This is the passion of his God that Ignatius wishes to imitate. In light of its paradox we can better appreciate why he glories in being bound with chains, which he refers to as his "spiritual pearls" (Eph. 11:2); and why he is so anxious not to be released from them, which would be tantamount to getting down from the cross. "Up till now I am a slave, but if I suffer [πάθω], I shall be a freedman of Jesus Christ" (Rom. 4:3).

Our task now is to specify more precisely the roles played by faith

---

59. Rom. 6:3; Smyr. 4:2; cf. Phil. 9:2.

and love within this mystery of συμπάθεια ("suffering with"). How do these two virtues, functioning in concert, enable the Christian to remain, so to speak, on the cross with Christ in order to share also in his resurrection? We begin with a passage quoted earlier.

> I perceived that you were established in an unshakable faith—as it were, nailed to the cross of the Lord Jesus Christ in both flesh and spirit—and firmly grounded in love in the blood of Christ. (Smyr. 1:1)

The adjective translated "unshakable" (ἀκίνητος) in this passage is the same word used as a substantive to denote the "serenity" (τὸ ἀκίνητον) of the bishop of Philadelphia (Phld. 1:2). The full conviction of faith gives the Christian serenity of mind and firm resolve. For the benefit of the Smyrnaeans, who are in danger of falling under the spell of docetism, Ignatius provides the longest of his creedal formulations, followed by two chapters of elaboration and commentary (Smyr. 1:1b–3:3). He places a strong accent on the historical reality and physical humanity of Christ, explicitly mentioning Jesus' "flesh" (σάρξ) in connection with the incarnation, the passion, and the resurrection. Jesus was "truly from the stock of David according to the flesh" (1:1), "truly under Pontius Pilate and Herod the Tetrarch nailed [to the cross] for our sake in the flesh" (1:2), and remained "in the flesh even after the resurrection" (3:1). Ignatius stresses that he knows and believes these things to be true (3:1). Indeed, this emphasis on *faith in the flesh of Jesus* continues throughout Smyrnaeans, for this is what grounds the various aspects of Christian existence: the corporal works of mercy, the eucharist, the visible hierarchy, and inclusion in the "catholic church" (6:2–8:2).

Ignatius also drops a number of hints to the effect that the Smyrnaeans will need to be ready to suffer for the faith, as if to wonder why anyone would suffer for a Lord who himself only "seemed" to suffer, and then he puts himself forward as an example: "I endure all things only in the name of Jesus Christ, in order to suffer with [συμπαθέω] him, while he who is the perfect man empowers me" (4:2). To endure "in the name of Jesus Christ" means to live out the orthodox faith in the historical and truly human Christ to the end. It is to look to the "perfect man," whose flesh-and-blood humanity was really glorified, as the source of one's strength. It is to be "mingled with him in his flesh and spirit" (3:2). The docetists err precisely in what they believe "regarding the grace of Jesus Christ that has come to us" (6:2). For them, grace is a disembodied, dehistoricized thing, involving speculation and arguments about "heavenly things and the glory of angels" (6:1). Their faith has been unmoored from the biblical revelation that has come through Moses, the prophets, the gospel of Jesus, and the apostles (5:1, 8:1), and they have detached themselves from the visible structure and communal life of the church (6:2). They need to "repent into the passion" (5:3) and "believe in the blood of Christ" (6:1).

While faith is associated especially with the Lord's flesh, Ignatius usually links love with the blood of Christ.[60] The frequency and precision with which he makes this pair of correlations suggest that it is not merely rhetorical but bears some theological significance for him. The foregoing discussion of *Smyrnaeans* already puts us well on the way toward understanding why Ignatius would link faith with flesh. Faith is confession of the historical and human Jesus and participation in the visible life of the church. We have also seen how closely linked love is with the passion of Christ, which is, of course, suggested by any reference to his blood.

Perhaps we should go one step further and correlate faith/flesh and love/blood with the two great moments of the Christ event: incarnation and paschal mystery, respectively.[61] This works particularly well if we think in Johannine categories. In the incarnation the Word became flesh (Jn 1:14), and on the cross he shed his blood (19:34). Christian faith confesses "Jesus Christ having come in the flesh" (1 Jn 4:2), and Christian love "even unto death" conquers "by the blood of the Lamb" (Rv 12:11). Indeed, Jesus himself is the "faithful witness" who showed his love for us by shedding his blood (1:5). Naturally these correlations should not be pressed too far. To link Christ's flesh exclusively with his incarnation, for example, would undermine Ignatius's polemic against docetism, which is certainly why he explicitly mentions the Lord's flesh not only in relation to the incarnation but also in relation to the passion and the resurrection. If, however, we think of the incarnation not simply as one moment in the Christ event but as extending forward from that moment throughout the life of Christ and right through the paschal mystery, the correlation works well. Jesus Christ came in the flesh precisely in order to suffer in the flesh (i.e., shed his blood), and be raised in the flesh.

---

60. *Smyr.* 1:2; *Tral.* 8:1; *Rom.* 7:3.
61. Richard A. Bower, "The Meaning of ΕΠΙΤΥΓΧΑΝΩ in the Epistles of St. Ignatius of Antioch," *Vigiliae Christianae* 28 (1974): 10.

The Beginning and the End

The real theological significance of all these correlations will emerge only if we draw into the discussion still one more of Ignatius's dyadic correlations: "the beginning and the end." Ignatius tells the Magnesians that if they ground themselves in the ordinances of the Lord Jesus and the apostles, they will prosper

> in flesh and spirit,
> in faith and love,
> in the Son and the Father and in the Spirit,
> in the beginning and in the end. (*Magn.* 13:1)

As we saw in chapter 3, the first three phrases in this formulation (apart from the reference to the Holy Spirit) correspond precisely to the three dyads found in *Magnesians* 1:2. And like that passage, this one is explicitly concerned with "union" (cf. ἕνωσις in 13:2). The phrase "the beginning [ἀρχή] and the end [τέλος]" seems therefore to denote still another dimension of unity. Moreover, Ignatius explicitly correlates this dimension to the virtues of faith and love when he says, "Faith is the beginning, and love is the end" (*Eph.* 14:1).

The terms ἀρχή and τέλος are expressive of Ignatius's teleological view of human temporality and of the economy of redemption. They are not merely chronological markers but together suggest that human life, under grace, has a structure and built-in direction. Guided by a first principle, it moves toward an ultimate goal. This is true of the historical economy as a whole, of the life of Christ, and of the life of the individual believer. We can observe Ignatius's teleological view of temporality on a relatively small scale by noting the way he speaks about his trip from Antioch to Rome.

> In bonds in Christ Jesus I hope to greet you, if indeed it is the divine will [θέλημα] that I be deemed worthy unto the end [εἰς τέλος]. For the beginning [ἀρχή] is in fact auspicious, if only I attain [ἐπιτυγχάνω] grace to reach my lot without being impeded. (*Rom.* 1:1b–2a)

This passage enables us to see that Ignatius's teleological view of temporality is closely caught up with his belief in divine providence, which he refers to just a few lines earlier as "the will [θέλημα] of the one who wills all things that are" (sal.). Here he attempts to discern this will in the present circumstances of his own life. The first part of his trip appears "auspicious" (εὐοικονόμητος; literally, "well-arranged"), a word that suggests that God has a "master plan" (οἰκονομία) for Ignatius's life, just as he has one for all of human history. Things seem to be tracking toward the goal (τέλος) that Ignatius so earnestly desires, and he is convinced that martyrdom in Rome is his appointed "lot." But providence is not a matter of inexorable fate. In the fullness of human freedom and out of a burning love for Christ, he prays for the grace to achieve that lot. The verb ἐπιτυγχάνω is the same one Ignatius frequently uses in speaking of his desire to "attain God," an expression that clearly indicates that he views life as having a single definitive goal toward which everything else is ordered.

This goal-oriented view of human life comes to its clearest expression in Ignatius's conviction that Christianity is fundamentally a matter of personal discipleship to Jesus Christ (χριστομαθία), a discipleship that has a "beginning" and must achieve "perfection."

> Though I am in bonds for the name, I have not yet been perfected in Jesus Christ. For now I possess the beginning [ἀρχή] of becoming a disciple and I address you as my fellow learners. (Eph. 3:1)

But what exactly is this "beginning"? An ἀρχή is not simply a temporal inception that recedes into the past as one moves toward the τέλος. It is a principle that guides one along the way and remains with one until the goal has been reached. Similarly, the τέλος does not suddenly appear at the chronological terminus. It too is present all along the way, but present in the modality of the ἀρχή. One already possesses the τέλος precisely to the extent that one actually lives as guided by the ἀρχή. Indeed, the τέλος is the way insofar as one really attains the goal by proceeding on the way. Now, this is exactly how Ignatius speaks of faith and love later in *Ephesians*. "Faith is your upward guide [ἀναγωγεύς], and love is the way [ὁδός] that bears you up to God" (9:1). Faith is the ἀρχή, and love is the τέλος.

The Christian life is fundamentally a matter of discipleship to the person of Jesus Christ, or "learning Christ" (χριστομαθία), and Jesus Christ himself is the supreme authority and definitive first principle (ἀρχεῖα) of that life (Phld. 8:2). This latter term is, of course, the one we translated as "archives" in our examination of the Philadelphia incident. Here I would call attention to its etymological relation and semantic proximity to the word ἀρχή. The Judaizers look to the Old Testament Scriptures as their supreme authority and guide, but Ignatius recognizes a person to be that principle, for he knows that person to be the Logos and definitive self-revelation of God. But because the Logos has taken flesh and has revealed the Father in his actions, there is no contradiction if he goes on to elaborate his claim by saying, "The inviolable archives are his cross and death, and his resurrection, and the faith that is through him" (8:2). Naturally, the person of Christ, his deeds, and the confessional content of faith (expressed in words) are not strictly identical, but the person is truly present and manifest in the deeds, and by grace the confession of the true faith terminates not simply in propositions but in realities, that is, in the person of Christ and in the deeds by which he has saved us. Thus, Jesus Christ is the definitive ἀρχεῖα of the Christian life, but it is also true that his redemptive acts, along with the faith by which we confess the reality of the person and his actions, constitute the ἀρχεῖα. Ignatius's identification of faith as the ἀρχή of Christian existence is thus very closely tied to his identification of Jesus Christ as the ἀρχεῖα.

Ignatius's teleological view of the Christian mystery, along with his identification of faith and love as its ἀρχή and τέλος, respectively, has deep affinities to various New Testament traditions. In Colossians Jesus Christ is the supreme ἀρχή, as principle of both creation and new creation (Col 1:15–20), and in him the eternal mystery of God has been revealed. The goal of Christian instruction is to "present every human being perfect [τέλειος] in Christ" (1:28), and "love" is "the bond of perfection [τελειότης]" (3:14). In the Johannine literature there is a close correlation between the eternal "beginning" (ἀρχή), when the Logos was with God, and the "beginning" (ἀρχή) of Jesus' signs. This correlation serves to indicate that the glory that the Son shared with the Father before the world existed is the same glory manifested in his miracles, to which the apt response is faith.[62] Jesus is "the one who is from the beginning" (ὁ ἀπ' ἀρχῆς), and the gospel is "that which you have heard from the beginning" (ὃ ἠκούσατε ἀπ' ἀρχῆς).[63] Jesus' mission is to "fully accomplish" (τελειόω) the works that the Father has given him to do.[64] This means loving his own "to the end" (εἰς τέλος), and this love is "consummated" (τετέλεσται) in his death on the cross.[65] Faith and love are intimately linked in the Christian life because "the message that you have heard from the beginning" is precisely the command to "love one

---

62. Jn 1:1, 2:11, 17:5. The first major portion of the Fourth Gospel is framed by two occurrences of the word ἀρχή (Jn 1:1, 2:11). The latter passage is a programmatic statement indicating the character and economic function of Jesus' signs.

63. 1 Jn 2:13–14, 24.   64. Jn 4:34, 5:36, 17:4.

65. Jn 13:1, 19:30.

another" in imitation of Jesus, and the goal of faith is to be "perfected in love" (τετελείωται ἐν τῇ ἀγάπῃ).⁶⁶ Similarly, the Epistle of James says that "faith is perfected [ἐτελειώθη] through works" (Jas 2:22).

Especially noteworthy in this regard is the Epistle to the Hebrews, where we find a parallelism and causal connection between the teleology of Jesus' life "in the flesh" and the lives of believers. Jesus was "faithful" (πιστός) over God's house, learned obedience through what he suffered, and "having been made perfect [τελειωθείς] became the cause of eternal salvation for all who obey him."⁶⁷ Unlike the Mosaic law, which "made nothing perfect," Jesus' self-offering cleanses and perfects the consciences of those who approach God through him.⁶⁸ The gospel of this salvation "received its principle [ἀρχή]" in the Lord's own teaching ministry, and "we are sharers in Christ if we hold the principle [ἀρχή] of the reality firm unto the end [μέχρι τέλους]."⁶⁹

For Ignatius and the author of the Epistle to the Hebrews alike, holding onto the principle of faith "unto the end" is essential for attaining eternal life. One's personal salvation can never be a settled matter prior to death. Just as Hebrews says that we partake in Christ "if" (ἐάν) we maintain the ἀρχή unto the τέλος, so Ignatius uses this eschatological "if" twice in *Ephesians* 14. First he assures the Christians of Ephesus that they will benefit from his exhortations "if" (ἐάν) they direct their faith and love "perfectly [τελείως] into Jesus Christ" (14:1). Then, after describing faith and love as "the beginning and end of life," he reminds his readers that "the work" of being a Christian consists not merely in making a public confession "but in the power of faith, if [ἐάν] one is found unto the end [εἰς τέλος]" (14:2). These statements are crucial for appreciating the role that faith and love play in Ignatius's soteriology. Like Paul, and the New Testament generally, Ignatius ascribes to faith a vital role in justification and salvation,⁷⁰ but faith can in no way achieve its goal apart from love. Ignatius would almost certainly concur with James that "faith without works is dead" (Jas 2:26), and with Thomas Aquinas when he says that "by love the act of faith is perfected and brought to its form" (*per caritatem actus fidei perficitur et formatur*).⁷¹ For Ignatius, faith is

---

66. 1 Jn 3:11, 4:18.
68. Heb 7:19, 9:9, 9:14, 10:1, 14.
69. Heb 2:3, 3:14. The author of Hebrews likens the rudiments of this ἀρχή to milk but wishes to nourish his readers with the solid food that belongs to the "mature" (τέλειοι; 5:12). Having already laid a foundation of faith in "the word of the principle [ἀρχή] of Christ," he wishes to move on to "maturity" (τελειότης; 6:1).
70. Phld. 5:2, 8:2; Smyr. 6:1.

67. Heb 3:1–6, 5:7–9, 7:28.

71. STh II-II, q. 4, a. 3.

not merely a disposition of trust but a "power" that works through love, and justification is not merely a status imputed by God but a condition attained by the believer. "Those who believe with love possess the imprint of God the Father through Jesus Christ" (*Magn.* 5:2).

This imprint, which Ignatius identifies with eternal life, is possessed already in this life but must be maintained unto the end if one is to attain final salvation. In other words, Ignatius's understanding of personal redemption affirms both realized eschatology and future eschatology. That is why he immediately qualifies his statement about the "imprint" by adding that "unless [ἐάν μή] we willingly direct *our dying* into his passion, his life is not in us" (5:2). The act of dying (τὸ ἀποθανεῖν) is decisive because the perfection of love is essential to salvation. Integral to Ignatius's flesh-and-spirit anthropology and his teleological view of human temporality is the notion that life has a specific, goal-oriented structure. It is *vita usque ad mortem*. Therefore it is the nature of the case that a human person can make a definitive act of love, which is essentially a matter of self-donation, only in death. Or rather, one can bring a lifetime of "believing with love" to perfection only through death. A near contemporary of Ignatius expresses a similar understanding when he eulogizes the Jewish martyr Eleazar in this manner: "O man of blessed age and of venerable gray hair and of law-abiding life, whom the faithful seal of death has perfected!"[72] Death seals the deal.

Both the notion that salvation is an imprint or condition and the notion that it is sealed by death are implicit in the many references that Ignatius makes to being "found" (εὑρεθῆναι), eschatologically speaking.[73] In an explicitly eschatological context, he exhorts the Ephesians "only to be found in Christ Jesus unto the true life" (*Eph.* 11:1). He reminds the Magnesians that we endure tribulations "in order that we may be found to be disciples of Jesus Christ" (*Magn.* 9:1), and he similarly tells the Trallians that if they submit to their bishop and presbyters they "will be found" to be in Jesus Christ "our hope" (*Tral.* 2:2). These and many similar expressions suggest that human beings come before God's judgment seat in something like an objectively verifiable condition relative to salvation. They will either be "found reprobate" (12:3) or "found blameless" (13:3). This sense of the objectivity of final judgment is also conveyed

---

72. 4 *Maccabees* 7:15 (ὃν πιστὴ θανάτου σφραγὶς ἐτελείωσεν) RSV.
73. The closest New Testament parallels are: Phil 3:9 ("found in him"), 1 Cor 4:2 ("found faithful"), 2 Cor 5:3 ("found naked"), and 2 Pt 3:14 ("found by him spotless and blameless"), all in eschatological contexts.

by a remarkable passage (*Magn.* 10:2) in which Ignatius likens authentic Christians to meat that is "salted" for preservation, while sinners and heretics are rotten foodstuffs that will be exposed for what they are by the stench they give off! We can now more readily appreciate why Ignatius expresses so much anxiety about his own eternal destiny. No proto-Pelagian, he recognizes his complete dependence on God's grace; but because he believes that salvation can only be reached by dying "into the passion" of Christ, he prays that "final" (τέλεια) grace will be given to him so that he might attain God (*Smyr.* 11:1). He does not allow the fact that he is bound in chains and headed for the Colosseum to breed complacency in him, but rather he "fears" for his salvation as long as he is "imperfect" (ἀναπάρτιστος), and he asks the Philadelphians to "perfect" (ἀπαρτίζω) him by means of their prayers.[74] Similarly, he asks the Roman Christians to pray that he will be "found" to be an authentic Christian or "faithful one" (πιστός), "found" to be a pure loaf, and "found" to be a sacrifice acceptable to God.[75]

Faith and Works

As noted near the beginning of this chapter, Ignatius has the reputation of having understood Paul only very imperfectly, and it should be apparent by now why it is especially in the realm of Paul's doctrine of justification by faith, and the relationship between faith and works, that some find Ignatius to have committed serious errors. Torrance goes as far as to maintain that Ignatius's understanding of justification "runs directly counter to the Gospel."[76] If we return once more to the "archives" passage, it is easy to see where Protestant scholars especially might find problems in Ignatius's understanding of justification.

> But to me Jesus Christ is the archives; the inviolable archives are his cross, death, and resurrection, and the faith that comes through him. It is by these, through your prayers, that I wish to be justified. (*Phld.* 8:2)

To say that justification comes through Jesus Christ, through his cross, death, and resurrection, and by faith, sounds Pauline enough and does not itself present a problem. It is generally understood that justification is accomplished objectively (i.e., once and for all) by Jesus Christ and his atoning sacrifice, and that it takes place subjectively (i.e., in the life of

---

74. *Phld.* 5:1; cf. *Eph.* 3:1.   75. *Rom.* 3:2, 4:1–2.
76. Torrance, *Doctrine of Grace*, 67.

the individual) by faith. Two difficulties emerge from Ignatius's formulation, however. First, it ascribes some sort of efficacy to the prayers of other Christians, such that the individual's own faith would not seem to be the sufficient cause of subjective justification. And this is by no means an isolated statement. The efficacy of intercessory prayer is a constant theme in Ignatius's letters, and he frequently expresses the hope that the prayers of other Christians will help him achieve salvation.[77] Second and even more problematic, *Philadelphians* 8:2 presents justification as something that has not yet definitively taken place in Ignatius's life but still lies in the future. In the one other passage in which Ignatius speaks in terms of justification (*Rom.* 5:1), he echoes a statement of Paul's—"I am not thereby justified" (1 Cor 4:4)—which he seems to interpret as meaning that a Christian should not be so presumptuous as to claim to have been justified while still in this life (cf. Rom 6:7). From these two passages it is tolerably clear that Ignatius does not expect to be justified prior to death and that he equates justification to becoming "perfect" or "attaining God."[78]

Moreover, since for Ignatius faith must be completed by love if one is to attain God, it is clear that one is not justified *sola fide*. Faith alone is not sufficient but must be completed by love, which is to say, by works. This is precisely where Torrance finds Ignatius to divert from the Pauline gospel egregiously: "Justification [for Ignatius] is a process bound up with his idea of faith that perfects itself in love leading finally to union with or attainment to God."[79] Torrance then turns to Ignatius's understanding of grace (χάρις), which he likewise judges to be discontinuous with authentic New Testament doctrine. For Ignatius grace is not the gratuitous divine judgment by which we are forgiven and justified, but a "principle of new life and power" that is "infused, and thus becomes associated with man's own φύσις [nature]." In other words, as Torrance views the matter, Ignatius lays "the groundwork for the [erroneous Catholic] doctrine of *gratia inhaerens et infusa*."[80]

In all this, no doubt, Torrance has interpreted Ignatius correctly. The

---

77. *Eph.* 11:2; *Rom.* 8:3; *Phld.* 5:1; *Smyr.* 11:1.

78. According to Schoedel, righteousness is "not an Ignatian theme" (*Ignatius of Antioch*, 222). But since he must acknowledge three exceptions in such a small corpus (*Rom.* 5:1; *Phld.* 8:2; *Smyr.* 1:1), one wonders whether his claim is justified (so to speak). If all we possessed of Paul's writings were 1 Corinthians, Colossians, and 1–2 Thessalonians (a collection roughly the size of the Ignatian corpus), we would find that δικαιοσύνη occurs only once (1 Cor 1:30), and we might conclude that righteousness is not a Pauline theme! In any case, Ignatius's use of δίκαιος ("righteous") and δικαίως ("rightly, righteously") should perhaps also be taken into account (*Eph.* 1:1, 15:3; *Magn.* 9:2, 12:1).

79. Torrance, *Doctrine of Grace*, 67.   80. Ibid., 76–77.

more debatable question is whether Ignatius's teaching is in fact incompatible with the Pauline gospel. The issues here are many and complex, and it will not be possible to deal with them adequately within the context of this study, as that would involve us more in the interpretation of Paul than of Ignatius. At the risk of stating the obvious, let me simply point out that Ignatius's understanding of justification and grace is less problematic from a Catholic dogmatic point of view, and perhaps still less problematic for Orthodox theology, than it is when viewed from within the Protestant tradition. The difficulties modern scholars have found with Ignatius's interpretation of Paul are at least to some extent attributable to the tendency to read Ignatius from the point of view of the Western theological tradition, and from the Protestant side of that tradition in particular. When Torrance notes that Ignatius has little to say about the forgiveness of sins but instead views redemption in terms of becoming like God and attaining God, this is not much more than to say that Ignatius is a Greek father, not a Latin father. And when Torrance says that Ignatius shares with the other apostolic fathers "a failure to realise that in relation to sin and guilt the death of Christ is a finished work, on the ground of which by a judgment of grace we pass from death to life," this is merely to say that Ignatius had not read Calvin or Luther.[81]

Furthermore, it has sometimes been supposed (though perhaps less often in recent decades) that as long as we operate with an interpretation of Paul that has been approved by modern biblical scholarship, which presumably gives us access to Paul's originally intended meaning, we are justified in holding Ignatius accountable to that interpretation. But this presupposition fails to recognize, first, that modern biblical scholarship has never been able to seal itself off from interpretive traditions (as if that were desirable), and, second, that modern biblical scholarship is constantly revising its conclusions, not least in the area of Pauline theology! Thus the reading of Paul upon which Torrance bases his critique of Ignatius might not seem as self-evident to New Testament scholars today as it did sixty-some years ago when Torrance wrote.

There are in any case passages in which Paul can reasonably be taken to speak of justification as an eschatological event, taking place on the day of judgment.[82] There is even a passage in which Paul refers to biolog-

---

81. Ibid., 66. I do not mean to suggest that reading Ignatius's letters from within a theological tradition is undesirable, or even avoidable, but simply that it is helpful to reflect on the fact that this is what we are doing.

82. E.g., Rom 2:13, 3:30, 5:19; Gal 5:5.

ical death as the moment at which one "has been justified [δεδικαίωται] from sin," which is to say, definitively freed from the power of sin (Rom 6:7). This may be an unusual use of the term δικαιόω for Paul, but it is one that resonates with Ignatius's thought. And even where Paul does speak of justification as already having taken place in this life (e.g., Rom 5:1), it is not so clear that he would have neatly separated this (initial) justification from sanctification and final judgment. One plausible way of putting together the various statements Paul makes about salvation is precisely to think in terms of a process that has a definitive beginning point in the individual's life but that is not complete short of "attaining God." At least Ignatius's view has the merit of not having to run circles around passages such as Philippians 2:12, where Paul exhorts his readers, "Work out your salvation with fear and trembling."

This statement and others like it make it clear that, for Paul, the road to salvation involves a human "work" that is not to be identified with "works of the law" and that is possible only by grace. Christians are able to "work out" (κατεργάζομαι) their salvation because God is "the one at work" (ὁ ἐνεργῶν) in them (2:13). Elsewhere, in a sharply polemical passage, Paul warns that those who attempt to be justified by works of the law "have fallen from grace," and then he contrasts such an attempt with the authentic approach to salvation.

> For we, by the Spirit and from faith, anticipate the hope of righteousness [ἐλπίδα δικαιοσύνης]. For in Christ Jesus neither circumcision nor uncircumcision has any efficacy, but faith working through love [πίστις δι' ἀγάπης ἐνεργουμένη]. (Gal 5:5–6)

Like most passages in the Pauline corpus, this one raises difficult exegetical and theological questions. Should we take the phrase "hope of righteousness" to mean "the hope of attaining righteousness" (objective genitive), or "the hope that righteousness gives" (genitive of source)? In other words, is this hope to be identified as the confidence that the righteousness received in initial justification will be completed by final justification, or is it the absolute certitude of a final salvation that is to crown a status of righteousness already perfectly possessed? One might also ask what exactly faith accomplishes through love. Is the "working" spoken of here intrinsically, or extrinsically, related to what Paul elsewhere calls justification by faith? Is love strictly essential to salvation as the perfection and "form" of faith, or is it essential only in the sense of demonstrating faith's genuineness?

One could legitimately debate how Paul would answer these questions, but there can be little doubt that for each of them Ignatius would opt for the first alternative and Torrence for the second. For Ignatius, justification (at least in its perfection) lies in the future, faith working through love is the way to arrive at this final justification, and there can be no certitude of salvation prior to biological death. Eternal life "lies before us" as a goal yet to be achieved, and there is a very real danger that the devil may divert us from the path to it (Eph. 17:1).

Whatever one may think of this doctrine, it is not one at which Ignatius would have arrived lightly, as if by way of a naive or unreflective reading of Paul. His letters suggest, on the contrary, that he had given serious thought, not only to the relationship between faith and love, but to the place of "works" within the whole structure of redemption. In order to tie together some of the threads of this discussion, and to conclude the chapter, I would like to examine the statements that bear witness to Ignatius's ergology, or theology of works. We begin with a sentence that, while not the most elegant Ignatius ever composed, does effectively express his gratitude to the Ephesians for sending an embassy to meet him at Smyrna.

As I have received your much beloved name, which you acquired by a nature righteous according to faith and love in Christ Jesus our Savior—being imitators of God and having inflamed yourselves in the blood of God, you have perfectly accomplished the connatural work. (Eph. 1:1)

The Ephesians' "name" is their reputation for authentic Christian identity and character. The grace of Christ is no merely imputed righteousness but has conferred on them a "righteous nature" (φύσις δικαία), so that to perform a charitable work is "connatural" (συγγένικον) to them. This transformation of nature, with the good works that flow from it, is by no means extrinsically related to the matter of one's eternal destiny but constitutes an integral dimension of the life of "faith and love" by which one attains God. Ignatius views charitable works, like everything else human, teleologically. As he says elsewhere, "Actions have a τέλος" (Magn. 5:1). In the present passage he emphatically states that the Ephesians have "perfectly accomplished" (τελείως ἀπηρτίσατε) the good deed, and he implies that this accomplishment contributes to their overall objective of achieving salvation. Indeed, the soteriological overtones in this passage are striking. The object of the Ephesians' faith and love is "our Savior." They are motivated to charity by the blood that he shed for them on the cross, which they receive in the eucharist, and their performance of a good work is nothing less than an imitation of his passion. Finally, the sequel to this sentence (*Eph.* 1:2) indicates that the special worth of their good deed lies in the contribution it makes to the success of Ignatius's martyrdom and thus to his own eternal salvation.

The elements of Ignatian ergology distilled from this passage are found throughout the letters. "To do good deeds" (εὖ πράσσειν or εὐποιΐα) is made possible by God's grace and constitutes a participation in God's life, so that only those who are spiritual can perform spiritual works.[83] When Christians do all things "in the unanimity of God," "according to God," and with the consciousness of being "indwelt" by God, they become capable of deeds that are "worthy of God" and "pleasing to God."[84] The performance of charitable deeds is so essential to Christian existence that Ignatius sometimes uses the phrase "the work" (τὸ ἔργον) almost as a synonym for Christianity (*Eph.* 14:2). "The work" achieves greatness when Christians are hated by the world and thus imitate Jesus' passion (*Rom.* 3:3), and paradoxically the "works" by which Christians endure abuse and persecution are the most efficacious in leading non-Christians to repentence, discipleship, and the attainment of God (*Eph.* 10:1–3). When Christians bring a good work to completion (ἀπαρτίζω), it belongs both to them and to God and becomes "an eternal work," a work that is "perfect [τέλειον] both on earth and in heaven."[85] It is "inscribed" to their credit and laid up as a "deposit" in heaven, something that can never be "lost."[86] These remarkable statements reflect not only Ignatius's teleological view of human temporality but also his flesh-and-spirit soteriological anthropology and his essentially historical understanding of the economy of redemption. That which is actually *done* in the flesh and in history matters. Human actions have eternal consequences (*Magn.* 5:1). This is supremely true of the deeds accomplished by Jesus Christ, deeds "worthy of the Father" (*Eph.* 15:1), but his followers can participate in the perfection of his deeds "if [they] perfectly direct [their] faith and love into Jesus Christ" (14:1).

In closing, let us consider Ignatius's fine adaptation of the Pauline armor of God motif, a passage that provides further insight into how faith and love fit into the structure of the Christian life, a life that has its source in baptism and that will be judged according to works.[87]

83. Smyr. 11:3; Poly. 7:3; Eph. 4:2, 8:2.
84. Magn. 6:1; Phld. 4:1; Eph. 15:3; Smyr. 11:3; Rom. 2:1; Poly. 6:2.
85. Poly. 7:3, 8:1; Smyr. 11:2.
86. Rom. 2:1; Poly. 6:2; Smyr. 10:1.
87. This passage is reminiscent of a number of Pauline texts (Rom 13:12; 2 Cor 6:7, 10:3–4;

Please the one whom you serve as soldiers, from whom you also receive your wages. May none of you be found to be a deserter. Let your baptism continue to serve as your weaponry: faith as a helmet, love as a spear, endurance as full armor. Your works are your deposit, in order that you may receive the savings you deserve. (Poly. 6:2)

This passage is anomalous among Ignatius's "faith and love" formulations in two noteworthy respects: its reference to baptism, and its adding of ὑπομονή ("endurance") to πίστις and ἀγάπη to form a triad of virtues. Ignatius presents baptism as the font of these virtues and thus of the Christian life. To associate baptism closely with faith is common in early Christian literature, for the baptizand makes a public confession of faith and is divinely illuminated. Ignatius recognizes that faith and its confession constitute the originary principle of eternal life, but he stresses that the true "power of faith" is realized in works of love "unto the end" (Eph. 14.2). In the present passage, Ignatius links baptism not only to faith but to love and endurance as well, in order to indicate once again the intrinsic relationship between faith and love and to suggest that works of charity, with which the passage is essentially concerned, flow from the same source of grace as does the gift of saving faith. And by adding "endurance" to his usual "faith and love," Ignatius indicates that faith and love move toward a goal and must be brought to perfection. The sequence of terms—baptism, faith, love, endurance—is, then, not haphazard but reflects the essential teleological structure of life in Christ. By framing faith and love with references to baptism and endurance, Ignatius accomplishes here roughly what he accomplishes elsewhere by identifying faith and love as the ἀρχή and τέλος of the Christian life (Eph. 14:1).[88]

Baptism, then, is the objective source of grace and, in a very real sense, determines the believer's eternal destiny. But the baptized Christian remains free and must choose between the two ways. He or she will either "please" the Lord or "desert" him. The grace of baptism must be lived out and must issue in works worthy of eternal life. While Ignatius recognizes the Pauline opposition between faith and "works of the law,"

Eph 6:11–17; 1 Thes 5:8; Ti 2:2). Polycarp, the letter's recipient, will himself employ the motif in Phil. 4:1.

88. Robert F. Stoops Jr. plausibly suggests that Ignatius took the name Theophoros ("God-bearer") at baptism, that it is "roughly equivalent to 'disciple,'" and that "its connotation of 'participant in a religious procession' suggests a dynamic understanding of faith" ("If I Suffer ...: Epistolary Authority in Ignatius of Antioch," *Harvard Theological Review* 80 [1987]: 170).

or what he calls "ancient practices" (*Magn.* 9:1), he sees no antithesis between faith and the "works" that are proper to the Christian life. Still less does he oppose good works to grace. The coming of Christ's grace into the world excludes any attempt at justification by means of the Mosaic law (*Magn.* 8:1), but "the grace of God" is fully compatible with "the law of Jesus Christ" (2:1). Ignatius's metaphorical references in *Polycarp* 6 to a soldier's "wages" (ὀψώνια) and "savings-with-interest" (ἄκκεπτα) adumbrate the theology of merit, but his doctrine is by no means Pelagian. He never for a moment entertains the notion that human beings could apart from God's grace accomplish something pleasing to God and worthy of a reward. In the very next chapter, he tells the Smyrnaeans, "I trust in grace that you are ready for a good deed in God's service."[89] The whole thrust of Ignatius's letters to the churches of Asia Minor is to oppose doctrines that distort "the grace of Jesus Christ that has come to us," whether by abstracting it from the historical economy and the realm of the flesh (docetism) or by reducing it to a mere addendum to the law of Moses (Judaization). Over against all such "heterodoxies" he insists that "the whole is faith and love, to which nothing is to be preferred" (*Smyr.* 6:1–2).

89. *Poly.* 7:3; cf. *Phld.* 8:1.

JUDAISM AND CHRISTIANITY

The Divine Economy and Its Historical Dimension

In the three previous chapters our exploration of the economy of redemption focused on three dimensions of unity, as suggested by the formulations found in *Magnesians* 1:2 and 13:1. The present chapter and the four that follow will consider the specifically historical dimension of the economy, in hope of disclosing what Ignatius means by referring to certain events of redemptive history as "mysteries," a term that he also applies to the eucharistic elements.[1]

Ignatius identifies Jesus Christ as "the door of the Father," through whom all who would enter "the unity of God" must do so, and he lists among those who have entered this unity "Abraham and Isaac and Jacob and the prophets and the apostles and the church" (*Phld.* 9:1). This catalogue suggests that a single people of God has been on pilgrimage down through history, at least since the time of Abraham. By naming the three patriarchs in chronological order, Ignatius hints at the way Israel's story unfolds generation by generation in the Old Testament. Rather than refer explicitly to Israel as a people, however, Ignatius singles out the prophets, for whom he seems to have a special affection (5:2). By distinguishing between "the apostles" and "the church," Ignatius does not, of course, exclude the former from the realm of the latter but rather indicates the apostles' unique status and historically foundational place within the church. He goes on to indicate that the decisive moment in salvation history consists of the "advent of the Savior, our Lord Jesus

---

1. *Eph.* 19:1; *Magn.* 9:1; *Tral.* 2:3.

Christ, his passion, and the resurrection" (9:2). The following outline of the historical economy thus emerges from this text.[2]

patriarchs → prophets → JESUS CHRIST → apostles → church

This schema prompts three sets of questions—namely, concerning Israel, concerning Jesus Christ, and concerning the church—to which I shall devote the remaining five chapters of this study. After some observations on Ignatius's view of the economy as a whole and a few other preliminaries, the present chapter will inquire into his understanding of the place of Judaism within the historical economy of redemption. How does he conceive of the relationship between the old covenant and the new covenant, between Israel and the church, between Judaism and Christianity? For the most part, modern scholarship has answered this question by filing Ignatius under "supersessionism." This classification, which tends to conflate a spectrum of views within early Christianity, does not do justice to what Ignatius actually says about Judaism. As usual, plenty of attention is given to his rhetoric, but he is not given his due as exegete and theologian. I shall endeavor to show that his teaching about the relationship between Judaism and Christianity, while not without lacunae, is carefully nuanced and theologically vital.

In chapters 7 and 8 we shall turn to the centerpiece of the historical economy: the Christ event. As I have already dealt with the basics of Ignatius's presentation of the Christ event at several points in earlier chapters, here I shall zero in on two specific topics. Chapter 7 will take up the paradox of word and silence, by which Ignatius conveys some of his most profound insights into the Christ event as God's self-revelation. We shall consider his description of the incarnation as the Word's having "come forth from silence" (*Magn.* 6:2), his teaching about the deeds "worthy of the Father" which Jesus performed "silently" (*Eph.* 15:1), and his puzzling reference to "three mysteries of a cry, wrought in the silence of God" (19:1). The paradox of word and silence also serves to illuminate the way believers appropriate and bear witness to God's self-revelation in Christ. Chapter 8 will focus on Jesus' baptism in the Jordan, which Ignatius references within two creedal formulae.[3] This "luminous mys-

---

2. The homily appended to the *Epistle of Diognetus* (chapters 11–12) contains a similar fivefold schema: "law ... prophets ... gospels ... apostles ... church" (*Diog.* 11:6). Describing how "the way of life" has been handed down, Irenaeus also employs a fivefold schema: "prophets ... Christ ... apostles ... church ... her children" (*Dem.* 98).

3. *Eph.* 18:2; *Smyr.* 1:1.

tery" can be viewed as a kind of hinge joining two panels of a diptych: the incarnation and the paschal mystery. And as such it discloses something of the unity of the Christ event. Moreover, by attending to the symbolism of the Lord's baptism and the lineaments of Ignatius's creedal formulations, we can also view this event as revelatory of the unity of the economy as a whole, inasmuch as it hearkens backward to the Old Testament story of creation, sin, and redemption, and forward to sacramental baptism and the life of the church.

Chapters 9 and 10 will take up two areas of Ignatius's theology that have been heavily criticized but not always well understood: ecclesiology and eschatology. Because Ignatius teaches no doctrine of apostolic succession, his ecclesiology is sometimes thought to lack a properly historical understanding of the church. He seems to prop up an excessively authoritarian view of ecclesial office by means of a Platonic or merely vertical schema. In order to correct this misperception, it will be necessary to proceed even more deliberately in chapter 9 than elsewhere, reviewing and critiquing recent scholarship and carefully examining a series of delicate ecclesiological issues. I will attempt to demonstrate that Ignatius actually has a well-rounded view of the church, according to which the Holy Spirit, the apostles, the word of God, the eucharist, and the threefold hierarchy all contribute to an ecclesial continuity between past and present, between heaven and earth, and between universal and local, each by virtue of its relationship to the person and event of Jesus Christ within the economy of redemption. In the realm of eschatology, Ignatius is sometimes thought to promote a radically realized and individualistic concept at the expense of the biblical understanding of eschatology as futuristic and communal. Corwin goes as far as to claim that he has abandoned the notion of Christ's second coming.[4] I shall address these issues in chapter 10, where I shall also draw together some of the principal threads of this study in order to demonstrate the inner coherence of Ignatius's understanding of the economy of redemption.

Twice Ignatius uses the word οἰκονομία in what was already becoming its technical sense, that is, to designate the "master plan" or "arrangement" by which God accomplishes the redemption of his creation.[5] Of course, Ignatius makes reference to the divine economy in

---

4. *St. Ignatius and Christianity*, 169, n. 20.

5. Eph. 18:2, 20:1. The word is used in a related sense in 6:1, and the cognate noun οἰκονόμος ("steward") is applied to Christians generally in Poly. 6:1. A related adjective, εὐοικονόμητος ("well arranged"), is found in Rom. 1:2. These are the only occurrences of this lexical root in the

many other ways throughout his letters, independently of this term, as for example when he employs creedal formulae. Though he never uses an expression such as "the Christ event," it is clear that he views the incarnation and the paschal mystery as demarcating a single event within a larger economy. Indeed it is the culminating and definitive event, the event that somehow subsumes the whole, such that the entire redemptive plan of God can be described as "the economy concerning the new man Jesus Christ" (Eph. 20:1).

Ignatius identifies Jesus Christ as "he who was with the Father before the ages and appeared at the end" (Magn. 6:1). This remarkably terse summary accomplishes three things simultaneously. First, while it distinguishes between θεολογία (that which eternally "was") and οἰκονομία (that which has taken place temporally according to God's plan), it places these alongside each other in such a way as to indicate their proper relation and the bond that unites them. The one who is eternally with the Father is the same one who has appeared in time. Second, though only one event in the entire economy is mentioned, the essential structure of the economy and the place of that one event within the whole are indicated. The economy has a teleological structure, and the appearing of the Son comes "at the end" (ἐν τέλει).[6] Naturally, this is not strictly or merely a matter of chronology. It indicates that the Christ event is the goal and point of perfection toward which the whole economy is oriented. Third, the specific nature and purpose of the economy is intimated: it is essentially a matter of the temporal manifestation of that which is eternal and invisible. Thus the entire Christ event is summed up by saying that "he appeared" (ἐφάνη). This is spelled out explicitly later in the same letter. The "one God" has "manifested himself [φανερώσας ἑαυτόν] through Jesus Christ his Son" (Magn. 8:2).

Taken out of context, Ignatius's creedal statements give the impression that the Christ event is the only event of any real consequence, or at least the only event of concern to Ignatius. That is not exactly correct. It is true that every other event finds its significance in its relation to the Christ event, but these other events do not thereby lose the quality of being true events. Every page in the Ignatian corpus bears witness to the

---

Ignatian corpus. Curiously, the two "strong" uses of the term οἰκονομία in Ignatius's *Ephesians* parallel the two "strong" uses in the New Testament, both of which are found in the Pauline Epistle to the Ephesians (1:10, 3:9).

6. Comparing *Magn.* 6:1 to 1 Pt 1:20 and *Shep.* 89:2–3 (= *Similitude* 9:12:2–3), Schoedel notes that the polarity between Christ's preexistence and his appearance in the last days "represented an early pattern for the bracketing of the world's history" (*Ignatius of Antioch*, 114).

moral and spiritual seriousness with which Ignatius regards human freedom and human action. The approach that he takes to his own martyrdom is an obvious case in point. At the same time, Ignatius by no means sets human freedom over against divine freedom. On the contrary, he is eager to submit his every plan to the divine "will" (θέλημα), from his plan to write a second letter to the Ephesians to his desire for martyrdom and eternal glory.[7] Ignatius discerns God's will at work everywhere: in the pleasant circumstances of Polybius's arrival at Smyrna (*Tral.* 1:1), as well as in the seemingly unfortunate circumstances that require him to set sail suddenly from Troas for Neapolis before he can finish writing to all the churches (*Poly.* 8:1). Man is truly free, but God's will encompasses every event and every use or abuse of human freedom. It is "the will of the one who wills all things that are" (*Rom.* sal.).

This all-embracing will of God gives the economy its unity and fullness. Certain events are prominent within the economy—above all, the Christ event with its pivotal moments—but the economy could hardly be limited to a certain number of events to the exclusion of others. It could not be one story among many, or one story within a larger story. Indeed, the economy is coterminous with the divine "will," which, as we have just seen, encompasses "all things." Better said, οἰκονομία and θέλημα are two ways to refer to the same reality. The theological tradition knows also a third term, not used by Ignatius: πρόνοια (*providentia*). And here it distinguishes two aspects: "providence" properly speaking, which resides eternally in the divine mind, and "governance," which is the temporal execution of providence.[8] This same distinction can be applied to either οἰκονομία or θέλημα as these terms are used by Ignatius. There is a "plan" or "will" in the divine mind eternally, and there is also the spatiotemporal execution of that plan or will.[9] In addition, Thomas Aquinas will emphasize the teleological character of divine providence. It is that by which God directs all created things to their particular ends and the entire universe to its final end.[10]

---

7. *Eph.* 20:1; *Rom.* 1:1; *Smyr.* 11:1.

8. Cf. *STh* I, q. 22, a. 3. In Scripture the term πρόνοια is used with reference to divine providence only in Wis 14:3—ἡ δὲ σή, πάτερ, διακυβερνᾷ πρόνοια (tua autem Pater gubernat providentia)—where one can already discern the aspects of "providence" proper and "governance." Among the apostolic fathers the term is used by Clement (1 *Clem.* 24:5) and Hermas (*Shep.* 3:4 [= Vision 1:3:4]).

9. The application of this distinction to the term οἰκονομία does not blur the prior distinction between θεολογία and οἰκονομία, for we still need to distinguish, within the eternal realm, between that which is strictly necessary (θεολογία) and that which is "willed" (οἰκονομία).

10. *STh* I, q. 22, a. 2.

These are later precisions, but they do no violence to Ignatius's thought. We sometimes find all three aspects—the eternal, the temporal, and the teleological—implicit in a single Ignatian formulation. For example, he describes the church at Ephesus as "predestined before the ages for enduring and unalterable glory forever, united and elect in true suffering [πάθος] by the will [θέλημα] of the Father and of Jesus Christ our God" (Eph. sal.). The master plan of God extends from eternity ("before the ages"), through the heart of the economy of redemption (union with Christ in his passion [πάθος]), and on to the eschatological goal of the economy ("enduring and unalterable glory forever"). These three elements, in a different order, are likewise found later in the same letter in a statement about the incarnation. When "God was manifesting himself humanly for the [eschatological] newness of eternal life," that which "had been [eternally] complete with God was receiving its [temporal] beginning" (19:3).

The divine self-manifestation in human form marks a great divide between two ages, the old and the new. The entrance of the "newness of eternal life" into the world nullifies the magic, ignorance, and malice of the "old kingdom" (19:3) and thus inaugurates the "last times" (11:1). With the advent of the incarnate Son, the eschatological τέλος of the economy is now already present in history. What this means for the economy as a whole is best appreciated in light of the fact that Christ is not only the τέλος but also the ἀρχή of all things, as the New Testament already affirms.[11] Ignatius's teaching seems to have helped Irenaeus of Lyons grasp this truth. Skillfully weaving together phrases from three Ignatian passages,[12] Irenaeus intimates that one can best approach the question of "why the advent of the Son of God occurred in the last times" (διὰ τί ἐπ' ἐσχάτων τῶν καιρῶν ἡ παρουσία τοῦ υἱοῦ τοῦ θεοῦ) by recognizing that in fact "the Beginning has appeared at the end" (ἐν τῷ τέλει ἐφάνη ἡ ἀρχή).[13] Ignatius himself is aware that the Jesus Christ who "appeared at the end" is also the divine Logos through whom and for whom all things are made.[14]

11. Col 1:18; Rv 3:14, 21:6, 22:13.
12. Eph. 11:1; Phld. 9:2; Magn. 6:1.
13. Haer. 1:10:3; SC 264.164. The verbal echoes are too striking to be the result of anything but Irenaeus's conscious borrowing from Ignatius's letters. For example, the use of παρουσία for the Lord's first advent (cf. Phld. 9:2) is rare in the second century (cf. BDAG, 781), and just a few lines earlier Irenaeus employs this word in the usual manner, i.e., to refer to the second coming, while using ἔλευσις for the first advent (Haer. 1:10:1). Moreover, throughout the chapter Irenaeus makes similar allusive use of various New Testament passages.
14. Magn. 6:1, 8:2; Eph. 15:1.

The definitive entrance of "the timeless one" (*Poly.* 3:2) into the temporal flux in the incarnation of the Logos is not only the decisive event within the historical economy, but also determines precisely what sort of historical character the economy as a whole will have. The economy is historical in the sense of unfolding along a temporal or "horizontal" axis, but it is not a mere chronological sequence of events. Its character is determined also by a "vertical" axis, which consists of God's *ad extra* activity and presence to his creatures. While this vertical dimension is most fully realized and manifested in the Christ event, it must not be confined to the Christ event, or even to a more inclusive series of discreet "interventions" of God within salvation history. Because God acts always and everywhere in the creation and conservation of creatures, and because his redemptive work is intimately and inseparably related to the order of creation, the entire economy of creation and redemption is imbued with this vertical dimension. Still, since "all things have been created through him and for him" (Col 1:16), it is the person and event of the incarnate Logos, "Son of Man and Son of God" (*Eph.* 20:2), who confers upon the economy of creation and redemption both its temporal-horizontal dimension and its transcendent-vertical dimension. The Christ event is both the decisive moment within time and the event that fills time with eternity. It is the *plenitudo temporis* (Gal 4:4).

Recent Scholarship on Ignatius's View of Judaism

The difficulty with which we shall have to wrestle in this chapter is one that has dogged Christian theology for two millennia. How are we to understand the place of biblical Israel, its religion, and its Scriptures within the economy of creation and redemption? Do these things belong to the old age, or to the new? At first glance, the answer seems obvious, at least for anyone who, like Ignatius, wishes to follow in the footsteps of the apostle Paul (cf. *Eph.* 12:2). Accordingly, Ignatius repeatedly uses the word "old" (παλαιός) to refer to the traditions and practices of Judaism, contrasting them with the "newness" that is Christianity, and his rejection of Judaism is based, at least in part, on the fact of its having already existed prior to the advent of Christ.[15]

Were this the whole story, however, everything associated with Judaism would be obsolete. Nothing of Israelite or Jewish origin would find

---

15. *Magn.* 8:1, 9:1, 10:2–3.

a place within Christianity. But this is not the case. As we have seen, while Ignatius qualifies the authority that the Scriptures of Israel possess for the church, he does not reject them outright (Phld. 8:2). In fact, he says that Christians ought to give heed to the law of Moses and the words of the prophets, and he quotes the books of Proverbs and Isaiah as Scripture.[16] Furthermore, he includes the patriarchs and prophets of Israel among those who have entered the unity of God and presents the prophets in an especially favorable light.[17] We might summarize Ignatius's position, then, by saying that he accepts the saints of Israel as members of the church and accepts the sacred books of Israel as authoritative Scripture for the church, but he rejects the practice of "Judaism" as something that has "grown old and sour" (Magn. 10:2). He claims that the Old Testament prophets were inspired by Christ's grace but insists that those who continue to practice Judaism (after the occurrence of the Christ event) act as if they have not received this grace (8:1–2).

Despite the apparent historical outline of the economy in Philadelphians 9:1 and Ignatius's positive statements about the prophets, Hans Conzelmann maintains that Ignatius's concept of οἰκονομία lacks a "salvation-historical perspective." He explains that in Ignatius's theology Israel's "prophets are simply claimed for Christianity," and "Judaism is simply replaced by Christianity."[18] Similarly, Schoedel writes, "'Judaism,' then, is not granted even a historically limited role in the unfolding of God's plan. Consequently Ignatius radically Christianizes the 'prophets.'"[19] While there is a large grain of truth in this opinion, it lacks proper nuance. I hope to show that Ignatius's theology does contain at least the rudiments of a salvation-historical perspective and that he does not view the relationship between Judaism and Christianity as a simple matter of "replacement." He does in fact accord Israel and Judaism a role in the unfolding of the divine economy. Moreover, while second-century orthodox Christian texts are often lumped together under the label "supersessionism," they actually display a range of approaches and viewpoints regarding the relationship between Judaism and Christianity. Whether Ignatius is correctly identified as a supersessionist depends, of course, on how one defines the term. It can be demonstrated, in any

---

16. Smyr. 5:1, 7:2; Eph. 5:3; Magn. 12:1; Tral. 8:2.
17. Magn. 8:2; Phld. 5:2, 9:1–2.
18. Hans Conzelmann, Gentiles—Jews—Christians: Polemics and Apologetics in the Greco-Roman Era, trans. M. Eugene Boring (Minneapolis, Minn.: Fortress Press, 1992), 259.
19. Ignatius of Antioch, 119.

case, that his view of Israel and Judaism differs in important respects from the views found in the *Epistle to Diognetus*, the *Epistle of Barnabas*, and Justin Martyr's *Dialogue with Trypho*, while it anticipates the incontrovertibly salvation-historical approach taken by Irenaeus in his *Demonstration of the Apostolic Preaching*.

In defending this thesis, however, I do not wish to associate myself with the claim that Ignatius takes a neutral view of Judaism. In an important recent study, Thomas A. Robinson rightly takes issue with those scholars who maintain that Ignatius's polemic against "Judaism" actually tells us nothing about his view of what *we* would call Judaism since it is directed solely at gentile Judaizers within the church.[20] According to Lloyd Gaston, for example, Ignatius sometimes refers to his opponents' doctrine as "Judaism" merely because they held a schismatic eucharist on Saturday (which happened to be the Jewish Sabbath) and supported their docetic Christology by appeal to the Septuagint (which happened to be the Bible of Hellenistic Judaism), practices that hardly qualify them to be labeled Jewish Christians, much less Jews.[21] Besides the fact that Gaston's interpretation depends on the dubious "one heresy" hypothesis, it fails to appreciate the rhetorical force of Ignatius's polemic. Critiquing Gaston's view, Robinson grants that gentile Judaizers within the church are the specific intended target of Ignatius's polemic, but he aptly notes that condemning their teaching and practices as "Judaism" is rhetorically effective only insofar as it involves a rejection of non-Christian Judaism too. "The stark and uncompromising language that Ignatius employs against Christian Judaizers of whatever stripe must carry over more broadly to Judaism as a whole if the language is to have the impact it is intended to have."[22]

There is, however, an element of truth in the view rejected by Robinson. Robinson rightly holds that Ignatius's polemic against the Judaizers can hardly be separated from his view of Judaism as such, but he is incorrect to suppose that the harsh rhetoric Ignatius uses to describe the Judaizers is simply transferrable to Judaism itself. He calls the Judaizers "treacherous wolves" (Phld. 2:2), "evil weeds" (3:1), and "tombstones" (6:1), but the worst he has to say about Judaism itself—in fact, the only

---

20. Thomas A. Robinson, *Ignatius of Antioch and the Parting of the Ways: Early Jewish-Christian Relations* (Peabody, Mass.: Hendrickson, 2009).

21. Lloyd Gaston, "Judaism of the Uncircumcised in Ignatius and Related Writers," in *Anti-Judaism in Early Christianity*, vol. 2, *Separation and Polemic*, ed. Stephen G. Wilson (Waterloo, Ont.: Wilfrid Laurier University Press, 1986), 38.

22. *Parting of the Ways*, 151.

negative thing he ever says about Judaism—is that it is "bad yeast, which has grown old and sour" (*Magn.* 10:2), a statement that I shall explain later in this chapter. At the same time, Robinson overlooks the fact that Ignatius has some rather positive things to say about Judaism, as for example when he calls the Old Testament priesthood "good" (*Phld.* 9:1). Ignatius's view of Judaism is neither purely positive nor purely negative. It is more complex than that. Robinson is closer to the mark when he says that, according to Ignatius, Judaism is "an actor whose part in the play is over."[23] What Ignatius condemns is not the practice of Judaism per se but the practice of Judaism "now" (*Magn.* 8:1).

Because Judaism's place in the economy of redemption is a complex matter, Ignatius cannot simply throw anti-Jewish rhetoric at the problem of Judaization within the church. Nor is he able to condemn his opponents merely by labeling their doctrine and practices as "Judaism," as if he could assume that his readers would hear that term pejoratively. In fact, it seems likely that the schismatics in Philadelphia and Magnesia were employing the term "Judaism" in a positive sense and making some headway in convincing other members of the community that the adoption of certain elements of Judaism by followers of Jesus was a good thing (see *Phld.* 6:1). Robinson convincingly argues that the Judaization of gentile Christians was a problem in the early church precisely because Judaism was to some extent still held in esteem and at least sometimes presented an attractive next step for former pagans who had come into contact with Jewish monotheism and morals via Christianity. "In some cases, converts to Christianity are likely to have found their curiosity about Judaism sparked, especially when, in the first three centuries, Judaism stood out impressively against the ragtag Christian movement."[24] Some early Christian leaders countered this threat by dismissing Judaism as "folly rather than piety" (*Diog.* 3:3), while others, such as Justin Martyr, resorted to outrageous blanket condemnations of the Jews.

> You have never shown yourselves to possess any friendship or love for God, or for the prophets, or for each other, but, as I am demonstrating, you are found always to have been idolaters and murderers of the righteous, so that you even went as far as to lay hands on the Christ. (*Dial.* 93:4)[25]

---

23. Ibid., 211.
24. Ibid., 65.
25. My translation of passages from the *Dialogue with Trypho* is based on the Greek text presented in Justin Martyr, *Dialogue avec Tryphon, édition critique*, ed. Philippe Bobichon, 2 vols., Paradosis 47 (Fribourg: Academic Press, 2003).

While Ignatius alludes to the fact that both the prophets and Jesus Christ "were persecuted," he does so using the passive voice (i.e., without identifying the persecutors) and without indulging in anti-Jewish rhetoric.[26] Instead, he constructs a carefully reasoned biblical argument aimed at convincing his readers that it is "incongruous" or "absurd" (ἄτοπον) for believers in Jesus to practice Judaism (*Magn.* 10:3). That this argument is rarely appreciated, or even understood, is attributable in part to the fact that modern scholars are, as a lot, not well disposed to expect serious exegesis and theology from Ignatius (due to the previously discussed unfair caricature of him as an amateur), and in part to the fact that the position that Ignatius takes with regard to the relationship between Judaism and Christianity will inevitably appear to be in bad taste when viewed from within a commitment to religious pluralism. Nonetheless, it is the burden of this chapter to give his argument a fair hearing.

Robinson has stepped into the fray of the debate over the question of "the parting of the ways" between Judaism and Christianity in order to clear the path for an honest interpretation of Ignatius's view of Judaism, a reading that is not distorted by "post-Holocaust and postcolonial supersensibilities."[27] He senses a hidden agenda behind interpretations that attempt to "sanitize" Ignatius's polemic, either by "muting" its harsh language or, failing that, by "deflecting" its reference away from Judaism itself and toward an aberrant form of Judaizing Christianity.[28] If it could be supposed that Ignatius was concerned only with ridding the church of Jewish practices while maintaining a "live and let live" attitude toward non-Christian Jews, the bishop of Antioch might even be claimed for the camp of those who, within the context of Jewish-Christian theological dialogue, advocate a "two-track" path to redemption: Jews are saved by following the law of Moses, while Christians are saved by faith in Jesus.

Whether we like it or not, this view of redemption would have made no theological sense to Ignatius. We can be quite certain that he would have regarded it as a trick of the devil (see *Phld.* 6:2). Jesus Christ is, and always has been, the "door of the Father," through whom one must enter the unity of God (9:1). Apart from Christ, it is not possible to come to eternal life (*Magn.* 9:2). The only hope of salvation that Ignatius would have held forth for non-Christian Jews is the same one he had for all human beings: "the hope of repentance" (*Eph.* 10:1), repentance "into

---

26. *Magn.* 8:2; *Tral.* 9:1.
27. Robinson, *Parting of the Ways*, 228, n. 89.
28. Ibid., 240, 223.

the unity of the church ... in order that they might live according to Jesus Christ" (Phld. 3:2). As Robinson correctly notes, when Ignatius says that "anyone who is called by any other name" than Christian "is not of God" (Magn. 10:1), he certainly does not intend to exempt non-Christian Jews![29]

Ignatius is the first writer we know of to use the word *Christianity* (χριστιανισμός), which either he or one of his contemporaries coined as a morphological analogue and semantic counterpart to the already existing word *Judaism* (Ἰουδαϊσμός). Ignatius sets the two terms opposite each other in order to make a sharp distinction between the two religions.[30] This fact by itself already suggests that his letters probably represent a significant moment in the story of the parting of the ways. This is an inconvenient truth for those who wish to suppose that the parting of the ways did not occur until at least the time of Constantine (i.e., two centuries after Ignatius's death) and who like to think of Judaism and Christianity, not under the metaphor of mother and daughter religions, nor even as older and younger siblings, but as "twins, joined at the hip."[31] What is most striking, and especially significant for the present inquiry, is the way Ignatius addresses the pressing pastoral issue of Judaization within the church, not only by making reference to Judaism as such, but by crafting a carefully nuanced theological argument about the historical-economic relationship between the two religions, an argument aimed at helping the Christians of Asia Minor to understand precisely why it is incongruous to confess Jesus Christ and practice Judaism.

Scripture's Salvation-Historical Perspective

Before proceeding to an analysis of Ignatius's argument, it is important to have a sense of why modern scholars would be concerned with a salvation-historical perspective in the first place, and why this might be a legitimate theological concern. To supply this sense, I shall sketch out two significant aspects of Ignatius's context within the history of Christian theology. First, I shall provide an overview of the place that a salvation-historical view of the economy has within the Old and New Testaments. While "salvation history" (*Heilsgeschichte*) is a modern construct, it rep-

---

29. Ibid., 151.
30. Magn. 10:3; Phld. 6:1. His only use of the term outside the anti-Judaizing polemic of Magnesians and Philadelphians is in Rom. 3:3, where it once again serves to mark out clearly the new religion, but this time over against "the world."
31. See Robinson, *Parting of the Ways*, 207–14.

resents an attempt—admittedly an imperfect one, open to misuse—to recover something essential to biblical revelation.[32] Second, I shall demonstrate that a spectrum of views of the relationship between Judaism and Christianity existed among orthodox Christian writers of the second century by surveying four representative texts: the *Epistle to Diognetus*, the *Epistle of Barnabas*, Justin Martyr's *Dialogue with Trypho*, and Irenaeus of Lyons's *Demonstration of the Apostolic Preaching*. These four texts afford us a panoramic view of the postapostolic church grappling with its identity vis-à-vis Judaism. In *Diognetus*, and to some extent also in *Barnabas*, we see how perilously close elements of the early church came to severing the Christian mystery from its roots in Israel and the Old Testament revelation. In the *Dialogue*, and more successfully in the *Demonstration*, we see serious theological attempts to preserve the real continuity between Judaism and Christianity, and between Israel and the church, without thereby compromising the definitiveness of God's redemptive self-revelation in Jesus Christ.

What do we mean by a "salvation-historical" perspective? A salvation-historical view accents the fact that redemption unfolds in time through the life of the community of believers and is deeply rooted in historical reality, as distinct from those views that tend to reduce redemption to a timeless truth, moral code, or sacramental system by which individuals achieve salvation. From a salvation-historical perspective redemption is perceived to have a narrative structure. Obviously Ignatius, as one who adheres to creedal Christianity, has this perspective at least insofar as he accents the fact that redemption was accomplished at a definite moment in history: "under Pontius Pilate and Herod the Tetrarch" (*Smyr.* 1:2). But does he also consider the historical events of the Old Testament to be constitutive elements of the economy of redemption? Does he view redemption as something that unfolds in stages leading up to the decisive event? And if so, how does he understand the events of Israel's encounter with God to be related to the Christ event?

The urgency of this question for contemporary Christian theology derives not only from the specific context of Jewish-Christian dialogue in the post-Holocaust era, but also from the widely held conviction that Christian theology must possess a salvation-historical perspective if it is to be authentically biblical, a conviction that is, in my opinion, one of the legitimate fruits of historical-critical biblical scholarship and its theo-

---

32. See Henning Graf Reventlow, *Problems of Old Testament Theology in the Twentieth Century* (Philadelphia: Fortress Press, 1985), 87–110.

logical appropriation. It is now generally recognized that ancient Israel habitually professed her faith in Yahweh by narrating his historical acts of covenant fidelity. These narratives, which are found throughout the Old Testament, admit of almost infinite variety but hover around a limited series of core events, especially the exodus from Egypt. As examples, one could point to the Song of the Sea in Exodus 15, the famous Wandering Aramean liturgical prayer of Deuteronomy 26, several "historical" psalms,[33] postexilic prayers of communal repentance in Nehemiah 9 and elsewhere, and Jesus Ben Sira's great catalogue of righteous ancestors in Sirach 44–50. Indeed, telling the big story seems to be the basic impulse behind the composition and compilation of Israel's Scriptures. Genesis through Kings constitutes a grand macronarrative of events from the creation of the world down to the exile, and the prophetic books are arranged in a roughly chronological order from Isaiah to Malachi, giving the Old Testament canon an overarching narrative framework, with non-narrative materials (law codes, wisdom literature, etc.) embedded or appended.

This basic salvation-historical structure of the economy carries over into the New Testament, where the Christ event is consistently presented as the great culmination of the Old Testament story and God's answer to the question with which Israel ended some of her most poignant communal laments: "How long, O Lord?"[34] Each of the evangelists has his own way to link the story of Jesus with Israel's story. Matthew, for example, employs a genealogy, a typological infancy narrative, a series of "fulfilled" prophecies, and a "new Moses" typology.[35] Luke-Acts, which may have been written by a gentile and for a gentile audience, embodies a sophisticated salvation-historical perspective, and the speeches of Stephen and Paul in Acts 7 and 13, respectively, suggest that the early church, at least when it addressed Jews and "god-fearers," presented its kerygma in the form of a narrative, beginning with the call of Abraham. In Romans, Paul introduces a three-era schema of salvation history, which will be taken up fruitfully by Augustine: from Adam to Moses (*ante legem*), from Moses to Christ (*sub lege*), and from Christ to the eschaton (*sub gratia*).[36] Even more strikingly, Paul's treatment of the question of Israel's place

---

33. Pss 78, 80, 89, 105, 106, 114, and 136.
34. Ps 89:46-51; Is 64:12.
35. See Dale C. Allison Jr., *The New Moses: A Matthean Typology* (Edinburgh: T. & T. Clark, 1993).
36. See Pamela Bright, "Augustine," in Jeffrey P. Greenman and Timothy Larsen, eds., *Reading Romans through the Centuries: From the Early Church to Karl Barth* (Grand Rapids, Mich.: Brazos Press, 2005), 69–71.

in the divine plan and her relationship to the church, in Romans 9–11, while not a narrative as such, has an implicit narrative framework: from God's promise to Abraham (9:7) to the eschatological salvation of "all Israel" (11:26), with the Christ event serving as the centerpiece (10:6–7).

It is important to recognize that the salvation-historical perspective of the biblical authors in no way reduces the economy to a mere series of contingent events, "history" in the positivist sense. Rather, the biblical authors of both testaments understand there to be a great *mysterium* at the heart of human history. This mystery is, of course, what we earlier called the economy's vertical dimension: the activity and presence of God, including his dealings with Israel. Already within Israel's Scriptures a kind of intratestamental typology points to the overarching unity that this vertical dimension confers upon the historical economy. Creation is a type of the exodus, and the return from exile is both a "new exodus" and a "new creation." Psalm 78 presents Israel's history as a riddle (v. 2), revolving around the seemingly endless friction between Israel's stubborn and rebellious "heart" (v. 8) and the merciful-wrathful fidelity of the Divine Shepherd (v. 52). This tension is finally resolved with the appearance of David, who shepherds Israel "in the perfection of his heart" (v. 72). As Israel passes through the crucible of the Babylonian captivity and, four centuries later, Antiochus IV's campaign of coerced Hellenization, it becomes increasingly clear that she will live out her vocation to be "a light to the nations" and attain the glory for which she is destined only by embracing the role of suffering servant.[37] The second chapter of Daniel introduces the word "mystery" (Aramaic *rāz*) into the biblical vocabulary and indicates that God will use something small and seemingly ineffectual—the purified remnant of Israel, presented as "a stone cut not by human hands" (v. 34)—to bring the long succession of arrogant and oppressive world empires to an end and establish his own kingdom on earth forever. The apocalyptic vision of Daniel 7 similarly presents the persecuted "saints of the Most High" collectively under the figure of "one like a son of man," who receives an everlasting kingdom from the Ancient of Days.

The biblical authors grasp the unity of the historical economy in a variety of ways. The patriarchal narratives of Genesis introduce the notion of promise and fulfillment, and the Priestly School frames the various Pentateuchal traditions within a schema of four covenants. The Deu-

---

37. The Servant of Yahweh's vocation is to be "a light to the nations" (Is 42:5, 49:6).

teronomic School will speak rather of a single covenant, the Mosaic one, setting the stage for Jeremiah's dramatic and fateful prophecy of a "new covenant," which is explicitly set over against "the covenant that I made with their ancestors on the day I took them by the hand to lead them forth from Egypt" (Jer 31:31–32). Repeating a single refrain twenty-six times, Psalm 136 drives home the point that Yahweh's "steadfast love" (*ḥésed*), which "endures forever," is the factor that holds together Israel's history. As we have already noted with respect to Psalm 78, Yahweh's steadfast love is matched in this regard only by Israel's persistent sinfulness, a point that is made also in a number of other prayers.[38] On the other hand, Jesus Ben Sira finds the coherence in Israel's story to lie in the virtues of the "men of steadfast love" (*'anšê ḥésed*) who have lived in every generation, from righteous Enoch down to Ben Sira's own contemporary, the high priest Simon, son of Onias (Sirach 44–50). Similarly but somewhat more mystically, the Wisdom of Solomon, which was composed in Greek near the very end of the Old Testament period, focuses on the activity of divine Sophia, who "in every generation passes into godly souls, making them friends of God and prophets."[39] In the New Testament the primary concern will be to demonstrate the continuity between Israel's story and the grace that has come into the world through Jesus Christ while at the same time indicating the radical "newness," perfection, and superiority of the latter. This goal is achieved by various appeals to prophecy and fulfillment, old covenant and new covenant, type and antitype, shadow and substance, and fear and love.

Drawing on the prophetic theme of the purification of the remnant of Israel (e.g., Zep 3:12–13), one also finds here and there in the New Testament intimations that all of God's seemingly futile efforts to "rear" Israel (cf. Is 1:2) have finally born fruit in "a people prepared" for the coming of the Messiah. Thus, in Luke's infancy narrative, Zechariah and Elizabeth (of priestly ancestry), Joseph and Mary (of the royal house of David), and Simeon and Anna (two prophets) embody the faithful remnant of Israel with its threefold office of priest, prophet, and king, while the ministry of John the Baptist represents a final stage in this long process of preparation (Lk 1:17). The notion that God actually "got somewhere" with Israel is admittedly a minor theme in either testament (both foreground the fact that most Israelites or Jews, especially the leaders,

---

38. Dn 9:4–19; Neh 9:6–37; Bar 1:15–3.8.
39. Wis 7:27; cf. 10:1–21.

were incorrigible), and this minor biblical theme will be all but drowned out in the Christian exegetical and theological tradition. It is, however, present in Irenaeus's view of human history as the long process of man's coming to maturity (*Dem.* 8–42), as well as in Aquinas's treatment of the old law, which makes much of Paul's reference to the Torah as "our pedagogue to Christ" (Gal 3:24–25).[40] This is the proper place within the theological tradition to locate what can be gleaned from modern biblical scholarship and the "history of religions" about Israel's theological and spiritual development within the Old Testament period. When the *Catechism of the Catholic Church* defines the "divine pedagogy" (a traditional category) in terms of God's revealing himself "gradually" and "by stages" in the Old Testament, leading up to his definitive self-revelation in Christ (CCC 53), it is providing a hermeneutical key for the theological appropriation of modern historical-critical insights.

When modern scholars such as Conzelmann speak of a "salvation-historical perspective," they probably have in mind a theological view of the economy that has integrated a positive appreciation for the various stages of Israel's development and that is cognizant of the distinctive character of Old Testament faith, a view that resists the temptation to conflate the religious consciousness of Israel's prophets with the postresurrection faith of the apostles. It would be anachronistic and unrealistic to expect exactly that from Ignatius or any other early Christian author, since they did not have the benefit of modern historical-critical tools and perspectives. Still, it is important to recognize that even the modern concept of *Heilsgeschichte* has biblical roots and a legitimate place within the theological tradition, and it is fair to ask whether, and to what extent, an author such as Ignatius is faithful to the biblical sense of salvation history and what sort of influence, negative or positive, his writings may have had on the church's ongoing attempt to understand its relationship to Israel and Judaism.

A Spectrum of Second-Century Views

When we turn to orthodox Christian writings of the late first and second centuries, we find that the New Testament's tendency to include at least some Old Testament events (beyond the creation of the world and man's original disobedience) as integral elements of salvation history

---

40. STh I-II, q. 91, a. 5; q. 98, a. 2 ad 1; q. 99, a. 6; q. 104, a. 3.

has dissipated to a remarkable degree and is present mostly by way of vestiges, as for example in the reference to "the holy vine of David your servant" in the eucharistic prayer preserved in the *Didache* (9:2). Broadly speaking, there are three types of reference to Old Testament materials in this body of literature. One type draws on Old Testament narratives, oracles, and especially parenesis as if they were directly addressed to the church, without in any way adverting to the fact that these texts first belonged to Israel. A second type aims to show how Old Testament passages prophesy or prefigure Christ, thus validating Christianity. And a third type draws on Old Testament condemnations of Israel in order to denigrate Judaism. Moreover, the culling of passages from the Old Testament quickly develops into a tradition of proof-texting that pays little regard to the Old Testament's narrative structure.

While these observations have some validity as generalizations, it is important to recognize that second-century Christian literature contains a spectrum of attitudes and approaches to the Old Testament and Judaism. In order to take proper stock of Ignatius's view, it will be helpful to sketch out this spectrum by describing the four texts previously mentioned, in the following order: the *Epistle to Diognetus*, the *Epistle of Barnabas*, the *Dialogue with Trypho*, and the *Demonstration of the Apostolic Preaching*.[41] At one end of the spectrum, *Diognetus* represents the approach that most decisively dissociates Christianity from its Jewish roots and concomitantly weakens the salvation-historical dimension of the divine economy. At the other end of the spectrum, Irenaeus's *Demonstration* represents the approach that most clearly embodies a salvation-historical perspective and strongly accents the continuity between old covenant and new covenant. While this schema is intended to illuminate a range of theological positions, rather than to measure anti-Jewish rhetoric, it is no coincidence that *Diognetus* is characterized by virulent anti-Jewish sentiment, while the *Demonstration* contains none at all.

Epistle to Diognetus

After dismissing all things Jewish as "ridiculous and not worth talking about," the anonymous author of the elegantly written *Epistle to Diognetus*

---

41. Obviously this is not an attempt to be exhaustive. Other texts, such as Melito's *Peri Pascha* and Tertullian's *Adversus Iudaeos*, might have been considered. Of the four texts chosen, only *Barnabas* is probably closely contemporary to Ignatius's letters. The *Dialogue* dates from the middle of the second century and the *Demonstration* from near its end. *Diognetus* is of uncertain date but is usually placed after A.D. 150.

launches into a tirade about the superstition, pride, and hypocrisy of the Jews (4:1).[42] He condemns the central practices of Judaism—Sabbath observance, circumcision as the sign of election, food laws and fasting, and liturgical seasons and feasts—ignoring the fact that the Old Testament presents all of these as divinely instituted. Indeed, he mocks the very idea that God would have commanded such things and concludes that "Christians rightly keep clear of the common triviality, deceit, fussiness, and boastfulness of the Jews" (4:2–6). The author never quotes the Old Testament, never mentions Abraham, Moses, David, or the prophets, and never so much as hints that there is any real connection or common history between Judaism and Christianity.

Inevitably, this theological severing of the church's ties to Judaism impacts the way the author views the divine economy and Christianity itself. Christians constitute a completely "new race," and their religion is a "new way of life" (1:1). Long ages ago God conceived "a great and inexpressible thought [ἔννοια]," which he confided to his Son but otherwise kept entirely secret, and he has revealed himself only quite recently and "all at once" (8:5–11). Prior to this event, no human being possessed knowledge of God (8:1). The author notes that God "seemed to neglect and show no concern for us" in ages past (8:10) and realizes that his addressee Diognetus will wonder why this new religion has appeared "now and not previously" (1:1). His answer to this question—God wanted us to recognize our inability to enter his kingdom on our own—is at root Pauline but has lost much of its force absent any reference to the giving of the law or the sending of the prophets (9:1).

The *Epistle to Diognetus* avoids outright Marcionism and retains some sense of a historical economy by rooting its understanding of the Christ event in the biblical doctrines of God, man, creation, and eschatology. Out of love, God the Father has created the cosmos and "subjected all things on earth" to human beings, whom he has "formed from his own image" and endowed with "reason" (λόγος). To them "he has sent his only-begotten Son," and he has promised to give "the kingdom in heaven to those who love him" (10:2).[43] Nonetheless, the Christ event itself

---

42. It is generally recognized that the epistle is preserved in chapters 1–10 (though its conclusion seems to be missing) and that chapters 11–12 constitute a homily on the Logos composed by a different author (Holmes, *Apostolic Fathers*, 689). Here we are concerned with the viewpoint of the author of the epistle only. For a dissenting view, affirming the literary unity of the entirety of *Diognetus*, see Horatio E. Lona, "Diognetus," in *Apostolic Fathers*, ed. Pratscher, 199–200.

43. This is arguably the only passage in the entire epistle that contains Old Testament echoes (i.e., of Psalm 8 and Genesis 1).

seems in danger of losing its historical moorings and concreteness. God sent "his Son" to reveal his love for us and "gave him up as a ransom" for our sins, "the righteous for the unrighteous, the imperishable for the perishable, the immortal for the mortal" (9:2). The author gives no indication of where or when this event occurred, does not mention any other persons involved (e.g., the virgin Mary or Pontius Pilate), never uses the name Jesus, never refers explicitly to Christ's crucifixion, much less to his flesh and blood, and does not so much as allude to his resurrection. The contrast to Ignatius's letters with their creedal formulae could hardly be starker.

Epistle of Barnabas

Next along our spectrum, the *Epistle of Barnabas* represents an approach that, while sharply dissociating Christianity from Judaism, and the church from the Jewish people, is able to retain and make extensive use of the Scriptures of Israel.[44] According to this author (whom, for the sake of convenience, we may call Barnabas), there is and always has been but one covenant.[45] This covenant was to be given to Israel through Moses, but since the Israelites showed themselves unworthy of it by worshipping the golden calf even before Moses had descended the mountain, they never actually took possession of it. They "lost" the covenant before they could receive it.[46] Moreover, Barnabas condemns the whole subsequent history of Jewish Torah observance as so much misinterpretation. For example, in declaring certain animals unclean, Moses "spoke in the Spirit," intending that we should not associate with people who are "like pigs," and so on, but the Jews foolishly took him literally to be prohibiting the use of these animals for food (*Barn.* 10:1-12). Similarly, God commanded Israel to "circumcise" their hearts and ears, but, led astray by "an evil angel," they continued to practice physical circumcision against God's will (9:1-5). Somewhat inconsistently, Barnabas maintains on the one hand that God never intended Israel to sacrifice animals to him, de-

---

44. For a general introduction, see Ferdinand R. Prostmeier, "The Epistle of Barnabas," in *Apostolic Fathers*, ed. Pratscher, 27-45.

45. For Barnabas's concept of covenant and interpretation of the Old Testament, see Oskar Skarsaune, "The Development of Scriptural Interpretation in the Second and Third Centuries— Except Clement and Origen," in *Hebrew Bible/Old Testament: The History of Its Interpretation*, vol. 1, *From the Beginnings to the Middle Ages (Until 1300)*, part 1, *Antiquity*, ed. Magne Sæbø (Göttingen: Vandenhoeck & Ruprecht, 1996), 384-87.

46. *Barn.* 4:8, 14:3-4; cf. Ex 32. Barnabas conveniently passes over Moses' intercession and the renewal of the covenant in Ex 33-34, as well as a thousand other passages that might have proven problematic for his theory!

siring instead the sacrifice of a contrite heart (2:4–10), while he claims on the other hand that the sacrifices of the Day of Atonement and the ritual slaughter of the red heifer prefigure the suffering of Christ (7:3–8:7).

Drawing on what was probably already traditional material, Barnabas employs a variety of typological and allegorical interpretive strategies in order to indicate that the Old Testament prefigures and prophesies Christ while it also gives spiritual commandments to Christians. Having inherited the one covenant, which Israel had forfeited, the Lord Jesus has given this covenant to his followers, thus establishing the church as "the people of inheritance" (14:4–5). Barnabas makes it abundantly clear that Israel and the church are two separate peoples, not one continuous people of God.[47] Just as his spiritual reading of the Torah entails the denial of the literal sense of many of its laws, so his affirmation of Christians as "the new people" involves a denial that Israel ever really was the people of God. Like Ignatius, Barnabas speaks positively of the patriarchs and Moses, and he even declares that the prophets received "grace" from Jesus Christ in order to foretell his coming.[48] These saints must, then, have been proto-Christians of some sort, and Barnabas does not clarify their relationship to the people of Israel as a whole.

Dialogue with Trypho

Occupying the next position on our spectrum is Justin Martyr's *Dialogue with Trypho*. Unlike Barnabas, Justin maintains that there are two covenants. Citing Jeremiah 31, he claims that Jesus Christ himself is the new covenant, whose arrival has rendered the old covenant obsolete (*Dial.* 11:2–4). As a result, the church is "the true spiritual Israelite stock" (11:5). Justin's interpretation of the Torah embodies a nascent distinction between the moral law and the ceremonial law.[49] The former is valid for all peoples of all times and is summed up in Christ's twofold commandment of love of God and love of neighbor, while the latter was imposed only on Israel and was temporary.[50] The ceremonial law has two distinct functions, however. Like Barnabas, and following in the same exegetical tradition, Justin interprets the various prescriptions of the ceremonial law as mystical prefigurements of Christ and the church. But unlike Barnabas, he maintains that these same prescriptions also had a literal meaning relevant to Israel's life prior to the coming of Christ. Thus, for example, the

---

47. Barn. 3:6, 5:7, 7:5, 13:1–6.   48. Barn. 8:4, 10:11, 5:6; cf. *Magn.* 8:2.
49. Skarsaune, "Development of Scriptural Interpretation," 400.
50. *Dial.* 93:1–3, 23:1–5.

Passover rite is both a temporary precept for Israel, recalling their deliverance from Egypt, and a type of Christ's passion.[51] The golden calf incident of Exodus 32 is a hermeneutical key for Justin, but not in the same way it is for Barnabas. The latter appeals to this event to justify his position that the Mosaic legislation had no real relevance to Israel's life (since they had forfeited the covenant), but Justin refers to the same event in order to indicate why God *did* give Israel the ceremonial law. Recognizing their hardness of heart and proneness to idolatry, God imposed temple worship and the sacrificial rituals in order to keep the Israelites from falling into further idolatry.[52] Somewhat surprisingly, Justin takes a permissive view regarding Jewish Christians who, "due to the weakness of their mind-set, wish to keep as many precepts of Moses as are still practicable ... while they also hope in this Christ" (*Dial.* 47:2).

Justin's explicit appeal to a dual sense of the ceremonial law (however incomplete or inconsistent his application of it might be) constitutes a crucial step within the Christian exegetical tradition, for it enables the church, in principle, to read the Pentateuch as Christian Scripture without thereby denying a literal sense to any part thereof. When it comes to the prophetic books and the Psalms, however, Justin maintains only a single sense (at least for certain passages). In order to demonstrate that Psalm 22, Psalm 72, and Isaiah 7 speak of Christ, he considers it necessary to deny that these texts can plausibly be taken to refer to David, Solomon, and Hezekiah, respectively, or to any other figure in Israel's history.[53] It does not occur to Justin to claim, as a modern theologian might, that a given prophecy has more than one level or stage of fulfillment within the divine economy. His exegetical procedure thus has the effect of weakening the salvation-historical dimension of large portions of the Old Testament. According to Justin, the Old Testament now belongs to the church, since Christians believe and obey it while Jews interpret it "carnally" (σαρκικῶς) and thus do not understand it.[54]

---

51. *Dial.* 40:1–3, 111:3–4.   52. *Dial.* 19:5–6, 22:1, 67:8.

53. See *Dial.* 97:4 (for Psalm 22), 34:7–8 (for Psalm 72), and 66:4 and 68:8 (for Isaiah 7). This becomes a stock argument among the apologists. Because certain Old Testament passages cannot plausibly be taken to have been fulfilled by any figure in Israel's history, they must refer to Christ (see Gregory Vall, "Psalm 22: *Vox Christi* or Israelite Temple Liturgy?" *The Thomist* 66 [2002]: 179). Even Irenaeus, despite his salvation-historical perspective, sometimes employs it (e.g., *Dem.* 49). Tertullian inverts the argument and makes it a principle for interpreting Old Testament prophecies: "If these things are coming to pass through Christ, they cannot have been prophesied of any other than him through whom we consider them to be accomplished" (*Adversus Iudaeos* 12:2; trans. Geoffrey D. Dunn, in *Tertullian*, Early Church Fathers [London: Routledge, 2004], 97).

54. *Dial.* 14:2, 29:2.

Justin perceives that the issue of the economic relationship between Judaism and Christianity, and between old covenant and new covenant, ultimately comes down to one question: Who is Israel? His answer to this question—namely, that the church is the true Israel—is more than enough to convince most scholars that he is a supersessionist, or as Oskar Skarsaune puts it, a "substitution" theologian.[55] Moreover, the *Dialogue with Trypho*, which, to be honest, is more of a harangue than a dialogue, breathes anti-Jewish sentiment almost from the first page to the last. It is hard to imagine the Christian reader who would not feel embarrassment at the abuse that Justin relentlessly heaps upon Trypho: "You are a people hardhearted, senseless, blind, and lame, sons in whom there is no faith" (27:4). Poor Trypho has fled from the Bar-Kochba Rebellion, which ended in A.D. 135 with Hadrian's decree forbidding Jews to step foot within Jerusalem, only to have Justin inform him that the whole reason circumcision was commanded for Abraham's descendants two thousand years earlier was to mark the Jews off from all other nations for the calamities they "now justly suffer"![56] What is to be noted here is not simply Justin's colossal lack of sensitivity, but the theological significance that Hadrian's decree has for him in conjunction with his millenarian expectations. Justin is convinced that the Jews have been providentially driven out of Jerusalem so that the church of all nations can quite literally *replace* them there upon Christ's return, which he expects to take place soon.[57]

Furthermore, according to Skarsaune, Justin supports his theology of replacement with a hermeneutics of replacement.

> Justin set a precedent for Christian hermeneutics with regard to the Jews and the Church that was to dominate for centuries to come: every negative and critical remark about Israel in the Bible was taken to describe in a timeless, almost ontological way, the very *nature* of the Jewish people. On the other hand, every positive saying about Israel was transferred to the Church, and the Gentiles were found to be believers almost by *nature* as well.[58]

To the extent to which this statement accurately summarizes Justin's hermeneutic, it certainly represents a dubious legacy with horrific consequences. I do not possess the expertise in this area to challenge Skarsaune's claim, and I suspect it contains at least a large grain of truth, in

---

55. Dial. 11:5, 123:5–7. Skarsaune, "Development of Scriptural Interpretation," 403. Similarly, R. Kendall Soulen, *The God of Israel and Christian Theology* (Minneapolis, Minn.: Fortress Press, 1996), 35.

56. Dial. 16:2–3, 19:2.   57. Dial. 80:1–2, 81:4.

58. "Development of Scriptural Interpretation," 404.

any case. But I would like to point out another element in Justin's view of the relationship between the Jews and the church, one that is easily overlooked and that to some extent counterbalances the replacement theme. Justin gives a second answer to the question "Who is Israel?" He interprets the "servant" prophecy of Isaiah 42:1–4 to mean that *Jesus Christ is Israel* and then goes on to note that Christians are members of Israel in and through Jesus Christ (Dial. 123:8–9). Ultimately this is the only answer to the question that can, from the point of view of Christian theology, do justice both to the unprecedented newness of the *novum* and to the real continuity between this *novum* and the *vetera*. We saw a similar idea in the *Epistle of Barnabas*, where it is said that Jesus Christ has inherited the covenant that Israel forfeited and that the church receives this covenant through Jesus Christ (Barn. 14:4–5). But Barnabas never explains why Jesus, humanly speaking, ought to have inherited the covenant intended for Israel. He never indicates any genealogical or historical continuity between the people of Israel and Jesus Christ. He never calls Jesus the "seed of Abraham" or "son of David"—in fact, he seems to deny outright that Jesus is the son of David (12:11)—and he never mentions the virgin Mary or the circumstances of Jesus' birth. For Justin, by contrast, Christ's physical origins from the virgin and, through her, from Abraham, Isaac, Jacob, and David, are quite important, not only because they indicate the fulfillment of prophecies such as Isaiah 7:14 and Micah 5:1–3, but particularly within the context of explaining in what sense Jesus Christ "is" Israel (Dial. 100:1–3).

Moreover, despite Justin's many references to Israel's hardness of heart, he is keenly aware of the fact that there were many righteous saints among the people of Israel during the Old Testament period and that since the proclamation of the gospel many Jews have entered the church. His interpretation of the apocryphal story about Isaiah being sawed in two—namely, as a prefigurement of the way Christ will divide the people of Israel into two parts, the worthy and the reprobate, at the final judgment (120:5)—seems to indicate that something more substantial than a tiny remnant of Jews will be saved. This recognition correlates with Justin's relatively positive view of the function of the Mosaic law within the life and history of Old Testament Israel. Not all the precepts were imposed in view of Israel's hardness of heart, he tells Trypho. Some were "ordained for the worship of God and the practice of righteousness" (44:2).

Since those who did the things that are universally, by nature, and eternally good are pleasing to God, they too will be saved through this Christ in the resurrection, as will the righteous who preceded them—Noah, Enoch, Jacob, and any others there were—along with those who acknowledge this Christ, the Son of God, who was before the morning star and the moon, and who to be born through this virgin of the stock of David submitted to being made flesh, in order that through this economy the serpent who gave wickedness its beginning and the angels who imitated him might be overthrown (45:4).

This passage is reminiscent of Ignatius's catalogue of those who enter the unity of God through "the door of the Father" (Phld. 9:1), for Justin clearly does not mean that righteous Israelites are saved by observing the law while Christians are saved by believing in Christ. Rather, he implies that those who by grace fulfilled the moral law participated in Christ, who is himself the eternal law. Elsewhere he says of those Jews who will attain salvation that "they are saved through him and have a share in him" (Dial. 64:3). Justin views Jesus Christ as the historical-economic link between faithful Israel and the church, who in the last analysis constitute a single people. Commenting on the promise given to Jacob, "In you and in your seed all the tribes of the earth will be blessed" (Gn 28:14), Justin explains to Trypho,

> He does not say this to Esau or to Reuben or to any other, but to those from whom the Christ was to come according to the economy that is through the virgin Mary. And if you were to study the blessing of Judah, you would see what I am saying. For the seed is divided after Jacob and descends through Judah and Perez and Jesse and David. And these things are a symbol indicating that some of your race will be found to be children of Abraham, and found to have a share in Christ. (Dial. 120:1–2)

It is clear from these passages that Justin's theology includes the rudiments of a salvation-historical perspective on the economy of redemption.[59] The *Dialogue with Trypho*, which will influence Irenaeus and Tertullian, and through them the entire theological tradition both east and west, contains both the most problematic and some of the more promising elements in early Christianity's attempt to understand its own relationship to Judaism. For better and for worse, it represents a mainstream position on this question.

---

59. Skarsaune theorizes that Marcion is the real intended target in chapters 56–60 of the *Dialogue* ("Development of Scriptural Interpretation," 408). Might not these other passages that accent the continuity between Israel and the church indicate that Justin is fighting on two fronts not only in chapters 56–60 but throughout the *Dialogue*?

Demonstration of the Apostolic Preaching

When we open Irenaeus's *Demonstration of the Apostolic Preaching*, we do not need to scour the text for intimations of a salvation-historical perspective on the economy of redemption.[60] The entire work is an embodiment of this perspective. After a few opening remarks about the *regula fidei* and the Trinity (*Dem.* 1–3a), Irenaeus recapitulates the Bible's own narrative of the divine economy, from the creation of all things to their restoration in Christ (3b–42a). His presentation of Israel's story is remarkably positive and devoid of anti-Jewish rhetoric. Physical circumcision is divinely instituted to signify Abraham's great faith (24). The golden calf incident, which figured prominently for Barnabas and Justin, is passed over in silence, and there is no hint that the laws of animal sacrifice constitute an accommodation to Israel's hardheartedness or proneness to idolatry.

On the contrary, Israel is a people designated for worship of the true God (21), and the tabernacle, with its vessels, altars, and ark, provides them with "a visible structure on earth of things that are spiritual and invisible in the heavens" (26), as does Solomon's temple later in their history (29). Of course, the tabernacle also prefigures Christ and the church (26), but since Christ *is* the heavenly Image come down to earth (97), there is a close organic connection between the significance that the tabernacle had for Israel's life during the Old Testament period and its prophetic significance for the church. The religious practices of Judaism are thus portrayed in a positive manner. Moreover, in recounting the passion of Christ, Irenaeus accents the fulfillment of prophecy and the Son's free cooperation with the Father's will, and he does not exaggerate or dwell on the role of the Jews (68–82).

As Irenaeus presents the history of redemption, its horizontal dimension (temporal unfolding) and vertical dimension (divine purpose and activity) are seamlessly interwoven. Israel's history is an integral and key element in the larger story of how God is leading fallen humanity back to communion with himself. Irenaeus acknowledges that many Israelites were guilty of sin and unbelief (27, 95), but he does not reduce their history to a foil for the church or to a mere series of prefigurements of Christ. Moses, the prophets, and John the Baptist did not simply foretell "the one who is to come"; their ministries were aimed at form-

---

60. Citations of this text, which has been preserved only in an Armenian version, are taken from Irenaeus of Lyons, *On the Apostolic Preaching*, trans. and intro. John Behr (Crestwood, N.Y.: St. Vladimir's Seminary Press, 1997). I have eliminated some of the excessive capitalization found in this translation. English translations of the *Demonstration* divide the text into chapters but not into verses.

ing and preparing the people of Israel for his advent.[61] By the action of the Holy Spirit "the prophets prophesied and the patriarchs learnt the things of God and the righteous were led in the path of righteousness" (6). But this high view of the *vetera* does not diminish the definitiveness and universality of the *novum*. "In the last times" the same Holy Spirit "was poured out in a new fashion upon the human race renewing man, throughout the world, to God" (6).

Since many of the theological emphases of the *Demonstration* seem to target Marcionism, there is little doubt that Irenaeus's positive depiction of Judaism, his extensive use of the Old Testament, and his accent on historical continuity in the economy of redemption are all intended to serve this apologetic purpose.[62] But these elements are far too deeply integrated into his overall theological understanding of redemption for us to suppose that they are mere apologetic devices. Besides, Irenaeus presents his account of the economy over against a variety of errors (*Dem*. 98–100), and twice he explicitly warns his readers against "turning back to the Mosaic legislation" (89, 95). Evidently Judaization was still a concern in the late second century. Accordingly, Irenaeus complements his focus on the unity of the historical economy with a detailed explanation of the sharp distinction between the old law and the "newness" of faith and love.[63] While he is obviously indebted to Paul here, Irenaeus makes effective use of several Old Testament passages as well, including the contrast between the "former things" and the "new thing" from Isaiah 43, the "new covenant" oracle of Jeremiah 31, and the "new heart" prophecy of Ezekiel 36.[64] The "new calling" accomplishes what the law never could: a "change of heart" (*Dem*. 94).

The contrast between the old and the new never becomes a dichotomy, however. Jesus, who has fulfilled the law, is himself "Lord of the law," and our faith in him is a recapitulation of the faith of Abraham (95). The beauty of the *Demonstration* lies in the way it shows forth both the definitiveness and superiority of the Christ event and its organic continuity with the Old Testament. This is not accomplished by means of a balancing act between two things that are in irreconcilable tension but by a proper understanding of their interrelation. The Mosaic law served a real salvation-historical function during the "intervening period," leading humanity by

---

61. *Dem*. 28, 30, 41.
62. Cf. Irenaeus, *Proof of the Apostolic Preaching*, trans. Joseph P. Smith (New York: Paulist Press, 1952), 22–27.
63. *Dem*. 87–96; cf. 35.   64. *Dem*. 89–90, 93.

means of fear back to the knowledge and worship of the Creator, whom they had abandoned and forgotten (8), but now that Christ has come, "we do not need the law as a pedagogue," since "we speak with the Father and stand before him" (96).

Irenaeus's exegesis of the story of Noah's three sons (Gn 9:18–27) conveys a profound insight into the relationship between Israel and the church. The curse upon Ham, who became the father of twelve nations dwelling in and around the Holy Land prior to Israel's arrival, represents the wickedness that proliferates among mankind (*Dem.* 20), but the "original blessing" given to Shem, which made him and his descendants worshipers of the true God, "flourished when it reached Abraham" and thence was passed down to the twelve tribes of Israel (21, 24). The blessing upon Japheth, that he should be "enlarged" and "dwell in the house of Shem," became fruitful much later when God "enlarged the call" to Japheth's descendants, the gentiles, through the ministry of the apostles. The "fruit" of this blessing is the Holy Spirit, by which the church receives the "rights of the firstborn" in Jesus Christ and "dwells in the house of Shem," which is to say, enters into the inheritance of the patriarchs (21, 42a). This does not mean that the church *replaces* Israel in the house of Shem, but rather that *in Christ* the one people of God has been enlarged to include both Jews and gentiles (51). Like Justin, Irenaeus says that Jesus Christ *is* Israel (97), thus establishing a clear economic link between Old Testament Israel and the church.

For Irenaeus, even more than for Justin, the virgin Mary plays an indispensable role in the economy of redemption. To fulfill this role she must not only be "of the race of Adam" but also "of the race of David and Abraham" (33, 59). As Adam was taken from the virgin earth, so Christ "received the same economy of enfleshment" from the virgin Mary in order that in him man might be restored to the image and likeness of God (32).[65] Her "virginal obedience" undoes the disobedience of Eve and complements the "obedience unto death" by which Christ recapitulates Adam (33–34). Since Christ's "economy of generation according to the flesh would be among the Jews" (58) and "his flesh would blossom from the seed of David" (30), Irenaeus places an extraordinary emphasis on

---

65. I have modified the translation slightly here to give a more literal rendering to the phrase οἰκονομία σαρκώσεως ("economy of enfleshment"), which Behr judges to have been in Irenaeus's original Greek. Behr's rendering is "arrangement of embodiment" (Irenaeus, *On the Apostolic Preaching*, 61), and Smith's is "scheme of his incarnation" (Irenaeus, *Proof of the Apostolic Preaching*, 68).

Mary's descent from Abraham and David.[66] She is the "shoot" from Jesse, and Christ's flesh is the "flower" from this shoot (59). In his passion, this flesh becomes "the fallen tabernacle of David," and in his resurrection it is "raised up" in fulfillment of Amos 9:11 (Dem. 38, 62). Christ's Israelite flesh is, in Tertullian's expression, the "hinge of salvation,"[67] and so in a very real sense the unity of the economy hinges on Mary the daughter of Israel. A theology in which Mary and Israel play such an essential role cannot in the last analysis be a theology of "replacement."

Supersessionism and Ignatius's Place on the Spectrum

If we define "supersessionism" as any theology that views Christianity as superior to Judaism—especially one that considers observance of the ceremonial laws of the Pentateuch to be obsolete, if they were ever in force to begin with—all four texts just surveyed qualify as supersessionist, as do Ignatius's letters. For that matter, the entire corpus of orthodox early Christian literature is at least implicitly "supersessionist" in this broad sense. It is impossible to be in real theological continuity with the New Testament and not consider Jesus Christ to be God's definitive self-revelation and thus the fulfillment of Israel's covenant with Yahweh. But it makes a very great difference for Christian theology—and, for that matter, for Jewish-Christian theological dialogue, though that is not our immediate concern—whether one dismisses Judaism as superstition, giving it no place whatsoever in the economy of revelation (as in *Diognetus*), or denies that Jewish Torah observance ever had any validity, while appropriating Israel's Scriptures for Christianity (as in *Barnabas*), or, again, casts aspersions on Jews and Judaism generally, while retaining some sense of economic continuity between Israel and the church (as in the *Dialogue*), or, finally, adopts an essentially positive view of Israel and Judaism, while holding that Jesus Christ has not only fulfilled the promises to Abraham and David, thus rendering Torah observance obsolete, but has "recapitulated all things" and thereby restored humanity to communion with God (as in the *Demonstration*).

However, if one defines "supersessionism" as any theology that views Christianity as having replaced Judaism, strictly speaking, and the church as having supplanted Israel as the people of God, none of the texts just surveyed quite qualifies. For the author of *Diognetus*, Christi-

---

66. Dem. 36, 40, 63.
67. *De resurrectione mortuorum* 8:2; CCSL 2.931.

anity is apparently the only divinely revealed religion and thus does not really *replace* anything. Similarly, since Barnabas holds that there is only one covenant and that Israel was disqualified before it could receive this covenant, thus depriving observance of the ceremonial Torah of any historical legitimacy, it is doubtful also in this case whether one can meaningfully speak of replacement. Meanwhile, in the Dialogue, and especially in the Demonstration, too much of Judaism is taken up into Christianity, and there is too much historical continuity and interpenetration between Israel and the church, for one to speak of replacement or supersession. This may seem to be a quibble over semantics, but if one's goal is to gain a proper biblical understanding of the mystery of redemption, it is an all-important distinction. Among second-century attempts to deal theologically with the relationship between Judaism and Christianity, Irenaeus's Demonstration represents the high-water mark, in my opinion, not simply because it lacks anti-Jewish rhetoric and is therefore likely to be somewhat less offensive to Jews than other attempts, but because it is arguably the most faithful to the New Testament and the most profound and cohesive theologically.

Where are Ignatius's letters to be located within the spectrum of second-century orthodox Christian views of the relationship between Judaism and Christianity? Since Ignatius treats the Old Testament as authoritative Scripture and considers Israel's patriarchs and prophets to be members of the people of God, his view is sharply distinct from that of Diognetus. Furthermore, as I shall demonstrate below, he considers the institutions of Judaism, including priesthood, Sabbath, and presumably circumcision, to have been divinely instituted, "good" per se, and in force right up till the advent of Jesus Christ. This distinguishes him not only from Diognetus but also from Barnabas. The relatively significant place in the divine economy that Ignatius assigns to the virgin Mary, and to Christ's descent from David through her, aligns his approach with those of Justin and Irenaeus while distinguishing him still further from Diognetus and Barnabas. Finally, in common with the Demonstration and over against the other three texts, Ignatius's letters are devoid of anti-Jewish rhetoric while at the same time indicating that Christians are not to observe the Mosaic legislation. Justin's opinion, according to which Jewish Christians (at least) may continue to observe the law, is one that Ignatius, like Irenaeus, would certainly reject. It is precisely the witness of Jewish Christians who have left behind the "old practices" of the law in order to "live according to Christianity" that Ignatius holds up to his gentile readers, so that they may see that it is "incongruous" to practice Judaism while confessing Christ.[68]

In sum, Ignatius's view of the relationship between Judaism and Christianity is most akin to that of the *Demonstration*. Admittedly, however, his presentation is less developed and contains significant lacunae. For example, while Ignatius indicates that Israel's prophets were inspired by the Holy Spirit and lived by the grace of Christ, he does not give us a sense of how God formed and prepared Israel as a people for the coming of Christ in anything like the way Irenaeus does.

Judaism and Christianity in Ignatius's Letters

A Response to Two Heresies

We may at this point return to the text of Ignatius's letters and begin our more detailed analysis by recalling that his teaching regarding the relationship between the Old Testament and the gospel, between Israel and the church, and between Judaism and Christianity was formulated within the context of his pastoral response to the two heresies that he found to be threatening the churches of southwestern Asia Minor: docetism and Judaization. Ignatius's polemic against the first of these, which is found in *Trallians* and *Smyrnaeans*, is well served by his comprehensive view of the divine economy as encompassing the entire cosmos of "things visible and invisible," the divinely willed sweep of temporal events from creation to eschaton, and the orders of creation and redemption. The challenge of countering docetism evidently led Ignatius to reflect deeply on man as a creature composed of "flesh and spirit," whose redemption would entail the sanctification of his entire being. As a result, man's interior thoughts and intentions but also his concrete bodily-temporal actions possess real moral and spiritual gravitas. Ignatius obviously gave serious thought, as well, to the church's creedal affirmations pertaining to Christology and soteriology, and he came to understand the divine plan of salvation precisely as "the economy concerning the new man Jesus Christ" (Eph. 20:1).

In response to the docetists' blasphemous failure to confess that Jesus Christ was "flesh-bearing" (*Smyr.* 5:2), Ignatius stresses that the nativity, passion, and resurrection of Christ "truly" happened, using the adverb ἀληθῶς a total of nine times in *Trallians* 9 and *Smyrnaeans* 1–2.

---

68. *Magn.* 9:1–10:3; cf. *Dem.* 89–96.

Over against the docetists' lack of adherence to the Old Testament and the gospel, their neglect of the corporal works of mercy, their failure to confess that the eucharist is the flesh of Christ, their consequent withdrawal from the eucharistic assembly and community prayer, and their disregard for the visible ecclesiastical hierarchy, Ignatius promotes attentiveness to the law of Moses and the prophets "and especially to the gospel," the practice of charity, sacramental realism, hierarchically sanctioned assemblies, and submission to the bishop (Smyr. 5–8). In every respect, in other words, Ignatius stresses the importance of what is visible, concrete, and actual in contrast to the docetists' tendency to reduce the Christian faith to something purely "spiritual." It may even be that the docetists who were attempting to infiltrate the churches of Tralles and Smyrna were already on the road to gnosticism, since Ignatius implies that they were overly concerned with speculations about heavenly beings and "puffed up" with a sense of their own knowledge.[69] Ignatius, for his part, was not in any danger of reducing Christianity to a form of gnosis or to a myth. He experienced the Christian faith in concrete ways: in his intimate fellowship with other believers, in the eucharistic flesh and blood of Christ, in the fetters and chains that held him (his "spiritual pearls"), and in his own body, which he kept as a temple of the Lord and which he was preparing to offer as a worthy sacrifice.[70]

Therefore, when Ignatius came to deal with the Judaizing heresy—the second major threat to the churches of Asia Minor, which he addresses in *Magnesians* and *Philadelphians*—simply lopping off the Old Testament, or the history it narrates, in order to declare Christianity independent of Judaism was not a viable option. He could not, in the manner of *Diognetus*, simply dismiss the practices of Judaism—circumcision, Sabbath, animal sacrifice, and the festival calendar—by ridiculing them as so much "superstition."[71] Nor could he, in the manner of *Barnabas*, retain the Old Testament as a sacred text while adopting an abortive view of Israel's history such that everything that occurred between the golden calf incident and the birth of Christ, apart from the actual writing down of the inspired texts, becomes entirely irrelevant to God's plan of redemption. Under such a view, the mystical sense of the Old Testament and the Christ event itself are both extrinsically related to the religious history that the Old Testament seems to narrate. Had Ignatius gone down either of these

---

69. Tral. 5:1–2; Smyr. 6:1.
71. Diog. 1:1, 3:1–4:6.

70. Eph. 11:2, 15:3; Phld. 7:2; Rom. 4:2.

paths, his conception of a comprehensive and unified divine economy would have collapsed, and his entire theology along with it, for the Pauline, Johannine, and Matthean writings and traditions upon which he had based his understanding of the Christian mystery all witnessed to an uninterrupted redemptive plan of God unfolding within history.

Nor could he have done full theological justice to the Christ event qua event. If the incarnation is the entrance of the Eternal into the temporal, such that Jesus' birth, death, and resurrection were events that truly involved God himself, in the most direct sense imaginable, as an actor within history, then this complex of events, this Christ event with its temporal thickness, must in some sense take up all other events into itself. It must be simultaneously the whole economy and one event within the economy. Ignatius does not speak of a "summing up" or "recapitulation," the way Paul already had (Eph 1:10) and Irenaeus later would (*Dem.* 6, etc.), but some such notion is implicit, as we shall see in the next chapter, in the way he relates the moments of the Christ event to each other and to the sacramental life of the church.

At the same time, a correct understanding of the Christ event likewise precluded any sort of compromise with the Judaizers. If Jesus Christ is the eternal Son and Logos of God, the timeless, invisible, intangible, and impassible one (*Poly.* 3:2), he cannot be simply another of the prophets, even the greatest of them, nor can his descent into the world be simply one event among others and on the same plane as other events. Had Ignatius answered the docetists by reducing Christ to a mere creature and making the events of his life but one more stage in the story of Israel and the world, he could not also have refuted the Judaizers. The observances of the Mosaic law would still be in force.

Ignatius was too deeply immersed in the apostolic traditions and understood them too well to be tempted either in a proto-Marcionite direction or in an Ebionite-like direction. He knew Matthew's theology of "fulfillment," John's doctrine of the enfleshed Logos, and Paul's theology of "newness," and, unlike some moderns, he did not find these to be mutually incompatible views.[72] In fact, facing the Judaizing and docetic heresies simultaneously probably helped Ignatius to clarify for himself how the various elements of the gospel cohere and how the various streams of the gospel tradition complement one another. It is necessary in principle to affirm both that the persons and events of the Old

---

72. *Smyr.* 1:1; *Magn.* 8:2, 9:1; *Eph.* 19:3.

Testament and the Christ event belong to one continuous and unified historical economy of redemption and that the Christ event is absolutely unique and definitive within that economy.[73] As Karin Bommes puts it, Ignatius's view of the relationship between the Old Testament and the gospel reflects "the fundamental tension of Christianity itself—the transcendent God becomes man and enters history."[74]

Old Testament Events

Granted, then, that Ignatius's view of the economy, coupled with his Christology, would permit him neither to dissolve the historical link between Judaism and Christianity nor to reduce the Christ event to the level of Old Testament events, it remains to be seen how exactly he does treat the history of Israel and the institutions of Judaism. For the moment, let us ask: Do his letters contain positive indications that he viewed the events narrated in the Old Testament as constitutive elements in the divine economy? We have already seen at least two statements from the letters that may point to an affirmative answer to this query. First, we heard Ignatius say that Christ "was with the Father before the ages and appeared at the end" (*Magn.* 6:1). While the expression ἐν τέλει ("at the end") is more teleological than strictly chronological, the statement as a whole probably implies a long temporal sequence of events in which Christ's advent represents the culminating point. Second, we noted Ignatius's reference to "the will of the one who wills all things that are" (*Rom.* sal.), on the basis of which it seemed safe to assume that he conceives the divine economy as encompassing the entire spatiotemporal realm. These two statements make it a priori likely that Ignatius would include, at the very least, God's creation of the world as an important event within the divine economy. It is somewhat surprising, then, to find that Ignatius makes only one clear reference to this event.

Still, that one reference tells us a great deal. Ignatius affirms clearly that Jesus Christ, our "one teacher," is he who in the beginning "spoke and it came to be" (*Eph.* 15:1). This statement, with its neat double allusion to Psalm 33:9 and Genesis 1:3, strongly suggests that Ignatius's view of creation is biblical, and specifically Logo-centric. By drawing God's act of creation-by-speaking into relation with the incarnate Son's

---

73. "He was faced by some who denied or ignored history, and by others who foreshortened history by resisting the genuinely new that could enter it" (Corwin, *St. Ignatius and Christianity*, 103).

74. *Weizen Gottes*, 118 ("die Grundspannung des Christentums selbst—der transzendente Gott wird Mensch und geht in die Geschichte ein").

revelatory activity as divine teacher, Ignatius hints that he views creation and redemption as integral elements in a single divine economy (as opposed to viewing creation and redemption as two extrinsically related dispensations). Indeed, the entire divine economy is unified in the person of Christ, whom Ignatius elsewhere identifies as God's Logos (*Magn.* 8:2). The paucity of explicit references to the creation of the world in Ignatius's letters reflects the fact that his exhortations to the churches of Asia Minor and Rome *presuppose* a biblical view of creation.[75] Even if we did not have *Ephesians* 15:1, we could assume that Ignatius regarded the creation of the world as an integral event in the divine economy. Such a view is presupposed in his references to "things visible and invisible," in the moral seriousness with which he constantly speaks of man as a creature composed of "flesh and spirit," and above all, in his polemic against docetism.

Ignatius's Logo-centric view of creation and redemption, in turn, makes it a priori likely that he also considered God's self-revelatory approaches to Israel in the Old Testament to be important elements in the divine economy. We should not be surprised, then, to find that Ignatius holds Israel's prophets in high regard, precisely as recipients of divine revelation. The "most godly prophets" were "inspired" by the grace of Christ (*Magn.* 8:2). They "awaited him righteously" and "expected him as their teacher" (9:2). Their preaching led up to his coming and anticipated the gospel, so that their writings are authoritative and should be carefully heeded by Christians.[76] But for Ignatius the prophets are much more than heralds of Christ's coming and authors of Sacred Scripture. They are our beloved brethren *in* Christ. Though they lived long before his advent, they were already "disciples" of Jesus "in the Spirit" and even "lived according to Christ Jesus."[77] They believed and hoped in him and, as such, "were saved," so that at his advent he himself "raised them from the dead."[78] Along with the patriarchs, the apostles, and the whole church, they have entered into the "unity of God" through "the door of the Father" (Phld. 9:1). Ignatius is emphatic in according the prophets full status within the "unity of Jesus Christ." Christians should "love the prophets" because they are "saints worthy of love and worthy of admira-

---

75. Camelot notes the contrast in this regard between Ignatius and his close contemporaries, Clement of Rome and Hermas, who seem to have felt a greater need to affirm explicitly God's creation of the cosmos (*Ignace d'Antioche*, 20).

76. Phld. 5:2, 9:2; Smyr. 5:1, 7:2.   77. Magn. 9:2, 8:2.

78. Phld. 5:2; Magn. 9:2.

tion" who have been "testified to by Jesus Christ" (5:2). Though the prophetic writings are subordinate to the gospel,[79] the prophets themselves have been "numbered together" with us "in the gospel of the common hope" (5:2).

The history of Israel during the Old Testament period does, then, have some prominence within the divine economy as conceived by Ignatius. Indeed, this period seems to be more than a mere preparation or prefigurement of the fullness to come. Not only does the Christ event reach forward to have its salvific effect upon the generations of the church, the "grace" of Jesus Christ also flows backward, as it were, from the Christ event to touch the lives of the Hebrew saints.[80] As we have seen, Ignatius sketches out a compelling diachronic diagram of one people of God, from Israel's patriarchs to the church of his own day, with Jesus Christ as the central figure and the prophets and apostles as authoritative pillars standing, as it were, on either side of Christ (Phld. 9:1).

This positive initial assessment of the place of ancient Israelite history within Ignatius's conception of the divine economy needs to be qualified, however. Apart from the one glancing reference to the creation of the world (Eph. 15:1), Ignatius does not mention a single discrete event from the Old Testament: no flood, no offering of Isaac, no exodus from Egypt or sojourn in the wilderness, no building of the temple, no exile or return from exile. In this respect the Ignatian corpus stands in marked contrast to the New Testament, where we find frequent references and allusions to the *magnalia Dei* recounted in the Old Testament. To some extent this may be accidental. We are, after all, dealing with a small corpus of parenetic letters, which, however theologically rich they may be, were not intended to provide a complete theological picture. Even in *Ephesians*, the longest and most ambitious of the seven, Ignatius claims only to have "begun" to describe "the economy concerning the new man Jesus Christ." His hope to write a second letter, which would fill out this description, was, as far as we know, never realized (20:1). Still, it is curious to note that, while Ignatius mentions several individual persons and groups of persons from the Old Testament (Abraham, Isaac, Jacob, Moses, David, the priests, and the prophets), he never so much as alludes to a specific event from any of their lives. For example, Ignatius refers to David five times, but in every case it is strictly a question

---

79. Smyr. 7:2; Phld. 8:2, 9:2.
80. Magn. 8:2; Phld. 5:2; cf. Barn. 5:6.

of Christ's human origins from the "seed" or "stock" of David.[81] There are no allusions to David's military career, his kingship, or his plans to build a temple. When it is a question of the birth, passion, and resurrection of Christ, Ignatius very strongly emphasizes that we are dealing with real, historical events, "truly and certainly accomplished by Jesus Christ" (*Magn.* 11:1), but when it comes to the place of the ancient Israelites within the divine economy, there is no such emphasis. This is where we must recognize a significant element of truth in Conzelmann's opinion that Ignatius's concept of οἰκονομία lacks a "salvation-historical perspective."[82]

Old Practices and Perfect Newness

Ignatius's treatment of the relationship between Judaism and Christianity in *Magnesians* 8–10 hinges on a carefully nuanced contrast between the "old" and the "new." The apostles and other Jewish Christians, who once "conducted their lives in accord with old practices," rightly gave these up, not because they were wrong ever to have lived this way, but because "they came to a newness of hope" (9:1). Judaism is "bad leaven," not because it always was so, or is so absolutely, but because it has "grown old and has soured," so that all persons should now turn to "the new leaven, which is Jesus Christ" (10:2).[83] Ignatius has prepared for this teaching with a series of creedal affirmations that present the Christ event as the pivotal moment in history: God's definitive self-manifestation in his incarnate Logos.[84] The real, historical accomplishment of the Christ event (11:1) means that Christians are living in the epoch of the "now" (νῦν), the time of fullness and grace.[85] The problem with Jewish observances is not that they are superstitious or that they represent mere accommodations to a stiff-necked people, but that they have served their function and their time has passed. They have given way to something "better" (7:1). "For if we are living according to Judaism even up till now [μέχρι νῦν], we are confessing that we have not received grace" (8:1). This is the guiding Pauline principle and central thesis statement of Ignatius's polemic against Judaization in *Magnesians*.

Immediately after making this statement, Ignatius forestalls the objec-

---

81. *Eph.* 18:2, 20:2; *Tral.* 9:1; *Rom.* 7:3; *Smyr.* 1:1.
82. *Gentiles—Jews—Christians*, 259.
83. Here Ignatius draws on 1 Cor 5:6–8, and perhaps also Mt 16:12 and Heb 8:13.
84. *Magn.* 6:1, 7:2, 8:2.
85. This use of the term "now" has deep roots in the New Testament and is especially characteristic of the Pauline letters (*TDNT* 4.1106–23, esp. 1116–18).

tion that by rejecting the present practice of Judaism he is thereby also rejecting the Old Testament. He eagerly confesses that Israel's "most godly prophets" were "inspired by [Christ's] grace" (8:2). By using the word χάρις in both 8:1 and 8:2, Ignatius seems to identify the "grace" of Old Testament prophetic inspiration with the "grace" that has become available historically in the fullness of time, and thus he leads us directly into the "fundamental tension" (*Grundspannung*) to which Bommes has referred. Ignatius is moving between a linear, chronological view of the divine economy and a transcendent or "vertical" view without attempting to resolve the inherent conceptual tension. Later in *Magnesians*, he will make the strongly worded point that it is "incongruous" (ἄτοπον) to "speak Jesus Christ and practice Judaism" simultaneously. Presumably Ignatius means that it is incongruous to do so *at the present time*, since he backs this affirmation up by appealing to a neat linear-historical view of the divine economy: "for Christianity did not come to believe in Judaism, but Judaism in Christianity" (10:3). This striking affirmation may imply that Judaism served as a preliminary stage that somehow prepared for Christianity. Judaism is clearly the lesser of the two religions, but as such it is at least something of positive value. All the same, if this statement reflects a salvation-historical perspective according to which Judaism and Christianity are two distinct but related stages within a single economy of redemption, Ignatius does not work out the ramifications of this perspective. In particular, he fails to explain why it was not likewise incongruous *for Israel's prophets* to proclaim Jesus Christ and practice Judaism simultaneously.

On the basis of what Ignatius does tell us, it may be instructive to pursue further this issue of the prophets' puzzling status relative to the two religions. If the prophets were already "disciples" of Jesus Christ (*Magn.* 9:2), why did they need circumcision, Sabbath, and the other observances of Judaism? And if the answer to this question is that they did not in fact need these, what positive role, if any, did such institutions play in the divine economy? Is there any essential difference, in Ignatius's view, between the dispensation of grace available to the Old Testament prophets and that which is available "now" in Jesus Christ? When he uses the phrase "to live according to Christ Jesus" to describe both the spiritual life of the prophets and that of Christians, and even says that the prophets "believed in" Jesus and "were saved," Ignatius seems to be at pains to eliminate any real difference.[86] This is, no doubt, what

---

86. *Magn.* 8:2; *Tral.* 2:1; *Phld.* 3:2, 5:2.

Schoedel has in mind when he says that Ignatius "radically Christianizes" the prophets.[87] On the other hand, Ignatius also emphasizes the prophets' chronological priority to the advent of Christ. They "anticipated" and "awaited" Christ (*Magn.* 9:2). Their preaching led "up to the gospel" (εἰς τὸ εὐαγγέλιον), and they awaited him in hope (*Phld.* 5:2). Indeed, their salvation was not really accomplished until he "came and raised them from the dead" (*Magn.* 9:2).[88]

By saying that the prophets waited for Christ "as their teacher" (9:2), Ignatius probably implies that they still had something to learn from him, that is, that their prophecies did not attain to the clarity and fullness of the gospel. This point is, in any case, made explicitly elsewhere.

> But the gospel has a distinct advantage [ἐξαίρετον ... τι], namely, the advent of the Savior, our Lord Jesus Christ, his passion, and the resurrection. The beloved prophets preached up to him, but the gospel is the completion of imperishability. (*Phld.* 9:2)

This is why Christians should "pay attention to the prophets, but especially [ἐξαιρέτως] to the gospel, in which the passion has been indicated to us and the resurrection has been brought to perfection" (*Smyr.* 7:2).

These statements are rather more carefully nuanced than is suggested by saying that the prophets are "simply claimed for Christianity" and that Judaism is "simply replaced by Christianity."[89] They reflect a fairly precise understanding of historical revelation. To say that the gospel is the "completion" (ἀπάρτισμα) of imperishability, or that in the gospel the resurrection "has been brought to perfection" (τετελείωται), indicates that what was being revealed to the prophets was good and true but not yet complete. The revelation was not yet complete because the historically unfolding plan of God had not yet arrived at its τέλος. Indeed, the sort of "fleshly and spiritual" salvation that Ignatius proclaims, as opposed to a docetic or gnostic concept of salvation, could not possibly have been fully revealed until it was fully accomplished in history. This is why Ignatius, even in a letter that is not targeting docetism, emphasizes so strongly that the nativity, passion, and resurrection of Jesus Christ occurred at a specific period in history and have been "truly and certainly accomplished" (*Magn.* 11:1). Ignatius's teleological understanding of

---

87. *Ignatius of Antioch*, 119.
88. Here Ignatius may be alluding to Mt 27:52–53 (cf. Lk 9:8), but, for another possible Jewish-Christian source of this tradition, see Grant, *Ignatius of Antioch*, 63–64.
89. Conzelmann, *Gentiles—Jews—Christians*, 259.

salvation may even imply that revelation during the Old Testament period was gradual and in stages, leading up to its culmination in the New Testament. Be that as it may, he does not seem to think of the prophets as having had a crystal ball vision of Jesus of Nazareth. Rather, they were his disciples "by the Spirit" (9:2). By this phrase Ignatius probably indicates a mode of discipleship that lacks the concrete historical and visible advantages enjoyed by the church: "the ordinances of the Lord and the apostles" (13:1), the sacraments, and the authoritative guidance of the bishop. All these have come about as a result of the Christ event, and that is the "distinct advantage" of the gospel.

Ignatius's view of the divine economy, then, combines a temporal-linear dimension with a dimension that transcends linear temporality, so that the Israelite prophets awaited the coming of Christ in hope, even while they already "lived according to Christ Jesus." This combination is achieved through what we might call historical teleology. History moves toward its τέλος, but because the Eternal is entering human temporality, history is never merely "history" in the positivist sense. It transcends itself at every stage, so that Israel's prophets can have been "inspired by his grace," the same grace that was still to come at a particular moment in history (8:1–2). But if history is transcended, it is not abolished. The actual arrival of grace through a series of historical events matters (11:1). In fact, the entrance of the Eternal into history is precisely what gives history real substance, so to speak, and confers on history its abiding significance. In holding on to both sides of the *Grundspannung*, Ignatius displays a well-developed theological instinct. He maintains an essentially historical view of the divine economy, and yet he recognizes equally clearly that the Christ event is far more than one item within a linear sequence. It is the transcendent *novum*, which encompasses and permeates everything. In this way Ignatius does, I think, possess the most fundamental elements of a salvation-historical perspective on the divine economy, and to that extent I disagree with Conzelmann's claim to the contrary. I hope also to have shown that the prophets are not "simply claimed for Christianity" in Ignatius's theology. The bishop of Antioch carefully nuances his statements about the prophets in such a way as to do justice both to their historical position within the divine economy and to their real relation to the τέλος that is history's self-transcending perfection: the Christ event.

Good and Better

Let us set the prophets to one side for the moment in order to take up a related question. What does Ignatius have to say about the other institutions and observances that comprise Judaism? Is Schoedel correct to say that he fails to grant them "even a historically limited role in the unfolding of God's plan"? In this regard, Ignatius gives us only a couple of brief remarks, but these remarks are highly suggestive. At least they will require us to qualify Schoedel's judgment to a significant extent.

First we have a statement strikingly reminiscent of the Epistle to the Hebrews.

A   The priests also are good, but better is the high priest,
B   who has been entrusted with the holy of holies,
C   who alone has been entrusted with the hidden things of God.
D   He is the door of the Father ... (Phld. 9:1)

Commentators agree that the "priests" referred to here (A) are Old Testament Jewish priests, not Christian presbyters.[90] According to Schoedel, "the priests of Israel are said to be good by way of concession: they are good, but the highpriest is better."[91] This is not strictly incorrect, but Ignatius's "concession" has perhaps more of a positive theological value than Schoedel recognizes. Obviously, it is not the sort of concession that is made in polite deference to one's interlocutors. Ignatius considers any persons who promote Judaism to the detriment of the true gospel of Jesus Christ to be "tombstones" and "graves of the dead," and he labels their doctrines "evil devices and traps" of the devil (6:1–2). He is unlikely to concede any point to such people, unless he is already convinced of its truth. Ignatius regards the priests of Israel to be "good" for one reason only. He recognizes that the old covenant was divinely instituted. How could such a covenant be anything less than good? The language of "good" and "better" is not so much a concession, in the rhetorical sense of the word, as it is a carefully chosen way of indicating the precise theological relationship between the *vetera* and the *novum*.

Identifying the "high priest" in Ignatius's compressed statement is a more delicate matter. At first glance it seems that the two relative clauses that modify "high priest" (B and C) constitute a redundancy, or perhaps a merely stylistic parallelism. Upon closer inspection, however, we recognize that these two clauses serve to unfold a typological-

---

90. Lightfoot, *Ignatius, Polycarp*, 2.274; Grant, *Ignatius of Antioch*, 106–7.
91. *Ignatius of Antioch*, 209.

Christological interpretation of the Levitical priesthood and of the Yom Kippur ritual in particular. Much as in the Epistle to the Hebrews, where the distinction *within* the old covenant between the many "priests" who enter the holy place and the one "high priest" who enters the holy of holies constitutes a "parable" prefiguring the relationship *between* the covenants (Heb 9:1–14), so here in *Philadelphians* the phrase "high priest" has two successive referents. According to the first relative clause (B), the "high priest" is not yet Christ but the Jewish high priest of the Mosaic covenant, who alone was permitted, on the Day of Atonement, to enter the holy of holies in the wilderness tabernacle or, later, in the Jerusalem temple. But the second relative clause (C) indicates that the old covenant high priest prefigures Christ and that the holy of holies is a type of "the hidden things of God" (τὰ κρυπτὰ τοῦ θεοῦ). This latter phrase refers to God's secret counsel, which the incarnate Logos reveals in the mysteries of the new covenant.[92]

That we are by this point in the text (C) concerned with Jesus Christ, the high priest of the new covenant, becomes all the clearer when Ignatius shifts to a quasi-Johannine image (D) and identifies this high priest as "the door of the Father, through which enter Abraham and Isaac and Jacob and the prophets and the apostles and the church, all these, into the unity of God" (*Phld.* 9:1). Obviously Ignatius wishes to present a unified vision of the economy of redemption. Jesus Christ, of course, is the primary unifying factor. He is the door through which all enter. But because Christ's redemptive work takes place in history, the entire economy possesses an essential historical dimension, which is also a unifying factor. It is not accidental, then, that Ignatius catalogs the members of the people of God in chronological order.

In his polemic against the Judaizers Ignatius exhorts his readers to "learn how to live according to Christianity" (*Magn.* 10:1). It is a question of understanding the true nature of the *novum* and all that it entails. At the end of *Philadelphians* 9, just after explaining the "distinct advantage of the gospel," he returns to the notion of the "good," while underlining once more the unity of the economy: "All things together are good, if you believe with love" (9:2). This carefully crafted axiom, which harkens back to Paul while looking forward to Augustine, concludes Ignatius's discussion of the Judaizing question in *Philadelphians*, and as his last word on the subject it deserves our careful attention. In context, "all things to-

---

92. According to Schoedel, this phrase refers to "exegetical secrets" (ibid.), but that interpretation trivializes what is really at stake here for Ignatius.

gether" must refer to the old *and* new covenants.⁹³ The somewhat abrupt shift to second-person direct address in the "if"-clause brings what has been a largely theoretical discussion back into the mode of exhortation, which Ignatius had left off near the beginning of 8:2. He wishes to reassure the Philadelphians that if they reject the overtures of the Judaizers and practice their faith "according to the learning of Christ" (8:2), they will not really be missing out on anything. If they have true faith in Jesus Christ and live it out in charity (ἀγάπη), they will possess the whole divine economy: "all things together."

Here Ignatius clearly indicates his unwillingness to deal with the Judaizing problem by denigrating the old covenant or any part thereof. If the priests are good, so too presumably is the temple cultus itself, as well as the other ceremonial observances of Judaism. But one must possess all things *together*, that is, within the unity of Jesus Christ and with the correct understanding that comes through the gospel. Clearly this does not mean that Christians are to observe the ceremonial precepts of Judaism, even so far as that was still possible after A.D. 70. Quite to the contrary! And yet, in the unity of the true "high priest" they somehow possess "all things together." The one thing that Ignatius never says explicitly but seems to imply throughout this discussion is that the old things are somehow taken up into the new. Clearly, *Philadelphians* 9 was not written by someone who thought in terms of Judaism being "simply replaced" by Christianity.

Sabbath and Lord's Day

With regard to the institutions of Judaism and their relationship to Christianity, there remains yet one more dense formulation to which we must attend. Returning to *Magnesians* 9, a passage that we have touched on already several times, let us note that Christians who once lived according to old rites but have come to new hope are "no longer observing Sabbath but living according to the Lord's day" (9:1). Whatever role the specific issue of Sabbath observance may have played in the Judaizing controversy of early second-century Asia Minor, presumably a significant one, Schoedel is certainly correct to say that Ignatius employs the parallel expressions "observing Sabbath" (σαββατίζοντες) and "living according to the Lord's day" (κατὰ κυριακὴν ζῶντες) "primarily to characterize two whole ways of life."⁹⁴ With respect to the former expression, the var-

---

93. Lightfoot, *Ignatius, Polycarp*, 2.276; Camelot, *Ignace d'Antioche*, 131; Grant, *Ignatius of Antioch*, 107.

94. *Ignatius of Antioch*, 123.

ious elements of Jewish life and religiosity, in the post-A.D. 70 diaspora more than ever, found their center and point of coherence in Sabbath observance. To "observe Sabbath" is to conduct one's life "in accord with ancient practices." That is, it is a mode of religiosity appropriate to the period of waiting for the Messiah. Correlatively, Ignatius can employ the phrase "living according to the Lord's day" as a way of summing up Christian existence because, like the council fathers of Vatican II, he recognizes the Sunday eucharist to be the source of the church's unity and the summit of its communal life.[95] If the community meets for a single episcopally sanctioned eucharist, *all that they do will be done* "validly" and "according to God."[96] As Sabbath observance characterizes the "old" and is appropriate to the period of waiting, living the Lord's day is for those who have "come to newness of hope" (*Magn.* 9:1). To assemble for eucharist on the Lord's day is to confess that grace has come into the world, whereas to continue to gather for prayer and Scripture on the Sabbath is to imply that it has not (8:1).[97]

Does this mean that the Lord's day has "simply replaced" the Sabbath? No. The shift from worshipping on the seventh day of the week to worshipping on the first day, which is also the eighth day, serves as a *Sinnbild* for the decisive historical moment of transition within the divine economy of redemption: the "coming" of Christ and of grace, when the *vetera* give way to the *novum*. This giving way is no mere replacement, however, for the *novum* comes ἐν τέλει and is itself both ἀρχή and τέλος, just as Sunday is both first day and eighth day. Upon its entrance into the world and into history, the *novum* permeates and transforms everything as it takes everything up into itself. If this seems to be reading a great deal into Ignatius's words, we should consider carefully the precise role that the phrase "no longer observing Sabbath but living according to the

---

95. *Lumen Gentium* 11 (*totius vitae Christianae fons et culmen*).
96. Phld. 4:1; Smyr. 8:1.
97. According to Pierluigi Lanfranchi, "Ignatius' purpose is to establish a sociological distinction between the Christians of pagan origin and the Christians of Jewish origin," and his promotion of the Lord's day over against the Sabbath is part of his "strategy" to "separate" the two groups. Recognizing an irreconcilable opposition between Judaism and Christianity, Ignatius is content to consign Jewish-Christianity to the side of Judaism. His manifest concern for "unity" is, then, only for "the unity of *his* Church," that is, the church of the gentiles ("Attitudes to the Sabbath in Three Apostolic Fathers: Didache, Ignatius, and Barnabas," in *Jesus, Paul, and Early Christianity: Studies in Honour of Henk Jan de Jonge*, Supplements to Novum Testamentum 130, ed. Rieuwerd Buitenwerf, Harm W. Hollander, and Johannes Tromp [Leiden: Brill, 2008], 256–57, emphasis added). This careless interpretation constitutes a profound distortion of Ignatian ecclesiology, which explicitly confesses that believers from among both "Jews" and "gentiles" are incorporated into the "one body" of Christ's church (Smyr. 1:2).

Lord's day" plays within the elaborately conceived (and admittedly tortuous) rhetorical question that constitutes most of *Magnesians* 9. Here is a literal translation of the entire chapter.

> If then those who once conducted their lives in accord with ancient practices have come to a newness of hope—no longer observing Sabbath but living according to the Lord's day, on which also our life dawned [ἀνέτειλεν] through him and his death, which some deny, through which mystery we have received the faith, and because of this we endure, in order that we may be found disciples of Jesus Christ our only teacher—how could we live apart from him, whom the prophets, being his disciples in the Spirit, anticipated as their teacher? And because of this, he whom they awaited righteously, when he came, raised them from the dead.

We should note the strong eschatological tenor of this passage and the paneling effect by which the two great periods of salvation history are placed alongside each other for the sake of comparison and contrast. The prophets' discipleship to Christ in the Spirit and the way they "awaited" his coming in history as their teacher is paralleled by the way Christians now "endure" in order to be "found" (i.e., *ante tribunal Dei*) to be true disciples of that same teacher. The Christ event, his paschal mystery in particular, stands as the centerpiece of salvation history and the dividing line between its two periods, but it also implicitly parallels and prefigures his second coming.[98] As the prophets awaited Christ's first advent, which turned out to be the moment of their eschatological resurrection, Christians endure in hope of their own resurrection to eternal life. Moreover, the salvation-historical passage from the old age to the new age, which is the basic temporal structure of the economy of redemption, is recapitulated at two other levels of temporality. First, it is summed up in the life's journey or personal salvation-history of those Jews and god-fearers who through their conversion to Christ have passed from the practices of Judaism to those of Christianity. Second, it is relived weekly in the passage from Sabbath to Lord's day. Those who worship on the Lord's day show that they are living in the new age.

Though he hardly exploits it to the full, Ignatius has a sense of the symbolic potential of the days of the week.[99] He associates the first day of the week with the rising of the sun (ἀνέτειλεν) and new life. The easiest way to employ this symbolism would have been to compare the sun's

---

98. Ignatius may be pointing to this prefigurement by using the participle παρών (here) and the noun παρουσία (Phld. 9:2) to refer to Christ's first coming.

99. Cf. Hugo Rahner, *Greek Myths and Christian Mystery* (New York: Harper & Row, 1963), 103–5.

rising to Christ's rising on the first day of the week. But Ignatius's procedure is more subtle and elliptical than that. His allusion to Christ's resurrection is indirect because his concern is to focus his readers' attention on "our life," which is the salient feature of the new age. By saying that this life has come into the world (on the first day of the week) "through him and through his death," Ignatius, in typical fashion, draws the events of Good Friday and Easter Sunday into close interrelation in order to present them as one "mystery." He might have filled out his sketch by suggesting that Christ fulfilled the Sabbath by "resting" in the tomb on Holy Saturday. There could be a hint along these lines in the reference to Christ's raising the prophets from the dead, where some scholars find an allusion to the *descensus ad infernum*.[100] But this is far from certain, and Ignatius shows no interest in Christ's descent among the dead elsewhere in his letters. What is much clearer and certainly more central to Ignatius's concerns is that Sabbath and Lord's day correspond to the two eras of the historical economy of redemption and sum up two successive modes of relationship to God, one imperfect and provisional, the other perfect and definitive.

Do the two eras of the historical economy of redemption also represent two distinct stages and levels of divine revelation, one partial and the other definitive? Ignatius's presentation in *Magnesians* 9 probably implies some such distinction, though he does not formulate this distinction with the clarity we find, for example, in Hebrews 1:1-2. Certainly Ignatius regards Jesus Christ as the definitive means by which God reveals himself to the world. He is "our only teacher." Because Israel's prophets awaited this same teacher, and as they were already his disciples even as Christians now hope to prove to be truly his disciples, the single revelation that comes through this one teacher serves to unite the two stages of the economy. Ignatius is evidently more concerned with the unity of revelation than with distinguishing sharply between the two eras in terms of the quantity or quality of revelation available to each. On the other hand, by referring to Christ as the one teacher, whom even the prophets themselves awaited, Ignatius clearly places Christ on a level above the prophets. Their role as instruments of revelation subserves the unique role of Christ. There is also a subtle but important difference between

---

100. Jean Daniélou, *The Theology of Jewish Christianity*, trans. John A. Baker (London: Darton, Longman & Todd, 1964), 236-37. Schoedel is certain that the verb παρών ("when he came") "must refer to a descent of Christ into Hades" (*Ignatius of Antioch*, 124). But this verb is more easily referred to the Christ event, globally conceived, as his coming into the world.

saying that the prophets anticipated Christ as teacher and saying that he is (already) our teacher. For them, the teacher was yet to come. For us, he is already fully present. Implicitly, we possess his definitive teaching in a more perfect way than they did. They were already his disciples, but "in the Spirit." We do not yet presume to be his disciples—prior to "enduring" to the end, we can, at best, claim that we have "begun to be" his disciples (Eph. 3:1)—but that is certainly not because we await some fuller revelation.

On the contrary, through the "mystery" of his passion and resurrection "we have received the faith" (ἐλάβομεν τὸ πιστεύειν; Magn. 9:1). This unusual phrase probably means both that we have received the true faith (with its essential objective content) and that we have received the grace to believe (subjectively). The fullness of revelation, along with the grace to accept this revelation, has come into the world through an event, a μυστήριον, at a specific moment in history. The situation of Israel's prophets vis-à-vis this event thus possesses two aspects, corresponding to the two dimensions of Ignatius's historical teleology (horizontal-temporal and vertical-transcendent). On the one hand, because they lived historically prior to Christ's advent, they do not appear to have enjoyed the full clarity of his revelation but still awaited him as teacher. On the other hand, the revelation that they have received cannot be other than, or extrinsic to, the one revelation that has come into the world definitively in and through Jesus Christ. Here too, Ignatius maintains both sides of the Grundspannung. But he does not address some of the most basic questions that this paradox raises. What exactly was the quality or nature of the prophets' faith? If "the faith" had not yet come into the world prior to the Christ event, how was it possible for the prophets to believe in Christ at all? And if the answer to this question is that Christ's grace, via history's transcendent dimension, somehow reached back to them and inspired them (Magn. 8:2), so that they "believed in him and were saved" (Phld. 5:2), how could their faith lack anything at all? And if the answer to this question is that it did not in fact lack anything, how does the gospel possess "a distinct advantage" (9:2)? We seem to be going in a circle at this point, and Ignatius offers us no way out.

The Old Testament and Christian Exegesis

Ignatius's presentation of the relationship between Judaism and Christianity is obviously not without its lacunae, some of which I have mentioned in the course of this chapter. But I hope also to have demonstrated that Ignatius's polemic against Judaization reflects a more carefully conceived and penetrating theological position than he is usually given credit for. By way of conclusion, I shall attempt to indicate more precisely both the basic weakness and the essential strength in Ignatius's approach, and to place these within the broad context of the church's centuries-long endeavor to understand her Old Testament roots. Obviously, in the present context this landscape must be painted with broad strokes.

The central problem with Ignatius's treatment of the *vetera* lies in his failure to relate Israel's prophets to their own religious context. He has gone to some lengths to indicate the prophets' economic relationship to Jesus Christ and the gospel, and to indicate how the practices and institutions of Judaism are economically related to Christianity, but he has not told us how Judaism and the prophets are related to each other. Ignatius presents the prophets as having such immediate access to the grace of Jesus Christ that they seem removed from the historical unfolding of the divine pedagogy by which Yahweh is teaching Israel during the various stages of Old Testament history. If a given prophet "lived according to Christ Jesus" (*Magn.* 8:2), was his life of faith merely extrinsically related to the institutions by which Israel as a whole was called to live in fidelity to the covenant, institutions such as circumcision, Sabbath, and temple cultus?[101] Ignatius never uses the word "covenant" and gives no indication of having wrestled with this issue, but it seems that any solution that would posit two extrinsically related covenants, or two species of covenant, to put the matter in Scholastic terms, would be inimical to his governing sense of a single unified economy of revelation and redemption.

The exegetical and theological tradition as a whole will look for a solution to this problem in the supposition that the institutions and observances of the old covenant were indeed important to the prophets but that they meant to them something quite different from what they meant

---

101. Donahue understands *Magn.* 9:1 to refer to the Old Testament prophets (not to the apostles or other Jews who converted at the time of Christ or later): "The prophets once lived 'according to Judaism,' then, after they had been inspired by the grace of Jesus Christ, they lived according to him ... even for the prophets, the ritual practices of Judaism had no value" ("Jewish Christianity," 88). This is improbable. However much Ignatius "Christianizes" the prophets, it seems unlikely that he would have envisioned them observing the Lord's day! Moreover, throughout the passage Ignatius is concerned with the historical transition from one era to another (10:3).

to run-of-the-mill Israelites. According to this view, which we found already in Justin's *Dialogue*, the Mosaic legislation and the institutions of Israel had a dual function. On the one hand, they represented a divine accommodation to a weak and carnal people, who, if they were not offering animals to the true God, would almost certainly be offering them to false gods. On the other hand, these same institutions were mystical prefigurements of Christ and the church. Most Israelites understood the precepts of the law according to the letter, even in a "carnal" fashion, but the prophets understood the same things spiritually. Thus the problem of how to understand the relationship between the covenants is sometimes redirected to the question of the relationship between the literal sense and the spiritual sense of the Old Testament. The two issues are in any case intertwined.

These observations also suggest that the problem is not simply to specify the relationship between the prophets and the *institutions* of Judaism but also to indicate the prophets' place among the *people* of Israel. Within the few lines of Ignatius's encomiastic treatment of the prophets in *Magnesians* and *Philadelphians*, one senses a gulf beginning to open between a relatively small handful of exceptionally righteous Old Testament "saints" and the *massa damnata* of recalcitrant Israel. When Ignatius tells us that the prophets were "persecuted" for their attempt to persuade "the disobedient" that there is only one God (*Magn.* 8:2), the allusion is no doubt to the way Moses, Elijah, Jeremiah, and other prophets suffered at the hands of their own people. Such a summary of the ministry of the prophets, moreover, can hardly be said to be unfaithful to the biblical record. Generally speaking, the Old Testament presents Israel as a "stiffnecked people," in any given generation of which one might be able to identify a few faithful souls (but see 1 Kgs 19:18).

For some later representatives of the exegetical tradition, the fateful hermeneutical misstep will consist in giving these biblical generalizations, which have a rhetorical and monitory function, the wrong sort of force and too much interpretive weight. Above we noted Skarsaune's claim that, in Justin's *Dialogue* and in patristic theology generally, the Bible's various denunciations of the Israelites were wrested from their context and "taken to describe in a timeless, almost ontological way, the very *nature* of the Jewish people."[102] But even where such an extreme view is not in evidence, one does find a tendency to underestimate the piety

---

102. "Development of Scriptural Interpretation," 404.

and theological development of Israel *as a people* while exalting that of the prophets to the point of making them proto-Christians. Increasingly, the fathers will look upon the patriarchs, Moses, Joshua, Samuel, David, Solomon, and the other prophets as a spiritual elite among the Israelites, men whose mystical knowledge of Christ was comparable to the evangelical understanding later possessed by the apostles, while the remainder of ancient Israel had a far inferior level of understanding and did well if they could but avoid idolatry.[103] Augustine captures the essence of this traditional view when he describes David as "a man *in* the Old Testament, but not a man *of* the Old Testament," and says that Moses and the prophets "dispensed the old covenant as was fitting for that time, while they in fact belonged to the new covenant."[104]

Because this same elite group of saints (excluding the patriarchs) was assumed to have written nearly the entire Old Testament, there was almost from the beginning the danger that a fissure would open, in practice even when not in theory, between the literal-historical sense of the Old Testament and its spiritual sense. Early Christians did not view the Old Testament as "the Scriptures of Israel," as we would think of them— the record of Israel's gradual theological and spiritual development within the historical and religious context of the ancient Near East—but as inspired oracles delivered through the agency of a handful of mystics. We have already seen the extreme case of this fissure in the *Epistle of Barnabas*, where Israel's religion is considered invalid from the beginning and thus most of its history rendered otiose, and where, as a result, the literal sense of the Old Testament is in part explicitly denied and for the remainder simply ignored. Fortunately, the exegetical tradition as a whole does not follow this example. But even where lip service is given to the dictum that the spiritual sense must be based firmly on the literal sense, few among the church fathers attempt to demonstrate in any given instance how the two are related.

Moreover, especially as one moves into the late patristic and medieval periods, there is a strong tendency to view the literal sense of the Old Tes-

---

103. See, for example, the discussion of this tendency—along with mitigating countertendencies—in the exegesis of Origen, in Henri de Lubac, *History and Spirit: The Understanding of Scripture according to Origen*, trans. Anne Englund Nash and Juvenal Merriell (San Francisco: Ignatius Press, 2007), 295–306.

104. Expositio epistolae ad Galatas 43; PL 35.2136–37 (homo in Veteri Testamento, sed non homo de Veteri Testamento); Epistola 140, 2:5; PL 33.540 (dispensabant ergo illi sancti pro congruentia temporis Testamentum Vetus, pertinebant vero ad Testamentum Novum); cf. Lubac, *History and Spirit*, 302.

tament as a kind of "husk," an easily understood historical record that can be summarized briefly and then set aside in order to get to the nutritious "ear of grain," that is, the spiritual sense. Knowledge of biblical Hebrew is rare among Christian exegetes of the first millennium, who nonetheless do not hesitate to judge the Old Testament to lack literary style and rhetorical sophistication, making it a fittingly humble vessel to hold the precious treasure of mystical meanings. As a result, the church carried on for the better part of her history with a significantly undervalued estimation of ancient Israel's religious life and a naively simplistic, at times condescending, view of the literal sense of the Old Testament.[105]

Modern biblical scholarship has challenged this patristic-medieval view in several respects. It has demonstrated convincingly that the Old Testament was not written by Moses, Samuel, David, and Solomon, but by a large number of mostly anonymous authors, nearly all of whom lived centuries after these famous worthies. It has brought to light the consummate literary skill with which most biblical Hebrew narratives and poems were composed. It has revealed the Old Testament to be an intricate interweaving of a whole range of sophisticated theological viewpoints. It has placed Israel within the rich cultural context of ancient Near Eastern civilizations. And it has given us a nuanced historical sense of Israel's religious development. From this new perspective, it no longer seems possible, or even desirable, to think of Abraham, Moses, and the prophets as possessing a Christian consciousness comparable to that of the apostles. Ancient Israel had its "saints" (ḥāsîdîm), to be sure, but their sanctity consisted in their fidelity to the ancient covenant that Yahweh had made with Israel, a covenant that had its own theological genius and spiritual wealth. The hermeneutical, exegetical, and theological challenge facing Christian interpreters of the Old Testament remains what it always has been, namely, to place the contents of the Old Testament in their proper relation to the Christ event. Today, however, we must reckon with new information and insights pertaining to those contents.

This new historical perspective has had a liberating and fecundating effect on much recent theology. Moreover, its positive influence can be felt almost everywhere in the documents of Vatican II, in recent papal encyclicals, and throughout the *Catechism of the Catholic Church*. But no one with a

---

105. For these trends, and notable exceptions, see Henri de Lubac, *Medieval Exegesis: The Four Senses of Scripture*, trans. E. M. Macierowski (Grand Rapids, Mich.: Eerdmans, 2000), 2.41–82.

serious commitment to the theological tradition and the rule of faith will consider modern biblical scholarship to have been an unmixed blessing. As this is not the place for anything like a comprehensive critique, let us simply note how unfortunate it is that modern biblical scholars, at least until recently, have tended toward a benign neglect, if not an arrogant dismissal, of patristic and medieval exegesis and theology.[106] This has been very much a case of throwing out the baby with the bath water. If there is in Ignatius's letters, and in the patristic-medieval tradition generally, a tendency to "Christianize" the prophets, modern biblical scholarship has responded by severing the Christological and economic link between the testaments, so that pre-exilic Yahwism, second-temple Judaism, early Christianity, and rabbinic Judaism appear to be connected by nothing more than the thin threads of historical contingency. To modern minds formed within the milieu of positivism, which rejects out of hand the very notion of a divine economy, and increasingly immersed in the ideology of multiculturalism, the claim that Israel's prophets "lived according to Christ Jesus" is scarcely intelligible and probably vaguely offensive. For theologians committed to historical Christianity, therefore, recovering what has been lost and articulating it in a manner that is intelligible to our contemporaries, and for that matter, to ourselves, is a multifaceted task of daunting proportions.

One vital aspect of this effort is the *recursus ad fontes*. The tendency to disengage the prophets from the religious life of ancient Israel and the concomitant undervaluation of the literal sense of the Old Testament are real deficiencies in the patristic-medieval exegetical tradition, but they are not the whole story. This same tradition holds inestimable riches for the renewal of biblical exegesis and theology in our day, not least in the realm of deepening our understanding of the economic relationship between Israel and the church, Judaism and Christianity, Old Testament and New Testament. I have already indicated where I think some of these riches lie with respect to Ignatius's letters, Justin's *Dialogue*, and Irenaeus's *Demonstration*. The writings of Origen, Augustine, Bonaventure, and Aquinas, among many others, also hold forth great promise. None of these authors enjoyed the advantages of our historical perspective on Israel's religious development, but they do offer us seminal insights, luminous principles, and a complementary perspective, without which we ourselves will not be able to reap the full theological benefits of modern

---

106. Cf. Pope Pius XII, Encyclical Letter *Divino Afflante Spiritu* (September 30, 1943), § 29.

scholarship. Even where ancient exegetes seem to us to have gotten off track a bit, we must be careful not to dismiss their statements before we have made an honest attempt to understand them. For example, when Ignatius says that the prophets "lived according to Christ Jesus," or when Augustine says that they "belonged to the new covenant," we must recognize that such statements are aimed at preserving an indispensable revealed truth about the unity of the economy of redemption and, as such, reflect an instinct native to the faith. The problem with these formulations is not that they are wrong but that they express only a partial truth.

I have granted that there is a significant element of truth in Conzelmann's opinion that Ignatius's view of the economy of redemption lacks a salvation-historical perspective. Not only does Ignatius lack the modern theologian's historical sense of the divine pedagogy as involving Israel's gradual religious development, but, as far as we can tell, he lacks even Irenaeus's sense of the events of the Old Testament as integral to the narrative of redemption. But upon closer inspection of the matter, Conzelmann's criticism has proved to be a superficial one and too easily dismissive of Ignatius. Ironically, the great strength undergirding Ignatius's treatment of the relationship between Judaism and Christianity turns out to be his profound understanding of the specifically historical aspect of the economy. His deep reflection on the Christ event led him to an appreciation of the economy's horizontal-temporal, vertical-transcendent, and teleological dimensions, thus giving him a far more theologically viable sense of history than we moderns tend to work with. Could it be precisely in the realm about which we are especially confident of our superior understanding, namely, history, that Ignatius and other ancient Christians have a great deal to teach us?

Writing *Magnesians* during his stopover at Smyrna, Ignatius described the relationship between Judaism and Christianity in terms of "old" and "new" (8:1–10:3). This is the most basic biblical way to construe the matter, having roots both in the prophets (Jeremiah, Ezekiel, and Deutero-Isaiah) and in the New Testament (Paul, Hebrews, Matthew), but the terminology of old and new is not without ambiguity. Many different kinds of relationship can be indicated by the words *old* and *new*, but when moderns who operate with a purely horizontal and positivist notion of history read an ancient Christian account of the relationship between Judaism and Christianity in terms of old and new, they inevitably judge it to be an expression of supersessionism. Thus, as we saw, Conzelmann maintains that in Ignatius's letters "Judaism is simply replaced by Christianity."[107] In any case, when Ignatius wrote *Philadelphians* and *Smyrnaeans* from Troas a week or two later, he employed two complementary ways of conceptualizing the relationship (both apparently drawn from the Epistle to the Hebrews): good and better, and imperfect and perfect.[108] Though a supersessionist interpretation might be forced upon these terms, in the context of Ignatius's presentation they are more naturally understood to indicate a significant degree of continuity and interpenetration between Judaism and Christianity, and between Israel and the church.

By filling out the fundamental Pauline distinction between old and new in terms of good and better, and imperfect and perfect, Ignatius's attempt to understand the relationship between Judaism and Christianity adumbrates in a striking manner Thomas Aquinas's treatment of the relationship between the *lex vetus* and the *lex nova* in the Prima Secundae. Heading off every tendency to denigrate the old covenant, Thomas insists, "Beyond all doubt, the old law was good."[109] The old law and the new law are distinct, not as two species of divine law, but "as perfect and imperfect in the same species." In other words, they differ from each other not as horse differs from ox but as boy differs from man.[110] Aquinas uses this image of boy and man to relate the distinction between imperfect and perfect to Paul's description of the Mosaic law as "our pedagogue to Christ" (Gal 3:24–25). The law is imperfect because it "brought nothing to perfection," but it did "dispose" Israel for the coming of Christ and the giving of the perfect law: *lex vetus disponebat ad Christum sicut imperfectum ad perfectum*.[111] This crucial distinction between disposing for perfection and actually bringing to perfection enables us to ascribe to the *vetera* their true role in the economy of redemption without in any way compromising the uniqueness and superiority of the *novum*.

This is the locus in the theological tradition into which we may funnel the insights gleaned from modern Old Testament scholarship regarding Israel's religious development, in order to see them bear real fruit. Ignatius indicates that the institutions of Judaism were "good" and had their place in the economy prior to the coming of Christ. But what was that place? What role did circumcision, Sabbath, and sacrifice play in the lives of the prophets and saints of Old Testament Israel? Ignatius does not tell us, but we see some progress in this regard already later

---

107. *Gentiles—Jews—Christians*, 259.
108. Phld. 9:1–2; Smyr. 7:2.
109. STh I-II, q. 98, a. 1.
110. STh I-II, q. 91, a. 5.
111. STh I-II, q. 98, a. 1 (cf. Heb 7:19); q. 99, a. 6.

in the second century in Justin's *Dialogue* and Irenaeus's *Demonstration*. Standing on the shoulders of Augustine, Isidore of Seville, Peter Lombard, Albert the Great—and Moses Maimonides!—Aquinas provides a grand summation of how the church accounts for both the literal *ratio* of the old law and its mystical significance. With the benefit of modern biblical scholarship, we might be able to build further on this edifice. Taking seriously the principle that the new is hidden in the old, we might even be able to glimpse how ancient Israel's prophets and saints already "lived according to Christ Jesus" and were "inspired by his grace" in and through their Yahwistic piety and their fidelity to the old covenant. Still, none of this would be possible apart from the fundamental historical-teleological understanding of the divine economy that Ignatius represents so well and at such an early stage in the church's theological development.

Without great exaggeration the Christian exegetical tradition can be viewed as an ongoing attempt to work out the ramifications of the apostle Paul's view of the relationship between old covenant and new covenant. While Ignatius did not work out these ramifications very far, he did understand the basic New Testament theology of the divine economy well, and he had a good instinct for how to steer between extreme views. Though one must be wary of excessive schematization when describing historical realities, it might be helpful to think of the two heresies that Ignatius encountered as representing a Scylla-and-Charybdis strait that Christian exegesis and theology would need to negotiate repeatedly down through the centuries. Docetism may be taken to represent those erroneous viewpoints that, out of concern to guarantee the transcendent nature of the faith, compromise the essential historical character of revelation. More or less extreme forms of this error, from Marcionism to the *Epistle to Diognetus*, dispense with the old covenant entirely. Ironically, this procedure undermines that which it was attempting to preserve, for without the old, the new is not truly new. It is simply a timeless idea. Broadly speaking, this danger is also present whenever the faith is reduced to a "message" or ideology, or transmogrified into a philosophical system. The Judaizing heresy, on the other hand, can be taken to represent any reduction of the gospel to something less than the definitive self-manifestation of the transcendent God. The form of Judaization that threatened the churches of Magnesia and Philadelphia in the early second century involved the subordination of the gospel to the law and the prophets (Phld. 8:2). A similar danger is present whenever Christianity is reduced to its "historical" dimension, which is to say, whenever history itself is reduced to its merely linear-temporal dimension. In such a case, the terms "old" and "new" designate only a chronological sequence or, at best, an accidental causal relationship within the realm of historical contingency. This Charybdis of historicism thus has something in common with the Scylla of ahistorical idealism. In neither case is the "new" any longer truly the historically transcendent *novum*.

WORD AND SILENCE

A Primer in Learning Christ

As Ignatius of Antioch sees it, the economy of redemption is fundamentally an economy of revelation. God has redeemed the world by "manifesting himself humanly for the newness of eternal life" (Eph. 19:3). When human beings appropriate God's self-revelation through faith and love, they become "children of the light of truth" (Phld. 2:1) and "imitators of God" (Eph. 1:1). And if they endure in this way of life to the end, they "attain God" (Magn. 1:3). Because God himself is unity, the unity of Father and Son in the Spirit, imitating God involves embracing unity in all its dimensions. Jesus Christ is the historical manifestation of this unity. In his life, death, and resurrection we see all the dimensions of unity in their perfection: the union of flesh and spirit, the union of faith and love, and, above all, Jesus' own union with the Father. To appropriate this multidimensional unity, therefore, Christians must "become imitators of Jesus Christ, even as he is of the Father" (Phld. 7:2). In its essence, then, redemption is a matter of χριστομαθία, or "learning Christ" (8:2).

The Ignatian letters are a kind of primer in χριστομαθία. Assuming the role of fellow student and teacher's aide, the bishop of Antioch exhorts his readers and himself, "Having become his disciples [μαθηταί], let us learn [μάθωμεν] to live according to Christianity ... we endure, in order that we may be found to be disciples [μαθηταί] of Jesus Christ, our only teacher."[1] The Christian already is a disciple, is learning to become a disciple, and hopes to prove to be a true disciple in the end.[2] But if Chris-

---

1. Magn. 10:1, 9:1.
2. Eph. 1:2, 3:1; Tral. 5:2; Rom. 4:2, 5:1 and 3.

tianity is χριστομαθία, not simply learning from Christ or about Christ but learning the very person of Christ, Jesus is not only our teacher but is also the truth that we are attempting to learn. We assimilate something of this truth by "adorning ourselves in the commandments of Jesus Christ" (Eph. 9:2), by learning and heeding "the precepts of the Lord and of the apostles" (Magn. 13:1). But even this recourse to his words is not enough. We must also have a personal encounter with the Lord himself. We must look to his life in the flesh, to the deeds by which he revealed the Father. It is not enough to possess "the word of Jesus" (λόγος Ἰησοῦ); we must also possess Jesus himself, the one who is God's Word (αὐτοῦ λόγος).[3] We encounter him personally in the eucharist, but the eucharistic flesh, Ignatius teaches us, is none other than the historical flesh that suffered and was raised (Smyr. 7:1). All roads, then, lead us back to the historical event of Jesus Christ. Surely we cannot "learn Christ" unless we know how to interpret the life of Christ. This is why Ignatius's primer is laced with interpretive creedal narrations of the Christ event.

To learn Christ, then, we must know how to interpret the Christ event, which is the centerpiece and summit of the historical economy. This chapter and the next will deal with the life of Christ as it is presented in Ignatius's letters, which is to say, under the aspect of mystery. A mystery is a historical event in which the incomprehensible God, without forfeiting any of his incomprehensibility, makes himself known and available to human beings. The Christ event, with its two great pillars of incarnation and paschal mystery, is the definitive μυστήριον by which "our only teacher" reveals the invisible Father and invites us to become his disciples (Magn. 9:1). Moreover, the dimension of mystery is located not only in the Christ event proper but in the whole ecclesial process by which that event communicates divine truth and life to us and finally brings us to God. If Christianity is a matter of imitating Jesus as he imitated the Father, our lives too must take on the dimension of mystery. As the *vita Iesu* brings the eternal mystery of God into the realm of human history, so the *vita ecclesiae* brings the mystery of the life of Christ into our lives. I will touch on aspects of how this happens in the present chapter but will defer a thorough examination of Ignatius's ecclesiology to chapter 9.

One of the ways Ignatius attempts to unfold the interlocking mystery by which the self-manifestation of the eternal God comes to us through the life of Christ and the life of the church is through the paradox of

---

3. Eph. 15:2, Magn. 8:2.

word and silence. He applies this paradox to the incarnation, referring to Jesus as "the Word come forth from silence" (*Magn.* 8:2), and also to the public ministry of Christ, which includes both the spoken "word" and deeds performed "silently" to reveal the Father (*Eph.* 15:1–2). An especially cryptic passage refers to three key moments within the Christ event as "three mysteries of a cry, wrought in the silence of God" (19:1). The paradox of word and silence carries over into our lives and into the dynamics of χριστομαθία. The disciple "who has truly taken possession of Jesus' word is able also to listen to his silence," and as a result there is a kind of harmony between that disciple's own words and silent deeds, a harmony of life that shows him or her to be an authentic Christian (15:2). Indeed, the paradox of word and silence is one of the chief ways Ignatius expresses his intense concern for authenticity. Jesus Christ is "the mouth that cannot lie, by which the Father has spoken truthfully," and "he will manifest" to the reader that Ignatius too, in the "few words" of his letters, "speaks truthfully" as a witness of Jesus Christ (*Rom.* 8:2). The need for authenticity takes on a special gravity in the life of one called to teach, such as a bishop: "Teaching is good, if the one who speaks acts accordingly" (*Eph.* 15:1).

Since the word-and-silence paradox is a significant expression of Ignatius's theology and has been the occasion of no little misunderstanding, it merits a thorough analysis.[4] Although the formulation of *Magnesians* 8:2, whereby Jesus Christ is described as God's "Word come forth from silence," has been interpreted as an expression of modalist emanationism, if not gnosticism, I hope to demonstrate that this formulation is in fact fully compatible with the New Testament and even reflects an inchoate understanding of orthodox Trinitarian theology. Likewise I will take issue with the view that Ignatius's commendation of "silent" bishops reflects an early stage in the development of the episcopacy during which the bishop was an administrator but not necessarily a teacher. This unfounded conclusion represents a failure to recognize that the Ignatian concept of the "silent" bishop has roots in the ideal of the "silent man" found in ancient Egyptian and Israelite wisdom literature, as well as an even more fundamental failure to appreciate Ignatius's insight into the very nature of ecclesial teaching, which he grounds in the Lord's own ministry as the "one teacher." Finally, by explicating what Ignatius means by saying that Jesus "silently" performed deeds "worthy of the Fa-

---

4. For a concise but keenly insightful treatment of this theme, see P. J. Ryan, "The Silence of God in Ignatius of Antioch," *Prudentia* 20 (1988): 20–27.

ther" (Eph. 15:1) this chapter will also lay some of the groundwork for chapter 8, where we will consider one such deed: the Lord's baptism in the Jordan.

The Word Come Forth from Silence

All the levels at which Ignatius finds the paradox of word and silence to be operative trace back ultimately to the mystery of Jesus Christ as the eternal and incarnate Word (λόγος) of God. Our investigation begins therefore with the one passage in which Ignatius refers to Christ by this Johannine title. Once again, we are dealing with a tightly woven creedal formula.

> ... there is one God,
> who manifested himself through Jesus Christ his Son,
> who is his Word [λόγος] come forth from silence [σιγή],
> who in all things pleased the one who sent him. (Magn. 8:2)[5]

The third line of this passage, with its striking terminology, has drawn comparison to the use of similar terms in gnosticism. For example, Irenaeus's account of the Valentinian myth begins this way.

> There is an unnamable dyad, of which one is called Inexpressible and the other Silence [σιγή]. Then from this dyad a second dyad emanated, of which one is named Father and the other Truth. And borne as fruit from this tetrad were Word [λόγος] and Life, Man and Church; and this was the first ogdoad.[6]

The fact that in this text Word is said to come forth, albeit indirectly, from Silence suggests the possibility that Ignatius and Valentinus, who was active in Rome in the middle decades of the second century, drew

---

5. On this passage and its textual criticism, see Lightfoot, Ignatius, Polycarp, 1.385–88, 2.126–27. Lightfoot argued so persuasively for the reading λόγος ἀπὸ σιγῆς ("Word from silence"), which is supported by the Armenian version and a quotation by Severus of Antioch (early sixth century), that it has been universally accepted by critical editions and commentaries ever since. Noting the tenuousness of the Armenian evidence, Boudewijn Dehandschutter dissents from this view and accepts the longer reading: λόγος ἀΐδιος οὐκ ἀπὸ σιγῆς ("eternal Word, not from silence"), which is found in the Greek Codex Mediceo-Laurentianus and the Anglo-Latin version ("Ignatius, Letter to the Magnesians 8:2 Once Again," in Jesus, Paul, and Early Christianity: Studies in Honour of Henk Jan de Jonge, Supplements to Novum Testamentum 130, ed. Rieuwerd Buitenwerf, Harm W. Hollander, and Johannes Tromp, 89–99 [Leiden: Brill, 2008]). Dehandschutter does not, however, deal with Lightfoot's stronger arguments (e.g., suitability to the context and coherence with Ignatius's thought), nor does he mention the fact that the shorter reading is now also supported by the Arabic version.

6. Haer. 1:11:1; SC 264.167–68.

upon a common source. A somewhat less impressive parallel is found in the *Apocryphon of John*, where an account of several emanations (Mind, Christ, Barbelo) coming to be "in silence [σιγή] and thought" is immediately followed by the statement that "the invisible Spirit wanted to make something through the Word."[7] According to Birger Pearson, the *Apocryphon* preserves a Sethian gnostic myth that may have emerged as early as the first century, and the Christianization of which is first attested with Saturninus of Antioch, a near contemporary of Ignatius.[8] Finally, Heinrich Schlier notes that Ignatius's choice of the verb προέρχομαι to refer to the Word's having "come forth" from silence (*Magn.* 8:2), or from the Father (7:2), finds a striking parallel in the frequent "soteriological" use of the same verb in the *Excerpts from Theodotus* compiled by Clement of Alexandria, whereas the Fourth Gospel consistently employs the verb ἐξέρχομαι (never προέρχομαι) when it speaks of the Son's coming from the Father.[9] Theodotus was a Valentinian gnostic of the late second century.

As I conceded in chapter 2, Ignatius's presentation of the gospel has terminological and even some conceptual affinities to gnosticism. This fact can be variously explained, and it is certainly possible that Ignatius drew upon currents of thought that were contributing, around the same time, to the early development of Christian gnosticism. Nevertheless, Ignatius's deepest theological affinities by far are to New Testament Christianity. The very parallels cited above indicate the profound differences between his theology and gnostic myth. Ignatius's confession of the "one God" (*Magn.* 8:2) and the "one Jesus Christ" (7:2) stands in stark contrast to gnosticism's fragmentation of God and Christ into dozens of divine and semidivine hypostases (Inexpressible, Silence, Father, Truth, Word, Life, Man, Church, Christ, Jesus, Mind, etc.). Moreover, Ignatius stresses that God has perfectly manifested himself in a historical event. There is no hint in *Magnesians* or anywhere else in the Ignatian corpus, not even in the passages that speak of "aeons" or "archontic constellations," of a mythological scheme of emanations. What Ignatius says about Jesus Christ is fully compatible with the Johannine Logos Hymn, which ends with these words: "No one has ever seen God; the only-begotten God, who is in the bosom of the Father, has declared him."[10]

---

7. Michael Waldstein and Frederik Wisse, eds., *The Apocryphon of John: Synopsis of Nag Hammadi Codices II,1; III,1; and IV,1 with BG 8502,2* (Leiden: E. J. Brill, 1995), 44–45.

8. Pearson, *Ancient Gnosticism*, 69, 99.

9. Jn 8:42, 13:3, 16:27–28, 17:8; Schlier, *Religionsgeschichtliche Untersuchungen*, 35.

10. Jn 1:18; Grant, *Ignatius of Antioch*, 62.

There can be little doubt that Ignatius learned the Christological use of the term λόγος from the Fourth Gospel, or at least from Johannine tradition, and even his surprising reference to eternal σιγή finds a far more meaningful parallel in the New Testament than in any gnostic text.[11] At the end of Paul's Epistle to the Romans we find (in most manuscripts) a doxology that articulates a theology of revelation similar to the one Ignatius presents in *Magnesians*.

To the one who is able to confirm you in my gospel and in the proclamation of Jesus Christ, according to the revelation of a mystery *kept in silence* [σεσιγημένου] for eternal ages *but now manifested* [φανερωθέντος δὲ νῦν] through the prophetic scriptures and made known to all nations, according to the command of the eternal God, for the obedience of faith—to the only wise God, through Jesus Christ, be glory unto the ages. Amen. (Rom 16:25–27)[12]

For the author of this text, as for Ignatius (*Magn*. 9:1), "mystery" designates, not what is utterly and forever unknowable, but that which, while remaining incomprehensible to human understanding, has nonetheless been revealed through the economic action of God. The Romans doxology multiplies lexemes suggestive of divine disclosure and annunciation ("revelation," "manifested," "made known," "gospel," "proclamation") in order to indicate that what was eternally hidden in the silence of God has really been communicated to the world in Jesus Christ and through the church. We have every reason to believe that Ignatius held a similar view. Moreover, for both authors, the revelation of this mystery is in some sense already present in the writings of Israel's prophets but has been definitively manifested only "now" in Jesus Christ and through the proclamation of the gospel to all nations.[13] In other words, the Romans

---

11. Pettersen is correct to distinguish sharply between gnosticism and Ignatius's New Testament–like Christianity, but he is too eager to dissociate the Ignatian God entirely from the concept of "silence" ("Sending Heretics to Coventry," 335–50). According to Pettersen, ἡσυχία is not a synonym of σιγή. The former term, not the latter, is "a primary characteristic of God." It means "stillness" or "tranquility" and in Eph. 15:2 and 19:1 refers to the "divine pacificity" (338–40). In *Magn*. 8:2, where Ignatius uses σιγή rather than ἡσυχία, "we need not find the association of silence with God" (339). Pettersen's argument is strained when he maintains that in this passage σιγή "refers not to God himself but to man's appreciation of God" (341). Are we to suppose, then, that in the incarnation the Logos "came forth from man's appreciation of God"? There are, of course, different shades of meaning between the terms σιγή and ἡσυχία, and they are not absolutely and always interchangeable (synonyms rarely are). But the way Ignatius uses the verb σιγᾶν with ἡσυχία in Eph. 15:1–2 argues against the sharp and artificial distinction that Pettersen makes between the two roots.

12. For the textual attestation of this passage and a brief discussion of its authorship and place within Romans, see Joseph A. Fitzmyer, *Romans: A New Translation with Introduction and Commentary*, Anchor Bible 33 (New York: Doubleday, 1993), 48, 753–56.

13. *Magn*. 8:2; *Phld*. 9:2; *Smyr*. 1:2.

doxology presupposes the sort of carefully nuanced economic relationship between "old" and "new" that we find in Ignatius's letters.

Whether Ignatius read the Romans doxology and drew upon it as a source, we cannot say. But comparison between this text and Ignatius's letters indicates at least that it was possible for early Christians to incorporate the notion of eternal silence into an authentically biblical theology of revelation. Having said this, it is important to note that Ignatius's use of σιγή in *Magnesians* 8:2 goes beyond what we find in the Romans doxology. Whereas the latter text employs the perfect participle σεσιγημένου to indicate the condition of the divine mystery prior to its being revealed—thus setting up a semantic opposition between two states: "kept in silence" versus "manifested"—Ignatius uses the noun σιγή and places it alongside the Christological term λόγος in such a way as to highlight the semantic tension between "silence" and "Word." The juxtaposition of λόγος and σιγή might, then, indicate that the latter term, like the former, denotes a personal being, not merely the state or condition of "silence." But if so, what exactly does Ignatius mean by the term? Is he using "Silence" as another name for the triune God? Or is he referring more specifically to the Father, the first person of the Trinity? A second, closely related question is whether the phrase "his Word come forth [προελθών] from silence" makes reference to the eternal generation of the Word, or to his economic mission.

According to Schoedel, the formulation of *Magnesians* 8:2 leaves one with "the impression that before Christ's coming the divine is conceived of as an undifferentiated unity."[14] In other words, Schoedel understands σιγή to refer, not to the Father, nor even to the Trinity, but to a non-Trinitarian or "undifferentiated" God. Moreover, he takes προελθών to refer, not to the Word's eternal generation, but to his coming into the world at the incarnation. More precisely, Schoedel seems to think that Ignatius is using the verb προέρχομαι in an emanationist sense, so that the advent of Christ is not really the incarnation of a preexisting Word. There was no distinct Word or Son prior to his coming into the world. The emanation of the Word and the mission of the Word are one and the same thing. Prior to this event, God was simply undifferentiated "Silence." In short, Schoedel understands Ignatius to be propounding a sort of modalism. He supports this interpretation of *Magnesians* 8:2 by reference to the similar use of λόγος, προέρχομαι, and σιγή in a fragment from the

---

14. *Ignatius of Antioch*, 120.

works of the fourth-century modalist Marcellus of Ancyra.[15] But because Ignatius says earlier in *Magnesians* that "Jesus Christ ... was with the Father before the ages" (6:1), and in our passage adds that Israel's prophets were "inspired by the grace of Christ" (8:2), Schoedel is compelled to admit that Ignatius's "modalism" is "not unmitigated." Strangely, he also maintains that Ignatius believed only in "the pre-existence of Christ ... not of the Son."[16]

There is an important grain of truth in Schoedel's interpretation of *Magnesians* 8:2, but the charge of (mitigated) modalism ultimately falls wide of the mark. To demonstrate both points, it will be necessary to sort through Schoedel's claims and to take a closer look at Ignatius's words. For starters, the fragment from Marcellus of Ancyra, while interesting, can be dismissed as irrelevant to the interpretation of *Magnesians*. As Lightfoot demonstrates, it is likely that Marcellus drew upon the Ignatian letters and manipulated their language to express his own theology.[17] Next, Schoedel's assertion that Ignatius believed in the preexistence of "Christ" but not of "the Son" is unsustainable, for it represents a strained interpretation of the passages in question. If "Jesus Christ ... was with the Father before the ages" (6:1) but was not yet the Son, how was the Father already the Father? If he did not yet have a Son and had not yet created the world, in what sense was he "Father"? Similarly, when Ignatius says that God "manifested himself through Jesus Christ his Son" (8:2), nothing in these words suggests that he was "Jesus Christ" prior to this manifestation but only became "his Son" by virtue of the manifestation.

Indeed, we might have expected Ignatius to say just the opposite, namely, that the Logos was already God's Son prior to the incarnation but only became the man Jesus Christ at the time of the incarnation. Ignatius could have said that, and such a formulation could be understood in an

---

15. Ibid.; see Eusebius, *De ecclesiastica theologia* 2:9 (for the relevant portion of the Greek text, see Lightfoot, *Ignatius, Polycarp*, 2.127). If I am reading Schoedel correctly, he is not taking Ignatius to be a nominalist modalist, that is, one who regards words such as "Father," "Word," and "Spirit" as merely designating the various economic actions of the one God. Rather, Schoedel seems to recognize that Ignatius makes a real distinction between the Father and the Word but maintains that for Ignatius this distinction has a beginning in time (i.e., Christ's coming into the world). The Word/Son would then be an emanation from the Silence/Father. Schoedel's comment is quite brief, however, and I may be looking for more precision in his thought than is actually there.

16. *Ignatius of Antioch*, 120.

17. Lightfoot, *Ignatius, Polycarp*, 2.126–27. Among the relevant differences between the two texts, one should note that whereas Ignatius is concerned with the incarnation (as I shall demonstrate), Marcellus transfers the reference to the creation of the world.

orthodox manner. But probably he avoids that sort of statement because he does not want to leave himself open to a misinterpretation that would take "the Son" and "Jesus Christ" to be two different subjects. Instead, he purposely speaks of "Christ" or "Jesus Christ" in the passages that most clearly indicate preexistence, and he does this in order to stress a fundamental continuity. The one who was "with the Father before the ages" and whose grace inspired the prophets of Israel is none other than the one who "appeared" in the flesh "at the end" as Jesus Christ (6:1). Though he does not have the benefit of the Christological categories that were to be developed by the fourth century, Ignatius already demonstrates an implicit understanding that the preexistent Son of God and the historical Jesus Christ are one and the same person.[18] This is not to say, of course, that the incarnation was inconsequential. Ignatius knows that a very important change took place at the time of the incarnation. Prior to this event, Christ was not yet in the flesh and had not yet "appeared" (6:1). That is why the prophets were his disciples "in the Spirit" (9:2). But nothing in *Magnesians* or any of the other letters suggests that Ignatius thought that Jesus Christ first became God's "Son" at the time of the incarnation.[19]

Whether Ignatius slips into modalism, or emanationism, when he describes Jesus Christ as God's "Word come forth from silence" is more difficult to determine since he employs the term λόγος as a Christological title only here (*Magn.* 8:2). With respect to this passage, we have still to decide what Ignatius means by "silence" and whether he is speaking here theologically, or economically, that is, whether "come forth" refers to the eternal generation of the Word, or to his coming into the world. In approaching these questions it will help to look first at still another creedal formula found earlier in *Magnesians* (7:2).

> All of you should hasten together to one temple of God, as to one altar, to one Jesus Christ, who came forth [προελθόντα] from one Father, and was toward one, and departed.

Ignatius expresses himself somewhat cryptically here, but his meaning can be teased out. Beginning at the end of the statement and working backward, we can be fairly certain that "departed" (χωρήσαντα) refers to the paschal mystery as Christ's departure from the world and return

---

18. That should not really surprise us, since the same could be said of John, Paul, and the author of Hebrews.

19. Ignatius's other references to Jesus Christ as Son of God are found in Eph. 4:2, 20:2; *Magn.* 13:1; Rom. sal. (bis), 7:3 (variant reading); and Smyr. 1:1.

to God.[20] The phrase "was toward one" (εἰς ἕνα ὄντα) evidently, then, refers to the fundamental orientation of Jesus' life on earth as directed "toward" the Father in obedience to his will.[21] This leaves the phrase "came forth from one Father" to refer to the incarnation. It does not, at least in its denotation, make reference to the eternal generation of the Word.[22] The thought of this passage is, as Camelot notes, reminiscent of the Fourth Gospel, where the Christ event is presented schematically as the Son's coming into the world to do the Father's will, followed by his departure from the world and return to the Father.[23]

Returning to *Magnesians* 8:2, we find that it too evokes this Johannine schema and is principally concerned with the Christ event.

> ... there is one God,
> who manifested himself through Jesus Christ his Son,
> who is his Word [λόγος] come forth from silence [σιγή],
> who in all things pleased the one who sent him.

Of the three "who"-clauses in this passage, the first and the third clearly refer to the divine economy, not to the inner life of the Trinity, at least not directly so. The first refers to the Christ event globally as God's self-manifestation in the Son. The third refers to the Son's economic mission and his life of obedience to the Father. Therefore the second "who"-clause, sandwiched as it is between two economic statements, is probably also economic rather than strictly theological. This likelihood is strengthened by the close verbal parallel to the creedal formula that we just examined in *Magnesians* 7:2, where the aorist participle of προέρχομαι rather clearly refers to the Son's coming into the world at the incarnation. We may, then, tentatively conclude that the phrase "his Word come forth from silence" refers directly to the incarnation rather than to the Father's eternal generation of the Son.[24] On this point, I agree with Schoedel.

---

20. Elsewhere Ignatius uses the verb χωρέω to refer to death as a departure from the world unto one's eternal destiny (5:1; Eph. 16:2; cf. Diog. 8:2). Alternatively one might take the verb to mean "yielded" or "accepted," as it does in Tral. 5:1 and Smyr. 6:1 (cf. συγχωρέω in Magn. 3:1). But this seems less likely, as χωρέω in this latter sense does not take a person as its object and does not take the object with εἰς.

21. Since the verb εἰμί has no aorist participle, it is legitimate in such a context to render the present participle with "was."

22. So Lightfoot, who however takes the middle phrase of 7:2 ("was toward one") as "describing the absolute eternal union of the Son with the Father," comparing Jn 1:18 (*Ignatius, Polycarp*, 2.123). It is that union, but as lived in and through his humanity.

23. *Ignace d'Antioche*, 86, n. 2; cf. Jn 16:28.

24. So Lightfoot (*Ignatius, Polycarp*, 2.127), who adds: "Ignatius however does not deny the pre-existence of the Word here, though he does not assert it" (127–28).

Next we need to specify, as nearly as possible, the referent of σιγή in *Magnesians* 8:2. The close verbal and structural parallel to 7:2 suggests some manner of correlation between "silence" and "one Father."

> ... the one Jesus Christ, who came forth from one Father (7:2)
> ... Jesus Christ his Son, who is his Word come forth from silence (8:2)

This is not to say, however, that Ignatius uses σιγή here as a formal title or proper name for the first person of the Trinity. The correlation between the two texts is not that strict. God the Father already has his place within the formulation of *Magnesians* 8:2 in the personal pronoun αὐτοῦ ("his"), and nothing in the grammar of the sentence indicates that "silence" has an anaphoric relation to "his." I suggest that by "silence" Ignatius refers to the eternal mystery of God's life and being, a mystery that originates in the Father but that is so fully shared with the Son that the latter is able to manifest it to the world. It is "silence" because it is hidden until the Son reveals it and remains mysterious even after he reveals it. Eternal "silence" for Ignatius is not the realm of the utterly unknowable; still less is it an ontological void cut off from the "being" of creatures. On the contrary, it is the fullness of being. The paradox of God's "Word come forth from silence" expresses the fact that Jesus Christ is the true and definitive revelation of God but that God loses none of his mystery in manifesting himself in this way.[25]

The Analogy of the Word and Trinitarian Theology

By combining the Johannine Christological title Logos with a description of the incarnation in terms of "coming forth from silence," Ignatius helps us to appreciate that λόγος is an analogical term. That is, the power of self-expression and truth-telling present in human linguistic rationality is a participation in the supremely transcendent Logos. There is therefore, on the one hand, an ontological bond between the two realities, but they remain, on the other hand, incommensurable. The coming forth of God's Logos is the transcendent perfection of self-expression and truth-telling. Therefore God can be spoken of truthfully in human words, but his mystery can never be reduced to human language and rationality. These truths are critical to Ignatius's theology of revelation. Jesus Christ himself is the "teacher," who has spoken divine truth in hu-

---

25. Broadly speaking, this is also the interpretation of Corwin (*St. Ignatius and Christianity*, 116–30, 268).

man language, but his revelation of the Father is by no means limited to, or exhausted by, what even he himself has said in human words. The mysteries he has accomplished "in the silence of God" are also "worthy of the Father."[26] This truth has, as we shall also see, important implications at the level of the church's proclamation of the gospel and the believer's subjective appropriation of the truth of revelation.

At this point it will be helpful to consider another aspect of the analogical use of the terms λόγος and σιγή. In some contexts and from certain perspectives "word" and "silence" are simply antithetical, as when a person must choose in a given circumstance between speaking (word) and refraining from speech (silence). In such a case, the silence with which we are concerned is the exterior silence that would be "broken" should the person opt to speak. But when we view speaking as a personal word of self-manifestation coming forth from interior silence, there remains a semantic tension between the terms "word" and "silence" but not a sharp opposition. In such a case, "silence" denotes the personal depths within which an unspoken word is formed and from which the corresponding spoken word issues forth. There is in this latter case more continuity than discontinuity between silence and word.[27]

If we are dealing with human speaking, of course, this continuity is quite imperfect. We are familiar with the incongruities that accompany human attempts at verbal self-expression. At one end of the spectrum, there are times when the exteriorization of the word, whether in speech or writing, seems to liberate and unfold the inchoate interior apprehension of the truth. In such a case the very act of articulation and of "bringing forth" the word seems concurrent with, perhaps even productive of, insight and understanding. Thus Augustine remarks that his task in writing the *De Trinitate* is one "not so much of discoursing with authority respecting things I know already, as of learning those things by piously discoursing of them."[28] At the other end of the spectrum, we sometimes have the experience that our exterior words do not do justice to that which we apprehend interiorly. And so the same Augustine elsewhere

26. Eph. 15:1, 19:1.
27. Bower correctly notes: "We may, of course, interpret this passage [*Magn.* 8:2] to mean that the divine silence was broken when the Word came forth. But more consistent with the rest of Ignatius' statements concerning σιγή is the interpretation that sees λόγος as an expression of σιγή. The divine silence is 'heard' (paradoxically) in the 'action' of the λόγος, i.e. in the obedience of Christ's Passion" ("The Meaning of ΕΠΙΤΥΓΧΑΝΩ," 12).
28. *De Trinitate* 1:5; CCSL 50.37 (non tam cognita cum auctoritate dissererere quam ea cum pietate disserendo cognoscere); translation: *Basic Writings of St. Augustine*, ed. Whitney J. Oates, 2 vols. (New York: Random House, 1948), 2.674.

complains, "My own speech nearly always disappoints me ... it saddens me that my tongue cannot do justice to my heart."[29]

When we speak analogically of God's bringing forth his own Word from eternal silence, however, we may assume the perfect identity of "interior" Word with "exterior" Word. The Word who comes forth into the realm of human finitude and temporality is the very Word who was "kept in silence for eternal ages." The economic Word neither improves upon nor falls short of the immanent Word. We may likewise assume that the immanent Word is already God's perfect self-knowledge and self-expression before it is sent forth economically. That is, there is an immanent conception of the Word that is not dependent for its reality upon God's *ad extra* act of sending forth the Word into the world. In God there is an eternal conception of the Logos analogous to the conception of the interior word in the human heart. God does not begin to know himself and express himself by means of his economic activity. The Word is not engendered by coming forth from a previously undifferentiated Deity.

Naturally, this is to view things with the hindsight of Trinitarian theology and dogma. I am not claiming that Ignatius, or anyone else in the second century, would have articulated the matter in quite this way. But Ignatius does clearly identify the one who "was with the Father before the ages," whom he elsewhere calls "the timeless one" (*Poly.* 3:2), with the one who "appeared" temporally in Jesus Christ (*Magn.* 6:1), and just a few lines later he refers to this same one as God's "Word come forth from silence" (8:2). Does not the sense of personal continuity between the preexistent and the economic that is expressed in the former passage carry over to the latter passage? Does not Ignatius's apparent familiarity with the Johannine Prologue (or at least Johannine tradition) suggest that he means λόγος to designate precisely the Word who "was in the beginning with God"? Within the context of *Magnesians*, does the image of the Word's coming forth from silence really leave one with "the impression that before Christ's coming the divine is conceived of as an undifferentiated unity"? Is it not rather the case that this image, which implicitly compares the incarnation to the speaking forth of a human word conceived in the silence of human interiority, implies the preexistence of the divine Word and thus strengthens the sense of continuity between the eternal and the economic that the reader has already gained from the formulation of *Magnesians* 6:1? One might, of course, conclude

---

29. *De catechizandis rudibus* 2:3; CCSL 46.122 (mihi prope semper sermo meus displicet ... contristor linguam meam cordi meo non potuisse sufficere).

otherwise, but only on the dubious prior assumption that the superficial similarity of *Magnesians* 8:2 to language found in later gnostic or modalist texts ought to bear more interpretive weight than its deep affinity to traditions and texts that were to find their way into the New Testament.[30]

Finally, is it unreasonable to suppose that Ignatius may even have possessed an inchoate knowledge of the Word's eternal procession? If he held that God had sent forth his Word into the world in order to "manifest himself" to human beings, and also held that this same Word was "with the Father before the ages," might it not have occurred to him that the Father already knew himself and, as it were, expressed himself "before the ages" in his Word? After all, it is only about a century after Ignatius's death that we find Tertullian attempting to elaborate a psychological analogy for the Trinity, in the course of which he says that God "has reason within himself even when he is silent, and in that reason a Word."[31] I suggest this merely as a possibility, having no desire to exaggerate Ignatius's explicit understanding of Trinitarian theology. In employing the Johannine term λόγος, his interest is primarily in the Son's economic mission as the one through whom the Father speaks, just as it is when he calls Christ "the mouth that cannot lie, by which the Father has spoken truthfully" (*Rom.* 8:2). And if Ignatius has only begun to work out the strictly theological implications of the title Logos, still less has he done this for the title Son. Far from confessing that the Son is "eternally begotten of the Father," he says that Jesus Christ is "unborn" with respect to his divinity (*Eph.* 7:2).

In sum, I agree with Schoedel on two points pertaining to the exegesis of the phrase "his Word come forth from silence": first, that this formulation refers to an economic action of God (the incarnation); and second, that "silence" here does not precisely designate the first person of the Trinity. But I disagree that this constitutes modalism or emanationism, even of a mitigated sort. Ignatius does not conceive of the divinity prior to Christ's advent as "an undifferentiated unity." Throughout his letters he maintains a clear distinction between God the Father and Jesus Christ his Son, and in at least one passage he explicitly indicates that this distinction preexists, not only the incarnation, but the creation

---

30. Jn 1:1–3; Rom 16:25–27. Already in the nineteenth century, Goltz adduced these two New Testament passages as evidence against a gnostic interpretation of *Magn.* 8:2 (*Ignatius von Antiochien*, 20).

31. *Adversus Praxean* 5:7; CCSL 2.1164 (habeat in se etiam tacendo rationem et in ratione sermonem).

of the world (*Magn.* 6:1). In fact, it is fair to say that the relational distinction between the Father and the Son within the unity of the "one God" permeates Ignatius's thought. He is far from being a modalist.[32] Modalist monarchianism, which emerged in the late second and early third centuries, attempted to explain the New Testament's sharp distinctions among Father, Son, and Spirit by reducing these to economic functions or "modes" of the one God. This is not at all the tendency of Ignatius's thought. Rather, he stands near the beginning of a process by which theology will work its way back through the mystery of God's economic activity to a serious consideration of his immanent relations. Ignatius's boldness of expression and willingness to embrace the paradoxical, in this case holding on to both the unity of God and the relational distinction between Father and Son, is compatible with later Trinitarian theology and in no way redolent of the naive rationalism of early modalism.[33]

In granting that the creedal formulae of *Magnesians* 7:2 and 8:2 refer to God's economic action, I qualified this admission by noting that it applies to the denotation or direct reference of Ignatius's words. In three respects the immanent life of God is also present in these passages, albeit indirectly. First, it is implicit contextually. Since Ignatius has already told us that Jesus Christ was "with the Father before the ages" (6:1), we bring that information with us when we read the subsequent statements about Jesus Christ's coming forth from the Father (7:2) or the Word's coming forth from silence (8:2). Second, God's immanent life is implicit in the ideas expressed by the words of the creedal formulae themselves. To say, for example, that God has "manifested himself" implies that there is some stable and prior reality of God ("himself") that is manifested, an eternal reality that is not dependent for its existence on his temporal self-manifestation. Third, and most importantly, whether or not Ignatius had any intention of referring to it, the immanent life of

---

32. Goltz, *Ignatius von Antiochien*, 15.

33. According to Jaroslav Pelikan, modalist monarchianism, as distinct from the later and more refined theology of Sabellius, was "an effort to provide a theology for the language of devotion" and constituted "a systematization of popular Christian belief" that was "rather naïve" and employed "simpleminded language" (*The Christian Tradition: A History of the Development of Doctrine*, vol. 1, *The Emergence of the Catholic Tradition (100–600)* [Chicago: University of Chicago Press, 1971], 178–79). However, this description may depend a little too uncritically upon Tertullian's caricature of the early modalists as *simplices* (*Adversus Praxean* 3:1; CCSL 2.1161). Other scholars hold that modalism arose "partly in reaction to the Gnostic theories of intermediate aeons and partly as a reaction to subordinationist tendencies of orthodox teachers" (P. J. Hamell, "Monarchianism," *New Catholic Encyclopedia*, 17 vols. [Washington, D.C.: The Catholic University of America Press, 1968], 9.1019). Basil Studer combines elements of both views (*Trinity and Incarnation: The Faith of the Early Church* [Collegeville, Minn.: Liturgical Press, 1993], 66–67).

God is truly present in *the economic realities* to which he does refer. "The Son of God ... communicates to his humanity his own personal mode of existence in the Trinity," so that "what was visible in his earthly life leads to the invisible mystery of his divine Sonship."[34] This is true objectively even if Ignatius lacks any subjective awareness of it.

In this context it might be worthwhile to recall the hermeneutic of understanding sketched out in the introduction. In his dense and suggestive theological affirmations Ignatius does not simply transmit his conceptual horizon to his readers. Rather, he proclaims a mystery that transcends his conceptual horizon and invites his readers to contemplate that mystery with him. Ignatius's horizon is vitally important, but it is not meant to stand alone. Understanding takes place when there is a conversation about the matter at hand and a fusing of horizons.

The development of Christology and Trinitarian theology is not merely the development of ideas, as Schoedel implies, but the unfolding of a mystery. From the beginning of its existence the church has possessed the mystery of God's immanent life hidden within the economic mystery of the Christ event (mediated through word and sacrament). The church has always possessed real knowledge of the immanent Trinity in and through the revelation of the economic Trinity. Initially this knowledge was mostly implicit, or tacit, and was expressed in dense formulas and symbols. Through centuries of reflection upon the Christ event, the church worked its way back into the mystery of the immanent Trinity, so to speak. This dynamic of theological development was determined by the nature of the economy itself. As John Chrysostom puts it, "For this is also how the reality was dispensed [ᾠκονομήθη]: First they saw him as a man on earth, and then they perceived that he is God."[35]

An Economy of Words and Deeds

Having taken a careful look at the formulation of *Magnesians* 8:2, we may now examine how the word-silence paradox plays out in the Son's economic mission, in the church's proclamation of the gospel, and in the believer's personal appropriation of divine revelation. One text that draws together all these levels and displays their interrelations is *Ephesians* 14–15, which is essentially an exhortation to Christian authenticity.

---

34. CCC 470, 515.
35. *Homiliae in epistolam ad Romanos* 1:2; PG 60.397 (οὕτω γὰρ καὶ τὸ πρᾶγμα ᾠκονομήθη· πρῶτον γοῦν εἶδον αὐτὸν ἄνθρωπον ἐπὶ τῆς γῆς, καὶ τότε ἐνόησαν θεόν).

Instead of attempting to expound the entire passage at once, I shall focus first on a dense Christological aphorism that is embedded within it.

There is one teacher, who spoke and it came to be; even the things he has done silently are worthy of the Father. (15:1b)

By calling Jesus Christ the "one teacher" Ignatius underscores his unique role as the revealer of the Father. This statement is thus closely related to the title Logos and to the image of Christ as "the mouth that cannot lie, by which the Father has spoken truthfully" (Rom. 8:2).[36] The Son plays the role of teacher already during the Old Testament period via the instruction that he gives to Israel's prophets "in the Spirit" (Magn. 9:2), and he realizes this role most perfectly in the Christ event, by which he definitively manifests the Father. But in Ephesians 15:1, and only here, Ignatius relates the Son's redemptive role as revealer of the Father to his role as creator of the world. The phrase "who spoke and it came to be" (ὃς εἶπεν καὶ ἐγένετο) is an allusion to God's act of creation as narrated in the Septuagint of Psalm 32:9 (αὐτὸς εἶπεν καὶ ἐγενήθησαν) and Genesis 1:3 (εἶπεν ὁ θεὸς ... καὶ ἐγένετο). The significance of this passing reference to creation lies in the way it suggests not only that the order of redemption is intimately linked to the order of creation within the unity of the one divine economy but also that the person of the Word is responsible for this unity. Because the cosmos is "spoken" into being by the Word, the cosmos itself is a revelatory "word" of God. The Logos begins the work of divine self-manifestation in the act of creation and builds upon this foundation in his redemptive mission. Here Ignatius displays a cohesive and fairly comprehensive theology of the Word. The very Word who was with the Father "before the ages" is he by whom the world was created and by whom the world is redeemed, and he unites the two principal stages of redemption by being the one teacher who makes "disciples" both of Israel's prophets and of Christians (Magn. 9:1–2). The new presupposes the old, redemption presupposes creation, and οἰκονομία presupposes θεολογία.

To refer to Jesus Christ as the "one teacher" evokes first of all his public ministry of the word.[37] The high regard in which Ignatius holds the Lord's teaching is evident in the numerous verbal echoes of Johannine discourses and Synoptic dominical logia found throughout his let-

---

36. Elsewhere in Ephesians Ignatius identifies Jesus Christ as "the mind-set [γνώμη] of the Father" (3:2) and "the knowledge [γνῶσις] of God" (17:2).

37. Corwin, St. Ignatius and Christianity, 105.

ters.[38] He exhorts Christians to "adorn" themselves "in the commandments of Jesus Christ" (Eph. 9:2) and to found their lives upon "the precepts of the Lord and of the apostles" (Magn. 13:1). But Ignatius extends Jesus' role as teacher to what he accomplished "silently" (σιγῶν), that is, through actions that were largely nonverbal.[39] To say that Christ's deeds are "worthy of the Father" probably means that they too are revelatory of the mystery of God. Recalling that the term λόγος is analogical, we might say that the incarnate Logos manifests the Father both in rational human discourse and in deeds that "bespeak" the Father. Both modes are λογικός insofar as they participate in the Logos and communicate the truth of God in ways intelligible to rational creatures. This way of viewing the Lord's public ministry is implicit in, and basic to, the canonical gospels, including the two upon which Ignatius seems to depend. As is well known, Matthew purposefully dovetails narrative material with discourse material in his account of the public ministry, and John presents Jesus' ministry as consisting of reciprocally illuminative "works" and "words," typically following the narration of a "sign" with a discourse that provides commentary on it (e.g., Jn 5:1–47).

Surprisingly, however, Ignatius never refers, or even alludes, to the healings, exorcisms, or other miracles of Jesus' ministry.[40] What "things done silently" by Jesus might Ignatius, then, have especially in mind? The answer to this question is found in the final chapters of Ephesians. Ignatius refers to the Lord having received perfumed ointment upon his head (17:1); to his conception, birth, baptism, and passion (18:2); and to his resurrection (20:1). And most importantly for our investigation of the word-silence paradox, Ignatius refers to Mary's virginity, her childbirth, and Jesus' death as "three mysteries of a cry [κραυγή], accomplished in the silence [ἡσυχία] of God" (19:1). Of the various attempts to explain this enigmatic statement, Schoedel's is perhaps the most plausible: "The unheralded events of salvation cry out their meaning to those who are able to grasp their significance."[41] This interpretation fits the context

---

38. For examples, see the section "Ignatius and the New Testament" in chapter 1.
39. One might compare the way Mark presents Jesus' exorcisms and other deeds of power as "a new teaching [διδαχή], with authority" (Mk 1:27).
40. Except possibly by referring to Jesus Christ as the "one healer" (Eph. 7:2). In any case, many of the miracles are performed with a word of command, e.g.: "Be still, and come out of him!" (Mk 1:25), "Be opened!" (7:34), "Lazarus, come out!" (Jn 11:43).
41. *Ignatius of Antioch*, 91. Alternatively, Ignatius may have in mind a "cry" uttered in connection with each mystery: with respect to Mary's virginal conception, either the angelic salutation (Lk 1:28) or Elizabeth's Spirit-filled greeting (cf. κραυγή in 1:42); Mary's cry of pain in childbirth (cf. κράζω in Rv 12:2); and Jesus' own cry at the moment of death (cf. κράζω in Mt 27:50;

nicely. Ignatius is concerned to present the events of the economy of redemption precisely as "mysteries," that is, as events that make manifest in the spatiotemporal realm that which is eternal and uncreated. Human words, to be sure, play an indispensable part in expounding the mystery of God, but as the latter is ineffable it cannot be communicated in words alone. Ignatius apparently finds great significance in the fact that the central moments in the Christ event are essentially nonverbal. The mysterious human silence that surrounds Jesus' conception, birth, and death reflects the fact that these events in a most profound manner bring into the spatiotemporal realm that which had been "kept in silence for eternal ages" (Rom 16:25). The events themselves "cry out" a truth that transcends human language.

Jesus' earthly life and ministry as "our only teacher" (*Magn.* 9:1) consisted, then, in deeds and words together, by which God was "manifesting himself humanly" (*Eph.* 19:3). This is in accord with the nature of the entire economy of revelation, which is "accomplished in deeds and words intrinsically interconnected."[42] Those who would receive this revelation, therefore, must be attuned not only to what Jesus teaches in words but to what he teaches nonverbally in his actions.[43] Indeed, if Jesus' words and deeds are intrinsically interconnected, it would be impossible to interpret one correctly without the other. Thus, immediately after mentioning "the things he has done silently," Ignatius adds, "The one who has truly taken possession of Jesus' word [λόγος] is also able to hear his silence [ἡσυχία]" (*Eph.* 15:2a). Presumably this capacity to "hear" Jesus' silence entails the cultivation of an interior life, so that the holy silence of Jesus' life finds a receptive counterpart in the soul of the believer (cf. *Barn.* 19:4). In fact, if the silent mysteries of the life of the incarnate Logos manifest the eternal "silence" from which the Logos has come forth, the believer finds a sort of access to this divine silence through prayerful meditation

---

and κραυγή in Heb 5:7, which, however, probably refers to the prayer in the garden). Either of these interpretations is probably preferable to the view that refers the "cry" to the church's proclamation, as in Holmes's translation: "three mysteries to be loudly proclaimed" (*Apostolic Fathers,* 197; cf. Lightfoot, *Ignatius, Polycarp,* 2.79–80). For this sense, Ignatius might have written τρία μυστήρια κερύγματος, though admittedly he does use the verb κραυγάζω to refer to the Spirit-inspired proclamation of the word in liturgical assembly in Phld. 7:1. Graydon F. Snyder seems to cut the Gordian knot by identifying "Jesus' birth, his baptism, and his death" as the three mysteries in question ("The Historical Jesus in the Letters of Ignatius of Antioch," *Biblical Research* 8 [1963]: 4), but this otherwise attractive hypothesis unfortunately ignores the plain sense of Ignatius's words.

42. *Dei Verbum* 2.
43. Corwin, *St. Ignatius and Christianity,* 106.

on the *mysteria vitae Iesu*. The attempt to assimilate one's interior life to the silence of Christ and thus to the divine silence will be developed in the East in the Hesychast tradition, the basic principle of which will be given succinct expression centuries later by the Spanish mystic John of the Cross.

> The Father spoke one Word, which was His Son,
> and this Word He always speaks in eternal silence,
> and in silence must It be heard by the soul.[44]

Admittedly, the great emphasis that Ignatius places upon prayer in his letters is driven more by practical than by theoretical or mystical concerns. As he is intensely interested in the concrete life of the community, his frequent exhortations to prayer refer almost without exception to communal intercessory petitions. Only in his exhortation of a fellow bishop does Ignatius directly touch on the cultivation of the interior life, and even here it is with the practical end of pastoral care for the church in view.[45] Still, it is hard to imagine that Ignatius's own intense personal devotion to Jesus Christ, his profound theoretical grasp of the faith, and his possession of charismata did not flow from a deep life of personal prayer. In any case, the real key to understanding how the word-silence paradox plays out in the life of the believer is to recognize that for Ignatius the practical and theoretical dimensions of Christian existence converge perfectly in its τέλος.

As noted above, *Ephesians* 14–15 is an exhortation to Christian authenticity, which for Ignatius is not only a matter of personal integrity but, above all, of living out the gospel "unto the end" (εἰς τέλος). He encourages the believers in Ephesus to direct their faith and love "perfectly" (τελείως) toward Jesus Christ, and then he explains that faith is the "beginning" (ἀρχή) and love the "end" (τέλος) of true life (14:1). As we learned in chapter 5, this means that an orthodox apprehension of the faith is a sort of theoretical principle (ἀρχή) without which one cannot get any traction in living out the Christian life, while love is the practical dimension and goal (τέλος) of Christian existence. But the theoretical and practical dimensions are so closely bound together that one

---

44. "Maxims and Counsels," no. 21 (*The Collected Works of St. John of the Cross*, trans. Kieran Kavanaugh and Otilio Rodriguez [Washington, D.C.: Institute of Carmelite Studies, 1979], 675). Another way to approach this is to say that divine silence and human silence meet in the person of the incarnate Word, specifically in the mystery of his human soul, and that the believer assimilates himself or herself to the *anima Christi* through silent prayer.

45. *Poly.* 1:3, 2:2.

cannot really possess the one without the other: "No one who professes faith sins."[46] This is so because the knowledge of divine truth that faith imparts is a kind of "power" at work in the believer's life, efficaciously moving that life toward its goal. The quality of one's profession of faith is evident in deeds and can only be judged from the perspective of the "end."[47]

> The tree is manifest from its fruit. Thus those who profess to belong to Christ will be seen through what they practice. For the work is not a matter of present profession but is carried out in the power of faith, if one is found faithful unto the end [εἰς τέλος]. (14:2b)

In sum, the verbal profession of faith is authentic and has value only if it is completed (synchronically) by deeds of love and (diachronically) by perseverance unto the end.

Next, Ignatius turns to the word-silence paradox in order to press the point: "It is better to remain silent and to be than to speak and not be" (15:1a). It is important to note here that he recommends silence as a relative, not an absolute, value. The absolute value, which relativizes the value of speech, is authenticity: to "be." The silence that Ignatius advocates is not antisocial, irrational, agnostic, or even apophatic. On the contrary, he wishes the followers of Christ to lead lives that "speak" the gospel. The authentic Christian *becomes* a "word of God" (λόγος θεοῦ), whereas one who merely "talks" the gospel without living it out unto the end is but a hollow "voice" (φωνή; *Rom.* 2:1). The Christian must present a rational and articulate witness to the world, but it is the whole life, the life that combines faith and love "perfectly" (τελείως), that possesses this quality of being an effective "word." One person may live such a life while speaking few words, whereas another may speak many words, perhaps even words that accurately represent the gospel, while not being a "word" himself. Thus Ignatius exhorts the Romans, "Do not speak Jesus Christ while desiring the world" (7:1).

The authentic Christian will actualize in his or her life what it means to be a true "man" (ἄνθρωπος; 6:2). Man is, already according to the order of creation, a rational (λογικός) creature made in the image of God (cf. *Diog.* 10:2). Within the order of redemption he realizes the supernatural end for which he was created by being incorporated into and empowered by "the perfect man" (τέλειος ἄνθρωπος), Jesus Christ (*Smyr.* 4:2),

---

46. *Eph.* 14:2a; cf. 8:2.
47. Cf. Sir 11:27 (Hebrew): "A man's end tells his story" (*sôp 'ādām yāgîd 'ālāyw*).

who is, of course, the incarnate Logos (*Magn.* 8:2). Such a person is a disciple of "the one teacher." He or she takes possession of the teacher's word and also learns how to listen to the teacher's silence "in order to be perfect" (τέλειος), that is, "in order to put into practice what he speaks about and to be recognized [as an authentic Christian] through what he does silently" (*Eph.* 15:2). With this last formulation Ignatius articulates rather precisely the interrelations between theory and practice, and between word and silence, in the Christian life. Speech gives birth to action, and silent action is a kind of word of witness. Once again, it is clear that silence as such is not the ideal. Perfection, or authenticity, is. And this perfection or authenticity will include of necessity the dimension of the word, both the spoken word and the silent "word."

Silent Bishops and True Life in Death

This last point is of particular relevance when we place the individual Christian life within its ecclesial context. Immediately after propounding the axiom, "It is better to be silent and to be than to speak and not be," Ignatius qualifies this statement with another aphorism: "Teaching is good, if the one who speaks acts accordingly" (*Eph.* 15:1). We must not underestimate the importance that the ministry of teaching has within Ignatius's understanding of the church. He grounds this ecclesial "good" in the ministry of the "one teacher" himself. Moreover, as noted above, Jesus Christ is not only the teacher but the content of instruction as well. Ignatius warns the churches not to listen to anyone who speaks to them "without Jesus Christ."[48] Such a person is, in effect, speaking without the Word. More dangerous still are those who disguise the fact that they are serving up their own ideas by mixing in a little bit of the truth of Jesus Christ, so that they are, as it were, "administering a lethal drug mixed with honeyed wine" (*Tral.* 6:2). Ignatius's letters, by contrast, are thoroughly Christocentric. Imitating his hero Paul, Ignatius has obviously decided to "know nothing" among the churches of Asia Minor "but Jesus Christ, and him crucified" (1 Cor 2:2). Though Ignatius is a creative and insightful theologian, his proclamation of Jesus Christ is thoroughly traditional in the best sense of the word. It has the "apostolic stamp" (*Tral.* sal.) because he clings to "the gospel" and "the apostles" (*Phld.* 5:1). If Ignatius eschews the title "teacher," it is certainly not

---

48. *Tral.* 9:1; *Eph.* 6:2; *Phld.* 6:1.

because he views himself as a mere "exhorter" or "pastoral theologian," as if such a role could be fulfilled without imparting solid doctrine.

In light of Ignatius's readiness to take up the role, if not the title, of teacher in his letters, and given the great importance that he places upon the episcopacy, it is curious to note how little he has to say about the bishop's responsibility to teach his flock. Instead, he extols the "silent bishop," who is reverenced all the more for his silence and who is to be held in the same regard "as the Lord himself" (Eph. 6:1). Such a bishop "can do more while remaining silent than can those who speak vain things" (Phld. 1:1).[49] "His very demeanor is a great lesson [μαθητεία], and his meekness is his power" (Tral. 3:2). As a bishop himself, Ignatius aspires to such meekness (4:2) and wishes to proclaim the gospel more with his life and death than with his words. Still, Christian charity does not permit him to remain completely silent, and so he undertakes to address the churches, more as their "fellow student" than as their teacher (Eph. 3:1–2). And just as he spoke aphoristically in the Holy Spirit when addressing the assembly in Philadelphia (Phld. 7:1–2), so in his letters he is circumspect to write "not according to the flesh, but according to the mind-set of God," as he addresses the churches "with few words."[50]

Ignatius's advocacy of "silent" bishops has sometimes been adduced as evidence that the episcopal office did not yet involve teaching as an essential responsibility in the early second century. It has been argued that Ignatius himself was exceptional in this regard and that the other bishops whom he mentions in his letters were administrators responsible for financial matters and the charitable distribution of goods, but not teachers.[51] This represents a rather wooden interpretation of Ignatius's words, ignoring precisely the theological function of the word-silence paradox that we have been examining in this chapter.[52] The sort of "silence" Ignatius has in mind is not at all the antithesis of "teaching" but represents rather the authentically Christ-like mode of teaching, that is,

---

49. I accept the reading λαλούντων ματαία with the Greek, Latin, and Coptic witnesses to the middle recension. Holmes omits ματαία with the Armenian version of the middle recension (Apostolic Fathers, 236).

50. Rom. 8:2–3; Poly. 7:3; Magn. 14:1.

51. Massey Hamilton Shepherd Jr., "Smyrna in the Ignatian Letters: A Study in Church Order," Journal of Religion 20 (1940): 141–59 (esp. 147); and Alistair Stewart-Sykes, "Prophecy and Patronage: The Relationship between Charismatic Functionaries and Household Officers in Early Christianity," in Trajectories, ed. Gregory and Tuckett, 165–89 (esp. 173–80).

52. Closer to the mark but still too reductive is the interpretation of Pettersen, which confines the "silence" of bishops to their "not speaking with the heretics" and "not discussing their heresy" ("Sending Heretics to Coventry," 346).

with few words and with actions that verify those words. Moreover, it is not the case that Ignatius has nothing at all to say about the bishop's responsibility to teach. In the one letter actually addressed to a bishop, he instructs Polycarp to give a "homily" or "public lecture" (ὁμιλία) on a certain subject (*Poly*. 5:1), employing a term closely related to the verb προσομιλέω ("address with a discourse"), which elsewhere refers to Ignatius's own didactic discourse to the churches via letters (*Eph*. 9:2).[53] More tellingly, Ignatius solemnly charges Polycarp to "exhort all, in order that they may be saved," and then immediately adds these words: "Vindicate your office" (*Poly*. 1:2). The clear implication is that "exhortation" is part and parcel of the episcopal office. Moreover, the verb translated "exhort" in this passage (παρακαλέω) is the same Pauline technical term that Ignatius frequently uses to describe what he himself is doing in his letters, which obviously involves imparting the central doctrines of the faith.[54]

Commentators have noted the Stoic coloring in Ignatius's description of the "silent" bishop, whose "freedom from anger" imitates God's own "mildness" and incompatibility with anger.[55] What has been overlooked is that Ignatius's promotion of "silence" also has deep roots in the biblical, and even prebiblical, wisdom tradition. The "silent man" of ancient Egyptian wisdom knows how to control his emotions and tongue, in contrast to the "hothead," who pours forth words in a fit of temper. The ideal here is obviously not total silence, for the "silent man" treasures up wise sayings in his heart and knows how to bring them forth at the right time. In fact, it is especially the person whose business is with words—the scribe, the teacher, the public official—who must aspire to be "truly silent."[56] This teaching passes into the biblical wisdom literature, beginning with the book of Proverbs, which warns against associating with "a man of heat" (*'îš ḥēmôt*) and advocates silence in the presence of fools.[57]

---

53. On the idiom ὁμιλίαν ποιεῖν with reference to a public lecture for instruction or persuasion, see Schoedel, *Ignatius of Antioch*, 271 (esp. n. 18), and BDAG, 705. I am not convinced by Stewart-Sykes's contention that Ignatius is merely telling Polycarp to "speak at the dinner table" ("Prophecy and Patronage," 173).

54. *Eph*. 3:2; *Magn*. 14:1; *Tral*. 6:1, 12:2; *Rom*. 4:1, 7:2; *Phld*. 8:2; *Poly*. 1:2, 7:3.

55. *Phld*. 1:2, 8:1; Lightfoot, *Ignatius, Polycarp*, 2.253; Schoedel, *Ignatius of Antioch*, 196.

56. The classic expression of this teaching is the "Instruction of Amen-em-ope," for which I depend on Miriam Lichtheim's English translation (William W. Hallo and K. Lawson Younger Jr., eds., *The Context of Scripture*, vol. 1, *Canonical Compositions from the Biblical World* [Leiden: Brill, 2003], 115–22).

57. Prv 22:24, 23:9.

> One who reviles his neighbor lacks sense,
> but a man of understanding is silent. (Prv 11:12b)
>
> One who shows restraint with his words possesses knowledge,
> and a man of understanding is cool of spirit. (17:27)

Likewise, the book of Sirach contrasts the rash and angry words of the fool with the well-chosen and timely words of the wise. Jesus Ben Sira issues frequent warnings against sins of the tongue and offers an elaborate contrast between the "silent" wise man and the prating fool.[58] At the same time, he is equally insistent that it is sinful for a wise man to hide his wisdom.[59] In the end, the wise man's responsibility is to "speak concisely, saying much with few words" (Sir 32:8). As we saw in chapter 2, it is exactly this *non multa sed multum* approach to teaching that characterizes Ignatius's epistolography, and we can be sure this is also what he had in mind in commending the "silence" of the bishops of Ephesus and Philadelphia. The "silent" bishop is by no means a nonteaching administrator but a Christ-like minister of the word.

Ignatius's appreciation for the biblical wisdom literature's advocacy of "silence" was no doubt reinforced by the closely parallel Hellenistic ideal of temperate and timely speech, which had the important civic function of preserving societal and political concord. Harry O. Maier illuminates Ignatius's remarks about silent bishops "against the backdrop of ancient denunciations of immoderate speech and exhortations to control speaking," which were "commonplace in pagan moral, philosophical, and rhetorical treatises."[60] He very plausibly relates this background to Ignatius's concern to foster "concord" (ὁμόνοια) and "good order" (εὐταξία) in the churches of Asia Minor and to the strategic role of the "silent" bishop in this regard.[61]

Another helpful suggestion comes from Henry Chadwick, who re-

---

58. Sir 20:5–8. The influence of this wisdom theme is evident not only in Ignatius's letters but elsewhere in early Christian literature (e.g., Jas 3:1–13; Barn. 19:4, 7–8).

59. Sir 4:23, 18:28–29, 20:30–31.

60. "The Politics of the Silent Bishop: Silence and Persuasion in Ignatius of Antioch," *Journal of Theological Studies* 55 (2004): 503–19 (quote from 506). Of course, these two backgrounds, biblical and Hellenistic, would have intermingled long before the time of Ignatius, especially in texts such as the Greek version of Sirach. Maier concentrates on pagan motifs because he thinks they provide "the closest resemblance to Ignatius' references to silence" (506, n. 11). The point is debatable. In any case, while it is an incontrovertible fact that Ignatius cites the biblical wisdom literature explicitly and authoritatively (*Eph.* 5:3; *Magn.* 12:1), Maier does not identify a single possible allusion in the Ignatian corpus to any of the pagan texts he marshals as examples of these motifs.

61. Maier, "Politics of the Silent Bishop," 516–19. See *Eph.* 4–6 and *Phld.* sal.–2.

lates Ignatius's advocacy of "silent" bishops to the ecclesiological typology by which Ignatius identifies the bishop as the earthly antitype (τύπος) of God (Tral. 3:1).⁶² By his "silence" the bishop is an "imitator of Jesus Christ, even as he is of the Father" (Phld. 7:2). Chadwick's treatment of this topic suffers, however, from a one-sided and underdeveloped view of Ignatius's ecclesiology. He makes the not uncommon mistake of supposing that, because Ignatius does not teach a doctrine of apostolic succession, his understanding of ecclesiastical authority must be ahistorical. According to Chadwick, Ignatius has taken over a "semi-gnostic conception of God as Silence" and "the familiar Hellenistic conception that things on earth correspond to things in heaven" and has applied these "whole-heartedly to his conception of the Church."⁶³ As I will attempt to demonstrate in chapter 9, however, Ignatian ecclesiology includes both vertical-transcendent and horizontal-temporal dimensions. The bishop's imitation of the divine "silence" cannot be separated from the historical mediation of revelation in the Christ event, the gift of the Spirit, the ministry of the apostles, the church's transmission of the spoken and written word of God, and the bishop's own teaching ministry.

Clearly Ignatius believes that the truth of revelation can be communicated effectively in human words. To proclaim the gospel is to "speak about Jesus Christ in truth" (Eph. 6:2). As we saw at the beginning of this chapter, however, Jesus Christ *is* the truth, and the good news is that in Christ we possess "the newness of eternal life" (Eph. 19:3). The extent to which Johannine and Pauline theology has penetrated Ignatius's thinking is evident in the way he regards the gospel, not merely as a moral code or "way," not merely as a doctrine of God or "knowledge," but above all as a vital power that transforms human persons, making them fit to live forever with God. Jesus Christ is the truth, and the truth is life. He is "our true life."⁶⁴

Ignatius recognizes the power of human words, for good and for ill. If the truth is life, the opposite of truth is not merely falsehood but death. Those who deny Jesus Christ are "advocates of death rather than of truth" (Smyr. 5:1). Authentic doctrine is "the only Christian nourishment," while heresy is an "exotic plant" from which one concocts a "lethal drug" (Tral. 6:1). Teachers of heresy are themselves "malignant offshoots that produce deadly fruit," whereas true teachers are like "branches of the

---

62. "The Silence of Bishops in Ignatius," *Harvard Theological Review* 43 (1950): 169–72.
63. Ibid., 172.
64. Smyr. 4:1; cf. Eph. 3:2, 7:2; Magn. 1:2.

cross" that bear "imperishable fruit" (11:1–2). Heretics are "beasts in the form of men" (Smyr. 4:1), or "rabid dogs" whose bite is "difficult to cure" (Eph. 7:1). The Judaizers are "tombstones and graves of the dead" (Phld. 6:1), while those who deny that Jesus Christ is "flesh-bearing" are themselves "corpse-bearing" (Smyr. 5:2). Heretical teaching gives off a "stench" like that of a decaying corpse (Eph. 17:1). This macabre imagery is not simply a rhetorical attempt to demonize one's opponents. It reflects Ignatius's deep conviction that words matter and that "bad doctrine" (9:1) is spiritually lethal.

The potency of words and the stark opposition between false doctrine and true gospel, therefore, present human beings with an existential choice between "death and life" (Magn. 5:1). The irony here is that Jesus Christ is "true life in death" (Eph. 7:2). His cross is the tree of life (Tral. 11:2), and we can possess "his living" within ourselves only if we "willingly direct our dying into his passion" (Magn. 5:2). In sum, "our life" comes about through "his death." It is through the mystery of Christ's death that the gift of the true faith has been made available to human beings (9:1). Jesus Christ endured crucifixion precisely so that we might come to "faith in God" (Eph. 16:2). But we appropriate this gift of faith and bear true witness to the Lord only through an imitative participation in his passion (Tral. 10:1).

Ignatius has "living water speaking within" him precisely because his desire has been crucified with Christ (Rom. 7:2), and he recognizes that all his words of preaching and teaching will mean nothing unless he seals his witness to the gospel by means of the martyr's death to which he has been called. If the Roman Christians grant his request and remain "silent" upon his arrival, he will become "a word of God," but if they interfere with his execution, he will be a mere "voice" (2:1). The church's "work" is not to convince the world through rhetorical "persuasion" but to be "hated by the world." Christianity achieves its true "greatness" only when it is lived out with such authenticity that it provokes persecution (3:3). Like the prophets before him, the Lord Jesus himself was "persecuted," and the church's principal and only essential witness to the world is to be "imitators of the Lord" in this regard.[65] Ignatius takes this nonverbal mode of proclamation so seriously that he includes "our individual sufferings" along with the law of Moses, the words of the prophets, and the gospel itself in a list of the modes of authoritative proclamation (Smyr. 5:1).

65. Magn. 8:2; Tral. 9:1; Eph. 10:3.

The Silence That Speaks

The paradox of word and silence is one of the principal ways by which Ignatius attempts to illuminate the mystery of redemption. This mystery comes forth from God and leads back to God. Eternal "silence" is the unfathomable mystery of the Trinity, the mystery of the Father who eternally brings forth his Word in the union of the Spirit. This mystery begins to speak for itself economically in the silent beauty of creation and in the rational discourse of man. It speaks more powerfully in the prophets and enters the world fully in the incarnation of the Word. Jesus proclaims the mystery in words and deeds "worthy of the Father" and achieves his greatest eloquence in his silent passion. The believer who truly possesses Jesus' word also knows how to listen to his silence. Through the action of the Holy Spirit, this silence becomes living water "speaking" within the believer, calling him or her to "come to the Father." Entrusted with the responsibility to teach and exhort others, that they may come to salvation, the bishop must imitate the mildness and silence of Christ while learning to "say much with few words." Words that truthfully proclaim Jesus Christ impart life, while words of heresy deal death. The essence of Christianity as *imitatio Christi* is most perfectly realized in the vocation of the martyr, whose suffering becomes a word of testimony to the Word himself. As bishop and would-be martyr, Ignatius of Antioch teaches and exhorts with few words and hopes to become an enduring "word" of witness through his own death.

A LUMINOUS MYSTERY

Ignatius of Antioch tells the Christians at Philadelphia that the gospel consists of three pillars: "the advent of the Savior ..., his passion, and the resurrection" (Phld. 9:2).[1] Similarly, he wants the Magnesians "to be fully convinced of the birth and the passion and the resurrection" of Christ (Magn. 11:1). This threefold schema appears to be basic for Ignatius, but he can elaborate it in a variety of ways to suit his purposes. In one text, the reference to the incarnation includes explicit mention of both the conception and the birth of Christ as distinct moments (Eph. 18:2). In another, the passion is broken down into three moments: persecution, crucifixion, and death (Tral. 9:1). In antidocetic contexts there are references to Christ's eating and drinking, whether prior to his death (9:1) or after his resurrection (Smyr. 3:3). Specific events in the life of Christ occurring between his birth and his death are, however, mentioned only rarely. Despite Ignatius's patent familiarity with the Synoptic tradition (in its Matthean form), we hear nothing of Jesus' miracles, exorcisms, or controversies with the Jewish leadership. In fact, apart from a glancing reference to the anointing at Bethany (Eph. 17:1), the only event between the nativity and the passion that merits mention in Ignatius's letters is the Lord's baptism in the Jordan by John, which is included within creedal formulations in Ephesians (18:2) and Smyrnaeans (1:1).

After a brief look at the way the Lord's baptism is presented in the gospels, the body of this chapter will be devoted to a thorough theologi-

---

[1]. An earlier version of this chapter appeared as Gregory Vall, "Lucis Mysterium: Ignatius of Antioch on the Lord's Baptism," Nova et Vetera 8 (2010): 143–60.

cal exegesis of these two Ignatian passages. The primary aim of this exegesis is to elucidate two important aspects of the divine economy: the interrelation of the distinct moments that comprise the Christ event, and the relationship between the Christ event and the events that precede and follow it in the temporal unfolding of the divine economy.[2] With regard to the first aspect, the baptism of the Lord can be viewed as a kind of hinge between the incarnation and the paschal mystery, helping us to grasp the soteriological unity of the life of Christ.[3] With regard to the second aspect, the baptism of the Lord is suggestive of how the Christ event is connected to the creation of the world, God's covenant with Israel, and the sacramental life of the church.

Pope John Paul II counted the Lord's baptism in the Jordan among the "luminous mysteries" (*lucis mysteria*) because of its capacity to illuminate "the total mystery of Christ" (*totum Christi mysterium*).[4] More recently Pope Benedict XVI, drawing on both modern biblical scholarship and ancient exegetical and liturgical traditions, has suggested some of the links between the baptism in the Jordan and the broader economy of redemption.[5] For Ignatius of Antioch, as we have seen, the Christian life is fundamentally a matter of χριστομαθία, or "learning Christ" (Phld. 8:2), that is, of entering into the mystery of Christ through a lifelong intellectual and moral process of personal discipleship. In his creedal formulae he places the Lord's baptism among the principal *mysteria vitae Iesu* in such a way as to suggest its mystagogical function, that is, its capacity to lead us into the mystery of Christ.[6]

---

2. "The mysteries of the faith form a mysterious structure in which we can, and should, relate them to each other and thereby form a rich account of the individual mysteries in the midst of all their connections" (Söhngen, "Analogy of Faith," 179).

3. Jean-Pierre Jossua offers a corrective to the view that posits two antithetical "theories" of redemption among the church fathers—a Greek "mystical" theory that ascribes an *immediate* soteriological efficacy to the incarnation, and a Latin "moral" theory that locates soteriological efficacy strictly in the paschal mystery. He demonstrates that, while there are various emphases among the fathers, they agree in viewing the incarnation and paschal mystery as an economic unity in which the theandrism of the former provides the foundation for Christ's redemptive action in the latter (Jossua, *Le salut*). The present chapter intends to show how the mystery of the Lord's baptism, as presented in the New Testament and in Ignatius's letters, may illuminate this economic unity.

4. Apostolic Letter *Rosarium Virginis Mariae* (October 16, 2002), § 21.

5. Joseph Ratzinger, Pope Benedict XVI, *Jesus of Nazareth: From the Baptism in the Jordan to the Transfiguration*, trans. Adrian J. Walker (New York: Doubleday, 2007), 9–24.

6. On the relationship between the *mysteria vitae Iesu* (plural) and the *mysterium Christi* (singular), see Christian Schütz, OSB, "The Mysteries of the Life of Christ as a Prism of Faith," *Communio* 29 (2002): 28–38.

From the Gospels to Ignatius's Letters

Aspects of the mystagogical capacity of the baptism in the Jordan are hinted at already in the New Testament.[7] First, it is an event in which all three persons of the Trinity are manifestly involved and in which something of the Trinitarian mystery is disclosed. At the Jordan God calls Jesus "my beloved Son," thus revealing himself as Father, while the Spirit descends from the Father and comes to rest upon the Son. Second, the Synoptic narratives of Jesus' baptism in the Jordan make various allusions to the Old Testament. The Father's voice from heaven and the hovering of the Spirit in the form of a dove over Jesus and over the waters of the Jordan may evoke the creation of the world as narrated in Genesis 1:1–3.[8] There may also be an allusion to the flood here, especially if Mark's statement that Jesus saw "the Spirit coming down to [εἰς] him like a dove" (Mk 1:10) is meant to recall the dove that came "to Noah" and "into [εἰς] the ark" (Gn 8:9 LXX).[9] If so, we should perhaps compare Jesus both to righteous Noah and to the ark itself, for these passed through the waters of death in order to bring the human race to a kind of rebirth or new creation.[10] The close narrative conjunction (especially strong in Mark) between the Lord's baptism by John and his forty-day testing in the wilderness may hint that in these events Jesus in some sense recapitulates the founding events of Israel's covenant with Yahweh: the crossing of the sea, the forty-year testing in the wilderness, and the crossing of the Jordan. The words spoken by the Father at the Jordan contain clear Old Testament echoes that indicate that Jesus is the Servant of Yahweh and the Davidic Messiah.[11] The brief allusion to Jesus' baptism as God's "anointing" of him "in the Holy Spirit and power" in Acts 10:38 points in a similar direction. The connection between Israel's historical covenant and the baptism in the Jordan is thematized in Matthew 3:15, where the Lord's words to John the Baptist,

---

7. For an exhaustive historical-critical study of the presentation of Jesus' baptism in the Synoptic Gospels, see Fritzleo Lentzen-Deis, *Die Taufe Jesu nach den Synoptikern: Literarkritische und gattungsgeschichtliche Untersuchungen*, Frankfurter Theologische Studien 4 (Frankfurt: Josef Knecht, 1970).

8. R. T. France, *The Gospel of Mark: A Commentary on the Greek Text*, NIGTC (Grand Rapids, Mich.: Eerdmans, 2002), 79.

9. Craig S. Keener considers it "likely" that "an allusion to Noah's dove as harbinger of new creation" is present in the tradition that lies behind both Jn 1:32 and the Synoptics (*The Gospel of John: A Commentary*, 2 vols. [Peabody, Mass.: Hendrickson, 2003], 1.460). France notes that the flood is a type of Christian baptism in 1 Pt 3:20–21, but he regards any link between Noah's dove and the dovelike Spirit of Mk 1:10 to be "obscure" (*Gospel of Mark*, 79).

10. Cf. Augustine, *De civitate Dei* 15:26.

11. John P. Meier, *A Marginal Jew: Rethinking the Historical Jesus*, vol. 2, *Mentor, Message, and Miracles* (New York: Doubleday, 1994), 106.

"Allow it for now, for it is fitting for us in this way to fulfill all righteousness," serve to draw this event into Matthew's programmatic theology of Old Testament fulfillment.[12] Third, two dominical logia in which Jesus refers to his approaching passion as a "baptism" that he must undergo (Lk 12:50; Mk 10:38–39) intimate a close connection between his baptism in the Jordan and the paschal mystery. Finally, the words of the Baptist, "I have baptized you with water, but he will baptize you in the Holy Spirit" (Mk 1:8), indicate the economic or salvation-historical relationship between John's baptism, on the one hand, and Christian sacramental baptism and the grace of the new covenant, on the other hand.[13] Jesus' own submission to John's ritual seems to transform it and in some manner prepares for or makes possible Christian baptism. In sum, the New Testament presents the baptism in the Jordan as a Trinitarian mystery that hearkens back to the creation of the world, the flood, and Yahweh's covenant with Israel, while it anticipates the death and resurrection of the Lord and sacramental baptism.

From early on, the baptism of Jesus in the Jordan gave rise to theological questions. Why did Jesus undergo a "baptism of repentance for the forgiveness of sins" (Mk 1:4)? Had *he* sinned? Did his submission to John's ritual indicate the latter's superiority over him? Do the descent of the Holy Spirit and the Father's proclamation, "You are my beloved Son," imply that Jesus was previously unaware of his divine Sonship, or even that he was not in fact the Son of God or Spirit-filled prior to this event? Further, it is evident that confusion over the relationship between John's ministry of baptism and Christian baptism continued for decades after the resurrection.[14] The gospel narratives were composed in such a way as to guide their readers toward a correct understanding of these issues. In Matthew, for example, the brief conversation between John and Jesus (Mt 3:14–15) indicates that the former was not in fact superior to the latter and that Jesus was baptized not because he was a sinner but in order to fulfill the requirements of righteousness on Israel's behalf. Matthew's slight alteration of the Father's proclamation, from "You are my beloved Son" (Mk 1:11) to "This is my beloved Son" (Mt 3:17), suggests that these

---

12. See Mt 1:22–23; 2:5–6, 15, 17–18, 23; 3:3; 4:14–16; 5:17; 8:17; 11:13–14; 12:17–21, 40; 13:14–15, 35; 15:7–9; 21:4–5, 13, 16, 42; 22:43–44; 23:39; 24:30; 26:31, 64; 27:9–10, 46. Of particular relevance is 5:17–20, which (like 3:15) combines the notions of "fulfillment" and "righteousness." Jesus' fulfillment of the law and the prophets enables his disciples to live a life of righteousness that exceeds that of the scribes and Pharisees.

13. See also Mt 3:11; Lk 3:16; Jn 1:26–27, 33 and 3:5; Acts 1:5, 11:16; 19:1–7.

14. Acts 19:1–7; Jn 3:22–30.

words were not spoken for Jesus' benefit but for ours. Luke, for his part, notes that the Holy Spirit overshadowed Mary at the annunciation such that the child conceived in her womb was already "Son of God" (Lk 1:35). He also virtually removes John from the scene of Jesus' baptism (3:20–21). Finally, John the Evangelist explains that Jesus Christ is the incarnation of God's coeternal Logos (Jn 1:1–18), sharply distinguishes between Jesus and the Baptist, and declines to narrate Jesus' baptism as such. Clearly the evangelists handled the whole affair with kid gloves.

It is, however, a crude reductionism to explain the gospels' treatment of Jesus' baptism in terms of "embarrassment" and "damage control," as John P. Meier does.[15] The four evangelists approached the Lord's baptism cautiously because of its potential for misinterpretation, but they also recognized its capacity to illuminate the mystery of Christ. Even the Fourth Gospel makes positive allusions to it (Jn 1:29–34). It is similarly unjustified to suppose, as Kilian McDonnell does, that Ignatius of Antioch found Jesus' baptism to be "problematic" and "a source of embarrassment" merely on the grounds that he alludes to Matthew 3:15 in one of his two references to this event (*Smyr.* 1:1) and hints at a relation to sacramental baptism in the other (*Eph.* 18:2).[16] Does one explain only in order to explain away? Ignatius was under no compulsion to include the baptism in his creedal formulations (most of which lack any reference to it), and it is likely that he had some positive reason to mention it when he chose to do so.[17] It is true that docetic gnostics beginning at least with Cerinthus (circa A.D. 100) interpreted the baptism of Jesus in a radically adoptionistic manner that cut at the very heart of the gospel,[18] and it is probable that Ignatius is consciously guarding his readers from some such interpretation.[19] But, as I will attempt to demonstrate, he also

---

15. *Marginal Jew*, 2.101–3.

16. *The Baptism of Jesus in the Jordan: The Trinitarian and Cosmic Order of Salvation* (Collegeville, Minn.: Liturgical Press, 1996), 19. McDonnell's treatment of the New Testament evidence is insufficiently critical of Meier's dubious methodology. Michael D. Goulder also parrots this approach when he finds "increasing defensiveness" in the gospel texts and "embarrassment" in Ignatius's two references to the Lord's baptism ("Ignatius' 'Docetists,'" *Vigiliae Christianae* 53 [1999]: 27).

17. According to Daniel Alain Bertrand, because he was citing traditional formulae, Ignatius was *compelled* to include two allusions to the baptism in the Jordan, but he was in fact entirely uninterested in—and did what he could to minimize the theological significance of—the Lord's baptism, which constitutes a "foreign body" in his argumentation (*Le baptême de Jésus: Histoire de l'exégèse aux deux premiers siècles*, Beiträge zur Geschichte der Biblischen Exegese 14 [Tübingen: J. C. B. Mohr, 1973], 26–32). The remainder of the present chapter should serve to refute this thesis.

18. For Cerinthus's interpretation of Jesus' baptism, see Irenaeus, *Haer.* 1:26:1; for that of the Valentinians, see 1:7:2 and 3:11:3; and for that of the Ophites, see 1:30:12–14.

19. Goulder, "Ignatius' 'Docetists,'" 26.

glimpsed theological riches in the Lord's baptism. After all, Ignatius polemicizes against the docetic interpretation of the passion as well,[20] but no one supposes that he viewed the passion as "problematic" or "a source of embarrassment"!

The Creedal Formula of *Smyrnaeans* 1

We may now proceed with the exegesis of the elaborate creedal formula found in *Smyraeans* 1:1b–2. Having spent time with the Christians in Smyrna, Ignatius recognizes that they are "fully convinced" that Jesus Christ is

> truly from the stock of David,
> Son of God according to will and power,
> truly born from a virgin,
> *baptized by John that all righteousness might be fulfilled by him,*
> truly, under Pontius Pilate and Herod the Tetrarch, nailed in the flesh for us,
> from whose fruit we are, from his divinely blessed passion,
> in order that he might raise a standard for the aeons through his resurrection
> for his holy and faithful ones, whether among the Jews or among the gentiles,
> in one body of his church.

Leaving aside for the moment the ecclesiological elements of this formulation, let us focus first on its Christological elements. Ignatius gives them in three pairs, introducing each pairing with the antidocetic adverb ἀληθῶς ("truly"). Simplified, they are as follows.

truly from the stock of David	(and)	Son of God
truly born from a virgin	(and)	baptized by John
truly nailed in the flesh ... passion	(and)	resurrection

Once we recall that the gospels associate the baptism in the Jordan with Jesus' divine Sonship, and that the New Testament likewise associates the resurrection with his divine Sonship, it is clear that once again Ignatius has used rhetorical symmetry to emphasize both Jesus' humanity ("from David ... from a virgin ... nailed in the flesh") and his divinity ("Son of God ... baptized by John ... resurrection").[21] But this is not the whole story. Each of the three pairings potentially displays a correlation between its two items as well as a contrast. The first pairing contrasts Jesus' human origins in the house of David with his divine Sonship; but

---

20. Tral. 10:1; Smyr. 2:1.
21. See Mt 3:17; Mk 1:11; Lk 3:22; Jn 1:34; Acts 13:33; Rom 1:4.

since "Son of God" is also a title of the Davidic Messiah, the pairing may suggest a close correlation as well.[22] Indeed, the fact that Ignatius qualifies the title "Son of God" with the phrase "according to will and power" suggests that he is thinking in economic rather than strictly theological terms here. The man Jesus is Son of God by virtue of an act of divine power that is part and parcel of the divine economy or "will" (θέλημα). But this affirmation need not be understood in an adoptionistic sense. In all likelihood the reference is precisely to the conception of Christ in his mother's womb, when a concrete humanity derived "from the stock of David" was united to the Logos. If this interpretation is correct, the creedal formula of *Smyrnaeans* 1:1b–2 is closely parallel to that of *Ephesians* 18:2, which likewise distinguishes between Christ's conception and his birth. As we shall see, the latter text qualifies its reference to the conception of Christ with the phrases "according to the economy of God" (cf. "according to will and power") and "from the seed of David" (cf. "from the stock of David"), while it pairs off the birth of Christ with his baptism in the Jordan (just as *Smyrnaeans* 1:1b does).

The second pairing of *Smyrnaeans* 1:1b–2, "born from a virgin" and "baptized by John," likewise suggests a close economic correlation between two events. The first of these phrases, following closely upon the reference to "the stock of David," completes an allusion to the famous prophecy of Isaiah 7:14, which Matthew 1:23 explicitly indicates to have been fulfilled by the birth of Jesus Christ. As we have seen, Ignatius qualifies the second phrase, "baptized by John," with an allusion to Matthew 3:15: "that all righteousness might be fulfilled by him." This indicates the fulfillment of Old Testament law and prophecy in a more general or comprehensive sense. Ignatius's formulation also sets up a suggestive parallelism between the virgin Mary and John the Baptist as key role players in the unfolding drama of salvation. Both are situated at the threshold between the old and the new. Later authors of the patristic period will discern further points of correlation between Christ's nativity and his baptism,[23] but as Ignatius presents these events in *Smyrnaeans* 1:1b, the accent is on Christ's fulfillment of the old covenant.

The third and final pairing of *Smrynaens* 1:1b–2, passion and resurrection, is one found frequently in Ignatius's letters, where it designates the two principal moments of the paschal mystery and suggests their close interconnection.[24] Here Ignatius continues the strongly historical cast

---

22. See 2 Sm 7:14; Pss 2:7, 89:27–28. 23. See McDonnell, *Baptism of Jesus*, 103–6.
24. Eph. 20:1; Magn. 11:1; Phld. sal., 9:2; Smyr. 7:2, 12:2; cf. Phld. 8:2.

of his creedal formula while he delicately transitions from Christological affirmations to ecclesiological and eschatological concerns. Having already mentioned David, Mary, and John, Ignatius now refers to Pontius Pilate and Herod the Tetrarch, thus grounding the story of salvation firmly in historical reality. The passion is the point at which the economy of redemption more directly pertains to "us"—Christ endured the passion "for us," so that "we" are its fruit—and through the resurrection the paschal mystery and the whole historically particular economy opens out into a universal and eschatological dimension. The reference to Christ's raising a "standard [σύσσημον] for the aeons" alludes to a whole trajectory of prophecies from the book of Isaiah.[25] According to these texts, Yahweh will raise a standard for the gentile nations, summoning them to himself at Jerusalem. One of these passages identifies the standard as "the root of Jesse," that is, the Davidic Messiah (Is 11:10), while another notes that the ingathered gentiles will be charged with the duty of bringing along with them Yahweh's scattered "sons and daughters," that is, the children of Israel (49:22). The eschatological people of God will thus consist, as Ignatius perceptively notes, of Jews and gentiles. The "one body of his church" takes up into itself, as it were, the two historical eras of redemption: the period of the old covenant, in which God sent his word to Israel; and the age of the new covenant, in which the gospel is proclaimed to all the nations. This is why Ignatius, like Paul, mentions the Jews ahead of the gentiles.[26]

It is his teleological view of the economy of redemption that enables Ignatius to grasp the unity of its temporal and transcendent dimensions. Formally the creedal affirmation of *Smyrnaeans* 1:1b–2 is concerned with the Christ event, which Ignatius here presents as comprised of five mo-

---

25. Is 5:26, 11:10, 49:22, 62:10. All four passages involve the Hebrew word *nēs* ("sign, battle standard"), which LXX normally translates σύσσημον. This word is not used in LXX Is 11:10, but it is found in the translations of that verse by Aquila and Symmachus (cf. Edwin Hatch and Henry A. Redpath, *A Concordance to the Septuagint and the Other Greek Versions of the Old Testament (Including the Apocryphal Books)* [Grand Rapids, Mich.: Baker, 1987], 1323). Each of the other three passages (in LXX) uses σύσσημον as well as some form of the verb αἴρω ("raise"), the same verb employed by Ignatius in *Smyr.* 1:2. As recent scholars have noticed, the canonical book of Isaiah, which contains the work of several prophetic authors living centuries apart, achieves a certain literary and theological unity by means of such trajectories, which unfold Isaiah's prophecies as they applied to Israel's situation in subsequent generations (cf. Brevard S. Childs, *Isaiah*, Old Testament Library [Louisville, Ky.: Westminster John Knox Press, 2001], 1–5). Ignatius's skillful allusion suggests to me that he was not simply scouring the book of Isaiah for proof-texts or cryptic passages that might be verbally referred to Christ but that he had a sense of the book as a whole and respected its literal meaning.

26. Rom 1:16, 3:29, 9:24; 1 Cor 1:23–24; cf. *Magn.* 10:3.

ments: conception, birth, baptism, passion, and resurrection. But through a series of carefully worded modifiers and biblical allusions Ignatius indicates that the Christ event fulfills and takes up into itself God's particular covenant with Israel while it opens out into a universal and eschatological reality: the church of Jews and gentiles. This understanding of salvation is thoroughly biblical and, in particular, Matthean and Pauline. Anyone who supposes that Ignatius was not a skillful exegete of the Old Testament, that his understanding of redemption lacks a salvation-historical perspective, or that his eschatology was confined to the redemption of the individual and dominated by the "realized" dimension, ought to pause carefully over this passage.

For present purposes, let us note that in this very carefully constructed creedal affirmation Ignatius has chosen to include one and only one event situated chronologically between Christ's birth and his death: the baptism in the Jordan. This moment in the life of Christ may, then, in some sense mediate between his conception-and-birth, on the one hand, and his death-and-resurrection, on the other hand. As such, it may illuminate the relationship between the incarnation and paschal mystery and help us to grasp the unity of the Christ event. Moreover, because John the Baptist is a threshold figure in the divine economy (Mt 11:13) and because Ignatius associates Jesus' baptism with "fulfillment" of the old covenant, it may even be that this *lucis mysterium* will shed light upon the relationship between "new things and old" (13:52).

The Creedal Formula of Ephesians 18

Turning now to Ignatius's one other reference to the baptism of the Lord, we find yet another tightly woven creedal formula.

> For our God Jesus Christ
> was conceived by Mary according to the economy of God,
> from both the seed of David and the Holy Spirit;
> he was born *and baptized*,
> in order that by the passion he might cleanse the water. (Eph. 18:2)

This statement comprises most of the same elements that we saw in *Smyrnaeans* 1:1b–2, and in roughly the same order, except that it contains no reference to the resurrection. In part, this is because Ignatius is concerned in the present context with the mystery of the cross in particular.[27]

---

27. See Eph. 18:1, 19:1.

Once again he employs rhetorical symmetry, but just where we would expect to find a reference to the resurrection, he mentions instead Christ's purification of the water. I shall defer for the moment the series of questions that this abrupt statement elicits (What water is meant? How has it become polluted? And how does Christ's passion effect its purification?). At this point it will suffice to note that Ignatius here makes an oblique but undeniable allusion to the Christian rite of baptism. Apparently he wishes to elucidate the relationship between this element of the *vita ecclesiae* and certain events in the *vita Iesu*, including the Lord's own baptism and his passion. A reference to the resurrection might have disrupted the balance of his formulation and unnecessarily distracted from the point he is making.

In this passage Ignatius refers to four moments in the Christ event: conception, birth, baptism, and passion. The cleansing of the waters is not presented as a fifth moment but as an effect of the passion. Jesus' conception receives a careful and fairly elaborate treatment, and once again Ignatius insists on both the human and divine origins of Christ. But our particular concern is with the very terse statement he makes about the birth, baptism, and passion, with its reference to the purification of the water and allusion to sacramental baptism.

We must note at the outset that Ignatius does not simply say that Christ cleansed the water by means of his baptism in the Jordan.[28] Some later church fathers make that claim,[29] and Thomas Aquinas will hold that Christ instituted the sacrament of baptism when he himself was baptized.[30] Be that as it may, Ignatius ascribes no direct efficacy in this regard to the Lord's baptism. Instead, he subordinates it to the passion. The baptism in the Jordan, like the nativity, is *for the sake of* the passion, and it is by means of the latter that Christ cleanses the water. This is hardly surprising given the centrality of the paschal mystery throughout Ignatius's letters. Of course, Ignatius does draw our attention to the parallelism between the Lord's baptism and our own, and he wishes us to discern a close economic connection between the two. But whatever that connection may be, it is not one that bypasses the mystery of the cross. For Ignatius, as for Paul, everything flows through the passion.

---

28. Expecting Ignatius to say this, Kirsopp Lake offers a highly improbable translation by which τῷ πάθει (normally rendered: "by the Passion") would refer to Jesus "himself submitting" to John's rite (Kirsopp Lake, trans., *The Apostolic Fathers*, 2 vols., Loeb Classical Library [Cambridge, Mass.: Harvard University Press, 1985], 1.193; cf. Corwin, *St. Ignatius and Christianity*, 100, n. 12).

29. McDonnell, *Baptism of Jesus*, 186, 197.

30. STh III, q. 66, a. 2.

Ignatius says that Jesus Christ "was born and baptized *in order that* by his passion he might cleanse the water." It is relatively easy to appreciate the force of the word ἵνα ("in order that") with respect to Christ's birth. His nativity is in a very practical sense necessary to his passion and thus to his cleansing of the water. If he is not born, he cannot do the Father's will as man. It is less obvious how the same purpose clause applies to Christ's baptism. Why is the latter necessary at all? By what sort of logic is Christ's baptism accomplished *for the sake of* his passion and his purification of the water? Perhaps the most straightforward and biblically defensible answer to this question comes through the simple recognition that the baptism in the Jordan inaugurates and empowers Christ's public ministry, a ministry that leads inexorably to Golgotha. If by means of his nativity the Son of God steps into the world of human action and historical causality, through his baptism he enters upon public life, so that what he does henceforth is done more fully in the sight of men and is in that sense more "on the record." This seems fitting for events that will be revelatory of the Father's universal redemptive will and that are to be proclaimed openly throughout the world and for all generations hence. Further, we might suppose that the descent of the Holy Spirit at the Jordan bestowed upon Christ's sacred humanity the particular charismata by which he would carry out his ministry of teaching, healing, and exorcism (see Acts 10:37–38). In short, Jesus Christ was baptized in order that he might carry out his public ministry, a ministry that culminates in the passion.

This answer is helpful as far as it goes but is not entirely satisfying. It begs the question why Christ's public ministry should begin with this particular gesture and why the Holy Spirit should descend in response to this particular action of Christ. And so we are led to consider the symbolic dimension of the event. Presumably John the Baptist, under the guidance of the Spirit of prophecy, chose a gesture that evoked key events in Yahweh's historical covenant with Israel (the crossing of the Red Sea and the crossing of the Jordan) while it also resembled the many ritual immersions required for "cleansing" by the priestly Torah.[31] And almost certainly John's ritual would have brought to the mind of the biblically literate Jew the story of Naaman, whose "baptism" in the Jordan, undertaken in obedience to a prophet, not only effected a cleansing

---

31. On the background to John's ritual, see Lentzen-Deis, *Die Taufe Jesu*, 59–76; and Lars Hartman, "Baptism," in David Noel Freedman, ed., *Anchor Bible Dictionary*, 6 vols. (New York: Doubleday, 1992), 1.583–84.

from "leprosy" but signaled a profound conversion of heart and mind (2 Kings 5).[32] Coupled with John's proclamation of imminent judgment, immersion in the Jordan symbolized Israel's eschatological repentance from sin. The Jews who submitted to John's ritual, then, would be indicating their own repentance through a sort of symbolic recapitulation of Israel's historical covenant with Yahweh.

For biblical Israel, and second-temple Judaism in particular, repentance was fundamentally a communal and historical matter. It involved personal remorse and amendment of life, of course, but it was never a merely individual and private affair. In the great communal prayers of repentance composed during the postexilic period, a righteous leader such as Ezra or Daniel speaks in solidarity with his sinful people, saying *"we have sinned,"* and confesses the sins of Israel's past generations as well as those of the present generation.[33] As Meier notes, Jesus fulfills a similar role of leadership and solidarity with his sinful people when he submits to John's baptism.[34] Indeed, we would want to say that Jesus undergoes baptism in solidarity not only with Israel but with the whole human race and even on behalf of the entire creation. In any case, it is impossible to say how many of these biblical resonances would have occurred to Ignatius. At a minimum, his allusion to Matthew 3:15 (*Smyr.* 1:1b) suggests that relating Jesus' baptism to Israel's past would not have been foreign to his thinking.

We may safely make one further assumption. Since Ignatius views Jesus' life and mission as fundamentally a matter of obedience to the Father's will, he would no doubt have viewed the baptism in the Jordan in those terms.[35] This is important theologically because it unites the baptism with the passion at the level of Jesus' voluntary human action "for us." Ignatius subordinates the baptism to the paschal mystery, but this does not mean that the baptism is merely a prefigurement or visual aid while the passion alone is "the real thing." Whatever symbolic value Ig-

---

32. The New Testament's use of the verb βαπτίζω to refer to quasi-ritualistic bodily immersion in the Jordan as a sign of repentance recalls the Old Testament use of the Hebrew verb *ṭābal* (which LXX normally renders with βάπτω or βαπτίζω) and its use in 2 Kgs 5:14 in particular. This text says that Naaman "went down and dipped [*wayyiṭbōl* (LXX ἐβαπτίσατο)] in the Jordan seven times according to the word of the man of God, and his flesh was restored, like the flesh of a little child, and he was clean." This is the climax of the narrative, after which Naaman acts with humility and confesses his knowledge of the God of Israel and his desire to serve him exclusively (cf. 5:15–17).

33. Ezr 9:9–15; Dn 9:3–19; Bar 1:15–3:8; Is 63:7–64:12.

34. *Marginal Jew*, 2.114–15. See also Martin Bieler, "The Mysteries of Jesus' Public Life: Stages on the Way to the Cross," *Communio* 29 (2002): 52–54.

35. See *Magn.* 7:1, 8:2, 13:2; *Smyr.* 8:1.

natius might or might not have recognized in Jesus' baptism, it seems likely that he would have viewed it first of all as an act of obedience to the Father and of love for man, an act having its own moral substance, so to speak.

The Lord's baptism has, to be sure, a type-antitype relationship to the paschal mystery, and its significance as type derives in large part from its symbolism. Christ's immersion in the Jordan anticipates his "immersion" in suffering,[36] his solidarity with his sinful people, perhaps even his descent among the dead, while his reemergence from the water to receive the Father's proclamation and the anointing of the Spirit foreshadows the glorification of his humanity in the resurrection. But it is crucial to view Christ's life as a unity and his saving action teleologically. His life and mission comprise a series of many acts of obedience and love that lead in a very definite direction and arrive at a "consummation" in his death. The act by which he lays down his life gathers up, as it were, all the "little" acts of obedience that precede and anticipate it and perfects them in an act of love εἰς τέλος, in finem (Jn 13:1), so that at the moment of death he can say τετέλεσται, consummatum est (19:30).

Lucis Mysterium

The passion is the antitype of the baptism and the definitive act of salvation by virtue of its place within this teleological structure, a structure that is determined to some extent by the basic structure of human life as vita usque ad mortem, but the passion does not stand in splendid isolation as the only redemptive act. Its special soteriological efficacy does not place it in an extrinsic relation to the baptism or to any other event in Christ's life. Each of Christ's actions is characterized by obedience and love, and so each participates in the whole and, in a sense, contains the whole, though not as perfectly as the passion does. Of the events of Christ's life, which are far too numerous to record (Jn 21:25), the early church preserved, and the evangelists narrated, a few that especially have the capacity to draw us into the mystery of the whole. These are events that indicate the direction of Christ's life, that show forth his revelation of the Father, that disclose the depth of his obedience and love. Among the events that fall between Christ's nativity and passion, the baptism in the Jordan arguably has this mystagogical capacity to an uncommon de-

---

36. Lk 12:50; Mk 10:38.

gree. It stands at a critical juncture in the life of Christ. As an act of divine humility and identification with sinners, it harkens back to the incarnation, disclosing the latter's character and purpose. As an act of filial obedience, it sets the Lord Jesus decisively upon the road that leads to the cross and so has a clear intrinsic relationship to the passion. And it possesses a remarkable symbolic potency that reinforces its significance within the life of Christ while shedding light upon the whole mystery of Christ and even upon the whole economy of redemption. It is indeed a luminous mystery.

To fill out this sketch of the mystagogical significance of the Lord's baptism somewhat, we may now turn to the three questions elicited by Ignatius's reference to Christ's cleansing of the water in *Ephesians* 18:2: What water is meant? How has it become polluted? And how does the passion effect its purification? On one level these questions are easily answered. "The water" is the water of the whole world. It has become polluted by human sin.[37] And the Christ event, which includes the incarnation as foundation, the baptism as an integral element, and the paschal mystery as culminating moment, has a redemptive effect not only upon men's souls but upon the whole creation, such that the elements of the physical world may serve a sacramental role under the new covenant. At least something of this sort seems to be presupposed by Ignatius's elliptical statement: "He was born and baptized, in order that by the passion he might cleanse the water." But this interpretation hardly penetrates below the surface. We should make some attempt to unfold the deeper rationale by which an ancient Christian such as Ignatius might view the divine economy of creation and redemption in this way. And here we face a hermeneutical gap, for the "logic" that underlies Ignatius's statement is largely foreign to the modern mind. Thus Schoedel speaks in this context of "the more or less magical idea that water was purified by Christ's baptism in the Jordan."[38] This smugly dismissive remark is characteristic of an approach that has no truck with metaphysical convictions. In what follows I will attempt to be a bit more empathetic.

Ignatius's statement presupposes the unity of creation and thus a kind of metaphysical solidarity among creatures. When man sins, his sin

---

37. According to many authors of the third and fourth centuries, the waters of the world were not only polluted by sin but infested by demons, who were vanquished when Christ descended into the Jordan (cf. Bertrand, *Le baptême de Jésus*, 31, n. 3), but it is not clear that Ignatius is implying this much when he refers to Christ's "cleansing" the water.

38. *Ignatius of Antioch*, 85.

has an adverse effect on all creation, rendering it "defiled" before God. In the incarnation the Son of God descends into his creation and unites it to himself in order to redeem and "cleanse" creation through the paschal mystery. Now, if we attend once more to the symbolism of Jesus' baptism in the Jordan, we may view it not only as the middle term between incarnation and paschal mystery but as a sort of epitome or "thumbnail sketch" of the entire Christ event, which the New Testament sometimes presents as a mystery of descent-and-ascent, followed by the descent of the Spirit. In the incarnation the Son of God descended from heaven into his creation—the *descensus de coelis* being, in a certain sense, completed in the *descensus ad inferos*—and when he had been exalted in his humanity through the resurrection and ascension, the Spirit descended upon the church to be the source of her sacramental life.[39] And it is this schematic view of the Christ event that draws our attention to similar contours in the Lord's baptism.[40] Christ's humble descent into the waters of the Jordan (at a geographical point that is very nearly the lowest spot on the surface of the earth)[41] recalls his incarnation while it also anticipates his death for sinners and descent among the dead. Similarly, his ascent from the Jordan, which is immediately followed by the descent of the Spirit to anoint his humanity with power for the public ministry (Acts 10:37–38), anticipates his resurrection and ascension, which makes possible the outpouring of the Holy Spirit and the ministry of the church. Moreover, the fact that the glorification of Christ's humanity constitutes the incipient redemption of all creation is reflected in the role now played by elements of the physical creation, such as water, in the new covenant's efficacious signs of God's grace. Thus Jesus' immersion in the *aqua Iordanis* purifies and sanctifies the waters of the whole world, not as an isolated

---

39. For the schema of descent and ascent, see Rom 10:6–7; Eph 4:8–10; Phil 2:6–11; Jn 3:13–14, 31; 6:38, 50–51; 62. For the descent of the Spirit following upon Christ's exaltation to glory, see Lk 24:49–51; Acts 1:8–9, 2:32–34; Jn 6:62–63, 7:39, 16:7.

40. "Jesus' descent into the river is at one and the same time solidarity with all who confess their guilt and dive into the waters of judgment and salvation, and—as solidarity—obedience to the voice of God that sounds forth from the prophet's voice, and thus obedience incarnated in history. Jesus' initiative attains immediately to its fulfillment, for he 'rises up' out of the waters, and his act of 'coming up from beneath' is answered by the 'coming down from above' of the 'Spirit (of God)': here we see that incarnation is the encounter, to the point of identification, of the Israel who has been made ready and the God of the covenant who descends to Israel" (Hans Urs von Balthasar, *The Glory of the Lord: A Theological Aesthetics*, vol. 7, *Theology: The New Covenant*, trans. Erasmo Leiva-Merikakis [San Francisco: Ignatius Press, 1989], 56).

41. The Jordan runs through the Rift Valley, a deep rut in the earth's surface that includes the Dead Sea basin and continues south to the Gulf of Aqabah. At nearly 1,300 feet below sea level, the water surface of the Dead Sea is the lowest spot on earth. The traditional site of Christ's baptism is near the southern end of the Jordan, close to where it empties into the Dead Sea.

event and certainly not by means of magic, but as an integral and revelatory moment within the broader mystery of redemption.

It should also be noted that Ignatius's view of the economy of redemption presupposes a hierarchical and teleological understanding of creation and implicitly identifies man as the creature in whom creation is summed up and reaches its τέλος. Not only is each creature ordered to its own end, but creation as a whole is ordered to a final end, an end that it cannot achieve apart from man. This end is the glory of God. The subhuman physical cosmos is not, of course, morally culpable for man's sin, but neither can it glorify God in the manner for which it was created as long as man remains alienated from the Creator.[42] The biblical category of "uncleanness" or "defilement," implicit in Ignatius's use of the verb "cleanse," serves him well here, for it does not necessarily suggest moral culpability but designates the condition of having been impeded from being "holy," that is, from being set apart for the purposes of God. Moreover, like all of Ignatius's statements about the divine economy, the formulation of *Ephesians* 18:2 presupposes that Jesus Christ is the one in whom man is summed up and reaches his τέλος. Christ is the "Son of Man" (20:2), "the new man" (20:1), "the perfect man" (*Smyr.* 4:2).[43]

Finally, let us note that the creedal formulation of *Ephesians* 18:2, like that of *Smyrnaeans* 1:1b–2, is fundamentally a statement about the Christ event, but one that opens out into something that is suggestive of a comprehensive view of the divine economy. Specifically, Ignatius's brief reference to the cleansing of the waters hearkens back to creation and the fall while it also points forward to sacramental baptism and the life of the church. The point is not simply to appreciate Ignatius's lapidary and elliptical style but to see that his creedal formulations reflect his Christocentric view of the divine economy. He is able to grasp the unity of the whole economy precisely in the Christ event with its interrelated moments. Moreover, it may well be that the baptism in the Jordan played an

---

42. The unified and teleological view of creation that informs Ignatius's interpretation of the economy of redemption is eminently biblical. To cite but two obvious examples, it is presupposed in the account of the fall in Genesis 3, where we read that the earth bears a curse "on account of" man (3:17), and also in the closely related passage in Romans 8, where Paul tells us that "the creation itself will be set free from the bondage of corruption for the glorious freedom of the children of God" (8:21). Anyone who wishes to describe the metaphysical convictions of Ignatius and the church fathers as "more or less magical" must say much the same with regard to the biblical authors.

43. On these Christological titles and their relationship to Ignatius's understanding of the divine economy and the mysteries of the life of Christ, see Ferdinando Bergamelli, "Cristo 'l'uomo nuovo' e 'l'uomo perfetto' in Ignazio di Antiochia (*Efesini* 20,1; *Smirnesi* 4,2)," *Studia Patristica* 26 (1993): 103–12.

important role in the development of Ignatius's thought in this regard. I do not suppose that he would have mentioned this event in the life of Christ at all, much less incorporated it into such carefully crafted statements, had he not previously devoted serious reflection to it. The baptism of the Lord is the sort of individual mystery into which one may gaze in order to espy something of the mystery.

9

CHRIST AND THE CHURCH

The vital relationship between pastoral purpose and theological instruction, present throughout Ignatius's letters, is nowhere more evident than in the realm of ecclesiology. Ignatius constantly brings doctrine to the service of his pragmatic pastoral concern to foster unity and right order within the churches. In one passage he virtually equates "good order" (εὐταξία) with "truth" (ἀλήθεια). To submit to the bishop is to "live according to the truth," which also means to tolerate no heresy but to listen only to one who "speaks about Jesus Christ in truth" (Eph. 6:2). The truth of doctrine concerns, above all, Jesus Christ, but it is also a question of possessing a right understanding of the universal church and of the constitution of the local church. Thus Ignatius does not simply exhort the faithful to obedience but attempts to help them understand why God has placed a bishop, a body of presbyters, and deacons over them. He does not simply *refer* to the church but gives explicit teaching *about* the church. It is in the area of ecclesiology that Ignatius most actively takes up the role of theologian and teacher, and according to Virginia Corwin, it is Ignatius's "vision of the church" that constitutes "perhaps his greatest service" to theology.[1]

Ignatius's ecclesiology has been variously interpreted, however, and sometimes harshly criticized by modern scholars, who have not always placed it in its proper relation to his broader understanding of the economy of redemption. Accordingly, a thorough reevaluation is in order. I have touched on Ignatius's view of the church at many points in the preceding chapters in order to indicate how it is interwoven with other

---

1. *St. Ignatius and Christianity*, 270.

aspects of his theology. Hopefully this has set the stage for taking up a series of more explicitly ecclesiological issues in the present chapter. After a flyover of Ignatius's favorite ecclesiological terms and themes, and a selective review and critique of twentieth-century scholarship, I will consider (1) the mission of the Holy Spirit and the gift of "imperishability," (2) the mission of the apostles and the "apostolic character," (3) the relationship between the "catholic church" and the local churches, (4) the "ecclesiological typology" by which Ignatius attempts to illuminate the threefold hierarchy of the local church, and (5) the appointment and validation of bishops.

Ecclesiological Terms and Themes

Ignatius employs a variety of terms to speak about the church. The most common by far is ἐκκλησία, which occurs a total of thirty-nine times and at least four times in each letter. This is a rather high concentration. By comparison, it is nearly double the number of occurrences found in the Acts of the Apostles, a book almost twice the length of the Ignatian corpus and one that has the church as its primary subject matter. Apart from the Apocalypse, the only New Testament books that instance the term ἐκκλησία as frequently as do the Ignatian letters are 1 Corinthians and Ephesians, Ignatius's two favorite Pauline letters. Ignatius's intense interest in ecclesial matters may in part explain why he was especially drawn to these letters, as well as to the Gospel of Matthew, which is the ecclesiological gospel par excellence. In most cases Ignatius uses ἐκκλησία to refer to a specific local "church" or to a plurality of local "churches," but at least six times this term refers to the universal church.[2] For the most part ἐκκλησία stands on its own, though we occasionally find the Pauline phrase "church of God" or more elaborate expressions such as "the church of God the Father and the Lord Jesus Christ."[3] Ignatius is the first person on record to use the phrase ἡ καθολικὴ ἐκκλησία ("the catholic

---

2. Eph. 5:1, 17:1; Phld. 9:1; Smyr. 1:2, 8:2; Poly. 5:1. Three other instances might be taken to refer to the universal church, depending on how the passages in question are interpreted (Tral. 2:3; Phld. 3:2, 5:1). The term occurs in the plural (ἐκκλησίαι) eight times (Magn. 1:2, 15:1; Tral. 12:1; Rom. 4:1, 9:3; Phld. 10:2; Poly. 8:1 [bis]). In Tral. 3:1 the singular refers to "a church," that is, any local church. Each of the remaining instances refers to a specific local church (Eph. sal., 5:2, 8:1, 21:2; Magn. sal., 14:1 [tris]; Tral. sal., 13:1; Rom. sal., 9:1; Phld. sal., 10:1 [bis]; Smyr. sal., 8:1, 11:1, 2; Poly. sal., 7:1). The church most frequently specified is Ignatius's own church in Syrian Antioch, which is mentioned at least once in each letter and eight times overall.

3. "Church of God": Tral. 2:3, 12:1; Phld. 10:1. More elaborate expressions: Phld. sal.; Smyr.

church"; *Smyr.* 8:2). We shall need to consider what precisely he means by this expression and how he understands the relationship between the church and the churches. Ignatius also employs τὸ πᾶν πλῆθος ("the whole multitude"), or similar expressions, to refer to the local church.[4] Interestingly, this usage is not found in Matthew, John, or Paul (Ignatius's clearest points of contact with the New Testament tradition) but is characteristic of Luke-Acts and may be related to a similar quasi-technical use of the Hebrew noun *rôb* ("multitude") found in the Qumran Community Rule.[5] Ignatius reserves the term κοινός ("common") for a positive and ecclesial use (never employing it in the pejorative sense of "profane"), to refer to the common endowment of Christians and especially to Jesus Christ himself as ἡ κοινὴ ἐλπὶς ἡμῶν ("our common hope").[6] Here he seems to echo Clement of Rome's phrase: τὸ κοινόν τῆς ἐλπίδος ("the common basis of hope"; 1 *Clem.* 51:1). The same adjective can refer to the local church in assembly,[7] while the substantive τὸ κοινόν can refer to the local church's common life (*Phld.* 1:1) or commonly held material resources (*Poly.* 4:3).

Three more or less biblical metaphors also factor significantly into Ignatian ecclesiology: body, temple, and tree. The Pauline image of the church as "one body" (ἓν σῶμα) or as "members" (μέλη) of Christ the "head" (κεφαλή) is found in contexts concerned with the unity of the universal church, but also in contexts concerned primarily with the unity of the local church, which Ignatius describes as possessing "its own bodily unity" (τὸ ἴδιον σωματεῖον).[8] As we shall see, some scholars feel that Ignatius has dangerously distorted Paul's body metaphor. In particular, his statement that "a head cannot be born by itself, without members" (*Tral.* 11:2) can seem to make Christ at least as dependent upon the church as vice versa. Ignatius uses the image of the ναός ("shrine, temple") with considerable flexibility and imagination. In a single passage (*Eph.* 9:1–2), he refers to Christians both as "shrine-bearers" (ναοφόροι) in a procession and as "temple stones" (λίθοι ναοῦ). Jesus Christ is, of course, the

---

sal. Of the seven New Testament occurrences of the phrase "church of God," four are found in 1 Corinthians (1:2. 10:32, 11:22, 15:9), Ignatius's favorite Pauline letter.

4. We find τὸ πᾶν πλῆθος in *Magn.* 6:1 and *Tral.* 1:1; τὸ ἐν θεῷ πλῆθος ("the multitude in God") in *Tral.* 8:2; and ἡ πολυπληθία ("the great multitude") in *Eph.* 1:3.

5. Cf. BDAG, 825–26; Lk 1:10, 19:37; Acts 4:32, 6:2 and 6:5, 15:12 and 15:30, 19:9; 1 *Clem.* 54:2; 1QS 5:2, 9, 22, 6:19. For the LXX background, see TDNT 6.276–78.

6. *Eph.* 1:2, 21:2; *Phld.* 5:2, 11:2.

7. *Eph.* 20:2; *Smyr.* 7:2, 12:2; cf. *Barn.* 4:10.

8. Universal church: *Smyr.* 1:2; *Tral.* 11:2. Local church: *Eph.* 4:2; *Smyr.* 11:2.

"one temple" to which Christians should "hasten together" (*Magn.* 7:2), but at the same time each Christian should regard himself or herself as a temple indwelt by God (*Eph.* 15:3) and thus should keep the flesh of that temple pure.⁹ These passages contain various Pauline echoes,¹⁰ but some of them also evoke pagan religious processions. Finally, in two passages Ignatius implicitly presents the cross as a tree of life and symbol of the church's unity. Christians are either "branches" of this tree, bearing imperishable fruit (*Tral.* 11:2), or are themselves the fruit of the tree (*Smyr.* 1:2). Strikingly, both passages combine this imagery with the metaphor of the church as Christ's body. Unlike heresy, which is an "exotic plant" furnishing a "lethal drug," the church is a "planting of the Father," which Jesus Christ himself cultivates.¹¹ The individual believer may also be thought of as a tree expected to bear the fruit of good works (*Eph.* 14:2).

Surely the most salient as well as controversial feature of Ignatius's ecclesiology is his vigorous promotion of a threefold hierarchy, along with the complex typology by which he attempts to elucidate and justify that hierarchy. Ignatius's letters provide the first unambiguous witness to the monepiscopacy. Whereas earlier texts (New Testament, 1 *Clement*, *Didache*) speak of plural ἐπίσκοποι ("overseers") in each church and sometimes use this term interchangeably with πρεσβύτεροι ("elders"),¹² Ignatius consistently refers to a single ἐπίσκοπος ("bishop") over each church and presents the πρεσβύτεροι as a distinguished body of elders (πρεσβυτέριον) or "bishop's council" (συνέδριον τοῦ ἐπισκόπου), with the deacons (διάκονοι) constituting a third rung of leadership.¹³ In a series of passages that evidence considerable variation, Ignatius compares the bishop either to God the Father or to Jesus Christ, compares the

---

9. Phld. 7:2; cf. Barn. 4:11.
10. E.g., Eph. 15:3 is strikingly reminiscent of 2 Cor 6:16.
11. Tral. 6:1–2, 11:1; Phld. 3:1.
12. Phil 1:1; Acts 20:17, 28; 1 Clem. 42:4–5, 44:4–5; Did. 15:1; see TDNT 2:615–20.
13. The noun ἐπίσκοπος occurs fifty-seven times (Eph. 1:3 [bis], 2:1 and 2, 3:2, 4:1 [bis], 5:1–3 [tris], 6:1 [bis], 20:2; Magn. 2:1 [bis], 3:1–2 [tris], 4:1, 6:1 and 2, 7:1, 13:1 and 2, 15:1; Tral. 1:1, 2:1 and 2, 3:1 and 2, 7:1 and 2, 12:2, 13:2; Rom. 2:2; Phld. sal., 1:1, 3:2, 4:1, 7:1 and 2, 8:1, 10:2; Smyr. 8:1 [tris], 8:2 [bis], 9:1 [tris], 12:2; Poly. sal., 5:2 [bis], 6:1 [bis]), along with its cognates ἐπισκοπέω ("oversee"; Rom. 9:1; Poly. sal.) and ἐπισκοπή ("oversight"; 8:3). The noun πρεσβύτεροι (always plural) occurs nine times (Magn. 2:1, 3:1, 6:1, 7:1; Tral. 3:1, 12:2; Phld. sal., 10:2; Poly. 6:1), and the collective noun πρεσβυτέριον thirteen times (Eph. 2:2, 4:1, 20:2; Magn. 2:1, 13:1; Tral. 2:2, 7:2, 13:2; Phld. 4:1, 5:1, 7:1; Smyr. 8:1, 12:2). The noun διάκονος occurs eighteen times (Eph. 2:1; Magn. 2:1, 6:1, 13:1; Tral. 2:3 [bis], 3:1, 7:2; Phld. sal., 4:1, 7:1, 10:1 and 2, 11:1; Smyr. 8:1, 10:1, 12:2; Poly. 6:1), and its cognate διακονία ("ministry, service") four times (Magn. 6:1; Phld. 1:1, 10:2; Smyr. 12:1). The phrase συνέδριον τοῦ ἐπισκόπου, apparently referring to the πρεσβυτέριον, occurs at Phld. 8:1 (cf. Magn. 6:1, 13:1; Tral. 3:1).

presbyters to the apostles, and usually, in one way or another, associates the deacons with Jesus Christ.[14] Scholars have generally found this ecclesiological typology problematic for three reasons. First, Jesus Christ can occupy two different positions in the typology, even within a single passage (*Tral.* 2:1–3:1). Second, when Jesus is associated with the deacons, he seems to be ranked below his own apostles. And third, the typology seems to ground ecclesial authority in a quasi-Platonic parallelism between a heavenly church and its earthly manifestation. We shall have opportunity to analyze Ignatius's ecclesiological typology carefully and sort through these issues later in this chapter.

At least four things link the church on earth to her exalted Lord: the Holy Spirit, the apostles, the word of God, and the eucharist. We considered Ignatius's pneumatology at some length in chapter 3, but we shall need to return to that topic here in order to examine how he relates the mission of the Holy Spirit to the life of the church. Surprisingly, this subject receives almost no consideration in scholarly treatments of Ignatian ecclesiology. As for the apostles, Ignatius makes sixteen distinct references to them in his letters.[15] Six of these occur in *Trallians*, including the first known Christian use of the adjective "apostolic" (sal.). The apostles form a "college" and heavenly "council," and Peter and Paul enjoy some sort of privileged status among them.[16] Overlapping these references to the apostles are Ignatius's many allusions to the word of God in written or oral transmission. He mentions "the prophecies and the law of Moses," the "gospel," the "law of Jesus Christ," the "commandment of God," the "commandments of Jesus Christ," the "precepts of the Lord and of the apostles," the "ordinances of the apostles," and Paul's letters.[17] Obviously Ignatius expects the church's life to be imbued with the word of God, which he also refers to as "Christian nourishment" (*Tral.* 6:1). Finally, Ignatius's highly developed teaching on the eucharist discloses the sacrament's many facets and places it near the center of his ecclesiology.[18]

---

14. The typology receives its fullest development in *Magnesians* (2:1–3:2, 6:1, 7:1, 13:2), *Trallians* (2:1–3:1, 12:2), and *Smyrnaeans* (8:1–9:1), but Ignatius evokes it here and there also in the other letters (*Eph.* 5:1, 6:1; *Rom.* 9:1; *Phld.* 5:1; *Poly.* sal., 8:3).

15. *Eph.* 11:2, 12:2; *Magn.* 6:1, 7:1, 13:1 and 2; *Tral.* sal., 2:2, 3:1 and 3, 7:1, 12:2; *Rom.* 4:3; *Phld.* 5:1; *Smyr.* 3:2, 8:1.

16. *Magn.* 6:1; *Tral.* 3:1; *Eph.* 12:2; *Rom.* 4:3; *Smyr.* 3:2.

17. "Prophecies and law of Moses": *Smyr.* 5:1. "Gospel": *Phld.* 5:1–2, 8:2, 9:2; *Smyr.* 5:1, 7:1. "Law of Jesus Christ": *Magn.* 2:1. "Commandment of God": *Smyr.* 8:1. "Commandments of Jesus Christ": *Eph.* 9:2; cf. *Rom.* sal.; *Phld.* 1:2. "Precepts of Lord and apostles": *Magn.* 13:1. "Ordinances of apostles": *Tral.* 7:1, cf. 3:3; *Rom.* 4:3; *Phld.* 5:1. Paul's letters: *Eph.* 12:2.

18. "L'Eucharistie nous apparaît donc comme un résumé de la théologie ignatienne. Parce qu'elle est la présence vivifiante de la passion-résurrection. Parce qu'elle est le centre unificateur

He relates the eucharist backward in time to the Christ event and, in the very same passages, relates it forward in time to eternal life.[19] He presents it as the meal around which the community gathers and in the same breath describes it in sacrificial and doxological terms.[20] The eucharist is, in other words, both a principle of ecclesial unity and an act of worship. Likewise, it is a weapon of spiritual warfare and a source of peace (Eph. 13:1–2). Ignatius ties the eucharist very closely to the episcopal ministry and to his own impending martyrdom.[21] I shall touch on Ignatius's theology of the eucharist at several points in this chapter.[22]

Naturally, to say that the action of the Holy Spirit, the continuing influence of the apostles, the proclamation of the word of God, and the celebration of the eucharist all put the church on earth in contact with the glorified and heavenly Christ presupposes the reality of grace. To get at the heart of Ignatius's ecclesiology, therefore, we must also pay careful attention to the way he speaks about grace and its presence in the church. R. M. Grant is mistaken when he claims that "there is not much emphasis on grace" in Ignatius's letters.[23] Ignatius uses the Pauline term χάρις ("grace") and its cognates (χαρίζω, χάρισμα) two dozen times.[24] Often he speaks of grace as something given to an individual, as for example to empower that person to carry out a specific ministry or task (Poly. 1:1, 2:2), but grace is always received within the church and for the church, and grace is that by which Christians gather as church (Eph. 20:2). Ignatius also notes that special graces and charisms are given to each local church.[25] Grace was already given to the Old Testament prophets, but as we have seen, even in that case it is none other than the grace that flows from Jesus Christ through the mystery of his coming into the world (Magn. 8:1–2). Grace is therefore an economic reality, which is to say, it is dispensed according to God's historical plan of redemption. It is "the grace of Jesus Christ that

---

de la communauté. Parce qu'elle est rattachée au martyre de telle façon que celui-ci est considéré comme 'Eucharistie'. Les hérétiques et les schismatiques, évidemment, le rejettent et meurent" (Sergio Zañartu, "Les concepts de vie et de mort chez Ignace d'Antioche," *Vigiliae Christianae* 33 [1979]: 327).

19. Eph. 20:2; Rom. 7:3; Smyr. 6:2–7:1. 20. Eph. 5:2, 13:1; Phld. 4:1.
21. Phld. 4:1; Smyr. 8:1; Rom. 4:1.
22. For a thorough treatment of Ignatius's eucharistic theology and its relationship to his Christology, soteriology, and ecclesiology, see Lothar Wehr, *Arznei der Unsterblichkeit: Die Eucharistie bei Ignatius von Antiochien und im Johannesevangelium*, Neutestamentliche Abhandlungen 18 (Münster: Aschendorff, 1987), 63–181.
23. *Ignatius of Antioch*, 25.
24. Eph. 1:3, 11:1, 17:2, 20:2; Magn. sal., 2:1, 8:1 and 2; Rom. sal., 1:2; Phld. 8:2, 11:1; Smyr. sal., 6:2, 9:2, 11:1, 12:1 and 2, 13:2; Poly. 1:2, 2:1 and 2, 7:3, 8:2.
25. Eph. 1:3; Magn. sal.; Rom. sal.; Smyr. sal.

has come to us" (*Smyr.* 6:2) and therefore "the present grace" (*Eph.* 11:1). There are actual graces that an individual receives, but fundamentally grace is an abiding reality both in the life of the individual, where it must come to perfection, and in the life of the church.²⁶ This abiding grace of the Holy Spirit's presence in the church is "the gift [χάρισμα] that the Lord has sent" (*Eph.* 17:2). Finally, although Ignatius sometimes accents the nomistic dimension of the gospel, he implies that there is no incompatibility or tension between "the grace of God" and "the law of Jesus Christ."²⁷

Ignatius uses a variety of other terms, all with New Testament antecedents, to speak of the same reality: the abiding principle of divine life and power that has been bestowed upon the church and is available to individuals as members of the church. It is, for example, "fullness," "power," and "the gift [δωρεά] of God."²⁸ Because this gift is distinct from the old covenant given to Israel, it constitutes "newness," a transformative "new leaven" that can keep one from perishing (*Magn.* 10:2). Evoking Pauline and Johannine expressions, Ignatius aptly terms it "the newness of eternal life" (*Eph.* 19:2).²⁹ Through Jesus Christ and his death "our life has dawned" (*Magn.* 9:1). This is the great paradox of "true life in death," which lies at the heart of the Christian mystery as Ignatius understands it (*Eph.* 7:2). The church possesses the living presence of Jesus Christ, who is himself "our everlasting life" (*Magn.* 1:2), "our unwavering life" (*Eph.* 3:2), and "our true life" (*Smyr.* 4:1). Like the Fourth Gospel, which presents "eternal life" as an eschatological reality that we already "have" (ἔχω) but that will be consummated in the resurrection "on the last day" (Jn 6:40), Ignatius affirms that we "have" (ἔχω) this true life now even as we await the resurrection of the body (*Tral.* 9:2). As we shall see in the next chapter, realized eschatology and future eschatology are fully compatible in Ignatius's thought. Because Jesus' life is already "in us," eternal life "lies before us" as something we can freely choose and hope to attain (*Magn.* 5:1–2).

26. Rom. 1:2; Smyr. 11:1; Poly. 8:2.
27. Magn. 2:1; cf. Rom. sal. Like certain passages in the New Testament (Rom 8:2; Gal 6:2; Jas 1:25), the formulation of Magn. 2:1 anticipates the somewhat paradoxical notion, so important to Christian theology, that the gospel of grace constitutes a "new law" (cf. Barn. 2:6; Justin, Dial. 18:3; Aquinas, STh I-II, q. 107). Curiously, in Smyrnaeans the recognition that grace is undeserved (11:1) is found in close proximity to the notion that grace can somehow itself be given as a "reward" (12:1). Such considerations will occasion precise distinctions in later theology (e.g., STh I-II, q. 112, a. 2).
28. "Fullness": Eph. sal.; Tral. sal. "Power": Eph. 14:2; Rom. 3:2; Smyr. 4:2. "Gift of God": Smyr. 7:1.
29. The phrase "newness of life" is Pauline (Rom 6:4), and the phrase "eternal life" is ubiquitous in the Johannine literature, though Paul also employs it occasionally (Gal 6:8; Rom 2:7, 5:21, 6:22–23).

Of special importance to Ignatius in this regard is the Pauline term ἀφθαρσία ("imperishability") and its cognate adjective ἄφθαρτος ("imperishable"). "Imperishability" designates a real participation in the Trinitarian life, which Jesus Christ has permanently "breathed into" his church, so that we can attain "the life that lies before us" (Eph. 17:1). It flows from the paschal mystery, so that the members of Christ's body can also be thought of as branches of the cross, bearing "imperishable fruit" (Tral. 11:2). Imperishability is mediated through the proclamation of the gospel, which (unlike the Mosaic law) is "the completion of imperishability" (Phld. 9:2), and through the eucharist, which is "the medicine of immortality" (Eph. 20:2) and "imperishable food" (Rom. 7:3). This mediation of ἀφθαρσία through word and sacrament is, however, inseparable from its mediation through the hierarchy. A local church that lives in unity with its bishop, presbyters, and deacons participates in the union of Jesus Christ with his Father and, as such, becomes "a type and teaching of imperishability" (Magn. 6:2). In other words, through such a church something of the heavenly life and the "newness of hope" (9:1) shines forth within the world. Here we gain a first glimpse as to what Ignatius is attempting to express through his ecclesiological typology, with its parallelism between heaven and earth. Like the phrase "eternal life," ἀφθαρσία designates the one eschatological reality under two aspects: as presently possessed by grace (Eph. 17:1), and as set before us as an eternal "reward" (Poly. 2:3).

Twentieth-Century Views of Ignatian Ecclesiology

Though it has received relatively little attention in the last quarter century, Ignatius's ecclesiology was the object of vigorous debate for most of the twentieth century. As this scholarship raises vital issues and makes some progress in dealing with them, a selective *Forschungsbericht* and a critique are in order.

A strong current in German-language scholarship views Ignatius as having "veered off into catholicism" by transforming Christianity into a cultic religion under the influence of Hellenistic and gnostic speculation, such that salvation is understood to be imparted "physically" via the institutional church with its threefold office of bishop, presbyters, and deacons.[30] This current has been fed by the *religionsgeschichtlich* hy-

---

30. Meinhold, *Studien zu Ignatius*, 57, summarizing earlier scholarship. Meinhold promises to subject this view to scrutiny but does nothing of the sort. Instead he simply accepts it as the starting point for his own critique of Ignatius's ecclesiology (57–66).

pothesis of Heinrich Schlier, according to which Ignatius's conception of the church is based not so much on the New Testament as on an early form of the Valentinian gnostic myth.³¹ Stressing the importance of *Trallians* 11:2, which seems to indicate that Christ the head could not be exalted to heaven apart from his members, Schlier understands Ignatius to present Christ as the gnostic redeemer who cannot possibly enter the Pleroma before gathering up the redeemed particles of light who by nature belong to him.³² The church is the heavenly σύζυγος ("partner, consort") of Christ, and together they form "the new Man."³³

Accepting Schlier's conclusions in the main, Peter Meinhold claims that Ignatius only narrowly avoids a thoroughly gnostic conception of the church by incorporating "historical realities" into his *Kirchenbegriff*, albeit in a nonhistorical manner.³⁴ The offices of bishop, presbyter, and deacon emerged in early Christianity as the result of strictly "historical" forces, but Ignatius claims divine sanction for them by combining "archetype-copy speculations" (*Urbild-Abbild-Spekulationen*) with an idealized picture of Christian history. In other words, Ignatius's legitimization of the institutional church weds an analogy between heavenly hierarchy and earthly authority to a second analogy, namely, "between the ideal apostolic era and the present day," conveniently obscuring the fact that the church's institutional structure is the accidental by-product of purely nontranscendent ("historical") factors.³⁵ Faced with troublesome "pneumatics" who oppose "spirit" to "office," and unable to deny that primitive Christian "pneumatism" is still having an effect within the church, Ignatius resorts to "the equation of office and spirit" (*die Gleichsetzung von Amt und Geist*).³⁶ The Pauline conception of the church as *pneumatischer Organismus* is thus transformed into the Ignatian conception of the church as *metaphysisches Organ*.³⁷

The *religionsgeschichtlich* view of Ignatius's ecclesiology has had a significant impact on English-language scholarship, though many Anglophone scholars have been critical of Schlier's hypothesis. Interpreting Ignatius's ecclesiology in the context of his polemics against the Judaizing and docetic heresies (a context almost entirely ignored in the German-

---

31. *Religionsgeschichtliche Untersuchungen*, 82–124.
32. Ibid., 90.   33. Ibid., 92.
34. *Studien zu Ignatius*, 62.
35. Ibid., 59, 65. Similarly, according to Henning Paulsen, "das ignatianische Verständnis von der Kirche als dem Antitypus der wahren Welt geschichtslos zu werden beginnt" (*Studien zur Theologie*, 150).
36. Meinhold, *Studien zu Ignatius*, 65–66.   37. Ibid., 58.

language treatments just outlined), C. C. Richardson finds Ignatius's understanding of the church to be more antignostic than gnostic.[38] To a large extent his argument relies on the claim that we do not need to take Ignatius's bolder statements too seriously. According to Richardson, Ignatius sometimes employs "extravagant phrases, characteristic perhaps of the milieu of Greek religion," and he has framed his argument for "ecclesiastical polity" in "somewhat Platonic terms," but one must keep in mind that "hyperbole is a marked feature of his overenthusiastic writing."[39] Ignatius is more "administrator" than "speculative theologian," and his purpose is the pragmatic one of solidifying the organization of the Christian communities in face of schism and heresy.[40] He insists only upon "a small but precise body of doctrine," and his understanding of the Christian religion is, in its essentials, faithful to Paul.[41] Still, Richardson notes that Ignatius's ecclesiology, unlike Paul's, has "very few affinities with the Old Testament or Jewish thought," and the dearth of eschatological references in his letters "raises the vital question of the relation of the church to history."[42]

T. F. Torrance provides an interpretation of Ignatius's ecclesiology that incorporates several key points from Schlier's hypothesis and is almost diametrically opposed to that of Richardson. Ignatius is "not concerned simply about good order" but "with a deep relation to God that is only attained within the unity of the Church." This represents "a movement away from the New Testament" and "in the direction of the view which thinks of the Church as an organism whose principle of life is infused grace, such that only by becoming members of this organism can we participate in the life of God."[43] According to Torrance, the apostle Paul understood the Holy Spirit to act directly upon the individual believer, so that *as a result* of this direct action the individual becomes a member of the church. For Paul (as Torrance reads him), the church thus has a secondary character and does not mediate the life of grace. But Ignatius, under gnostic influence, has developed a doctrine according to which "Christ and the Church together in union form the New Man," such that "Christ can only be the Head in a reciprocal relation to the Church."[44] This doctrine removes the emphasis from "the individual's faith and

---

38. Cyril C. Richardson, "The Church in Ignatius of Antioch," *Journal of Religion* 17 (1937): 429.
39. Ibid., 432, 436, 437.   40. Ibid., 429–30.
41. Ibid., 430, 433.   42. Ibid., 441–42.
43. *Doctrine of Grace*, 72.
44. Ibid., 73–74. Like Schlier, Torrance takes Smyr. 11:2 quite literally.

love" and places it upon membership in the church, which alone "brings one into touch" with the Spirit of Christ.[45]

Corwin gives a reading of Ignatius's ecclesiology that in effect splits the difference between Richardson and Torrance while making progress beyond both viewpoints. Like Torrance, she holds that Ignatius is not especially concerned with administrative matters but genuinely believes that human beings can attain salvation only within the church.[46] On the other hand, she subjects Schlier's hypothesis to a point-by-point critique and concludes that Ignatius's ecclesiology is neither gnostic nor positively influenced by gnosticism.[47] Schlier is correct to hold that, for Ignatius, the church is "ontologically" united to Christ, has "cosmic significance," and "cannot be explained simply on sociological grounds," but Schlier's analysis does not account for the "down-to-earth quality" of much of what Ignatius says about the church, and still less does it do justice to the way Ignatius's entire theology is firmly rooted in the historical Christ event.[48] Corwin points to the significant place that the apostles occupy in Ignatius's ecclesiology and especially in the typology by which he draws a correlation between the church's heavenly leadership and its earthly leadership. The apostles are historical figures who have attained a "supra-historical" status. Where German scholarship saw "idealized history," Corwin sees "the reverent imagination of the church as it looks back to the great leaders of its earliest days" and perceives their "continuing place in the universal church." The point of Ignatius's typology is not to set up "a strict heavenly-earthly parallelism" of a Platonic sort, and still less to legitimate ecclesiastical authority by reference to a gnostic myth, but to indicate the "real continuity" between the church's "visible ranks and those that are invisible."[49]

Several of the scholars whose interpretations of Ignatian ecclesiology we have just surveyed point out that Ignatius's typology combines a primary correlation between earthly church and heavenly church with a secondary correlation between the church's present and its (idealized) past. William R. Schoedel claims that a third correlation factors into Ignatius's complex typology, namely, one between local church and universal church. Taking Corwin's critique of Schlier as his starting point, Schoedel argues that the prominence of the apostles in Ignatius's ecclesiology precludes "any strict parallelism between the earthly and heaven-

---

45. *Doctrine of Grace*, 75–76.
46. *St. Ignatius and Christianity*, 189.
47. Ibid., 199–204.
48. Ibid., 203–4.
49. Ibid., 195–97.

ly realms." In fact, since most of the figures on the apparently "heavenly" side of the analogy, namely, Jesus Christ and the apostles, are historical personages understood to exercise a continuing influence over the whole church, "it is primarily the universal and local, then, which [are] being compared by Ignatius rather than the heavenly and earthly," and "the universal is rooted (at least in part) in an idealized past."[50] Schoedel clearly wishes not merely to exculpate Ignatius from the charge of gnosticism, but to dilute as much as possible the theological force of his heavenly-earthly analogy. The apostles are "venerable personages whose presence is still a reality," but this presence is mediated by the precepts that they laid down. Schoedel emphatically rejects the idea that "Ignatius meant to present God, Christ, or the apostles as mystically present in the ministry" of bishop, presbyters, or deacons.[51] He is thus swimming very much against the current of German scholarship, in effect denying that Ignatius's ecclesiology has "veered off into catholicism" (as the parties in the discussion would understand that term).

Much of value can be derived from modern scholarship's cumulative effort to understand Ignatian ecclesiology if we subject this scholarship to a brief critique. Since Schlier has set the agenda for this effort, we should begin by asking whether his hypothesis has any merit. As Corwin and Schoedel demonstrate with regard to many particulars, Schlier's hypothesis is vulnerable to critique on methodological grounds, and so it may well be that Meinhold and Torrance have accepted certain of his conclusions too uncritically.[52] Still, there are important elements of truth in Schlier's hypothesis and especially in the development it receives at the hands of Meinhold and Torrance. As I have noted more than once, Ignatius's conceptual world is not strictly limited to biblical categories and does have striking affinities with the *Denkboden* out of which gnosticism grew. Further, while there is no solid evidence that Ignatius adapted

---

50. Schoedel, *Ignatius of Antioch*, 113.

51. Ibid., 113–14.

52. Corwin and Schoedel challenge Schlier's gnostic reading of Ignatius throughout their works, not only in the area of ecclesiology. My own observation is that Schlier applies a crass double standard in assessing possible sources of influence on Ignatius's thought. When it comes to apparent echoes of the Pauline letters (a group of texts to which Ignatius makes explicit reference in *Eph.* 12:2), Schlier exercises extreme skepticism. For example, despite a series of impressive verbal, conceptual, and thematic parallels, Schlier will not allow that the New Testament Epistle to the Ephesians had any formative influence on Ignatius's ecclesiology (*Religionsgeschichtliche Untersuchungen*, 88–92). But when it is a question of considerably later Valentinian sources such as the *Excerpts from Theodotus*, or still later Mandaean sources, Schlier throws caution to the wind and indulges in parallelomania. Even a modest amount of terminological overlap suffices to posit a common mythological background (84–87).

a gnostic myth, his daring development of the head-and-members metaphor and his "new man" language (both of which are likely derived from the Pauline Ephesians) can fairly be said to give expression to an understanding of the church as "metaphysically" united to Christ and as the dispenser of grace. Torrance is very much on target in taking Ignatius to mean that the individual can only receive the principle of new life in and through the church and its sacraments. Further still, as I hope to demonstrate later in the chapter, Meinhold is quite correct to suppose that Ignatius not only sees no contradiction between "office" and "Spirit" but actively promotes their full compatibility. In sum, I have no objection to describing Ignatius's ecclesiology as "catholic," but whether this constitutes a departure from the New Testament depends, of course, on how one interprets the latter.

Ignatius's ecclesiological typology, with its heavenly-earthly analogy, serves the important theological function of pointing to the vertical or transcendent dimension of the economy of redemption as it manifests itself in the ecclesial sphere. It is wrongheaded to reduce the typology's function to a rhetorical or political one. For Richardson, Ignatius's "extravagant" and "overenthusiastic" language represents an administrator's benign attempt to consolidate the Christian communities against heresy, so that we would be mistaken to read his letters as serious speculative theology. For Meinhold, something more insidious is going on. Ignatius is wielding *Urbild-Abbild-Spekulationen* as an ideological weapon in order to hoodwink the laity into thinking that the church's authority structure has been divinely instituted. Schoedel, for his part, takes Ignatius's ecclesiological typology quite seriously, carefully analyzing its permutations, and his discovery of an analogy between universal church and local church within the typology represents a real breakthrough, but his attempt to make this analogy the true focal point of the typology is unconvincing. He wishes to deflect attention away from the heavenly-earthly analogy because he is manifestly uncomfortable with the vertical-transcendent dimension of ecclesiology to which it points.

Apart from Schlier, each of the authors we have surveyed calls attention to a historical dimension within Ignatian ecclesiology. This is a crucial point, for it is impossible to understand this ecclesiology if we attempt to detach it from Ignatius's broader understanding of the economy of redemption, which lays such stress on the Christ event as "truly and surely accomplished" within history. Moreover, the apostles, who have a certain prominence in Ignatius's letters, and in particular within the ecclesiological typology, seem to form a kind of bridge between the historical Christ event and the present life of the church. One might even say that for Ignatius the apostles constitute a crucial link between Christology and ecclesiology. True, he articulates no doctrine of apostolic succession, but we should not for that reason ignore what he does say about the apostles. Vague references to "idealized history" are not especially helpful in this regard. Corwin's reference to "reverent imagination" is a less objectionable description of how apostolic traditions seem to have been preserved in the early church. To this Schoedel adds the simple but crucial observation that when Ignatius speaks of apostolic authority and of the apostles' continuing influence upon the church, he has in mind above all their concrete "ordinances" and "precepts."[53] The church's careful transmission of these, whether in writing or orally,[54] would have supplied a degree of real historical continuity and objectivity and would have tempered even "reverent imagination."

The real trick, then, to gaining a firm hold on Ignatius's ecclesiology will be just what it was when we looked at the relationship between Judaism and Christianity, and also when we considered the Christ event as *mysterium*, namely, to disclose the proper relationship between the horizontal-temporal and the vertical-transcendent dimensions of the divine economy. (The only difference is that in the present case we must also take into account the relationship between the universal and the local.) The twentieth-century effort to understand Ignatian ecclesiology represents, I believe, a helpful but ultimately flawed attempt to deal with this challenge. The flaw lies once again in an impoverished notion of human temporality. If we begin with a positivistic view of "history," namely, one that excludes transcendence and teleology a priori from the realm of human temporality, the two dimensions that we are attempting to place in their proper relation, the vertical and the horizontal, will have been set in irreconcilable opposition to each other from the outset. Under such conditions, if Ignatius should tell us, for example, that the bishop is "the type of the Father" (Tral. 3:2) and "presides in the place of God" (Magn. 6:1), we will inevitably hear this as so much metaphysical mumbo-jumbo.

The one thing that unites nearly all the scholars we have looked at is that they do not quite know what to make of Ignatius's references to a transcendent dimension *within* the terrestrial church. For Schlier they reflect elements of gnostic mythology, for Meinhold Urbild-Abbild-

---

53. Tral. 7:1; Magn. 13:1.
54. See Eph. 12:2; Phld. 5:1.

Spekulationen, for Richardson "extravagant language," and for Torrance a dangerous departure from the authentic New Testament doctrine of grace. Schoedel, for his part, must ultimately deny that Ignatius's heavenly-earthly analogy has any real theological importance, for, if it did, it could only mean that God, Jesus, or the apostles were "mystically present in the ministry itself," a conclusion that Schoedel clearly finds unpalatable.[55] Thus, at one end of the spectrum we have Schlier, who ignores the historical element entirely and thus reduces Ignatius's ecclesiology to its vertical dimension, while at the other end we have Schoedel, who places all the emphasis on the horizontal dimension, to the point of very nearly denying the vertical. Only Corwin comes close to disclosing the true interrelation between vertical and horizontal dimensions, and only she rightly concludes that Ignatius's ecclesiological typology is meant to show forth "real continuity." Here we begin to glimpse the heart of the matter. Ignatius's ecclesiology amounts to a vision of ecclesial unity, between past and present, visible and invisible, hierarchy and laity, universal and local, those who have attained God and those who are still living in hope.

The Gift That the Lord Has Truly Sent

The trajectory of scholarship that we have just surveyed places before our eyes what Richardson aptly terms "the vital question of the relation of the church to history."[56] Though every scholar in our survey other than Schlier finds Ignatius to have preserved at least some element of history in his ecclesiology, all but Schoedel demonstrate some concern that Ignatius has dangerously weakened the historical element. Even Corwin grants that Ignatius's ecclesiological typology represents "a step in the direction of the Platonic or more immediately the Philonic view of the world."[57] Now, no one can deny that the clearest and firmest point of contact with history in Ignatius's theology is to be found in his creedal narrations of the Christ event, which consists of those things "truly and surely accomplished by Jesus Christ ... in the time of the governorship of Pontius Pilate" (*Magn.* 11:1). What I find amazing is that not one of these scholars, who have devoted such careful attention to Ignatius's ec-

---

55. *Ignatius of Antioch*, 114. Throughout his commentary Schoedel attempts to mitigate the force of any expression in Ignatius's letters suggestive of mystical union between God and man.
56. "Church in Ignatius," 442.
57. *St. Ignatius and Christianity*, 197.

clesiology, directly addresses the question: How does Ignatius conceive of the relationship of the church to the Christ event? Specifically, does Ignatius think of the church as having received its principle of new life from Christ and through his historical actions? Even more surprising, given the way early Christian literature as a whole links church and Spirit, is the similar failure in the scholarly literature to inquire carefully into the relationship between pneumatology and ecclesiology in Ignatius's letters. These are the two gaping lacunae in twentieth-century scholarship's effort to understand Ignatian ecclesiology: the church's relation to the Christ event, and its relation to the gift of the Holy Spirit.

These two lacunae are reducible to a single omission, of course, since the Christ event and the sending of the Spirit are themselves intimately linked within the economy of redemption. In fact, the sending of the Spirit can be viewed as the final moment in the Christ event. Not surprisingly, this point too is neglected by the scholars we have surveyed. A reader with no prior knowledge of early Christianity would never guess on the basis of Meinhold's statements about *Geist* and *urchristliches Pneumatismus* that major contributors to the New Testament think of the Holy Spirit's quickening of the church first and foremost as an event within the historical economy.[58] John and Luke, each in his own way, present the passion and exaltation of Christ as the economic trigger, so to speak, that releases the outpouring of the Holy Spirit upon the apostles.[59] And Paul, for his part, draws an unmistakable correlation between the mission of the Son and the mission of the Spirit (Gal 4:4–6).[60] Ought we not at least to ask whether the letters of Ignatius contain evidence of a similar view? Does Ignatius anywhere present the church as having been brought to life by an infusion of the Holy Spirit that comes as a direct result of the Lord's death and resurrection? This question, it seems to me, is the obvious place to begin an inquiry into his ecclesiology.

While Ignatius never speaks of an outpouring of the Holy Spirit in so many words, two passages in his letters directly link the spiritual quickening of the church to the paschal mystery. The first of these is *Ephesians* 17:1–2.

---

58. *Studien zu Ignatius*, 65–66. Ironically, while charging Ignatius with gnosticism, Meinhold himself seems to favor an ahistorical view of the church.

59. Jn 7:39, 16:7, 19:30, 20:22; Acts 2:32–33.

60. Admittedly, however, Paul does not clearly present the sending of the Spirit upon the church as a single historical event, closely linked to the paschal mystery, in the way Luke and John do. Both here in Galatians and also in Romans (5:5, 8:15) the Spirit is sent by God the Father into the "hearts" of believers rather than to the church as such. The two perspectives are, of course, complementary.

To this end the Lord received myrrh upon his head: that he might breathe imperishability into the church. Do not anoint yourself with the malodorous teaching of the ruler of this aeon, lest he take you captive, away from the life that lies before you! Why are we not all wise, having received the knowledge of God, which is Jesus Christ? Why do we foolishly perish, failing to recognize the gift that the Lord has truly sent?

This brief midrashic reflection on the anointing at Bethany should be interpreted in much the same way we dealt with Ignatius's references to the Lord's baptism in the Jordan. By meditating upon a single moment in the life of Christ in its interrelations with other moments, Ignatius glimpses vital aspects of the Christian mystery as a whole. *Ephesians* 17 is a piece of mystagogy, and a profound one. To characterize it as a "flight of fancy," as Richardson does, smacks of cultural chauvinism.[61]

Ignatius's apparent starting point for his reflection is Matthew's account of the anointing at Bethany, the only New Testament version to identify the ointment simply as "myrrh" and the only one to contain the precise phrase ἐπὶ τῆς κεφαλῆς αὐτοῦ ("upon his head").[62] In Matthew (as also in Mark and John) the anointing at Bethany inaugurates the passion narrative and anticipates Jesus' death and burial. All three gospel accounts stress the fact that Jesus welcomed the gesture, over against the protestations of some present, and called attention to the way it foreshadowed his burial. By simply saying that the Lord "received" (ἔλαβεν) the perfumed oil, Ignatius alludes to Jesus' willing acceptance of the passion. Immediately before and after this passage he makes reference to the cross, and this part of *Ephesians* is clearly focused on "the death of the Lord" as μυστήριον.[63] Why then does Ignatius refer to the anointing at Bethany at all? Why not simply speak about the passion? As we have noted in previous chapters, Ignatius views the Lord's life, just as he views his own life and every human life, as a teleological whole: *vita usque ad mortem*. The essential characteristic of the Lord's mission, the char-

---

61. "Church in Ignatius," 433.
62. Mt 26:7. We are concerned here only with the three New Testament accounts of the anointing that took place at Bethany in the last week of Jesus' life (Mt 26:6–13; Mk 14:3–9; Jn 12:1–8). The anointing recounted in Lk 7:36–50, though it has points of contact in the tradition with the other accounts, is not located in Bethany, occurs earlier in the Lord's ministry, and is not said to anticipate his burial. Mark and John must be understood to use the word μύρον generically for "perfumed ointment" since they specify that it is made of νάρδος ("spikenard"; Mk 14:3; Jn 12:3; cf. Keener, *Gospel of John*, 2.863). Since Matthew has simplified this to a reference to μύρον, perhaps to invite the reader to correlate it with the myrrh (σμύρνα) given to Jesus by the Magi (Mt 2:11), the word μύρον in his account, as in that of Ignatius, may refer to ointment made of myrrh.
63. Eph. 16:2, 18:1, 19:1.

acteristic that is present throughout his life and is most perfectly realized in his death, is his obedience to the Father's will, an obedience that "manifests" his eternal union "with the Father" and is "pleasing to the one who sent him."[64] In Jesus' serene acceptance of the myrrh Ignatius glimpses certain facets of this precious mystery.

Oil of myrrh and other perfumes were applied to corpses to mask the stench of corruption.[65] This fact suggests to Ignatius that the myrrh poured upon Jesus' head might symbolize both his death and the gift of "incorruption" (ἀφθαρσία) which that death brings into the world. A theologian with Ignatius's sense of symbolism, and captivated as he is with the wondrous paradox of "true life in death" (Eph. 7:2), would find this interpretation irresistible. To this symbolism Ignatius connects the Johannine idea that through the paschal mystery, if not in the very act of dying, Jesus "handed over the Spirit" or "breathed" it upon the apostles.[66] While Ignatius does not retain John's word ἐνεφύσησεν ("he breathed into"; Jn 19:30), which constitutes a strong verbal echo of Septuagint-Genesis 2:7 (and probably also an allusion to Ezek 37:9), the verb he uses in its place, πνέω ("to breathe"), evokes both the "breath of life" (πνοὴ ζωῆς) of Genesis 2:7 and the gift of the "Spirit" (πνεῦμα). Furthermore, he strengthens the allusion to the Genesis narrative by putting "the church" in the dative case (τῇ ἐκκλησίᾳ), so that Jesus breathes imperishability "into" the church, even as God the Creator breathed the breath of life into the first man.[67] Ignatius thus presents the church as the new Adam. This may strike us as odd, since we are accustomed to thinking of Christ himself as the new Adam and the church as the new Eve, but Ignatius here is developing the teaching of the Pauline Ephesians (2:15), which says that Christ, by bringing his members into union with himself, their head, forms the church "into one new man" (εἰς ἕνα καινὸν ἄνθρωπον).[68] Writing his own *Ephesians*, Ignatius is concerned to present above all "the economy concerning the new man [εἰς τὸν καινὸν ἄνθρωπον] Jesus Christ" (20:1).

---

64. *Magn.* 6:1, 7:1, 8:2, 13:2.   65. Keener, *Gospel of John*, 2.865.
66. Jn 7:39, 19:30, 20:22.
67. The idiom πνέω τινί τι means to "instill something into someone" (BDAG, 838). The correct rendering of τῇ ἐκκλησίᾳ is therefore: "into the church," as in Bart D. Ehrman, ed. and trans., *The Apostolic Fathers*, 2 vols., Loeb Classical Library (Cambridge, Mass.: Harvard University Press, 2003), 1.237, not "upon the church," as one finds in most other translations.
68. The identification of the church as the new Eve combines two Pauline ideas: Christ as the new Adam or "last Adam" (Rom 5:12–21; 1 Cor 15:45–48), and the church as the bride of Christ (Eph 5:24–32). It is also hinted at in the Johannine literature, where Mary the mother of the Messiah is presented as an Eve-like figure as well as a symbol of Israel/church (Rv 12:1–18; Jn 2:1–11, 19:26–27).

It is not that Ignatius confuses the church with its divine Lord but that he wishes to show how intimately and truly the two are united, a truth that he has been at pains to clarify throughout *Ephesians*. The church is "mingled with" (ἐγκεράννυμι) Jesus Christ, "even as Jesus Christ is with the Father" (5:1), so that we may "always participate [μετέχω] in God" (4:2). This is the aspect of Ignatius's ecclesiology that many modern scholars, rooted as they are in the Protestant theological tradition, find disturbing. Torrance gives these statements their full force, grants that Ignatius views the church as "an organism whose principle of life is infused grace," and concludes that this constitutes "a movement away from the New Testament."[69] Richardson and Schoedel, each in his own way, attempt to justify not taking these same statements at face value, presumably because they too feel that such a view of the church would constitute a "veering off" into "Catholicism," if not gnosticism. I do not share their concern, because I do not think Ignatius's catholic ecclesiology is at odds with the New Testament. In any case, we should understand the first sentence of *Ephesians* 17 to mean that through the paschal mystery the Lord Jesus has imparted his Spirit to the church as a permanent endowment and principle of imperishable life, thus drawing the members of his body into a real participation in divine life.

Somewhat elliptically, Ignatius next contrasts the church's infused gift of imperishability with the "malodorous teaching" of the devil (17:1). This step in his reflection may have been prompted by John's remark that "the house was filled with the aroma of the ointment [μύρον]" (Jn 12:3). It has even been suggested that Ignatius, like some later patristic authors, would have taken "the house" here as a figure for the church.[70] Be that as it may, the contrast between the aroma of ecclesial imperishability and the stench of heresy implies both that the former consists, at least in part, in orthodox teaching and that the latter is a kind of corruption, an agent of death.[71] Elsewhere, Ignatius connects the dots more or less explicitly. True doctrine is "nourishment," but heresy is a "lethal drug" (Tral. 6:1). Those who preach the gospel impart "imperishability" (Phld. 9:2), but heretics are "advocates of death rather than of the truth" (Smyr. 5:1). This pair of equations, while remaining mostly implicit, is foundational to Ignatius's thought.

$$\begin{aligned} \text{truth/orthodoxy} &= \text{life/imperishability} \\ \text{falsehood/heterodoxy} &= \text{death/corruption} \end{aligned}$$

69. *Doctrine of Grace*, 72.
71. Schoedel, *Ignatius of Antioch*, 82.
70. Grant, *Ignatius of Antioch*, 47.

That *Ephesians* 17:1 should be taken to imply this pair of equations is confirmed by its immediate context. What Jesus Christ has brought into the world through his life-giving death is both πίστις θεοῦ ("faith in God"; 16:2) and γνῶσις θεοῦ ("knowledge of God"; 17:2).[72] As we learned in chapter 5, Ignatius accents the objective doctrinal content of faith, which comes to us through God's self-manifestation in Christ, but the act of faith does not, for that reason, terminate in mere doctrines or propositions. Faith puts us in touch with divinely revealed realities, indeed with God himself. That is why Ignatius, in the present passage and also just a bit earlier in *Ephesians*, links faith so closely to "life." Faith is, in fact, "the principle of life" (ἀρχὴ ζωῆς) because it brings us into a communion of love with the one who is himself in perfect communion with the Father (14:1). But this life-giving contact with the Trinity is corrupted when heterodoxy distorts the content of faith. A heretic "corrupts [φθείρω] faith in God by his evil teaching" (16:2), and the devil uses such a person to lead us into captivity, "away from the life [τὸ ζῆν] that lies before us" (17:1). Ignatius says all of this in a remarkably efficient while highly provocative manner. Our Lord Jesus allowed himself to be anointed with the myrrh that betokened his suffering so that he might confer upon his church the knowledge of God that is life itself, and therefore we should be careful not to let ourselves be "anointed" with corrupt doctrines and thus "perish" (17:1-2).

Ignatius concludes the chapter by chiding any of his readers who might have failed to recognize "the gift that the Lord has truly sent" (17:2). This simple expression is of the greatest importance for understanding Ignatius's ecclesiology. The "Lord" to whom he refers is, of course, the risen Christ, and the "gift" (χάρισμα) that the Lord has "sent" is the Holy Spirit's abiding presence in the church. It is both "imperishability" and "knowledge of God," for the Holy Spirit is both "life-giver" and "Spirit of truth," the one who leads the church into all truth.[73] The affirmation that the glorified Lord Jesus himself has "sent" the Holy Spirit from heaven has deep roots in New Testament tradition.[74] Ignatius does not say that Jesus "sends" (present tense), or even that he "sent" (aorist tense), but that he "has sent" the gift of the Spirit (πέπομφεν, perfect tense). He uses the perfect tense to indicate an action that was completed

---

72. Ignatius's thought, imagery, and wording in this passage merit comparison with Paul's in 2 Cor 2:14-16.
73. Jn 6:63, 16:13.
74. Lk 24:49; Jn 15:26, 16:7; Acts 2:33; 1 Pt 1:12.

at a definite time in the past and has brought about a situation that endures right up to the present.[75] It is true that God gives his Spirit personally to each believer, but he does not need to send his Spirit into the world over and over again, in each age, to each local church, to each individual. The Lord has "breathed" this gift "into the church" once and for all, and this gift belongs to the church as a lasting possession. The mission of the Spirit is an economic event, and as such it is intimately linked to the other key events in salvation history. By saying that the Lord Jesus has "truly" (ἀληθῶς) sent the gift of the Spirit, Ignatius invites us to regard this event as one among those things that the Lord has "truly" accomplished.[76] One might even think of the sending of the Spirit as the final moment in the Christ event. Like the incarnation and the resurrection, it has the quality of being both truly temporal and fully transcendent.

The second key text pertinent to the relationship between the paschal mystery and the spiritual quickening of the church is *Smyrnaeans* 1–3. As this passage is rather long, I will summarize most of it and quote only the most pertinent section. Wishing to strengthen the Smyrnaeans' adherence to the most essential aspects of the gospel in face of the docetic heresy, Ignatius gives his lengthiest presentation of the Christ event. He affirms Jesus Christ's human and divine origins, his birth from a virgin, baptism by John, crucifixion under Pilate and Herod, and resurrection (1:1–2). The really distinctive feature of this creedal formula is, however, its ecclesiology. From beginning to end, Ignatius shows how believers are united to Christ and his paschal mystery precisely as members of the church, and he achieves this through a remarkable meditation on the cross itself. Through faith and love the Smyrnaeans are "nailed" to the cross with Jesus Christ. The cross is a tree of life, and they are its fruit. Through Christ's resurrection, the cross has been lifted up as a "battle standard," visible "to the aeons," so that "his holy and faithful ones, whether among the Jews or among the gentiles," might be gathered into "the one body of his church" (1:1–2). The cross is the sacrament of the church, and the church is the sacrament of the cross. That is, the cross is the efficacious sign of the church's life and unity, and the church becomes the "sign of the cross" in the world. She is the visible presence of Christ to all peoples of all ages.

In chapters 2–3 Ignatius directly addresses the teaching of the docetists, who claim that Jesus only "seemed" to die and rise from the

---

75. See BDF § 340.
76. *Magn.* 11:1; *Tral.* 9:1–2; *Smyr.* 1:1–2:1.

dead and that what appeared to the disciples was a "bodiless phantom" (δαιμόνιον ἀσώματον). He warns that it is in fact these "unbelievers" who merely "seem to be" and that in the end they will find *themselves* "bodiless and phantasmal" (2:1). We shall have opportunity in the next chapter to consider how this statement factors into Ignatius's eschatology. For the present, it will suffice to note that fundamentally what renders all unbelievers "bodiless" is the fact that they do not belong to "the one body of his church." To "be," in the fullest sense of the word, is to possess the true life that comes from Jesus Christ and is available within the unity of the church. To have this life, one must be united to Christ, and it is the church that enjoys this union with Christ. Ironically, it was precisely through his fleshly death and resurrection, the very reality that the docetists deny, that Jesus Christ bestowed upon the church this life-giving union with himself.

> And when he came to those around Peter, he said to them, "Take, handle me, and see that I am not a bodiless phantom." And immediately they touched him and believed, being mingled with his flesh and spirit. (3:2)

After his resurrection, according to this passage, Jesus did not merely "appear." Rather, he "came" (ἦλθεν) in the flesh, so that his disciples might have living contact with him (cf. Jn 20:19, 24). He came, moreover, not simply to some disciples who happened to be together, but to "those around Peter," that is, to those united around the one whom Jesus himself had established in authority, to "the college of apostles" (*Tral.* 3:1). The command to "take" (λάβετε), which could also be translated "receive," has eucharistic overtones (cf. Mt 26:26), but in context it recalls even more readily the parallel scene in the Gospel of John (20:22), where Jesus says to the apostles, "Receive the Holy Spirit" (λάβετε πνεῦμα ἅγιον). In either case, Jesus is handing *himself* over to the apostles. The expression "handle me and see" (ψηλαφήσατέ με καὶ ἴδετε), which Ignatius has taken verbatim from Luke 24:39 or from a similar noncanonical account, might by itself suggest an ephemeral experience. But when this phrase is supplemented with the Johannine λάβετε, the Lord's words suggest that he is conferring upon his disciples a new and lasting mode of union with himself. He will be present to his church henceforth through the action of the Holy Spirit and through the eucharist. This impression is confirmed by the characteristically Ignatian phrase, "being mingled with his flesh and spirit." Elsewhere Ignatius uses a strengthened form of the same verb (κεράννυμι) to refer to the way the universal church is "mingled" with Jesus Christ and the local church is "mingled" with the bishop (Eph. 5:1). What Ignatius wishes for all the churches is precisely "union with the flesh and spirit of Jesus Christ" (Magn. 1:2).

Two final observations about this remarkable passage from *Smyrnaeans* merit mention in the present context. First, this text recounts the same event as *Ephesians* 17, namely, the Lord's gift of "imperishability" to his church. Christ's coming to the apostles in the cenacle enabled them to "scorn death," so that in the end "they were found to be beyond death" (Smyr. 3:2). Second, the passage is laced with eucharistic overtones, from the reference to Jesus' flesh and blood in 1:1 to the reference to his postresurrection eating and drinking with the apostles in 3:3. Here Ignatius prepares for the explicit eucharistic teaching that he will give later in the letter. By identifying the eucharistic flesh with Jesus' historical flesh, which suffered and was raised, he will insist on the strongest possible bond between the paschal mystery and the church's sacramental life (6:2). The eucharist is the means by which the apostles' Easter Sunday encounter with the risen Lord remains with the church permanently. It is the mode by which the Lord Jesus "comes" to believers of all ages, so that they may "take, handle, and see" him and thus ultimately be found "beyond death." It is the "medicine of immortality" (Eph. 20:2). The presence of the Spirit and the sacrament of the eucharist, together with the word of God, constitute the gift of imperishability that the Lord Jesus, through his paschal mystery, has conferred upon his body the church.

The Apostolic Character

In this chapter we are attempting to understand Ignatian ecclesiology by placing its vertical-transcendent and horizontal-temporal dimensions in their proper interrelation. The church, to be truly herself, must possess both these dimensions. In order to bestow eternal life and real hope upon her members, she must have access to divine truth and life and at the same time be a real historical presence within the world. The fundamental bond between heaven and earth, that which gives the church both her access to the divine and her historical grounding, is of course the person and event of Jesus Christ, the incarnate Logos. But since the Christ event has its own specific locus in history, the "real continuity" between heaven and earth must also include continuity between the past of the Christ event and the present of the church. This fact, therefore, requires us also to consider the relationship between the *vita Iesu* and the *vita ecclesiae*. We began to do just that in the previous section by looking at how the Lord Jesus, through the paschal mystery, breathed the enduring gift of imperishable life into his church. This sending of the Spirit is the most fundamental link between the life of Christ and the life of the church, for the church does not possess the true life that comes from Jesus apart from the gift of the Holy Spirit. But there are, and must be, other dimensions to the continuity between past and present. A church in which the Holy Spirit's presence constitutes the only element of continuity between past and present would be a purely charismatic church. Ignatius's understanding of the church includes a strong charismatic dimension, but it also includes the complementary dimension of a visible authority structure. Nearly all the scholars surveyed in our *Forschungsbericht* recognize that Ignatius attempts to ground this authority structure, in part, by reference to the apostles as historical, or quasi-historical, figures. While Corwin and Schoedel make some helpful observations in this regard, it seems to me that we still lack a satisfactory theological account of the role that the apostles play in Ignatius's ecclesiology. It is to this important piece in the puzzle that we now turn.

Ignatius tells the Magnesians that "the Lord did nothing apart from the Father, being united to him, either by himself or through the apostles" (*Magn.* 7:1). When and how did the Lord Jesus act "through the apostles"? Ignatius may have in mind the mission given to the twelve during the course of the Lord's own public ministry, as recounted in Matthew 10, but more likely he is thinking in Johannine terms of the Lord's postresurrection "sending" of the apostles into the world, just as the Father had sent him into the world.[77] It is in *Magnesians* especially that Ignatius develops the Johannine doctrine according to which the incarnate Logos accomplishes our salvation essentially by doing the Father's will. In the present passage he indicates that the Lord's accomplishment of the Father's will, in a very real sense, extended beyond his own time on earth and into the period of the apostles' postresurrection ministry. Naturally, to speak of the risen Lord's having acted "through the apostles," and to mean this as a serious theological statement, presupposes both that the apostles remained obedient to the Lord's will and that such obedience to the Lord

---

77. Jn 17:18, 20:21. Cf. Grant, *Ignatius of Antioch*, 61. Corwin jumps the gun, passing right over the apostles' earthly ministry, and finds in this passage a reference to "some suprahistorical reality which [Ignatius] envisages, in which the Apostles have [a] continuing place in the universal church" (*St. Ignatius and Christianity*, 196).

was tantamount to obedience to the Father. And this is exactly what Ignatius affirms later in the same letter when he says that Jesus Christ submitted "to the Father" during his earthly life and that the apostles submitted "to Christ and to the Father" (13:2).

Statements found elsewhere in the letters suggest that the postresurrection ministry of the apostles, at least of Peter and Paul, was of some interest and theological significance to Ignatius, and that he possessed reliable historical traditions in this regard. In particular, he knew that Paul had a close relationship with the church at Ephesus, had written several letters, and had died for the faith (Eph. 12:2). He was also aware that both Peter and Paul had instructed the Christians in Rome, and probably knew that they had been martyred in that city (Rom. 4:3). In any case, by saying that the apostles "scorned death" (Smyr. 3:2), Ignatius implies that most, if not all, of them suffered martyrdom. Having been found to be "beyond death" (3:2), they were reunited to their risen Lord, who is now "beyond time" (Poly. 3:2). In heaven they form a "college" or "council" and are worthy of special "honor."[78] Ignatius describes Paul as having been "declared holy, testified to, and worthy of blessing" (Eph. 12:2), that is, in much the same terms he applies to the Old Testament prophets (Phld. 5:2). Presumably he would describe the other apostles in a similar manner. To be honest, it escapes me how any of this constitutes "idealized history." The details that Ignatius supplies concerning the apostles' earthly ministry are quite sober and do not go beyond what we find in the New Testament and 1 Clement. As for the heavenly honor Ignatius accords them, this is likely to sound "idealized" only to those who would first call into question the essential tenets of the Christian faith.

The historical ministry of the apostles can, therefore, be viewed as extending the Lord's own mission into the portresurrection history of the church, but only by a few decades. Does this dimension of "real continuity" extend any farther forward in time? And if so, by what means? Ignatius clearly thinks of the apostles as distinguished members of the universal church, now ensconced in heaven. Are they somehow still present to the earthly members of the body of Christ, present *from heaven*? And if yes, how is this presence mediated? Ignatius believes that when a Christian "attains God" he or she remains somehow in spiritual communion with the church on earth. He anticipates this in his own case and presumably would understand it to be true of the apostles as well.[79] Given the

---

78. *Magn.* 6:1; *Tral.* 3:1, 12:2.
79. *Eph.* 11:2; *Tral.* 13:3; *Poly.* 6:1.

tremendous seriousness with which he takes intercessory prayer, it is not inconceivable that he would think of the apostles in heaven as praying for the church on earth, and it may even be that he sought their intercession. But when Ignatius speaks of the apostles' continuing influence upon the earthly church, he seems primarily to have something more tangible and specific in mind. The apostles continue to instruct and command the church through the "precepts" and "ordinances" that they have left behind, whether in writing or orally.[80] Ignatius evinces no concern with apostolic succession as such, but when he praises the Ephesian Christians for having "always lived in accord with the apostles in the power of Jesus Christ" (Eph. 11:2), he witnesses to one church's unbroken continuity of life and doctrine with the apostolic age.

It is important to note in this regard that Ignatius does not view the teaching of the apostles as mere words, as if doctrine or moral exhortation were extrinsically related to other elements of ecclesial life such as the grace of the Holy Spirit or the eucharist. One lives in accord with the apostles' teaching "in the power of Jesus Christ" (11:2). The teaching of the apostles is a sure "refuge" (Phld. 5:1), authentic "nourishment" (Tral. 6:1), a means of being "confirmed" in the true faith (Magn. 13:1) and of remaining in union with God (Tral. 7:1). Ignatius views the apostles as occupying a position within the economy of redemption parallel to that of the Old Testament prophets (Phld. 9:1). Much as the prophets seem to have a personal living presence within the church in and through their writings (5:2), so the apostles seem to be personally present to the church largely through their words (Eph. 12:2). Finally, the apostles' words are intimately linked with those of the Lord himself (Magn. 13:1) and together with the gospels and the books of the prophets form a unified deposit of doctrine (Phld. 5:1–2).[81]

At this point it will be instructive to ask how Ignatius views his own ministry vis-à-vis that of the apostles. The short answer to this question is that, while he never explicitly associates the office of bishop with the apostles, he seems to waver between claiming and forswearing quasi-apostolic authority for himself in his letters. Much hinges on what we take Ignatius to mean by greeting the church at Tralles ἐν ἀποστολικῷ χαρακτῆρι (Tral. sal.). There is no justification for the translation "in apostolic authority," which is found in a recent commentary written in

---

80. Magn. 13:1; Tral. 7:1.
81. Hill, "Ignatius and the Gospels," 267–85.

the "Catholic apologetics" vein.[82] The meaning "authority" is unattested for the word χαρακτήρ. At most, possessing the "apostolic character" (whatever that turns out to mean) might be a *basis* for speaking with authority. On the other hand, Lightfoot's minimalist interpretation, according to which Ignatius is simply claiming to compose his greeting "after the manner of the apostles," that is, in imitation of the epistolary style of the Pauline letters,[83] while lexicologically sound, is hardly plausible in this context. Leaving aside the fact that the Ignatian salutations are really not much like the Pauline in terms of style or vocabulary, what does characterize them is their great solemnity and their focus on the divine blessings bestowed upon author and addressees alike. Are we to suppose that Ignatius has inserted such a trivial, irrelevant, and self-conscious remark into one of these solemn salutations? Taken as a reference to epistolary style, the phrase ἐν ἀποστολικῷ χαρακτῆρι would represent quite a thematic descent from the phrase that immediately precedes it: ἐν τῷ πληρώματι ("in the fullness"). Lightfoot himself notes that this latter phrase (which likewise modifies "I greet") refers to "the sphere of the Divine graces," and he accordingly observes, "It is no mundane salutation which the writer sends."[84]

The phrase ἐν ἀποστολικῷ χαρακτῆρι introduces one of the central leitmotifs of *Trallians*. Ignatius will refer to the apostles five more times in the course of the letter.[85] Having felt the fatal attraction of heretical teaching, a "lethal drug" mixed with "honeyed wine," the Trallians have become "puffed up" and are in grave peril of being estranged from their bishop, from "the ordinances of the apostles," and thus from Jesus Christ himself (6:2–7:1). They need to "regain" themselves in authentic faith and love (8:1). In such a context, Ignatius's claim to greet this church (which, as far as we know, had no prior contact with him) "in the fullness" and "in the apostolic character" is best understood as his solemn assurance that the teaching and pastoral admonishment he is about to deliver to them is the unadulterated gospel of Jesus Christ, and that he is writing out of genuine Christian love. His words have the "apostolic stamp," as it were, with respect to faith and love (though not necessarily with respect to literary style). This is not a formal appeal to his episcopal office, which he never mentions in this letter and which he

---

82. Kenneth J. Howell, *Ignatius of Antioch: A New Translation and Theological Commentary* (Zanesville, Ohio: Coming Home Network International, 2008), 84.
83. Ignatius, *Polycarp*, 2.152; Grant, *Ignatius of Antioch*, 71; Schoedel, *Ignatius of Antioch*, 137.
84. Ignatius, *Polycarp*, 2.152.   85. Tral. 2:2, 3:1 and 3, 7:1, 12:2.

never explicitly correlates with the apostolic office. It is actually a much bolder and, one might say, more charismatic claim. While reticent to issue orders "as an apostle" (3:3), Ignatius does not shy away from claiming that he speaks "in the voice of God," or rather that the Holy Spirit speaks through him (Phld. 7:1–2). He begins every letter by identifying himself as "God-bearer" (Θεοφόρος), never by identifying himself as a bishop. In addressing the Christians at Tralles, who are near to being seduced by the error of docetism, he is especially eager to affirm that one who has a living share in the suffering love of Jesus Christ proclaims the gospel to them. He writes, "I exhort you, not I but the love of Jesus Christ, to take only Christian nourishment" (Tral. 6:1), and again, "My bonds exhort you, which I bear about for the sake of Jesus Christ, asking to get to God" (12:2).

To speak "in the apostolic character" means to speak with authentic Christian faith and love, and in the context of Ignatius's response to docetism the close interrelation between πίστις and ἀγάπη takes on a precise nuance. What makes the apostles so significant to Ignatius is their historical contact with, and faith in, the crucified and risen flesh of Jesus ("they touched him and believed"), and what makes them so worthy of emulation is the love by which they joined themselves to his passion.[86] Apostolic faith is to believe in the death of Jesus "for us" (Tral. 2:1), and apostolic love is to "suffer with him" (Smyr. 4:2). Faith is "the flesh of the Lord," and love is "the blood of Jesus Christ" (Tral. 8:1). But each depends on the other. Ignatius poses the same question in both Trallians (10:1) and Smyrnaeans (4:2): If Jesus only seemed to suffer, why would Ignatius allow himself to be led away in chains to be fed to the beasts at Rome? He intends his martyrdom, like that of the apostles, to be an act of faith and love, and an enduring authentic witness to the whole reality of Jesus Christ (Tral. 10:1). This is why he appends the phrase "our individual sufferings" to a list of permanent documents that bear witness to Jesus Christ: the "prophecies," the "law of Moses," and the "gospel" (Smyr. 5:1).[87] When the adjective ἀποστολικός makes its next appearance in early Christian literature, it will be used in a similar context, to describe the martyr Polycarp as "an apostolic and prophetic teacher, bishop of the catholic church in Smyrna" (Mart. 16:2).

Speaking of Polycarp, it is interesting to note in this context Ignatius's reference to the Smyrnaean bishop's "mind-set [γνώμη] in God,"

---

86. Smyr. 3:2; Eph. 12:2.

87. The phrase τὸ εὐαγγέλιον ("the gospel") presupposes one or more written gospels, or at the very least, a specific and permanent content to the oral kerygma.

which is "founded as upon an immovable rock [ἡδρασμένη ὡς ἐπὶ πέτραν ἀκίνητον]" (Poly. 1:1). The latter phrase recalls Ignatius's description of Polycarp's flock as established "in an unshakable faith" (ἐν ἀκινήτῳ πίστει) and "founded in love" (ἡδρασμένους ἐν ἀγάπῃ; Smyr. 1:1). As we learned in chapter 5, the term γνώμη refers to a firm resolve based on one's knowledge of revealed truth and is closely connected to Ignatius's teaching about faith and love. Presumably, then, the "immovable rock" of Ignatius's metaphor refers to the "unshakable faith" of a man who is "fully convinced" of the truth of the church's creedal affirmations about Jesus Christ (1:1–2). If that is the case, Ignatius's metaphor should probably also remind us of two passages from his favorite gospel. In one, the person who hears and lives by Jesus' words is likened to a prudent man who built his house "upon the rock" (ἐπὶ τὴν πέτραν), so that it would not be shaken by wind and rain (Mt 7:24–25). In the other, Jesus gives Simon the name Πέτρος and promises to build his church upon the "rock" (πέτρα) of Peter's faith (16:18). Polycarp's "mind-set" and therefore his episcopal ministry are built upon the unshakable rock of Petrine and apostolic faith (cf. Smyr. 3:2).

For Ignatius, the truth of the Christian faith could never be reduced to mere ideas. Real faith makes a divine "imprint" (χαρακτήρ) on the believer, and that is why faith can only be lived out "with love." Moreover, because faith confesses the one who suffered for us, love must be a voluntary participation in his passion (Magn. 5:2). Spoken or written words from someone who has an experiential knowledge of these realities will have the "stamp" of apostolic authenticity—not only conformity to apostolic doctrine, though that is essential, but also the mark of apostolic love. Christians do not merely receive doctrine but are "handed over" to a "pattern of teaching" (τύπος διδαχῆς) in order to obey it "from the heart" and to be transformed by it (Paul, Rom 6:17). When this happens, they themselves become a "pattern and teaching [τύπος καὶ διδαχή] of imperishability" (Magn. 6:2). They become, as it were, an epistle "written not with ink but with the Spirit of the living God ... known and read by all men" (2 Cor 3:2–3). Near the end of the *Demonstration of the Apostolic Preaching*, wishing to assure his addressee Marcianus that he has composed for him an authentic summary of the *regula fidei*, Irenaeus of Lyons writes,

This, beloved, is the preaching of the truth, and this is the *character* of our salvation, and this is the way of life, which the prophets announced, Christ confirmed, the *apostles* handed over, and the church in the whole world hands down to her children. (*Dem.* 98)

The foregoing interpretation of the phrase ἐν ἀποστολικῷ χαρακτῆρι is not contradicted by the two passages in which Ignatius says that he does not "issue commands like an apostle."[88] Ignatius evinces no doubt whatsoever that what he is proclaiming is the true apostolic faith, and he constantly protests that his motive for writing letters to the churches is authentic Christian charity.[89] He distinguishes himself from the apostles in only one respect and cites this as his only reason for not using full apostolic authority: He has not yet reached the goal of martyrdom. "They are apostles, I am condemned. They are free, but I am up till now a slave" (*Rom.* 4:3). It is not a question of rank or office, but of teleology and personal eschatology. The salient difference between the apostles and Ignatius is a temporary one. He does not say, "They rank far above me, and so my words could never bear the stamp of their teaching. The best I can do is to imitate their epistolary style." He simply recognizes that he is "still in danger" of losing his salvation and thus thinks it would be presumptuous to assume the tone of authority of those who have already "attained God."[90] Still, he sincerely hopes and anticipates that this situation will not last for long. "But if I suffer, I [too] will be a freedman of Jesus Christ, and I will rise free in him" (*Rom.* 4:3). Naturally, this way of reducing the difference between the apostles and himself to a single factor has a certain rhetorical quality. I am certainly not suggesting that Ignatius expected to be enrolled in the college of the apostles after his death! At the same time, it is perfectly reasonable to suppose that he intended his letters to be read and reread after his martyrdom, when they would instruct and exhort the churches with even greater efficacy, having been fully validated by the shedding of his blood.

Within Ignatian ecclesiology the apostles provide a key element of continuity between past and present, between heaven and earth, and between universal and local. It is far too simplistic to make Ignatius the early church's "spokesman" for a "vertical" and "charismatic" understanding of apostolic authority over against the "horizontal" model of apostolic succession advocated by Clement of Rome and Cyprian, leaving it to Hippolytus and Irenaeus to achieve the desired Hegelian synthe-

---

88. *Tral.* 3:3; *Rom.* 4:3.
89. *Eph.* 3:2, 21:1; *Magn.* 6:1, 11:1; *Tral.* 3:3, 6:1, 8:1; *Phld.* 5:1; *Smyr.* 4:2.
90. *Tral.* 13:3; *Eph.* 3:1.

sis of the two.[91] The apostles are real historical figures, who continue to instruct the church through their writings and the example of their lives. Because they received the gift of imperishability in the cenacle and have attained glory through martyrdom, they are also heavenly members of the church who continue to intercede for their brothers and sisters who are still *in via*. There is no contradiction, or even tension, between the horizontal-temporal and vertical-transcendent dimensions, since the whole effect of the economy of redemption is to bring into the earthly realm a gift of divine life that leads human beings to heaven. Though Ignatius does not teach a doctrine of apostolic succession, this does not mean that his ecclesiology reduces the apostles to Platonic archetypes of charismatic authority. He draws on sober historical traditions when he affirms that the church at Ephesus has "always lived in accord with the apostles" (Eph. 11:2) and when he expresses his own aspiration to walk "in the footsteps" of Paul (12:2). As a bishop who appreciates the full compatibility of office and charism, and the interpenetration of doctrine and life, he is confident that his own faith and love bear the "stamp" of apostolic authenticity.

Catholic Church and Local Churches

This may be the opportune place to consider what Ignatius intends by referring to "the catholic church," and more generally, how he conceives of the relationship between the church and the churches. The adjective καθολικός ("pertaining to the whole, general, generic, universal") is used frequently in ancient Greek, but Ignatius is the first on record to apply it to the church.

> Wherever the bishop appears, there let the multitude be;
> just as, wherever Christ Jesus is, there is the catholic church. (Smyr. 8:2)

It is certainly no coincidence that, after this occurrence, the phrase ἡ καθολικὴ ἐκκλησία shows up next in the *Martyrdom of Polycarp*, a document produced by the church of Smyrna some forty years after Ignatius's death.[92] In that context it is already used as a technical term designating the universal and orthodox church over against more or less well defined heretical groups. The meaning Ignatius intended for ἡ καθολικὴ

---

91. Pace Niels Christian Hvidt, *Christian Prophecy: The Post-Biblical Tradition* (Oxford: Oxford University Press, 2007), 231.
92. Mart. sal., 8:1, 16:2, 19:2.

ἐκκλησία earlier in the second century has been the subject of debate, however.

Lightfoot understands καθολικός to mean "universal" in *Smyrnaeans* 8:2 and restricts its referent to the church's geographical extension. This, he claims, is the term's primary meaning, to which the ideas of right doctrine and unity were only later added.[93] The first part of this interpretation is plausible, since Ignatius does sometimes speak of the church as having something like universal geographical extension, as for example when he refers to "the bishops who have been appointed throughout the world [κατὰ τὰ πέρατα]."[94] But perhaps we should not be too hasty to exclude the idea of unity from an ecclesiological statement made by the Doctor Unitatis himself! Corwin maintains that Ignatius does not think of the universal church as having "a particular institutional structure,"[95] and that does seem to be true with regard to the universal church *on earth*. Ignatius never speaks of the world's bishops as forming a college, and considerable exegetical imagination is required to make his letter to the *Romans* support the idea of the primacy of the Roman church.[96] But if one thing should be clear from Ignatius's letters, it is that he would never dream of limiting the scope of the church or its leadership to its visible earthly members. The universal church, as he conceives of it, most certainly does have an authority structure, but the members of its hierarchy—God the Father, Jesus Christ, and the apostles—are all enthroned in heaven. In any case, it has been pointed out that the idea of "wholeness" or organic unity is a more natural and better attested sense for καθολικός than is the idea of geographical extension,[97] and it would be more in accord with Ignatius's usual priorities and preoccupations, and more germane to the context of *Smyrnaeans* 8, for him to refer to the church's wholeness and unity than to its geographical extension as such.

If Ignatius uses the phrase ἡ καθολικὴ ἐκκλησία to refer to the church's wholeness and unity, we should also be cautious about excluding the idea of orthodox doctrine too quickly, for these notions are hard-

---

93. Ignatius, *Polycarp*, 2.310–12.
94. *Eph.* 3:2; cf. *Magn.* 10:3.
95. *St. Ignatius and Christianity*, 190.
96. E.g., Ray, *Upon This Rock*, 135–44. More cautious and nuanced is the discussion of this point by Howell (*Ignatius of Antioch*, 41–43), though he goes too far in saying, "There can be no doubt that the claim to the primacy of the Roman church is consistent with the evidence in Ignatius' *Letter to the Romans*" (43; emphasis added).
97. Schoedel, *Ignatius of Antioch*, 243.

ly separable in his ecclesiology. True, it would be anachronistic to suppose that he is using the phrase in its later technical sense, as specifically referring to the orthodox church over against identifiable "churches" of heretics. At the same time, this use of the term, which is attested already in the Martyrdom of Polycarp (16:2), may well have grown organically out of the Smyrnaean church's reading of the letter that Ignatius had addressed to them.[98] In the immediate context of his statement about "the catholic church," Ignatius warns against individuals or groups who teach false doctrines, withdraw from the eucharistic assembly, and perform baptisms and love-feasts that have not received episcopal sanction (Smyr. 6:2–8:2). These people have forfeited their place in the local church, since they are in effect serving the devil (7:2, 9:1), and so neither do they belong to the "catholic church."

Running directly counter to Lightfoot's interpretation of Smyrnaeans 8:2 is that of the Orthodox theologian John Zizioulas, who absolutely excludes the idea of geographical extension from Ignatius's use of the phrase ἡ καθολικὴ ἐκκλησία.[99] According to Zizioulas, καθολικός means "whole" but only in the sense of "generic," not in the sense of universal. Smyrnaeans 8:2 does not involve a comparison between local church and universal church. Both parts of Ignatius's statement refer to the local church, which is distinguishable from the "whole" church only as the concrete particular is distinguishable from the generic. The particular "is in no way a segment of" the whole, "but constitutes its actual concrete form."[100] The point of the passage, according to Zizioulas, is that "the local Church constitutes a reality exactly the same as that of the catholic Church," for the former is "the concrete form in space and time of the whole body of Christ ... each local Church forms the incarnation of the whole Christ and the Church as a whole."[101] The local church is the whole church by virtue of the eucharist, which "incarnates" the "whole historical Christ" within her, and therefore also by virtue of her bishop, under whose presidency "the eucharistic synaxis and communion of all

---

98. According to André de Halleux, the phrase ἡ καθολικὴ ἐκκλησία in Smyr. 8:2 means nothing more than "l'Église dans sa totalité," without any special ecclesiological significance, and only "une coïncidence purement verbale" connects Ignatius's use of this phrase to its later history ("'L'Église catholique' dan la lettre ignacienne aux Smyrniotes," Ephemerides Theologicae Lovanienses 58 [1982]: 23–24). To some extent this is a foregone conclusion, given Halleux's methodological decision to abstract Ignatius's statement from its context in the ecclesiological tradition and to adopt "une approche plus strictement philologique" that deals with it "dans sa singularité," as befits a historical rather than a theological hermeneutic (5–6).

99. Eucharist, Bishop, Church, 107–20.   100. Ibid., 109–10.
101. Ibid., 112, 117–18.

the members" takes place.[102] Finally, since "each local Church having its own bishop is catholic *per se*," it does not need to be complemented by the other local churches.[103] The local churches do not together form a whole that is greater than any one of its parts.[104]

I confess that I find Zizioulas's interpretation of *Smyrnaeans* 8:2 scarcely intelligible. He seems to be saying that the "whole" church has no concrete existence except as it is incarnated in each local church. But if there is no other "whole" church than that which each local church incarnates, what sense does it make to predicate of the local church that it *is* the whole church? How is this not a pure tautology? Moreover, even so far as Zizioulas's view is intelligible, it seems to fly in the face of much of what Ignatius says in his letters. Granted that Ignatius views each local church as possessing a certain "fullness" of ecclesial grace and a unity of its own—granted, in other words, that he does not view the local churches as *mere* parts of a larger whole—does this mean that he considers them *in no sense* parts of a larger whole? When Ignatius says, earlier in *Smyrnaeans*, that the cross has been raised as a standard "to the aeons" in order to summon all of Christ's "holy and faithful ones, whether among the Jews or among the gentiles," into "the one body of his church" (1:2), is he not affirming precisely that all believers in all places and times together form a single body of Christ? Is not the same truth implied when Ignatius speaks of Christians as "temple stones" that are being hoisted up to take their place in "the edifice of God the Father" (*Eph.* 9:1), or again, in the passage about believers of every age entering the "unity of God" through the one "door of the Father" (*Phld.* 9:1), or yet again, when Ignatius says that in Christianity "people of every language have come to believe and have been gathered to God" (*Magn.* 10:3)?

Does Ignatius encourage each local church to think of itself as the whole church, such that it does not in any way need the other churches? Does he not rather ask each church to "bedew" the others with their prayers and love (14:1)? When an ambassador from the church at Philadelphia travels to the church at Antioch "in order to congratulate [συγχαρῆναι] them in their assembly and to glorify the name" with them (*Phld.* 10:1), is not the church of Antioch in some sense augmented by his presence? Certainly the individual from Philadelphia does not for

---

102. Ibid., 115, 117.
103. Ibid., 117, 120.
104. Essentially the same interpretation of Ignatian ecclesiology is found, perhaps not coincidentally, in John S. Romanides, "The Ecclesiology of St. Ignatius of Antioch," *Greek Orthodox Theological Review* 7 (1961–1962): 53–77 (see esp. 65–66).

that period of time cease to be a member of the church at Philadelphia and become instead a member of the church at Antioch, for he comes as a representative of the church at Philadelphia. Is not the point of the gesture precisely to strengthen bonds of Christian fellowship among the churches? The Ignatian corpus, especially when read together with Polycarp's *Philippians*, witnesses to a remarkable coordination of efforts and pooling of spiritual resources by at least ten churches stretching from Syria to Italy: Antioch, Tarsus, Philadelphia, Smyrna, Ephesus, Magnesia, Tralles, Troas, Philippi-Neapolis, and Rome.[105] Ignatius's interaction with the churches along his route—receiving their representatives, speaking in their assemblies in the Holy Spirit, writing them pastoral letters, coordinating their embassies to the church at Antioch—is utterly unintelligible apart from some sense that the local churches *together* form the "whole" church. He is in chains "for the *common* name and hope," and that is why the churches are eager to see him (*Eph.* 1:2). They welcome him "for the name of Jesus Christ" and do not regard him as a mere "passerby" (*Rom.* 9:3).[106]

What, then, is the relationship between the whole and the parts, between the church and the churches? Zizioulas's interpretation of *Smyrnaeans* 8:2 represents a sincere attempt to secure a very important truth, namely, that the local community of Christians in union with the bishop does in fact constitute a "church." The flesh and blood of Jesus are fully present in their eucharist, and they enjoy the full benefit of the gift of imperishable life in the Holy Spirit. They possess in its fullness that which makes the church "church." Ignatius can refer to the Christians in a given locality as "the faithful there" (*Eph.* 21:2), or "the brethren who are in Troas" (*Phld.* 11:2), and so he might have addressed his letters to "the faithful" or to "the brethren" in such and such a city. The fact that, instead, he identifies his addressees by reference to the local ἐκκλησία in the salutations of all seven letters (including *Polycarp*), and goes on to use this word several more times in each letter, suggests that he wants his addressees to think of themselves as "church"—a church among the churches and within the universal church—and to reflect on what this

---

105. I include Tarsus since "Philo the deacon from Cilicia" (*Phld.* 11:1) was presumably from that church. In any case, more than ten churches must have been involved (cf. 10:2; *Poly.* 8:1).

106. "Ein immanent universaler, geographischer Aspekt im Begriff καθολικός legt sich auch nahe, wenn die sich in den Ignatianen überall zeigende intensive Kommunikation zwischen den einzelnen Kirchen berücksichtig wird, mit denen immer auch ganz reale, diakonisch-soziale Aktivitäten gemeint sein können" (Reinhart Staats, "Die katholische Kirche des Ignatius von Antiochien und das Problem ihrer Normativität im zweiten Jahrhundert," *Zeitschrift für die neutestamentliche Wissenschaft und die Kunde der älteren Kirche* 77 [1986]: 252).

means. Ignatius uses the word ἐκκλησία analogically, that is, to refer to entities that are not merely similar but that participate in the same reality according to a certain proportion.

The precise relationship between catholic church and local churches is admittedly complex and difficult to specify. While Ignatius sometimes uses the word ἐκκλησία to refer to one or more local churches and sometimes uses the same word to refer to the universal church, there are still other passages where one would be hard-pressed to exclude either sense of ἐκκλησία. For example, Ignatius writes that deacons are "servants of the ἐκκλησία of God" (Tral. 2:3). Does ἐκκλησία here refer to the local church, or to the universal church? Obviously deacons are, in a special way, servants of their local church, since the diaconate by its very nature places them under the authority of a particular bishop, but they do not cease to be deacons or to serve the ἐκκλησία of God when they interact with members of the body of Christ who belong to other churches.[107] They are simultaneously servants of the catholic "church of God" and of the local "church of God." This fluid, analogical use of ἐκκλησία is Ignatius's way of indicating that the local ἐκκλησία is not merely *a* church but is, in a very real sense, *the* church. On a certain level, then, I agree with Zizioulas that the whole church is present in the local church, especially when it gathers with its bishop for the eucharist. But, whereas for Zizioulas this means that the local church is in no way a "segment" of the whole church, I would say just the opposite: The whole church is present in the local church precisely because the latter is part of the former. This is true at all times, of course, not only during the eucharistic assembly, but it is the eucharist that most intimately unites the local church to all the members of Christ in heaven and throughout the world.

During Ignatius's stopover at Smyrna at least five bishops were present—Onesimus of Ephesus, Damas of Magnesia, Polybius of Tralles, Polycarp of Smyrna, and Ignatius of Antioch—along with presbyters and deacons from various churches. To meet with these bishops is to have "the churches of God present with me," Ignatius claims.[108] He comments on the bond of spiritual "fellowship" (συνήθεια) that quickly developed between himself and Onesimus (Eph. 5:1), and several passages attest to his special love for Polycarp.[109] He writes a letter "on behalf of" Polybius (Tral. 3:3), and Polycarp is entrusted with writing several letters in Ignatius's stead (Poly. 8:1). Is there no hint of episcopal collegiality

---

107. See Eph. 2:1; Phld. 11:1–2; Smyr. 12:1.   108. Tral. 12:1, cf. 1:1–2; Eph. 1:3; Magn. 2:1.
109. Eph. 21:1; Magn. 15:1; Poly. 2:3.

in all of this? In all likelihood the five bishops offered the eucharist together at least once at Smyrna, and it is almost impossible to imagine that they did not on that occasion have a sense of the unity and complementarity of the churches, and therefore of "the church as a whole" (ἡ καθολικὴ ἐκκλησία). Might it not even be that reflection on this experience of catholicity at Smyrna led Ignatius, when composing his letter to the Smyrnaean church, to coin the phrase "catholic church"?

By addressing each local church as ἐκκλησία, Ignatius is able to accent both that congregation's full participation in the church and its unique geographical and spiritual identity, as for example when he greets "the holy church that is in Tralles of Asia, chosen and worthy of God" (Tral. sal.). In writing to the churches in Ephesus and Rome, Ignatius is especially effusive in praise of them, and at several points he alludes to their respective ecclesiastical histories.[110] According to Zizioulas, the epithets that Ignatius applies to each church simply express what is true of the "whole" church, that is, of the church generically.[111] This is manifestly untrue of certain expressions—for example, "you Ephesians, a church that is famous to the aeons" (Eph. 8:1), "the thoroughfare of those who are being put to death for God, fellow initiates of Paul" (12:2), and "presiding in the place of the region of the Romans" (Rom. sal.)—and in any case misses the point. Ignatius understood himself to have a divine mandate to write to as many churches as possible.[112] That he chose to write an individual letter to each church, when it would have been far easier, especially under the circumstances, to compose a single encyclical letter and have copies distributed to the various churches (in the manner of 1 Peter), is significant. Not only did this enable him to address specific issues of concern to each church, but it gave him the chance to "sing the praises of the churches" (Magn. 1:2). The salutations and closing instructions of the letters indicate that Ignatius wanted each church to recognize its full membership in the church, its unique endowments and identity as a local church, and its responsibilities toward the other churches. In every letter he attempts to foster bonds of love and a sense of unity among the churches.[113]

Along with 1 Clement and Polycarp's Philippians, Ignatius's letters to the Ephesians and to the Romans witness to a growing sense that certain

---

110. Eph. sal., 8:1, 11:2–12:2; Rom. sal., 3:1, 4:3.
111. Eucharist, Bishop, Church, 113.
112. Rom. 4:1; Poly. 8:1.
113. Eph. 21:1; Magn. 14:1, 15:1; Tral. 12:1, 13:1; Rom. 9:1–10.1; Phld. 10:1–11:2; Smyr. 11:1–12:1; Poly. 7:1–8:1.

churches possess a privileged spiritual patrimony, if not yet an official status, by virtue of their direct historical contact with one or more apostles. We should not be surprised if Irenaeus, growing up in Smyrna during the final years of Polycarp's long tenure as that city's bishop, acquired a strong appreciation for this. In any case, Ignatius's letters generally convey the sense that the various churches, individually and in their interrelations, constitute a rich treasure belonging to the whole church. His recognition of the individual character of each church actually contributes to a sense of solidarity among the churches.

Let us now return to Ignatius's statement about "the catholic church" in *Smyrnaeans* 8, this time taking into account a bit more of the context, to see if we can get the proper sense of it. Ignatius is concerned that "no one perform, without the bishop, any of those actions that pertain to the ἐκκλησία" (8:1). In this statement, he does not clearly distinguish between local church and universal church. Baptism, love-feast, and eucharist are actions that pertain to the whole church, inasmuch as they are performed by all churches throughout the world, but they are usually performed at the level of the local church. In the next statement, however, wishing to make a sharp distinction between local church and universal church, Ignatius puts aside his analogical language for the moment. He uses τὸ πλῆθος ("the multitude") to refer to the local church and ἡ καθολικὴ ἐκκλησία to refer to the church as a whole.

> Wherever the bishop appears, there let the multitude be;
> just as, wherever Christ Jesus is, there is the catholic church. (8:2)

The first part of this sentence employs the Greek third-person imperative (ἔστω) to express a command, while the second part grounds that command in what is taken to be an established fact (albeit expressed in a new way), namely, that the church exists qua church by virtue of the person and event of Jesus Christ. In this context the comparative conjunction ὥσπερ ("just as") serves not merely to indicate a comparison but to suggest that the local community's act of congregating for worship ought to imitate the broader and certainly more basic reality of the catholic church's union with Jesus Christ its head. In other words, the "multitude" ought to act, not simply as a multitude, but as ἐκκλησία. They are to gather around their "one bishop" (*Phld.* 4:1), just as the catholic church, in heaven and on earth, is united to the "one Jesus Christ" (*Magn.* 7:2).

The truth spoken of in *Smyrnaeans* 8:2 is also expressed when Ignatius blesses those Ephesians who have been "mingled" with Onesimus their bishop "as the church is with Jesus Christ and as Jesus Christ is with the Father" (*Eph.* 5:1). The correlation between Jesus Christ and the bishop is important for Ignatius, but we can only understand it if we first grasp the relationship of Jesus Christ to the church. And we can only understand this latter relationship if we keep in mind that it enables the church to have an economic participation in the preeconomic union between the Father and the Son. And none of this will make any sense unless we constantly remind ourselves of the fundamental place that the Christ event occupies in Ignatius's ecclesiology. The union between "Jesus and the Father" in the Holy Spirit is the "most essential" union (*Magn.* 1:2), and through his incarnation and paschal mystery Jesus Christ has conferred upon the church a graced participation in this union by establishing a union between the church and himself. He established this union by breathing the gift of imperishability into the church, such that head and members now form "one new man" (*Eph.* 17:1, 20:1). He established it by taking flesh, dying in the flesh, rising in the flesh, and feeding the church with his flesh in the eucharist (*Smyr.* 1:1–3:2). In the eucharist the church eats and drinks, as it were, with her risen Lord "as in a fleshly manner, even though he remains spiritually united to the Father" (3:3).

I have frequently called attention to the great significance of the description of Jesus Christ as the one "who before the ages was with the Father and appeared [ἐφάνη] at the end" (*Magn.* 6:1). In the present context we should note that this brief summary of the Christ event is embedded within an ecclesiological parenesis that shares the same basic concern as *Smyrnaeans* 8, namely, that the local church (πλῆθος in both texts) "do everything" in union with its bishop, so that it might become "a type and teaching of imperishability" (*Magn.* 6:1–2). Now, if we bear in mind that gathering for eucharist on "the Lord's day" is the summative act by which the local church puts itself in touch with the "mystery" of Jesus' death, the death through which "our life" has come into the world (9:1), we can begin to appreciate why Ignatius ascribes such great importance to the bishop. The "one bishop" presides over the "one eucharist" precisely as the earthly and local representative of Jesus Christ, whose "one flesh" the eucharist is (*Phld.* 4:1). Because the bishop has been sent by the Lord Jesus, "it is necessary for us to receive him as we would receive the sender himself" and "to look upon the bishop as one looks upon the Lord himself" (*Eph.* 6:1). Thus, the *missio episcopi* not only runs parallel to the *missio Filii* but, in a sense, extends the latter into the life of the local church. Under a figure, Ignatius even describes the sending of the bishop in "economic" terms. The divine "householder" (οἰκοδεσπότης) sends the bishop "to dispense the goods of the house on his behalf" (εἰς ἰδίαν οἰκονομίαν; 6:1). And it is especially in the eucharist that the bishop does this. In light of these observations, it is striking to note that *Smyrnaeans* 8 first explicitly teaches that a eucharist is valid only if the bishop, or someone designated by the bishop, presides over it, and then refers to the bishop's presence in the eucharistic assembly as an *appearing*: "Wherever the bishop appears [φανῇ], there let the multitude be" (8:1–2). Reading this ecclesiological formulation in light of the Christological ἐφάνη of *Magnesians* 6:1, might we not think of the eucharist as a sacramental reenactment of the Christ event, at which the bishop "appears" as the representative of Jesus Christ?

We shall revisit the question of the bishop's relationship to Jesus Christ below, when we consider Ignatius's ecclesiological typology. But before turning to that topic, I wish to expound one further aspect of the "catholic church," an aspect to which I have alluded more than once in this chapter, namely, its orientation to heaven. Here, once again, we must attend carefully to the relationship between the horizontal-temporal and vertical-transcendent dimensions of the divine economy, lest we erroneously conclude that Ignatius is dabbling in gnostic myths or Platonic speculations. When Ignatius speaks of the "catholic church," he refers to a reality that comprises, not only all the local churches "throughout the world" (*Eph*. 3:2), but also, and even primarily, the heavenly members of the church, beginning with Jesus Christ, the prophets whom he has raised from the dead (*Magn*. 9:2), and the apostles who have been "found to be beyond death" (*Smyr*. 3:2). This primacy of the heavenly church, far from being the result of any loss of the biblical sense of salvation history or eschatology, is rooted in a correct appreciation of precisely these dimensions of the divine economy.

Jesus Christ is the heavenly head of the church, not as a gnostic redeemer, but as the incarnate, crucified, and risen Lord whose return in glory the church awaits. Let us consider once again the magnificent creedal affirmation from the *Letter to Polycarp* (3:2).

Take note of the times. Await the one who is beyond time, the timeless one, the invisible one, who for us became visible; the intangible one, the impassible one, who for us became subject to passion, who in every manner endured for us.

As the eternal Son of God, Jesus Christ is "timeless" (ἄχρονος), and by entering our temporality, he transformed it. By rising from the dead in the flesh that he had assumed and in which he had suffered, he created a new bond between the eternal and temporal realms. As the exalted Son of Man he is "beyond time" (ὑπὲρ καιρόν), but he will come again in glory at the end of time. By enduring suffering for us he perfected his own humanity, and when we "endure all things" in order to "suffer with him," he who is "the perfect man" fills us with his power and transforms our humanity (Smyr. 4:2). Through him it is possible now for us to "attain God." The prophets and apostles have already achieved this goal and now form the "council of God" and the "college of apostles," seated around the throne of Jesus Christ in heaven.[114]

Ignatius sees the church as a dynamic and teleological reality. The church moves through history and is headed toward a goal. The gift of imperishability, which makes her what she is, descends to her from her heavenly head (by way of the Christ event) and leads her up to him in heavenly glory. Jesus Christ is her ἀρχή and her τέλος. The church's dynamic character and orientation to heaven is nicely caught in Ignatius's version of the biblical church-as-temple image. Christians are "temple stones prepared for the edifice of God the Father, borne up to the heights by the crane of Jesus Christ, which is the cross, making use of the Holy Spirit as a cable" (Eph. 9:1). The church is fundamentally a heavenly "edifice" (οἰκοδομή; cf. 2 Cor 5:1), and the overriding concern of Christians should be to take their proper place in that structure by "attaining God." The church's ascent is not a purely vertical or gnostic one, since she moves through time toward the eschaton (and each of her members must live out his or her *vita usque ad mortem*), but it is a true ascent, not merely the hope for "a better world." In any case, Ignatius often thinks of the church's members as moving together toward a goal. The Christian life is a "racecourse" (δρόμος), and Christians are "those who run to God" (θεοδρόμοι) upon it.[115] They are "fellow pilgrims" (σύνοδοι) in a religious procession (Eph. 9:2), and they "run together [συντρέχω] as to one temple of God, as to one altar, to one Jesus Christ" (Magn. 7:2).

The Ecclesiological Typology

In union with the Lord Jesus, the Christian faithful, both in heaven and on earth, constitute the "one body of his church" (Smyr. 1:2). The supreme authority for the church is first of all God the Father, then Je-

---

114. Tral. 3:1; cf. Rv 4:4.
115. Poly. 1:2; Phld. 2:2.

sus Christ, who submitted to the Father in his earthly life, and finally the apostles, who submitted "to Christ and to the Father" (*Magn.* 13:2). Correspondingly, the local church possesses its own "bodily integrity" (σωματεῖον) and its own threefold hierarchy of bishop, presbytery, and deacons (*Smyr.* 11:2, 8:1). Presbyters are to "yield" to their bishop, and deacons are to "submit" both to the bishop and to the presbyters (*Magn.* 2:1–3:1). A community of Christians that does not have this structure "is not called a church" (*Tral.* 3:1), whereas a community that acts in unity with its bishop forms "the whole church" (πᾶσα ἡ ἐκκλησία), which is to say, the *local* church in its proper wholeness (*Eph.* 5:2). When Christians show reverence and love for one another and "are united with the bishop and with those who preside," they evidence a wholeness and unity that is a "type and teaching" of the imperishable life that makes the catholic church what it is (*Magn.* 6:2). The gift of imperishability, which flows from God and leads back to God, gives the church a heavenly center of gravity, as it were. The church consists of members of Christ who are either already in heaven or attempting to get to heaven. The local church, which is on earth, is a "type" of this heaven-oriented catholic church insofar as the united faith, mutual love, and proper order of its members offer evidence that they already possess the gift of imperishability. The life they live is a foretaste of the life of heaven.

Ignatius attempts to explain, and to some extent perhaps to justify, the threefold hierarchy of the local church by way of an elaborately conceived series of analogies, which I have been referring to collectively as his ecclesiological typology. Since the heavenly-universal hierarchy consists of three levels—God the Father, Jesus Christ, and the apostles—and the earthly-local hierarchy likewise consists of three levels—bishop, presbyters, and deacons—Ignatius might have constructed his typology by way of a simple one-to-one correspondence. Thus the bishop would be associated with God the Father, the presbyters with Jesus Christ, and the deacons with the apostles. But instead, Ignatius associates the bishop sometimes with God the Father but at other times with Jesus Christ, associates the presbyters with the apostles, and usually (but not always) associates the deacons with Jesus Christ. Allowing for further variations and complicating factors, we can summarize Ignatius's typology as follows.

bishop	→	God the Father, or Jesus Christ
presbyters	→	apostles
deacons	→	Jesus Christ

The difficulties that this scheme presents will be obvious from a cursory examination of one of the key passages in which it is found, *Trallians* 2–3. First Ignatius counsels submission to the bishop "as to Jesus Christ" and submission to the presbytery "as to the apostles of Jesus Christ," and he identifies the deacons as ministers "of the mysteries of Jesus Christ" (2:1–3). Thus far, the typology presents no special difficulty. Jesus is mentioned at all three levels of the typology, but only the bishop is directly compared to him. Moreover, the deacons are not explicitly compared to anyone but are simply said to be "ministers" (διάκονοι) of the mysteries of Christ rather than of mere food and drink.[116] But in the very next verse Ignatius gives a second version of the typology. All should show reverence for the deacons "as for Jesus Christ," for the bishop because he is "a type of the Father," and for the presbyters "as for the college of the apostles" (3:1). If we place the two versions side by side, the difficulties become apparent.

		Trallians 2	Trallians 3
bishop	→	as Jesus Christ	type of Father
presbyters	→	as apostles of Jesus Christ	as college of apostles
deacons	→	of mysteries of Jesus Christ	as Jesus Christ

The second version presents a difficulty even on its own terms, since it seems to rank Jesus below the apostles, and it is further problematic insofar as it seems to contradict the first version. There is also the more basic interpretive question of what force we should give to words such as ὡς ("as") and τύπος ("type"). Are we dealing here with rhetorical comparisons, poetic metaphors, or analogies that indicate some sort of metaphysical relationship?

It is probably safe to say that most scholars have found Ignatius's ecclesiological typology to fall somewhat short of pellucidity. According to Corwin, the "fluid and changing" character of Ignatius's analogies indicate that he was struggling to clarify his own speculations.[117] Lightfoot suggests that Ignatius combined more than one analogical scheme but, because he composed his letters in "extreme haste," did not even notice the incongruities that resulted from this redactional procedure.[118] Other scholars have developed this suggestion into a historical hypothesis, ac-

---

116. The reference is probably to the eucharistic elements, which the deacons may have distributed to the laity in the liturgical assembly (Grant, *Ignatius of Antioch*, 73; Schoedel, *Ignatius of Antioch*, 141).
117. *St. Ignatius and Christianity*, 194.
118. *Ignatius, Polycarp*, 2.159.

cording to which the threefold hierarchy emerged in the early church when two systems of ecclesiastical authority, each with its own origins, were combined. Originally, the Pauline churches had "bishops and deacons" (Phil 1:1), while the Jewish-Christian congregations were led by a "council" (συνέδριον) of "elders" (πρεσβύτεροι).[119] Presumably these two systems were merged first in the mixed Jewish-gentile community of Antioch, and the resulting hybrid system was then introduced into Asia Minor. The "apparent illogicality" of Ignatius's typology, then, is the result of his having combined traditional speculations that were rooted in two originally distinct systems of authority.[120]

Whatever the merits of this hypothesis as a historical explanation of the origin of the threefold hierarchy, it hardly suffices as an exegesis of the passages in question. Do we not have here the old fallacy of historicism, according to which an ancient text is not intelligible in its own right but only once its hypothetical sources have been separated out? It is scarcely plausible, in any case, to explain the suppleness and complexity of Ignatius's train of thought in these passages by claiming that he has borrowed and woodenly combined two separate speculative schemes without recognizing their incompatibility. In presenting his ecclesiological typology, Ignatius interweaves various sorts of comparison, approaches the object of his meditation from multiple angles, and argues on more than one level.[121] This is not the sort of discourse that one elucidates by demonstrating that it is not reducible to a tidy system, nor does such a demonstration warrant the conclusion that the author did not quite know what he was saying. The rich complexity of Ignatius's thought, here as elsewhere, is due to the fact that he is gazing upon a mystery of inexhaustible abundance and writing about it with insight and creativity. As I suggested in chapter 2, our best chance to discern the intelligibility of his theology is to sit alongside him, respectfully considering the same reality, and to operate on the assumption that he might just be able to teach us something. Ignatius's ecclesiological typology is not an ad hoc rhetorical scheme, or clumsy combination of schemes, that, while easily recognized by modern readers to be incoherent, probably sufficed to persuade credulous second-century Christians to toe the line. The typology flows, rather, from the same comprehensive vision of

---

119. Grant, *Ignatius of Antioch*, 21.
120. Hammond Bammel, "Ignatian Problems," 75.
121. Schoedel's careful analysis demonstrates some appreciation for this complexity (*Ignatius of Antioch*, 113–14), but he also stresses "the tentative character of all such comparisons" in Ignatius's letters (141).

the divine economy that has engendered all other aspects of his theology. We must, therefore, attempt to interpret it as an integral part of that whole.

Let us begin with the correlation between the bishop and God the Father. The word ἐπίσκοπος literally means "overseer," and—along with its cognates ἐπισκέπτομαι ("to look after, visit, care for"), ἐπισκοπέω ("to exercise oversight"), and ἐπισκοπή ("oversight, care")—its ecclesiological use has deep roots in the Septuagint. Of special note are those prophetic oracles that link the verb ἐπισκέπτομαι with the imagery of shepherding. The Lord sets "shepherds," that is, leaders, over his people to "look after" them on his behalf, but when he grows dissatisfied with their job performance he promises to "look after" his own flock.[122] Ignatius likewise thinks of the bishop as a "shepherd" whom the "sheep" should "follow."[123] Referring to the flock that he has left behind in Antioch, he writes, "In my stead, it has God as its shepherd, and Jesus Christ alone will look after [ἐπισκοπήσει] it" (Rom. 9:1). There are passages in the Septuagint in which ἐπισκοπή (translating Hebrew pĕqûdâ) approaches the idea of divine providence (e.g., Jb 10:12), to which we may compare Ignatius's exhortation to the Smyrnaean church to "remain in the unity and care [ἐπισκοπή] of God" (Poly. 8:3). In yielding to the bishop, one in fact yields to God the Father, who is "the bishop [ἐπίσκοπος] of all" and "the one who willed us" (Magn. 3:1–2). The latter phrase recalls Ignatius's description of divine providence as "the will of the one who wills all things that are" (Rom. sal.). As God is provident over the whole universe and over the universal church, so the bishop exercises a kind of providence over the local church (Eph. 6:1). Polycarp 1:2–5:2 makes it especially clear that Ignatius expects the bishop's oversight to extend far beyond liturgical matters.

God is the "invisible" bishop, and the ἐπίσκοπος is his visible representative, the local church's "bishop in the flesh."[124] The bishop "presides in the place [τόπος] of God" (Magn. 6:1) and is even "a type [τύπος] of the Father" (Tral. 3:1). These statements require careful interpretation. The bishop is God's representative but does not *replace* God or Jesus in the lives of the laity, as if the latter had no intimacy with God of their own. Thus Ignatius exhorts a fellow bishop, "Let widows not be neglected. *After the Lord*, you are to be their caretaker [φροντιστής]" (Poly. 4:1). The bish-

---

122. Zec 10:3; Ezek 34:11–12; Jer 23:1–4; cf. Nm 27:16–17.
123. Phld. 2:1; Smyr. 8:1.
124. Magn. 3:2; Eph. 1:3.

op's ministry is *one* of the ways in which the Lord's love and providence becomes tangibly present in the lives of Christians. Moreover, Ignatius's distinction between the invisible Father and his visible τύπος reflects a sacramental view of reality, not a Platonic one. Ignatius expects the bishop to mediate spiritual wisdom and divine oversight to his flock by bridging the realms of flesh and spirit within his own person and in his episcopal ministry. He explains to Polycarp, "To this end you are made of flesh and spirit: that you might coax along the matters that appear before your face. As for the invisible things, ask that they may be made manifest to you, that you may lack nothing but abound in every charism" (2:2).

This vocation is lived out by virtue of a unique spiritual bond that exists between God and the bishop. If God is "the bishop of all" (*Magn.* 3:1), he is in a special sense the bishop of the bishop. The earthly ἐπίσκοπος is "overseen [ἐπισκοπήμενος] by God the Father and the Lord Jesus Christ" (*Poly.* sal.). He bears up all, even as the Lord bears him up (1:2). The efficacy of this bond is not magical but requires spiritual maintenance, as it were. The letter to *Polycarp* manifests Ignatius's conviction that even the best bishop needs to be exhorted to ever greater diligence, spiritual insight, and fidelity to the Lord's will. He does not possess clairvoyant knowledge of God's will merely by virtue of his office. On the contrary, Ignatius challenges Polycarp, whom he obviously holds in high esteem, "Vindicate your office [τόπος] in all fleshly and spiritual solicitude" (1:2), which is to say, "Prove that you are the right man for the job!" Apparently Ignatius thinks that Polycarp could stand to spend more time in prayer, so that he can acquire a deeper level of spiritual perspicacity (1:3, 2:2).

Unlike some modern scholars, Ignatius does not consider office and charism to be antitheses. Indeed, they require each other. Addressing the concern of those Ephesian Christians who find Onesimus, as well as the sort of monepiscopal authority that Ignatius is espousing, insufficiently charismatic, Ignatius extols Onesimus's "inexpressible love" and pronounces a blessing upon the God who has "graced" (χαρισάμενος) the Ephesians with "such a bishop," encouraging his readers to see in the one who holds episcopal office a kind of charismatic endowment of their community (*Eph.* 1:3).

In addition to office and charism, a third element is also necessary for the bishop's authority to constitute an effective link between past and present, between heaven and earth, and between catholic church and local church. This element is the word of God. The bishop can only effectively communicate God's mind-set to the rest of the church if he himself is seeking and living out that mind-set in all things. "Let nothing be done without your approval [γνώμη], but neither must you do anything apart from God's mind-set [γνώμη]" (4:1). Developing a "mind-set toward God" that is "virtuous and perfect" requires knowing and living in harmony with "the commandments" (Phld. 1:2). Naturally, the bishop must also "speak about Jesus Christ in truth" (Eph. 6:2). These passages, and many others, presuppose an objective standard of faith and morals derived from Scripture and ecclesial tradition. Effective episcopal authority is a three-legged stool, combining office, charism, and what is elsewhere called "the standard of truth" (ὁ κανὼν τῆς ἀληθείας) or "the standard of our tradition" (ὁ τῆς παραδόσεως ἡμῶν κανών).[125]

Like everything else in the divine economy, the bond between God the Father and the bishop is, of course, mediated by Jesus Christ, who is "the mind-set [γνώμη] of the Father" (Eph. 3:2). This is why Ignatius can interchangeably correlate the bishop with Jesus Christ (Tral. 2:1) or with God the Father (Smyr. 8:2). Everything that God wishes to give to the church—revelation, unity, imperishable life—he gives by sending his Son into the world. Thus the local church is united to its bishop, as the catholic church is to Jesus Christ, and as Jesus Christ is to the Father (Eph. 5:1). This is the complete chain, and all of its links are presupposed even when not all of them are supplied explicitly. The passages that draw a direct line from the bishop to the Father give, as it were, a foreshortened or contracted view, but in doing so they indicate how perfect the mediation accomplished by Jesus Christ really is. It gives the church true access to the Father, for Jesus is "the door of the Father" (Phld. 9:1). Ignatius moves effortlessly back and forth between the two conceptions, bishop as type of the Father and bishop as type of Christ, not because he is still trying to clarify his own speculations but because he is quite clear about who Jesus Christ is and what he has accomplished.[126]

Christians are to obey Jesus Christ as he obeyed the Father (Heb 5:8–9), or, as Ignatius puts it, they are to "be imitators of Jesus Christ, even as he is of the Father" (Phld. 7:2). These formulations help us to see that when we consider Jesus Christ as mediator, we can view him from either of two sides: as he relates to us, or as he relates to the Father. As such, he is both the object and the model of obedience. As the *object* of obedience, he corresponds to the bishop. Christians "submit to the bishop as

---

125. Irenaeus, *Haer.* 1:9:4; Clement of Rome, 1 *Clem.* 7:2.
126. *Tral.* 2:1, 3:1; *Rom.* 9:1; *Smyr.* 8:1–2.

to Jesus Christ" (*Tral.* 2:1). But as the model of obedience, he corresponds to all those who are called to submit to the bishop. Ignatius places Christ in precisely this role in three passages. "Just as the Lord did nothing apart from the Father ... so neither are you to do anything apart from the bishop and the presbyters" (*Magn.* 7:1). "Submit to the bishop and to one another, as Jesus Christ submitted to the Father when he was in the flesh" (13:2). "You must all follow the bishop, as Jesus Christ followed the Father" (*Smyr.* 8:1). Now, because Ignatius also thinks of deacons as models of obedience and of selfless service to the church,[127] he has good reason to compare the deacons to Jesus Christ, the one who "came not to be served but to serve [διακονῆσαι]" (Mt 20:28). The deacons are "most sweet" to Ignatius because they have been "entrusted with the ministry [διακονία] of Jesus Christ" (*Magn.* 6:1).

As Ignatius understands it, the threefold hierarchy does not represent a straightforward "chain of command." Deacons are not so much authority figures as they are images of Jesus Christ in their humble service to the church. Unlike bishops and presbyters, deacons are never said to hold "office" (*Magn.* 6:1), and seldom does Ignatius present them along with bishop and presbyters as objects of obedience.[128] Much more often he counsels submission to bishop and presbyters, either placing the deacons on the side of those who are to submit or not mentioning them at all.[129] Thus the laity should "follow" the bishop and his presbyters, but they should "reverence" the deacons as they do Jesus Christ.[130] In their unique capacity as images of Jesus Christ the servant of all, deacons are models for all Christians to imitate. All should strive to "imitate" a deacon such as Burrhus, who is "an exemplification of the service [διακονία] of God" (*Smyr.* 12:1). This is true even, perhaps especially, of the bishop, who has received, not "power," but a special "ministry" (διακονία) to the local church (*Phld.* 1:1). Though he is a bishop himself, Ignatius readily identifies with the deacons and calls them his "fellow slaves,"[131] and he constantly refers to himself as the "last" member of the church in Antioch.[132] Though he says a great deal in his letters about himself and his vocation as a Christian, we would not even know that Ignatius held the episcopal office apart from two brief allusions to this fact in *Romans* (2:2; 9:1). This reticence to mention his own office does

---

127. *Magn.* 2:1; *Phld.* 1:1.
128. Only *Phld.* 7:1 and *Poly.* 6:1.
129. *Eph.* 2:2, 5:3, 20:2; *Magn.* 2:1, 7:1; *Tral.* 2:1–3, 13:2.
130. *Smyr.* 8:1; *Tral.* 3:1.
131. *Magn.* 2:1; *Phld.* 4:1; *Smyr.* 12:2.
132. *Eph.* 21:1; *Tral.* 13:1; *Rom.* 9:2; *Smyr.* 11:1; cf. *Magn.* 14:1.

not indicate that it is unimportant to him but that he does not want his ego to become inflated (*Smyr.* 6:1).

Once we recognize that the position of deacons within the threefold hierarchy is not so much a question of "rank" as it is a call to exemplify "the διακονία of Jesus Christ" to which all Christians are called, the fact that some versions of Ignatius's ecclesiological typology seem to place Jesus "below" his own apostles ceases to be a problem. This placement may even have a special appropriateness, since Jesus presented himself as the servant of his own apostles, saying, "I am in your midst as the one who serves [ὁ διακονῶν]" (Lk 22:27). The fact that Jesus Christ can occupy either of two positions in Ignatius's ecclesiological typology is a function of good Christology, not a by-product of sloppy redaction. Because he is the eternal Son, sent into the world to represent the Father, Jesus is the *object* of our obedience and, like the Father, can be aligned with the bishop. Christians should "submit to the bishop as to Jesus Christ" (*Tral.* 2:1). Because he took flesh in order to "please the one who sent him in all things" (*Magn.* 8:2), Jesus is also our *model* of service and obedience (13:2) and can be aligned with the deacons (6:1). Christians should "show reverence for the deacons as for Jesus Christ" (*Tral.* 3:1). It is no coincidence that Ignatius appends one of his most significant Christological affirmations directly to a description of the deacons. "And the deacons, who are most sweet to me, have been entrusted with the ministry of Jesus Christ, who before the ages was with the Father and has appeared at the end" (*Magn.* 6:1).

It remains to say a word about the presbyters. As the "college of apostles" in heaven constitutes a "council of elders" (πρεσβυτέριον) for the whole church, so within the body of the local church the presbyters occupy "the place of the council of the apostles."[133] Unlike the deacons, who are a plurality but are never described as forming a body, the presbyters are often spoken of in this way. Indeed, Ignatius uses the collective term "presbytery" (πρεσβυτέριον) more often than the plural "presbyters" (πρεσβύτεροι). He makes a sharp distinction between bishop and presbyters, and defines the office of presbyter in terms of its special relationship to the office of bishop. The presbyters constitute a "bishop's council" and thus presumably give advice to the bishop (*Phld.* 8:1). Those who are literally "elders" (πρεσβύτεροι) may be tempted to take advantage of a younger bishop, but "holy presbyters" show themselves

---

133. *Tral.* 3:1; *Phld.* 5:1; *Magn.* 6:1.

"wise in God" by "yielding to him" (*Magn.* 3:1). Presbyters have a special responsibility to "refresh" the bishop (*Tral.* 12:2) and to remain "in tune" with him "as strings with a lyre" (*Eph.* 4:1). If deacons represent the universal call to service, presbyters symbolize the responsibility of all Christians to act in union with their bishop. When renegade presbyters convoke assemblies without the bishop's knowledge or consent, this threatens the local church's very unity (*Smyr.* 8:1–9:1).[134] Christians are unified when they are "one with the bishop and with those presbyters who stand with him [τοῖς σὺν αὐτῷ πρεσβυτέροις]."[135] Still, the Lord is ready to forgive schismatics, provided they "repent into the unity of God and the council of the bishop" (*Phld.* 8:1).

It is especially as they are seated around the bishop in eucharistic assembly that the presbyters symbolize the church's unity. Allen Brent plausibly proposes that their horseshoe-like seating arrangement suggested to Ignatius the image of the presbyteral council as a "worthily plaited spiritual wreath" (*Magn.* 13:1).[136] In any case, it is remarkable how often Ignatius mentions the bishop with his presbyters (and sometimes also the deacons) in contexts concerned with the church's "coming together" in "one sanctuary" to break the "one bread" of the eucharist.[137] In this setting the presbyters would easily bring to mind the apostles, both as the latter reclined around the Lord in the cenacle and as they are now enthroned with him in the heavenly sanctuary. Ignatius either directly compares or loosely associates the presbyters with the apostles in no less than seven passages.[138] Like the eucharist itself, the presbyters are a sign both of the church's origins and of her eschatological goal.

The Appointment and Validation of Bishops

In a passage that we examined briefly in chapter 5, Ignatius expounds the interlocking unity of the divine economy as the communication of God's "mind-set" (γνώμη) to believers via Jesus Christ and the bishops of the church. God the Father makes his mind-set available to the whole

---

134. When the bishop delegated someone to convoke the eucharist on his behalf, it was presumably a presbyter, and according to Ignatius such a eucharist would be valid (8:1).

135. *Phld.* sal.; cf. *Polycarp, Phil.* sal.

136. *Ignatius of Antioch*, 86.

137. *Eph.* 20:2; *Magn.* 7:1–2; *Tral.* 7:2; *Phld.* 4:1; *Smyr.* 8:1.

138. *Magn.* 6:1, 7:1, 13:1–2; *Tral.* 2:2, 3:1, 12:2; *Phld.* 5:1. The comparison between the presbytery and "the law of Jesus Christ" (*Magn.* 2:1) may be a related association, since the apostles transmitted this law. *Trallians* 7:1 is the one passage in which the apostles seem to be more closely associated with the bishop than with the presbyters.

church in Jesus Christ, and because "the bishops designated throughout the world are in the mind-set of Jesus Christ," they are able to communicate this mind-set to their respective flocks. Thus the Christian faithful at the local level are able to "run together in the mind-set of God" precisely by "running together in the mind-set of the bishop" (Eph. 3:2–4:1a). According to this passage, then, the divine mind-set is transmitted as follows.

God the Father → Jesus Christ → the bishop → the local church

This schema is obviously streamlined, eliding some of the crucial factors we have discussed in this chapter, such as the gift of the Holy Spirit and the role of the apostles. Still, this passage from *Ephesians* serves to highlight the fact that Ignatius views the bishop as a vital link in the line of communication by which the Father's mind-set is transmitted to the faithful. It also raises important questions about Ignatius's understanding of episcopal authority and its establishment within the church. What does Ignatius have in mind when he speaks of bishops being "designated"? How can he be so sure that the bishops of the universal church are in fact "in the mind-set of Jesus Christ"? Does his emphasis on submission to the bishop diminish the lay believer's intimacy with, and personal responsibility to, Jesus Christ? Though the letters give us relatively little to go on in answering these questions, they do not leave us entirely in the dark, and it is important to say what we can. Failure to do so would leave us to fall back on tired caricatures of Ignatius's ecclesiology as "authoritarianism."[139] Accordingly, I will conclude this chapter with a brief look at what Ignatius says about the appointment and "validation" of bishops and a few related observations about his anxiety for the church of Antioch.

By referring to the bishops of the universal church as "designated" (ὁρισθέντες), Ignatius surely means that they have been appointed by God (Eph. 3:2). In the New Testament and the writings of the apostolic fathers the verb ὁρίζω almost always refers to the fixing of something by divine decree,[140] and that is also true of Ignatius's use of the related

---

139. Grant faults Ignatius's ecclesiology for being "exaggerated in the direction of authoritarianism" and "deficient in regard to the Holy Spirit and its activities" (*Ignatius of Antioch*, 25). This assessment is itself an exaggeration. It is, however, closer to the truth than Walter Bauer's description of Ignatius's concept of episcopacy as the "dictatorship" of a "strong man" who has "absolute control of the whole group" (*Orthodoxy and Heresy*, 62).

140. Lk 22:22; Acts 2:23, 10:42, 17:26 and 31; Rom 1:4; Heb 4:7; 1 *Clem.* 40:2 and 3, 41:4; *Barn.* 19:1; *Shep.* 6:5 (= Vision 2:2:5). The only exceptions seem to be Acts 11:29 and *Diog.* 5:10.

verb προορίζω ("foreordain") earlier in *Ephesians* (sal.). Later in the letter he says that a church must receive its bishop as "sent" by the Lord Jesus himself (6:1), and he blesses God for having "graced" (χαρίζομαι) the Ephesians with such a bishop as Onesimus (1:3). Naturally, Ignatius understands that in these matters the divine will manifests itself through a human process of discernment and selection. This is implied in another letter when he says that bishops, presbyters, and deacons "have been appointed according to the mind-set of Jesus Christ," who has "confirmed them in validity by his Holy Spirit" (Phld. sal.), and then begins his commendation of the bishop of Philadelphia in these words:

> I know that it was neither from himself nor through men that your bishop acquired the ministry pertaining to the common life, nor was it in vainglory, but in the love of God the Father and the Lord Jesus Christ. (1:1)

Though this statement echoes Paul's emphatic protestation that his apostleship was "not from men, nor through a man" (Gal 1:1), it is unlikely that Ignatius means that the bishop of Philadelphia has received his appointment literally without the agency of any other human being. The point seems to be rather that his elevation to the episcopacy was not driven by his own initiative ("from himself"), nor was it a crassly political act ("from men"). The motivation behind it was not the sort of vainglory that worldly persons seek for themselves or bestow upon each other, but authentic Christian charity. This is not a purely charismatic view of leadership, to be sure, but it does look for evidence of the Spirit's guidance of the church in the spiritual and moral qualities of men who have been appointed to ecclesiastical office. Accordingly, Ignatius goes on to say how impressed he is with this particular bishop's "mildness" and describes his "mind-set toward God" in some detail, highlighting, as an objective criterion, his being "in tune with the commandments" (Phld. 1:1–2).

As Ignatius knew well, some members of the church in Philadelphia were not acting as if their bishop had been divinely designated.[141] To counter this, he does not say, "Look, your bishop was appointed ac-

---

141. Phld. 4:1, 7:1–8:1. According to Meinhold, the Philadelphian bishop's opponents were "pneumatics" who were opposed to office as such (*Studien zu Ignatius*, 27). Conversely, Stewart-Sykes thinks that Ignatius's argument in Phld. sal.–1:2 presupposes opponents who favor the "human election" of leaders over against Ignatius's more charismatic idea that the bishop has received his office from God ("Prophecy and Patronage," 178). Both views are simplistic. Ignatius's argument presupposes a common recognition that, while the bishop was selected through a human process, this process represented an attempt to discern God's will in the matter.

cording to proper ecclesiastical procedure and therefore must be accepted as God's choice." But neither does he say, "Your bishop was designated by such and such a prophet and therefore must be heeded as the oracle of God." Instead, he appeals to the man's godlike character as the most important indicator that he has been confirmed "in validity" (ἐν βεβαιωσύνῃ) by the Holy Spirit (Phld. sal.). Ignatius thinks it reasonable to ask a bishop to "vindicate" his appointment to office (Poly. 1:2). He does not require his readers to submit to their bishop without also expecting the bishop to prove himself worthy of their obedience.

At the same time, it is the responsibility of all Christians, not bishop or clergy alone, to know the "commandments of Jesus Christ" (Eph. 9:2) and the "ordinances of the apostles" (Tral. 7:1) and to be "validated" by obeying them. The whole picture comes into focus in the following passage.

Be eager therefore to be validated [βεβαιωθῆναι] in the precepts of the Lord and of the apostles, in order that in all that you do you may prosper, in flesh and spirit, in faith and love, in the Son and the Father and in the Spirit, in the beginning and in the end, with your most worthy bishop and the worthily plaited wreath that is your presbytery and the godly deacons. Submit to the bishop and to one another, as Jesus Christ submitted to the Father according to the flesh, and as the apostles submitted to Christ and to the Father, in order that your unity might be both fleshly and spiritual. (Magn. 13:1–2)

At first glance this exhortation seems to suggest something like a direct chain of command: Jesus submitted to the Father, the apostles to Jesus, the bishop to the apostles, the presbyters to the bishop, and so on. But a closer look reveals that it is not really that simple. Ignatius is careful to say that the apostles submitted to Christ "and to the Father," as if to discourage the notion that their relating to God *through Jesus Christ* has placed them at one remove from the Father (cf. Jn 14:8–10). Nor does Ignatius suggest that the church's reception of the Lord's precepts *through the apostles* places the church at one remove from Jesus Christ. Rather, the church is to obey both the Lord's precepts and those of the apostles. Most significantly, Ignatius's formulation here steers clear of any conception of the laity as spoon-fed children or unthinking automatons. The bishop's mediation of God's will is one integral element in an ecclesial existence that brings every member of the church into an intimate (which is not to say unmediated) relationship with the Holy Trinity. Finally, we should not overlook the way Ignatius qualifies his command to submit to the bishop by adding the phrase "and to one another" (καὶ ἀλλήλοις), as if to suggest that subordination to episcopal authority is but one aspect of a mode of life that is more broadly characterized by humility and mutual deference (cf. Paul, Eph 5:21). Earlier in the same letter Ignatius says that, since all have received the same godly manner of life (ὁμοήθεια θεοῦ), all should "reverence one another" and "love one another" (*Magn.* 6:2). His view of the church is far from egalitarian or democratic, and obviously it is not "presbyterian," but neither is it the rigidly authoritarian and purely hierarchical ecclesiology it is sometimes taken to be.

When there was an episcopal vacancy in one of the churches of early second-century Syria or Asia Minor, how was a new bishop chosen? Presumably Ignatius's first readers knew the answer to this question, and so he supplies us with no information. My guess is that the church fasted and prayed, and that the presbyters were primarily responsible for discerning the Holy Spirit's choice. In most cases he would have been a man from their own number, or perhaps a deacon. Probably the whole process normally took but a few days. As we have seen, Ignatius clearly believes that the Holy Spirit guides and protects the church in these decisions, for he describes her bishops as divinely "designated" and as carrying out their ministry "in the mind-set of Jesus Christ" (Eph. 3:2). We have no way of knowing whether his convictions in this regard were ever tested by a heretical or grossly immoral bishop, and if so, how he may have dealt with such a situation. He does not seem to sense the potential conflict between his warnings against heresy and immorality, on the one hand, and his exhortations to do everything in union with the bishop, on the other hand, but this may simply reflect his confidence that the bishops of Ephesus, Magnesia, Tralles, Philadelphia, and Smyrna, whatever their personal shortcomings, are all solid men of the church who can be relied on to teach and live the true gospel. In any case, if Ignatius has anything like a belief in the church's infallibility, it is not such as to breed complacency in him. He exhorts the churches to fidelity to the gospel as a matter of the greatest urgency and seriousness, and there is nothing pro forma about his exhortation of a fellow bishop in the *Letter to Polycarp*. In sum, everything we know about Ignatius suggests that he would consider the choosing of a new bishop to be a critical moment in the life of any local church, certainly not something to be taken for granted.

These reflections may have some bearing on the much debated issue of the situation that Ignatius left behind in Antioch. In each of the four letters written from Smyrna, Ignatius asks for prayers for "the church in Syria" in an anxious tone but without indicating explicitly the cause of his concern.[142] Having received in the interim a report that the church in Antioch is now "at peace," in the three letters written from Troas he expresses joyful relief over this news and gives instructions for each church to send a delegation to Antioch to "congratulate" the church there in liturgical assembly.[143] The length and adamant tone of these latter three passages suggest that this delegation was a matter of considerable importance to Ignatius. It would not be an exaggeration to speak here of his dying request. As I noted in chapter 2, the slender evidence we possess does not warrant elaborate hypothetical reconstructions of the situation in Antioch. Many aspects of it must remain shrouded in mystery. But, whatever the circumstances surrounding Ignatius's arrest were, whatever party politics may have been at play within the church at Antioch, and whatever Ignatius's approval rating as bishop may have been before or after his arrest, of this much we can be quite certain: Ignatius left his church without an earthly bishop (Rom. 9:1), and even under the best of circumstances he would have regarded this as a cause for great concern and an excellent reason to request intercessory prayers from other churches.[144]

This simple observation has great explanatory power when it comes to the seven passages referred to above. To the Ephesians Ignatius writes, "Pray for the church in Syria, whence I am being led in bonds to Rome" (Eph. 21:2). In the same breath with which he asks for prayers for his community, he mentions his own absence from them. Similarly, to the Romans he writes, "Remember in your prayer the church in Syria, which in my stead has God as its shepherd. Jesus Christ alone, and your love, will look after [ἐπισκοπήσει] it" (Rom. 9:1). This passage expresses Ignatius's conviction that Jesus Christ is, in the truest sense, the church's one bishop, while at the same time reflecting his well-formed ecclesiological understanding that each local community of Christians ought to have also a "visible" bishop (Magn. 3:2), a "bishop in the flesh" to represent Christ on earth (Eph. 1:3). Without one, a community does not possess the full structure of a "church" (Tral. 3:1). Whatever the cause of Ignatius's concern, it must have been resolved within a matter of days,

---

142. Eph. 21:2; Magn. 14:1; Tral. 13:1; Rom. 9:1–2.
143. Phld. 10:1–2; Smyr. 11:1; Poly. 7:1–8:2.
144. Grant, *Ignatius of Antioch*, 107–8, 124; Frederic W. Schlatter, "The Restoration of Peace in Ignatius' Antioch," *Journal of Theological Studies* 35 (1984): 465–69.

or a week or two at most, after his departure, since the courier from Antioch was able to catch up to his entourage. Especially if we assume that there were more or less serious divisions within the church at Antioch, as many scholars do, no development could have so swiftly brought the situation to a new equilibrium and given Ignatius confidence that his church was once again "at peace" than for a capable leader to have taken the helm. In fact, it is hard to imagine that Ignatius would have claimed that the Antiochene Christians had "regained their proper greatness" and had "their proper bodily integrity restored to them" (Smyr. 11:2) unless a new bishop had been chosen.

Ignatius's concern for the church at Antioch and his anxiety over whether he will achieve martyrdom are closely bound together in his mind, for both have been occasioned by his arrest and both pertain to salvation.[145] The faithful need a bishop to exhort and lead them "that they may be saved" (Poly. 1:2), and Ignatius needs to seize this unique opportunity to "attain God" (Rom. 2:1). Writing from Smyrna, he views his arrest as a propitious development and a sign of God's mercy toward him, but he worries that the devil may yet impede him, in one way or another, from achieving martyrdom.[146] Once he learns that a new bishop has been chosen to replace him, he is "more encouraged, with a freedom from anxiety that comes from God," though hardly complacent about his own situation (Poly. 7:1).[147] In other words, the fact that his brothers and sisters in Antioch have experienced "good weather" and "have already reached harbor" seems a good omen for his own success (Smyr. 11:3). It is interesting to note that when Ignatius employs this metaphor again, it is explicitly a bishop who is compared to "favorable winds" and a "harbor" (Poly. 2:3). So in the present case, the Antiochene church has presumably attained the safe haven of having a bishop over them once again.

This hypothesis—namely, that the good news that reached Ignatius in Troas was that a new bishop had been chosen in Antioch—also makes good sense of Ignatius's insistence that as many churches as possible

---

145. Magn. 14:1; Rom. 9:1–2; Smyr. 11:1.

146. Rom. 1:2, 9:2, 7:1; Tral. 4:2.

147. Cf. Phld. 5:1. Willard M. Swartley overstates the point: "When Ignatius knew that the church over which he was bishop attained unity, then his own concern about being worthy, being a true disciple, attaining God, etc. appears to be relieved and virtually non-existent!" ("The Imitatio Christi in the Ignatian Letters," *Vigiliae Christianae* 27 [1973]: 93). Swartley misconstrues the word ἐάνπερ in Poly. 7:1 (which should be rendered: "if indeed [ἐάνπερ] through suffering I attain God") and overlooks the explicit statement of Phld. 5:1 ("being in bonds, I fear all the more, since I am not yet perfect").

send delegations, or at least letters, to the church in Antioch. And this is especially the case if there was any sort of unrest or factionalism within that church. By having other churches publically recognize the new bishop and congratulate the Antiochenes on his installation, Ignatius helps secure his lasting authority. Were the church at Antioch to keep his appointment a mostly private matter, a rival candidate backed by one of the factions could more easily challenge the decision after the fact. There would then be real doubt among the churches about who had been chosen, and this could contribute to a full-fledged schism within the church at Antioch.[148] Ignatius's desire to involve the other churches in the affairs of Antioch, first by requesting their prayers during the period of discernment and then by calling for delegations, indicates once again his sense of the unity and complementarity of the local churches within the one catholic church.

An Ecclesiology of Continuity

In this chapter I have attempted to clarify how the Holy Spirit, the apostles, the word of God, the eucharist, and the threefold hierarchy all contribute to the ecclesial continuity between past and present, between heaven and earth, and between universal and local, each by virtue of its relationship to the person and event of Jesus Christ within the economy of redemption.[149] At every step it has been important to discern the re-

---

148. If this is Ignatius's intent, however, it is difficult to understand why he does not mention the new bishop by name and give him a brief commendation (in the letters sent from Troas). I must admit that this is a point of vulnerability in my hypothesis.

149. Ignatius's ecclesiology is in this sense decidedly Christocentric. It is also and at the same time centered on the eucharist. I have purposely avoided giving the eucharist its own section in this chapter in order to show how the various other elements in Ignatius's ecclesiology converge in the eucharist. Writing from an Orthodox perspective, Kenneth Paul Wesche goes much further, identifying the eucharist as the sum and substance of Ignatian ecclesiology ("St. Ignatius of Antioch: The Criterion of Orthodoxy and the Marks of Catholicity," Pro Ecclesia 3 [1994]: 89–109). According to Wesche, the congregation with its bishop cannot be identified as the church, for nothing human is constitutive of the church "except the deified humanity of Christ's life-giving body and blood" (98). The eucharist is the church, and the church is the eucharist. "[T]he church is the body and blood of Christ in a concrete, physical way" (97). Nor do Scripture, proclamation, dogma, or episcopacy in any real sense make Christ present to his people. (No "theology of the word" for Wesche!) All these elements of ecclesial life "point beyond" themselves to the eucharist, but the eucharist in no sense points beyond itself, for it is not "significatory" (ibid.). This reading of Ignatius tends to collapse the Christ event, salvation, and eschatology into the eucharist: "The eucharist of the catholic church, as the actual accomplishment of our salvation, as Christ's passion and resurrection, as the true living body and blood of Christ, as the crucified and risen Jesus Christ himself, is the consummation of faith's love; it is the mystical union for which faith longs; it is the beloved God himself" (102).

lationship between the vertical-transcendent and horizontal-temporal dimensions of this economy. The sending of the Spirit is an event within history and at the same time a gift of divine imperishability. Having received this gift, the apostles have attained a life beyond death and now exercise their authority over the church from heaven. At the same time, they are historical figures who maintain a concrete presence to the church on earth through the witness they bore to Christ and the body of doctrine they have bequeathed to the church. Enlivened by the Holy Spirit and having studied the writings of Matthew, John, and Paul, a leader such as Ignatius can exhort the churches "in the apostolic character" as he attempts to follow in the footsteps of the apostles by embracing martyrdom. The local church, with its threefold hierarchy, is a living image of the church as a whole. Deacons exemplify the humble, selfless service by which all Christians are called to imitate the Lord Jesus. Presbyters recall the church's origins in the cenacle, where the apostles received both the eucharist and the gift of the Spirit, and at the same time they point the church toward her eschatological goal in heaven, where the apostles now surround their exalted Lord. The bishop, by virtue of his intense spiritual life, his adherence to the word of God, and the grace with which he has been "clothed," exercises his office in order to lead others to salvation (Poly. 1:2). As head of the local church, he is the visible representative of God the Father and the Lord Jesus. It is difficult to overstate the importance of the bishop in Ignatius's ecclesiology, but it is simplistic to describe his view of the church as authoritarian.

10

UNITY AND ESCHATOLOGY

Unity and History

"God promises union, which is himself" (*Tral.* 11:2). Like many of Ignatius's aphorisms, this one may be read as a summary of the gospel. What God offers to man—namely, "union"—is a participation in God's own life. The entire economy of creation and redemption flows forth from the primordial Trinitarian unity and leads rational creatures to an eschatological participation in this same unity. The intrapersonal and interpersonal unity that God promises is at the same time also unity from God and unity with God. The economy comes from God and leads back to God, for he is ἀρχή and τέλος. More specifically, redemption is accomplished in history when Jesus Christ comes forth from the Father and returns to the Father, and for each believer it is accomplished in and through the cross of Christ, by which the Holy Spirit leads the believer "to the Father."[1] One might therefore, with some reservations, follow Ferdinando Bergamelli in describing Ignatian theology as "a single grand vision" in which God the Father is presented as the primal source and ultimate end of all things.[2]

Ignatius of Antioch views the economy of redemption as a *mysterium unitatis*. In chapters 3 through 5 we explored various dimensions of unity. We saw that the eternal union of the Father and the Son in the Spirit has

---

1. *Magn.* 7:2; *Eph.* 9:1; *Rom.* 7:2.
2. "Dal Padre al Padre: Il Padre come principio e termine del Cristo e del cristiano in Ignazio di Antiochia," *Studia Patristica* 36 (2001): 168–76 (quote from 176: "un'unica grandiosa visione"). All but missing from this "grand vision," of course, is an explicit doctrine of creation. It is no coincidence that the texts that Bergamelli marshals present the Father as both principle and end for Jesus Christ but as end alone for the Christian. Despite *Eph.* 15:1, Ignatius never clearly speaks of creatures coming forth from God, much less from God the Father.

manifested itself definitively in the event of Jesus Christ, and we learned that even in the case of Christ himself the intrapersonal unity of flesh and spirit is a dynamic and teleological reality. The humanity assumed by the Word in the incarnation has been transformed and glorified through the paschal mystery, so that the grace of imperishability might be conferred upon human beings through the ministry of the church. Ignatius's view of the human person as composed of flesh and spirit reflects his biblical sense for the goodness of creation but also expresses an essentially soteriological anthropology. Human beings achieve the divinely promised intrapersonal and interpersonal unity when the whole human person and the whole of human life is spiritualized by the newness of eternal life made available in Jesus Christ. This imperishable "life" (ζωή) is possessed already in the present "life" (βίος)—it is therefore called "the present grace" (Eph. 11:1)—but because human life has a temporal and teleological structure, the effects of grace can only be fully realized and definitively secured when a human person passes through the mystery of death and attains glory. Ignatius's robust realized eschatology only makes sense in conjunction with his appeals to future eschatology. We also saw that the teleological character of the gift of unity is reflected in the complementarity of faith and love, which are the "beginning and end of life" (ἀρχὴ ζωῆς καὶ τέλος; Eph. 14:1). Faith "works" through love (Gal 5:6). This is not a Pelagian view of redemption, since the believer depends on grace from beginning to end,[3] but one that respects the essentially historical and eschatological nature of the economy.

In chapters 6 through 9 we focused on the historical aspect of this same economy of unity, attending carefully to the relationship between its vertical-transcendent and horizontal-temporal dimensions in order to recover the biblical sense of *mysterium* implicit in Ignatius's presentation of the economy. Because God's self-manifestation in Jesus Christ comes both "at the end" and "as the goal" (ἐν τέλει; Magn. 6:1), it divides the historical economy into two distinct and successive stages—old and new, good and better, imperfect and perfect, Judaism and Christianity—while at the same time it confers a transcendent dimension upon all of history, so that the grace of Jesus Christ was available even to those "disciples" who lived chronologically prior to the Christ event.[4] Judaism gives way to Christianity but is not simply replaced by it, since the old is taken up into the new and perfected by it. Out of "silence," that is, the

3. Rom. 1:2, 3:2; Smyr. 11:1.
4. Magn. 8:2; Phld. 9:1.

unfathomable mystery of God's Trinitarian life, the Logos comes forth into the world in order to reveal the Father both in spoken words and in silent deeds.[5] One such deed is his baptism in the Jordan, a richly symbolic gesture that serves as a kind of hinge between the incarnation and the paschal mystery, harkening back to Israel's covenant and anticipating the sacramental life of the church, illuminating the whole economy from creation to eschaton. In Ignatian ecclesiology the mission of the Spirit, the ministry of the apostles, the spoken and written word of God, the eucharist, and the threefold hierarchy together establish a real historical and transcendent bond between the *vita Iesu* and the *vita ecclesiae*, between the church in heaven and the church on earth, and between the catholic church and the local churches. That which makes the church what it is—faith, love, and imperishability—comes down from heaven through the Christ event and leads the earthly members of the church upward to their heavenly goal.

This brief summary of the ground we have covered in this volume underscores the importance of teleology and eschatology in Ignatius's conception of the economy of redemption while it begs the question: What exactly is Ignatius's understanding of eschatology? If we limit eschatology to apocalyptic scenarios, it will seem to be of very minor concern to Ignatius; but if we define eschatology more broadly to include references to death as a threshold, post-mortem judgment, and everlasting life, we shall find that he is intensely interested in the subject. Ignatius is sometimes thought to favor a Hellenized concept of realized eschatology over the traditional Jewish concept of future eschatology and to emphasize greatly the personal dimension of eschatology over its communal dimension. The principal goal of this final chapter is to demonstrate that this assessment entails false dichotomies that obscure Ignatius's teaching. Once we have established that his eschatology does in fact have a future orientation and a communal dimension, we can ask whether it also has a properly historical dimension. After treating Ignatius's eschatology, I will conclude the volume with a final attempt to show that his letters provide us with a cohesive vision of the divine economy.

Eschatology: Realized and Future, Personal and Communal

Ignatius frequently uses the noun ζωή or the articular infinitive τὸ ζῆν to refer to the principle of supernatural "life" that is available to believers

---

5. *Magn.* 8:2; *Eph.* 15:1.

already in this life. This "true life," which is the grace of the new covenant and the principle of salvation, is thus the "newness of eternal life" or "salvation and eternal life."[6] It has come into the world through the death of Jesus Christ, who is thus identified as the source of life.[7] The Ignatian theme of life already discloses the fundamental inseparability and complementarity of realized and future eschatology.[8] The life in question is possessed now and already has the quality of being "the life that is forever" (*Magn.* 1:2), but it is not simply identical with life after death, nor does it entail the absolute assurance of personal salvation. Life is also "set before" believers as something yet to be attained, a goal from which the devil attempts to divert them (*Eph.* 17:1). Indeed, both death and life are "set before" us, and we can hold on to the life we already possess and definitively secure it only by willingly associating our own dying with Jesus' passion (*Magn.* 5:1–2). This is why "endurance" unto death is a leitmotif throughout the Ignatian corpus.[9]

Note how Ignatius combines realized and future eschatology when he describes the eucharist as the "medicine of immortality, the antidote that enables us not to die but to live forever in Jesus Christ" (*Eph.* 20:2). Elsewhere, similarly, he combines the idea of the present possession of "true life" with the hope of resurrection (*Tral.* 9:2). This is the authentic biblical and especially Johannine notion of realized eschatology.[10] Properly understood, there is no tension whatsoever between realized and future eschatology, for it is the very nature of the "life" possessed now that it leads one to eternal life, as Ignatius indicates when he describes the indwelling Holy Spirit as "living and speaking water in me, saying from within, 'Come to the Father!'" (*Rom.* 7:2).[11]

If the principle of salvation is τὸ ζῆν, forfeiting this principle is τὸ ἀποθανεῖν, spiritual "death" (*Tral.* 2:1, 6:2). Those who have received the

---

6. Eph. 11:1, 19:3, 18:1.
7. Magn. 9:1; Eph. 3:2, 7:2.
8. Goltz, *Ignatius von Antiochien*, 40.
9. Eph. 3:1; Magn. 1:3, 9:1; Tral. 1:1; Rom 10:3; Smyr. 4:2, 9:2, 12:2; Poly. 3:1, 6:2.
10. See Jn 5:24–29, 6:40 and 50–58.
11. According to Albert Osger Mellink, "realized eschatology stands alongside future eschatology without conflict" in the Ignatian letters (*Death as Eschaton: A Study of Ignatius of Antioch's Desire for Death* [Amsterdam: University of Amsterdam, 2000], 332). On the same page, however, Mellink points to a "tension" between present and future aspects of eschatology that is a "fundamental element" in Ignatian soteriology. He seems to be referring to the existential tension experienced by the believer who already possesses "life" but has not yet attained its fullness in the resurrection, a tension to which Paul too refers (Rom 8:23). My point is not to deny this existential tension but to note that it entails no real theological tension as long as one recognizes, as Ignatius surely does, that "present grace" is "unto true life" (Eph. 11:1). In the words of Aquinas, "Grace is nothing other than a certain beginning of glory in us" (STh II-II, q. 24, a. 3, ad 2).

knowledge of God may yet "perish" in their folly (Eph. 17:2), as also may anyone who becomes puffed up and begins to boast (Tral. 4:1). Indeed such a person has already "been corrupted" and has "perished" (Poly. 5:2). Similarly, one who partakes of the "death-bearing fruit" of heresy "dies immediately" (Tral. 11:1). We might call this "realized perdition" since the principle of salvation has really been lost and a principle of death has taken its place. But just as the attainment of salvation cannot be finalized prior to biological death, the same is true of damnation. As long as we remain in this life, "we still have opportunity to repent into God" (Smyr. 9:1). For those who live out their faith with love and endurance, biological "dying" (τὸ ἀποθανεῖν) is the pathway to God and therefore not to be looked upon with dread (Magn. 5:2). It can even be viewed as a "birth" into new life (Rom. 6:1). Spiritual death is the real "dying" (likewise τὸ ἀποθανεῖν), which one can, however, "escape" by believing in Jesus' death (Tral. 2:1). Taken out of context, Ignatius's description of salvation as an escape from death, or as a "nondeath" (Eph. 20:2), can sound like a failure to take human temporality and biological death seriously, but it is actually his way of teaching his readers that separation from God is the one "death" that they should really dread.

Ignatius believes that the Lord Jesus forgives the sins of anyone who repents (Phld. 8:1), but he does not teach a doctrine of imputed righteousness. Speaking for himself, he does not claim to "have been justified" already (Rom. 5:1) but hopes to "be justified" in the future (Phld. 8:2), presumably in a post-mortem judgment. As we saw in chapter five, redemption entails an objective transformation of the human person. In order to be "saved,"[12] one must be "sanctified" (Eph. 2:2), "perfected" (3:1), and "found blameless" at the judgment (Tral. 13:3). Those who are "reprobated" by God (Rom. 8:3) or "found reprobate" (Tral. 12:3), however, "will not inherit the kingdom of God" but instead "depart into unquenchable fire" (Eph. 16:1–2). In either case, it is the objective condition of the human person before God that determines his or her eternal destiny (Magn. 10:2). Each of us will render an "account" before God, "who knows the hidden things" of our lives.[13] That is why it is so important "not only to be called Christians but to be such" (Magn. 4:1). This does not, however, mean that Ignatius substitutes a doctrine of justification by works for the Pauline doctrine of justification by faith. He understands faith to have an indispensable role in the redemption of the human person. One is justi-

---

12. Smyr. 2:1, Poly. 1:2, Phld. 5:2.
13. Magn. 3:2; cf. Eph. 15:3.

fied and saved by faith in Jesus Christ, and those who fail to "believe in the blood of Christ" face condemnation.[14] But as we learned in chapters 5 and 7, faith is intrinsically related to love and endurance, so that a person must "believe with love" and persevere to the end in order to be saved.

According to Virginia Corwin, Ignatius's references to "the coming wrath" (*Eph.* 11:1) and "unquenchable fire" (16:2) are little more than the "trappings of Jewish eschatology," and the fact that they are interspersed among expressions of realized eschatology reflects his "state of uneasy indecision" between two concepts of judgment: the Johannine concept of realized eschatology, according to which "men exclude themselves from unity with God" by their "present refusal" of grace, and the traditional Jewish notion of an "objective future testing."[15] She finds evidence of Ignatius's indecision especially in the following passage.

> The last times are here. For the remainder, let us be ashamed and fear the long-suffering of God, in order that it not become a judgment against us. For let us either fear the coming wrath or love the present grace, one of the two, only to be found in Christ Jesus for true life. (*Eph.* 11:1)

As Corwin reads this text, Ignatius is telling his readers that they can understand judgment in either of two ways. According to the first way, one judges himself in this life by accepting or refusing grace; but according to the second way, one is judged by God after death. Ignatius does not really know which of these views is correct, but he is "able to endure" this indecision "because he is utterly certain that the matter is not an essential part of the Christian gospel." His last word on the subject amounts to "a denial that notions of eschatology are important."[16]

This interpretation of the passage, and of Ignatius's eschatology generally, is sorely mistaken. He certainly thinks that we decide our own fate by choosing either life or death, God or "the world," and that we do so in the flesh, by the way we live and die. But he would never separate this perspective from the idea of God's objective, post-mortem judgment of us. Our faith and love, or their absence, determine whether we bear God's "imprint" or the world's, and this makes all the difference (*Magn.* 5:1–2). In *Ephesians* 11:1, Ignatius is not offering his readers two different doctrines or concepts of eschatology and leaving it up to them to choose the one they prefer. That would be completely out of character for him. Rather, he is offering them two different ways to motivate themselves to live

---

14. Phld. 5:2, 8:2; Smyr. 6:1.
16. Ibid., 174.

15. *St. Ignatius and Christianity*, 173–74.

out an authentic Christian existence. They are invited to consider either the present effects of grace or the prospect of future wrath. The contrast he poses is, however, not only between future wrath and present grace but between fear and love. Underlying his formulation is a biblical principle: "The fear of God is the beginning of loving him" (timor Dei initium dilectionis eius; Sir 25:16). Fear of judgment is the primary motivation of novices in the faith, whereas the proficient are motivated more and more by love of God, until finally "perfect loves casts out fear" (1 Jn 4:18).[17] Ignatius considers the Ephesian church a generally mature group of Christians and appeals to their love for the God who indwells them by grace, but he recognizes that there are some members of their community who still need to be motivated by the salutary fear of future judgment.[18] This does not at all mean that either present grace or future judgment can stand on its own as a concept of eschatology. Properly understood, the two ideas imply each other.

Richard A. Bower offers a similar misreading when he observes that Ignatius's eschatology is "not futuristic in the apocalyptic sense" and concludes on this basis that for Ignatius "final salvation or perfection can be realized immediately" in this life.[19] As we have seen, Ignatius does hold to realized eschatology in the sense that the principle of "life" that brings us to eternal salvation is received now, in this life. But to say that "final" salvation can be realized "immediately" is a contradiction in terms. The defect in Bower's argument is in supposing that the relative paucity of apocalyptic imagery and the abundance of expressions of realized eschatology in Ignatius's letters amount to a concept of eschatology that is not futuristic in any sense. But in fact, Ignatius's eschatology lays a heavy emphasis on the future. In some respects his eschatology is more future-oriented than even that found in the Pauline letters. We have already seen that he speaks of being "justified" and "saved" as that which is yet to come, and we have not even touched on his many references to "hope," to "attaining God," and to the "resurrection" of believers.

Now, it remains to be seen whether his focus is entirely on personal eschatology, such that the future in view is simply that which lies ahead of each individual, or whether his eschatology includes also a historical and "general" component. But that is another question. Even if the only

---

17. Augustine deftly combines the two biblical statements into a single axiom: "Piety begins with fear and is perfected in love" (De vera religione 17:33; CCSL 32.207; pietas timore incohatur, caritate perficitur).
18. He appeals to their love for God in Eph. 9:2 and 15:3 and warns of judgment in 16:1–17:2.
19. "Meaning of ΕΠΙΤΥΓΧΑΝΩ," 13.

futuristic element in Ignatian eschatology turns out to be that of the individual—that is, his or her post-mortem judgment and resurrection—it would be wrong to describe such eschatology as "realized" in the sense that Bower gives that term. The whole Ignatian corpus, which is dominated by the author's anxious concern for his own salvation and that of his readers, stands opposed to the idea that one can attain final salvation immediately. Ignatius explicitly says that the essential "work" of Christianity is not accomplished in the "present profession" of faith (νῦν ἐπαγγελία) but must be lived out "unto the end" (εἰς τέλος; Eph. 14:2). By framing the question of eschatology as a choice between "futuristic in the apocalyptic sense" and "realized" in a radical sense, Bower takes no account for Ignatius's teleological view of human temporality and the great importance that he places on biological death as the individual's one "opportunity" (καιρός) to seal the deal on his or her eternal destiny (Rom. 2:1).

With respect to the question of whether Ignatius's eschatology is personal or communal, Bower correctly recognizes that this is a false dichotomy, pointing out that, for Ignatius, the individual can "attain God" only "within the unity of the Church."[20] Ignatius does not expect to attain God on his own, without the love and prayers of other Christians.[21] Still, given Ignatius's enthusiastic promotion of ecclesial unity, the degree to which his eschatology focuses on the destiny of the individual is somewhat surprising, at least at first glance. One must recall, however, that the grace of Christ is the cause both of intrapersonal and of interpersonal unity, and that these two require and reinforce each other. To live according to Jesus Christ is to grow into the fullness of humanity in all its dimensions. By placing before man "both death and life," the mystery of redemption discloses the teleology of human action and calls forth the full dignity of the individual.

Employing what seems to have been a standard formula, Ignatius indicates the gravity and ultimacy of human freedom when he affirms that "each will depart to his own place" (Magn. 5:1). This might be a "place" of perdition (Acts 1:25), or a "deserved place of glory" (1 Clem. 5:4).[22] In the

---

20. Ibid.
21. Cf. Eph. 1:2, 3:1; Magn. 14:1; Tral. 12:3; Rom. 8:3; Phld. 5:1, 8:2; Smyr. 11:1.
22. Clement also calls this "the holy place" (1 Clem. 5:7) and in another eschatological context refers to "a place among the godly" (50:3). Polycarp assures his readers that Ignatius and his fellow martyrs are now "in the place deserved by them, with the Lord" (Phil. 9:2). Wishing to remove from Ignatian eschatology any hint of belief in an intermediate state of the blessed, Mellink much too facilely dissociates Magn. 5:1 from this impressive series of near-contemporary

latter case, however, one's "own place" is certainly not a place of isolation but a place within the unity of the church in heaven, for Ignatius expects the interpersonal communion now enjoyed among the members of the church on earth to continue on the other side of death.[23] Christians are "temple stones" prepared to be raised up and to take their place in "the edifice of God the Father" (Eph. 9:1). This is also the sense of the controversial parabolic saying according to which "a head cannot be born separately, apart from the members" (Tral. 11:2). The point is not to make Jesus Christ dependent on his church but to indicate that the humanity of Jesus Christ and the humanity of all his disciples are glorified according to a single "plan" or "arrangement," the "οἰκονομία concerning the new man Jesus Christ" (Eph. 20:1), so that together they form "one body" (Smyr. 1:2).

The Historical Dimension of Eschatology

Thus far we have determined that Ignatius's eschatology includes complementary realized and future dimensions, as well as complementary personal and communal dimensions. But does it also have a properly historical dimension? Because Ignatius focuses on the way the drama of Christian existence plays out within the context of *vita usque ad mortem* and presents biological death as the portal through which believers must pass in order to attain God, it is not immediately apparent whether the future unfolding of universal human history retains any real importance in his eschatology. Ignatius obviously anticipates his own eschatological horizon and that of other believers, but does he also anticipate an eschatological horizon for universal history? And if so, do the second coming of Christ, a general resurrection, and a final judgment have a place within this expectation? The seven letters provide us with just enough evidence to answer these questions affirmatively, but admittedly the properly historical dimension of eschatology is mostly implicit and plays a relatively minor role in Ignatius's presentation of the divine economy.

As we have seen throughout this study, for Ignatius the decisive point of reference within the historical economy of redemption is the Christ event, and this applies also to eschatology. It is Jesus Christ's appearance "at the end" (*Magn.* 6:1) that situates Ignatius and his readers within the

---

"place" texts and forces upon it an interpretation that makes Ignatius refer only to "this-worldly consequences of one's actions" (Death as Eschaton, 338, cf. 328–29).

23. Eph. 2:2; Tral. 13:3.

"last times" (*Eph.* 11:1). Israel's prophets anticipated Christ's first coming within history, which turned out to be their eschatological resurrection from the dead (*Magn.* 9:2). Presumably Ignatius refers here to a bodily resurrection and not merely a spiritual one (cf. Mt 27:52–53), and that would make the prophets a conspicuous exception with regard to any concept of a future general resurrection that Ignatius may have held. He also stresses the importance of Christ's first advent by referring to it with the participle παρών (*Magn.* 9:2) and the related noun παρουσία (*Phld.* 9:2). The latter word, as is well known, usually serves as a technical term in early Christian literature with reference to the second coming. Ignatius's transference of it to the context of the first advent seems to be purposeful.

Corwin is on the right track when she says that Ignatius's use of παρουσία with reference to the first coming reflects "his belief that this was a definitive and absolute event fully consummated," but she draws the wrong conclusion when she adds, "It also shows his abandonment of the notion of the second coming."[24] The Christ event is indeed definitive and absolute, but as I have noted repeatedly it is precisely this definitiveness that bestows a transcendent character and real significance upon the entire historical economy and upon each of its moments. The definitiveness of the first coming is what creates the expectation of a second coming and makes that coming necessary. In any case, Ignatius's reference to ἔσχατοι καιροί ("last times"), together with his relatively frequent references to future judgment and future resurrection, implies the expectation of a further consummation of history—not one that is more definitive than the Christ event, to be sure, but one that participates in the definitiveness of the Christ event while having its own integral importance within the historical economy. Moreover, Ignatius does make one passing but tolerably clear allusion to Christ's second coming, when he instructs Polycarp, "Study the times [καιρούς]. Await [προσδόκα] the one who is beyond time" (*Poly.* 3:2). As noted in chapter 6, Ignatius presents a kind of parallelism between the way the Old Testament prophets "awaited" (προσεδόκων) Christ's first advent and the way Christians "endure, in order that we may be found to be disciples of Jesus Christ" at the last judgment (*Magn.* 9:1–2). This parallelism reflects Ignatius's biblical sense for typology, whereby he discerns and displays something of the coherence of the historical economy of redemption. Within his the-

---

24. *St. Ignatius and Christianity*, 169, n. 20.

ology he certainly subordinates the second coming to the first coming, and also to personal eschatology, but this by no means amounts to an "abandonment" of the very notion of the second coming.

Ignatius employs the traditional language of "resurrection" (ἀνάστασις, ἀναστῆναι), not only when referring to Christ's resurrection, but also when he speaks of the hope of Christians.[25] Though he does not elaborate on what "resurrection" will mean for Christians, it is a priori unlikely that someone whose theology has been so profoundly influenced by the Pauline epistles would use this language to refer to a merely "spiritual" resurrection or to express a radically "realized" eschatology.[26] The great importance that Ignatius places on the fact that Jesus was still "in the flesh" after his own resurrection makes it even less likely that he would anticipate anything other than bodily resurrection for those who prove to be Jesus' disciples. Indeed, Ignatius explicitly says that God the Father will raise those who believe in Jesus "in a similar manner" (κατὰ τὸ ὁμοίωμα) to the way he raised Jesus from the dead (Tral. 9:2). Unbelievers, by contrast, will end up "bodiless and phantasmal" (Smyr. 2:1). While this statement may be in tension with the traditional notion of a "resurrection of both the righteous and the unrighteous,"[27] it coheres with the Ignatian soteriological anthropology we explored in chapter 4. If redemption is the "unity of flesh and spirit"—that is, the full integrity of the human person—it makes sense that damnation would be an absence of such fullness and integrity. If the spiritualization of the fleshly dimension transforms and glorifies it, the failure to spiritualize the flesh should result in a condition that amounts to a mere shadow of the true self.

Ignatius's apparent belief in a general resurrection of the body raises the question of an intermediate state. Charles E. Hill aptly observes that many of Ignatius's expressions of hope convey the expectation that those who endure to the end will enter into the presence of God immediately after death. Hill points in this regard to Ignatius's anticipation of entering a realm of "pure light" (Rom. 6:2), to the aphorism, "Near the sword, near God; in the midst of beasts, in the midst of God" (Smyr. 4:2), and especially to Ignatius's frequently expressed hope to "attain God."[28] Though the vast majority of these passages refer to Ignatius's attainment

25. Eph. 11:2; Tral. sal.; Rom. 4:3; Smyr. 5:3, 7:1–2; Poly. 7:1.
26. See 2 Tm 2:18; 1 Cor 15:12–58.
27. Acts 24:15; cf. Jn 5:29.
28. *Regnum Caelorum: Patterns of Millennial Thought in Early Christianity* (Grand Rapids, Mich.: Eerdmans, 2001), 87–90.

of the special "lot" marked out for him as a martyr, Hill rightly rejects the idea that Ignatius holds forth the hope for immediate entry into God's presence only in the case of martyrs while believing that other Christians will have to wait for the general resurrection to "attain God."[29] More likely, Ignatius holds that all authentic Christians enjoy some sort of spiritual access to God's presence immediately after death (as opposed to being detained in Hades) and that all await the consummate glorification of their humanity in the general resurrection.

Three of Ignatius's formulations can plausibly be read as implying a distinction between the two stages.

> ... if indeed through suffering *I attain God*,
> so that I may be found to be your disciple in the resurrection. (Poly. 7:1)

> It is good to set *from the world to God*,
> in order to rise to him. (Rom. 2:2)

> But if I suffer, *I shall be a freedman of Jesus Christ*,
> and shall rise free in him. (Rom. 4:3)

Each passage begins with a reference to suffering and death and ends with a reference to resurrection (presumably at the end of time), and in each passage the italicized phrase can be taken to refer to the soul's intermediate state of blessedness in God's presence. I suggest this merely as an intriguing possibility. Other interpretations of these passages are admittedly possible.[30] In any case, neither the gap between biological death and the general resurrection nor the delay of the parousia seems to trouble Ignatius. What matters is that one live out faith and love "perfectly" (τελείως) and thus "be found unto the end" (εὑρεθῇ εἰς τέλος; Eph. 14:1–2). Biological death is the point at which one either definitively secures or definitively forfeits the redemption of his or her humanity.

Since the seven letters were written by a man who anticipated his

---

29. Tral. 12:3; Rom. 1:2; Phld. 5:1; Hill, *Regnum Caelorum*, 85–87. Wayne Willis, on the other hand, citing evidence from the mid-second to the mid-third century, understands Ignatius to have believed in the martyr's special eschatological privilege ("Martyr Eschatology: Ignatius' Use of Epitugchanō," *Restoration Quarterly* 10 [1967]: 81–88).

30. Ignoring them is another matter, however. In his discussion of a possible intermediate state in Ignatian eschatology, Mellink makes no reference to Poly. 7:1 or Rom. 4:3. He touches on Rom. 2:2 briefly but only in order to paraphrase it in terms of "setting from the world and rising to God," thus collapsing Ignatius's curious formulation into a bland two-part schema of death and resurrection (*Death as Eschaton*, 338). By "bypass[ing] the whole problem of an intermediate state," Ignatius stands apart from his contemporaries Clement and Polycarp and closer to Luther and Barth as "a witness of evangelical teaching on death" (339, 342). According to Mellink, because God's eternity transcends human time, "death and eschaton, as it were, collapse into a single moment" (342).

own death within a matter of weeks, we can forgive their author if he places an inordinate emphasis on personal eschatology.[31] Ignatius anticipates his own redemption and also (sometimes in the same breath) expresses fear that he may fall short and be condemned,[32] but he expresses similar hopes and fears for his readers and others.[33] Likewise, he speaks frequently of his own hope to "attain God" but makes it clear that this is the goal of every Christian (Magn. 1:3). While he never explicitly refers to a general resurrection or a universal final judgment, his various eschatological statements are best understood to presuppose these. The fact that Ignatius has borrowed the phrase "will not inherit the kingdom of God" from Paul hardly constitutes evidence that he did not own or understand the concept.[34] Even the somewhat off-handed remark that Jesus Christ "will not be ashamed of" the Smyrnaeans probably reflects anticipation of a final judgment.[35] Ignatius's lack of interest in apocalyptic scenarios and his reserve with regard to the futuristic dimension of historical eschatology should in any case be viewed as points in his favor within the context of second-century theology. Unlike Justin, Irenaeus, and Tertullian, the bishop of Antioch does not appear to have been tempted down the path to chiliasm.[36]

"Hope" (ἐλπίς, ἐλπίζω) is Ignatius's most comprehensive eschatological concept, and one that in its own way reflects the coherence of the truths of the faith. Ignatius speaks of hope in such a way as to indicate both the definitiveness of the Christ event and the historical continuity of old and new within the economy of redemption. The "newness of hope" is distinctive of Christianity over against Judaism (Magn. 9:1), but because Israel's prophets already "hoped" in Christ they are "numbered together with us in the gospel of the common hope" (Phld. 5:2). Indeed, Jesus Christ is hope's past, present, and future. Hope has come into the world through the Christ event and is now available in Christ and in the life of the church, and it is Jesus Christ "the perfect hope" who will either "honor" or "be ashamed of" those who stand before him at the final judgment.[37] Ignatius thus frequently identifies the person of Jesus

---

31. Goltz, Ignatius von Antiochien, 38–39.
32. Eph. 11:2; Tral. 12:3; Rom. 8:3.
33. Eph. 11:1, 16:1–2; Tral. sal., 9:2; Smyr. 6:1, 7:1; Poly. 4:3.
34. Eph. 16:1; Phld. 3:3; cf. 1 Cor 6:9–10, 15:50; Gal 5:21; Eph 5:5.
35. Smyr. 10:2; cf. Mk 8:38.
36. The upshot of Hill's argument in *Regnum Caelorum* is that those who, like Ignatius, did not embrace chiliasm were in this respect in continuity with the New Testament, whereas chiliasm represents a real aberration within the early development of the theological tradition.
37. Phld. 11:2; Smyr. 10:2.

as "our hope" or "our common hope."[38] As used in the Ignatian letters, "hope" combines eschatology's realized and future dimensions, as well as its personal and communal aspects. If we "conduct our lives" now in him who is our hope, "we shall be found" to be in him after death (*Tral.* 2:2). This is no guarantee of final salvation, however, since one may still "be turned away" from Christ anytime prior to biological death (*Magn.* 11:1). An individual such as Ignatius "hopes" to attain God, but he hopes to do so through the prayers of others Christians, so that Jesus Christ is "the common name and hope" (*Eph.* 1:2). It is especially when Christians come together liturgically that they experience the "one hope" that unites them (*Magn.* 7:1). This "common hope" for life beyond death does not amount to a denial of the goodness of the material creation but rather reflects the unity of the human person, for Christians "hope" in Jesus "with flesh, soul, and spirit" (*Phld.* 11:2). Nor does the fact that Christians possess this hope as something that unites them over against "the world" indicate a lack of appreciation for the essential solidarity of the human race and the universality of God's saving will. Believers in Christ not only possess hope for themselves but hold forth the "hope of repentance" for those outside the church (*Eph.* 10:1).

An Economy of Life, Truth, and Unity

In this volume I hope to have shown that the seven authentic letters of Ignatius of Antioch contain a sophisticated, cohesive, and substantially complete theology. After dealing with Ignatius's approach to Scripture and other prolegomena (chapters 1 and 2), I explored his relatively advanced Christology and nascent Trinitarianism (chapter 3), his soteriological flesh-and-spirit anthropology and understanding of spiritual warfare (chapter 4), his authentically biblical aretology of faith and love and teleological view of redemption (chapter 5), his nuanced presentation of the relationship between Judaism and Christianity (chapter 6), his utilization of the word-and-silence paradox (chapter 7), his insight into the Christ event as "mystery" (chapter 8), his multifaceted ecclesiology (chapter 9), and his fairly well-rounded eschatology (the present chapter). Throughout, I have attempted to demonstrate both Ignatius's fundamental continuity with the New Testament and some of the ways in which he adumbrates the patristic and Scholastic theological tradition.

---

38. *Magn.* 11:1; *Tral.* sal., 2:2; *Eph.* 21:2; *Phld.* 11:2.

If some readers find all this to amount to a maximalist interpretation of the letters, I readily admit that I have intended it to be at least a generous and sympathetic one. For centuries Ignatius has been underestimated by his admirers and vilified by his foes. It seemed to me that the time had come for someone to make the best possible case for regarding him as a theologian to be reckoned with. By way of conclusion, I would like to make a final attempt to demonstrate the coherence of his presentation of the divine economy by drawing together three of its most salient themes: life, truth, and unity.

As presented by Ignatius of Antioch, the mystery of redemption is fundamentally an economy of life. When we looked at his soteriology in chapter 5, we saw that he rarely speaks in terms of the forgiveness of sins and is much more apt to conceive of redemption as a principle of new life that delivers the believer from spiritual death. The Christ event itself is a mystery of "true life in death" (Eph. 7:2), and so the life of the believer becomes a kind of parallel mystery, as he or she "suffers with" Christ in order to participate also in his life.[39] Likewise, in the present chapter we have seen that Ignatian eschatology is at root a matter of life and death. Those who believe in Jesus have already received "his life," but they must secure it as an everlasting possession by directing their own biological death into his passion (Magn. 5:2). At the same time, however, throughout this study we have learned from Ignatius that the economy of redemption is essentially a matter of God's self-revelation or "manifestation" in Jesus Christ.[40] The divine plan of salvation is therefore at its core an economy of truth. Because Jesus Christ is God's Word, "the mouth that cannot lie, in whom the Father has spoken truthfully" (Rom. 8:2), it is crucial to know the things that Jesus has "truly accomplished" (Magn. 11:1) and to "speak about Jesus Christ in truth" (Eph. 6:2). Authentic Christians are thus "children of the light of truth" (Phld. 2:1) who possess an "intense desire for the truth" (Poly. 7:3). The mystery of redemption is therefore simultaneously an economy of life and an economy of truth.

How do these two aspects of the economy cohere? In chapter 9 I touched on the fact that Ignatius virtually equates the truth of orthodox doctrine with the new life or "imperishability" that the risen Lord has breathed into his church, while he correspondingly identifies the false doctrine of heretics as a principle of death and corruption. Indeed, the largely implicit equation between truth and life is an integral aspect of the

---

39. Rom. 6:2–3; Smyr. 1:1, 4:2.
40. Eph. 19:3, Magn. 6:1, 8:2.

Johannine substratum of Ignatian theology. Its effects are felt everywhere. It is present, for example, in Ignatius's "flesh and spirit" anthropology and his "faith and love" aretology. By faith, one lays hold of the truth of revelation with the intellect, but because this revelation is not simply an idea but a life—a truth that is life—a person only truly possesses it by living it out concretely "in a fleshly and spiritual manner," that is, by "believing with love."[41] At the same time, it is impossible to live a life of Christian charity without knowing and adhering to the objective truth of the gospel. Christianity is neither a purely vertical gnosis nor a merely horizontal ethic. It is rather a *mysterium*, that is, a divine self-communication that has come to us in the midst of our temporality and the history of our race, conferring on that temporality and history a transcendent dimension. The gospel is truly God's word, which descends from on high, but this descent is mediated by a concrete history of salvation—Moses, the prophets, Jesus Christ, the apostles, the church—and it must be appropriated and lived out "unto the end" within the teleological temporality of one's life and the eschatologically oriented history of the church.

The truth that is life is also and at the same time "unity." It begins with the eternal Trinitarian union of "Jesus and the Father" in the Holy Spirit, and it is communicated to the world through the economy of creation and redemption. Coming forth from the "silence" of this eternal mystery, the Logos begins to speak forth the mystery of God in the creation of the world and through Israel's prophets, and he manifests it "humanly" in a personal and definitive manner through his own "union of flesh and spirit" in the mysteries of his incarnate life.[42] Ignatius describes himself as "a man constituted for unity" (Phld. 8:1), but in an important sense every human being is already constituted for unity according to the order of creation. As a rational creature, man is made to "hear" God's self-communication in all its modalities. As a creature of flesh and spirit whose life is embedded in temporality, man is made for concrete "actions" (πράγματα) that have a τέλος (Magn. 5:1). As members of the brotherhood of humanity (Eph. 10:1–3), human beings are made also for interpersonal unity, though they are to love God above all (9:2). While Ignatius never speaks directly of a primal fall, he is keenly aware of the problem of sin—emphasizing vices such as pride, anger, selfish ambition, and lust, which work against intrapersonal and interpersonal unity—and he has personal experience of the diabolical "envy" that would

---

41. Magn. 5:2; Phld. 9:2; Eph. 10:3; Smyr. 13:2.
42. Eph. 19:3; Magn. 1:2.

keep human beings from attaining the goal for which they have been created (*Tral.* 4:2). Satan attempts to sow seeds of falsehood among the members of the church in order to "torment" and divide them, but when Christians come together often for eucharist they thwart Satan's destructive ways by their "unanimity in the faith."[43]

The truth, life, and unity that constitute God's redemptive self-communication are fully present in the person and event of Jesus Christ. As definitive revealer of the Father, he is the "one teacher," and he himself is the truth that he teaches (*Eph.*15:1). The essential practice of Christianity is thus χριστομαθία, learning the person of Christ (*Phld.* 8:2), and the goal of our lives is "that we may be found to be disciples [μαθηταί] of Jesus Christ our only teacher" (*Magn.* 9:1). Because this revelation has come to us in the mystery of Christ's earthly life, knowing the truth of that mystery is a matter of vital importance. In order to become "perfect," the believer must possess Jesus' word and listen to his silence (*Eph.* 15:2). The gospel consists of the objective fact of Christ's advent, passion, and resurrection (*Phld.* 9:2), but it also includes his commandments and those of the apostles (*Magn.* 13:1). And so it calls for a concretely lived response with a moral dimension. The gospel is the "perfection of imperishability" (*Phld.* 9:2) and the "newness of eternal life" (*Eph.* 19:3), but because this life is also truth, faith is not "pure Pauline trust" but has an objective intellectual content. That is why heresy "corrupts" the true faith that has come to us from God (16:2).

Since God's self-revelation has come into the world in the concrete historical event of Jesus Christ, it is transmitted from generation to generation and made available to men and women in and through a concrete historical church. Though Ignatius has developed no doctrine of tradition or theory of apostolic succession, he knows that the churches must remain "always in accord with the apostles" if they are to be in union with Jesus Christ (11:2). Because Jesus revealed his eternal union with the Father by submitting to the Father in the somatic concreteness of his historical existence, and because the apostles received this revelation by submitting "to Christ and to the Father," the local church must have its own authority structure, and its members must "submit to the bishop and to one another" (*Magn.* 13:2). Ignatius does not view the threefold ecclesiastical hierarchy as a necessary evil but as a blessing from God and an integral aspect of the divine economy.[44] But because the truth of

---

43. *Eph.* 8:1, 9:1, 13:1.
44. *Eph.* 1:3, 5:1, 6:1.

revelation is no mere doctrine but also a principle of divine life, and because the bishop and his presbyters are to exercise no merely human authority, the risen Lord has breathed into his church "the gift" of the Holy Spirit (*Eph.* 17:1–2). The apostolic doctrine must be taught, received, and lived "in the power of Jesus Christ" (11:2); the bishop must be "clothed with grace" (*Poly.* 1:2) and "abound in every charism" (2:2); and all must live out the true faith in concrete acts of charity that demonstrate that they have assimilated the "mind-set of God" (*Smyr.* 6:2). Finally, because the truth and life that God communicates to human beings is fundamentally a participation in his own Trinitarian unity, this gift can only be received and lived out within the communal life of the church. When Christians reverence and love one another and allow nothing to divide them but remain united to their bishop, their church becomes a "type and teaching" of the "imperishability" that comes forth from God and leads back to God (*Magn.* 6:2).

BIBLIOGRAPHY

Aland, Kurt, ed. *Synopsis Quattuor Evangeliorum: Locis parallelis evangeliorum apocryphorum et partum adhibitis*. 14th ed. Stuttgart: Deutsche Bibelgesellschaft, 1995.
Allison, Dale C., Jr. *The New Moses: A Matthean Typology*. Edinburgh: T. & T. Clark, 1993.
Augustine of Hippo. *Basic Writings of St. Augustine*. Edited with an introduction and notes by Whitney J. Oates. 2 vols. New York: Random House, 1948.
Balthasar, Hans Urs von. *Convergences: To the Source of the Christian Mystery*. Translated by E. A. Nelson. San Francisco: Ignatius Press, 1983.
———. *Explorations in Theology*. Vol. 1, *The Word Made Flesh*. Translated by A. V. Littledale with Alexander Dru. San Francisco: Ignatius Press, 1989.
———. *The Glory of the Lord: A Theological Aesthetics*. Vol. 7, *Theology: The New Covenant*. Translated by Erasmo Leiva-Merikakis. San Francisco: Ignatius Press, 1989.
Barnard, L. W. *Studies in the Apostolic Fathers and Their Background*. New York: Schocken Books, 1966.
Bartsch, Hans-Werner. *Gnostisches Gut und Gemeindetradition bei Ignatius von Antiochien*. Gütersloh: Bertelsmann, 1940.
Bauer, Walter. *Orthodoxy and Heresy in Earliest Christianity*. Edited by Robert A. Kraft and Gerhard Krodel. Translated by a team from the Philadelphia Seminar on Christian Origins. Philadelphia: Fortress Press, 1971.
Bauer, Walter, Frederick William Danker, W. F. Arndt, and F. W. Gingrich, eds. *Greek-English Lexicon of the New Testament and Other Early Christian Literature*. 3rd ed. Chicago: University of Chicago Press, 2000.
Beale, G. K. *The Book of Revelation: A Commentary on the Greek Text*. New International Greek Testament Commentary. Grand Rapids, Mich.: Eerdmans, 1999.
Beatrice, Pier Franco. "The 'Gospel according to the Hebrews' in the Apostolic Fathers." *Novum Testamentum* 48 (2006): 147–95.
Benedict XVI, Pope. *Church Fathers: From Clement of Rome to Augustine*. San Francisco: Ignatius Press, 2008.
Bergamelli, Ferdinando. "Cristo 'l'uomo nuovo' e 'l'uomo perfetto' in Ignazio di Antiochia (*Efesini* 20,1; *Smirnesi* 4,2)." *Studia Patristica* 26 (1993): 103–12.
———. "Dal Padre al Padre: Il Padre come principio e termine del Cristo e del cristiano in Ignazio di Antiochia." *Studia Patristica* 36 (2001): 168–76.

———. "'Fede di Gesù Cristo' nelle lettere di Ignazio di Antiochia." *Studia Patristica* 40 (2006): 339–51.

Bertrand, Daniel Alain. *Le baptême de Jésus: Histoire de l'exégèse aux deux premiers siècles.* Beiträge zur Geschichte der Biblischen Exegese 14. Tübingen: J. C. B. Mohr, 1973.

Bieler, Martin. "The Mysteries of Jesus' Public Life: Stages on the Way to the Cross." *Communio* 29 (2002): 47–61.

Blass, F., A. Debrunner, and Robert W. Funk. *A Greek Grammar of the New Testament and Other Early Christian Literature.* Chicago: University of Chicago Press, 1961.

Boersma, Hans. *Nouvelle Théologie and Sacramental Ontology: A Return to Mystery.* Oxford: Oxford University Press, 2009.

Bommes, Karin. *Weizen Gottes: Untersuchungen zur Theologie des Martyriums bei Ignatius von Antiochien.* Theophaneia: Beiträge zur Religions- und Kirchengeschichte des Altertums 27. Cologne: Peter Hanstein Verlag, 1976.

Bower, Richard A. "The Meaning of ΕΠΙΤΥΓΧΑΝΩ in the Epistles of St. Ignatius of Antioch." *Vigiliae Christianae* 28 (1974): 1–14.

Brent, Allen. "Ignatius and the Imperial Cult." *Vigiliae Christianae* 52 (1998): 30–58.

———. *Ignatius of Antioch and the Second Sophistic: A Study of an Early Christian Transformation of Pagan Culture.* Studien und Texte zu Antike und Christentum 36. Tübingen: Mohr Siebeck, 2006.

———. *Ignatius of Antioch: A Martyr Bishop and the Origin of Episcopacy.* London: T. & T. Clark Continuum, 2009.

Bright, Pamela. "Augustine." In *Reading Romans through the Centuries: From the Early Church to Karl Barth*, edited by Jeffrey P. Greenman and Timothy Larsen, 59–80. Grand Rapids, Mich.: Brazos Press, 2005.

Brown, Milton Perry. *The Authentic Writings of Ignatius: A Study of Linguistic Criteria.* Durham, N.C.: Duke University Press, 1963.

Brown, Raymond E. *The Birth of the Messiah: A Commentary on the Infancy Narratives in the Gospels of Matthew and Luke.* 2nd ed. Anchor Bible Reference Library. New York: Doubleday, 1993.

Brown, Raymond E., and John P. Meier. *Antioch and Rome: New Testament Cradles of Catholic Christianity.* New York: Paulist Press, 1983.

Bruce, F. F. *The Epistle to the Galatians: A Commentary on the Greek Text.* New International Greek Testament Commentary. Grand Rapids, Mich.: Eerdmans, 1982.

Burghardt, Walter J. "Did Saint Ignatius of Antioch Know the Fourth Gospel?" *Theological Studies* 1 (1940): 1–26, 130–56.

Burke, Patrick. "The Monarchical Episcopate at the End of the First Century." *Journal of Ecumenical Studies* 7 (1970): 499–518.

Camelot, P.-Th. *Ignace d'Antioche, Polycarpe de Smyrne: Lettres, Martyre de Polycarpe: Texte Grec, introduction, traduction et notes.* 4th ed. Sources chrétiennes 10. Paris: Cerf, 1969.

Catechism of the Catholic Church. 2nd ed. Vatican City: Libreria Editrice Vaticana, 1997.

Chadwick, Henry. "The Silence of Bishops in Ignatius." *Harvard Theological Review* 43 (1950): 169–72.

Childs, Brevard S. *Isaiah.* Old Testament Library. Louisville, Ky.: Westminster John Knox Press, 2001.

Conzelmann, Hans. *Gentiles—Jews—Christians: Polemics and Apologetics in the Greco-Roman Era*. Translated by M. Eugene Boring. Minneapolis, Minn.: Fortress Press, 1992.

Cooper, Michael. "Virginia Corwin Brautigam, 95, Pioneer in Comparative Religion." *New York Times*, August 24, 1996. Available online at http://www.nytimes.com/1996/08/24/us/virginia-corwin-brautigam-95-pioneer-in-comparative-religion.html.

Corwin, Virginia. *St. Ignatius and Christianity in Antioch*. New Haven, Conn.: Yale University Press, 1960.

Cranfield, C. E. B. *A Critical and Exegetical Commentary on the Epistle to the Romans*. International Critical Commentary. Edinburgh: T. & T. Clark, 1979.

Daniélou, Jean. *The Development of Christian Doctrine Before the Council of Nicaea*. Vol. 1, *The Theology of Jewish Christianity*. Translated by John A. Baker. London: Darton, Longman & Todd, 1964.

Davies, Stevan L. "The Predicament of Ignatius of Antioch." *Vigiliae Christianae* 30 (1976): 175–80.

Dehandschutter, Boudewijn. "Ignatius, Letter to the Magnesians 8:2 Once Again." In *Jesus, Paul, and Early Christianity: Studies in Honour of Henk Jan de Jonge*, Supplements to Novum Testamentum 130, edited by Rieuwerd Buitenwerf, Harm W. Hollander, and Johannes Tromp, 89–99. Leiden: Brill, 2008.

Dietze, Paul. "Die Briefe des Ignatius und das Johannesevangelium." *Theologische Studien und Kritiken* 78 (1905): 563–603.

Donahue, Paul J. "Jewish Christianity in the Letters of Ignatius of Antioch." *Vigiliae Christianae* 32 (1978): 81–93.

Dostal, Robert J., ed. *The Cambridge Companion to Gadamer*. New York: Cambridge University Press, 2002.

Dunn, Geoffrey D. *Tertullian*. Early Church Fathers. London: Routledge, 2004.

Dunn, James D. G. *A Commentary on the Epistle to the Galatians*. Black's New Testament Commentaries. London: A. & C. Black, 1993.

Ehrman, Bart D., ed. and trans. *The Apostolic Fathers*. 2 vols. Loeb Classical Library. Cambridge, Mass.: Harvard University Press, 2003.

Evagrius Ponticus. *The Praktikos, Chapters on Prayer*. Translated by John Eudes Bamberger. Cistercian Studies 4. Kalamazoo, Mich.: Cistercian Publications, 1981.

Farrer, Austin. *The Revelation of St. John the Divine: A Commentary on the English Text*. Oxford: Clarendon Press, 1964.

Figal, Günter. "The Doing of the Thing Itself: Gadamer's Hermeneutic Ontology of Language." In *The Cambridge Companion to Gadamer*, edited by Robert J. Dostal, 102–25. New York: Cambridge University Press, 2002.

Fitzmyer, Joseph A. *Romans: A New Translation with Introduction and Commentary*. Anchor Bible 33. New York: Doubleday, 1993.

Foster, Paul. "The Epistles of Ignatius of Antioch and the Writings That Later Formed the New Testament." In *The Reception of the New Testament in the Apostolic Fathers*, edited by A. F. Gregory and C. M. Tuckett, 159–86. New York: Oxford University Press, 2005.

France, R. T. *The Gospel of Mark: A Commentary on the Greek Text*. New International Greek Testament Commentary. Grand Rapids, Mich.: Eerdmans, 2002.

Freedman, David Noel, ed. *Anchor Bible Dictionary.* 6 vols. New York: Doubleday, 1992.
Gadamer, Hans-Georg. *Philosophical Hermeneutics.* Translated and edited by David E. Linge. Berkeley and Los Angeles: University of California Press, 1976.
Gaston, Lloyd. "Judaism of the Uncircumcised in Ignatius and Related Writers." In *Anti-Judaism in Early Christianity,* vol. 2, *Separation and Polemic,* edited by Stephen G. Wilson, 33–44. Waterloo, Ont.: Wilfrid Laurier University Press, 1986.
Goltz, Eduard Freiherrn von der. *Ignatius von Antiochien als Christ und Theologe: Eine Dogmengeschichtliche Untersuchung.* Leipzig: J. C. Hinrichs, 1894.
Goulder, Michael D. "Ignatius' 'Docetists.'" *Vigiliae Christianae* 53 (1999): 16–30.
Grant, Robert M. *Ignatius of Antioch.* Vol. 4 of *The Apostolic Fathers: A New Translation and Commentary,* edited by Robert M. Grant. Camden, N.J.: Thomas Nelson & Sons, 1966.
———. "Scripture and Tradition in St. Ignatius of Antioch." *Catholic Biblical Quarterly* 25 (1963): 322–35.
Gregory, Andrew F., and Christopher M. Tuckett, eds. *The Reception of the New Testament in the Apostolic Fathers.* New York: Oxford University Press, 2005.
———. *Trajectories through the New Testament and the Apostolic Fathers.* New York: Oxford University Press, 2005.
Grillmeier, Aloys. *Christ in Christian Tradition.* Vol. 1, *From the Apostolic Age to Chalcedon (451).* 2nd ed. Translated by John Bowden. Atlanta: John Knox Press, 1975.
Grondin, Jean. "Gadamer's Basic Understanding of Understanding." In *The Cambridge Companion to Gadamer,* edited by Robert J. Dostal, 36–51. New York: Cambridge University Press, 2002.
Hall, Robert G. "Astonishment in the Firmament: The Worship of Jesus and Soteriology in Ignatius and the *Ascension of Isaiah.*" In *Jewish Roots of Christological Monotheism: Papers from the St. Andrews Conference on the Historical Origins of the Worship of Jesus,* Supplements to the Journal for the Study of Judaism, edited by Carey C. Newman, James R. Davila, and Gladys S. Lewis, 148–55. Leiden: Brill, 1999.
Halleux, André de. "'L'Église catholique' dan la letter ignacienne aux Smyrniotes." *Ephemerides Theologicae Lovanienses* 58 (1982): 5–24.
Hamell, P. J. "Monarchianism." In *New Catholic Encyclopedia,* 19 vols., 9.1019–20. Washington, D.C.: The Catholic University of America Press, 1967–1996.
Hammond Bammel, C. P. "Ignatian Problems." *Journal of Theological Studies* 33 (1982): 62–97.
Hartman, Lars. "Baptism." In *Anchor Bible Dictionary,* 6 vols., edited by David Noel Freedman, 1.583–94. New York: Doubleday, 1992.
Hatch, Edwin, and Henry A. Redpath. *A Concordance to the Septuagint and the Other Greek Versions of the Old Testament (including the Apocryphal Books).* 2 vols. and suppl. Grand Rapids, Mich.: Baker, 1987.
Haykin, Michael A. G. "'Come to the Father': Ignatius of Antioch and His Calling to Be a Martyr." *Themelios* 32 (2007): 26–39.
Hill, Charles E. "Ignatius and the Apostolate: The Witness of Ignatius to the Emergence of Christian Scripture." *Studia Patristica* 36 (2001): 226–48.
———. *Regnum Caelorum: Patterns of Millennial Thought in Early Christianity.* Grand Rapids, Mich.: Eerdmans, 2001.

———. *The Johannine Corpus in the Early Church*. Oxford: Oxford University Press, 2004.

———. "Ignatius, 'the Gospel,' and the Gospels." In *Trajectories through the New Testament and the Apostolic Fathers*, edited by A. F. Gregory and C. M. Tuckett, 267–85. New York: Oxford University Press, 2005.

Hoffman, Daniel. "The Authority of Scripture and Apostolic Doctrine in Ignatius of Antioch." *Journal of the Evangelical Theological Society* 28 (1985): 71–79.

Holmes, Michael W., ed. and trans. *The Apostolic Fathers: Greek Texts and English Translations*. 3rd ed. Grand Rapids, Mich.: Baker Academic, 2007.

Howell, Kenneth J. *Ignatius of Antioch: A New Translation and Theological Commentary*. Zanesville, Ohio: Coming Home Network International, 2008.

Hvidt, Niels Christian. *Christian Prophecy: The Post-Biblical Tradition*. Oxford: Oxford University Press, 2007.

Irenaeus of Lyons. *Proof of the Apostolic Preaching*. Translated and annotated by Joseph P. Smith. New York: Paulist Press, 1952.

———. *On the Apostolic Preaching*. Translated and introduced by John Behr. Crestwood, N.Y.: St. Vladimir's Seminary Press, 1997.

John of the Cross. *The Collected Works of St. John of the Cross*. Translated by Kieran Kavanaugh and Otilio Rodriguez, with introductions by Kieran Kavanaugh. Washington, D.C.: Institute of Carmelite Studies, 1979.

John Paul II, Pope. Apostolic Letter *Rosarium Virginis Mariae*. Issued October 16, 2002.

Joly, Robert. *Le dossier d'Ignace d'Antioche*. Université libre de Bruxelles, Faculté de philosophie et lettres 69. Brussels: Éditions de l'Université de Bruxelles, 1979.

Jossua, J.-P. *Le salut: Incarnation ou mystère pascal, chez les Pères de l'Église de saint Irénée à saint Léon le Grand*. Paris: Éditions du Cerf, 1968.

Justin Martyr. *Dialogue avec Tryphon, édition critique*. 2 vols. Edited by Philippe Bobichon. Paradosis 47. Fribourg: Academic Press, 2003.

Keener, Craig S. *The Gospel of John: A Commentary*. 2 vols. Peabody, Mass.: Hendrickson, 2003.

Kelly, J. N. D. *Early Christian Creeds*. 3rd ed. New York: Continuum, 2006.

Kinzig, Wolfram, and Markus Vinzent. "Recent Research on the Origins of the Creed." *Journal of Theological Studies* 50 (1999): 535–59.

Kittel, Gerhard, Gerhard Friedrich, and Geoffrey W. Bromiley, eds. *Theological Dictionary of the New Testament*. 10 vols. Grand Rapids, Mich.: Eerdmans, 1964–1976.

Lake, Kirsopp, trans. *The Apostolic Fathers*. 2 vols. Loeb Classical Library. Cambridge, Mass.: Harvard University Press, 1985.

Lanfranchi, Pierluigi. "Attitudes to the Sabbath in Three Apostolic Fathers: Didache, Ignatius, and Barnabas." In *Jesus, Paul, and Early Christianity: Studies in Honour of Henk Jan de Jonge*, Supplements to Novum Testamentum 130, edited by Rieuwerd Buitenwerf, Harm W. Hollander, and Johannes Tromp, 243–59. Leiden: Brill, 2008.

Lentzen-Deis, Fritzleo. *Die Taufe Jesu nach den Synoptikern: Literarkritische und gattungsgeschichtliche Untersuchungen*. Frankfurter Theologische Studien 4. Frankfurt: Josef Knecht, 1970.

Lichtheim, Miriam, trans. "The Instruction of Amen-em-ope." In *The Context of Scripture*, vol. 1, *Canonical Compositions from the Biblical World*, edited by William W. Hallo and K. Lawson Younger Jr., 115–22. Leiden: Brill, 2003.

Liddell, Henry George, Robert Scott, and Henry Stuart Jones. *A Greek-English Lexicon*. Oxford: Clarendon Press, 1968.

Lieu, Judith M. *Image and Reality: The Jews in the World of the Christians in the Second Century*. London: T. & T. Clark Continuum, 1996.

Lightfoot, J. B. *The Apostolic Fathers*, part 2, S. Ignatius, S. Polycarp. 3 vols. 2nd ed. London: Macmillan, 1889.

Logan, Alastair H. B. *Gnostic Truth and Christian Heresy: A Study in the History of Gnosticism*. Peabody, Mass.: Hendrickson, 1996.

Löhr, Hermut. "The Epistles of Ignatius of Antioch." In *The Apostolic Fathers: An Introduction*, edited by Wilhelm Pratscher, 91–115. Waco, Tex.: Baylor University Press, 2010.

Lona, Horacio E. "Der Sprachgebrauch von σάρξ, σαρκικός bei Ignatius von Antiochien." *Zeitschrift für katolische Theologie* 108 (1986): 383–408.

———. "Diognetus." In *The Apostolic Fathers: An Introduction*, edited by Wilhelm Pratscher, 197–213. Waco, Tex.: Baylor University Press, 2010.

Lotz, John-Paul. *Ignatius and Concord: The Background and Use of the Language of Concord in the Letters of Ignatius of Antioch*. Patristic Studies 8. New York: Peter Lang, 2007.

Lubac, Henri de. *History and Spirit: The Understanding of Scripture according to Origen*. Translated by Anne Englund Nash and Juvenal Merriell. San Francisco: Ignatius Press, 2007.

———. *Medieval Exegesis: The Four Senses of Scripture*. Vol. 2. Translated by E. M. Macierowski. Grand Rapids, Mich.: Eerdmans, 2000.

Luz, Ulrich. *Matthew 1–7: A Commentary*. Translated by Wilhelm C. Linss. Minneapolis, Minn.: Augsburg Fortress, 1989.

MacDonald, Margaret Y. "The Ideal of the Christian Couple: Ign. Pol. 5:1–2 Looking Back to Paul." *New Testament Studies* 40 (1994): 105–25.

Maier, Harry O. "The Politics of the Silent Bishop: Silence and Persuasion in Ignatius of Antioch." *Journal of Theological Studies* 55 (2004): 503–19.

Marshall, John W. "The Objects of Ignatius' Wrath and Jewish Angelic Mediators." *Journal of Ecclesiastical History* 56 (2005): 1–23.

Martin, Francis. *The Feminist Question: Feminist Theology in the Light of Christian Tradition*. Grand Rapids, Mich.: Eerdmans, 1994.

———. *Sacred Scripture: The Disclosure of the Word*. Naples, Fla.: Sapientia Press of Ave Maria University, 2006.

Martin, José Pablo. "La pneumatología en Ignacio de Antioquia." *Salesianum* 33 (1971): 379–454.

Maurer, Christian. *Ignatius von Antiochien und das Johannesevangelium*. Abhandlungen zur Theologie des Alten und Neuen Testaments 18. Zurich: Zwingli Verlag, 1949.

McConnell, Timothy. "Ignatius of Antioch: Death Wish or Last Request of a Condemned Man?" *Studia Patristica* 45 (2010): 385–89.

McCue, James F. "The Roman Primacy in the Second Century and the Problem of the Development of Dogma." *Theological Studies* 25 (1964): 161–96.

McDonnell, Kilian. *The Baptism of Jesus in the Jordan: The Trinitarian and Cosmic Order of Salvation.* Collegeville, Minn.: Liturgical Press, 1996.

Meier, John P. "Matthew, Gospel of." In Anchor Bible Dictionary, 6 vols., edited by David Noel Freedman, 4.624. New York: Doubleday, 1992.

———. *A Marginal Jew: Rethinking the Historical Jesus.* Vol. 2, Mentor, Message, and Miracles. New York: Doubleday, 1994.

Meinhold, Peter. *Studien zu Ignatius von Antiochien.* Wiesbaden: Franz Steiner Verlag, 1979.

Mellink, Albert Osger. *Death as Eschaton: A Study of Ignatius of Antioch's Desire for Death.* Amsterdam: University of Amsterdam, 2000.

Menken, Maarten J. J. "The Source of the Quotation from Isaiah 53:4 in Matthew 8:17." *Novum Testamentum* 39 (1997): 313–27.

Mitchell, Matthew W. "In the Footsteps of Paul: Scriptural and Apostolic Authority in Ignatius of Antioch." *Journal of Early Christian Studies* 14 (2006): 27–45.

Moffatt, James. "Ignatius of Antioch: A Study in Personal Religion." *Journal of Religion* 10 (1930): 169–86.

Norris, Frederick W. "Ignatius, Polycarp, and 1 Clement: Walter Bauer Reconsidered." *Vigiliae Christianae* 30 (1976): 23–44.

O'Keefe, John J., and R. R. Reno. *Sanctified Vision: An Introduction to Early Christian Interpretation of the Bible.* Baltimore: Johns Hopkins University Press, 2005.

Paulsen, Henning. *Studien zur Theologie des Ignatius von Antiochen.* Göttingen: Vandenhoeck & Ruprecht, 1978.

Parvus, Roger. *A New Look at the Letters of Ignatius of Antioch and Other Apellean Writings.* Bloomington, Ind.: iUniverse, 2008.

Pearson, Birger A. *Ancient Gnosticism: Traditions and Literature.* Minneapolis, Minn.: Fortress Press, 2007.

Pelikan, Jaroslav. *The Christian Tradition: A History of the Development of Doctrine.* Vol. 1, The Emergence of the Catholic Tradition (100–600). Chicago: University of Chicago Press, 1971.

Pettersen, Alvyn. "Sending Heretics to Coventry? Ignatius of Antioch on Reverencing Silent Bishops." *Vigiliae Christianae* 44 (1990): 335–50.

Pius XII, Pope. Encyclical Letter *Divino Afflante Spiritu.* Issued September 30, 1943.

Polanyi, Michael, and Harry Prosch. *Meaning.* Chicago: University of Chicago Press, 1975.

Pratscher, Wilhelm, ed. *The Apostolic Fathers: An Introduction.* Waco, Tex.: Baylor University Press, 2010.

Prostmeier, Ferdinand R. "The Epistle of Barnabas." In *The Apostolic Fathers: An Introduction,* edited by Wilhelm Pratscher, 27–45. Waco, Tex.: Baylor University Press, 2010.

Rahner, Hugo. *Greek Myths and Christian Mystery.* New York: Harper and Row, 1963.

Ratzinger, Joseph. Pope Benedict XVI. *Jesus of Nazareth: From the Baptism in the Jordan to the Transfiguration.* Translated by Adrian J. Walker. New York: Doubleday, 2007.

Ray, Stephen K. *Upon This Rock: St. Peter and the Primacy of Rome in Scripture and the Early Church.* San Francisco: Ignatius Press, 1999.

Reis, David M. "Following in Paul's Footsteps: Mimēsis and Power in Ignatius of

Antioch." In *Trajectories through the New Testament and the Apostolic Fathers*, edited by Andrew F. Gregory and Christopher M. Tuckett, 287–305. New York: Oxford University Press, 2005.

Reventlow, Henning Graf. *Problems of Old Testament Theology in the Twentieth Century*. Philadelphia: Fortress Press, 1985.

Richardson, Cyril Charles. "The Church in Ignatius of Antioch." *Journal of Religion* 17 (1937): 428–43.

———. *The Christianity of Ignatius of Antioch*. New York: AMS Press, 1967. First published in 1935 by Columbia University Press.

———, trans. and ed. *Early Christian Fathers*. New York: Macmillan, 1970.

Robinson, Thomas A. *Ignatius of Antioch and the Parting of the Ways*. Peabody, Mass.: Hendrickson, 2009.

Romanides, John S. "The Ecclesiology of St. Ignatius of Antioch." *Greek Orthodox Theological Review* 7 (1961–1962): 53–77.

Ryan, P. J. "The Silence of God in Ignatius of Antioch." *Prudentia* 20 (1988): 20–27.

Schlatter, Frederic W. "The Restoration of Peace in Ignatius' Antioch." *Journal of Theological Studies* 35 (1984): 465–69.

Schlier, Heinrich. *Religionsgeschichtliche Untersuchungen zu den Ignatiusbriefen*. Giessen: Alfred Töpelmann Verlag, 1929.

Schoedel, William R. "Ignatius and the Archives." *Harvard Theological Review* 71 (1978): 97–106

———. "Are the Letters of Ignatius of Antioch Authentic?" *Religious Studies Review* 6 (1980): 196–201.

———. *Ignatius of Antioch: A Commentary on the Letters of Ignatius of Antioch*. Hermeneia. Philadelphia: Fortress Press, 1985.

Schütz, Christian. "The Mysteries of the Life of Christ as a Prism of Faith." *Communio* 29 (2002): 28–38.

Shepherd, Massey Hamilton, Jr., "Smyrna in the Ignatian Letters: A Study in Church Order." *Journal of Religion* 20 (1940): 141–59.

Sibinga, J. Smit. "Ignatius and Matthew." *Novum Testamentum* 8 (1966): 263–83.

Sieben, Hermann Josef. "Die Ignatianen als Briefe: Einige formkritische Bemerkungen." *Vigiliae Christianae* 32 (1978): 1–18.

Skarsaune, Oskar. "The Development of Scriptural Interpretation in the Second and Third Centuries—Except Clement and Origen." In *Hebrew Bible/Old Testament: The History of Its Interpretation*, vol. 1, *From the Beginnings to the Middle Ages (Until 1300)*, part 1, Antiquity, edited by Magne Sæbø, 373–442. Gottingen: Vandenhoeck & Ruprecht, 1996.

Snyder, Graydon F. "The Historical Jesus in the Letters of Ignatius of Antioch." *Biblical Research* 8 (1963): 3–12.

Söhngen, Gottlieb. "The Analogy of Faith: Unity in the Science of Faith." Translated by Kenneth Oakes. *Pro Ecclesia* 21 (2012): 56–76, 169–94.

Soulen, R. Kendall. *The God of Israel and Christian Theology*. Minneapolis, Minn.: Fortress Press, 1996.

Spicq, Ceslas. *Theological Lexicon of the New Testament*. Translated and edited by James D. Ernest. 3 vols. Peabody, Mass.: Hendrickson, 1994.

Staats, Reinhart. "Die katholische Kirche des Ignatius von Antiochien und das Problem ihrer Normativität im zweiten Jahrhundert." *Zeitschrift für die neutestamentliche Wissenschaft und die Kunde der älteren Kirche* 77 (1986): 126–45, 242–54.

Stewart-Sykes, Alistair. "Prophecy and Patronage: The Relationship between Charismatic Functionaries and Household Officers in Early Christianity." In *Trajectories through the New Testament and the Apostolic Fathers*, edited by Andrew F. Gregory and Christopher M. Tuckett, 165–89. Oxford: Oxford University Press, 2005.

Stoops, Robert F., Jr. "If I Suffer . . . : Epistolary Authority in Ignatius of Antioch." *Harvard Theological Review* 80 (1987): 161–78.

Story, Cullen I. K. "The Christology of Ignatius of Antioch." *Evangelical Quarterly* 56 (1984): 173–82.

Streeter, Burnett Hillman. *The Primitive Church: Studied with Special Reference to the Origins of the Christian Ministry*. New York: MacMillan, 1929.

Studer, Basil. *Trinity and Incarnation: The Faith of the Early Church*. Collegeville, Minn.: Liturgical Press, 1993.

Svigel, Michael J. "The Center of Ignatius of Antioch's Catholic Christianity." *Studia Patristica* 45 (2010): 367–71.

Swartley, Willard M. "The Imitatio Christi in the Ignatian Letters." *Vigiliae Christianae* 27 (1973): 81–103.

Tarvainen, Olavi. *Glaube und Liebe bei Ignatius von Antiochien*. Schriften der Luther-Agricola-Gesellschaft 14. Joensuu, Finland: Pohjois-Karjalan, 1967.

Thiselton, Anthony C. *New Horizons in Hermeneutics: The Theory and Practice of Transforming Biblical Reading*. Grand Rapids, Mich.: Zondervan, 1992.

Torrance, Thomas F. *The Doctrine of Grace in the Apostolic Fathers*. Edinburgh: Oliver and Boyd, 1948.

Trebilco, Paul. "Christian Communities in Western Asia Minor into the Early Second Century: Ignatius and Others as Witnesses against Bauer." *Journal of the Evangelical Theological Society* 49 (2006): 17–44.

———. *The Early Christians in Ephesus from Paul to Ignatius*. Grand Rapids, Mich.: Eerdmans, 2008.

Trevett, Christine. "Prophecy and Anti-Episcopal Activity: A Third Error Combatted by Ignatius?" *Journal of Ecclesiastical History* 34 (1983): 1–18.

———. "Approaching Matthew from the Second Century: The Under-Used Ignatian Correspondence." *Journal for the Study of the New Testament* 20 (1984): 59–67.

———. "The Other Letters to the Churches of Asia: Apocalypse and Ignatius of Antioch." *Journal for the Study of the New Testament* 37 (1989): 117–35.

Vall, Gregory. "Psalm 22: Vox Christi or Israelite Temple Liturgy?" *The Thomist* 66 (2002): 175–200.

———. "Lucis Mysterium: Ignatius of Antioch on the Lord's Baptism." *Nova et Vetera* 8 (2010): 143–60.

Villiers, Pieter G. R. de. "Ignatius of Antioch in His Pagan Context." *Studia Historiae Ecclesiasticae* 33 (2007): 399–411.

Wachterhauser, Brice. "Getting It Right: Relativism, Realism, and Truth." In *The Cambridge Companion to Gadamer*, edited by Robert J. Dostal, 52–78. New York: Cambridge University Press, 2002.

Wagner, Walter. *After the Apostles: Christianity in the Second Century*. Minneapolis, Minn.: Fortress Press, 1994.

Waldstein, Michael, and Frederik Wisse, eds. *The Apocryphon of John: Synopsis of Nag Hammadi Codices II,1; III,1; and IV,1 with BG 8502,2*. Leiden: Brill, 1995.

Wehr, Lothar. *Arznei der Unsterblichkeit: Die Eucharistie bei Ignatius von Antiochien und im Johannesevangelium*. Neutestamentliche Abhandlungen 18. Münster: Aschendorff, 1987.

Weinandy, Thomas G. "The Apostolic Christology of Ignatius of Antioch: The Road to Chalcedon." In *Trajectories through the New Testament and the Apostolic Fathers*, edited by Andrew F. Gregory and Christopher M. Tuckett, 71–84. New York: Oxford University Press, 2005.

Wesche, Kenneth Paul. "St. Ignatius of Antioch: The Criterion of Orthodoxy and the Marks of Catholicity." *Pro Ecclesia* 3 (1994): 89–109.

Winslow, Donald F. "The Idea of Redemption in the Epistles of St. Ignatius of Antioch." *Greek Orthodox Theological Review* 11 (1965): 119–31.

Willis, Wayne. "Martyr Eschatology: Ignatius' Use of *Epitugchanō*." *Restoration Quarterly* 10 (1967): 81–88.

Zahn, Theodor. *Ignatius von Antiochien*. Gotha: Perthes, 1873.

Zañartu, Sergio. "Les concepts de vie et de mort chez Ignace d'Antioche." *Vigiliae Christianae* 33 (1979): 324–41.

Zizioulas, John D. *Eucharist, Bishop, Church: The Unity of the Church in the Divine Eucharist and the Bishop during the First Three Centuries*. Translated by Elizabeth Theokritoff. Brookline, Mass.: Holy Cross Orthodox Press, 2001.

INDEX OF PRIMARY SOURCES

Old Testament

Genesis
 1.1–3: 286
 1.3: 272
 2.7: 318
 8.9: 286
 9.18–27: 227
 28.14: 224
 37.5–11: 130–31

2 Kings
 5.1–27: 294–95

Job
 10.12: 345

Psalms
 1.2–3: 50–51
 2.2: 136
 22: 221
 33.9: 49n53, 272
 72: 221
 78: 214
 136: 215

Proverbs
 3.34: 43n38, 49n53
 11.12b: 280
 17.27: 280
 18.17: 43n38, 50n53
 22.24: 279n57
 23.9: 279n57

Wisdom
 1–19: 131–33, 215
 1.14: 133n24
 2.24: 133, 152
 3.9: 176
 7.21: 131
 7.26: 131
 7.27: 215n39
 7.29–30: 131
 13.2: 131
 14.3: 204n8
 18.4: 132
 18.13–24: 132

Sirach
 11.27: 276n47
 18.29: 55
 20.5–8: 280n58
 25.16: 365
 32.8: 280
 44–50: 213, 215

Isaiah
 5.26: 291n25
 7: 221
 7.9: 22
 7.14: 223, 290
 11.10: 291
 42.1–4: 223
 43: 226
 43.18–19: 35
 49.22: 291
 52.5: 43n38
 53.4: 42n33
 62.10: 291n25

Jeremiah
 23.1–4: 345n122
 31: 220, 226
 31.22: 138
 31.31–32: 215

Ezekiel
 34.11–12: 345n122
 36: 226
 37.9: 318

Daniel
 2: 214
 7: 214

Hosea
 11.1: 135

Amos
 9.11: 228

Micah
 5.1–3: 223

Zephaniah
 3.12–13: 215

Zechariah
 10.3: 345n122

New Testament

Matthew
 1–28: 41–42, 50, 75, 84, 213, 302
 1.20: 113
 1.23: 290
 2.1–15: 134–35
 3.13–17: 286–88
 3.15: 41, 286–87, 290, 295

Matthew (cont.)
  7.24–25: 329
  10.16: 41
  11.13: 292
  12.33: 42
  13.52: 292
  15.13: 42
  16.18: 329
  19.12: 42
  20.28: 348
  26.6–13: 317
  26.26: 145n42, 322
  27.52–53: 238n88, 368

Mark
  1.4: 287
  1.8: 286
  1.9–11: 286–88
  10.38–39: 287
  shorter ending: 48

Luke
  1–2: 215
  1.17: 215
  1.35: 288
  3.21–22: 286–88
  9.8: 238n88
  12.50: 287
  22.27: 349
  24.39: 48, 322

John
  1–21: 42–43, 273
  1.1: 189n62
  1.1–18: 288
  1.18: 260n10
  1.29–34: 288
  2.11: 189n62
  3.8: 42
  4.10: 149n47
  4.23: 149n47
  4.34: 189n64
  5.1–47: 273
  5.19: 43n36, 47n47
  5.29: 369n27
  5.36: 189n64
  6.33: 43n35, 149n46
  6.38: 107
  6.40: 307
  6.55: 149n46
  7.38: 43n35
  8.14: 42n34, 43
  8.28: 43n36, 47n47
  8.29: 43n37
  10.7: 9, 43n35
  10.11–14: 43
  10.18: 184
  12.3: 319
  13.1: 189n65, 296
  14.6: 43n35
  14.8–10: 353
  17.4: 189n64
  17.5: 189n62
  17.11: 94n14
  17.21: 94n14
  19.30: 189n65, 296, 318
  20.19–23: 47–48
  20.22: 145n42, 322
  20.24–29: 48

Acts
  1.25: 366
  10.37–38: 298
  10.38: 286
  24.15: 369n27
  27.34: 44

Romans
  1–16: 213
  6.7: 195
  6.17: 329
  8.15: 149n47
  9–11: 213–14
  11.17–24: 135
  16.25–27: 261–62, 274

1 Corinthians
  1–16: 40, 43, 302
  1–2: 127
  2.2: 277
  3.1–4: 122, 123
  3.4: 124
  4.4: 193
  11.1: 47n48
  13.13: 176
  15: 59
  15.45: 102

2 Corinthians
  2.14–16: 320n72
  3.2–3: 329
  4.4: 128
  5.1: 341
  6.16: 304n10
  10.1: 183

Galatians
  1.1: 352
  3.1: 153
  3.24–25: 216, 253
  4.4–6: 35, 316
  4.4: 206
  4.6: 149n47
  5.4: 153
  5.5–6: 195–96
  5.6: 176, 360
  5.25: 56

Ephesians
  1.3–14: 57
  1.10: 232
  2.15: 318
  3.9–10: 129
  4.4–6: 90
  4.20: 45
  5.1: 46n46
  5.21: 354
  5.25: 62, 174

Philippians
  1.1: 344
  2.3: 45
  2.6–11: 45
  2.10: 59
  2.12–13: 195

Colossians
  1–4: 69
  1.15–20: 189
  1.16: 206
  1.28: 189
  3.14: 189

1 Timothy
  1–6: 69
  1.4–5: 176–77
  3.3: 183

Hebrews
  1–13: 57, 190, 253
  1.1–4: 35, 245
  2.3: 190n69
  3.1–6: 190n67
  3.14: 190n69
  5.7–9: 47n49, 190n67, 347
  6.1: 181
  7.19: 190n67
  7.28: 190n67
  9.1–14: 60, 241
  9.9: 190n68
  9.14: 190n68
  10.1: 190n68
  10.14: 190n68

James
   2.22: 190
   2.26: 190

1 Peter
   1–5: 337
   1.20: 203n6
   2.23: 184

1 John
   1–5: 69
   2.9–11: 56n12
   2.13–14: 189n63
   2.15–17: 149
   2.24: 189n63
   3.6: 56n12
   3.11: 190n66
   3.15: 56n12

4.2: 186
4.18: 190n66, 365
4.20: 56n12

Revelation
   1.5: 186
   2–3: 69
   11.15: 135
   12.1–17: 136–39
   12.11: 186

Non-Canonical

4 Maccabees
   7.15: 191n72

1 Qumran Serek
   5–6: 303

Apostolic Fathers

Barnabas
   1–21: 212, 219–20, 228–29, 231, 249
   2.4–10: 220
   2.6: 307n27
   3.6: 220n47
   4.8: 219n46
   5.6: 220n48
   5.7: 220n47
   7.3–8.7: 220
   7.5: 220n47
   8.4: 220n48
   9.1–5: 219
   10.1–12: 219
   10.11: 220n48
   12.10: 99n25
   12.11: 223
   13.1–6: 220n47
   14.3–4: 219n46
   14.4–5: 220, 223
   18.1: 46n44
   19.4: 274, 280n58
   19.7–8 280n58

1 Clement
   1–65: 77, 83, 152n54, 234n75, 304, 325, 330, 337–38
   3.4: 152n54
   5.4: 366
   5.7: 366n22
   7.2: 347n125
   9.1: 152n54
   10.4–6: 130n19
   20.3: 130n17
   24.5: 204n8

   50.3: 366n22
   51.1: 303

2 Clement
   3.1: 108n43
   20.5: 108n43

Didache
   1–16: 77, 83, 84, 304
   1.1: 46n44
   9.2: 217

Diognetus
   1–10: 212, 217–19, 228–29, 231
   1.1: 218
   3.3: 209
   4.1–6: 218
   8.1: 218
   8.5–11: 108n43, 218
   8.10: 218
   9.1: 218
   9.2: 219
   10.2: 218, 276
   11–12: 218n42
   11.2: 108n43
   11.6: 201n2

Ignatius of Antioch
Ephesians
   1–21: 73–75, 90–91, 126
   sal.: 205, 352
   1.1: 46n46, 196–97
   1.2: 197, 335, 372
   1.3: 345n124, 346, 352, 355
   2.1: 175

   2.2: 74, 363, 367n23
   3.1: 7, 86, 188, 246, 278, 363
   3.2–4.1a: 179, 351
   3.2: 13, 174, 278, 332n94, 340, 347, 351, 354
   4.1: 347, 350
   4.1b–2: 180–81
   4.2: 138, 319
   5.1: 112, 124, 319, 323, 336, 339, 347
   5.2: 306n20, 342
   5.3: 43n38, 49n53
   6.1–9.2: 100
   6.1: 74, 278, 339–40, 345, 352
   6.2: 74, 277n48, 281, 301, 347, 373
   7.1: 74, 282
   7.2: 15, 16, 98, 99–103, 169, 269, 282, 307, 363, 373
   8.1: 74, 126, 128, 337, 375n43
   8.2: 15, 123, 155, 178
   9.1–2: 303
   9.1: 58n16, 74, 114, 169, 173, 188, 334, 341, 367, 375n43
   9.2: 142, 172, 257, 273, 279, 341, 353, 374
   10.1–3: 56n14, 141–42, 156–57
   10.1: 210, 372

Ephesians (cont.)
10.2: 181
10.3: 46n46
11.1: 7, 191, 307, 360, 364–65, 368
11.2: 184, 326, 331, 375–76
12.2: 325, 326, 331, 337
13.1–2: 140, 305
13.1: 165, 306n20, 375n43
14.1: 24, 111, 167, 173, 175–76, 181, 187, 190, 197, 275, 320, 360, 370
14.2: 42, 56n12, 163, 173, 177, 190, 197, 276, 304, 366, 370
15.1–2: 56, 258
15.1: 25, 37, 57, 67, 197, 233–34, 267, 272–73, 276, 277, 375
15.2: 157n3, 274, 277, 375
15.3: 172, 304
16.1–2: 74, 170, 363–64, 371nn33–34
16.2: 320, 375
17.1–2: 316–21, 362, 376
17.1: 196, 282, 308
17.2: 14, 31, 58n16, 114, 139, 307
18.1: 127, 139, 169
18.2: 25, 58n16, 113, 114, 127, 137, 202n5, 284, 292–300
19.1–3: 32, 126–39
19.1: 127–28, 267, 273–74
19.2: 128, 307
19.3: 106, 108n43, 170, 205, 256, 375
20.1: 74, 93, 120, 162, 171, 202n5, 203, 299, 318, 339, 367
20.2: 15, 17, 99n25, 165, 206, 299, 306, 308, 362, 363
21.2: 355

Magnesians
1–15: 72–73
1.1: 181
1.2–3: 91–92
1.2: 92–96, 112–13, 175, 323, 337, 339, 362
1.3: 119, 140, 371
2.1–3.1: 342
2.1: 50, 199, 307n27
3.1–2: 345
3.1: 346, 350
3.2: 345n124, 355, 363n13
4.1: 363
5.1–2: 141, 155–56, 282, 307, 362, 364
5.1: 46n44, 196, 97, 366, 374
5.2: 173, 176, 177, 181, 184, 191, 329, 363, 373
6–8: 43, 106
6.1: 32, 97, 112, 203, 233, 263–64, 268–70, 325n78, 339–40, 345, 348–49, 360, 367
6.2: 308, 329, 339, 342, 354, 376
7.1–2: 90
7.1: 43n36, 113, 324, 348, 372
7.2: 16, 106–7, 260, 264–66, 270, 304, 338, 341
8–10: 236–38, 252
8.1–2: 207, 239
8.1: 199, 209, 243
8.2–9.2: 114
8.2: 25, 31, 43n37, 106–8, 203, 234, 247–48, 258–71, 349
9.1–2: 57, 242–46, 272, 368
9.1: 12, 14, 31, 46, 50, 72, 170, 191, 199, 247n101, 256n1, 257, 339, 371, 375
9.2: 234, 237–39, 272, 340, 368
10.1: 46n45, 116, 211, 241, 256n1
10.2: 192, 207, 209, 307, 363

10.3: 171, 210, 211n30, 334
11.1: 72–73, 164, 236, 238, 284, 372, 373
12.1: 14, 43n38, 51
13.1–2: 165n17, 353–54
13.1: 14, 50–51, 50n53, 95–96, 115, 187, 257, 273, 326, 350
13.2: 107, 122, 133–34, 325, 348–49, 375
14.1: 278n50, 334, 355n142
15.1: 15–16, 58n16

Trallians
1–13: 64–66
sal.: 40, 326–31, 337
1.1: 204
1.2: 46n46
2–3: 343
2.1: 46n45, 124, 169, 347–49, 362–63
2.2: 191, 372
2.3: 336
3.1: 322, 325n78, 342, 345, 349, 355
3.2: 140, 157, 175, 278
3.3: 328, 330n88, 336
4.1: 49, 363
4.2: 140, 142, 152, 173, 278, 375
5.1: 59, 65, 162
5.2: 15, 56, 59, 65, 76
6.1–2: 65
6.1: 29n6, 162, 174, 281, 305, 319, 328
6.2–7.1: 327
6.2: 277, 362
7.1: 7, 165n17, 353
8.1: 16, 66, 173n31, 186n60, 327
8.2: 43n38
9.1–2: 16, 58–59
9.1: 128, 277n48, 284
9.2: 307, 362, 369
10.1: 59, 328
11.1–2: 65–66, 281–82
11.1: 42, 363
11.2: 16, 111, 113, 116, 169, 282, 303–4, 308, 309, 359, 367
12.1: 336n108

12.2: 325n78, 328, 350
12.3: 87, 175, 191, 363
13.1: 355n142
13.2: 172
13.3: 165, 191, 363, 367n23

Romans
1–10: 68, 125–26, 142–54
sal.: 98, 151, 163, 187, 204, 233, 337, 345
1.1–2: 187–88
1.2: 150, 151, 154
2.1: 150, 157, 197n86, 276, 366
2.2: 143, 146, 173, 348, 370
3.1: 150, 153, 156
3.2: 143–44, 166, 178, 192n75
3.3: 143–44, 156–57, 197, 211n30, 282
4.1–2: 192n75
4.1: 145–46, 151, 306n21
4.2: 46n45, 83, 145–46, 157n63
4.3: 142, 173, 184, 325, 330, 370
5.1: 193, 363
5.3–6.2: 124
5.3: 36, 140, 146, 153
6.1: 147–48, 155, 169, 363
6.2: 125, 142–43, 151–52, 153, 157, 276, 369, 373n39
6.3: 7, 46n46, 87, 154, 184n59, 373n39
7.1: 147, 150–51, 154, 182, 276
7.2: 14, 43n35, 142, 148–49, 150, 153–54, 173, 282, 362
7.3: 43n35, 143, 147, 173n32, 186n60, 306n19, 308
8.1: 124–25, 147
8.2–3: 278n50
8.2: 31, 106, 170, 258, 269, 272, 373
8.3: 150, 363

9.1: 28, 345, 348, 355
9.2: 157n63
9.3: 335

Philadelphians
sal.: 58n16, 114, 142, 350n135, 352–53
1.1–2: 182–84, 352
1.1: 124, 278, 348
1.2: 279n55, 347
2.1–2: 43, 117, 178
2.1: 27n3, 162, 345n123, 373
2.2: 208, 341n115
3.1: 42, 208
3.2: 29, 46n45, 210–11
3.3: 27n3, 182, 371n34
4.1: 27n2, 243n96, 306nn20–21, 338, 339
5.1: 173, 192n74, 326, 349n133
5.2: 32, 50n53, 87, 171, 234–35, 238, 246, 326, 371
6.1–2: 240
6.1: 27, 208, 211n30, 277n48, 282
6.2: 173, 182
7.1–2: 123, 278, 328
7.1: 42, 114–15
7.2: 28n5, 45, 46–47, 57, 124n8, 171, 256, 347,
8.1: 28n5, 29, 45, 88, 110, 112, 165, 279n55, 349, 350, 363, 374
8.2: 14, 16, 23, 28–33, 44–46, 51, 169, 170, 188–89, 192–93, 242, 256–58, 285, 363, 375
9.1–2: 38, 50n53, 59–61, 200–1, 253n108
9.1: 43n35, 45, 110, 170, 171, 209, 234, 240–41, 334
9.2: 33, 73, 234n76, 238, 241–42, 246, 284, 308, 319, 368, 375
10.1–2: 355n143
10.1: 334

11.1: 158
11.2: 175, 371n37, 372

Smyrnaeans
1–13: 185–86
sal.: 172
1–3: 321–23, 339
1.1–2: 25, 101, 164, 289–92, 329
1.1: 41, 173n31, 181, 185, 373n39
1.2: 50n53, 168, 171, 185, 186n60, 212, 304, 341, 367
2.1: 103n34, 168, 369
3.1–3: 103
3.1: 165, 185
3.2: 47, 144–45, 168, 185, 325, 340
3.3: 113, 115, 339
4.1: 29n6, 281n64, 282
4.2: 184n59, 185, 276, 299, 328, 341, 369, 373n39
5–8: 231
5.1: 14, 50, 168, 186, 281, 282, 319, 328
5.2: 142, 230, 282
5.3: 16, 29n6, 169, 186
6.1: 42, 59, 129, 169, 175, 185–86, 199, 349, 364n14
6.2–8.2: 185, 333
6.2–7.1: 180
6.2: 143–44, 174, 185–86, 199, 306–7, 323, 376
7.1: 14, 43n35, 168, 173, 257
7.2: 50n53, 238, 253n108
8.1–9.1: 350
8.1: 186, 243n96, 306n21, 338, 340, 342, 345n123, 348
8.2: 25, 173n32, 331–41
9.1: 363
10.1: 197n86
10.2: 371n35
11.1: 192, 355n143
11.2: 197n85, 303n8, 342, 356
11.3: 56, 356

INDEX OF PRIMARY SOURCES

Smyrnaeans (cont.)
12.1: 348
12.2: 104, 110–11
13.2: 181

Polycarp
sal.: 346
1.1: 182, 306, 329
1.2–5.2: 345
1.2–4.3: 56
1.2: 173, 279, 341n115, 346, 353, 356, 358, 376
1.3: 42, 55–56, 346
2.2: 41, 306, 346, 376
2.3: 308, 356
3.1: 56, 182
3.2: 16, 97, 102, 105, 184, 206, 268, 340–41, 368
4.1: 345
4.3: 173
5.1–2: 61–64
5.1: 174, 279
5.2: 172, 363
6.1: 90
6.2: 175, 197–99
7.1–8.2: 355n143
7.1: 356, 370
7.2: 174
7.3: 63, 197n85, 199n89, 278n50, 373
8.1: 182n54, 197n85, 204, 336
8.3: 63, 110, 345

Polycarp of Smyrna
Philippians
1–14: 40, 50, 77, 83, 335, 337–38
sal.: 350n135

4.1: 198n87
9.2: 184n59, 366n22

Martyrdom of Polycarp
sal.: 331n92
8.1: 331n92
16.2: 328, 331n92, 333
19.2: 331n92

Shepherd of Hermas
3.4: 204n8
89.2–3: 203n6

Fathers and Doctors

Anselm of Canterbury
Proslogium
I: 19, 22

Augustine of Hippo
De catechizandis
2.3: 268n29

De magistro
11: 22n34

De Trinitate
1.5: 267n28

De vera religione
17.33: 365n17

Epistola 140
2.5: 249n104

Exp. in Galatas
43: 249n104

Eusebius of Caesarea
De eccles. theologia
2.9: 263n15

Historia eccles.
3.36: 27n1
4.1–4: 39n26

Evagrius Ponticus
Chapters on Prayer
60: 22n35

Gregory of Nyssa
Adv. Macedonianos
16: 35

Irenaeus of Lyons
Against Heresies
1.9.4: 347n125
1.10.1: 205n13
1.10.3: 205n13
1.11.1: 259n6

Demonstration
1–100: 212, 217, 225–30
6: 226, 232
8–42a: 216
8: 227
20–34: 225–27
36–42a: 226–28
51: 227
58–63: 227–28
68–82: 225
87–100: 225–27
92: 99n25
98: 201n2, 329–30

John Chrysostom
Hom. in Romanos
1.2: 271n35

John of the Cross
Maxims and Counsels
21: 275

Justin Martyr
Dialogue with Trypho
1–142: 212, 220–24, 228–29
11.2–5: 220
14.2: 221n54
16.2–3: 222n56
19.2: 222n56
19.5–6: 221n52
22.1: 221n52
23.1–5: 220n50
27.4: 222
29.2: 221n54
34.7–8: 221n53
40.1–3: 221n51
44.2: 223
45.4: 224
47.2: 221
64.3: 223
66.8: 221n53
67.8: 221n52
68.8: 221n53
78.9: 135n29
80.1–2: 222n57
81.4: 222n57
93.1–3: 220n50
93.4: 209
97.4: 221n53
100.1–3: 223
111.3–4: 221n51
120.1–2: 224
120.5: 223

123.5–7: 222n55
123.8–9: 223

Origen of Alexandria
In Canticum
    prol. 2.36: 148

Tertullian
Adversus Iudaeos
    12.2: 221n53

Adversus Praxean
    5.7: 269n31

De resurrectione
    8.2: 155n59, 228n67

Catechism
    53: 216
    114: 39n28
    374–76: 35n20
    470: 271n34
    515: 271n34

Thomas Aquinas
Summa theologiae
    I, q. 1, a. 7: 4n4, 19
    I, q. 22, a. 2: 204n10
    I, q. 22, a. 3: 204n8
    I-II, q. 91, a. 5: 216n40, 253
    I-II, q. 98, a. 1: 253
    I-II, q. 98, a. 2 ad 1: 216n40
    I-II, q. 99, a. 6: 216n40, 253
    I-II, q. 104, a. 3: 216n40
    II-II, qq. 1–16: 168n23

Magisterial

689–90: 35n21
1812–13: 177

Dei Verbum
    2: 274n42
    11: 19n25

II-II q. 1, a. 2, ad 2: 20, 163
II-II, q. 1, a.3, ad 1: 177n48
II-II, q. 2, a.2: 177n47
II-II, q. 2, a. 9, ad 3: 166n22
II-II, q. 4, a. 3: 190
II-II, q. 4, a. 7: 177n47
II-II, q. 24, a. 3, ad 2: 36, 362n11
III, q. 66, a. 2: 293

Divino Afflante Spiritu
    29: 251n106

Lumen Gentium
    11: 243n95

INDEX OF GREEK WORDS AND PHRASES

ἀγάπη, ἀγαπητός, ἀγαπάω, 87, 117, 142, 151, 159, 172–77, 180, 190, 198, 242, 328–29
ἀδελφοί, 141
αἰών, 78, 128
ἀκίνητος, τὸ ἀκίνητον, 182, 185, 329
ἀληθῶς, 59, 73, 230, 289, 321
ἀνάστασις, ἀναστῆναι, 369
ἀνέστησεν ἑαυτόν, 103
ἀνέτειλεν, 244
ἀνθρωπίνως, 106, 108n43
ἄνθρωπος, 118, 122, 124–25, 143, 145, 276
ἀόργητον, τὸ, 182
ἀπάθεια, ἀπαθής, 104, 184
ἀπαρτίζω, ἀπάρτισμα, 192, 197, 238
ἀποθανεῖν, τὸ, 191, 362–63
ἀπὸ θεοῦ ὄν, 115
ἀποστολικός, 326–28, 330
ἀρχεῖα, 28, 32, 188–89
ἀρχή, 24, 96, 167, 181, 187–90, 198, 205, 243, 275, 320, 341, 359–60
ἀρχὴ ζωῆς καὶ τέλος, 320, 360
ἄρχων τοῦ κόσμου τούτου, 128
ἄτοπον, 210, 237
ἀφθαρσία, ἄφθαρτος, 308, 318
ἄχρονος, 105, 340

βασκανία, βασκαίνω, 150, 153–54
βίος, 62, 121, 147, 360

γέγραπται, 29, 43
γεννητὸς καὶ ἀγέννητος, 98
γνώμη, 106, 160, 178–82, 272n36, 328–29, 347, 350
γνῶσις (θεοῦ), 78, 106, 178, 272n36, 320

δαιμόνιον ἀσώματον, 48, 322
διάκονος, διακονία, διακονέω, 304, 343, 348–49

δίκαιος, δικαιοσύνη, δικαιόω, 193n78, 195–96
δοκεῖν, τὸ, 71–72
δρόμος, θεοδρόμοι, 341
δωρεά, 43, 307

ἐάν, ἐὰν μή, 190–91
εἰς ἕνα ὄντα, 106, 265
εἰς τέλος, 187, 189, 190, 275, 276, 296, 366, 370
εἰς τὸ εὐαγγέλιον, 238
εἰς τὸν καινὸν ἄνθρωπον, 318
εἷς, μία, ἕν, 90
εἷς καὶ ὁ αὐτός, 16
ἐκκλησία, 302, 318, 335–38
ἐλπίδα δικαιοσύνης, 195
ἐλπίς, ἐλπίζω, 175, 303, 371
ἐμπνεόμενοι, 114
ἐν ἀποστολικῷ χαρακτῆρι, 326–27, 330
ἐν τέλει, 96, 203, 233, 243, 360
ἑνότης, ἑνόω, 89, 90n5
ἑνότης θεοῦ, 96, 110–12
ἕνωσις, 63, 89, 90n5, 91, 95, 187
ἐξαίρετόν τι, ἐξαιρέτως, 61, 238
ἐπὶ (τὴν) πέτραν, 329
ἐπιείκεια, 182–83
ἐπιθυμία, ἐπιθυμεῖν, 63, 142, 149, 150, 172–73
ἐπισκοπέω, ἐπισκέπτομαι, 345
ἐπίσκοπος, ἐπισκοπή, 63, 304, 345–46, 355
ἐπιτυγχάνω, 95n16, 187–88
ἔργον, τὸ, 197
ἐριθεία, 44–46
ἔρως, ἐράω, 142–43, 148, 172–73
ἔσχατοι καιροί, 368
εὐοικονόμητος, 187, 202n5
εὑρεθῆναι (εἰς τέλος), 191, 370
εὐταξία, 280, 301
ἐφάνη, φανῇ, 108n43, 203, 205, 339–40

ζῆλος, ζηλόω, 152-53
ζωή, τὸ ζῆν, 94, 117, 121, 318, 320, 360, 361, 362

ἦλθεν, 47, 322
ἡσυχία, 261n11, 273-74

θέλημα, 147, 179, 187, 204-5, 290
θέλω, 146-48
θεολογία, 3, 20, 34, 36, 38, 203, 204n9, 272
θεός, 97-98
θεοῦ ἀνθρωπίνως φανερουμένου, 108n43
θεοῦ ἐπιτυχεῖν, 95n16
Θεοφόρος, 81-82, 328
θυσία, 83, 145

Ἰουδαϊσμός, 211

καθολικὴ ἐκκλησία, ἡ, 302, 331-33, 337-38
καιρός, 156-57, 366, 368
καλός, 60, 143, 155
κατὰ κυριακὴν ζῶντες, 242
κατὰ σάρκα, 122, 123, 172
κεράννυμι, ἐγκεράννυμι, 319, 322
κοινός, 303
κόσμος, 125-26, 140, 156
κυριώτερον, 94

λάβετε, 47, 145n42, 322
λόγος, 31, 79, 132, 218, 257-69, 273-74, 276
λόγος ἀπὸ σιγῆς προελθών, 79, 259n5

μαθητεία, μαθητεύω, 156, 157, 278
μαθητής, 46, 256, 375
μανθάνω, 156, 256
μετέχω, 95, 319
μηδὲν κατ' ἐριθείαν, 44-45
μιμηταὶ Χριστοῦ, 46-47, 57
μύρον, 317n62, 319
μυστήριον, 31, 246, 257, 317

ναός, ναοφόροι, 303
νῦν, μέχρι νῦν, 236
νῦν ἐπαγγελία, 366

οἰκοδεσπότης, 340
οἰκοδομή, 341
οἰκονομία, 3, 20, 34, 36, 126, 177n46, 188, 202-4, 207, 227n65, 236, 272, 340, 367
οἰκοφθόροι, 170
ὁμιλία, προσομιλέω, 61, 279
ὁμοήθεια, 91n9, 354

ὁμόνοια, 91n9, 165, 175, 180, 280
ὁρατά τε καὶ ἀόρατα, 15
ὁρίζω, προορίζω, 351-52
ὃς εἶπεν καὶ ἐγένετο, 272
οὐδὲν φαινόμενον καλόν, 143

παθητός, πάσχω, 104, 184
πάθος, 39, 205, 293n28
παλαιός, 206
πάντα, τὰ, 129-30, 132
παρακαλέω, 44-45, 65, 279
παρουσία, παρών, 205n13, 244n98, 245n100, 368
πεισμονή, 56
πέπομφεν, 320
πέτρα, Πέτρος, 329
πιστεύειν, τὸ, 170n26, 246
πίστις, πιστεύω, 159-60, 170-71, 176-77, 180, 195, 198, 320, 328
πίστις δι' ἀγάπης ἐνεργουμένη, 176, 195
πίστις θεοῦ, 170, 320
πιστοὶ ἐν ἀγάπῃ, 176
πιστός, 159nn1-2, 165-66, 176, 190, 192
πλῆθος, 303, 338, 339
πληροφορέω, 165
πλήρωμα, 78, 327
πνεῦμα, 93n12, 105, 115, 118, 121-22, 318, 322
πνευματικός, πνευματικῶς, 93n12, 100-101, 104, 121-23, 155
πνευματικῶς ἡνωμένος τῷ πατρί, 103, 113-15
πνέω, πνοὴ ζωῆς, 114, 318
πράγματα, 155, 374
πραότης, πραϋπάθεια, 65n23
πράσσειν, 44-45, 156, 197
πρεσβύτεροι, πρεσβυτέριον, 304, 344, 349-50
προέρχομαι, προελθών, 79, 260, 262, 264, 265
πρόκειται, 29
πρόνοια, 204
προσδοκέω, 368
πῦρ φιλόϋλον, 142

σαββατίζοντες, 242
σαρκικός, σαρκικῶς, 93n12, 100, 101, 103, 104, 120-23, 155, 221
σαρκικὸς καὶ πνευματικός, 100, 104
σαρκικῶς καὶ πνευματικῶς, 120, 155
σαρκοφόρος, 98, 125, 142
σάρξ, 93n12, 105, 118, 121-25, 185
σεσιγημένου, 261-62

σιγή, σιγῶν, 79, 132, 182, 259–62, 265–67, 273
συγγένικον, 196
συγκατάβασις, 35
σύζυγος, 309
σύμβιος, 62
συμπάθεια, συμπαθέω, 87, 160, 184–85
σύμφωνος, 90, 180
συνδιδασκαλίται, 86, 90
συνέδριον, 304, 344
σύνοδοι, 90, 341
συντρέχω, 90, 179, 341
σύσσημον, 291
σῶμα, σωματεῖον, 121, 303, 342

ταραχή, 132
τέλειος, τελείως, 56, 78n57, 182, 189–90, 192, 196–97, 275–77, 370
τέλειος ἄνθρωπος, 78n57, 276
τελειόω, 189–90, 191n72, 238
τέλος, 24, 96, 155, 167, 173, 176–77, 181, 187–90, 196, 198, 205, 238–39, 243, 275–76, 296, 299, 341, 359–60, 366, 370, 374
τετέλεσται, 189, 296

τόπος, 345–46
τοὺς περὶ Πέτρον, 48
τύπος, 281, 329, 343, 345–46
τύπος καὶ διδαχή, 329

ὕλη, 125, 142
ὑπὲρ θάνατον, 105
ὑπὲρ καιρόν, 105, 341
ὑπομονή, 175, 198

φανερώσας ἑαυτόν, 108, 203
φύσις, 193, 196
φωνή, 276

χαρακτήρ, 141, 173, 181, 326–30
χάρις, χαρίζω, 193, 237, 306, 346, 352
χάρισμα, 14, 306–7, 320
χορός, 132
χριστιανισμός, 211
χριστομαθία, 44–46, 76, 188, 256–58, 285, 375
χρῶμα Θεοῦ λαβόντες, 180
χωρέω, 264, 265n20

ψηλαφήσατέ με καὶ ἴδετε, 48, 322

GENERAL INDEX

Allison, Dale C., Jr., 213n35
anointing at Bethany, 317–20
anthropology, 93, 118–25, 155–56, 191, 369
Antioch, situation in, 75, 80–81, 84–85, 354–57
aphorisms, 54–57, 61, 64, 65, 241–42, 272, 277, 359
apostles, 64, 200–201, 305, 311–14, 322–31, 342–43, 349–50, 353, 357–58, 375
"archives": dispute over, 27–32
attaining God, 88, 92, 95n16, 119, 140, 193. *See also* eschatology
authenticity, Christian, 46, 75, 124–25, 144, 178, 192, 258, 275–77
authority, ecclesial, 13–14, 80, 164–65, 346–47, 353–54

Balthasar, Hans Urs von, 17, 31n17, 298n40
baptism, sacramental, 197–98, 287, 293
baptism of the Lord, 25, 127, 284–300, 361
Barnard, L. W., 77, 122, 160
Bartsch, Hans-Werner, 77, 129n15
Bauer, Walter, 82n80, 83n83, 351n139
Beale, G. K., 136n31
Beatrice, Pier Franco, 48n50
Benedict XVI, Pope, 47n49, 88n1, 285
Bergamelli, Ferdinando, 20n29, 170n27, 299n43, 359
Bertrand, Daniel Alain, 288n17, 297n37
Bieler, Martin, 295n33
bishop: appointment of, 350–54; obedience to, 179; office of, 345–48; representative of Christ, 339–40; "silence" of, 258, 277–81. *See also* ecclesiological typology; monepiscopacy, origin of
bishop of Philadelphia (unnamed), 28–29, 182–84, 352

Boersma, Hans, 20n30
Bommes, Karin, 79n58, 233, 237
Bower, Richard A., 186n61, 267n27, 365–66
Brent, Allen, 11n11, 23, 53n3, 54, 57n15, 79–85, 87, 350
Bright, Pamela, 213n36
Brown, Milton Perry, 40n29
Brown, Raymond E., 84n88, 134n26
Bruce, F. F., 153n57
Burghardt, Walter J., 42n34
Burke, Patrick, 82n80

Camelot, Pierre-Thomas, 54, 98n23, 152n53, 234n75, 242n93, 265
Cerinthus (gnostic), 288
Chadwick, Henry, 280–81
Chalcedon, Council of, 16–17
chiasmus, 99–100, 103
Childs, Brevard S., 291n25
Christ event, 59–60, 73; cosmic significance, 127–39; as mystery, 109, 257–58, 273–74, 284–300; place in historical economy, 203, 205–6, 232–33, 239; relation to church, 316–18, 339–40; and second coming, 367–69; as source and object of faith, 168–71
Christology, 16–17, 96–105, 261–71, 289–90, 349
church, 301–58; as body of Christ, 303, 367; catholic and local, 331–41; and Christ event, 316–19; oriented to heaven, 340–41; quickened by Holy Spirit, 315–23; as temple, 303–4; as tree, 304
communicative intention: author's, 2, 5–14, 18
Conzelmann, Hans, 207, 216, 236, 238n89, 239, 252–53

397

Corwin, Virginia, 54, 67n28, 68n29, 76n47, 77, 79, 84n87, 89n4, 93, 102n33, 111–13, 121n5, 161, 202, 233n73, 266n25, 272n37, 274n43, 293n28, 301, 311–12, 314, 315, 324, 332, 343, 364, 368
cosmology, 119, 126–39
Cranfield, C. E. B., 44
creation, theology of, 37, 120, 126–28, 131–34, 137–39, 233–34, 272, 297–99
creedal formulae, 16, 58–61, 72–74, 97, 99–103, 127, 164–65, 169, 185, 259, 264–65, 270, 284–85, 289–94, 299, 321, 340–41

Damas of Magnesia, 70, 81, 336
Daniélou, Jean, 245n100
Davies, Stevan L., 27n1
deacons, 348–49
desire: purification of, 142–43, 146–49, 172–73, 184
Dietze, Paul, 42n34
divine pedagogy, 216, 247, 252–53
docetism, 58–59, 64–66, 69–73, 103–4, 125, 143–44, 185–86, 230–31, 254, 288–89, 321–22, 328
Donahue, Paul J., 29–31, 67n28, 69n32, 247n101
Dunn, James D. G., 153n56

ecclesiological typology, 281, 304–5, 311–15, 341–50
ecclesiology, 25, 37–38, 202, 281, 301–58, 361; apostles, 323–31; catholic church and local churches, 331–41; hierarchy, 341–57; Holy Spirit, 315–23; terms and themes, 302–8; in twentieth-century scholarship, 308–15
economic participation, 31–32, 111, 178n51, 339
economy, divine, 33–40, 359–61, 372–76; and cosmology, 139; historical dimension, 60, 76, 171, 200–206, 360–61; Judaism's place in, 206–55; as *mysterium unitatis*, 88–89; of words and deeds, 271–74. *See also* Christ event; horizontal and vertical dimensions
Ehrman, Bart D., 318n67
endurance unto death, 191, 198, 362–64, 366
envy, diabolic, 152–54
eschatology, 25–26, 244, 359–72; absence of chiliasm, 371; general resurrection, 369–70; intermediate state, 369–70; personal and communal, 141, 366–67; realized and future, 191, 361–66; second coming, 367–69. *See also* attaining God; hope
eucharist, 66, 145, 148–49, 180, 231, 243, 305–6, 323, 333, 336, 339–40, 350, 357n149
extratextual realities, 7, 9, 19–20, 86

faith, 160–68; analogy of, 3, 20, 39–40, 91; apostolic, 327–29; and Christ event, 168–71; and imperishable life, 320; and love, 175–92; objective content, 21–22; of prophets, 246; rule of, 21–22, 58, 329, 347; seeking understanding, 19, 21–22; subjective act, 22–23; and works, 192–99
Farrer, Austin, 136n31
Figal, Günter, 6n6
Fitzmyer, Joseph A., 261n12
flesh and spirit, unity of, 92–94; anthropological, 120–25; Christological, 100–105
flesh as hinge of salvation, 155, 228
Foster, Paul, 40n30, 42n34
France, R. T., 286n8

Gadamer, Hans-Georg, 2, 4, 6–7, 12, 17, 18, 19n26, 22
Gaston, Lloyd, 208
gnosticism, 76–79, 118, 125, 128n13, 231, 259–60, 261n11, 308–13, 314, 340
Golz, Eduard Freiherrn von der, 36n23, 76n47, 79n58, 161n7, 269n30, 270n32, 362n8, 371n31
Goulder, Michael D., 288n16
grace, 192, 193–99, 237, 306–7; and glory, 36, 360
Grant, Robert M., 32n19, 77, 129n15, 148n45, 152n53, 238n88, 240n90, 242n93, 260n10, 306, 319n70, 324n77, 327n83, 343n116, 344n119, 351n139, 355n144
Grillmeier, Aloys, 16, 100n27, 102n31
Grondin, Jean, 2n2, 7n9, 22n33

Hall, Robert G., 130n16, 133n23
Halleux, André de, 333n98
Hamell, P. J., 270n33
Hammond Bammel, C. P., 29n8, 53n3, 82n80, 129n14, 344n120
Hartman, Lars, 294n31
Haykin, Michael A. G., 55n10, 158n64

Hellenism and biblical faith, 183–84, 280–81, 308–11, 361
heresies, 68–75. *See also* docetism; Judaizers
hermeneutics, 6–11, 18–23
hierarchy, ecclesiastical. *See* ecclesiological typology
Hill, Charles E., 28n4, 41n30, 42n34, 50n54, 64n22, 326n81, 369–70, 371n36
historical-critical method, 2, 5, 8–10, 52–53, 85, 250–52
historical theology, 5–9, 75–76, 85–87
historicism, 10–11, 255, 314, 333n98, 344
Hoffman, Daniel, 31n12
Holmes, Michael W., 3n3, 63n20, 93n11, 148n43, 153n58, 218n42, 274n41, 278n49
Holy Spirit: economic mission, 35, 114–15, 315–24; and the flesh, 123; at Jesus' baptism, 287, 294; as living water, 14, 148–49, 283, 362; within the Trinity, 114–15
hope, 175, 195, 371–72
horizons: fusion of, 4, 8, 271
horizontal and vertical dimensions, 78, 206, 214, 225, 237–39, 246, 252, 281, 313–15, 323–24, 330–31, 340–41, 358, 360–61, 374
Howell, Kenneth J., 327n82, 332n96
humanity of Christ: fleshly and historical, 59, 63, 72–74, 98–99, 185; glorified in resurrection, 102–4, 134, 144–45, 298, 367; mediating redemption, 142–43, 144–45; representative of creation, 134–35, 138
Hvidt, Niels Christian, 331n91

ideological criticism. *See* sociocritical approaches
Ignatius of Antioch: agenda, 79–87; biblical view of reality, 120; brevity of expression, 16–18, 29, 55, 66–67; conceptual horizon, 2–5, 12–13, 271; mode of discourse, 15–18, 54–68, 344; place in history, 1–2, 16–18; 39–40, 108; reuse of sources, 44–49; temperament, 54–55, 66, 79, 82n80; theological lacunae, 36–39; theological praxis, 34, 67, 86–87, 164, 277–78, 301, 344
imitation of Christ, 46–47, 95, 140, 141, 145, 146, 171, 184, 197, 256, 282, 283
imperishability, 308, 317–20
inclusio (framing device), 59, 60, 65, 183
"infolded" theology, 17–18, 39–40
intellect and will, 168, 177–79

Israel, people of, 130–32, 135–37, 206–8, 212–55, 286, 291, 294–95

Jesus Christ: God's self-revelation, 106–9, 116–17, 272–74; high priest, 240–41; teacher, 106, 116. *See also* Christology
Johannine theology, 1, 42–43, 74, 94, 101, 105–6, 114, 172, 189, 259–61, 265, 281, 324, 362; fused with Pauline elements, 47, 125, 128, 149, 156–57, 307, 318
John Paul II, Pope, 285
Joly, Robert, 39n27, 67n27
Jossua, Jean-Pierre, 86, 129n15, 285n3
Judaism and Christianity, 24, 50, 200–255; good and better, 240–42, 253; imperfect and perfect, 253; old and new, 236, 252; in recent scholarship, 206–11; second-century views of, 216–30
Judaizers, 27–30, 59–60, 69–73, 75, 153, 208–11, 226, 231–33, 236–37, 241–42, 254
justification by faith, 190–91, 192–96, 363–64

Keener, Craig S., 286n9, 317n62, 318n65
Kelly, J. N. D., 58n16, 100
Kinzig, Wolfram, 58n16

Lake, Kirsopp, 293n28
Lanfranchi, Pierluigi, 243n97
learning Christ, 14, 16, 18, 45–46, 76, 116, 156, 188, 242, 256–58, 285
Lentzen-Deis, Fritzleo, 286n7, 294n31
Lichtheim, Miriam, 279n56
Lieu, Judith M., 11n12
Lightfoot, J. B., 27n1, 39n26, 42n33, 44n39, 48n50, 52–53, 69–72, 77, 83n82, 98n23, 125, 148n45, 152n53, 182n55, 183, 240n90, 242n93, 259n5, 263, 265n22, 265n24, 279n55, 327, 332, 333, 343
Lightfoot-Zahn consensus, 52–53
Logan, Alastair, H. B., 77n52
Logos, 36–37, 131, 233–34, 259–62, 265–275
Löhr, Hermut, 41n31, 53n4
Lona, Horacio E., 93n12, 218n42
Lotz, John-Paul, 91n9
love, 172–75; unity of faith and, 94, 159–60, 175–99, 327–29
Lubac, Henri de, 249n103, 250n105
Luz, Ulrich, 134n25

MacDonald, Margaret Y., 10n10, 62n18
Maier, Harry O., 280
Marcellus of Ancyra, 263
marriage and celibacy, 62–64, 174
Marshall, John W., 71–72, 76
Martin, Francis, 31n16, 52n1
Martin, José Pablo, 15n16, 93n12, 113n57
martyrdom, theology of, 92, 139, 140, 142, 145–54, 157–58, 282–83, 328, 330
martyr procession, 80–82, 92, 158, 175, 198n88
Matthew: Ignatius's dependence on, 41–42, 134–35, 290, 317
Maurer, Christian, 42n34
McConnell, Timothy, 150n48
McCue, James F., 38n25
McDonnell, Kilian, 288, 290n23, 293n29
Meier, John P., 75n46, 84n88, 286n11, 288, 295
Meinhold, Peter, 32, 308n30, 309, 312–13, 314, 316, 352n141
Mellink, Albert Osger, 362n11, 366n22, 370n30
Menken, Maarten J. J., 42n33
mildness, 182–83
mind-set, 178–82, 346–47, 350–52
mission of the Son, 35, 105–9, 271–74
mission of the Spirit, 35, 114–15, 315–24
Mitchell, Matthew W., 28n4, 31n14, 31n18, 40n30, 116n63
modalism, 262–64, 269
Moffatt, James, 54
monepiscopacy: origin of, 80–83, 304
mysteria vitae Iesu, 109, 273–75, 285
mystery, 109–10, 257, 261; biblical-patristic category, 20; exceeding author's horizon, 12–13, 271; Israel's history as, 214

Nelson, E. A., 17n21
New Testament: Ignatius's use of, 1, 40–49
Nicaea, Council of, 17
Norris, Frederick W., 83n83

O'Keefe, John J., 30
Old Testament: in exegetical tradition, 246–52; and gospel, 28–29, 32–33, 50–51, 61, 71n37; Ignatius's use of, 29–30, 49–51, 60, 130–33, 290–92; in modern scholarship, 250–52
Onesimus of Ephesus, 74, 81, 122, 124, 182, 336, 338–39, 346, 352

pagan religious imagery, 80–83, 304
paradox: the cross, 184; divine self-revelation, 108–9, 246; Ignatius's fondness for, 144, 270; integrity through disintegration, 145–46; overcoming evil by enduring abuse, 138–39, 140, 197; true life in death, 15, 169, 282, 307, 318; word and silence, 25, 201, 256–83
Parvus, Roger, 53n3
Pauline theology: continuity with, 122–25, 161–63, 192–96, 281, 309–10, 313; creative adaptation of, 43–47, 62, 90, 174, 175–77, 181, 197–99, 303–4, 313; fused with Johannine elements, 47, 125, 128, 149, 156–57, 307, 318
Paulsen, Henning, 79n58, 309n35
Pearson, Birger A., 75n46, 77n52, 260
Pelikan, Jaroslav, 270n33
Pettersen, Alvyn, 141n38, 261n11, 278n52
pneumatology, 113–15. See also Holy Spirit
Polanyi, Michael, 6–7
Polybius of Tralles, 64–65, 70, 81, 140, 204, 336
Polycarp of Smyrna, 42, 81, 83, 182, 279, 328–29, 336, 338, 346
prayer, 22–23, 193, 274–75
presbyters, 349–50
priests, Israelite, 240–41
prophets, Israelite, 32, 109, 200–201, 207, 225–26, 234–35, 237–39, 244–51
Prosch, Harry, 6n7
Prostmeier, Ferdinand R., 219n44

Rahner, Hugo, 244n99
Ratzinger, Joseph. See Benedict XVI, Pope
Ray, Stephen K., 38n24, 332n96
recursus ad fontes, 40, 251
Reis, David M., 11n11, 117n66
Reno, R. R., 30
repentance, 156, 295, 363
revelation, theology of, 106–9, 116–17, 170, 238, 245–46, 256, 261–62, 266–67, 373–76
Reventlow, Henning Graf, 212n32
rhetoric, 11, 13; in anti-Judaizing polemic, 208–10, 229; and gospel, 56; in *Romans*, 68, 151–54
Richardson, C. C., 13, 54–55, 160–62, 310–11, 313, 315, 317, 319
Robinson, Thomas A., 61n31, 61n33, 73, 82n80, 208–11
Romanides, John S., 334n104
Ryan, P. J., 258n4

Sabbath and Lord's day, 242–45
salvation-historical perspective, 60, 207–8, 211–16, 224, 225, 239, 244, 252, 291–92
Sasse, Hermann, 128n13
Satan, 126–28, 133, 136–40, 147, 152–54, 182, 319–20, 375
Saturninus of Antioch, 75, 76, 260
schema of five distinctions, 3–4, 20, 34–38
Schlatter, Frederic W., 355n143
Schlier, Heinrich, 77, 260, 309–15
Schoedel, William R., 16n17, 28n4, 31, 40n30, 43n38, 48n50, 53n3, 55, 56n13, 62n18, 77, 94–95, 110–11, 129, 142, 143–44, 148n45, 150–51, 152nn53–54, 154, 157, 163–64, 183, 193n78, 203n6, 207, 238, 240, 241n92, 242, 245n100, 262–63, 265, 269, 271, 273, 279n53, 279n55, 297, 311–15, 319, 324, 327n83, 332n97, 343n116, 344n121
Schütz, Christian, 109n45, 285n6
Scripture, 31–33, 51, 305
second coming, 205n13, 244, 367–69
Shepherd, Massey Hamilton, Jr., 278n51
Sibinga, J. Smit, 41n32
Sieben, Hermann Josef, 65n24
Skarsaune, Oskar, 219n45, 220n49, 222, 224n59, 248
Snyder, Graydon F., 176n44, 274n41
sociocritical approaches, 10–11, 75–76, 243n97
Söhngen, Gottlieb, 20, 285n2
Soulen, R. Kendall, 222n55
Spicq, Ceslas, 45n43
spiritualization of matter, 146, 155
spiritual warfare, 91–92, 119, 126–28, 138–40, 147, 152
Staats, Reinhart, 335n106
Stewart-Sykes, Alistair, 278n51, 279n53, 352n141
Stoicism, 182–84, 279
Stoops, Robert F., Jr., 14n15, 198n88
Story, Cullen I. K., 135n29
Streeter, B. H., 54–55, 82n80
Studer, Basil, 270n33
suffering with Christ, 184–85
supersessionism, 37, 201, 207, 222, 228–29, 252–53
suspicion, hermeneutic of, 10–11
Svigel, Michael J., 21n32
Swartley, Willard M., 356n147
sympathy for divine things, 86–87

Tarvainen, Olavi, 17, 159n3
teleology, 91–92, 139, 155–56, 167, 171, 187–92, 196–98, 203, 204–5, 239, 252, 275–76, 296, 299, 341, 360–61, 366
temporality and eternity, 105, 203, 205–6, 233, 340–41
Theodotus (gnostic), 260
theological interpretation, 18–23
theological tradition, 2–3, 5, 17–18, 216, 253–54
theological virtues, 177
Thiselton, Anthony C., 10n10
three spiritual enemies, 119, 147
topical discourses, 61–64
Torrance, T. F., 160, 192–94, 310–13, 315, 319
Trebilco, Paul, 74n45, 83n83
Trevett, Christine, 41n32, 69n31, 137n32
Trinitarianism, nascent, 114–15, 268–71
truth and life: equation of, 281, 319–20, 373–74

understanding, hermeneutic of, 2, 5–12, 18–23, 271
unity, 88–96, 359–60, 374–76; of faith and love, 94, 159–60, 175–99, 327–29; of flesh and spirit, 92–94, 100–105, 118–25; of God, 110–17; of humanity and divinity in Christ, 99–104, 113; of Jesus and the Father, 94–108, 112–16, 339

Villiers, Pieter G. R. de, 83n86
Vinzent, Markus, 58n16
Virgin Mary, 126–28, 133, 135–38, 223–24, 227–29, 273, 289–90
vita usque ad mortem, 155, 191, 296, 317, 367

Wachterhauser, Brice, 19n26
Wagner, Walter H., 16n6
Weinandy, Thomas G., 17
Wesche, Kenneth Paul, 357n149
will, divine, 204–5
Willis, Wayne, 370n29
Winslow, Donald F., 16n17
wisdom literature, 279–80
word and silence, 25, 256–83
works, theology of, 196–99
world: Christians in, 140–42, 156–58; as spiritual enemy, 119, 147, 149

Zahn, Theodor, 52–53
Zañartu, Sergio, 305n18
Zizioulas, John D., 83, 333–37

LEARNING CHRIST: IGNATIUS OF ANTIOCH AND THE MYSTERY OF REDEMPTION WAS DESIGNED IN QUADRAAT AND QUADRAAT SANS AND COMPOSED BY KACHERGIS BOOK DESIGN OF PITTSBORO, NORTH CAROLINA. IT WAS PRINTED ON 55-POUND NATURES RECYCLED AND BOUND BY SHERIDAN BOOKS OF ANN ARBOR, MICHIGAN.

www.ingramcontent.com/pod-product-compliance
Lightning Source LLC
Chambersburg PA
CBHW020313010526
44107CB00054B/1822